P9-CMX-973

DISCARD
T. W. PHILLIPS LIBRARY
BETHANY COLLEGE
BETHANY, WV 26032

ALFRED MARSHALL: PROGRESS AND POLITICS

Also by David Reisman

ADAM SMITH'S SOCIOLOGICAL ECONOMICS
RICHARD TITMUSS: Welfare and Society
GALBRAITH AND MARKET CAPITALISM
STATE AND WELFARE
THE ECONOMICS OF ALFRED MARSHALL

ALFRED MARSHALL
Progress and Politics

David Reisman

St. Martin's Press New York

Scholarly & Reference Division,
St. Martin's Press, Inc., 175 Fifth Avenue, New York, NY 10010

First published in the United States of America in 1987

Printed in Hong Kong

ISBN 0–312–00773–6

Library of Congress Cataloging-in-Publication Data
Reisman, David A.
Alfred Marshall, progress and politics.
Bibliography: p.
Includes index.
1. Neoclassical school of economics. 2. Marshall,
Alfred, 1842–1924. I. Title.
HB98.2.R44 1987 330.15′5 87–4811
ISBN 0–312–00773–6

Contents

1 Introduction

Marshall's great books on progress and politics were never written. His fourth major work was to be *Progress: Its Economic Conditions*, but he never found time in his crowded life to convert the notes into the treatise. The third volume of his *Principles*, he announced in 1907, was to deal with 'the economic functions of Government', thereby indicating his conviction that, alongside micro ('the modern conditions of industry and trade') and macro ('credit and employment')[1] the student of economics should in some measure also be a student of political economy. As, of course, Adam Smith and so many of the English classicals had been. And Plato, who, as Keynes reminds us, inevitably captured the imagination of the philosopher missionary: 'One day in his eighty-second year he said that he was going to look at Plato's *Republic*, for he would like to try and write about the kind of Republic that Plato would wish for, had he lived now.'[2] But the great interdisciplinary account of Economy and Polity, Ethics and Society, had in the event this in common with the path-breaking dynamical synthesis of Growth and Betterment, Upgrading and Evolution, that it too never saw the light of day.

The books were never written but that does not mean that the ideas were lost. On the contrary; and it is the thesis of the present volume that a very great deal indeed is known about Marshall's views on progress and politics precisely because he assigned so much importance to these topics as to discuss them extensively even in books and articles ostensibly concerned primarily with other themes. This is entirely to be expected, for Marshall's maximand was human well-being (as opposed to economic welfare) and his time-period absolutely continuous (as opposed to the eternal *stasis* of the stationary state). As we allocate, Marshall reasoned, so we grow; as we grow, so we grow different; and what renders legitimate such upheaval and such mutation is the fact that such change is not random and kaleidoscopic but purposive and improving, a movement from alcohol to tea and not tea to alcohol. Where, moreover, the invisible hand is demonstrably inadequate for the task of uplifting and upgrading, then the visible hand must be enlisted in the service of the tone of life, as if guided by a hectoring moral philosopher and an ethically-informed political economist anxious to do good. Market mechanism and State intervention, Marshall believed, are but instruments, to be selected or rejected on grounds of expediency rather than dogma. What matters most of all is attainment of the end. And that end is the uplifting and upgrading of the tone of life.

2 Human Betterment

Alfred Marshall did not look backward with regret to some 'Golden Age' before the Fall but rather forward to the future with cautious optimism and a reasonable amount of hope: 'There is then need to guard against the temptation to overstate the economic evils of our own age, and to ignore the existence of similar and worse evils in earlier ages.'[1] We should not be romantics but nor should we be fatalists; and while quite sensibly avoiding the 'potent medicines' and 'impatient insincerity' of what Adam Smith would have called the 'man of system' (and what Marshall dismisses as the 'charlatan'), we are duty-bound also to avoid the evil of 'that moral torpor which can endure that we, with our modern resources and knowledge, should look on contentedly at the continued destruction of all that is worth having in multitudes of human lives, and solace ourselves with the reflection that anyhow the evils of our own age are less than those of the past'.[2] But there are good grounds for a moderate degree of complacency nonetheless; for, Marshall stressed, situating himself in that way far more on the side of the Polyanna than on that of the Cassandra, the truth is that 'we never find a more widely diffused comfort alloyed by less suffering than exists in the western world to-day'.[3]

Many have been critical of that complacency. Joseph Schumpeter, for example, who wrote as disparagingly as one suspects the aristocratic and luxury-loving Pareto would have done of Marshall's 'mid-Victorian morality, seasoned by Benthamism', and who suggested that Marshall's ideal world of property, frugality, enterprise, energy, initiative, calculativeness, exchange, individualism, deferred gratification, industrious self-reliance is (however functional from the economist's perspective) a somewhat boring and antiseptic middle-class utopia that 'knows no glamor and no passion.'[4] Jacob Viner, similarly, like Schumpeter writing in the dark days of the Second World War, was sharply critical of Alfred Marshall on human betterment: 'Marshall's economics is now distinctly that of a generation which is past, and is increasingly *not* that of our own . . . .

Both the Victorian complacency with respect to the present and the Victorian optimism with respect to future progress are now utterly inappropriate. As a social philosopher, Marshall is not yet merely a period piece. If he should become so in the near future, it would properly be a matter for concern, but not for surprise.'[5]

Our own view is moderately more sympathetic to an author who, looking back over more than a century of unprecedented economic, social and technological development, called for more of the same: living standards for most (albeit not all) Englishmen had improved, character-patterns had been upgraded, the negative side of change was in no sense threatening enough to undermine the ever more attractive superstructure that was continuously being constructed on the healthy basis of market capitalism; and growth and betterment would in addition appear to be inextricably and symbiotically linked, each both feeding and feeding off the other. These arguments constitute the pillars of Marshall's theory of human betterment. They also constitute the subject-matter of this chapter and the next. Before, however, proceeding to examine in more detail the moralisations and prognostications of a complex author with whom even close associates such as Keynes *père* ('Marshall said a good many silly things')[6] and Keynes *fils* ('He was an utterly absurd person')[7] on occasion found it difficult not to lose patience, the following comment by way of defence must first be registered. One can disagree with Marshall's values (his neglect of joyful spontaneity, for example, or his eulogy of the future-orientation to the detriment of the present pleasure); one may regard his evolutionary growth-path as value-laden to the point of wishful thinking not least because his evidence is anecdotal to the point of selectivity (his neglect of the mugger and the con-man, for instance, in favour of the generous blood-donor and the responsible Strutt of Derby); and one might even argue, more controversially perhaps, that the sentimental liberalism of the Marshallian type contains the seeds of its own destruction (as where increasing altruism leads to increased institutionalisation of the gift-relationship and therewith to the substitution of bureaucratic for entrepreneurial rationality as part of a campaign to assist the less privileged by direct means). What one cannot disagree with is the strength of Marshall's convictions and of his desire to demonstrate that economic science is useful because – and only because – it makes a genuine contribution to the process of human betterment. Speculation on social trends, reflection on the evolution of institutions, concern with the wider picture, are all characteristics of Marshall's economics. They are not characteristics of all of economics today. Yet there are, when all is said and done, few more important tasks for the contemporary economist than to look, with Alfred Marshall, at the broad sweep of historical processes and to ask in what way economic growth is related to individual and to social improvement.

2.1 WANT-SATISFACTION

We live in an era of rising productivity, a period in which improving methods of production have a tendency continuously to 'increase the produce of each man's labour when aided by a given amount of capital'.[1] Many forces have boosted output per unit of input, and one of the most important of these is technological advance: 'We all know that the progress of science and invention has multiplied enormously the efficiency of labour within the last century.... Even in agriculture the returns to labour have much increased.'[2] Increasing efficiency, whatever the cause, is, in a market economy, ultimately passed on via competition to the final consumer, and this cheapening of goods in the shops represents a *de facto* rise in real wages which Marshall much welcomed: 'The increase of the national dividend owing to the growth of capital and invention is certain to affect all classes of commodities; and to enable the shoemaker, for instance, to purchase with his earnings more food and clothes, more and better supplies of water, artificial light and heat, travel, and so on.'[3] Even where this process of boosting and cheapening initially affects only the luxuries of the rich (and 'such cases are rare'), nonetheless the rich consumer of today can only be seen as the harbinger of what is to come: 'Improvements, designed for the luxuries of the rich, soon spread themselves to the comforts of other classes.'[4] The welfare gain, it must be stressed, presupposes the market mechanism, and that is why the British consumer is in an enviable position when compared with his German counterpart – since in Germany high tariffs and strong cartels mean that producers in effect have the power to 'charge so high prices at home that the people do not get their just share of the benefits which should have resulted from those wonderfully efficient processes of modern manufacture'.[5] Rising productivity and cheapening of goods in the shops simply do not go hand in hand when I perversely refuse to share my gain with you.

Given competition, however, redistribution from producer to consumer then follows as a matter of course.

Rising productivity not only means cheapened consumables. It also means rising money incomes, both for those who continue to sell their existing skills and *a fortiori* for those who are able to turn to their own advantage the secular 'increase in the number of the higher industrial grades relatively to the lower',[6] which in itself is a characteristic of economic progress. What is increasingly being demanded is increasingly being supplied, and the principal cause of this development would seem to be 'the diffusion of education and prudent habits among the masses of the people': 'The growth of general enlightenment and of a sense of responsibility towards the young has turned a great deal of the increasing wealth of the nation from investment as material capital to investment as personal capital. There has resulted a largely increased supply of trained abilities, which has much increased the national dividend, and raised the average income of the whole people.'[7] Yet that very increase in supply 'has taken away from these trained abilities much of that scarcity value which they used to possess, and has lowered their earnings, not indeed absolutely, but relatively to the general advance';[8] while, simultaneously, the reduction in the pool of the unskilled which occurs when you and I move out and into higher grades has led to a rise in the average earnings of those who do not enjoy the benefits of upward social mobility. Thus it happens that economic progress raises the incomes of 'all the ranks of the wages receiving classes, but especially the lower ranks'.[9] Meanwhile, the accumulation of capital which made so great a contribution to the rise in productivity has meant redistribution of income away from the capitalist classes – since 'a rapid growth of capital' means in effect that that input is forced by competition 'to accept a lower rate of interest', with the consequence that it then leaves 'a larger share of a larger produce to be distributed among the different grades of labour'.[10] As those labourers become more affluent, moreover, they are able themselves to become moderate capitalists, so great nowadays are 'the opportunities which the new methods of business offer for the safe investment of small capitals';[11] and they thus have the chance in that way to increase their money incomes still further, through the reaping of a reward to which they, before the rise of the modern joint stock company with its limited liability and its salaried managers, simply had no access. While the position of the wealthy urban landowner whose rents rise so rapidly in the course of economic progress as to redistribute the national income in his favour is undeniably the exception,[12] the rule would seem to be that almost all money incomes rise with growth but that the money incomes of relatively less advantaged groups increase the fastest. Thus, statistics 'all indicate that middle class incomes are increasing faster than those of the rich; that the earnings of artisans are increasing faster than those of the professional classes, and that the wages of healthy and vigorous unskilled labourers are increasing faster even than those of the average artisan.'[13] Not only does each of us receive a larger piece of a larger cake, in other words, but growth also redistributes, reallocates and restructures our relative shares. Specifically, important underlying factors in an improving economy 'are telling on the side of moderate incomes',[14] and such a trend is a good thing: 'Social and economic forces already at work are changing the distribution of wealth for the better.'[15] Even if they were not, incidentally, the very fact that money incomes are rising across the board is in itself a solvent of social tensions since it permits of a divorce between absolutes and relatives and an escape from the nastiness of the zero sum game: clearly, 'when the aggregate income is stationary, and any one class gets a better share than before, it must be at the expense of the others'.[16]

With rising incomes goes rising consumption, and here Marshall was pleased to be able to cite instance after instance where economic growth had brought about rising standards of living. As in the case of fuel: 'During the middle ages the cottagers could generally, though not always, get the little brushwood fire needed to keep them warm as they huddled together round it in huts which had no chimneys through which the heat could go to waste .... (Coal) is now so cheap that even the comparatively poor can keep themselves warm indoors without living in an unwholesome and stupefying atmosphere.'[17] And housing: 'The modern suburban artisan's cottage contains sleeping accommodation far superior to that of the gentry in the middle ages; and the working classes had then no other beds than loose straw, reeking with vermin, and resting on damp mud floors.'[18] And the environment: 'London air is full of smoke; but it is probably less unwholesome than it was before the days of scientific sanitation';[19] 'school playgrounds have multiplied; ... commons are now kept in good order; and ... electric tramways and railways enable an ever-increasing number of artisans, and even of unskilled labourers, to take their families out of London occasionally during the summer'.[20] And food: 'A century ago very little meat was eaten by the working classes; while now, though its price is a little higher than it was then, they probably consume more of it, on the average, than at any other time in English history.'[21] Free trade measures contributed much 'to raise four-fold, or more, the amount of good bread which a labourer could purchase with his weekly earnings'.[22] Improved transport lowered the cost of imported perishables such as strawberries and increased 'the period of time during which different kinds of food are available'.[23] Scientific techniques upgraded the character of consumables and rendered them of better quality: 'An ox or sheep weighs now twice as much as it did not very long ago: of that weight a larger percentage is meat; of the meat a larger percentage is prime meat.'[24] In case after case economic growth and rising standards of living have moved together, and the latter development is an important source of legitimation for the former.

With rising incomes goes rising consumption; but Marshall made clear that he was able to report past and to predict future progress that was of a qualitative as well as of a quantitative nature. Marshall distinguished in particular between a straightforward improvement in comfort ('a term that may suggest a mere increase of artificial wants, among which perhaps the grosser wants may predominate') and a genuine improvement in standard of life: 'A rise in the standard of life implies an increase of intelligence and energy and self-respect; leading to more care and judgement in expenditure, and to an avoidance of food and drink that gratify the appetite but afford no strength, and of ways of living that are unwholesome physically and morally.'[25] Marshall did not preach asceticism (despite the fact that he seems personally to have practised it); but he did argue that the better kinds of consumer goods were not those which simply satisfied man's existing wants but rather those which actually contributed to the 'development of his activities, physical, mental, and moral'.[26] Such consumer goods 'attain in the highest degree the end of all production: for they then raise the tone of human life'.[27] It must therefore have been a source of great satisfaction to him to be able to point, in the England of his own times, to the triumph of 'higher' wants over the 'bad' desires represented by 'artificial comforts and luxuries',[28] and to write as follows concerning the new consumption patterns which, he believed, were emerging: 'Doubtless some indulgences are positively harmful; but these are diminishing relatively to the rest . . . Most of that expenditure which is not strictly economical as a means towards efficiency, yet helps to form habits of ready resourceful enterprise.'[29] Marshall, a believer both in freedom of consumer choice and in morality of consumables chosen, would have found himself in a serious quandry had the sovereign consumer opted with his effective demand not for healthy food and durable boots but for opium and pornography instead – a quandary which the mathematical economist and unitarian clergyman Wicksteed encapsulated as follows in 1888 in his tract on *Getting and Spending*: 'To have ministered to a want that ought not to exist, to have fostered and stimulated a destructive passion, to have given vice its trappings and instruments and enabled guilty or reckless folly to have its way, this is to have supplied human wants and made money. Is it a work on which a good man can ask God's blessing in the morning and for success in which he can thank him at night? . . . This stands out clearly enough, that no man can appeal simply to men's wants, and justify himself by declaring that he supplied them, if he knows all the while that it would have been better had they not been supplied at all. It is not enough to make what *is* money. We must make what *ought* to be money also.'[30] Marshall did not find himself in this quandary born of the disparity between *is* and *ought*, between negative freedom (to do as I like with my own) and positive freedom (to unfold my essence in such a way as to enjoy a truly noble and worthy life), and the reason is quite simply the optimistic confidence with which he approached the momentum inherent in matter. Marshall was entirely in agreement with Arnold Toynbee's perspective on the relationship between earning and consuming, which was in effect that 'high wages are not an end in themselves. No one wants high wages in order that working men may indulge in more sensual gratification. We want higher wages in order that an improved material condition, with less of anxiety and less uncertainty as to the future, may enable the working man to enter on a purer and more worthy life.'[31] What Marshall also believed, however, was that better consumption-patterns were even now breeding and forming better men, and that the evolutionary economist cannot but rejoice at the direction in which events are even now moving: 'There is a constant improvement in the way in which wages are spent. As a cup of salt water increases thirst, so an ill-spent rise in wages deepens misery. But in the main increased wages are used to improve the physical, mental, and moral strength of the present and the rising generation. In so far as they are so used, high wages are a cause of that efficiency and 'social morality' which enable wages to be permanently high.'[32]

Better consumption-patterns breed and form better men, but the proposition is reversible since better men also demand better things.

Thus we note that that part of the English working classes is 'rapidly lessening' who 'have no ambition and no pride or delight in the growth of their faculties and activities, and spend on drink whatever surplus their wages afford over the bare necessaries of a squalid life';[33] and it is important to remember that the cause of this improvement is material, not ideal. As Marshall explained as early as 1873, a man compelled to long hours of 'hard corporeal work' is likely to be too exhausted by evening for anything more challenging than 'the coarse pleasures of the public house': 'If his toil has been fierce, and so his brain is dulled, he is apt to seek there only the coarser pleasures – drink, ignoble jests, and noise.'[34] If therefore such men are guilty of 'using their bodies as furnaces for the conversion of alcohol into fumes', they ought not personally to be too severely censured for that which is in truth the result of strenuous exertion and physical fatigue, of 'unduly sustained work that is heavy': 'these things have formed the men', for 'the rougher the work of the body, the lower the condition of the mind'.[35] And the circumstances of life when not at work are to blame as well. Among the low-paid in overcrowded London slums, for example, 'even when their houses are whitewashed, the sky will be dark; devoid of joy, they will . . . tend to drink for excitement'[36] and to escape 'the sadness of London'.[37] A man dwelling in a congested urban district faces 'an incessant strain on his nervous strength', he is unlikely to see much of 'the fresh air and bright sunshine of the countryside', he tends to forget 'the blessedness of repose', he is 'scarcely ever completely refreshed', and in such a state it is no surprise that he turns for relief and release not to knowledge, art and uplifting conversation but to gin: 'He is apt to seek for excitement by the paths of least resistance, and the excitements to which they lead are seldom altogether pure and healthy.'[38] The problem is material, the solution economic – by mechanising rough work, raising wages and reducing hours; through slum clearance and decentralisation of industry. And the beneficial impact of growth on wants is already to be observed: 'Speaking generally, we may say that every increase in the wealth of the working classes adds to the fulness and nobility of human life, because it is used chiefly in the satisfaction of real wants.'[39] Applied to the specific case of the demon drink, sound evidence of genuine improvement is at hand: 'Those drinks which stimulate the mental activities are largely displacing those which merely gratify the senses. The consumption of tea is increasing very fast, while that of alcohol is stationary.'[40] Alas, the same cannot be said for gambling (which appears to be the 'chief exception' to the general tendency towards greater wisdom with respect to consumption),[41] and the account of the discussion at the Industrial Remuneration Conference in 1885 actually reported Marshall as describing 'the gambling spirit that had invaded the most progressive countries of the world' as 'a greater evil for the future than drunkenness; for though not as great an evil now, it was likely to increase while drunkenness diminished'.[42] Marshall is reported as having been shocked by the extensiveness of reckless gambling among working men in Germany ('He had high ideas of what the Germans would do with their leisure; to his horror he found that a great many of them spent a great part of it in petty gambling') and he apparently maintained, speaking of what he clearly regarded as a 'great evil', that 'advancing education did not stop it'.[43] Perhaps, however, Marshall expected that, like drunkenness, 'those amusements which constitute the miserable creature who is called the sporting man'[44] would one day wither away with the degradation which gives rise to the craving for such morbid forms of excitement.

The idea that better men will demand better things is not, moreover, applicable to the poorer classes alone. It applies to the upper classes as well, as the decreasing incidence of conspicuous consumption will serve to demonstrate: 'In the upper grades, though the dress of women is still various and costly, that of men is simple and inexpensive as compared with what it was in Europe not long ago, and is to-day in the East. For those men who are most truly distinguished on their own account, have a natural dislike to seem to claim attention by their dress; and they have set the fashion.'[45] And even among women there is an increasing concern with the character under the clothes, and a relative decrease in the importance assigned to extravagant ostentatiousness: 'A woman may display wealth, but she may not display only her wealth, by her dress; or else she defeats her ends. She must also suggest some distinction of character as well as of wealth.'[46] Thus her dress – which, to be honest, 'may owe more to her dressmaker than to herself' – must be 'beautiful', durable, and 'well-adapted' to the situation as well as merely being costly. But if she is able conspicuously to make intelligent choices of this nature, her action then 'belongs to the same class, though not to the same rank in that class, as the painting of a good picture';[47] and it is her powers of taste and judgement which come to win her approbation. With social evolution, in other words, people 'become not only more efficient producers but also wiser consumers, with greater knowledge of all that is beautiful, and more care for it':[48] 'A time may come when it will be thought absurd for a woman to display her wealth by carrying about a great quantity of expensive materials and embroidery; just as a painter who advertised the price he had paid for the paints on his picture would be thought vulgar.'[49] Marshall, like Marx never entirely adverse to accelerating the momentum inherent in matter, expressed the hope that public opinion would come to reward popular tastes of the healthy kind with additional approbation and to stigmatise spurious and wasteful expenditures on clothes which wear out too quickly, fashions which alter too frequently, and luxuries which are bought exclusively for 'silly show':[50] 'We need to turn consumption into paths that strengthen the consumer and call forth the best qualities of those who provide for consumption.'[51] But it is doubtful if much is needed in the way of moral guidance in view of the extent to which the upgrading of tastes is already in evidence – a process guided, one is tempted to add, as if by an invisible hand.

Wants initially lead to activities, but it is then activities which take over the role of the independent or causal variable: 'Speaking broadly therefore, although it is man's wants in the earliest stages of his development that give rise to his activities, yet afterwards each new step upwards is to be regarded as the development of new activities giving rise to new wants, rather than of new wants giving rise to new activities.'[52] So in that sense 'it is not true . . . that "the Theory of Consumption is the scientific basis of economics"', since an evolutionary economics finds itself confronted in the last analysis not with the *same* men satisfying the *same* wants but with quite *different* men satisfying quite *different* wants. As Talcott Parsons puts it: 'The satisfaction of known wants supplies the only possible norm in terms of which the desirability or efficiency of an economic process can be judged. Once ends themselves come to vary as a function of the process of their attainment, the standard no longer exists; the argument becomes circular.'[53] And Frank Knight: 'If it is the intrinsic nature of a thing to grow and change, it cannot serve as a scientific datum. A science must have a "static" subject-matter; it must talk about things which will "stay put"; otherwise its statements will not remain true after they are made and there will be no point to making them.'[54] Success is extremely difficult to define in an environment where ends as well as means are variant over time; the economist *qua* economist cannot be sure that *more* means *better*; and it was no doubt considerations of this nature that brought out the moral philosopher and even the Old Testament prophet that were so much a part of Marshall's personality.

A richer society offers more opportunity to earn and spend. It also offers more opportunity not to work, to take potential income in the form of leisure and relaxation. Just as exertion has in past years been on the increase, so it seems now to be passing its zenith, and that is a good thing: 'In all grades of work except the very highest, people are getting to prize relaxation more highly than before, and are becoming more impatient of the fatigue that results from excessive strain; and they are perhaps on the whole less willing than they used to be to undergo the constantly increasing "discommodity" of very long hours of work, for the sake of obtaining present luxuries.'[55] Marshall's rather hesitant formulation (a man who speaks of 'perhaps on the whole' is unlikely to win many prizes for rigorous decisiveness) no doubt reflects his own awareness of countervailing forces (the upgrading of tastes, as opposed to satiation with 'present luxuries'; the reduction in the proportion of work which 'tires without educating'[56] and therewith in the 'discommodity' or disutility of labouring; the increasing willingness on the part of ever larger sections of the population to 'incur present ills for the sake of future benefits');[57] but his general conclusion on the direction of change would seem to be that 'it is doubtful whether we can now trace a continued increase in the amount of exertion'.[58] This does not mean that the national income will then automatically be less than it would otherwise have been since, as Marshall never tires of emphasising, efficiency and energy are in many cases actually undermined by hard work, long hours, 'excessive strain on muscles',[59] and overall fatigue. In such cases (and we are speaking most of all of 'the lowest grade of honest workers',[60] whose stamina and productivity are most impaired by excessive wear and tear of body and mind), a greater recognition that 'leisure, rest and repose . . . are among the necessaries for efficiency' might, if it led to a diminution in the hours of labour, have a beneficial impact on the workers: 'Their increased energy, intelligence and force of character would enable them to do as much as before in less time; and thus, even from the point of view of material production, there would be no ultimate loss.'[61] But even if there were a loss, first principles teach that 'severe strain . . . is itself an evil',[62] while rest, relaxation and recreation are good things in their own right: 'Though it is true that a shortening of the hours of labour would in many cases lessen the national dividend and lower wages: yet it would probably be well that most people should work rather less; provided that the consequent loss of material income could be met exclusively by the abandonment by all classes of the least worthy methods of consumption; and that they could learn to spend leisure well.'[63]

Both provisos are admittedly rather restrictive. One would have to accept Marshall's underlying premise concerning the continuous improvement in consumer preferences ('A sage might suggest a little improvement here and there, but on the balance there seems no great matter for regret')[64] to accept *ex ante facto* that the incidence of a marginal reduction in disposable income would fall, as Marshall suggested it ought to do, on anti-social modes of consumption taking the form of those things which, he believed, 'do little or nothing towards making life nobler or truly happier'.[65] And, regarding the wholesome use of leisure, the reader is unlikely to derive much reassurance from the following: 'In every age, in every nation, and in every rank of society, those who have known how to work well, have been far more numerous than those who have known how to use leisure well.'[66] But in spite of this, Marshall remained a man of hope. Theoretically speaking, his reason was the educative function of learning by doing: 'It is only through freedom to use leisure as they will, that people can learn to use leisure well: and no class of manual workers, who are devoid of leisure, can have much self-respect and become full citizens.'[67] Besides that, there is solid empirical evidence that leisure is in its nature less and less passive (i.e. 'idle stagnation that is not rest'),[68] more and more active (as where it is used 'for school and for such kinds of play as strengthen and develop the character'):[69] 'Leisure is used less and less as an opportunity for mere stagnation; and there is a growing desire for those amusements, such as athletic games and travelling, which develop activities rather than indulge any sensuous craving.'[70] Mechanisation, the exploitation of new sources of power, the extended usage of the shift system (which facilitates the efficient utilisation of plant while at the same time ensuring that 'even the lowliest of human operatives need work only during short hours; though with energy while at work'[71] – all of these factors have made possible a shortening of 'the hours of manual labour',[72] and increased the quantum of time available for creative leisure: 'Perhaps the percentage of artisans who are so tired at the end of the day's work as to be disinclined to use their minds actively, is not a tenth as great as it was a century ago; and meanwhile the abundance and cheapness of periodical and other literature, adapted to their requirements, and even specially devoted to their interests, have increased very fast.'[73] Improvements in 'cheap and artificial light' permit men to read rather than drink and are thus an important complement to active recreation: necessary for man's work, they are also – 'what is of higher moment' – necessary 'for the good use of his evening leisure'.[74] Improvements in transportation permit men to garden rather than to gamble and have the additional benefit of strengthening family-feeling by uniting husband, wife and children in the shared cultivation of a common allotment. Even in the case of want-satisfaction via active recreation, it would appear, material change and social progress may confidently be expected to move in step.

2.2 CONDUCT AND CHARACTER

Marshall praised historical inquiry and other manifestations of the comparative method for demonstrating with evidence what he had long suspected *a priori*, that 'man himself is in a great measure a creature of circumstances and changes with them',[1] and for drawing attention to the extensiveness of much mutability: 'The study of economic history has done good service . . . in proving that habits and institutions which had been assumed to be inherent in human nature are comparatively of modern growth.'[2] Marshall's economics is replete with qualifying clauses such as 'while human nature remains as it is',[3] or 'as human nature is constituted',[4] and the reason is, quite frankly, that even human nature itself is to a considerable degree the product of time and place. Thus, 'while the earlier economists argued as though man's character and efficiency were to be regarded as a fixed quantity, modern economists keep constantly in mind the fact that it is a product of the circumstances under which he has lived'.[5] It is indeed particularly appropriate that economists should, avoiding the temptation to regard man as 'so to speak, a constant quantity',[6] begin to take an interest in the variations in human nature that are brought about by changes in circumstances. These changes in circumstances, after all, include a very large component which is uniquely economic: 'The character of man affects and is affected by the prevalent methods of the production, distribution and consumption of wealth'[7] and, indeed, 'man's character has been moulded by his every-day work, and the material resources which he thereby procures, more than by any other influence unless it be that of his religious ideals'.[8]

The modern economist cannot but perhaps be somewhat jealous of the naive over-confidence of his forebears 'at the beginning of the century';[9] for the men of Ricardo's time, content to ignore history and statistics and happy to assume that most people were or ought to be like modern urban Englishmen, could then proceed to develop generalisable economic theories which they were able to regard as being of virtually universal applicability. Thus it was 'the same bent of mind, that led our lawyers to impose English civil law on the Hindoos' which also 'led our economists to work out their theories on the tacit assumption that the world was made up of city men'.[10] That tacit assumption is no longer tenable: 'The changes in human nature during the last fifty years have been so rapid as to force themselves on the attention.'[11] Even the individual cannot be assumed to have a deep-seated essence independent of the existential situation – an environment in which tastes and character both alter, so do 'the habits and institutions of industry',[12] and the economist has no choice but to eschew the mechanical, the mathematical and the physical in favour of the biological and especially the historical if he is truly to capture the dynamism of that which is evolving around him. History at least picks up flow and process and seeks to show 'not only what human nature was at any time, but also how it has developed. It offers us therefore great aid towards estimating the direction and the rate of growth of human nature in the future.'[13]

Marshall was deeply interested in 'the pliability of human nature'.[14] Convinced as he was that 'man is himself largely formed by his surroundings',[15] he sought to predict 'the changes in man himself'[16] that were likely to come about in the course of economic development. These, after all, are more than anything else the force which renders economic growth legitimate and good: 'The progress of man's nature . . . is, I conceive, the centre of the ultimate aim of economic studies',[17] logically so since 'the true key-note of economic progress is the development of new activities rather than of new wants'.[18] Conduct and character is a far more important topic than that of want-satisfaction: 'If either, more than the other, may claim to be the interpreter of the history of man . . . it is the science of activities and not that of wants.'[19] The topic being an important one, our task must now be to seek to identify those improvements in man himself which Marshall believed to be associated with a nation's economic growth.

(1) Honesty

Looking at the historical record, we do not find that man has grown 'harder and harsher than he was';[20] what we do find is 'strong proof of the marvellous growth in recent times of a spirit of honesty and uprightness in commercial matters'.[21]

One might have expected modern businessmen to be less honest rather than more honest. After all, the advance of technical knowledge 'has rendered possible many new forms of adulteration', many new ways 'of making things appear other than they are',[22] and the fact 'the opportunities for knavery are certainly more numerous than they were' is reinforced by the fact that the opportunities for retribution are also more reduced: 'The producer is now far removed from the ultimate consumer; and his wrong-doings are not visited with the prompt and sharp punishment which falls on the head of a person who, being bound to live and die in his native village, plays a dishonest trick on one of his neighbours.'[23] A similar separation of action and reaction may be found in the modern joint stock company, where the 'leading officers' are exposed to 'the vast temptations to fraud which lie in their way' and need have no fear of the shareholders, these being nothing more than paper tigers – numerous, indifferent, ill-informed and, 'save in a few exceptional instances, almost powerless'.[24]

And yet, a tribute to the high degree of probity in modern business life, these managers even now yield remarkably seldom to the temptation to substitute individual for collective interests, managerial for capitalist-orientated goals. Had they frequently misbehaved, 'their wrong uses of the trusts imposed in them would have been on so great a scale as to *prevent the development* of this democratic form of business'.[25] Yet they did not normally misbehave, partly due to 'the progress of trade morality' (that is why, even though management already functions efficiently, it still functions 'not indeed as cheaply as it may ... in the future when men's collective instincts, their sense of duty and their public spirit are more fully developed'),[26] partly due to an extension of past and present external constraints having the character of selective material incentives to be good (specifically, 'a diminution of trade secrecy and ... increased publicity in every form').[27] These benefits then become cumulative external economies which feed the process of growth – and seem to be the precondition for it, since few verbal contracts on the Stock or Cotton Exchanges would be made if there were not an assumption that they would be honoured.[28] Thus, 'even the most purely business relations of life assume honesty and good faith; while many of them take for granted, if not generosity, yet at least the absence of meanness, and the pride which every honest man takes in acquitting himself well'.[29]

It seems to be matter in motion which generated this free good and wrought this welcome change in mind. At least, 'modern methods of trade imply habits of trustfulness on the one side and a power of resisting temptation to dishonesty on the other, which do not exist among a backward people'.[30] Witness how few dependable persons with 'strong moral character' can be found in under-developed countries (where foreign labour must be imported not only because of its stock of scarce skills but also because native labour is simply not worthy of trust), or how much the merchants of the middle ages were dominated by egotism and driven by greed: 'Adulteration and fraud in trade were rampant in the middle ages to an extent that is very astonishing, when we consider the difficulties of wrong-doing without detection at that time.'[31] Our modern economy, based as it is upon extensive specialisation and extended division of labour, would hardly function very smoothly if the customer feared exploitation and mendacity at every stage in every transaction; even 'detection' and the associated sanctions of public opinion would appear, historically speaking, deterrents to dishonesty partial and imperfect at best; and the conclusion to be reached is that there is no substitute in the sophisticated modern economy for honesty as a Kant-like ethical *ne plus ultra*, a moral principle which constitutes an absolute end in its own right that is conceptually distinct from the utility of outcome to which it also serves as a means. Each of us indeed has come to take for granted such 'just treatment' (analogous to the Scholastic concept of the 'just price'): 'If a carpenter has made a box, or a surveyor has made a map of some land for us, we consider that he acts fairly by us, if he does not attempt to take advantage of our not having made a bargain beforehand, or of our ignorance, or of any special hold he may have over us.'[32] The very fact that it is increasingly rational for us, in contemporary economic conditions, to expect such men to behave towards us with honesty rather than deceit, is in itself an interesting illustration of the proposition that, in economic morality as in market economics, demand creates its own supply.

(2) Respect for persons

Half a century later, looking back on his paper of 1873 on 'The Future of the Working Classes', Marshall commented that it 'bears marks of the over-sanguine temperament of youth'.[33] Perhaps it does, but there is in it one key concept on which Marshall never compromised, and that is the strong emphasis on equality of respect: 'The question is not whether all men will ultimately be equal – that they certainly will not – but whether progress may not go on steadily if slowly, till the official distinction between working man and gentleman has passed away; till, by occupation at least, every man is a gentleman. I hold that it may, and that it will.'[34]

The distinction between the two nations within one nationality is not between those who work and those who do not (even sculptors and military officers work, and yet they are not considered working class). Nor is it between those who supply labour-power and those who supply capital (since the two groups, in Marshall's view, are unified by virtue of the fact that what they really supply is subjective sacrifice). Rather, the distinction between the two nations that sadly still coexist within the bosom of a common citizenship is properly between those whose character is normally debased through economic activity and those whose character is normally enhanced: 'Is it not true that when we say a man belongs to the working classes we are thinking of the effect that his work produces on him rather than of the effect that he produces on his work? If a man's daily task tends to give culture and refinement to his character, do we not, however coarse the individual man may happen to be, say that his occupation is that of a gentleman? If a man's daily task tends to keep his character rude and coarse, do we not, however truly refined the individual man may happen to be, say that he belongs to the working classes?'[35]

Some occupations demand and supply 'powers and activities of mind' such as 'directly promote culture and refinement' and also stimulate sympathy and 'fellow-feeling with men far off and near':[36] 'They demand the faculty of maintaining social intercourse with a large number of persons; they demand, in appearance at least, the kindly habit of promptly anticipating the feelings of others on minor points, of ready watchfulness to avoid each trivial word or deed that may pain or annoy. These qualities are required for success, and they are therefore prepared in youth by a careful and a long continued education. Throughout life they are fostered and improved by exercise and by contact with persons who have similar qualities and require them of their associates.'[37] Through formal education, through informal contacts at work and beyond, through intellectual interests and artistic pursuits, through the challenge and responsibility of his occupation in its own right, the gentleman develops and is perceived to possess character patterns which make him a focus for admiration and emulation. He will no doubt acquire some wealth as well – but the wealth is the proxy for the focus and not the focus itself: 'It is to (the) effects on character that the chief attractiveness of wealth is due.'[38]

Some occupations, sadly, demand and supply something less appealing; and the gentleman will find little in common with 'those vast masses of men who, after long hours of hard and unintellectual toil, are wont to return to their narrow homes with bodies exhausted and with minds dull and sluggish'.[39] Exhausting physical work in unpleasant surroundings uses up a man's vitality at such a prodigious rate as to dull his 'higher energies'[40] and produce 'stupefaction of his intellect'[41] (as in the case of 'the rough work of the miners').[42] Such work has a subtle but powerful effect in 'dwarfing the growth of the man'.[43] It 'crushes a man's life';[44] for it provides no outlet for ambition (and thus no incentive for rational upward striving), no chance to develop that 'manly respect for themselves' (together with 'courteous respect for others')[45] which results from independent and self-motivated activity, no opportunity to learn 'how glorious a thing it is to be able to think and to feel about things and with many men'[46] (as opposed to the permanent isolation of the other-directed automaton), no hope of ever grasping the fundamental truth (so important for any genuine sense of human dignity) that he and his co-workers 'are men, and not producing machines'.[47] Such work is wrong in itself (since no man's 'inner life' ought to be repressed to the point of atrophy) and it is wrong in addition because it produces a divided society in which the sheep and the goats share no common language or common culture.

Marshall's opinion was that no man 'should have any occupation which tends to make him anything else than a gentleman'.[48] He also believed that economic evolution was steadily producing the kind of society which he welcomed, a society 'where the opportunities of a noble life may be accessible to all',[49] a society based on the 'equality of conditions' (the 'true kernel of democracy') that he was convinced he had seen in the relatively classless environment of the United States. Addressing the Cambridge Moral Science Club on 17 November 1875, he reported that 'with the exception of a few immigrants, I met no one, man or woman, in America whose appearance indicated an utterly dull or insipid life'; 'I did not see a single American face full of that gross deathly coarseness which is to be seen in the lowest and most stagnant classes not only of England, but even of Germany'; no one seemed to be lost in 'the fog of a glum sensuality' or to act on the basis of impulses that are 'simply animal'; and the reason for this remarkable lack of conspicuous debasement would appear to lie essentially in the wide diffusion in America of 'knowledge, energy and conscious power'[50] that results from universal State education combined with equality of opportunity and the *carrière ouverte aux talents*. Ranks and grades do exist in America, Marshall conceded, and not all contestants in life's race run equally far or equally fast, but the important point is that in America each runner perceives the runner next door as being made of the same stuff as himself, as *deserving* one vote precisely because he *is* one man: 'Where all receive nearly the same school education, where the incomparably more important education which is derived from the business of life, however various in form it be, yet is for every one nearly equally thorough, nearly equally effective in developing the faculties of men, there cannot but be true democracy.'[51]

Education in place of ignorance, meritocracy in place of birth, are important steps on the road to one-nationhood and the therewith associated respect for persons; and they indeed operate in the same direction as three other social forces which we have already encountered, namely rising incomes, upgraded wants, and improved use of leisure. Even so, for all of this to happen, it is important that men should not only have the will and the chance to rise up from degradation but that there should also exist an increasing number of higher-level slots for them to occupy. Should those slots be 'positional goods' in strictly limited supply, of course, then the outcome of aspiration is inevitably frustration; for, as Hirsch puts it, in such circumstances 'what each of us can achieve, all cannot'.[52] Should economic growth, moreover, presuppose de-skilling within the working population and the 'mental mutilation' which Adam Smith believed to be the inescapable concomitant of division of labour,[53] then economic development need not lead to cultural homogeneity via *embourgeoisement* – since, in Smith's perspective, 'the habits . . . of order, oeconomy and attention, to which mercantile business naturally forms a merchant'[54] cannot but distinguish him radically from the factory operative whose repetitive and unchallenging tasks in the pin-factory not only make him 'exceedingly stupid',[55] but actually render him 'as stupid and ignorant as it is possible for a human creature to become'.[56] Marshall would have sympathised strongly with Tawney's impassioned *plaidoyer* for respect for persons: 'Social well-being does not only depend upon intelligent leadership; it also depends upon cohesion and solidarity. It implies the existence, not merely of opportunities to ascend, but of a high level of general culture, and a strong sense of common interests, and the diffusion throughout society of a conviction that civilization is not the business of an *élite* alone, but a common enterprise which is the concern of all.'[57] Marshall would also have recognised clearly the threat to respect for persons that is represented by the Hirsch problem (of being dressed up with nowhere to go) and the Adam Smith dilemma (that because *we* grow, therefore *you* sink). Crucial to his optimistic view of social progress is therefore his confident belief in the increasing premium on skill and in the increasing mechanisation of those tasks which are dull, monotonous and brutalising: 'As civilisation advances the relative importance of mental to manual labour changes. Every year mental labour becomes more important, and manual labour less important. With every fresh invention of machinery work is transferred from the muscles, or vital force, to natural force.'[58] Nothing but good can come from such a process: 'machinery takes over sooner or later all monotonous work in manufacture',[59] 'complex machinery increases the demand for judgement and general intelligence',[60] and the social benefits are both material (higher pay for more demanding, more skilled jobs) and cultural (since 'hard bodily toil' develops 'scarcely any valuable qualities save those of patience and endurance'[61] and in any case 'poverty causes degradation'[62] such as drives a not inconsiderable wedge between Them and Us). Technology, Marshall believed, was liberating and upgrading. Already, he noted, 'all ranks of society are rising; on the whole they are better and more cultivated than their forefathers were'.[63] The process of change was rapid to say the least – the ratio of skilled to unskilled actually doubled in the quarter-century after 1850, Marshall declared in 1887[64] – and the net result would soon be a society inhabited essentially by cultural equals, not by classes but by gentlemen. In that enviable situation, 'since there will be nothing tending to render the individual coarse and unrefined, there will be nothing to render society coarse and unrefined'.[65] Some men would still not be included (the residual or hard-core poor, for example) but they would be in the minority; for in the society of gentlemen 'everyone who is not a gentleman will have himself alone to blame for it'.[66]

Some theorists have sought to produce an integrated society by means of an appeal to Christian ethics (the idea that all men are children of God, created in His image and equal in His sight). Others have pointed to mass consumption as a standardising and therefore a unifying force; while still others have praised the shared institutions of the modern Welfare State for creating an overlap in life-experiences and in that way the perception of a shared identity. Marshall's answer to the question of how best to engineer a society of equal citizens who know they are equal was more work-centred than any of these three approaches; for he substituted for them economic growth, occupational upgrading, and the romance of steel.

Respect for persons has a further dimension, and it is the international one. Materially speaking, we all know that the early voyages of discovery such as that of Vasco da Gama were 'the beginning of the economic unification of the world';[67] that because of the telegraph and telephone 'inflations and depressions of industrial activity are becoming increasingly international';[68] that steam transport and freedom of trade have created 'a single wheat market for the two hemispheres'[69] such as permits superfluity in one area rapidly to relieve famine in another; and that 'those nations have made most progress, which have had the largest opportunities for absorbing the best qualities of other nations, and for assimilating their most fertile thoughts: those nations have, in general progressed most rapidly whose trade has afforded them the widest intercourse with other nations'.[70] What we must not forget is that the gains from international intercourse are cultural as well as concrete, in the sense that commerce (via shared thoughts and feelings as well as complementarity of interests) 'has worked without ceasing to give nations that knowledge of each other, which alone can afford a solid basis for friendship'.[71] It is accordingly emotions as well as interests which lies at the root of the contemporary move towards international co-operation in economic and other affairs: 'It is of course true that international agreements are now spreading over all fields of commerce and politics, to an extent which would have been thought impossible even a generation ago: and a few generations hence the psychological force of international opinion may be sufficient to support almost any agreement which is generally approved.'[72] If I increasingly care what you think of me, the inference is that I increasingly regard you not only as a problem to be solved but as an end in your own right. The inference, in other words, is that I increasingly regard you as a person – even if, through no fault of your own, a foreign person – and therefore as worthy of respect.

Marshall believed that respect for persons had an international dimension and that even foreigners in the era of intercourse and interdependence will come to command as well as to deserve such respect. Not equally so, however, since blood is thicker than water. That is why, although we have an Empire, we should not neglect our kith and kin by moving away from freedom of trade towards a system of Imperial Preference:

> Since the Empire is not geographically continuous, Imperial federation could not have the economic advantages which resulted from the German Zollverein. But it is a high aim in itself; while material wealth is merely a means towards ends. And yet, in my humble judgement, it is far from being our highest aim and it is being pushed in direct hostility to our highest aim. That highest aim is, I submit, the development of a common feeling and of common interests throughout our race . . . The United States contain many more of our race than do all our colonies and dependencies together . . . Our true ideal is to be found not in little Anglosaxondom, but in great Anglosaxondom.[73]

This is not to deny the material advantages that are associated with the present system. A common external tariff would mean higher food prices (a burden which falls disproportionately on lower income groups), it might lead to American retaliation against our goods, and there is also the military consideration that 'England cannot permanently hold both the Atlantic and the Pacific against all comers' and that 'the United States will be in a short time the dominant power in the Pacific'.[74] Even so, the material should not be allowed to obscure the ideal nor guns speak louder than genes; and the fact is that we have more in common with the Americans than we do with the Indians, the Chinese and the other races who live in our Empire. We can respect these persons, but not as much as we can respect the Americans.

And, of course the Germans, who when all is said and done are branches off the same venerable tree as ourselves. The Germans, Marshall conceded in August 1914 in the course of a heated exchange of letters in *The Times* with a correspondent signing himself simply 'Union Jack', are undeniably more likely than are Englishmen to fall victim to 'the hectoring militarism which is more common there than here', but that is still no reason for them to be scorned and hated (as opposed to being fought): 'As a people I believe them to be exceptionally conscientious and upright, sensitive to the calls of duty, tender in their family affections, true and trusty in friendship. Therefore they are strong and to be feared, but not to be vilified.'[75] Marshall, who was in Berlin in the Franco-Prussian War and had kept in touch with Germany, knew that trade breeds respect for persons – and that this is never so true as when the persons in question are, like the Germans, in essence already very much like ourselves.

(3) The pursuit of excellence

Talking about want-satisfaction we noted that a rise in incomes is causally associated with a betterment in that which is demanded. Talking now not of tastes and preferences but of conduct and character we are compelled to note that a rise in incomes is causally associated as well with an improvement in that which is supplied, with an upgrading in the quality of work and an increasing concern with excellence as an end in its own right on the part of ever more groups and groupings in society: 'The desire for excellence for its own sake, is almost as wide in its range as the lower desire for distinction. Just as the desire for distinction graduates down . . . so the desire for excellence for its own sake graduates down from that of a Newton, or a Stradivarius, to that of the fisherman who, even when no one is looking and he is not in a hurry, delights in handling his craft well.'[76] Nowadays, in short, more excellence is supplied as an end in its own right, just as more excellence is coincidentally also demanded due to betterment of wants: 'It is . . . the desire for the exercise and development of activities, spreading through every rank of society, which leads not only to the pursuit of science, literature and art for their own sake, but to the rapidly increasing demand for the work of those who pursue them as professions.'[77]

Marshall, as we have indicated, was convinced that activities become relatively more important, wants relatively less important, in the course of social evolution, and praised the classical economists (who, after all, made much of the labour theory of value and wrote – like Marshall himself – far more fully about supply than about demand) for having been aware of the fundamental truth that *homo* is essentially *faber*: 'It is important still to assert the great truth on which they dwelt somewhat too exclusively; viz. that while wants are the rulers of life among the lower animals, it is to changes in the forms of efforts and activities that we must turn when in search for the keynotes of the history of mankind.'[78] Put in other words, where the job is not so brutalising, debasing, monotonous and routine as to 'stunt the mental growth, preventing people from rising out of old narrow grooves of thought and feeling',[79] where the job instead offers an outlet for creativity, novelty and 'the vigorous exercise of faculties' ('the main aim of every man' in such a situation[80]), there the worker will take pleasure and pride in performing it well – as we can indeed increasingly see before our very eyes, in an economy in which men increasingly 'delight' in the training and exercise of their faculties:[81] 'Many artisans are becoming artists, who take a proud interest in the glories of their art, are truly citizens, are courteous, gentle, thoughtful, able, and independent men.'[82] As operatives increasingly become gentlemen, so the pursuit of 'mere material wealth' is likely to be 'reduced to its proper, and very small, proportions',[83] and the pursuit of excellence (in the sense of the unfolding of man's active and higher self) is likely to become of ever greater significance. A dimension of social evolution, needless to say, which Marshall, who stated categorically in the *Principles* that 'the most economic use of man as an agent of production is wasteful if he is not himself developed by it',[84] was bound much to welcome and even to identify with the philosopher's *Summum Bonum*:[85] 'There has always been a substratum of agreement that social good lies mainly in that healthful exercise and development of faculties which yields happiness without pall, because it sustains self-respect and is sustained by hope.'[86]

Marshall took the view that 'work, in its best sense, the healthy energetic exercise of faculties, is the aim of life, is life itself',[87] and argued in addition that the chief responsibility of the teacher is to reinforce this process of progressive unfolding: 'The schoolmaster must learn that his main duty is not to impart knowledge, for a few shillings will buy more printed knowledge than a man's brain can hold. It is to educate character, faculties and activities.'[88] If, however, a process of progressive unfolding is genuinely taking place, and if 'the healthy exercise of faculties' is truly nothing less than 'the aim of life', 'life itself', then it is not clear what remains of Marshall's 'real cost' approach to the upward-sloping supply curve, which focuses on compensation for subjective disutility experienced.[89] Parsons concludes that Marshall 'simply did not think through' the implications of what would appear to be an over-determined model – a model in which I work because I am I *and* because I am paid.[90] Pointing out that few observers would treat the bearing and rearing of children *wholly* as a sacrifice ('It is, at the same time, one of those "activities" whose development is the aim of social progress'),[91] Parsons reminds the reader that essentially the same conclusion must be reached, given Marshall's premises, concerning the production of goods and services as that concerning the production of people: 'Any sense of the sordidness of economic acquisition as such is totally absent. Indeed, it can be said that on the whole Marshall saw the field of business enterprise as the principal opportunity for the exercise of what he considered the noblest traits of human character. The wealth acquired in the process was not the aim, but rather a by-product.'[92] I work well because it is in my nature to work well and material change increasingly generates the outlets which I require in my ongoing struggle to pursue excellence through my activity.

Material change contributes in other ways as well to the pursuit of excellence. For one thing, a gentleman polices himself, being fully cognisant of the 'private and public duties of a citizen';[93] his very sense of personal responsibility is a precondition for the successful introduction of advanced technology (since modern machinery is 'too subtle and expensive'[94] to be entrusted to the loutish, the backward and the indolent); and thus the up-skilling and upgrading that are so much a part of economic growth make their own contribution to the betterment of product by virtue of the fact that they make so substantial a contribution to the betterment of self-image. Then there is an important point to be made about the non-pecuniary reward of status in an era of ever-improving communications – the reason why, in large joint stock companies, while corporate bureaucrats on a salary tend *ceteris paribus* to be sleepy and fearful of change, yet 'the modern intercourse of expert officials with one another is bringing into the business world some part of that great progressive force which pure science has long derived from the approbation awarded to successful research by audiences fit though few'.[95] The fact is that 'the motives which induce business men to compete for wealth are not altogether as sordid as the world in general, and I am forced to admit, economists in particular, have been wont to assume',[96] and that many among them value 'high prestige for business ability',[97] and 'a reputation for able leadership'[98] even more than they value monetary payment *per se* – which indeed they treat chiefly as a trophy, as 'evidence of their organizing genius. As arts and sciences flourish best where their followers work for the approval of brethren of the craft, and not for the sake of money: so business flourishes most where the aim of the business man is not to shine in elegant society, but to be held in respect by those who are the best judges of his special form of strength.'[99] The pursuit of excellence in the interest of praise and distinction is, of course, morally inferior to the pursuit of excellence as an end in its own right; but, given competition and our modern modes of publicity, it is nonetheless a significant cause of improved standards of workmanship.

It would be unusual to speak of excellence in economic activity without reference to competition and Marshall, as we have seen, does not do so. Competitive markets by their very nature, Marshall stressed, are highly favourable to betterment of product: 'The action of competition, and the survival in the struggle for existence of those who know best how to extract the greatest benefits for themselves from the environment, tend in the long run to put the building of factories and steam-engines into the hands of those who will be ready and able to incur every expense which will add more than it costs to their value as productive agents.'[100] Nor should the extremely beneficial impact of competition on human character be neglected, as Marshall explained in a letter to John Hilton written not long before his death: 'My notion that it is an essential stimulus for many forms of activity was developed long ago in a racquet court. I found that if my friend – & opponent – came late, I could knock about the balls by myself for some ten minutes without discomfort. But then I got tired; & became lively again when he arrived to compete. I did not care whether he won or I did: I enjoyed the competition; & I think it did me good.'[101] As with competition in sport, so with competition in business; and improvement is the result, the consumer the beneficiary.

(4) Generosity

Marshall believed in the functionality of altruism in the animal kingdom: 'We find that among so-called social animals, such as bees and ants, those races survive in which the individual is most energetic in performing varied services for the society without the prompting of direct gain to himself.'[102] Marshall also took the view that altruism is no less functional among human beings: 'The struggle for existence causes in the long run those races of men to survive in which the individual is most willing to sacrifice himself for the benefit of those around him; and which are consequently the best adapted collectively to make use of their environment.'[103] Generosity, unselfishness, self-sacrifice and a sense of personal responsibility towards others may thus frequently be preached by men of ideals, by priests, prophets, visionaries and politicians; but they are also, it would appear, useful and necessary if the social organism is properly to adapt to the imperatives of its material situation. Individualism rather than patriotism is of little benefit in a war; peacetime challenges such as 'contests with famine and disease'[104] typically require a greater concern for and kindliness towards others than the model of self-interest narrowly-defined would normally incorporate; and it is therefore good to know that man with economic growth is actually becoming less 'sordid or selfish',[105] more open to 'the social possibilities of economic chivalry',[106] than ever before. The alternative, after all, is far from attractive – since, as Fred Hirsch puts it, classical liberalism 'was predicated on an underlying moral-religious base',[107] and without that even private property itself would not be secure from 'the first entrepreneur to be able to raise enough credit to buy the judge'.[108] Robin Matthews has vividly demonstrated the essential instability of a market economy in which individual participants act exclusively on the basis of the self-interested egotism of the *bellum omnium contra omnes* in his example of a primitive society where 'neither competition nor legal redress is an adequate safeguard if your partner in the hunt decides at the critical moment that, all things considered, his utility will be maximized by leaving you to be eaten by the tiger. If you know he is liable to behave in this way, the whole tiger-hunting enterprise will fail to be undertaken, with detriment to Pareto-efficiency.'[109] Robin Matthews would accordingly, one suspects, welcome Marshall's stress on the other-regarding alongside the self-centred orientation in economics, even if he would not in the event go as far as Marshall does in predicting the continuing advance of the former norm relative to the latter.

Marshall's position is that man's progress is unambiguously in the direction of separating the *quid* from the *quo*: 'A higher notion of social duty is spreading everywhere. In Parliament, in the press and in the pulpit, the spirit of humanity speaks more distinctly and more earnestly.'[110] And so it should, for both our knowledge of and our involvement in the condition of others evolves with affluence: 'However wise and virtuous our grandfathers had been, they could not have seen things as we do; for they were hurried along by urgent necessities and terrible disasters.'[111] Clearly, when men are hungry and poor, it is understandable that they will tend to be indifferent and insensitive to the welfare of others (this is presumably the reasoning behind Marshall's anecdotal observation that 'no traders are more unscrupulous in taking advantage of the necessities of the unfortunate than are the corn-dealers and money-lenders of the East',[112] and it is certainly the logic behind Adam Smith's declaration that 'if our misery pinches us very severely, we have no leisure to attend to that of our neighbour',[113] but we today simply cannot legitimately defend selfishness by reference to material distress: 'We must judge ourselves by a severer standard . . . The nation has grown in wealth, in health, in education and in morality; and we are no longer compelled to subordinate almost every consideration to the need of increasing the total produce of industry.'[114]

Nor do we do so. Looking at modern Britain, it is highly significant that 'that country which is the birthplace of modern competition devotes a larger part of its income than any other to charitable uses'[115] (some public, some private), and this growth of an increasingly other-regarding consensus in turn calls into question the validity of the narrower formulations of public choice theory. After all, the Treasury is now becoming demonstrably more concerned than it used to be with mitigating and lessening 'the ignorance, the disease, and the sufferings of the poor'[116] – whereas 'if the present age were as selfish as it is often represented to be, we should find that the chief expenditure of public money for improving the conditions of life and work had accrued to the benefit of those who can enforce their will at the polling-booth'.[117] Again, and writing in 1907 in the shadow of the reforming Liberal Government of Asquith, Marshall noted with apparent satisfaction that 'our age has reversed the old rules that the poor paid a larger percentage of their income in rates and taxes than the well-to-do'.[118] While a sceptic, a cynic or a supporter of the economics-of-politics approach might point out that 'our age' had also seen a dramatic widening of the franchise (and that Marshall's discovery of a 'growing opinion that it is an ignoble use of wealth to leave large fortunes mainly to relations',[119] could well indicate only that many of the have-nots likely to be the greatest beneficiaries of the fiscal free gifts in question were for the first time in a position to vote for them), the fact is that Marshall did not make use of this explanation but rather of a broader, more chivalrous one – one which makes much of our 'delight in succouring those who need a helping hand'[120] and of our 'sympathy with those who are strangers to us' ('a kind of deliberate unselfishness, that never existed before the modern age').[121]

Unselfishness has, of course, long existed within the family (even among, for that matter, the most predatory of species of wild animals, which survive precisely because they are prepared altruistically 'to exert themselves for the benefit of their offspring').[122] The point about modern society, however, is that nowadays 'the ties of family are in many ways stronger than before' and 'the obligations of family kindness become more intense'.[123] Man, being 'more unselfish', is today 'more inclined to work and save in order to secure a future provision for his family';[124] and it is this greater sense of responsibility towards the young (accompanied, naturally, by an upgrading in self-respect, future-orientedness, 'general enlightenment' and 'intelligence, wisdom and forethought')[125] which has increasingly caused parents of all classes (not just of the commercial and professional classes) to make greater financial sacrifices in order via education to promote their sons into a higher estate. Through their willingness to labour and then to abstain from present consumption so as to benefit discrete (if known) others, parents clearly demonstrate a tendency towards benevolence and an ability to separate the *quid* from the *quo*.

Employers too separate the *quid* from the *quo*, as where a businessman deliberately over-pays a half-starved worker (thereby acting *as if* he had a statutory duty to obey a minimum wage law)[126] or consciously over-invests in the formation of fully transferable skills (thereby acting *as if* he had a statutory duty to supply the public good of occupational training despite the fact that in a non-slave society the abilities inculcated 'will be the property of the workman himself: and thus the virtue of those who have aided him must remain for the greater part its own reward'[127]). The duty is not a statutory one, needless to say, but it is a real duty nonetheless, and one which is widely acknowledged, most notably by those efficient entrepreneurs 'who are aiming at leading the race, and whose ambition it is to turn out the best work by the most advanced methods': 'The character that fits them to take the lead in the arts of production is likely also to make them take a generous interest in the wellbeing of those who work for them.'[128] Once upon a time, in the early stages of industrialisation, 'the capitalist employer, untrained to his new duties, was tempted to subordinate the wellbeing of his workpeople to his own desire for gain'.[129] Increasingly, however, we as a community are 'learning the importance of insisting that the rich have duties as well as rights in their individual and in their collective capacity'[130] and we are therefore pleased to discover even now that 'there is much nobility to be found in business'.[131] Obviously, businessmen are still 'comparatively few' who acknowledge the existence of a normative constraint superior to 'that which the traffic will bear', but the future is full of hope in view of the fact that 'the number of such employers is increasing'.[132]

It is bound to increase still further. Commercial chicanery, for one thing, is likely more and more to be eroded by economic chivalry, as Marshall clearly indicates by the conspicuous use of the word 'still' when speaking, in *Industry and Trade*, of the self-interest axiom: 'The present volume is in the main occupied with the influences which *still* make for sectional and class selfishness: with the limited tendencies of self-interest to direct each individual's action on those lines, in which it will be most beneficial to others; and with the *still* surviving tendencies of associated action by capitalists and other business men, as well as by employers, to regulate output, and action generally, by a desire for sectional rather than national advantage.'[133] And again, precisely because 'railway shareholders belong to the class of people most of whom wish to do something practical for the London poor', they may, if made aware of the unhealthy conditions in crowded urban agglomerations, confidently be expected to put pressure on the directors of the railways to operate more trains than would be strictly economic in order to 'enable an ever-increasing number of artisans, and even of unskilled labourers, to take their families out of London occasionally in the summer': 'There is scarcely any other direction in which a very little unselfishness will purchase so much good for others; will cause so much happiness unalloyed by any harm; will do so much to raise the quality of human life.'[134] The railway shareholder does not, it must be emphasized, rank the utility of the London poor so much above his own that he is, like the monk and the martyr, prepared to sacrifice all he has in the pursuit of his ideal. What he does, however, is to recognise that the utility-function of Ego incorporates *to some extent* the utility-function of Alter, and that to make decisions exclusively on the basis of self-interest narrowly-defined is frequently to expose oneself to the comments and criticisms of the Smithian 'man within the breast' – the hypothetical being who, speaking with the voice of conscience, frequently calls to us 'that we value ourselves too much and other people too little, and that, by doing so, we render ourselves the proper object of the contempt and indignation of our brethren'.[135] The railway shareholder, in other words, occupies that middle ground between Gradgrind and Christ which Edgeworth in *Mathematical Psychics*, not unlike Sidgwick in *Methods of Ethics*, describes as follows: 'Between the two extremes Pure Egoistic and Pure Universalistic there may be an indefinite number of impure methods; wherein the happiness of others as compared by the agent (in a calm moment) with his own, neither counts as nothing nor yet 'counts for one', but *counts for a fraction*.'[136] Marshall was in no doubt as to the direction of social change but he would have been deeply distressed if the railway shareholder suddenly deserted the middle ground in favour of total and complete other-directedness of orientation: 'If every one always found his greatest happiness in trying to do that which was best for others, the world would have no theory of Normal values . . . Some such Communism as that which prevailed among the early Christians would be the basis of economic theory. But in this world, as it is, the chief *active* principle in business is the desire of each man to promote the material interests of himself and his family.'[137] Our era is characterised by increasing altruism on the part of business-men, Marshall argued; but he also took the view that there could be too much generosity as well as too little in economic affairs.

Generosity on the part of capital is being matched by generosity on the part of labour, and this development is illustrated by the important fact that many unions nowadays deliberately make a free gift to future cohorts in the same trade by refusing to hold out for a wage so high that the employer will one day have no alternative but to substitute machines for men.[138] Individual workers too, one would hope, will come increasingly to develop responsible attitudes with respect to the spillovers, the externalities, the social costs, the neighbourhood effects that are involved in the course of action which they select for themselves. There are, for example, 'a few narrow occupations in which blind people can earn in full self-respect a moderate living: if people whose eyesight gives them a larger choice moved into these occupations, the harm done to the blind would outweigh socially any slight gain that consumers might get from the cheapening of the products of those occupations.'[139] The sighted worker knows that he can earn more in occupation *A* than in occupation *B*. He also knows that the blind worker can earn nothing in occupation *B* and something in occupation *A*. Microeconomics pushes him in one direction, ethics in another, but Marshall was in no doubt that moral sentiments and sympathy would ultimately speak louder than invisible hands and greed – even where the actual outcome turns out in the last analysis to be economically sub-optimal when seen from the narrow perspective of allocation and growth.

All in all, therefore, the conclusion must be reached that economic altruism is a force of growing relevance both for the economy and for economics:

> Economics has a great and an increasing concern in motives connected with the collective ownership of property, and the collective pursuit of important aims. The growing earnestness of the age, the growing intelligence of the mass of the people, and the growing power of the telegraph, the press, and other means of communication are ever widening the scope of collective action for the public good; and these changes, together with the spread of the co-operative movement, and other kinds of voluntary association are growing up under the influence of various motives besides that of pecuniary gain.[140]

Clearly, 'voluntary committees',[141] charities and similar philanthropic organisations may reasonably be regarded as indicators of progress on the road to altruism, just as the co-operative form may be taken as a welcome instance of collective self-help (it is not for nothing that Marshall described as 'brilliant' Kropotkin's book on *Mutual Aid*[142]); and, indeed, 'there are already faint signs of a brighter time to come, in which there will be a general willingness to work and save in order to increase the stores of public wealth and of public opportunities for leading a higher life'.[143]

Such a collective orientation is fully legitimate, for (unlike the compulsory collectivism of former times and less advanced cultures, which is imposed via the straightjacket of tradition and the threat of external sanctions) our modern orientation of each *to some extent* to all is in every sense the product of free individual action and conscious rational choice. It is for that reason also genuinely moral, since it presupposes the pre-existence not of pre-programmed social automatons but rather of thinking human beings, creatures alone 'endowed with reason and speech'[144] and capable of intelligently weighing alternatives at margins without sinking into the conventional morass of reacting without reflecting. Sociability and other-orientatedness are in such an environment deliberately selected, and genetics comes to the aid of affluence in making the process cumulative; for factual evidence suggests 'that those races, whose members render services to one another without exacting direct recompense, are not only the most likely to flourish for the time but most likely to rear a large number of descendants who inherit their beneficial habits'.[145] Since Marshall elsewhere states that the efficient are *ceteris paribus* more likely to limit births than are the poor and the feckless,[146] it is not clear precisely what weight should be assigned to this factual evidence concerning the upgrading that is born of selecting the right parents, but it does enable him to make very decisive predictions with respect to that future state of things when generosity will ultimately have come to outweigh interest. Then 'private property, the necessity for which doubtless reaches no deeper than the qualities of human nature, would become harmless at the same time that it became unnecessary',[147] and what we would be left with is a society, purified of lust for cash and fear of the constable, with 'no rights but only duties; where everyone shall work for the public weal with all his might, expecting no further reward than he in common with his neighbours shall have whatever is necessary to enable him to work well, and to lead a refined and intellectual life'.[148]

Religion reinforces this trend; and Marshall, however lapsed a Christian as anti-Christian'[150]). More significantly, however, Marshall Knight's observation that 'if there is anything on which divergent interpretations would have to agree, it would be the admission that the Christian conception of goodness is the antithesis of competitive'[149] (even if, arguably, moderately less sympathy with Tawney's declaration that the capitalist system itself is 'not so much un-Christian as anti-Christian'[150]). More significantly, however, Marshall took the view that religious ideals themselves are 'raised and purified'[151] by our present-day process of economic growth and social betterment. A rich country, after all, both depends upon and improves the 'health and strength' of its citizens – physical, mental, but also moral, as is the case with 'force of will, and strength of character'.[152] This trend upwards in the momentum inherent in matter is thus much to be welcomed by the believer in religious values (doubly so, of course, if he is also a scarcity-economist whose trough runneth under): 'This strength of the man himself, this resolution, energy and self-mastery, or in short this "vigour" is the source of all progress: it shows itself in great deeds, in great thoughts and in the capacity for true religious feeling.'[153] It is also worth making the point that it is infinitely easier to love one's neighbour as oneself, to offer him the milk of human kindness in an attempt to assuage his plight, if there is enough of a family resemblance to convince both parties that each was genuinely created in God's image; and in that sense the greater cultural convergence, the greater respect for persons, which are inescapably associated with economic growth acquire a dimension that is sacred alongside that which is secular.

Let us conclude our discussion of generosity by saying that

Marshall, who like Hirsch believed strongly in the functionality of altruism, took the view that competitive, acquisitive capitalism was to be congratulated for having increasingly generated precisely those non-competitive, non-acquisitive background values which are in the event essential for the viability and even the survival of the market-exchange system. Marshall stressed at all times that 'ethical forces are among those of which the economist has to take account'[154] and expressed his satisfaction that moral upgrading accompanies economic growth. This is not to suggest that there is no longer any room for improvement: 'No doubt men, even now, are capable of much more unselfish service than they generally render: and the supreme aim of the economist is to discover how this latent social asset can be developed most quickly, and turned to account most wisely.'[155] Room for improvement there may still be, but even the most dismal of philosophers would have to concede, Marshall was convinced, that a remarkable amount of improvement has already taken place.

(5) Deliberateness

Marshall believed that men increasingly adopt an economising posture when selecting means with a view to the attainment of ends, and not just in economic affairs: 'There is a sense in which it may be argued that business operations are merely one drift of a tendency to adapt means to ends, which is universal throughout all forms of life.'[156] Marshall went so far as to say that 'it is deliberateness, and not selfishness, that is the characteristic of the modern age'.[157]

Deliberateness to Marshall means being able rationally to formulate a plan of campaign and then having the moral fibre and strength of purpose required to carry that plan through to a successful conclusion. It implies, in other words, two separate and discrete stages. Initially there is deliberateness at the level of projection, which involves those quasi-aesthetic sensibilities which thinkers from Plato to Adam Smith had identified with maximal suitability and of which Marshall spoke as follows in a lecture delivered in 1877: 'I do not suppose, I do not hope, that we shall ever cease to be a nation of manufacturers and merchants, of artisans and shopkeepers: but I do hope and think that we may become a nation of artists, of men who glory in their work, because it is the best work that their heads and hands can do; because they have tried to make it satisfy their notions of fitness and adaptation to its purpose, of grace and beauty better than anything of its kind that has gone before.'[158] Subsequently there is deliberateness at the level of execution, which involves 'the firm will, the iron resolution, the absorption in definite serious aims of the mature man' which are greatly to be admired in the Romans: 'They shaped their own lives for themselves with a deliberate choice that had never been known before. They were strong and daring, steady of purpose and abundant in resource, orderly in habit, and clearsighted in judgement; and thus, though they preferred war and politics, they had in constant use all the faculties required for business enterprise.'[159]

Deliberateness, needless to say, is not a quality which we would expect from a poor, benighted savage: 'Whatever be their climate and whatever their ancestry, we find savages living under the dominion of custom and impulse; scarcely ever striking out new lines for themselves; never forecasting the distant future, and seldom making provision even for the near future; fitful in spite of their servitude to custom, governed by the fancy of the moment; ready at times for the most arduous exertions, but incapable of keeping themselves long to steady work.'[160] Nor, for that matter would we expect it from an under-developed Irish smallholder: 'The Irish Cottier is a poor and uneducated peasant who rents a small plot of land either directly from its owner or from a middleman, who makes a living by subletting land. He has not the English habits of foresight and self-control; and a great injury was done him when free competition and free contract for the hire of land were forced upon him. They were excellent things in themselves: but he was *not ready* for them. He recklessly offered rents that it was not possible for him to pay, and thus put himself at the mercy of the landowner, or more often the middleman from whom he rented his plot.'[161] The Irish smallholder, like the benighted savage, is not a hopeless case in himself, but the fact is that he is *as yet* unschooled and inexperienced in the exercise of deliberateness and cannot therefore be expected to display the same virtuosity with respect to 'commercial habits'[162] that one looks for – and finds – in the more advanced modern Englishman, the product of generations of learning by doing in economic and social conditions ever more favourable to industry and trade.

The modern Englishman, for one thing, is increasingly free of that oppressive 'yoke of custom'[163] which ridicules and punishes as an enemy any bold spirit who, substituting creativity for conformity, 'should set himself up to be wiser than his ancestors':[164] 'Every designer in a primitive age is governed by precedent: only very daring people depart from it.'[165] Nowadays, however, 'we change our customs more quickly than our forefathers did';[166] 'everyone feels free to make a new departure';[167] and this means greater opportunities for innovation, initiative and originality than would exist in a more stagnant and culturally self-reproducing society. In that sense, therefore, the changefulness that is characteristic of modern Britain is to be welcomed precisely because it is changefulness: 'A perfect adjustment is inconceivable. Perhaps even it is undesirable. For after all man is the end of production; and perfectly stable business would be likely to produce men who were little better than machines.'[168] Stationary smacks of somnolence and somnolence was anathema to a dynamic thinker who advocated change precisely because change smacks of challenge – at least in the free enterprise system of the market economy, where men have the way as well as the will to make the most of that challenge. Such an opportunity for moral education is denied them in the rigidly-traditionalised conditions of a savage society (which is therefore backward morally as well as materially) and the same 'sterilizing influence on those mental activities which have gradually raised the world from barbarism'[169] is to be found in those contemporary schemes which involve extensive State direction and intervention: 'I am convinced that, so soon as collectivist control has spread so far as to narrow considerably the field left for free enterprise, the pressure of bureaucratic methods would impair not only the springs of material wealth, but also many of those higher qualities of human nature, the strengthening of which should be the chief aim of social endeavour.'[170] The same threat to freedom and enterprise can, of course, arise in the private sector as well, as in the case of giant corporations with their inflexible organisational charts or, for that matter, trades unions which make unscrupulous use of restrictive practices in order to frustrate the attempts of an able man to better his condition by entering a new grade or trade: 'Under the pretext of repressing anti-social competition, they deprive him of the liberty of carving out for himself a new career.'[171] In so doing they deprive society of the cheapened comforts which would presumably have been the fruits of a more competitive economy; and they also deprive society of that improved stock of character-patterns which would have almost certainly accrued to it had competitive conditions been permitted to widen men's horizons and inculcate in them a desirable firmness, elasticity, 'energy and strength of character'[172] which then becomes for the rest of the community an external economy and a public good. Activities as well as wants evidently speak loudly in favour of policies designed to favour and foster changefulness and challenge – a not unimportant illustration of the proposition that 'human will, guided by careful thought, can so modify circumstances as largely to modify character'.[173] That having been said, however, a very great deal of changefulness and challenge now exists in modern Britain, and has contributed a very great deal to the development of deliberateness.

The modern Englishman, increasingly free of the yoke of custom, is also increasingly aware that the doors are open to merit, and the presence of hope, like the absence of other-directedness, is a further stimulus to purposive action: 'For the future, as for the past, the chief lever of all is hope, hope for a man's self and hope for those dear to him.'[174] The frustration of the slave breeds melancholy, melancholy saps vigour and is 'as wasteful as disease',[175] and the breaking of the mould of caste and class thus upgrades both the individual's character and in consequence his nation's economy via 'the energizing influence of hope':[176] 'Freedom and hope increase not only man's willingness but also his power for work.'[177] In a more fluid economy with increased equality of opportunity, each man of genuine talent and/or exceptional assiduity can realistically aspire to upward social mobility; and the perceived fact that the cream increasingly rises to the top in itself helps to breed and form the desirable quality of deliberateness. Nor should we neglect the beneficial impact on character of geographical alongside occupational mobility, both internal (e.g. from the provinces to London) and international (e.g. from the metropolitan countries to new colonies): 'A shifting of places enables the more powerful and original minds to find full scope for their energies and to rise to important positions',[178] and that is why (together with the fact that it tends to be the more adventurous and the more enterprising who have the imagination to hope for something better and the courage and the fortitude to act on that dream) it is so frequently the case that 'a disproportionately large share of the best energy and enterprise is to be found among those who were born elsewhere'.[179] Evidently security – although security of person and property is, of course, a precondition for freedom and growth alike – must not be so great as to stifle hope and change: 'Changes of work, of scene, and of personal associations bring new thoughts, call attention to the imperfection of old methods, stimulate a "divine discontent", and in every way develop creative energy.'[180]

The modern Englishman, moreover, is in a strong position to

manifest deliberateness at the levels of perception and execution for the important reason that his nation has a long history of progress with respect to the development of institutions favourable to calculative rationality. Even in the Middle Ages, Marshall recorded, it was England which 'took the lead in converting labour dues into money payments, a course which must (have) increased the power of everyone to steer his course in life according to his own free choice.'[181] The precise explanation which he gives for these important strides is, as it happens, such as would seem to make the English experience with voluntary contracts, monetary valuation and market exchanges more a series of fortunate but fortuitous once-for-alls than a general theory of historical evolution – the particular 'qualities' of the English national character *ante* as well as *post* the wealth of nations ('The strength of character which in later times made England the leader of manufacturing progress, showed itself at first chiefly in politics, in war, and in agriculture'; and even the English *archer*, it would appear, had 'indomitable perseverence', 'free independence', 'self-control' and 'discipline');[182] the Black Death (when rural depopulation led to rising wages and thereby undermined custom); the emergence of centralised royal power under the Tudors (which increased internal security).[183] Selective and anecdotal his account of the rise of calculative rationality may be but the fact remains that the requisite institutions did develop.

The modern Englishman, finally, is not ashamed to demonstrate imaginativeness accompanied by self-mastery since there exists in his country a high social valuation of deliberateness. The ancient Greeks tended to show a definite lack of sympathy with 'the anxious cares and plodding work of business';[184] the ancient Romans went further and showed 'public disdain';[185] and no sensitive man would wish to get involved in an activity which would cost him the respect of others and perhaps even his own self-respect as well. Low status can also mean low efficiency as when, in the Middle Ages, workers, 'even when permitted to manage their own local affairs', were consistently stigmatised as lowly and second-rate – and in consequence thereof 'were often wanting in the courage, the self-reliance, and the habits of mental activity, which are required as the basis of business enterprise'.[186] We are, in modern Britain – unlike the Greeks, the Romans and the 'social superiors'[187] who dictated trends and values in the Middle Ages – far more appreciative of our business men. More generally, we tend to reward with approbation all those, whether businessmen or not, who show deliberateness in their way of life; and this is yet another reason for believing that we are making progress 'towards the distant goal of ideally perfect social organisation'.[188]

2.3 CHANGE - THE NEGATIVE SIDE

Alfred Marshall was an optimist who believed that organic growth and evolutionary change meant material and moral improvement: 'In every age of the world people have delighted in piquant stories, which tell of some local or partial retrogression; but, if we look at the broad facts of history, we find progress.'[1] At the same time, however, he was aware of the darker side of the growing and changing economy; and he saw that even a seamless web is not always entirely free from moths, tears and wrinkles which no invisible hand is prepared to iron out.

In some cases Marshall's views on the social costs of economic growth must be inferred from casual and often tantalising asides (as where, for example, Marshall, reflecting that it is those classes least able to adapt which would seem to be most prone to breed, comments that 'progress may be hastened . . . by the application of the principles of Eugenics to the replenishment of the race from its higher rather than its lower strains'[2]). In other cases the less pleasant features of our historical highway are treated to explicit and occasionally even detailed analysis. Four aspects of negative human betterment appear in particular to have caused Marshall a moderate amount of concern.

(1) Want-satisfaction

Marshall did not advise that we should adopt the Buddhist objective of serenity or predict that we would one day gravitate to the Stoic ideal of *stasis*. What he did do was to express the value judgement that commodities should be aesthetic in nature, morally and/or materially improving, and untainted by the 'personal vanity' and the 'envy' that inevitably stain and spoil the enjoyment of the status symbol in the zero-sum game. Thus, he said, 'so long as wealth is applied to provide for every family the necessaries of life and culture, and an abundance of the higher forms of enjoyment for collective use, so long the pursuit of wealth is a noble aim; and the pleasures which it brings are likely to increase with the growth of those higher activities which it is used to promote'.[3] If, however, he warned, 'instead of seeking for a higher standard of beauty, we spend our growing resources on increasing the complexity and intricacy of our domestic goods, we gain thereby no true benefit, no lasting happiness'.[4] Marshall's point is that 'true' benefit and 'lasting' happiness (what *I* think you *need*, in other words, as opposed to what *you* think you *want*) are linked to the composition of output and not exclusively to aggregate stock[5] – and that is why his acknowledgement that there exist even in an affluent society men who are little more than 'dandyfied perambulating machines, for the display of the cheaper triumphs of the haberdasher and the tailor'[6] must inevitably raise the question of whether the withering away of the perversions of poverty (including the 'morbid development of the taste for drink'[7]) might not be counterbalanced by the flowering of the perversions of plenty (including those luxuries and frivolities to which Marshall is referring when he speaks of 'those forms of expenditure which serve no high purpose'[8]).

That the danger exists that richer men might not after all consume better things is not to be denied. Marshall branded as an unambiguous 'misuse' of affluence the 'tendency among commercial nations to think too much of wealth and to use it for the purposes of display'[9] and he showed particular anxiety concerning the ephemeral fads and transient fashions of which he believed the dominion to be on the increase: 'The rule of fashion is spreading, till it will soon have little ground left to conquer. Neighbours are becoming strangers to one another as persons: but in matters of etiquette, even country-folk look to the arbitrament of the larger world, and in matters of costume they now learn quickly what passes there.'[10] Nowadays, with the spread of literacy and the mass media, 'newspaper dealers in working-class districts, find that a very large portion of their business is in cheap fashion journals',[11] and the cause of this expanded popular interest is something far more tangible than idle curiosity and the vicarious thrill: 'Until a little while ago it was only the rich who could change their clothing at the capricious order of their dressmakers. But now all classes do it.'[12] This development is much to be regretted. If a thing is beautiful there is no reason for it rapidly to be scrapped, if a thing is ugly there is no reason for it ever to be adopted, and one is bound therefore to conclude that 'everyone who changes the material of her dress simply at the bid of fashion, sins against the spirit of art'.[13] Besides that, rapid changes in fashion involve wastage of resources, partly because durable objects are discarded before their physical serviceability is at an end, partly because the pursuit of excellence is seldom compatible with the premium on speed which is an essential part of the trend-setting process: 'In every such movement there is much exercise of skill and taste of a high order: but since everything is done hastily, the effects are generally cruder than those which people of a lower mental quality would have evolved by the patient method of ancient custom.'[14] Nor should the social waste involved in excessive advertising and salesmanship be neglected, so important is the fact that those who control changes in fashion 'have always a general interest in causing anyone, who wishes not to be out of fashion, to discard the costumes of last season'.[15] Much of the appeal of the persuaders, needless to say, will be to conspicuous consumption, base ostentation and 'the large opportunities for display of wealth and of alertness by those who discard the declining fashion most promptly and completely';[16] and such an appeal cannot but reinforce the present-day development of 'that unwholesome desire for wealth as a means of display'[17] which Marshall evidently contemplated with considerable reservations.

Marshall did not believe that advertising and salesmanship were likely to lead to large-scale bamboozlement or to the total replacement of consumer by producer sovereignty. It would be wrong to assert, however, that he regarded the sales effort as having no impact whatsoever on the nature of the wants that cry out to be satisfied, or that he was entirely happy with marketing strategies that (going beyond the mere provision of essential information) seek to influence desires by means other than an honest appeal to calculative rationality. The following passage shows that Marshall (to whom, it must be remembered, product differentiation and therefore the search for intelligence were variables of the greatest significance[18]) was fully aware of considerations such as these:

> The combative force of mere capital obtrudes itself in the incessant iteration of the name of a product, coupled perhaps with a claim that it is of excellent quality. Of course no amount of expenditure on advertising will enable any thing, which the customers can fairly test for themselves by experience (this condition excludes medicines which claim to be appropriate to subtle diseases, etc.), to get a permanent hold on the people, unless it is fairly good relatively to its price. The chief influence of such advertisement is exerted, not through the reason, but through the blind force of habit: people in

general are, for good and for ill, inclined to prefer that which is familiar to that which is not.[19]

Such lavish advertising is not constructive and must therefore be treated, together with other, similar activities in the field of marketing, as a clear case of 'social waste': 'A great part of marketing consists of bargaining, of manoeuvring to get others to buy at a high price and sell at a low price, to obtain special concessions or to force a trade by offering them. This is, from the social point of view, almost pure waste; it is that part of trade as to which Aristotle's dictum is most nearly true, that no one can gain except at the loss of another . . . It is the only part of honest trade competition that is entirely devoid of any enobling or elevating feature.'[20] Such lavish advertising can indeed be positively destructive, since a further 'element of social waste, caused by bold displayed advertisements' is inevitably 'the relative obscurity into which they are designed to throw, and do throw, the smaller advertisements of less wealthy men; some of whom may have high constructive faculty'.[21] In the limiting case, therefore, advertising and salesmanship might successfully persuade me, *via* 'incessant iteration', to buy a second-rate brand of typewriter made and marketed by a large firm while simultaneously causing me to neglect the first-rate alternative produced but poorly publicised by its smaller competitor; and to the extent that I fall victim to this form of social waste, the consequent loss in welfare is hardly a strong argument for human betterment.

Marshall offers little comfort to the social critic who is concerned about the wasteful nature of advertising and salesmanship. Rather the opposite, in fact, as when, increasingly concerned about economies of large size and increasingly sceptical about the rise-and-fall theory in a world of corporations which stagnate but do not die, he observed late in life that 'in the present age the tasks of marketing offer ever increasing scope for vast aggregations of capital'.[22] With regard to the abominations of affluence that are represented by fashion, display of wealth and conspicuous consumption, however, he was able to provide much reassurance. For one thing, the 'dandyfied perambulating machines' turn out to be 'few'[23] in number (and, one would guess, will be fewer still in a one-class society of educated gentlemen where the cultural change associated with being *nouveaux riches* becomes that much less drastic and dramatic). And there is the power of public opinion: 'Laws against luxury have been futile; but it would be a gain if the moral sentiment of the community could induce people to avoid all sorts of display of individual wealth.'[24] Such social pressures have considerable potential for good as they can play an important part in helping to bring about an economic environment in which spending-patterns would come to reflect 'chivalry in using wealth': 'Expenditure for the sake of display, however disguised by an aesthetic atmosphere, would be thought vulgar. He who devoted his energies to buying good pictures, especially by artists not yet known to fame, and gave them to the public at his death, if not before, would have reaped a good return from his wealth.'[25] For public opinion to work such wonders, of course, two conditions must be satisfied. First, the 'moral sentiment' of the community must genuinely rank poetry over pushpin, laud good things and stigmatise bad ones; since while consensus can hypothetically be corrective of an aberrant minority (the case which Marshall presumably has in mind when he says 'gradually, it may be hoped, public opinion may be worked up to the point at which a rich man who lives idly will be despised'[26]), there is no way by definition that it can be corrective of itself (the case where public opinion favours gin, despises tea, and thereby reinforces popular preference-patterns which Marshall himself would stubbornly have refused to recognise as compatible with evolution and progress). Second, peer-group pressures and collective constraint (the informal sanctions of approbation and disapprobation which Marshall regarded as eminently effective in normal circumstances) must be operative; and Marshall did acknowledge in a not unimportant footnote the erosion of mutual moral support that could result from geographical mobility and the anonymity of the new (presumably urban) environment. There he reflects (much, one is bound to say, in the spirit of *natura non facit saltum*) that 'change may be carried to excess; and when population shifts so rapidly, that a man is always shaking himself loose from his reputation, he loses some of the best external aids to the formation of a high moral character'.[27] This footnote seems to echo impressions which Marshall had formed in America – a 'restless' society – in 1875 and which he described as follows to the Cambridge Moral Science Club upon his return:

> The instability of the conditions of industrial life in America affects the development of moral character in some ways not only indirectly but also directly. Money is a more portable commodity than a high moral reputation. The doctrine that honesty is the best policy is at a disadvantage when it submits itself to the judgement

of a man whose associates would continually be changing even if he were stationary; who knows that if he makes money but loses his reputation, he can pack up his money and make it help him to earn a new reputation amid new surroundings, but that if he starts by building up a good reputation it is not unlikely that he may want to migrate into a new career to which but little of his reputation will follow him. It cannot, I think, be denied that a short-sighted man is thus exposed to great temptations in America.[28]

But *anomie* or the breakdown of normative constraint in a mobile society is not on balance a major concern with Marshall; and, to return to 'the display of individual wealth', Marshall was normally confident that the power of public opinion would be sufficient to stem this potential danger.

There is a final point which must be mentioned if our discussion of Marshall's views on the negative side of change with particular reference to want-satisfaction is to be complete, and that involves the Malthusian spectre of physical limits of growth. At present, Marshall declared with some relief in 1907, the problem seems to be in abeyance: owing to improvements in international transportation and agricultural technology, 'wages in Britain are now but very little affected by the rate of growth of population and the pressure on the means of subsistence'.[29] The prospects for the future, however, are somewhat less rosy and somewhat more Ricardian: 'The world is really a very small place, and there is not room in it for the opening up of rich new resources during many decades at as rapid a rate as has prevailed during the last three or four. When new countries begin to need most of their own food and other raw produce, improvements in transport will count for little. From that time onward the pressure of the Law of Diminishing Return can be opposed only by further improvements in production; and improvements in production must themselves gradually show a diminishing return.'[30] Marshall, like Malthus and Ricardo, was concerned about the eventual diminution of returns to the fixed factor of land (the quantity of which cannot be much altered even in the long-run when seen from the perspective of the world as a whole); but his examples in the event extend beyond agriculture and fisheries[31] to embrace resource depletion in other areas of 'nature's storehouse' as well.[32] The most notable among these areas, and despite the fact that Marshall did not share the extreme anxiety concerning early exhaustion that had been demonstrated by Jevons in *The Coal Question*, involved the national stock of non-replaceable fossil fuel. Marshall was aware that economic progress was likely to generate new sources of energy which could well prove close substitutes for existing ones (tidal and solar energy are two examples which he cites[33]) but in spite of that he took the view that, because of finite supplies in the ground and diminishing returns in the mines, Britain could simply not afford to export any of her scarce coal: 'The position which Britain will hold in the world some centuries hence will depend largely on the care with which she has husbanded her stores of it: any generation which exports it, in order to pay for those manufactures in the production of which Britain should hold her own, will inflict an injury on coming generations.'[34] Marshall could have recommended that we as a nation economise on our scarce supplies of natural resources by means of voluntary limitation of our birth-rate, our growth rate, or both. It is a matter of record that, at least with respect to his own country, he made no such recommendation. There is accordingly no guarantee in his system that physical limits to growth will not, at some unspecified date in our national future, constitute a major stumbling-block in our on-going march towards want-satisfation.

(2) The family

Marshall felt sadly compelled in extreme old age to admit that, despite the general atmosphere of social progress, yet the family was at risk. The problem was first and foremost that more and more women were coming to neglect their domestic duties and were even developing a 'selfish desire . . . to resemble men'.[35] Writing to a friend at the time of the Suffragettes, he reflected that 'an optimistic tone . . . fills my voice more and more as I grow old . . . in nearly all matters *except* the relations of family life under the influence of aggressive womanhood'.[36]

Woman's place, Marshall believed, was by and large in the home, and her primary economic function was to constitute a part of the social infrastructure (analogous, perhaps, to roads and schools) which is so essential if the economic functions of others are to be properly performed. Part of the cost of production of a man's labour is undeniably 'the service which women render as mothers, as wives and as sisters';[37] and in that sense women's work ought correctly to be understood as an input in the formation of an input.

Men depend on 'the women who are fitted to make their homes

happy, and to bring up their children vigorous in body and mind, truthful and cleanly, gentle and brave'[38] – and women for their part should not underestimate the importance of feminine work of this nature. A man returning exhausted from work looks forward to 'a tranquil and restful evening in a healthy and happy home'[39] such as both grants him utility of the highest order and restores his productive energies for the next bout in the arena of life. A woman would accordingly be ill-advised to deprive him of both the consumption and the investment benefit by getting involved in 'masculine work': she would in that way 'destroy that balance and mutual supplementary adaptation of masculine and feminine character, which enabled a man to secure rest and repose by marriage; though he might have probably been worried beyond endurance by the lifelong incessant companionship of another man'.[40]

Then there are the children: 'The elevation of the ideals of life ... is due on the one side to political and economic causes, and on the other to personal and religious influences; among which the influence of the mother in early childhood is supreme.'[41] More important than any other single influence, Marshall seems to have believed, 'the character of a nation depends chiefly on that of the mothers of the nation – on their firmness and gentleness and sincerity. It is in childhood, and at home, that the workman must learn to be truthful and trusty, cleanly and careful, energetic and thorough, to reverence others and to respect himself.'[42] It would evidently be difficult to praise motherhood too highly. As Marshall put it in 1883: 'Man is the perfection of nature, but woman is one step further still. Progress in general and the abolition of poverty depend above all things on the strength and gentleness and purity and earnestness of the women of England. It is they that form character when it is most plastic. If the mothers of a nation are ignoble that nation must fall; if they are noble it must rise.'[43] And that being the case, there are strong grounds for saying that women ought at the very least to avoid rough and brutalising toil: 'If we compare one country of the civilized world with another, or one part of England with another, or one trade in England with another, we find that the degradation of the working-classes varies almost uniformly with the amount of rough work done by women. The most valuable of all capital is that invested in human beings; and of that capital the most precious part is the result of the care and influence of the mother, so long as she retains her tender and unselfish instincts, and has not been hardened by the strain and stress of unfeminine work.'[44] Mechanisation and occupational upgrading will do something to alleviate the burden of toil *per se* but they are powerless to deal with the more fundamental problem that a women who is at work is a woman who is not with her children: 'If the mother were not working for wages, she would be doing work at home that would promote the health, and the moral, if not the intellectual education of her children. While she is earning wages, some of this work will be neglected, and she will have to spend part of her wages on hiring others to do the rest of it.'[45] The reference to 'hiring others' reminds us that Marshall was aware of the *economic* significance of the unpaid labour of the housewife and took the view that some imputed measure of its value ought in strict logic to be included in any statistical estimation of the national product: 'There is . . . some inconsistency in omitting the heavy domestic work which is done by women and other members of the household, where no servants are kept.'[46] Far more significant than the reference to a net benefit inferior to the gross benefit due to the need to hire and remunerate surrogates is, however, the admission that even then some of the mother's domestic tasks 'will be neglected' if delegated to representatives and mercenaries. Such neglect is the reason why, despite higher wages and better hospitals, infant mortality is not, as one would have expected, generally lower in the towns than in the countryside. On the contrary, 'it is generally higher, especially where there are many mothers who neglect their family duties in order to earn money wages'.[47] To paraphrase an observation once made by Kenneth Boulding, would you in these circumstances want your son to marry an economic woman?

Wages for women are rising, and this is 'a great gain in so far as it tends to develop their faculties; but an injury in so far as it tempts them to neglect their duty of building up a true home, and of investing their efforts in the personal capital of their children's character and abilities'.[48] Evidently, there is at work here both an income and a substitution effect, in the sense that higher wages overall both make the second income that much less necessary and the opportunity cost of not-working that much higher. Cross-sectional data at the present time would seem to suggest that, the further we proceed up the income scale, the greater is the probability that the mother will be 'able to give more of her time to the care of her family';[49] but the concern which Marshall expresses with regard to women's present-day desires to win liberation from the home is itself a significant reminder that *what is* cannot always be taken as an infallible guide to *what will be*. Whether or not women will elect to perpetuate the evils of the eighteenth century (when the sudden upsurge of economic activity *de facto* 'unfitted mothers for their duties'[50]) or whether they will, more sensibly, put their 'maternal and . . . household duties' before the attractions of the wage packet,[51] is uncertain; but Marshall's advice to an enlightened age is clear enough.

Marshall is in favour of women's liberation from work outside the home but he in no way wants women to be emancipated from productive activity – for women as for men 'the aim of life', 'life itself'.[52] What he does want to do is to narrow the range of jobs undertaken by women to those specifically related to family affairs; but within the limits of that domain he is only too pleased that women should seek to 'develop their faculties' as such betterment would represent a 'great gain' to domestic and thence to national husbandry. Marshall seems to have regarded the jobs done by the housewife as by no means simple ones, and perhaps here once again we are confronted with an instance of character in a system of division of labour being upgraded by (and subsequently upgrading) the productive function. He certainly seems to have had considerable admiration for those expert housewives who consistently made the most of their calculative rationality when it came to making the most of a limited budget: 'Much depends on the proper preparation of food; and a skilled housewife with ten shillings a week to spend on food will often do more for the health and strength of her family than an unskilled one with twenty. The great mortality of infants among the poor is largely due to the want of care and judgement in preparing their food; and those who do not entirely succumb to this want of motherly care often grow up with enfeebled constitutions.'[53] What matters in such cases, Marshall is stressing, is not simply the aggregate *quantum* of resources at the family's disposal but also the extent to which genuinely constructive use is made of such scarce resources as it has – as is illustrated by the enviable position of the Frenchman: 'His income is generally smaller than that of the Englishman; but his wife is an economical manager, and turns inexpensive food to good account.'[54] Our women are obviously letting the side down. Given that 'the power of rightly using such income and opportunities, as a family has, is in itself wealth of the highest order, and of a kind that is rare in all classes',[55] there is a powerful premium on good wifebandry, and that in turn points in the direction of organised instruction in the principles of home economics: 'Something like the whole imperial revenues, say 100 millions a year, might be saved if a sufficient number of able women went about the country and induced the other women to manage their households as they themselves did.'[56] The powerful premium on good wifebandry, it must be added, certainly does not point in the direction of such frills as Cambridge degrees for women.

The family is important for the well-being of the man, the child, and presumably also the woman; and not least because of the character-traits which it demands and supplies. It is, after all, in essence a consumer co-operative which has the beneficent function of reviving 'the old collective tendencies' that went seriously into eclipse in the earlier stages of modern individualism.[57] Family affections are as 'pure a form of altruism' as we are likely to find in contemporary conditions,[58] and it is encouraging to note that even if the ties of neighbourhood and extended family are weaker now than in primitive society, the ties of the nuclear family are actually stronger: 'In a modern society the obligations of family kindness become more intense . . . Family affection leads to much more self-sacrifice and devotion than it used to do.'[59] All in all, it would be no exaggeration but simply the re-statement of a very great truth to describe the affections of the family as 'the richest and fullest of earthly feelings': 'Perhaps there never has been before any material texture at once so strong and so fine, with which to build up a noble fabric of social life.'[60] Women should accordingly remember that it is their duty to rock the cradle, not the boat.

A child needs his father as well as his mother, however, and men should keep their own responsibilities in mind: 'Able workers and good citizens are not likely to come from homes, from which the mother is absent during a great part of the day; or from homes, to which the father seldom returns till his children are asleep.'[61] Clearly, society as a whole, insofar as it is actively committed to the family as a unit, must also take an interest in the 'curtailment of extravagantly long hours of duty away from home':[62] 'The coming generation is interested in the rescue of men, and still more in that of women, from excessive work.'[63] Mechanisation and upgrading of tasks, of course, are likely to mean in any case that men less and less return home too exhausted to enjoy the pleasures of family life; and higher pay at the very least makes possible (even if, in Marshall's formulation, not inevitable) the institution of shorter working days than would otherwise have been the norm. Economic evolution itself, in brief, would appear to make a significant contribution to the emergence of a situation where the father has more energy, more time and more money to devote to his family; and this suggests that he is not a prime threat to its health and strength.

That having been said, there is one aspect of economic evolution which must almost without exception have negative implications for family life, and that is the process of change *per se*. Marshall does not say a great deal about this problem. He was, however, fully aware of its existence, and pointed with some concern to 'those social discords that arise, when the skill of middle-aged and elderly men is rendered almost valueless by improved methods'.[64] Change means that rapid adaptability come to be more highly valued than long experience, a development which tends *ceteris paribus* to favour the young. Besides that, a changing economy is normally one in which customary entry-barriers are breaking down (allowing children and even women access to trades formerly closed to them). Nor should the upgrading impact of education and training be neglected. All of these factors cause the pay of young people (and of women) to rise not only absolutely but also relative to that of men – which in turn enables 'boys, and even girls, to set their parents at defiance and start in life on their own account'.[65] Marshall did not approve of children setting their parents 'at defiance' and certainly he would have – had he been asked to give a talk or perhaps a sermon on this subject – instructed young people to make more responsible use of the increased resources which economic growth had put at their disposal. We can but guess what the young people in question would have made of a social philosopher who attempted so decisively to lean against the prevailing winds and who sought to set 'at defiance' the momentum inherent in matter. Perhaps they would have been impressed by the very audacity of his idealism. After all, as Keynes so eloquently says, 'the youth are not satisfied, unless their Socrates is a little odd.'[66]

(3) Speculation

Some forms of speculation are entirely beneficial – as where 'professional purchasers' exercise a 'steadying influence' on markets such as those for rare coins or unique paintings where prices would otherwise fluctuate wildly around the normal level,[67] or where the 'speculative builder' ('in the honourable sense of the term') 'sets out to erect honest buildings in anticipation of general demand': he 'bears the penalty of any error in his judgement' and, 'if his judgement is approved by events, benefits the community as well as himself'.[68] The work of the speculator is entirely in the national interest in a case such as this, where an expert professional who 'anticipates the future correctly' ultimately 'renders a public service by pushing forward production where it is wanted, and repressing it where it is not'.[69]

Some forms of speculation, however, are anything but constructive – as where unscrupulous and fraudulent promoters become 'associated with anti-social strategy, and even with evil manipulation of the sources from which ordinary investors derive their guidance';[70] or where 'powerful joint stock companies' amass great wealth through the abuse of their great strength in 'speculative ventures on the stock exchange';[71] or where an 'astute knave' employs 'subtle devices for misleading the public' because he is convinced he can 'induce others to believe they have a good chance of success, though he himself suspects they have none; and who is careful to clear out from them before they collapse';[72] or where a well-organised rogue, taking advantage of international time-differences, employs agents 'acting secretly on his behalf'[73] to boost prices in Chicago by spreading rumours and suggestions to the effect that a scarcity is developing in Liverpool. Or, for that matter, where cliques and 'strategic combinations' are formed specifically 'for the purpose of moving the price':[74] 'Manipulative speculation has many forms and many degrees. Its chief method is to create false opinions as to the general conditions of demand and supply. A clique will lead the market generally to believe that they are working for a fall, when really they are buying quietly and by indirect means much more largely than they are selling; and conversely they will buy openly, when they are really speculating for a fall.'[75] Economically speaking, destructive speculation feeds on destructive speculation to such an extent that the accelerating process of pyramiding paper cannot but end in tears: 'Sensational success in great speculation tends to strengthen the nervous, confident temper in which it originated. It engenders rashness in venturing, and an even more dangerous inability to recognize defeat. In fact a great speculator has scarcely ever rested on his victory: he has nearly always persisted till overtaken by disaster.'[76] Morally speaking, destructive speculation constitutes yet another manifestation of the 'gambling spirit' which, encouraged in America 'even among little children, who would bet on races', had the deleterious impact on character and productivity which was only to be expected in persons who had been infected by evil habits: even working men in America, Marshall reported with regret, 'were being tempted away from the noble opportunities before them, and were speculating largely in mines; even servant girls were doing it'.[77] Nor should the wasteful and destabilising impact of 'illegitimate speculation' on the national economy be neglected, as when it increases the amplitude of trade cycles and macroeconomic fluctuations by means of credit-expansions based on recklessly short-run expectations: 'When prices are likely to rise, people rush to borrow money and buy goods, and thus help prices to rise . . . When afterwards credit is shaken and prices begin to fall, everyone wants to get rid of commodities and get hold of money which is rapidly rising in value; this makes prices fall all the faster.'[78] Trading on borrowed money itself tends *ceteris paribus* to have a disruptive effect – since, quite simply, a businessman making use of a capital not his own does not have the same incentive to cut his losses that he would have had had the funds been his alone. Where a businessman trades on borrowed money, it is, after all, his creditors who will pay the penalty for his 'semi-fraudulent inertness' (as opposed to 'deliberate fraud', always a further option open to an irresponsibly self-seeking borrower 'should his standard of honour not be high'): 'If he withdraws at once he will have lost all he has of his own; and if he allows the speculation to run on, any additional loss will fall on his creditors; and any gain will come to himself.'[79]

Some forms of speculation are entirely beneficial – as where well-informed experts, 'professional dealers who make a living by speculative purchases and sales . . . render great public services by carrying risks that would otherwise need to be borne by people whose special aptitudes lie in other directions'.[80] Some forms of speculation, however, are anything but constructive – as where even ordinary professionals find themself at a disadvantage 'relatively to great financiers in anticipating those wayward moods of the money market that conform to no rule: for indeed those moods are themselves largely fashioned by the great operators'.[81] Marshall for his part saw clearly that the unhealthy forms of speculation were as dangerous to the community as the healthy were productive of advance; but he also took the optimistic view that economic evolution had a tendency, as if guided by an invisible hand, to discriminate in favour of those modes of speculation which were compatible with sustained expansion – and against those which constituted brakes on quantitative advance and indices of negative human betterment. Three aspects of economic evolution in particular would seem to be of particular significance.

First, improvements in the generation of dependable economic information and commercial intelligence, either within the business sector itself (which presupposes in turn lifting the veil of 'needless secrecy'[82] so that the constructive sharing of knowledge can take place, as was indeed apparently the practice even in Marshall's time[83]) or outside it. Thus Marshall reflected that he could 'see no reason why a body of able disinterested men, with a wide range of business knowledge, should not be able to issue predictions of trade storm and of trade weather generally, that would have an appreciable effect in rendering the employment of industry more steady and continuous'.[84] The preparation of a tabular standard of value (especially where accompanied by indexation of contracts) would be a further means of protecting output and employment from the vicissitudes of a credit cycle caused in no small measure by speculation in conditions of considerable uncertainty.[85] At a more microeconomic level the trade press has a role to play in ferreting out details about precisely what is happening in individual markets: greedy men who know of a market-swing beforehand 'because they have contrived it'[86] are only in a strong position to reap their ill-gotten speculative gain so long as the rest of us remain in the dark. Matter is in motion and the trade press is even now doing good work in combatting ignorance in areas such as this.

Second, improvements in the diffusion of 'the very little that is already known'[87] such as are associated with the communications and transportation revolutions of modern times. It is, for instance, reassuring to discover that 'in spite of the increasing complexity of business, commercial panics are now much milder than they were; and this is chiefly due to the timely warnings given by the press'.[88] The media are not perfect (their influence can indeed 'fail at critical times') but they are nonetheless an increasingly important means of combatting the instabilities and inequities that are born of 'false news' and 'false suggestion': 'In all such matters opinion is under influence from a public press, in which wise and honest counsels have the upper hand in ordinary times.'[89] Thus it is that 'the course of progress is hostile to the fraudulent promoter . . . The detective forces of organized knowledge in the public press and elsewhere grow cumulatively, and the new elements in his guiles are less in each generation than in the preceding.'[90] Clearly, 'publicity generally helps honest dealings; and puts difficulties in the way of some crude forms of dishonesty'.[91] It does this, incidentally, not merely by informing and influencing public opinion with respect to phenomena but also by arousing and mobilising moral outrage in the case of abuse committed by persons or institutions – a sanction, as it happens, of considerable value in view of the fact that 'they are seldom willing to sacrifice their reputation for the sake of a temporary gain'.[92] The efficacy of this sanction at the multinational level is not quite so certain, however; and all in all the growth of 'international speculative combinations ... is the source of some of the gravest practical problems with which the coming generation will have to deal'.[93]

Third, improvements in the quality of human character in the course of economic growth. Men are today more honest and upright, more altruistic and other-regarding than they were in the past; and this means that they are *ceteris paribus* less likely to fall victim to the temptations offered by the less attractive aspects of the speculative propensity. Laws to defend the public interest against the anti-social contrivances of destructive speculators reinforce this upgraded collective consciousness and thereby do much good: they admittedly 'plod with heavy steps some way in the rear' but they are nonetheless 'gaining ground relatively to the wayward progress of the evil-doers'.[94] They would be more effective still, Marshall suggests, if punishment for fraud and corruption in business were to be proportioned (as is already the practice in criminal cases) to the harm actually done: 'Given two acts of commercial dishonesty, similar in other respects, but of which one causes injury only to a few, while the other, like the Glasgow Bank failure, spreads desolation through thousands of homes, the latter ought to be far the more heavily punished.'[95] The love of gambling remains a genuine problem, however, being a source of considerable economic disruption which is also stubbornly resistant to the normal causal factors of social progress: 'Legitimate speculation benefits trade in the long run; but mere gambling in business is a great and growing evil. Unfortunately, intellectual education, which is a slow but sure cure for drunkenness, is not so sure a cure for the spirit of gambling; though it may show the folly of playing against loaded dice.'[96] And here it must be said that, in his search for a solution, Marshall is not shown off to his own best advantage. Eschewing the idea of prohibition by law, and ignoring the proposal made by Walras and others that Stock Exchange speculation should be restricted to a limited number of licensed professionals, Marshall falls back on reiterating the end without naming the means: we need, he says, 'to encourage the growth of moral feeling against gambling, especially amongst the young'.[97] His only proposal of substance is in fact a negative one, that a system of premium bonds not be introduced since the State would in that way 'in effect become the holder of a gaming table. Surely this would be a grave error . . . We have inherited a great birthright; shall we sell it for a very small mess of pottage?'[98] That the example set by the State in this way would be uplifting is not in question. Whether it would significantly repress the love of gambling in our society – and the destructive speculation which emanates from that love of gambling – is, however, another matter.

Marshall believed that 'the more wasteful forms of speculation and of competition'[99] were great evils in themselves. He also shared with contemporary socialists a certain anxiety that the 'openings which the present industrial system offers of amassing great wealth by sustained good fortune in speculation'[100] might lead to excessive and even unjustifiable distributional inequalities. Looking at the Britain of his own times, Marshall was happy to be able to report that great wealth remained 'exceptional'[101] and, indeed, that he could find no support for the hypothesis that the rich were growing richer at a faster rate than were the rest of us: 'The aggregate income of the very rich is perhaps not a larger part of the whole in England now than in earlier times.'[102] Even so, and even in England, however, Marshall felt compelled to admit that 'many of the largest fortunes are made by speculation rather than by truly constructive work',[103] a state of things which gives cause for concern on two grounds – that inequalities founded on speculative gains might actually become greater as the opportunities for speculation expand and that speculative activity (as distinct from 'truly constructive work') is in itself barren, sterile, and (where destructive) anti-social. Looking across the Atlantic to the United States, Marshall was able to identify an economic experience which if anything strongly reinforced such anxieties as he entertained concerning speculation and inequality at home: 'In America the aggregate value of land is rising fast; the higher strains of the working population are yielding ground to lower strains of immigrants; and great financiers are acquiring vast power: and it may possibly be true that the aggregate income from property is rising relatively to that from labour, and that the aggregate income of the very rich is rising fastest of all.'[104] In America, Marshall reported, there had been considerable concentration of capital and therewith the emergence of a 'relatively small group of men' who possess 'vast wealth' and want to show a 'Napoleonic faculty in its use'[105] – and policy measures adopted had done little to resolve the problem of great gains married to great influence: 'No banking reform can remove some of the dangers which are inherent in the power of very rich men, who have not retired into the quietude which is preferred by most of the wealthy families of old countries, but are still eager for the excitements of the chase in the hunting ground of Wall Street.'[106] Marshall for his part took the view that the problem required a solution. He also admitted that he had no clear idea what form that solution should take: 'A remedy is not easy, and may never be perfect. Hasty attempts to control speculation by simple enactments have invariably proved either futile or mischievous: but this is one of those matters in which the rapidly increasing force of economic studies may be expected to render great service to the world in the course of this century.'[107] Marshall, it must be said, normally travelled in hope even when, as in the present case, he never actually arrived.

(4) Competition

Peaceful, friendly, honest competition is a valuable and a good thing, both in so far as it promotes efficiency in the field of want-satisfaction and because it makes an important contribution to the upgrading of conduct and character. No moral philosopher who believes that duties ought to eclipse rights can feel entirely comfortable with a normative orientation which assigns pride of place not to the *quo per se* (as ideally it should) but to the *quid pro quo* (a permanent reminder of the Fall of Man), but Marshall was nonetheless prepared to make himself the champion of the second-best for the simple reason that no superior alternative was in practice on offer: 'In "competition", as it is commonly understood, I find something crude, ugly, harsh; but with this evil, which can and ought to be diminished, I find very much good that has hitherto been attained by no other route. Till another route has been found, I think it is dangerous and even wrong to speak of competition as though it were an evil touched with good.'[108] We must all most devoutly wish, naturally enough, for an economic system legitimated by beneficence of intention and not merely (as in the case of competition) by optimality of outcome. Whatever the future may, however, hold, there can be no doubt that 'a grateful memory will always attach to the excellence of the work, which free exchange has done and is doing, in turning to account the combative and predatory energy of the present crude nature of man'.[109] Obviously, 'if competition is contrasted with energetic co-operation in unselfish work for the public good, then even the best forms of competition are relatively evil; while its harsher and meaner forms are hateful' – but 'in the responsible conduct of affairs, it is worse than folly to ignore the imperfections which still cling to human nature',[110] and thence the eulogy of the second-best.

Second-best is acceptable. Third-best is not. Marshall in looking at competition in a period of change, made no secret of his concern that second-best might well degenerate into one of two aberrations, neither of which we really want. The first of these is too much competition. The second is too little.

Consider first the case of *too much competition*. Excessive ambitiousness, unprincipled competitiveness, selfish aggressiveness, together with cold indifference to others are, Marshall maintained, manifestations of the market mentality which can only be regarded as malign, as the 'ordeal of economic freedom' of late eighteenth-century Britain so dramatically illustrates. Then 'free competition, or rather, freedom of industry and enterprise, was set loose to run, like a huge untrained monster, its wayward course. The abuse of their new power by able but uncultured business men led to evils on every side; it unfitted mothers for their duties, it weighed down children with overwork and disease; and in many places it degraded the race.'[111] The crude and greedy manufacturers and merchants of the early part of the nineteenth century were not much better: 'They were, no doubt, often inclined to regard business as a species of warfare, in which every man's hand must be against his neighbour; and they sometimes found more pleasure in the empty defeat of competitors than in an increase of solid prosperity, which was shared by all.'[112] Obsessed with riches to the exclusion of ease or pleasure, driven on by 'bitter contentiousness' and the pursuit of trophies and scalps won in zero-sum games, such men were trapped in an over-competitive market environment which ultimately destroyed in them precisely that which they should instead have learned to value most highly – 'the finer sensibilities and nobler aspirations'.[113]

Such men fortunately belong to the past, not to the present. Of course there were cut-throat practices and an atmosphere of general nastiness in the abnormal period of accelerated transition known as the Industrial Revolution, but the vast majority of us in the early twentieth century have long since outgrown such execrescences of upheaval: 'The representative British business man of the present century has a broader mind and a more generous character . . . His progress in mind and character towards higher things during recent generations is one of the most notable changes on record.'[114] Competition still involves struggle for the positional good of success for without struggle it would not be competition; but the men of today have increasingly learned to make haste slowly and to temper acquisitiveness with restraint – as where a conscientious employer defines a superfluous worker as a fixed overhead because of a sentimental reluctance to part with old associates,[115] or where a perfect competitor who is sensitive to respect and self-respect deliberately eschews a profit-maximising bout of price-cutting in order specifically to avoid 'incurring odium from other producers for spoiling the common market'.[116] More generally, widespread social disapprobation may reasonably be expected constructively to discipline such few remaining buyers and sellers as do not yet grasp that markets involve rights as well as duties: thus it is that economists today 'look to the extension of the new force of public opinion as a means of eliminating much of the evil effects of competition, while retaining its good effects'.[117] A return from unrestrained individualism to individualism constrained by consensus need not and must not mean a return to 'the cruelty of the yoke of custom and rigid ordinance'[118] which freedom of enterprise displaced so brutally because so rapidly. What it does mean is a loose acceptance of ethical norms which could, theoretically speaking, retard advance but which, looking at the facts, are in practice entirely favourable to it: 'Some of the beneficial effects of custom are cumulative. For among the many different things that are included under the wide term 'custom' are crystallized forms of high ethical principles, rules of honourable and courteous behaviour, and of the avoidance of troublesome strife about paltry gains; and much of the good influence which these exert on race character is cumulative.'[119] Modern capitalism (and, specifically, modern *British* capitalism) has evidently evolved in an eminently healthy manner – since it has apparently come successfully to steer a middle course between excessive individualism (which is cut-throat and nasty, 'crude, ugly, harsh') and excessive constraint (which stifles initiative and treats the innovator as a leper to be shunned). One of the principal reasons for the successful adoption of this middle course, it must be added, would appear to be the fact that modern capitalism is characterised by transition that is gradual rather than accelerated; since only where change is evolutionary and not revolutionary can the businessman enjoy the enviable degree of ethical support from which he would appear able to benefit in present-day conditions. He who is exercised about excessive competition should therefore be reminded that *natura non facit saltum* and neither should human society.

Consider now the case of *too little competition*. Just as a glut of competitiveness is likely to cause an abnormal incidence of economic instability, so a dearth of competitiveness is likely to lead to an unwelcome loss of allocative and dynamic efficiency; and that is why every one concerned with England's future prosperity must also be concerned about 'the short-sighted selfishness which has developed the evil practice of stinting output (whether by trade unions or by employers' associations on the cartel model)'.[120] Market power benefits those who enjoy it but it also imposes a considerable burden on the rest of the community – and, when all is said and done, even the actors in the drama of the market-place should themselves see that 'the energy and resourcefulness of their rival is a social gain'.[121]

Neglect of social in favour of particular gain is nonetheless not uncommon in contemporary economic conditions; and Marshall (most forcefully in his later years) would definitely have instanced in this connection the restrictive practices and conflictual militancy of certain trades unions. The trouble with the unions, he seems increasingly to have believed, is that they had outlived their time, grown too strong, and begun to impose diminishing marginal productivity on the economy of which they were a part: 'Their good is diminishing, because there are less evils to contend with. (Largely a result of their own action). . . . And their evil is increasing in some trades, because they have a greater power to spread habits of making work over a larger area.'[122] Marshall's deep sympathy with the working classes clearly did not extend to the institutionalised shirking represented by these make-work practices, which, as he wrote to the Master of Balliol in 1897, he saw as a threat to character as well as efficiency: 'Leisure is good, if it is well used. But the laborious laziness, which has come into many English Government workshops, and some private ones, engenders a character to which leisure is useless.'[123] Nor was he much in sympathy with the 'unenlightened selfishness of workmen' in retarding the introduction of the productivity-boosting shift system – nor with their 'careless and dishonest maltreatment of machinery'[124] – nor with their tendency to 'look askance' at an exceptional man who 'makes the machine diligent':[125] 'An operative, who worked more strenuously than was the custom, was always likely to be rebuked by his shopmates. But now he is likely to be called to account at a trade-union meeting, and incur grave censure: for it is argued that his example will tend to make a bad precedent.'[126] Nor was he particularly friendly to the 'obstacles' put by the interested conservatism of organised labour in the way of 'improvements in machinery or technique'[127] – obstacles which are by no means uncommon in an old country where 'those who have acquired special manual skill are inevitably somewhat jealous of technical improvements that tend to narrow the sphere of their special usefulness. There are in fact very few occupations, in which every operation performed by skilled workers makes demands on their special skill.'[128] Which reminds us that Marshall was not much more in sympathy with artificially-drawn lines of demarcation, man-made partial monopolies in the field of labour, and 'such trade-union regulations as restrict particular classes of work to those, who have acquired their skill in it under the auspices of the appropriate craft':[129] such measures keep you out of the trade (thereby 'stinting output' to the community as a whole) while giving me a vested interest in the preservation of an obsolete skill, laboriously acquired (a clear case of 'sectional selfishness'[130] and one bound to reduce potential welfare of all consumers, the vast bulk of whom are 'the working classes, as a body'[131] and many of whom are actually members of trades unions).

Marshall had great admiration for British working men, for 'the general nobility and generosity of their character' (something that 'appears not to be surpassed, even if it is equalled, among the corresponding classes of any other country').[132] He also had great respect for the best of British unionism – which, he felt, protects weak employees from exploitation by powerful employers, which inculcates desirable habits of mutual care and co-operative action, which imparts a valuable familiarity with both business techniques and participatory democracy, and which makes an independent contribution to higher standards via collective constraint and guaranteed training. His quarrel was neither with British working men nor with the best of British unionism but with the new and more aggressive unions of the 1880s and 1890s (which, he felt, approached 'class consciousness' with 'an almost religious fervour'[133] and which accordingly focused on shares to the exclusion of advance), together with the rules and regulations, the bureaucratisation and regimentation which the institutionalisation of collective bargaining had tended to generate (and which, he felt, was more conducive to ossification than it was to enterprise). As an illustration of his attitude towards unions which seek redistribution rather than expansion his confidential comments in 1897 to a privileged correspondent on the subject of the Amalgamated Society of Engineers may usefully be cited: 'I am wholly a trade-unionist of the old stamp. For the sake of trade unionism, and for that of labour as a whole, I hope that the employers will so far get the better of the leaders of the modern unionism, that the rank and file of the workers will get to see the futility as well as the selfishness of the policy which their new leaders are pressing. Everywhere the tried men, who had made modern unionism the greatest of England's glories, have been pushed aside – sometimes very cruelly. For a time the Engineers adhered to moderate and unselfish courses. But lately they have used their grand prestige, I hold, for England's ill . . . Unless the A.S.E. *bona fide* concedes to the employers the right to put a single man to work an easy machine, or even two or more of them, the progress upwards of the English working classes, from the position of hewers of wood and drawers of water, to masters of nature's forces will, I believe, receive a lasting check.'[134] As an illustration of his attitude towards bureaucratisation and regimentation, consider the case of the Common Rule – which, intended to simplify wage-settlements by classing together similar workers for purposes of similar payment, had the unintended side-effect of creating involuntary unemployment amongst those who were sub-normal within their class but still prohibited by the logic of the Rule from volunteering to accept employment at a reduced wage. The Common Rule in such cases has latent consequences which in some measure reduce the benefit from administrative convenience: by 'refusing to allow an elderly man, who can no longer do a full standard day's work, to take something less than standard wages', it both imposes the 'harsh and anti-social' penalty of enforced idleness on the elderly gentleman himself and also 'lowers the national dividend'[135] as compared with what it would have been if the worker had been permitted to accept work at a rate of payment determined by supply and demand and little else. A phenomenon which, as Clark Kerr points out, is by no means unheard of even today: 'Several decades and countless studies later, the wisdom of Marshall largely stands. The standard rate has replaced personal rates in unionized and many non-union employments and has certainly often gone beyond, as Marshall feared it would, equalizing the rates of workers of equal efficiency.'[136] Such a state of affairs, Marshall argued, is unacceptable – a clear case of not enough competition.

Marshall identified the unions as one cause of not enough competition. Trusts, cartels, monopolies, and similar instances of market imperfection he identified as another,[137] and he also expressed concern lest the joint stock corporation *per se* prove 'a source of danger to social progress': as it spreads, so 'a tendency to ossification of the social organism might therefore be feared as the result of bureaucratic habits of shirking troublesome initiative'.[138] The man on a salary is more likely *ceteris paribus* than is the old-style owner-entrepreneur to be lacking in 'that zeal which is continually laying schemes by which greater profit may be obtained, or expense saved, and which is ever anxious about small gains and small savings';[139] he is more likely to eschew challenge, originality and the Schumpeterian 'perennial gale of creative destruction'[140] in favour of stability and the quiet life; and he is less likely to make an energetic and informed selection and deployment of manpower.[141] The man on a salary is, of course, likely to be honest, dutiful and conscientious in our immensely upgraded present-day conditions, but something is nonetheless lacking where it is a man's study to conserve what he has rather than imaginatively and energetically to take risks. Marshall's views on this matter were, however, mixed, and it must be added that the conclusions to be drawn are more ambiguous where he, disaggregating, contrasted the best of managers with the worst of entrepreneurs. Thus he observed, concerning the British steel industry, that much technology had become antiquated because many entrepreneurs had become sleepy: 'Many of the British steel plants which were at work before the German steel industry became prominent, were in the hands of men who had inherited the material, but not the intellectual resoures of those who had set them up: and family traditions hindered the infusion of energetic new blood.'[142] In such circumstances there might well be a strong case to be made out for management by propertyless meritocrats – men who, for their part, welcome the growth of joint stock companies precisely because of the extent to which that development 'offers great opportunities to those who have business power, to obtain the control over capital.'[143] The question is not simply whether our own best managers are more efficient and more up-to-date than our own worst capitalists, however, but also how they stand relative to the normal run of capitalists in our main competitor-nations, and here the example of the steel industry confirmed to Marshall that our organisation men were likely to face formidable opposition indeed: 'In Germany . . . the control of steel businesses, partly because they were new, was mainly in the hands of men, who had been nurtured in frugal habits, and expected to work for eight or ten hours a day, and for three hundred days in the year, very much as had those who created the British steel industry two generations earlier.'[144] Given such formidable opposition, not enough competition at home can all too easily translate itself into not enough competitiveness abroad, and therewith a serious threat to Britain's position in the world: 'She may rapidly fall from her high place, if she becomes slack in any respect.'[145]

A nation which could count on peace and which was not heavily committed to exportation in order to procure for itself large quantities of imported food and primary produce could perhaps afford the luxury of not enough competition. Britain therefore could not. Marshall, as he grew older in the troubled years which led to the First World War, became increasingly concerned about German militarism and about the 'decline in our willingness to exert ourselves', not least because of the close links which exist between defence and opulence:

> We are no longer at the high premium at which we were for those operations in iron works etc. which require exceptional powers of endurance; and in manual skill we have been nearly overtaken by several nations who were far behind us. . . . We should quickly be passed by rivals still some way behind us, if their productive energy were a little greater than our own, and their mode of living a little more sparing . . . . If similar changes continue for long, and go much further, our surplus of revenue over expenditure, available for naval and military use will be less than that of Germany.[146]

Writing as early as 1901, Marshall reminisced about the days of his youth when Britain was truly Great ('Fifty years ago nine-tenths of those changes, which have enabled the working classes to have healthy homes and food, originated in England'[147]) and lamented Britain's relative decline. Once, he argued, Britain was the workshop of the world, and deservedly so: 'We owed our leadership partly to accidental advantages, most of which have now passed away. But we owed it mainly to the fact that we worked much harder than any continental nation. Now, on the average, we work less long and not more vigorously than our fathers did: and, meanwhile, the average amount of thoughtful work done by the German has nearly doubled; and a similar though less marked improvement is to be seen in other countries. Americans and Germans jeer at the way in which many of our business men give their energies to pleasure, and play with their work . . . It is, I believe, a fact that there is scarcely any industry, which has not changed its form during the last ten years, in which we are not behind several countries; and that every Teutonic country, whether behind us or in front of us, is on the average growing in vigour of body and mind faster than we.'[148] A negative aspect of change certainly, and one all but inevitable in a nation 'a little spoilt by prosperity'[149] and no longer as imbued with the spirit of youthful pioneering as once it was. A negative aspect of change, however, which an open economy in a world of aggressive nationhood must make every effort to reverse: 'It is specially incumbent on Britain to strive against the stiffness of the joints that is almost inevitable in each old country.'[150] The social organism evolves as if guided by an invisible hand but there is still, it would appear, some room for conscious action in the service of human betterment.

3 Growth and Betterment

It is frequently asserted that the neo-classical economists were principally concerned with topics in the field of comparative statics (and specifically with microeconomic questions such as those involving rational choice between alternative options, efficient allocation of scarce resources, constrained maximisation of utility and profit) and that it was the classical authors who wrote most fully about macroeconomic dynamics, aggregation, growth and development. If the 1870s did indeed witness such a paradigm-switch, then it is not easy to know precisely in which camp to situate Alfred Marshall, who in the 1880s and 1890s made an unprecedented contribution to the pure theory of partial equilibrium – but also warned that 'the general conditions of life are not stationary',[1] declared that time 'is at the centre of the chief difficulty of almost every economic problem',[2] and stressed that we in the West are nowadays 'moving on at a rapid pace that grows quicker every year; and we cannot guess where it will stop'.[3] Of course the neo-classical box of tools is there, but so too is the perception that time is 'absolutely continuous',[4] reality quintessentially dynamic, the wealth of nations to be assigned pride of place in an approach to the economic system 'permeated', as Dennis O'Brien puts it, 'by a concern over growth. The post-Walrasian view of Marshall is totally misleading because it fails to appreciate that, for Marshall, economic phenomena were observed not at rest but in the course of growth . . . He was impressed by England's industrial leadership, and after more than a century of growth, was concerned for the maintenance of both that growth and of England's premier position; and in this he was wholly classical.'[5]

Stigler says that 'almost every important subject in the *Principles* receives its exposition in terms of evolutionary change',[6] and the operative word here is evolutionary – since phenomena in Marshall's economics not only grow but, more significantly, also grow better. Economic growth itself means that less is superseded by more; the associated process of human betterment involves (with the undeniable exception of certain negative aspects) a sustained improvement both in want-satisfaction and in patterns of conduct and character; and the relationship between growth and progress is in addition fundamentally symbiotic, each both feeding and feeding off the other. Growth normally leads to progress. Progress normally leads to growth. Growth (like the hectoring of the moral philosopher) is an input in the process of human betterment. Betterment (like the allocative efficiency of the neo-classical microeconomist) is an input in the process of economic growth. It is with these two sides of the circular flow of economic phenomena – with, respectively, the economic veins and the economic arteries – that we shall be concerned in the two sections of this Chapter.

3.1 FROM GROWTH TO BETTERMENT

Marshall never developed a formal growth model as such but it would be very wrong to conceive of his system as being concerned exclusively with allocation and maximisation subject to the constraint of a fixed endowment of scarce means.[1] Growth is present even if the model is not, and it is the task of the sympathetic reader to reconstruct the edifice out of the wealth of hints, suggestions and insights provided by a master architect who never found the time fully to communicate all the details of his Grand Design.

(1) The constants

Economic evolution involves adaptation to environment, but to an environment not entirely of our own choosing. When a nation's economy grows, in other words, it grows against a background of certain fundamental and underlying constants with which it must come to terms before it can begin to blend in its variables. The following inter-related causal constants would seem to be of particular significance in Marshall's perception of the environment which constrains the economy.

First, climate. A very warm climate 'is destructive of energy'[2] while a relatively cool (but not a severely cold) climate is favourable to hard work: 'While man is altering the face of nature, nature is ever-changing the quality of man. A healthy invigorating climate is one of the most important of the gifts that nature bestows . . . England is fortunate in having a climate in which men can work with vigour out of doors almost all the year round; and which, by thus fostering energetic and steady habits of labour, contributes much to her greatness.'[3] Besides that, a very warm climate renders nature bountiful and life therefore lacking in challenge: one of the reasons why the ancient Greeks 'at last . . . sank into frivolity' was the fact that 'a genial climate slowly relaxed their physical energies: they were without that safeguard to strength of character which comes from resolute and steadfast persistence in hard work' – for which deficiency not the niggardliness of nature was to blame but rather an over-bounteous climate, which showered upon them 'the material requisites for a perfect life' and which, to their own detriment, 'absolved them from the need of exhausting work'.[4] Climate influences economic activity *via* its impact on man's character ('Climatic conditions have controlled the nature of man almost as much as that of vegetables'[5]) and on social institutions ('In India the climate has caused a limp habit of body and mind, which has made people submit to the rule of despotic kings, and more despotic custom'[6]), and there is in addition a rather obvious point to make about seasonal unemployment: 'In many places even in the temperate zones work is almost entirely suspended during the extreme heats of summer. And in some parts of America men are not only prone to take a holiday during "the heated term", but are also prevented from doing such work as that of carpenters in the open air during the extreme severity of winter.'[7] Where it is often too hot or too cold to supply labour, there economic growth will, other things being equal, proceed at a slower pace than in nations with a more moderate climate.

Second, race. Each of us inherits a genetic endowment which differentiates in appearance the Javanese from the Congolese and which distinguishes in 'tone of thought' the Jew from the Englishman: 'The faults and virtues of Ricardo's mind are traceable to his Semitic origin; no English economist has had a mind similar to his.'[8] In the case of England, our race is itself a sound one, and it has been made even better by the addition of new blood from abroad, particularly since invasion by 'successive hordes of immigrant warriors'[9] has meant that this country came to be 'peopled by the strongest members of the strongest races of northern Europe; a process of natural selection brought to her shores those members of each successive migratory wave who were most daring and self-reliant'.[10] It is, of course, not easy to disentangle the genes from the culture which those genes produce; but the end product of the process would appear, in the case of England, to be unambiguously beneficial in view of the fact that 'the adventurous races who peopled her shores brought with them a spirit of enterprise which has been transmitted to their descendants'.[11] There is in us quite literally much of the 'sturdy resolute Norse character';[12] and the conclusion to be reached is that, in the case of England at least, not only race but the mixture of race has proven a particularly valuable asset. Even so, however, the student of race should take care to avoid excessive complacency or fatalism: 'The physical power and energy of man is of course partly dependent upon inherited race-qualities. But modern science shews that the character of a race may be greatly modified by changes in its habits of living, in diet, in cleanliness, in house-room, etc. Thus the physical vigour of a race depends partly on its wealth.'[13] Good nurture clearly has a role to play alongside the gifts of nature but, when all is said and done, strong superstructures require firm foundations; and therefore, *ceteris paribus*, it would be reasonable to expect that 'to him that hath, to him is given'.[14] You are what you eat. You are even more what you are.

Third, goegraphical location. Inland powers have to maintain large standing armies, with the inevitable result that the enterprise of the nation's 'most restless spirits' is 'crushed down by discipline'[15] – which is a good reason for saying that Britain is fortunate to be an island. Besides that, 'being entrenched by the sea she has escaped the devastating wars which have discouraged the accumulation of capital on the Continent'[16] and has been able to devote more of her resources to more productive pursuits, much encouraged in that direction by an abundance of navigable waterways conducive to the expansion of trade. Commercial activity, needless to say, then helped to breed and form those character-traits which are most functional for the purposes of adaptation to a changing environment: 'Her seas and rivers have promoted commerce, and with it that flexibility of habits which is caused by free intercourse with distant places.'[17]

Fourth, national character. Nations differ for many reasons (notably such causal factors as climate, race, geographical location and, prominently, economic experience). Recognising that, we must assign due weight to the contribution of collective traits to economic growth, as in the case of 'the early faculty of the Anglo-Saxon temperament for ordered freedom'[18] (accompanied, needless to say, by 'firm will, self-determination, thoroughness, fidelity'[19] and 'sustained energy':[20] 'Self-restraint in the statement of claims, and resolute persistence in those which have been finally approved, have generally enabled Anglo-Saxon peoples to move forwards steadily: retrogressions have occurred, but they have been rare.'[21] Some nations have a 'love of order'[21] (the Prussians, for example), others are notorious for 'disdaining hard manual work'[22] (the Portuguese have not always been blameless in this respect), and that reminds us of the essential functionality as an economic input of the British *via media*: 'The English had combined order with freedom, and therefore had lived strenuous lives longer than any other nation, unless it was the Dutch.'[24] Of course national character can evolve slowly over time. Our present point, however, is a dual one – that the change is so gradual as to render national character *de facto* a constant for the purposes of short-term analysis, and that there is in the event an exceptionally high degree of stability in national character over quite lengthy time-periods indeed: 'It is . . . worth while to insist that the energies of Englishmen have always had the same fundamental character . . . The English archer was the progenitor of the English artisan.'[25] Such stability is to be expected; since while our economic institutions have undoubtedly altered as compared with 1066, when we consider influences such as climate, race and geographical location, one thing is clear, that *natura non facit* anything in particular.

Fifth, natural resources. Human resources, Marshall believed, are of greater importance than natural resources: 'In the long run, national wealth is governed by the character of the population more than by the bounty of nature.'[26] The following illustration vividly demonstrates the primacy of the human input: 'In the course of generations man works on the face of nature, and improves her gifts, or wastes them. The patient industry of the Dutch has turned their barren sands into fertile meadows; while the wasteful carelessness of the slave-owning cotton-planters of Southern America has turned some of the richest districts of the world into a wilderness.'[27] Even the best endowment of natural resources can prove barren and sterile where the 'liberality of nature' is not complemented by the wisdom and activity of man. But obviously a country does have *ceteris paribus* a better start if it has a good stock of potential wealth – potential wealth, it must be added, which 'consists not only in her gifts of fertile land and rich mines, but also in a convenient arrangement of her gifts. Before the invention of railways, a district could not have a prosperous trade unless it had easy means of communication by river or by sea. Iron mines are of comparatively little value if there is no coal near them. England's present position in the world is in a great measure due to the fact that she not only has coal mines and iron mines, but also her coal and iron mines are near together.'[28] The magnitude of the endowments and their proximity to one another were fortuitous accidents – as was the fact that Britain's endowments lent themselves to exploitation in a manner which was conducive to economies of large size: 'Her rich mines of coal and iron have given prominence to those industries in which . . . production on a large scale is at the greatest advantage, in which large capitals have the best chance of becoming larger, while small capitals are in great risk of becoming smaller.'[29] As was the fact that, with respect to food and other farm produce, Britain was exceptionally well-placed to benefit from the 'original and indestructible powers of the soil' in that 'her climate has been singularly favourable to rapid changes in agriculture'.[30] It must be stressed, however, that fortuitous accidents in and of themselves are not productive of economic growth. Their potential must first be harnessed, must first be 'turned to full account': while a non-replicable fixed endowment (say, of unique human talent) cannot be increased in quantity, it can all too easily be under-exploited where 'free gifts of nature'[31] such as the scarce skills of the extraordinary barrister, singer, jockey or entrepreneur are allowed (in whole or in part) to go to waste. Again, and even in the classical case of land, Marshall argued, man is active as well as passive in that, unable as he is to control the area of the earth (which is fixed), he can nonetheless, by means of ingenuity in the improvement of fertility and productivity, 'make almost any land bear large crops'; even now (and such improvements 'are likely to be carried out more extensively and thoroughly in the future than in the past') 'the greater part of the soil in old countries owes much of its character to human action; all that lies just below the surface has in it a large element of capital, the produce of man's past labour'.[32] Man is in similar fashion at the mercy of fortuitous accident with respect to a fixed stock of fossil fuel; man can nonetheless, in the Jevonian as in the Ricardian case, exercise his ingenuity to surmount his constraints (as where, faced with rapidly-depleting supplies of coal, he seeks out good substitutes and strives to develop 'new methods of distributing power by gas and petroleum and electric engines')[33]; and this reminds us yet again, despite the undeniable significance of natural resources for economic growth, of the primacy of the human input.

(2) The infrastructure

For an economy given its constants to make the most of its inputs, a certain number of basic infrastructural institutions must have evolved and reached a reasonably high level of sophistication. Three such institutions are of particular importance.

First, the rule of law. Marshall believed that sustained economic growth was unthinkable without an environment of law and order and took the view that vital activities such as saving and investing presuppose, seen from the perspective of any rational individual, that 'Government should protect his property from fraud and violence':[34] 'The thriftlessness of early times was in a great measure due to the want of security that those who made provision for the future would enjoy it.'[35] Such security must evidently be perceived as obtaining in the future as well as in the present (precisely because saving and investing, more so than most other activities in economics, are inter-temporal in orientation) but for it genuinely to constitute a 'necessary condition'[36] for enterprise and progress it must have a dual nature: 'Capital, as well as industry, requires to be protected *by* the Government and *from* the Government.'[37] Security from the *bellum omnium contra omnes* must be paid for but the price must not be the 'shackles of political despotism'[38] that for so long retarded economic growth on the continent. In this respect as in others, however, Britain has been fortunate, and her development has truly been much facilitated by 'her easy maintenance of liberty in conjunction with firm order and the rigid enforcement of equal laws'[39] – and by the fact that our rulers regard themselves as our servants and not our masters. Like Adam Smith before him, Marshall pointed to the impossibility of extensive industry and trade in the insecure political environment of the Middle Ages, when 'people generally, and traders in money in particular, had learnt by experience that a prince who found it inconvenient to discharge a debt, which he had incurred, simply set it aside: or, as the saying goes, "threw his sword into the scale" to make up the balance of his payments against his obligations'.[40] Far more attractive than this, far more conducive to manufacturing and commerce, is the later compromise that was made by William III: 'William's shrewdness, as well as his honesty, induced him to lay stress on the fact that the commercial credit of a constitutional government was that of the parliament and not the king.'[41] All in all, therefore, while it would be fair to assert that 'commercial security and habits of confidence are a product of civilization, and grow with it',[42] yet it must immediately be added that they are also in some measure a precondition for the civilising process; and that, historically speaking, 'the broadening of civil liberty has enabled individual enterprise and originality to flourish, even in the centre of a great inland and military power'.[43]

Second, market freedom. Merchants and manufacturers most benefit the community when they are given maximal opportunity to show initiative and make choices – to 'select from many markets the fittest and the most opportune for the sale of any particular ware', to 'buy quickly and sell quickly' so as thereby to minimise the capital 'locked up in idleness',[44] to make full use, without let or hindrance, of those valuable 'powers of insight and imagination'[45] (with respect, say, to new plant and machinery and new modes of business organisation) which are so essential for sustained economic progress. This means that the Government should not seek to direct operations which ought in the interests of economic efficiency to be delegated to the decentralised decision-making of market competition, but it also means freedom from abuse of concentrated power on the part of unions of firms and/or of unions of households – that, in short, 'all classes and groups, eschew all practices which tend to raise the market value of their services or products by making them relatively scarce'.[46] Given genuine freedom to exchange, however, the benefits in terms of economic efficiency are clear and result from the automaticity of 'forces constantly at work tending so to readjust the distribution of resources between their different uses, that any maladjustment will be arrested before it has gone far'.[47]

The argument for market freedom extends to inputs as well as to outputs. It is, for example, the self-corrective interaction of supply and demand which proportions, as if guided by an invisible hand, the relative remuneration of skilled and unskilled workers to their respective levels of marginal productivity; since, clearly, ' if A will do twice as much work as B, an employer on the margin of doubt as to whether it is worth his while to take on additional workers, will make just as good a bargain by taking on A at four shillings as by taking on B and another at two shillings each'.[48] The argument for market freedom, furthermore, is of international and not merely of domestic relevance. Thus Britain was able to import a plentiful supply of foreign-grown raw produce at a low price once she renounced the Corn Laws and went over to a system of free trade; while she was able to reap significant economies of large size in production by virtue of the fact that foreigners apparently did not impose prohibitive tariffs on the commodities which she exported to them. Venice at an earlier stage did impose such tariffs – and from that time on began to decline: 'The heat of the day continues to increase for some little time after the sun has begun its downward course: and the impetus which Venice had obtained from enterprise, fostered by freedom and only tempered by regulation, carried her onwards for a while, even after excessive regulation and the want of stimulating competition had begun to lower her vitality.'[49] Protection, it is clear, was not beneficial to Venice (nor, indeed, to Spain, whose economic ruin followed hard on the heels of her adoption of the Venetian system), which 'excluded the products of foreign skill and forbad her own artisans to emigrate; and at last she ceased even to learn': 'The history of Venice would seem to lend some support to the opinion that external competition tends to stimulate and to maintain the resource and energy of a nation's industries.'[50]

Market freedom is beneficial but it cannot be absolute; and Marshall, like Adam Smith aware of 'the frequent opposition that there is between private interests and the public good',[51] drew attention to the case for *constrained* competition where pure self-interest demonstrably does not lead to maximum happiness (as perceived by the philosopher). In *constrained* competition the constraints take two forms, the political and the normative.

With respect to the State, Marshall recognised that errors can easily be made in a market economy, both of commission (such as the repression of healthy rivalry through action by 'a privileged class of producers, who often use their combined force to frustrate the attempts of an able man to rise from a lower class than their own'[52]) and of omission (such as the failure of free enterprise to generate an adequate supply of roads, canals, schools and other essential services). Marshall argued accordingly that where such shortcomings were to be identified, there State intervention might be desirable in order to bend the bent rod so as to make it straight again. Such intervention could take the form of prescription (say, of standardised units – a step towards homogeneity which, historically speaking, gave a great if unexpected boost to mass production), of inspection (say, of factories and sanitary conditions), of regulation (say, of occupancy-rates in slum-dwellings); or, more actively, of subsidisation (say, of industries experiencing increasing returns) and even of provision (say, of schooling allocated by merit rather than effective demand, or of a tabular standard of value). In all cases the State should proceed with caution in view of the undeniable costs to the economy that are associated with any form of other-directedness, however well-intentioned. Nor should the State neglect the unintended spillovers and externalities that might arise as a direct consequence of its actions – not all of them as beneficial as the encouragement to industry and trade that resulted from the construction of 'great highways . . . made chiefly for political and military purposes'.[53] Nor should the State act as if it and it alone must pick up the pieces consequent upon market failure (witness the extensive contribution that has been made by private philanthropy to improvements in the housing conditions of the urban poor). But when all is said and done, the State bears ultimate responsibility and government remains an important input in Marshall's model of – constrained – market freedom.

With respect to background values, Marshall's position is a cautious one. Absolutely rigid custom stifles any improvement which involves a break with tradition and is thus a great social evil, being the friend of stagnation and the enemy of freedom. Plastic and elastic custom is another matter, however, as it offers no more than a broad unifying matrix, a set of rules of the road which inhibit but do not crush within the innovator and the creator 'the desire to humour his own fancy, or his love of novelty, or his inclination to save trouble by a rather better adjustment of implements to the work done'.[54] Plastic and elastic custom constitutes nothing more repressive than a 'body of general design, on which each fresh mind might try to make some variation for the sake of economy of effort, of increased utility, or more pleasing effect',[55] subject only to the need to make haste slowly, precisely because public opinion,like a glacier which ultimately changes its shape to suit its changed surroundings, refuses to be hurried in its adjustments. Of course absolutely rigid custom is the enemy of dynamic market capitalism – indeed, 'it is probable that this has been the most important of all the causes which have delayed the growth of the spirit of free enterprise among mankind'.[56] Yet too aggressive, too self-seeking a mode of competitiveness is an aberrant thing as well, sacrificing as it does the crucial social objective of progress to the ethically less significant objective of growth. Competition unshackled is like a 'fierce monster', 'terrible to deal with';[57] and that is why Marshall, in arguing strongly in favour of market freedom, nonetheless came down in favour of self-interest loosely constrained by public opinion, moral consensus, and shared normative orientation.[58]

Third, transportation and communications. Marshall believed that

England had benefited very greatly indeed from improvements and developments in these areas: 'Probably more than three-fourths of the whole benefit she has derived from the progress of manufactures during the nineteenth century has been through its indirect influences in lowering the cost of transport of men and goods, of water and light, of electricity and news: for the dominant economic fact of our own age is the development not of the manufacturing, but of the transport industries.'[59]

Consider first the case of transportation. At the level of imports, an expanding railway network complemented by larger, faster steamships, has opened up new sources of supply of primary produce – in America, for instance – such as have shifted the 'margin of cultivation' from the Pennines to the Prairies and have provided a significant counterbalance to the tendency *ceteris paribus* towards diminishing returns in agriculture at home: 'The bleak hill-sides, up which the wheat-fields were laboriously climbing in Ricardo's time, have returned to pasture; and the ploughman works now only where land will yield plentiful returns to his labour.'[60] Modern methods of transportation facilitate the mass consumption of cheapened products not only 'out of place' (as opposed to the inferior substitute of which the unique attraction is that it is 'near at hand') but also 'out of season'[61] (since improved shipment in bulk ensures regular supplies with reduced uncertainty from an ever-increasing range of distant nations) and in that way yield considerable benefit to the consumer as compared with the situation in the past, when 'even the well-to-do were forced to eat but sparingly of fresh meat in winter; and, until quite recently, fresh sea fish was not to be had far from salt water. Fruit seldom travelled far.'[62] At the level of exports, meanwhile, expanded international trade made possible by better and cheaper transport has meant increased sales abroad of our manufactures (our clothing and our hardware, for example) and therewith the spillover benefit to the domestic purchaser which one indeed would have expected from the economies of size associated with more extensive markets: 'Production on a large scale of these things for consumers beyond the sea cheapened them for him.'[63] There is in addition much to be gained on all sides from an international division of labour based on comparative advantage but possible only if good transport is available – and, of course, if the community's merchants (as is likely) show 'the same energy of character, that makes a nation eminent in industry' in manifesting their alertness 'to seize every opportunity of bringing the products in which she excels, to the notice of countries that cannot produce those things with as much relative ease and efficiency as they can other products'.[64] At the level of domestic intercourse, finally, improvements in transportation (including roads, canals and the motor-car) widen the geographical boundaries of a 'market' (a stimulus to economies of size and a threat to producers anti-socially exploiting a local monopoly); they reduce the average cost and increase the accessibility of supplies (before the Duke of Bridgewater's canal was constructed, 'in winter, when the roads were bad, Manchester was like a beleagured town'[65]); and they make possible the de-urbanisation both of production and of population. Industry benefits through a reduction in the overhead cost of rent: 'The high value of land in large cities tends to drive away those branches of production which have been taken over by massive machinery, and especially those which must be accommodated in low wide spreading sheds.'[66] Labour benefits through a diminution in degradation and a consequent increase in productivity which comes about when sunlight and fresh air become accessible even to men who continue to work in overcrowded towns: 'New facilities for traffic are enabling large numbers of those, who work in them, to have their homes in suburbs, where the children can play in fresh air: and the same facilities are giving to the residents in such suburbs advantages that are beyond the reach of country folk.'[67] At the level of imports, at the level of exports and at the level of domestic intercourse, it is clear, the contribution of improvements and developments in transportation has been valuable indeed.

Consider now the case of communications. Marshall said (and few would disagree) that 'knowledge is our most powerful engine of production; it enables us to subdue Nature and force her to satisfy our wants'.[68] Implicit in his statement, however, is a tacit but essential subsidiary clause to the effect that knowledge only unlocks the door to economic growth where information and intelligence are adequately diffused among the relevant households and firms; and it is therefore not surprising that he welcomed contemporaneous improvements in the transmission of news (improvements in the telephone, the telegraph, the postal services, the printing press, the specialist press, the generalist press) not least because of the specifically economic benefits which they conferred. Thus, given that 'perfect competition requires a perfect knowledge of the state of the market',[69] the communications revolution renders the not inconsiderable service to buyers (who thereby avoid paying over the odds) and to sellers (who thereby avoid taking less than they could get) of making common property an awareness of the going market price; while up-to-date information (even if, in a dynamic and future-orientated world, by its very nature never complete) is in itself infinitely preferable to the frequently destabilising guesstimates of the speculator. Improvements in communications are in addition at the root of the growing internationalisation of markets, both in commodities (such as wheat) and in financial assets (such as debentures, government bonds, and quoted shares); and this 'growing tendency of intercommunication'[70] (as in the case of cotton, where the exchanges of New York, New Orleans and Liverpool 'may for some purposes be regarded almost as a single market'[71]) is indicative of better organisation and more efficient market conditions. Better intelligence complemented by improved transportation reduces the amplitude of price-fluctuations by communicating news of a local scarcity to an area able to rush in stocks due to a local surplus – or able at least ('a strong testimony to the consolidation of economic nationality'[72]) to respond rapidly to the distress signals of international supply and demand by means of generating such a surplus (as where 'bad conditions of the crops in the Northern hemisphere are reported by telegraph in the Southern in time to increase the sowings of grain, that will be reaped during the Northern spring'[73]). Better intelligence complemented by improved futures – markets, banking and storage facilities plays an important role in the 'subdivision and specialization of the risks of constructive speculation' such as would previously have been unthinkable and such as today makes a significant contribution to the process of rational allocation: 'The farmer can now either sell his wheat, and set all his capital in it free at once: or he can store it, if he expects its price to rise, and meanwhile borrow money on it.'[74] Nor should the impact of improved communications on standards be neglected – as where 'the railway and the printing-press have enabled members of the same trade in different parts of the country to communicate easily with one another, and to undertake and carry out broad and far-seeing lines of policy';[75] or where more extensive publicity provides a disincentive to wrong-doing on the part of a businessman concerned about his reputation, together with an incentive to right-doing in the case of a sensitive inventor or innovator anxious to win the approbation of his peers.

The communications revolution is of particular significance where it undermines business secrecy and accelerates the transmission of ideas, concepts and techniques. Nowadays, 'the most important improvements in method seldom remain secret for long after they have passed from the experimental stage',[76] and such compulsory sharing is on balance a good thing: 'One great hindrance to knowledge is the excessive secrecy of traders. When everyone else keeps his business as secret as possible, no one likes to make his own public. But if no one had secrets, everyone would be better off than he is now.'[77] The communications revolution in that sense contributes to economic growth precisely because it erodes a previous obstacle and improves access to useful information. Nowadays, as it happens, and with increasing rapidity, 'the improvement of methods spreads from its first home all over the country, all over the world; and the private gain which results from it to the inventor is seldom a hundredth part, sometimes not even a millionth part of the social gain'.[78] The 'social gain' is reaped by a wide constituency indeed, it must be said – since while some of 'those ideas which make for industrial progress' have been known to originate in smaller countries, yet normally 'the chief initiative seems likely to lie with countries whose great size, rich natural resources, and accumulated capital enable them to concentrate large and highly organized mental and material appliances on the translation into practice of the architectonic ideas of the scientific student and the inventor'.[79] Nowadays, however, and thanks to the communications revolution, the new ideas, wherever they might originate, rapidly become the 'common property' not only of all firms within a given country but 'of all countries of the Western world'.[80]

Which is not to say that the transfer of technology is automatic, frictionless and total, the free gift of improved consumables and machines (embodying 'advanced industrial ideas and methods' such as have a powerful 'educative influence'[81] on would-be competitors) combined with better trade-papers and a greater supply of specialised journals. Technology, whether within a nation or between nations, does not, after all, transfer itself, and for that reason the communications revolution can never be more than permissive. The distinction between the necessary and the sufficient condition (between leading the horse to water, on the one hand, making him drink, on the other) is a vital one and is most easily illustrated by examples of a comparative nature – instances which demonstrate the truth of the fundamental proposition that one nation's discovery only becomes another nation's external economy where businessmen in the later-to-arrive state not only 'have adequate resources and opportunities' but also (a separate point) have the will to devote their energies to developments 'in which they nevertheless lag behind best practice that can be found elsewhere'.[82] Thus it is of interest to learn that 'the best English ideas have nearly always been accessible to Americans', but of equal importance to learn that the Americans were actually prepared to take advantage of those ideas, to seize their opportunities with an alacrity which is in effect to be expected from an economy 'worked in a temperate climate by a mixture of races of great energy and alertness'.[83] The Americans have in that respect much in common with the people of Japan: 'She is eager to adopt western methods that require a larger capital than she yet possesses. And though her people are poor . . . yet they are so alert, so closely in touch with western thought, and so full of independent enterprise, that her manufactures for export are growing rapidly.'[84] Both the Americans and the Japanese, one suspects, will make a conscious effort both to minimise adoption-lags (lest the advances in question in the interim become obsolete[85]) and to adapt the transferred technology to local conditions (something which is seldom if ever a ready-made externality). The same cannot, however, be said of the Indians, who live in a society dominated by tradition and convention to such an extent that it 'has not yet awakened';[86] and the moral of the story is that if in some cases British technological advances have enjoyed greater popularity abroad than at home, the countries in question (the countries from which British businessmen therefore have most to learn) are more likely to be America and Japan than to be nations such as India, where social inflexibilities and cultural resistances are bound to make even the most extensive improvements in communications powerless to effect change.

(3) The variables

Given the constants and the infrastructure, the final step is to examine the nature and contribution of the three inputs which vary over time and which in that way play their part in the drama of economic growth.

First, labour. Marshall, at least with respect to the Britain of his own times, was not in essence a Malthusian: 'Persons in any rank of life who are not in good physical and mental health have no moral right to have children. But in spite of popular Malthusianism, though not in opposition to Malthus' principles, we may affirm that those who bring up a large healthy family with a thoroughly good physical, mental, and moral training relatively to their own rank of life, do a service to their country.'[87] More population means more labour, more labour means more output, and all in all 'the restriction of births from selfish motives'[88] is much to be deplored: 'The rather violent checks to population, which have recently appeared in some strata of some Anglo-Saxon peoples, seem to be partly caused by a selfish devotion to "sports" and other amusements on the part of men: and partly to a selfish desire among women to resemble men.'[89] Such selfishness is in itself indicative of unhealthy social attitudes and a general 'weakening of individual, and therefore of national character';[90] and, by breeding a retardation in the growth of population, it also imposes an artificial limit on the quantity supplied of an important input. There is, admittedly, much talk of 'enforced idleness', and undeniably 'inconstancy of employment is a great evil' – but, to be frank, despite the 'rapidity of invention', the 'fickleness of fashion' and the 'instability of credit', yet 'there seems to be no good reason for thinking that inconstancy of employment is increasing on the whole'.[91] Some trades even record an increase in the percentage of employees offered annual contracts (as opposed to being hired by the day or the week). Since these trades include those linked to transport and related activities (areas, it must be stressed, 'in some respects, the representative industries of the second half of the nineteenth century, as the manufacturing trades were of the first half'[92]), the inference is clearly that surplus population and under-full employment are no more likely to exist in the foreseeable future than they do in the present. Less so, in fact, since the rapidly expanding tertiary sector is (in contrast to agriculture and industry, where 'ever increasing supplies' are being produced 'without requiring any considerable increase in the number of people who tend the machines'[93]) exceptionally labour-intensive. The income-elasticity of demand is high for post-industrial activities such as 'the service of Government, central and local; education of all grades; medical service; musical, theatrical and other entertainments, besides mining, building, dealing and transport by road and railway';[94] 'in none of these is very much direct help got from new inventions: man's labour is not much more efficient in them now than it was a century ago';[95] and such structural changes in an economy already showing an automatic tendency towards full employment as analysed by an economist with a strong belief in Say's Law would seem to assign a definite importance to an increase in the quantity of labour in the interests of economic growth.

What matters is not simply the quantity of labour, of course, but also its quality; and one of the principal ways in which this can be improved is through education and training, through the inculcation of skills and attitudes in schools and universities and on the job. Brute strength may suffice among uncivilized races, but in an advanced society sustained growth is becoming more and more dependent upon the diffusion of education among all classes. This is true even where the recipient does not in the event enjoy significant occupational upgrading as a direct result of the development of his mental potential, his judgement and his resourcefulness: 'Indeed a thorough general education, together with a special training for some particular employment, is becoming more necessary to the working man every year . . . A man does work that does not need skill all the better if he knows more than is actually required for him. Education makes him quick to understand whatever directions may be given to him: if his machinery gets out of order, or the plan of his work miscarries in any other way, he can set things to right at once and thus prevent much loss. In this and other ways, every increase in the intelligence of the workman diminishes the amount of supervision required from the employer and his foreman.'[96] But still greater benefits (both private and social) undeniably stand to be reaped where the recipient does in consequence of his education and training become the proprietor of valuable acquired capabilities on which he promises himself a return having much of the character of 'profits on capital invested'.[97] Marshall took the view that a nation requires for sustained growth 'human resources of high energy and varied faculty';[98] he stressed that 'human faculties are as important a means of production as any other kind of capital';[99] he predicted that with the increasing delegation of simple tasks to the 'properly guided mechanical slave'[100] there would increasingly be an overall demand for upgraded labour to the detriment of the less trained; and he reached the conclusion that a movement upwards was in both the private and the social interest. Assisted where appropriate by State-sponsored educational institutions, 'the children of unskilled workers need to be made capable of earning the wages of skilled work: and the children of skilled workers need by similar means to be made capable of doing still more responsible work'.[101] A nation which sets itself the goal of sustained growth simply cannot afford to waste scarce human potential or to under-provide equality of opportunity at the level of education and training – or to provide an open road to merit in the classroom without at the same time developing assiduously 'the channels by which those who are endowed with high faculties of thought and invention, of enterprise and administration, may rise rapidly to posts of responsibility commensurate with their qualities'.[102] Education without the opportunity to make use of it does little to raise the effective productivity of the human machine and it also generates intense feelings of frustration. Such feelings, fortunately, are least likely to be found in the meritocratic environment of the modern market economy, in which to an extent without precedent in history 'the relations between the various industrial strata ... are based on reason, rather than tradition'.[103] Equality of opportunity in life is an all but essential complement to equality of opportunity at the level of education and training if investment in skills and attitudes is to make its maximal contribution to economic growth.

Education and training undeniably have a sector-specific component in view of the fact that economic growth is fed not only by quantity and quality but by division of labour as well. Specialisation of knowledge and expertise boost average productivity through their contribution to improved dexterity and discernment; frequent repetition and long practice save time by converting much of the decision-making component in human action into the quick intuitive reflex; and there is, economically speaking, much to be said in favour of the system adopted by the Dutch shipwrights (a system not dissimilar to that which obtained among Petty's watch-makers and in Smith's well-known pin factory), who came to 'specialize themselves on different classes of work so that one man shall be always and only employed in the manufacture of keels of one and the same dimensions; another of ribs, another of beams, another of rudders, and so on'.[104] Admittedly there can be costs as well as benefits associated with the division of labour, as where, in industry, 'the effects of taking away from the operative any duty, save that of carrying out his instructions carefully, are not likely to be altogether good'[105] should his 'mental vision' be 'thereby dulled'.[106] Even where the mind remains 'active', moreover, monotonous and concentrated work is unambiguously 'work that has no elevating character' [107], as where, in banking, the clerk faces 'a prodigious amount of routine work, which does little towards the development of the higher faculties; and it does not tend directly, as the open air work of railway men does, to improve the physical vigour of the race'.[108] That the benefit of economic advance for all might be purchased at the cost of the mental mutilation of some is evidently a real possibility and Marshall was quick to recognise the threat: 'Not all of those characteristics of manufacture, to which its importance is owing, are of high quality. The substitution of repetition of work in massive standardized production, even though it be true to a thousandth part of an inch, is not an advance, from the human point of view, over skilled handicraft: it increases man's power over matter: but it may diminish his power over himself.'[109] Marshall, however, as a man of balance, felt compelled to point out that there can be mutilation even without mechanisation ('in places', for example, 'where nearly all furniture is made by hand, there is much monotonous weary work, without interest or initiative'[110]) and that even skilled handicraft can be ugly, unimaginative, and singularly lacking in 'high artistic excellence' (witness the work of the tradition-bound wood-carvers of the Tyrol, who 'carve toys by the cartload, many of which are crude, ill-shaped reproductions of a pattern that has been set to them'[111]). More significantly, perhaps, Marshall, as an economist with a strongly evolutionary perspective, was able to draw attention with evident satisfaction to the manner in which the accumulation of capital not only raises the average efficiency of labour (to which it acts as a complement) but also reduces the extent to which the division of labour potentially requires 'the sacrifice of the individual to the exigencies of society as regards the production of material wealth'.[112] In the case of the routine work of the bank-clerk, what this means is that 'possibly the demand for the most mechanical parts of it may be considerably checked by the further development of automatic tabulating, reckoning and printing machines',[113] while in the case of the 'dull heavy work'[114] of the factory-operative, such tasks are even now being passed to 'semi-automatic machines' which 'have taken on themselves some of the responsibilities which used to weigh heavily on artisans in the larger staple manufactures':[115] 'Machinery constantly supplants and renders unnecessary that purely manual skill, the attainment of which was, even up to Adam Smith's time, the chief advantage of the division of labour.'[116] This is not to say that mechanisation will completely eradicate the 'incidental evils' to which Smith with his 'philosophic insight'[117] had drawn attention, and in certain instances the process positively breeds de-skilling, as Marshall admitted in 1887: 'Some of those trades which had from the first to do with machinery require now not more than half or even one-fourth of the skill which they did twenty or thirty years ago.'[118] Marshall's view, simply, was that such instances were the exceptions, not the rule, in the modern era, where the division of labour accompanied by the employment of complex new plant places a premium on the exercise of the higher faculties which indeed such activity helps to breed and form: 'The machine is intricate and costly, and the person who minds it must have an intelligence, and an energetic sense of responsibility, which go a long way towards making a fine character.'[119] Specialisation accompanied not by the mutilation of 'mental vision' but by the formation of 'a fine character' is likely itself to go a long way towards promoting economic growth.

Specialisation is an important ingredient in the cake of growth. So too is mobility (both occupational and geographical); and it is important to remember that in Marshall's perspective the *yin* of 'increasing subdivision of functions'[120] is inseparable from the *yang* of barriers between trades and grades (in contrast to the 'deep and broad partitions' of the medieval guilds or the caste system) nowadays 'so slight that a man thrown out of work in one subdivision could pass into one of its neighbours without any great loss of efficiency'.[121] Thus it happens in modern economic conditions that 'the division of labour sometimes enables a man to pass easily between trades which used to be totally distinct. A country watchmaker could not easily become a gun-maker or vice versa; but many of the men in a large watch factory could easily find employment in a large rifle factory, and vice versa. When the late American war came to a close, a famous rifle factory devoted itself to making sewing machines.'[122] Such occupational mobility is an important asset to an individual who wishes to avoid the risk of long-term unemployment associated with excessive specialisation (since, clearly, 'a man whose skill can be turned to account in only one trade is likely to suffer much when that trade is depressed, or his skill is displaced by machinery'[123]) and it also enables the economy as a whole more rapidly to adapt to the imperatives of a continuously changing set of parameters – and it is on the increase: 'If we compare those industrial qualities which are Non-specialised, and can be turned to account in many trades, with those which are Specialised to one trade, we shall find that the former are rising in importance relatively to the latter. . . . Those qualities which enable men to decide rightly and quickly in new and difficult cases, are the common property of the better class of workmen in almost every trade; and a person who has acquired them in one trade can easily transfer them to another.'[124] The trend towards increased occupational mobility is reinforced by infrastructural upgrading (as where the cheap popular press and widespread literacy ensure diffusion of news concerning job-opportunities) and by institutional reform (notably the decay of guilds, apprenticeships and similar restrictions on entry); and it is complemented by a simultaneous trend towards greater geographical mobility (a trend which reflects both improvements in transport and a psychological preparedness to seize new opportunities). Those persons who opt to move (most noticeably so where the move involves international migration) are self-selected natural adapters, 'on the average bolder, sturdier, and more fertile of initiative than those who stay at home';[125] their exceptional ambition and industry makes them want not merely to move on but to move up ('the hope of rising in the world is one of the chief inducements to energetic action, and to thrifty habits' and,[126] as the torpor and indolence of the slave clearly demonstrates, 'without hope there is no enterprise'[127]); and the very act of moving has a valuable educative function in so far as it trains character to rise to challenges rather than simply conforming to traditions. Nor should it be forgotten that mobility in response to market signals is an essential precondition for optimal allocation of human resources in a system of decentralised decision-making: 'The fluidity of labour is sufficient to make it true that the wages of labour of the same industrial grade or rank tend to equality in different occupations throughout the same western country.'[128] Excessive mobility, of course, is a clear instance of having too much rather than too little of a good thing, and no one who believes that *natura non facit saltum* can have any real sympathy for change so rapid that it becomes counter-productive – as when, for example, 'the extreme hopefulness and restlessness of those who wander to new countries lead to much waste of effort in half acquiring technical skill, and half finishing tasks which are speedily abandoned in favour of some new occupation'.[129] The believer in gradual evolution is unlikely also to be an advocate of violent revolution any more than he is likely to be a supporter of the fixities and inflexibilities of tradition and stagnation. What he is likely to propose – and what Marshall did propose – is a compromise solution and a middle way with respect to the tolerable range of mobility, as with respect to most other matters lying in the field of economic and social philosophy. Those limits once established, however, the mobility of labour 'from trade to trade and from place to place'[130] must then be recognised, alongside quantity of labour, quality of labour and division of labour, as an important independent cause of sustained economic growth.

Second, capital. The input of capital involves intertemporality as well as instrumentality (in the sense that it is 'devoted mainly to securing benefits in the future rather than in the present'[131]) and consists in essence of 'the factory and the business plant of a manufacturer; that is, his machinery, his raw material, any food, clothing, and house-room that he may hold for the use of his employees, and the goodwill of his business'.[132] Capital goods are employed because of their 'productiveness',[133] because of the service they render in boosting output per unit of labour input, and their employment is on the increase. While 'there is no universal rule that the use of roundabout methods of production is more efficient than direct methods',[134] such is obviously very frequently the case as otherwise that increase would not have taken place. It is much to be welcomed: 'An increase of material capital causes it to push its way into new uses; and though in so doing it may occasionally diminish the field of employment for manual labour in a few trades, yet on the whole it will very much increase the demand for manual labour and all other agents of production. For it will much increase the national dividend, which is the common source of the demand for all; and ... by its increased competition for employment it will have forced down the rate of interest.'[135] The accumulation of capital is evidently entirely beneficial to the community: it raises the productivity of labour, expands employment opportunities, contributes to economic growth and in addition brings about redistribution in favour of the less advantaged (since the fall in the rate of interest – itself an incentive to further investment induced by the cheapening of the inanimate input – means that 'the joint product of a dose of capital and labour will now be divided more in favour of labour than before'[136]).

The act of investment presupposes a prior act of saving, and such an act in turn presupposes that two complementary conditions are satisfied. The first of these conditions involves the wherewithal, since it is reasonably clear that 'the power to save depends on an excess of income over necessary expenditure'.[137] To that extent today's growth lays the foundations for tomorrow's advance. Nor is any redistribution of income consequent upon the falling rate of interest likely significantly to discourage the supply of savings in view of the fact that all classes in an affluent society are saving classes: 'Any change in the distribution of wealth which gives more to the wage receivers and less to the capitalists is likely, other things being equal, to hasten the increase of material production ... It will not perceptibly retard the storing-up of material wealth.'[138] Then, distinct from the availability of the wherewithal, the second of the conditions involves the will to be 'wise and thrifty'[139] (as opposed to extravagant and short-sighted), the desire as well as the ability to be prudent and frugal, the capacity of 'distinctly realizing the future and providing for it'[140] (a capacity 'at once a chief product and a chief cause of civilization'[141]), the valuation of deferred gratification such as is 'seldom fully developed except among the middle and upper classes of the more cultivated nations'.[142] Such future-orientated self-control is the product of many causes, including a conscious attempt to make provision for anticipated contingencies such as illness, the hope of bettering one's social station, the desire to conform to religious traditions and/or social conventions (external constraints of this nature being at least partly the reason why the Anglo-Saxons are among the more 'steadfast and self-disciplined races'[143]), 'family affection' ('the main motive of saving'[144]), and not least the incentive to postponement of consumption that is represented by the rate of interest (since 'the higher the rate of interest, the larger the amount of future enjoyment which can be obtained by sacrificing a given amount of present enjoyment'[145]). Yet the rate of interest shows a long-term tendency to fall, and he who argues *ceteris paribus* might be tempted to draw the inference that prospectiveness with respect to saving may be expected to decline with it. Such an inference would be entirely fallacious since the fact is that we live in an 'age of abundant capital'[146] precisely because of the numerous causes which stimulate the act of saving, and of which the attraction of interest is only one among many. Put in other terms, 'capital is growing at least twice as fast as population' in 'modern England';[147] the increasingly abundant supply of loanable funds relative to demand means that savers 'are so eager to lend it out that they will accept a constantly lower and lower rate of interest for it';[148] and the fall in the rate of interest thus reveals itself to be not so much a disincentive to save as the product of a number of other forces such as have provided an exceptional stimulus, in Britain at least, to the supply of savings. He who argues *ceteris paribus* will reflect that 'a rise in the rate of interest offered for capital, *i.e.* in the demand price for saving, tends to increase the volume of saving'[149] and will voice fears concerning the adequacy of that volume should interest-rates genuinely fall, as Marshall predicted they would, to no more than two per cent within a century.[150] Marshall's reply to such an argument would have been reassuring – that any movement to the left along a given supply curve is likely to be dwarfed in magnitude by a simultaneous shift outward to the right in the schedule, and that there is therefore no real grounds for concern: 'Speaking generally, an increase in the power and the willingness to save will cause the services of waiting to be pushed constantly farther.'[151]

The supply of savings is on the increase due to the fact that man today has both a greater capacity and a greater desire to save than was the case at lower levels of economic evolution. The demand for savings, meanwhile, is also on the increase, and on all sides there are to be seen 'openings . . . all of which will tend to change the character of our social and industrial life and . . . enable us to turn to account vast stores of capital in providing new gratifications and new ways of economizing effort by expending it in anticipation of distant wants.'[152] For the surplus savings of future-orientated income-earners to be made available 'to any business that is able to turn them to profitable account',[153] however, it is plain that a sophisticated capital market must first have come into existence; and the development of institutions such as can promptly and delicately mobilise and transfer funds cannot but be regarded as a separate and an important ingredient in the cake of economic growth. Thus it is, in Britain, to the credit of 'the ease and elasticity of her banking system'[154] that finance has been made available 'from rich districts to those which hunger for it'[155] – some of them overseas, since 'many new countries are still in urgent need of capital'.[156] Due weight must also be assigned to the benefits to be derived from institutional specialisation and the division of labour, in this as in other areas of economic life. Consider the buying and selling of bills of exchange and other kinds of commercial paper. Such activity requires a considerable amount of 'special and wary study', so numerous are the industries and even the nations involved; but where – as is very often the case – a would-be borrower does not have an established reputation at a bank, such a trader can nonetheless discount his bills (albeit 'at a relatively high rate') with 'a broker, who gives his whole thought to the material and personal details of that particular market in which the trader moves: and the broker re-discounts them, after endorsement, at a bank or other financial house which does a more general business'.[157] The potential borrower is no doubt much indebted to the specialist broker for thus improving his relative attractiveness in the eyes of the ultimate lender, but the saver benefits as well from institutional specialisation. Clearly, 'a man who saves, hopes that he and his family may enjoy in security the fruits of his saving', which means in effect that 'if he or those whom he leaves behind him are unwilling or unable to employ the capital in business themselves, they must be able to lend it out to others and live in quiet on the interest of it'[158] –

which means in turn that the saver and his family will much welcome the contribution of expertise and specialisation to the processes of risk-minimisation and return-maximisation. More generally, the saver and his family are likely also to welcome the greater variety of savings instruments that are in an increasingly complex financial system increasingly on offer. Should I not wish to put my money on deposit with a bank, I nowadays have a range of other options, including the purchase of 'shares of very small amounts'[159] issued by joint-stock companies in an effort to attract the smaller saver and/or the compulsive diversifier. Should I not wish to leave my savings in low-return domestic credit markets, I nowadays have the unprecedented opportunity of scouring the world for more attractive outlets – an opportunity, needless to say, which is 'largely the product of the electric telegraph and international civil law'.[160] Not only has a sophisticated capital market come into existence, it would appear, but that capital market is becoming increasingly sensitive to the unique requirements of discrete sub-groups with special needs, both among investors and among savers. Whether at the aggregative or at the more microeconomic level, it must be concluded, the significance of this match-making function for economic growth simply cannot be underestimated.

Savings and investment are flows; flows involve the passage of time; and time in the case of capital involves invention and innovation, change and improvement, to such an extent that the machines being installed today are not only additional to the machines installed yesterday but of a qualitatively different vintage as well. The continuous upgrading of plant is a further ingredient in the cake of economic growth, and a significant one as well – since 'one new idea, such as Bessemer's chief invention, adds as much to England's productive power as the labour of a hundred thousand men'.[161] The modern inventor is, of course, fortunate in that he is able to stand upon the shoulders of giants and to build upon the cumulative and irreversible intellectual advances made by previous generations. Human knowledge, after all, is the crucial factor in production: 'It has been well said that if all the material wealth in the world were destroyed by an earthquake, leaving only the land, knowledge, and food enough to sustain life till the next harvest, mankind would in a generation or two be nearly as prosperous as before; but, if accumulated knowledge were destroyed, while the material wealth remained, several thousand years might be needed to recover lost ground.'[162] The storage and transmission of existing knowledge thus provides the foundation for future developments and the generation of additional knowledge: 'The progress of the science of business, as of all other sciences, depends largely on the clearness and precision with which the achievements of one generation are recorded so as to form starting points for those of the next.'[163] Education and communications put researchers in touch with up-to-date information on the current state of the art and with one another, but so much learning can also have its negative side: 'In modern science so much knowledge is required for originality, that before a student can make his mark in the world, his mind has often lost the first bloom of its freshness.'[164] Be that as it may, it cannot be denied that our researchers have in practice surmounted the obstacle of their erudition and have made a valuable contribution to our economic growth. There would also appear to be quite a wide range of researchers nowadays actively involved in the work of improvement. There is, for example, the entrepreneur who innovates in order to cut the costs of his operations: 'Thus he will obtain increasing return and also increasing profit: for if he is only one among many producers his increased output will not materially lower the prices of his goods and nearly all the benefit of his economies will accrue to himself.'[165] Then there is the professional student (say, the university teacher) 'in the pursuit of knowledge for its own sake':[166] motivated most of all by intellectual ambition and the love of approbation from the 'brother-experts'[167] in his peer-group, such a man makes important discoveries, ensures that his work is 'promptly published in the general interest',[168] and generates in that way valuable external economies for the nation and even the world as a whole. Yet another source of new ideas, given greater industrial specialisation, would appear to be the capital goods sector itself: 'The leaders of improvement now are often not machine-users but machine-makers.'[169] Whatever the source of the new ideas, the important inference to be drawn is that, in a dynamic economy, technology, like savings, like investment, is most realistically treated when treated as a flow, not as a stock.

Much technological advance nowadays originates within large firms – organisations capable by virtue of their very size of supporting the heavy overheads associated with research and development. These firms are able to spread the fixed cost of maintaining a staff of highly paid, highly skilled technocrats to conduct experiments; to pool the risks and the losses with the successes and the gains; to cover legal fees involved in patents and litigation. Nor are advantages with respect to technological advance the only economies of size that become accessible to the firm as it grows large. A large firm can also spread large outlays on plant (the case of the railways) and on marketing (via techniques including advertising, salesmanship, the employment of commercial travellers) over a large number of units of output; it can narrow the field of specialisation both of men and of machines while ensuring (precisely because of the large scale at which it produces) that all are constantly employed despite the extensive sub-division of tasks; it can exercise its power to obtain quantity discounts from suppliers and reduce its risk-levels by building up a recognisable and trustworthy trade-name such as Coats; and it can even afford to take advantage of recent developments in accountancy and in scientific management to identify aptitude and reward merit while simultaneously weeding out the somnolent and the incompetent. High overheads, in short, both necessitate and facilitate production on a more massive scale; but large is beautiful where internal economies of size set in and average cost falls as a result. Scale in this way, by boosting average productivity, by raising average efficiency, makes a contribution of its own to the process of economic growth. The exploitation of such economies of size, it must be added, has been considerably favoured by 'the great nineteenth century principle of interchangeable parts'[170] (which presupposes a high degree of homogeneity and is conducive to long production-runs), but retarded by a lack of standardisation on the demand side: 'In most of those trades in which the economies of production on a large scale are of first-rate importance, marketing is difficult... Though the production itself might be economically increased very fast, the sale could not.'[171] Economies of size might even be counterbalanced by concomitant diseconomies where large organisations become sluggish and inflexible, afraid of new initiatives, wasteful of resources and insensitive to potential talent; but Marshall's conclusion would appear to be that large size on balance is favourable to economic growth.

Whether it is large or small, each firm in a given industry might nonetheless be in a position to benefit from external even if not internal economies; since there exist nowadays a number of cost-reducing developments which are a function of the size of the industry, not the size of the individual firm. Thus trade papers spread intelligence on developments in a specialised area of activity. provided only that that area of activity is large enough to warrant such publications; while the concentration of businesses of a similar character in a particular locality provides a stimulus to the growth in that region of subsidiary industries and the concentration in that region of specialist labour. Intelligence that can be bought at the news-stand does not have to be internally generated, the internal economies of implement-makers are likely to become the lowered average cost curves of the parent-industry which buys the inputs, the availability of skilled labour reduces the time and expense of search; and in all of these cases the reduction of costs comes to the firm irrespective of its own expansion and output. Admittedly there might here too be diseconomies – as where the growth of our town pushes up site values, or where our exceptional dependence on a limited range of activities makes us unnecessarily vulnerable to interruptions in the supply of raw materials. But the diseconomies here too would appear to be less significant than the economies. Size of industry as well as size of firm then becomes yet another factor which has a contribution to make to the process of economic growth.

Third, organisation. More and better labour does not automatically and spontaneously join up with more and better capital so as thereby to generate, as if guided by an invisible hand, the social benefit of more and better output. Inputs must actively be brought together and consciously assigned tasks to perform, and for such work nothing less than the visible hand of the organiser and the entrepreneur will suffice. An economy can if need be substitute labour for capital at the margin or replace coal with new sources of energy. What it cannot do is to find a viable alternative to the qualities of imagination and vision, alertness and insight, adaptability and assiduity, calculative rationality combined with intuitive understanding, which are the characteristics of the business leader driven to make a decisive breach with habit and impelled by the very nature of his perennial discontent to act as the motor of change. Such a man eschews the mental bureaucratisation of routine in favour of 'bold creative enterprises' and,[172] recognising as he must that 'great progress can be attained only by bold daring',[173] he bravely shoulders the burden of 'anxiety and risk'[174] which is the constant companion of the new departure. Such a man, however, being a captain of industry rather than a gamester and a gambler, simultaneously collects information on normal outcomes, constructs alternative scenarios, involves himself in 'forecasting probable future events',[175] and in that why reveals himself to be a man of science as well as a man of hunch. Such an individual displays, in short, qualities which are not very common (yet another reason for the *carrière ouverte aux talents*, so as to minimise the wastage of rare entrepreneurial talent) and which are the essential prerequisites for sustained economic growth: 'The dark spots of western Europe are not agricultural. They are the homes of those manufactures which are divorced from initiative.'[176] Central planning is thus antithetical to economic advance precisely because it seeks to replace initiative by directive.[177] A nation which wants sustained economic growth would be well advised to delegate the making of business decisions to the unique aptitudes of a distinct factor of production, and one which is as dynamic and revolutionary as its polar opposite, land, is passive and inert.

More specifically, the choices made by the businessman would appear to fall into three main groups.

The organiser, to begin with, must select the commodity that is to be produced. Here he seeks to anticipate consumer's future wants in an effort to maximise his own rewards, but he does so in an economic environment of considerable uncertainty in view of the fact that tastes and preferences might subsequently alter and also because he is ignorant of the plans and strategies of his rivals. In order to minimise that uncertainty the organiser must frequently become something of a salesman, selecting not only the commodity itself but also the most appropriate mode of demand creation: 'A progressive business must sometimes rouse an interest in its improved and new-fashioned products: and if they are very expensive, as for instance electrical power plants are, the marketing side of the business must be very strong and enterprising and courageous: he who can discharge these functions adequately must include among his qualities and aptitudes those of a great merchant.'[178] His decision in such a case is quite clearly dual, not only what to produce but also how best to sell it.

The organiser, in addition, must select his inputs, substituting one for another at the margin until he is convinced that payment in each case is proportional to net product: 'A chief function of business enterprise is to facilitate the free action of this great principle of substitution.'[179] It is in addition the organiser who actually performs the dividing of labour, which means that he must be capable both of identifying potential economies to be made through a rearrangement of the organisational chart (a topic in scientific management) and of ensuring 'that all men are put on work for which they are fit'[180] (a topic in individual psychology and the art of 'reading the characters of strong men'[181]). With all of this he must not merely be a leader but be seen to be a leader, since 'the trust, esteem and affection of his staff are a valuable business asset'[182].

The organiser, finally, must select his techniques and must keep himself abreast of new developments. He must, in other words, demonstrate a 'high faculty for appreciating new inventions',[183] together with a decisiveness in adopting them without delay should they promise well. The organiser must, evidently, know something about the scientific and technological aspects of his trade if he is to make a shrewd and perceptive assessment of the latest discoveries. He must know something, but there is no point in knowing too much; since just as the member of the Cabinet moves from ministry to ministry 'without any great loss of efficiency' (his field of expertise being politics and not, say, agriculture or education), so the 'judgement and sagacity'[184] of the business leader is highly mobile from trade to trade depending most of all on relative rates of profit and least of all on sector-specific education (his field of expertise being business broadly defined, within which category, however, 'the peculiarity of his mind does not lie in doing any one thing in particular'[185]). The organiser must therefore steer a middle course with respect to his current line, learning just enough to be able intelligently to select techniques and assess developments while at the same time collecting information on alternative trades with different techniques and developments which might nonetheless offer an attractive home to a man of ability with an above-average endowment of 'the broad and non-specialized faculties of judgement, promptness, resource, carefulness and steadfastness of purpose'.[186] His success in steering such a middle course is in itself proof that he possesses truly entrepreneurial qualities.

The organiser spends his life in searching and selecting, dividing and combining, efficiently allocating and creatively destroying; and it is evident that such a man simply has no place in the theory of equilibrium, either partial or general. The organiser spends his life in responding to stimulus after stimulus in a time period which is absolutely continuous and in an economic environment which is continuously changing. The organiser thus constitutes the bridge between microeconomics and macroeconomics; and most of all between the theories of resource allocation with which Marshall's name is inextricably linked and the theories of economic growth of which the master architect regrettably never found the time to provide more than the shadow on the wall.

3.2 FROM BETTERMENT TO GROWTH

Economic growth is an input in the process of human betterment. Human betterment is an input in the process of economic growth. Each process is both causal and caused, both independent and dependent, and it is logical that an organicist and a functionalist such as Alfred Marshall should have found this to be the case. In the previous section we examined the nature of the ingredients in the cake of economic growth (while reflecting that the master baker never found the time to supply the precise recipe or formula by which the discrete parts are to be converted into a unified whole). In the previous Chapter we considered the numerous ways in which economic growth is related to individual and to social improvement (and concluded that the meta-principle in Marshall's economics is not the ever fuller trough of the ne'er-to-be-satisfied pig but rather the continuous betterment of tastes and preferences, conduct and character). In the present section we must complete the circuit by demonstrating that betterment not only comes from growth but also reinforces and accelerates it – to such an extent, indeed, that the more superstitious of readers may suspect the beneficent intervention of an Invisible Hand that had penned no Cambridge examination papers and yet knew enough to place the nose just above the mouth so as thereby to enable us to enjoy the smell as well as the taste of our food.

(1) Want-satisfaction

Marshall was pleased to report that money wages had risen while the cost of foodstuffs and a wealth of other consumables had fallen, with the result that living standards had reached unprecedented levels: 'Improvements in manufacture and in transport, aided by Free Trade, enable England to supply her own requirements as regards food, clothing, etc., at the cost of a continually diminishing percentage of her whole exports. Her people spend a constantly diminishing percentage of their income on material commodities; they spend ever more and more on house-room and its attendant expenses, on education, on amusement, holiday travel, etc.'[1] Due not least to the increasing complement of expensive and complicated machinery per unit of labour employed, 'there is no doubt that real efficiency wages have risen; that is, the exertion of a given amount of strength, skill and energy is rewarded by a greater command over commodities than formerly'.[2] What must be stressed is that a higher 'national dividend' means higher real incomes for all classes ('the larger it is, the larger, other things being equal, will be the share of each agent of production'[3]), including that majority of the population which is represented by the workers: 'It is to be hoped that in time the wages of manual labour will rise all over the world, mainly through increased production; but partly also in consequence of a general fall in the rate of interest.'[4] The rise results from greater productivity, greater prudence and occupational upgrading and is therefore fully justifiable; whereas, of course, 'methods of raising wages, which make for a higher standard of comfort by means that lessen rather than promote efficiency, are so anti-social and shortsighted as to invoke a speedy retribution'.[5] What the militancy of the unions cannot do, the beneficence of the growing economy can; but higher living standards then return the compliment by making a contribution of their own to subsequent growth. Poor peasant proprietors put in 'very long hours' but 'do not get through much work' not least because they 'feed themselves worse than the poorest English labourers'.[6] Yet food is fuel to the human machine; 'any stinting of necessaries is wasteful';[7] and such proprietors are a good illustration of the proposition that 'the poverty of the poor is the chief cause of that weakness and inefficiency which are the cause of their poverty'.[8] Such persons (having initially 'neither the necessaries nor the decencies of life') 'can hardly fail to get some increase of vitality and energy from an increase of comfort'[9] should some increase in efficiency occasion some increase in remuneration; and that increase of 'vitality and energy' (the result of improved health and strength due to the better diet, housing, clothing, fuel which only money can buy) then makes a feedback contribution to the process of economic growth as well as legitimating yet another increase in remuneration. Such persons, meanwhile, increasingly freed by higher pay born of higher productivity from 'dirt and squalor and misery . . . physical suffering . . . mental and moral ill-health',[10] are in an increasingly advantageous position to pass on the benefits of higher living standards to their children, thereby tending to render the improvement cumulative: 'We conclude then that an increase of wages, unless earned under unwholesome conditions, almost always increases the strength, physical, mental and even moral of the coming generation.'[11] A man's desire to secure 'a good position'[12] for his children is a noble thing but also an empty gesture in the absence of hard cash: 'In regard to popular education it is to be remembered that drinking troughs are in vain supplied for horses, if their bearing-reins are kept so tight that they cannot reach the water. Therefore, if education in any broad meaning of the word is to become a reality, reasonable conditions of life are necessary.'[13] Reasonable conditions of life, it would appear, are not only the result of past economic growth but a not unimportant cause of future economic advance as well.

A low 'standard of comfort' was associated by the Mercantilists with the wealth of nations and by Marshall with poverty, lethargy and sluggishness: 'When a person's whole energies are strained to procure him the necessaries of life, he becomes the slave, not indeed of wealth, but of subsistence... When the body is not properly nourished the spirit is in general faint and weak.'[14] A rising 'standard of comfort' was accordingly associated by Marshall with rising productivity both of the present generation and of the next. Such quantitative change, he added, was further to be welcomed because of the qualitative change which it produced – qualitative change, it must be stressed, which continues to yield its benefits long after that threshold has been reached beyond which higher incomes *per se* cease to have a significant impact on economic growth via their impact on health and strength. The benefits arising from the physical upgrading arising from a rising 'standard of comfort' are finite and accrue to the hungry and the poorly housed who cannot afford to keep their children long at school. The benefits arising from the upgrading of tastes and preferences arising from a rising 'standard of life' are not similarly constrained and circumscribed: 'A rise in the standard of life for *any* one trade or grade will raise their efficiency.'[15] In all classes of society in the course of economic growth, the pattern is the same, that better men consume better things and then do better work as a result. Because of evolution, different consume different; but the outcome is philosophically acceptable when seen in the light of the symbiotic relationship between the two desirable developments of betterment and growth. Thus the fact that increasing affluence produces an increasing 'avoidance of food and drink that gratify the appetite but afford no strength'[16] (that, for instance, 'the consumption of tea is increasing very fast, while that of alcohol is stationary'[17]) will have a strong appeal to the student of progress who wishes to nurture the economy as well as the body: 'The prevalence of intemperate habits in a country diminishes both the number of days in the week and the number of years in his life during which the bread-winner is earning full wages. Temperance increases a man's power, and generally increases his will to save for the benefit of his children, and also to bring them up well, and invest Personal capital in them.'[18] Drunkenness imposes cumulative diswelfares on future generations and is incompatible with maximal economic efficiency in this, and the same observation may be made concerning overwork: 'Overwork of every form lowers vitality; while anxiety, worry, and excessive mental strain have a fatal influence in undermining the constitution, in impairing fecundity and diminishing the vigour of the race.'[19] Such a loss is a luxury which a nation committed to economic growth simply cannot afford, and it is therefore a welcome development that with increasing affluence goes a tendency towards a substitution of leisure for labour. Shorter hours are a desirable end in their own right ('Since, after all, production is for men, and not men for production, it may be better to have shorter hours even if this should entail some loss of wealth to the whole community and some loss of wages also') and they, like temperance, are in addition frequently the means to the attainment of a further end: 'In many trades even shorter hours would increase efficiency in several ways, among others by enabling the worker to hold himself better in hand, and therefore to manage more delicate and complex machinery.'[20] Illustrated by the cases of temperance and leisure, Marshall's position is clear – that while economic growth can be associated with individual preferences that are dysfunctional from the point of view of sustained expansion (as in the case of gambling) and with commodity-characteristics that are in essence afunctional (the increasingly aesthetic sensibilities of the contemporary consumer, for example), nonetheless a rise in the 'standard of life' and an improvement in economic efficiency normally go hand in hand.[21]

A growing economy is a changing economy – an economy which displays 'an ever increasing tendency towards the substitution of new things . . . for old'[22] – and for that reason it would be true to say that growth itself is a significant cause of further growth. Novelty and variety represent utility in their own right, being antidotes to that boredom and loss of charm which is 'the result of familiarity';[23] and they introduce into social life an element of dynamism and even excitement 'without which men become dull and stagnant, and achieve little though they may plod much'.[24] Men who sought only to reproduce their traditional standard of living would not exert themselves to rise to new challenges or contend with new difficulties in order to obtain something more and/or something different, but would strive merely to obtain their 'accustomed enjoyments'[25] and thereupon cease their exertions. Such men, trapped in conventional ruts and blinkered by limited horizons, would have no incentive to develop those qualities of activity and enterprise which Marshall regarded as essential for economic advance and social progress, and they would furthermore be the harbingers of the generally stationary state in which 'there will be no new important wants to be satisfied'.[26] The fact that 'there seems to be no good reason for believing that we are anywhere near a stationary state'[27] must therefore be taken as a welcome indication that such men of little imagination are in the minority; and that a change in supply is likely to be associated with the change in demand which it deserves. Even so, however, change must not be too rapid – as in the case of 'the desire for transient luxuries' or,[28] worse still, 'the evil dominion of the wanton vagaries of fashion'[29] – lest it lead to wastage of scarce resources (where consumables, say, come to be scrapped long before their serviceability is at an end) and perhaps also to destabilising economic fluctuations (reinforced, no doubt, by sharp-eyed speculators whose business it is to anticipate non-rational whims and non-calculative fads). Fortunately, Marshall was able to report, the commodities which consumers increasingly demand in a growing economy tend increasingly to be durable, less and less to reflect transient tastes and passing fashions. Such upgrading of consumer behaviour thus comes to make a contribution of its own to the process of economic growth.

(2) Conduct and character

Alfred Marshall tended to regard patterns of conduct and character as flows, not as stocks: 'Economics cannot be compared with the exact physical sciences: for it deals with the ever changing and subtle forces of human nature.'[30] The social individual, he believed, is to a significant extent the product (once 'personal peculiarities of temper and character'[31] have been netted out by means of the law of large numbers) of his social environment; and that social environment, he was convinced, is to a considerable extent conditioned (once due allowance has been made for other causal variables such as racial endowments and religious ideals) by the nature and functioning of the economic system. Patterns of conduct and character, Marshall believed, emanate in no small measure from economic activity, just as 'bodily and mental health and strength are much influenced by occupation';[32] and those patterns of conduct and character, he was convinced, then have a feedback effect on economic activity such as to generate accelerated economic growth. The argument is circular – logically so, for 'man himself is the chief means of the production of that wealth of which he is the ultimate aim'.[33] It is also eminently optimistic – since 'the average level of human nature in the western world has risen rapidly during the last fifty years'.[34] It is also profoundly Spencerian – since the great free trader, far from being obsessed with maximum gratification from limited inputs, had himself unambiguously assigned pride of place to improvement and development: 'The end which the statesmen should keep in view as higher than all other ends, is the formation of character.'[35] It is also fully functionalist with respect to the twin processes of betterment and growth – since Marshall's argument in effect is that progress tends to mould and shape human nature in precisely such a manner as to render that progress self-sustaining. Growth leads to betterment. Betterment leads to growth. Change is not random but systemic, systematic and upwards – as may be demonstrated by examining once again, but this time as means rather than as ends, the five aspects of adaptive upgrading in conduct and character which we considered in Chapter 2.

First, honesty. Marshall stated bluntly that 'uprightness and mutual confidence are necessary conditions for the growth of wealth':[36] it being impossible for all of us at all times to watch each, publicity and public opinion only being operative as sanctions once the abuse has been brought to light, the division of labour being a major obstacle to the layman's assessment of the specialist's evaluation, Marshall reasoned, there is simply no substitute in modern economic conditions for self-restraint and self-discipline, a sense of duty and a commitment to truthfulness. Consider the example of the joint-stock company, where managers enjoy a multiplicity of opportunities to defraud shareholders and yet resist such 'gross iniquity'[37] (together with the bribery, corruption and nepotism that characterised the great trading companies of the Mercantilist period) precisely because of the 'great improvement' in the morality and uprightness of the average man'[38] that has accompanied the process of economic growth. That 'great improvement' is clearly a valuable externality to the economy as a whole. Where such background values are absent, the consequences can be grave indeed – as may be illustrated by the high interest rates, the involuntary unemployment, the sequential bankruptcies that may be brought about by a businessman trading irresponsibly with borrowed funds:

> A man trading with his own capital has every motive for exerting himself to discover whether he is carrying on his business at a loss. But the man working with borrowed capital has not such strong motives. If his moral sense is not very active he may, without intending any deliberate fraud, carry on a losing business so long as to cause heavy losses to his creditors. If he has not a strict sense of honour, and finds himself in difficulty, he may plunge into rash speculations: for if they succeed,the gain will be his; and he may not care whether he fails for a large or a small sum.[39]

The problem nowadays is that business trust and confidence are normally not reinforced by peer group pressures and collective constraint, as they would have been in a small, static and settled community; 'most of those on whose actions anyone relies are personally unknown to him'; and there is accordingly a genuine need for the public good of 'social credit' – where 'social credit' (analogous in some respects to personal and commercial credit) is to be defined as 'trust in the character of society', including trust in 'the probity and reasonableness of people generally, and especially business men and legislators'.[40]

Such 'social credit' normally subserves the public interest. Normally but not invariably, as is demonstrated by the case of a cartel formed to exclude interlopers and to raise prices. Each oligopolist has an economic incentive to cheat, thereby unintentionally bending the bent rod so as to make it straight again. Thus 'an agreement among English cotton manufacturers to limit supply might raise the price appreciably in a time of great commercial activity; but since every one wants to make hay while the sun shines, every one would be anxious to get a large share of the abnormally high profits that were then being made, and the combination would almost certainly be broken through'.[41] In such a case, where there is a reasonably large number of reasonably dispersed firms in the cartel, the informal sanctions of disapprobation and ostracism are likely to prove insufficient to prevent greed from conferring unintended benefits on the consumer. In such a case, however, honesty and self-policing may come to the rescue of the restrictive practice. Where there is honour in the nation as a whole, there is likely to be honour even among thieves; and to that extent morality and welfare point in opposite directions.

Second, respect for persons. Self-respect is the enemy of perceived degradation and the friend of self-motivated industriousness; and it is important to remember that Britain, developing her economic potential later than the Dutch, soon became a leader 'mainly because her people had never been inclined or compelled to look to authority for instructions. Each man settled his own affairs, subject to but little discipline save that of custom. And since the shackles of custom were not felt, they merely narrowed the range of action of individuality: they did not destroy it. So individuality accomplished great things, with ever-enlarging scope.'[42] Respect for oneself is in addition the valuable first step in the direction of respect for others: 'He, who respects his own individuality, is unlikely to be a tyrant: he may be wanting in tact, and in quickness to assimilate that which is good and helpful in the temper and habits of others. But he is sure to be frank, and likely to respect the individuality of others: refusing to be regimented, he is unlikely to regiment others.'[43] Employers of such openness and tolerance are unlikely to treat their workers as underlings and inferiors, a race apart; and are likely instead to search out and to promote merit, to seek to turn to economic advantage 'THE waste product', namely 'the higher abilities of many of the working classes; the latent, the undeveloped, the choked-up and wasted faculties for higher work, that for lack of opportunity have come to nothing'.[44] The employee, for his part, happy to be regarded 'not merely as a hand, but as a thinking and thoughtful human being'[45] and pleased with the triumph of achieved over ascribed status, then experiences heightened interest in and attachment to the purposes of the organisation. This shows itself in good times (*via* the contribution of *morale* to productivity) but also in bad, as is shown by the incidence of labour disputes in the late nineteenth century: 'It is noteworthy that this trouble was most conspicuous in parts of the country in which the social distinctions between employers and employed have been greatest.'[46] Assimilation of living standards and a diminution of perceived social distance would appear to bear a return of an economic as well as a cultural nature; and this illustrates the manner in which respect for persons can contribute to growth.

Third, the pursuit of excellence. It is, Marshall believed, only the 'more ignorant and phlegmatic of races and of individuals'[47] who regard work as the curse of Adam and a veil of tears. In the earliest stages of human development man toils because toil he must, but thereafter – a fact full of hope for the future of self-sustaining economic growth – man 'delights in the use of his faculties for their own sake . . . The religious, the moral, the intellectual and the artistic faculties on which the progress of industry depends, are not acquired solely for the sake of the things that may be got by them; but are developed by exercise for the sake of the pleasure and the happiness which they themselves bring.'[48] It is, it would appear, in man's nature to strive and struggle in order to overcome difficulties, to succeed in the performance of challenging and worthwhile tasks, to find new outlets 'for vigorous and creative intellect' in 'adapting means to ends, and devising new means and new ends', to pursue, in short, 'excellence for the sake of excellence'.[49] It is this pursuit of excellence which explains much of the activity of the most outstanding among captains of industry: 'Those business men, on whose work the progress of industry most depends, care for wealth more as an indication of successful achievement than for its own sake.'[50] It is this Veblenesque 'instinct of workmanship' which lies at the root of the bulk of the principal scientific advances of our times: 'There are many kinds of laboratory experiments which a man can be hired to make at a few hundred pounds a year, but the epoch-making discoveries generally come from men who love their work with a chivalrous love.'[51] Work, Marshall believed, is 'the aim of life', 'life itself';[52] and such commitment cannot but make a significant contribution to the process of economic growth. Of course money matters and matters quite a lot: 'The steadiest motive to ordinary business work is the desire for the pay which is the material reward of work.'[53] Marshall's point is simply that not *only* money matters, that not *all* incentives are pecuniary, that 'the love of money is only one among many'[54] – and that the love of a job well done is significantly on the increase in an affluent society in which it is increasingly possible for men to devote time and money to creativity and craftsmanship because they increasingly regard good work as an end in its own right. You and I, needless to say, can *via* our approbation help to accelerate the inevitable: 'We need to foster fine work and fresh initiative by the warming breath of the sympathy and appreciation of those who truly understand it.'[55] Our approbation is a reward like any other; and 'partly for that reason it may be trusted to act steadfastly'.[56] Even so, however, the supply of high-quality workmanship must not be regarded as a straightforward appeal for approbation any more than it is a straightforward appeal for money. It is at least in part a reflection of that pursuit of excellence which first emanates from economic growth and then reinforces it.

Fourth, generosity. Marshall, reflecting on the incidence of free gifts, observed that 'whenever we get a glimpse of the economic man, he is not selfish'[57] and took the view that economic man in the course of economic growth was becoming less selfish still. Such generosity is the product of past growth but also the cause of future – as where employers provide training and apprenticeships even for workers likely subsequently to move on[58] and introduce measures for their men which 'aim at developing their ability and intelligence in ways, some of which are likely to promote their efficiency as employees: and some, which are desired only as contributing to their higher well-being, are among the best fruits of the larger sense of social duty which is characteristic of the present age'.[59] Employers further demonstrate the generosity of their sentiments by typically seeking actively to place elsewhere, without a demoralising and wasteful spell of unemployment, those workers whom they make redundant through the introduction of new technologies and automation: 'When an employer displaces by a machine the special skill which men have spent their lifetime in acquiring, and which constitutes their whole capital, he generally exerts himself to prevent their sinking down to the level of unskilled labourers: if this were universally done the last plea for resistance to machinery would be removed.'[60] While it might be objected that some of the instances of 'latent chivalry' and the 'finer sympathies'[61] in business life which Marshall cites would appear to be positively dysfunctional with respect to economic growth (as where a benevolent employer stubbornly refuses despite changes in market conditions to cut the 'normal wage' for the job because of 'notions of fairness',[62] 'a desire to "do what is right" '[63] and 'ethico-prudential considerations'[64]), the point to stress is that Marshall did not draw this conclusion. Arguing characteristically that 'much of that care for employees, which has been prompted in the past mainly by altruistic motives, is commercially profitable',[65] Marshall tended to adopt the position that good intentions and good business are normally complements rather than substitutes. Economically as well as ethically, he tended to maintain, altruism matters and matters quite a lot; and for that reason it would be wrong to classify him without further qualification amongst those perhaps rather short-sighted nineteenth century economists who wrote as if 'nothing more were to be expected in business transactions than that a man should avoid dishonesty and pursue his own interests'.[66]

In any case, even those thinkers who assume that maximisation of personal material advantage is the principal goal of modern man in competitive capitalistic economic conditions would be prepared to make an exception by assigning some role to altruism within the family unit – and Marshall, not surprisingly, strongly championed such self-denying devotion to the subjective welfare of others: 'In fact the Normal supply of all grades of industry, except perhaps the lowest, depends on the unselfish sacrifice by parents of their own pleasures for the benefit of their children.'[67] It is parental altruism which causes responsible adults to limit family-size (an other-regarding instance of the broader proposition that 'regard for the future induces many individuals to control their natural impulses'[68]). It is 'a higher notion of their duties to their children'[69] which causes increasingly affluent parents to sink increasing sums of money in good food and clothing, housing 'more consistent with refinement' than the slum tenement, greater access to fresh air and sunshine, all of which tend to reduce infant mortality in the here-and-now while also representing a long-term investment in the health and strength of the labour-force. It is 'family affection' which more than any other single factor stimulates alert and ambitious parents to abstain from present consumption – and, indeed, then to plunge a significant proportion of the resultant savings in the formation of scarce skills: 'The middle and especially the professional classes have always denied themselves much in order to invest capital in the education of their children.'[70] It is accordingly such parental altruism which accounts for much of our contemporary occupational mobility: the formation of human capital by parents nowadays increasingly means (although subject to the time-lag normally associated with training) that 'sons are less frequently found in their father's occupation'[71] than was the case when our society was poorer and our national stock of generosity still underdeveloped. Clearly, however, 'an increase of population may go with a rapid rise in average wages, if the children of each grade are brought up with the intelligence, self-command, and vigour that now belong to the grade above them';[72] and growing parental altruism therefore gives us good grounds for optimism concerning economic growth in the future.

In a meritocratic society such as ours is increasingly becoming, the 'stronger and more strenuous' rise to higher fortunes – but the 'weak and the dissolute'[73] simultaneously sink into the *residuum*. Fortunately, an increasingly generous society increasingly provides the safety net of private philanthropy to catch these unfortunates and to reintegrate them into constructive economic life. Marshall, his ideas reflecting in some measure what Beatrice Webb described as 'a new consciousness of sin among men of intellect and men of property',[74] had great respect for the initiative of Ebeneezer Howard, the work of the Garden City Movement, the activity of the Charity Organisation Society – all of them indications of the kind of welfare society which is likely to emerge as increasingly other-regarding individuals increasingly come together in groups.[75] Ours, more generally, is an era of corporatism and grouping, and that development is much to be welcomed, satisfying as it does a human need to manifest generous sentiments through constructive actions: 'He who lives and works only for himself, or even only for himself and his family, leads an incomplete life; to complete it he needs to work with others for some broad and high aim.'[76] Admittedly such groups can become particularist, narrow-minded and inward-looking, other-regarding within but self-seeking without; and it must be conceded that the development of charitable associations (formed to assist the needy) has been coincidental with the development of trades unions (formed to assist their members). Marshall, as is well known, privately entertained in later life certain doubts concerning the unions; but his more usual view was that the modern trades union increasingly demonstrates that very 'gravity, self-restraint, dignity and forethought'[77] which we would indeed expect in an era of increasing generosity. Nowadays unions are normally involved in 'an effort to obtain conditions of life consistent with true self-respect and broad social interests, as much as a struggle for higher wages'[78] – a significant upgrading of their behaviour which parallels the 'growing power and intelligence of the manual labour classes'[79] and which dates at least from the repeal of the Combination Laws: 'With freedom came responsibility. Violence and the intimidation of Non-Unionists, which had lost all excuse, soon went out of favour; and workmen generally chose for their leaders able and far-seeing men, and under their guidance the modern organization of Unions has been rapidly developed.'[80] Unions exercise countervailing power on behalf of labour (but higher pay can be self-validating where it induces higher productivity); they seek to render members independent of charity via the provision of Benefit and Provident funds which involves an insider's inspection of the cause, voluntary or involuntary, of the state of dependency); they seek to enforce standards (not least by punishing members who are frequently out of work due to drunkenness); and they in these and other ways play their part in the drama of economic growth. They are able to play that part because they are a self-help group which educates the worker in the value of other-regarding actions: 'When the interests of his republic appear to clash with his own, his "patriotism" teaches him to bear and forbear: in adversity he will suffer hunger, in prosperity he will decline his own advancement.'[81] Unions are in addition able to play their part in the drama of economic growth because of the 'self-restraint' which they increasingly show, because of the concern with 'broad social interests' which they increasingly demonstrate. Exceptions can be found (the occasional violent and disruptive strike is one and resistance to the adoption of shift-working is another), but exceptions are exceptions and the rule is the rule – the rule being that unions, like most of the other groups and groupings which characterise our era, serve the cause of economic growth in no small measure because of the generosity of sentiments which increasingly informs their actions.

Fifth, deliberateness. Deliberateness is on the increase, both at the level of projection and at that of execution. It shows itself in 'energy and initiative, and a high sense of the value of time',[82] in imagination, determination, and 'resourceful inventiveness',[83] in that telescopic foresight combined with resolute prudence which is an essential feature of those 'men of vigorous and enterprising faculty'[84] who are destined to become the leaders of our industry. Creative imaginativeness is, naturally, a desirable quality in its own right, and so too is self-control: 'Strong men are getting more and more to recognize that a deep full character is the only true source of happiness, and that it is very seldom formed without the pains of some self-compulsion and some self-repression. Those who from childhood upwards have been able to gratify every whim are apt to be poor in spirit.'[85] Apart from their value as ends, however, creative imaginativeness and self-control also have considerable significance as means with respect to the objective of economic growth.

Consider the case of the inter-temporal transfer. The habit of mind of 'distinctly realizing the future' is 'as yet not very common'[86] but is is becoming more common as men become more capable of conceptualising future pleasures and discounting them against present pains. As with perception, moreover, so with execution; for not only does man today increasingly possess the intellective power 'of realizing the future and bringing it clearly before his mind's eye'[87] but he is also more willing to act on the basis of that information. Man, in other words, 'though still somewhat impatient of delay, has gradually become more willing to sacrifice ease or other enjoyment in order to obtain them in the future . . . He is more prudent, and has more self-control.'[88] Higher incomes by themselves, it must be stressed, are a necessary but not a sufficient condition for deferred gratification and capital formation. They generate the economic ability to save but they equally generate the economic ability to spend on drink and the casino. The conscious decision to be frugal must accordingly originate in some other source, and here the upgrading of conduct and character consequent upon economic growth comes to the rescue: 'A rise in wages leads in the course of time to an increase in the will to save, as well as in the power to save.'[89] This upgrading, in fact, is all but inevitable in the course of economic evolution: 'Children and nations in an early stage of civilisation are almost incapable of realising a distant advantage; the future is eclipsed by the present . . . . But when the child or the race grows up to maturity, it learns to exert itself for the sake of the future, as well as for the sake of the present.'[90] As with children and savages, of course, so with the poor, who 'are careless about the distant future both of their children and of themselves; for they have not a vivid imagination; they are ruled by custom and not by the deliberate use of their reason'.[91] For poor people as well as poor nations, however, the future is full of hope – since rising incomes are likely to generate those very qualities of creative imaginativeness and self-control which then lead to an even more rapid rise in incomes.

Consider now the market for land. The landowner in the past has been known to make important economic decisions on the non-rational basis of social, political and even religious considerations (to the detriment not only of civil rights but of allocative efficiency); whereas nowadays such 'evils' are 'rapidly diminishing'[92] and the landowner increasingly makes decisions in the light of calculative rationality (a vote both for social tolerance and for economic growth). Similarly, the landowner in the past has been prevented by the 'constraining force of custom and public opinion'[93] from varying tenures and rents in accordance with supply and demand; whereas nowadays 'the moral sense of all around him' (together with his own personal moral sense) is less and less outraged by behaviour-patterns reflecting contract rather than tradition. This is not to deny that the market price of land is in the event abnormally high relative to its economic return because of the fact that it yields non-pecuniary benefits as well in the form of 'social status',[94] a 'way into good society',[95] 'social amenity and political influence'.[96] On the contrary – since these and other influences (economic and non-economic) on the demand-function for the commodity demonstrably influence its price in our present-day free market system and, sadly, did not do so in that earlier period when weighing at the margin and optimal adaptation were constrained and stifled by the force of habit and the tyranny of the done thing.

Consider finally the case of geographical mobility. Movement from areas of surplus to areas of scarcity is an important part of the process of economic growth but it seldom if ever demonstrates the automaticity of the knee-jerk reflex. The reason is that the mobility of labour is another name for the mobility of the labourer; and 'the unwillingness to quit home, and to leave old associations, including perhaps some loved cottage and burial-ground, will often turn the scale against a proposal to seek better wages in a new place. And when the different members of a family are engaged in different trades, and a migration which would be advantageous to one member would be injurious to others, the inseparability of the worker from his work considerably hinders the adjustment of the supply of labour to the demand for it.'[97] Much of immobility is fully rational – as where some men 'prefer London life'[98] and consciously count location alongside pay in computing the net advantage of their employment. Some forms of immobility are, however, less rational – as where men fail to seize attractive opportunities due to 'apathy and ignorance',[99] 'ignorance and indifference',[100] 'lack of information'[101] and straightforward 'lethargy'.[102] That part of immobility which is fully rational is likely to survive; and despite pay differentials such considerations as the 'expense and trouble of moving'[103] will always deter certain born calculators from pulling up stakes. The spread of deliberateness, however, to the extent that it is even now undermining the non-rational foundations for inertia and equilibrium, has a not inconsiderable impact on the market for labour; 'new developments of critical and analytical faculties have caused men increasingly to submit their instinctive tendencies to the cold arbitrament of numerical estimates';[104] and where this then leads to greater mobility in pursuit of pay, such calculative rationality, here as elsewhere, makes a valuable contribution to sustained economic growth.

(3) Change - the negative side

Preferences and traits emerge in the course of economic evolution as outputs which become inputs and which help to render economic development cumulative. Change is, however, not without its negative side, and the question then becomes whether that which is morally undesirable is also undesirable when seen from the perspective of economic growth.

First, want-satisfaction. Conspicuous consumption and unnecessary changes in fashion squander scarce resources; and for that reason men and women who turn themselves into 'dandyfied perambulating machines'[105] not only sin against the spirit of art but against betterment and growth as well. Rapid change in tastes means shopkeepers are likely to be left with excess stocks of unsaleable goods; a great part of marketing is 'almost pure waste'[106] where demand is neither created nor destroyed but merely redistributed as between competing brands; the pursuit of excellence is incompatible with built-in obsolescence and frequent model-changes, just as the norm of rationality is incompatible with non-rational consumer behaviour reflecting nothing more than the blind force of habit and the iteration of a name; and there is also a danger that too much luxury at home will render us soft, sluggish and therefore insufficiently competitive abroad. This danger was undeniably uppermost in Marshall's thinking when, towards the end of the First World War, he wrote as follows in a letter to *The Economist* on 'The Need for More Taxation': 'Almost every great increase in a nation's wealth and prosperity has been preceded by a period of hard living. And there is therefore some little justification for the boast of the Germans that they are working as hard as we are and consuming much less; that, therefore, their resources are not being diminished as rapidly relatively to ours as might have been anticipated, and that the hardships which they are enduring are a better preparation for energetic work after the war than are the unwonted luxuries which some of us are enjoying at the expense of mortgaging the future for the benefit of the present.'[107] You are to a non-trivial extent what you eat and what you wear. England is happy for you to enjoy some luxuries but also expects you to keep your personal cost of production within reasonable limits. To the extent that you become lax in that respect, your high personal cost of production represents an entirely unwarranted tax on your fellow-citizens, and one which is gleefully collected by our foreign competitors.

Second, the family. A good home has, in Marshall's view, a significant impact not only on the growth of the child from boy to man but also on that of his nation from poor to rich: 'A man's physical and moral qualities depend chiefly upon the character of his home in youth. If he was well fed and housed, if his father, and what is perhaps more important, if his mother had energy and kindness and honesty, he is pretty sure to have those physical and moral qualities which are a necessary condition of industrial efficiency.'[108] Economic growth is clearly favoured by a good home. Whether economic growth is equally favourable to a good home is less clear. Growth, accompanied as it is by capital accumulation, and occupational upgrading, tends to raise the productivity and pay of the woman while simultaneously reducing the real cost embodied in the toil which she performs for money: 'The progress of science and machinery is opening out to women many new occupations in which very little physical strength is required. Telegraphy is a good instance of these.'[109] Here, because of change and mechanisation, the woman comes to earn higher wages for lighter work and is not so exhausted by her paid labour that she is unable to spend a constructive evening's leisure with her husband and children. Yet the fact remains that a woman who is in the factory or the office is a woman who is not at home; and the truth is that as paid labour becomes lighter and wages higher, so women have *ceteris paribus* a greater incentive to accept outside employment. This tendency is reinforced by the spread of education (which makes women able to do more challenging and better paid jobs) and by the decay of prejudice, apprenticeship regulations and trade union restrictions such as once discriminated against them (this decay reflecting the profit-orientated economic rationality and the meritocratic commitment to equality of opportunity which are so characteristic of our enlightened times). Peasants are poor, but at least 'agricultural families in new countries . . . work together so that the family life is not broken up, and the physical, mental and moral well-being of the children is well cared for'.[110] The temptation faced by women in rich countries increasingly to substitute filthy lucre for family responsibilities gives rise to legitimate concern with respect to the quality of our own offspring. To the extent that it sinks because of women's wish to resemble men, to that extent economic growth breeds and rears its own nemesis.

This might happen but it need not happen – since men (and, still more, women) can via their ideals and attitudes influence the course of events, as seems to have been the case in Germany: 'The German woman, though well educated, is in no way emancipated from the old ideals of patient devotion to family cares. And the intense interest, which parents take in the schoolwork of their children, is in the first rank among the sources of German progress.'[111] That progress is in addition the cause of still further progress where rising living standards cause children to be better 'fed and housed' than would otherwise have been the case (since children thrive on 'cleanliness, comfort and sobriety'[112] and wilt in the absence of it); and progress, associated as it is with an improvement in the 'energy and kindness and honesty' of both men and women, could conceptually even lead to women refusing jobs outside the home, to men turning down voluntary overtime in order to invest time and care in the next generation. Less labour is in such a case supplied today (at some cost to the rate of economic growth) but better labour is supplied tomorrow (a definite benefit). Given the upgrading of moral sentiments in general and the power of public opinion in particular, the conclusion must be reached that a good home might be threatened by the process of economic growth but that economic growth itself might in practice generate the appropriate countervailing forces that are needed to protect the important input of a healthy family life.

Third, speculation. Constructive speculation is an important part of the normal work of the entrepreneur and represents a genuine contribution to the process of economic growth: 'When a man has superior knowledge that the supply of anything is likely to run short in any particular country or in the world generally; and buys it either outright or for future delivery; then, on the assumption that his judgement is right, his action is to be regarded as constructive speculation. Such work adds to the world's wealth, just as diverting a stream to work a watermill does, for it tends to increase the supply of things where and when they are likely to be most wanted, and to check the supply of things where and when they are likely to be in less urgent demand. This is its most conspicuous service.'[113] Destructive speculation is another matter. Fraud, false news, rumour-mongering, manipulation, cliques, corners, reckless gambling, inadequate capitalisation and similar evils, Marshall maintained, constitute a real threat to the stability (both microeconomic and macroeconomic) of the economy as well as being morally reprehensible in their own right: business failures, financial upheavals, and 'an exceptionally rapid succession of disastrous commercial crises'[114] are hardly the stuff of which the wealth of nations is made. Yet the very fact that Marshall adopted an evolutionary perspective when examining the problem suggests that, here as elsewhere, he was moderately optimistic about the course of change – as in the following: 'It has been generally agreed that the vehement fury of speculation during most of the eighteenth century in the few stock exchange securities which were accessible, indicates that *the time had not arrived* at which more gain than loss was likely to arise from opportunities offered to the general public to hand over the control of their capital directly to businesses, of which they had no personal or technical knowledge.'[115] *The time had not arrived* – but forces such as improved honesty and greater publicity increasingly evolve in a growing economy which favour the healthier and more functional kinds of speculation while containing the power of the malign to cause harm – and it is therefore likely that the time is every day arriving a bit more.

Fourth, competition. Competition in itself is entirely beneficial to the growth process. Marshall had a strongly utopian streak and was fond of indicating that 'in ideal freedom there is no competition, except perhaps emulation in doing good for its own sake'.[116] As a realist, however, he saw that the institution of private property and the maximisation of personal gain were necessary stimuli to human nature at the present stage of social evolution. Simply, he argued, there must obtain, in this as in other arenas of life, a certain degree of moderation. Too much competition is not functional with respect to growth and progress. Nor is too little.

The problem of too much competition is the problem of 'bitter contentiousness' and frenzied conflict. Trade in such an environment tends to degenerate into a 'species of warfare', men become obsessed with the desire to win the prizes of financial success and social esteem in zero-sum games which other men must lose, and qualities such as honesty and generosity come to be seen as second-best alternatives compared to trickery and strategy. The oligopolist, for example, does not love interloping new entrants as himself but employs instead 'ferocious and unscrupulous methods to compass their undoing';[117] and he is equally nasty to his partners in the cartel, conspicuously keeping his prices constant but surreptitiously making 'improvements of service'[118] in an attempt to cheat them of their agreed market-shares. Such conduct is a threat to 'high ethical principles' and – because such principles are an input as well as an end – to orderly economic growth as well. Market freedom, Marshall believed, is a valuable thing, but only if constrained by background values, social conventions and a perception of duty – and 'the great evil of our present system . . . lies in the fact that the hope and ambition by which men's exertions are stimulated have in them too much that is selfish and too little that is unselfish'.[119] It is in such circumstances all too easy for competition to destabilise the economy, render the pace of change intolerably rapid, contervail the process of human betterment, and in these ways reveal itself as dysfunctional with respect to sustained economic growth.

The problem of too little competition is the problem of 'a few large firms',[120] of 'vast joint stock companies, which often stagnate, but do not readily die,'[121] of giant corporations with economies of size so great that they become bureaucratised within and dominant without: 'Continued rivalry is as a rule possible only when none of the rivals has its supply governed by the law of increasing return.'[122] The problem is in addition that of cartels, trusts and collusive arrangements which impede dynamic change and new entry, which reward military discipline and penalise entrepreneurial flair, which – last but not least – misuse their market power by ruthlessly 'restricting their supplies to the home consumer, in order to compel him to pay an artificially high price for them'.[123] And the problem is that of strong but irresponsibly militant unions which resist cost-cutting new techniques lest these 'render their skill obsolete',[124] which insist on 'cruel apprenticeship regulations'[125] such as exclude men capable of expanding the supply of high-class work from entry into a trade for which they have an aptitude (only one of many 'anti-social contrivances for stinting output'[126] of which far too many unions are now enamoured), which become involved in 'laborious laziness', make-work policies, rigid and inflexible demarcation of tasks and other devices which dull initiative, diminish the adaptability of the economy and ultimately cause capital to emigrate. Our workers nowadays even exert informal pressures on one another not to raise the norm – pressures so great that they are in truth adversely affecting the competitiveness of British goods in world markets: 'The appeal to a strong worker not to work so hard as to cast reflections on others who are less able, or even less industrious, is a chief cause, so far as the employees are concerned, of the vastly inferior *per capita* output of British industries to those of America.'[127] As with America, so with Germany, where 'the long hours of more or less intensive work'[128] to which her labour-force is accustomed (reinforced in the case of that country by a high cultural valuation of obedience) have tended to render British goods relatively less attractive to final consumers. Newly industrialising countries such as America and Germany are forced by the logic of their new-boy situation to adopt the best techniques and the best machinery. In England, however, we are accustomed to customs and unjustifiably complacent that the sun will never set on the workshop of the world; and it is, sadly, our recent experience that 'the spirit, if not the formal regulations, of the old guilds offered a more or less open opposition to the introduction of new methods that tended to lower the value of the knowledge and the skill obtained by long training.... American manufacturers, who have travelled in England and in Germany, appear to be unanimous in their opinion that a modern American machine is less likely to be worked grudgingly and to less than its full capacity in Germany than in England.'[129] Britain is falling behind in sunrise areas of industrial advance such as important branches of electrical engineering and chemicals,[130] Marshall noted in 1903, and limping economic growth can in an unharmonious world all too easily have unpleasant political consequences: 'Our real danger is that we shall be undersold in the product of high class industries, and have to turn more and more to low class industries. There is no fear of our going backwards absolutely, but only relatively.... This might be tolerable if peace were assured; but I fear it is not. Here I am very sad and anxious.'[131] In the extremely long run, of course, there remains the background threat of physical limits to economic growth due to increasing world population and (despite improvements in agricultural techniques, transport and communications) world diminishing returns. But it is hard to be a Ricardian in the shadow of the Kaiser; since perhaps in the extremely long run we shall all be not growing and progressing but – quite literally – dead.

4 Collective Action

One model of collective action is that which relies on unintended outcomes of egoistic action for the static welfare and the dynamic upgrading of the social organism as a whole – which argues that private vices are public virtues where adaptation to environment and the consequent collective progress are concerned. This model sees the normal relationship between citizens in a society as being based not upon benevolence and stranger-gifts but rather upon self-interest and the exchange of the *quid* for the *quo*. The orientation is perhaps sordid but the co-ordinated collective action which results, as if guided by an invisible hand, is not: because I demand your deer I must supply your beaver and not your pin-factory, much as the function of the heart is to pump blood and not breath. This is the model of collective action that was presented by Herbert Spencer when, in the shadow of Smith and the footsteps of Darwin, he reached the following conclusion concerning the primacy of individual action in an inescapable future which he was only too happy to welcome: 'The ultimate man will be one whose private requirements coincide with public ones. He will be that manner of man, who, in spontaneously fulfilling his own nature, incidentally performs the functions of a social unit; and yet is only enabled so to fulfill his own nature, by all others doing the like.'[1] Spencer's most eloquent defence of maximal personal responsibility, minimal governmental direction, may be found in the four essays which he contributed to the *Contemporary Review* of 1884 and which, appearing soon thereafter in book form under the important title of *The Man Versus The State*, did much to advance the libertarian cause at a time when Spencer's influence upon the Victorian mind was at its zenith.

It was in the year of those four essays that Alfred Marshall joined Jowett's Balliol for what was to prove a single season prior to taking up the Chair of Political Economy at Cambridge; and while there Spencer's ideas and predictions must have constituted the meat and potatoes of more than one High Table exchange of views. Unable to participate was T. H. Green, whose short life (1836–82, as opposed to Spencer's lengthy if not always happy one, 1820–1903) had exhausted itself two years earlier, but whose influence lived on in its intellectual home – and far beyond. As Richter puts it: 'Between 1880 and 1914, few, if any, other philosophers exerted a greater influence upon British thought and public policy than did T. H. Green.'[2] Alfred Marshall was not exempt from that influence and from the 'politics of conscience' to which it pointed. Both he and Mary Paley, after all, had been exposed at an impressionable age to an Evangelical upbringing so strict that even an agnostic such as Marshall later became can never entirely escape the moral baggage of his past. It was to precisely such souls in the torment of limbo that the doctrines of Philosophical Idealism had the greatest appeal. In Richter's words:

> The fortunes of Idealism were determined by the intellectual situation which challenged the grounds for belief of a generation brought up under the discipline of evangelical piety. Green adapted Idealism to the needs of those who wanted justification for the moral code and values of their parents: he gave conscience a political and social meaning, and gave an outlet to the strong sense of duty and obligation to serve, so characteristic of his generation. . . . His work had an avowed religious purpose. He sought to replace fundamentalist Evangelicalism by a metaphysical system that would transform Christianity from a historical religion into an undogmatic theology. This would turn the attention of those disciplined in Evangelical families away from the means of personal salvation in the next world to improving the condition of this one. In politics as in theology, the doctrine of citizenship and reform developed by Green can best be understood as a surrogate faith appealing to a transitional generation.[3]

In the work of Green we encounter a second model of collective action and one very different in character from that of the methodological individualist. Where the Philosophical Radical spoke of self-interest, the Philosophical Idealist spoke of self-denial and self-sacrifice. Where the libertarian spoke of individualism, the corporatist spoke of belonging and solidarity. Where the student of Bentham spoke of utility, the student of Kant spoke of duty and commitment. Where the economist spoke of outcome (and suggested that unappealing motives are legitimated by attractive results), the moralist spoke of intent (and maintained that only good can lead to good). Where, finally, the political minimalist spoke of *laissez-faire* and the invisible hand, the social reformer called for deliberate action and State intervention to help correct the abuses born of class snobbery and unequal development – co-ordinated collective action on such a scale, indeed, that Richter goes so far as to call it 'something close to a practical programme for the left wing of the Liberal Party.'[4] Individual action via private philanthropy naturally remains of great importance (and good works such as participation in settlement houses in the East End, in boys' clubs, in voluntary hospital visiting, in private charities, are much to be welcomed as indicative of genuine inner-worldly piety, correctly channelled). But sometimes it is not enough, and then the integrated citizen imbued with Christian values has no choice but to call for collective action via State intervention if he is himself to sleep soundly in his bed: 'This is a civic religion which Green taught . . . He asked the privileged to sacrifice their selfish advantages so that the poor and weak might be given the chance to realise their potentialities. In return, the privileged would gain the release from bad conscience and more: that moral development which comes from living in a moral society where all men are treated as agents, each of whom is an end equally to himself and to others.'[5]

Alfred Marshall was acquainted with the theories both of Spencer and of Green and with the centuries of debate on the nature of collective action which they reflect. It is with his own views on collective action (action which, of course, he saw both as cause and effect of evolutionary upgrading in a world where, as in that both of Spencer and of Green, the clock never stops and time never stands still) that we shall be concerned in the four sections of this Chapter. We begin with Marshall's rejection of socialism and end with his praise of co-operation. In the two central sections we examine his attitudes to the orchestration of mutual aid and self-help on a national scale by our men in Westminster and Whitehall. No clear picture emerges and no clear conclusion can be drawn – Alfred Marshall was far too cautious for that – and the reader remains free to guess in which direction the invisible finger points.

4.1 SOCIALISM

In the preface to *Industry and Trade* Marshall in 1919 turned his mind once again to the days of his youth and declared that he had then 'developed a tendency to socialism': 'For more than a decade I remained under the conviction that the suggestions, which are associated with the word "socialism", were the most important subject of study, if not in the world, yet at all events for me.'[4] The decade in question is not identified by name; but an examination of the tenor of his various writings would seem to place it roughly between 'The Future of the Working Classes' in 1873 (when Marshall was thirty-one) and the paper to the Industrial Remuneration Conference in January 1885.

The term 'socialism' means different things to different people. To Marshall it seems to have involved three characteristics.

First, a concern with greater equality of outcome as well as of opportunity. Marshall even as a youngish man came to the conclusion that inequalities in remuneration were less arbitrary or accidental than was commonly thought and could indeed be explained in terms of 'natural' causes – but he also took the view that, despite the unquestioned existence of such natural constraints, men still remained in some measure the masters of their own collective destiny: 'I believed that the causes of these causes were not wholly beyond human control; and that they might probably be so modified as to bring about a nearer approach to equality of conditions, and a better use of the products of human effort for the benefit of humanity.'[2] Greater equality of outcome, needless to say, has a sociological as well as an economic dimension in that it normally brings with it that greater overlapping of life-experiences which obtains when a society is not made up of rich and poor but only gentlemen capable of participating equally in a culture common to all.

A concern with levelling is indeed a characteristic of socialism, Marshall believed, but he also made clear that avowed socialists are by no means unique in advocating redistribution of wealth and income. As he wrote to Lord Reay in 1909: 'I do not know what "socialistic" means. The *Times* has just said that it means taking away *property* from individuals and giving it to the State. But the Budget proposes to take *money*: and if, say, £M150 have to be levied by taxation, the Budget, *whatever its form*, must be accordingly Socialistic to the extent of £M150, neither more nor less.'[3] Redistribution *per se* is a socialistic act because it involves central direction (the second of the three characteristics of socialism that may be identified in the thought of Alfred Marshall). *Levelling* redistribution is therefore doubly socialistic, marrying as it does the element of compulsion to the pursuit of equality.

Second, a commitment to paternalism and State direction: 'My own notion of Socialism is that it is a movement for taking the responsibility for a man's life and work, as far as possible, off his shoulders and putting it on to the State.'[4] Such limitation of autonomy may be found, say, in the case of Germany's methods for dealing with its 'Residuum': 'In my opinion Germany is beneficially "socialistic" in its regimentation of those who are incapable of caring for themselves.'[5] Socialism is here being linked explicitly to direction by others and, more generally, it is *central* direction which in common parlance is widely taken to be the essential feature of socialism. In common parlance, Marshall wrote in 1907, the label 'socialist' is extensively applied to 'everyone who strenuously endeavours to promote the social amelioration of the people . . . at all events, if he believes that much of this work can be better performed by the State than by individual effort. In this sense nearly every economist of the present generation is a Socialist. In this sense I was a Socialist before I knew anything of economics; and, indeed, it was my desire to know what was practicable in social reform by State and other agencies which led me to read Adam Smith and Mill, Marx and Lassalle.'[6] Note, however, that State direction is not to be confused with State ownership – nor, therefore, 'socialists' with 'collectivists'. The latter are quite a different breed of animal, seeing as they are to be defined specifically as 'those who would transfer to the State the ownership and management of land, machinery, and all other agents of production'.[7] Marshall tells us that he had a tendency to socialism. He does not say that he had a tendency to collectivism.

Third, a conviction that altruism is morally superior to egotism. Marshall declared that 'true Socialism' is 'based on chivalry'[8] and indicated that men in an ideally socialistic environment would, theoretically speaking, 'work for the general good with all the energy, the inventiveness, and the eager initiative that belonged to them'[9] without any thought of the *quid pro quo*: 'Men would think only of their duties; and no one would desire to have a larger share of the comforts and luxuries of life than his neighbours.'[10] Of course, 'in a world in which all men were perfectly virtuous, competition would be out of place; but so also would be private property and every form of private right' – and this inevitably leads one to speculate on the possibility that 'energetic co-operation in unselfish work for the public good'[11] and an associated eagerness to rank duties significantly above rights might ultimately engender a form of back-door collectivism such as may be implicit in Marshall's definition of socialism but is nowhere and never explicit.

Marshall in his thirties had a 'tendency to socialism'. Marshall as he grew older grew increasingly hostile. The following statement made in 1909 is indicative of the strength of his feelings: 'I regard the Socialistic movement as not merely a danger, but by far the greatest present danger to human well-being.'[12] If anything it seems to have been the very spread of socialistic ideas and working class movements which pushed Marshall to the right and caused him in 1902 to issue the following warning: 'Now that democratic economics are so much more popular than they were a generation ago; now that the benefits of socialistic and semi-socialistic action are so much more widely advertised, and its dangers so much underrated by the masses of the people, I think it is more important to dwell on the truths in Mill's *Liberty* than on those in his *Essays on Socialism*.'[13] Ironically, it was to those same *Essays*, when originally published in the *Fortnightly Review* of 1879, that Marshall attributed a significant formative influence on his earlier 'tendency to socialism'.[14]

Marshall's objections to socialism (which, it must be said, closely resemble those raised by Herbert Spencer) fall into four categories. Those four classes of objections to socialism are as follows:

First, socialists are dreamers, utopians and poets, men with little or no understanding of how resources are allocated and business life is organised. Even at the peak of his flirtation with socialism, Marshall said in 1919, he had nonetheless known that the authors he was reading with such admiration were capable of feeling intensely but not always of thinking clearly: 'The writings of the socialists generally repelled me, almost as much as they attracted me; because they seemed far out of touch with realities.'[15] And indeed, as early as 1881 he had in actual fact declared publicly that 'wild rhapsodies' are no substitute for scientific analysis – as when, looking back in that year, he reported: 'I read the Socialists: and found much with which anyone who has a heart at all must sympathise, and yet I found not one Socialist who had really grasped economic science.'[16] Yet without economic science we cannot expect economic growth, and without economic growth we can expect neither social change nor human betterment.

Historically speaking, socialists have become imbued with 'the wild deep poetry of their faiths' to such an extent that they, ignoring the laws of nature and not troubling to take the practicable into account, have 'recklessly suggested means which were always insufficient and not seldom pernicious – recklessly, because their minds were untrained, and their souls absorbed in the consciousness of the grandeur of their ends'.[17] Needless to say, where men 'have not had a training in thinking out hard and intricate problems', where they do not see the difficulties which actualities and events throw in the path of 'creeds and catechisms',[18] the outcome of schemes such as those of the socialists is more or less what we would expect: 'The greater part put forth hastily conceived plans which would often increase the evils that they desire to remedy.'[19] One reason for the generally low level of economic awareness among socialists, incidentally, would seem to be the fact that 'the greater part'[20] of authors writing in the socialist tradition are Germans (together with Americans and others 'much under German influence'[21]): citizens of more nearly an agricultural than an industrial commonwealth, men with all too little exposure to free enterprise as opposed to State directive, it is no surprise that socialist authors are remarkably naive when it comes to comprehending precisely how a sophisticated economic system really operates.

Second, socialists speak of man as he *ought to be*, not of man as he *is*, in any society known to us, when they speak of sustained social action emanating exclusively from other-regarding motivation. Socialists tend to exaggerate the incidence of generosity in real-world social conditions due to their propensity to attribute to every man 'an unlimited capacity for those self-forgetting virtues that they found in their own breasts'[22] – Marshall wrote those words as early as 1873 – and the result is a distorted picture of human nature as it is *now*: 'History in general, and especially the history of socialistic ventures, shows that ordinary men are seldom capable of pure ideal altruism for any considerable time together.'[23] Yet, clearly, 'in the responsible conduct of affairs, it is worse than folly to ignore the imperfections which still cling to human nature'.[24]

The word 'still' is important and reminds us of the extent to which Marshall, like the socialists, accepted that man could be chivalrous and was indeed in the process of becoming increasingly so. Unlike the socialists, however, Marshall took the view that the clay was still coarse and that the time was therefore not right at the present for the suppression of material incentives. Conviction, he argued, is by itself simply not adequate to justify running the risks that would be involved in the introduction of the new (even if indeed the higher) civilisation that the socialists have in mind: 'Those who believe that all commerce of the world will ere long be carried through the air should make a few aeroplanes carry heavy cargoes against the wind before they invite us to blow up our railway bridges.'[25] Certainly when one looks at the outcome of the projects which socialists have already undertaken the evidence on the efficacy of voluntary self-sacrifice is not encouraging. Scheme after scheme seems to have failed because of 'the belief on the part of some of the members that others were doing less than their share of hard and disagreeable work, or were getting insidiously more than their share of the comforts and amenities of life'.[26] Voluntary self-sacrifice, sadly, presupposes unselfish and earnest volunteers, men who welcome the opportunity to 'bring out latent powers of goodness in human nature'[27] – and therefore withers away in the face of agents too lazy to volunteer, too 'frail and faulty'[28] to eschew the benefits of free ridership. Socialism is in sum inexpedient so long as most men are what they are, namely unprepared to 'work energetically and accumulate (property) unless they have some privileges with regard to it';[29] and socialist authors should therefore not underestimate the extent to which the success of their proposed projects is put in jeopardy by the simple fact that your 'unselfish love of humanity' and mine is hardly 'as eager and unalloyed as their own'.[30]

Third, socialists do not grasp the important relationship between individual freedom and individual initiative – and it is in this (and not in 'its tendency towards a more equal distribution of income, for I can see no harm in that') that the 'chief dangers' of the socialist system are to be found: 'I think that the chief dangers of Socialism lie . . . in its sterilizing influence on those mental activities which have gradually raised the world from barbarism.'[31] The socialists, tending as they do to 'regard economic progress as a thing that goes almost by itself', have ignored 'the intimate dependence of progress on the right taking of risks'[32] and have in particular underestimated 'the functions of the undertaker of business enterprises' with respect to the difficult work involved in modern industrial and commercial activity: 'They seem to think too much of competition as the exploiting of labour by capital, of the poor by the wealthy, and too little of it as the constant experiment by the ablest men for their several tasks, each trying to discover a new way in which to attain some important end.'[33] The socialists are, in short, singularly weak on the *how to* when it comes to imagination, innovation and those outlets by which the flair of the 'constructive genius' is under the present system enabled to 'work its way to the light':[34] 'No socialistic scheme, yet advanced, seems to make adequate provision for the maintenance of high enterprise, and individual strength of character; nor to promise a sufficiently rapid increase in the business plant and other material implements of production to enable the real resources of the manual labour classes to continue to increase as fast as they have done in the recent past, even if the total income of the country be shared equally by all.'[35]

Nor is it only the potential self-help of the entrepreneur which is repressed where freedom is replaced by coercion. If socialistic schemes have failed, a not insignificant reason must inevitably be their consistent denial to the worker of freedom of choice with respect to his own job: 'The schemes of the socialists involved a subversion of existing arrangements, according to which the work of every man is chosen by himself and the remuneration he obtains for it is decided by free competition.'[36] Such a subversion of autonomous choice brings with it misallocation of scarce resources and stunts the development of human character. Paternalism may be acceptable where the Residuum is concerned. The rest of us, however, want and need a looser rein if we are to maximise our contribution to change and improvement.

Fourth, socialists advocate sudden change whereas Marshall was the quintessential gradualist: 'I fear that socialists would refuse to admit me into their fold because I believe that change must be slow',[37] he told the Industrial Remuneration Conference in 1885. A year later, in his lectures on 'Socialism and the Functions of Government', he warned his students at Cambridge that sudden change is likely also to be violent change, both because socialist leaders frequently believe that the end justifies the means and because their personal ambitions are such as not to preclude recourse to force of arms. Violent revolution had little appeal to a peaceful evolutionist who believed strongly that *natura non facit saltum* and neither should we. Projects for great and sudden change were foredoomed to failure, he stressed, and the safest course in the circumstances was not to move so rapidly that our new plans of life altogether outrun our instincts: 'It is right to look eagerly far ahead: but it is not wise to move hastily on to perilous ground. Eagerness in testing progress is a duty: but the larger the venture, the more cogent is the rule *Festina lente*.'[38]

Marshall, to summarise, ultimately turned away from socialism despite an early tendency in that direction. It would be a mistake, however, to confound the position of the quintessential gradualist, the peaceful evolutionist, with that of the stolid reactionary who has no feel for history-to-come – or to forget that in Marshall's view human nature itself is a variable, not a constant. The mutability of human nature is one of those 'shrewd observations and pregnant suggestions' which Marshall shared with the socialists and which indeed led him in 1885 to praise socialist thinkers for their speculations 'about the hidden springs of human action of which the economists took no account'.[39] Such mutability (the direct opposite of the economists' timelessness and universality) introduces a whole new dimension into his discussion of socialistic ideas and constructs and makes his position in the mid-1880s appear precisely what it was – contingent and not absolute.

Thus it is that Marshall in 1919, looking at the world in the wake of the Great War, reached the conclusion that changes in human nature would seem if anything to have increased the scope for socialistic activity: 'I see on all sides marvellous developments of working-class faculty: and, partly in consequence, a broader and firmer foundation for socialistic schemes than existed when Mill wrote.'[40] With growth and advance go altruism and chivalry, and the inference is that 'the future may be made brighter than the past by greater community of thought, action and sympathy' such as these forces are likely to continue to engender:

> When man has been raised to a level far higher than he has yet attained, he will have raised the State also to far higher possibilities than it has yet reached: and then industry is likely to be recast on some plan not yet in sight. For human nature has developed new possibilities in almost every generation under quiet and orderly conditions; and it has progressed very fast in this country during the last fifty years... One indication of this progress is the increasing solidity and breadth of socialistic schemes.[41]

As we develop economically, Marshall is saying, so we develop morally – so, in other words, we develop that 'fuller recognition of the dignity of man', that 'cordial cooperation among all the various ranks of industry'[42] which are not initially so much the results as the causes of genuine collective action. The passage of time, here as elsewhere in Marshall's work, is clearly visible on the horizontal axis and provides the key to statements such as the following which would otherwise be profoundly difficult to interpret: 'Social disaster would probably result from the full development of the collectivist programme, unless the nature of man has first been saturated with economic chivalry.'[43] The *caveat* 'unless' to the optimistic evolutionist has the force of the reassuring 'until' and looks forward to betterment induced by growth in precisely the same manner as Marx does when he warns, as is so frequently the case in his work, against premature revolution – as in the following: 'No social order is ever destroyed before all the productive forces for which it is sufficient have been developed, and new superior relations of production never replace older ones before the material conditions for their existence have matured within the framework of the old society. Mankind thus inevitably sets itself only such tasks as it is able to solve.'[44] If there is ambiguity in Marshall's 'untils', it lies not in his view that the success of socialistic institutions presupposes antecedent human betterment as in his reservations concerning the successful workings even of the private sector itself in the absence of other-regarding motivation: 'The world under free enterprise will fall far short of the finest ideals until economic chivalry is developed. But until it is developed, every great step in the direction of collectivism is a grave menace to the maintenance even of our present moderate rate of progress.'[45] Selfish *as well as* non-selfish economics, it would appear, presupposes for its success the moral upgrading that results, as if guided by an invisible hand, from material improvement; and it is in effect because of this *double* contention that Marshall's attitude to the income elasticity of demand for socialism is shrouded in a certain degree of ambiguity.

That having been said, there is no doubt that Marshall himself consistently found much to admire in the ideals and proposals of the socialists. Their concern with social justice, for example: 'An absolutely fair rate of remuneration belongs to Utopia: but there is much to be learnt from trying with the socialists to ascertain how far it is thinkable, and how far it is attainable.'[46] Their benevolence, their altruism, their generosity: 'I have watched with admiration the strenuous and unselfish devotion to social well-being that is shown by many of the able men who are leading the collectivist movement.'[47] Their emphasis on duty alongside interest: 'All socialist schemes, which have any claims to be practical, avowedly involve a compromise: they do not venture to dispense entirely with material reward as an incentive to industrial energy; though they rely less on it, and more on the sense of duty than our present system does.'[48] As early as 1885 Marshall, aware that all his fellow citizens were not yet gentlemen, felt compelled to ask the following question: 'Why should it be left for impetuous socialists and ignorant orators to cry aloud that none ought to be shut out by the want of material means from the opportunity of leading a life that is worthy of men?'[49] As late as 1909 he felt compelled to supply the following answer: 'Morally everyone is a trustee to the public – to the All – for the use of all that he has.'[50] That statement, with its overtones both of Hegel and of

Green, reminds the reader in turn of Marshall's important declaration on the subject of obligation which was made to the Industrial Remuneration Conference: 'In one sense indeed I am a socialist, for I believe that almost every existing institution must be changed. I hold that the ultimate good of all endeavour is a state of things in which there shall be no rights but only duties.'[51]

Marshall retained throughout his life two of the three attributes of a socialist – a concern with equality and a belief in altruism. Not, however, the other, namely a commitment to control, to paternalism, to State direction, which he felt were far inferior to 'the energizing work of competition' (subject, needless to say, to 'the regulating force of public opinion'[52]) when it came to promoting national economic vigour. Precisely because we want material and moral upgrading, Marshall seems to be saying, we do not want the State.

And yet we do – for Marshall both calls for State action (with respect, say, to the correction of unwarranted inequalities in the distribution of income[53]) and specifies that such action would only be tolerable if 'it were possible to effect that change without danger to freedom and to social order'.[54] The fact that he recommends it shows that he thinks it can be done. So even if not a simple-minded socialist, neither was the mature Marshall a hard-hearted market liberal. The reader who conceives of the mature Marshall as a man with a tendency to social democracy will probably be nearest the mark. Even the mature Marshall, however, stressed that 'economic institutions are the products of human nature, and cannot change much faster than human nature changes'[55] – but that human nature was itself continuously being upgraded and improved. What was true of the present might accordingly have to be modified at some time in the future.

4.2 MARKET AND STATE

Alfred Marshall, as is well known, wrote extensively about automaticity and entrepreneurship, competition and adaptation, and clearly regarded these forces as both economically and ethically beneficial. He also wrote extensively about state intervention, but typically along the lines of the following ringing *credo* from his Presidential Address in 1890 to Section F: 'We believe that a private company which stands to gain something by vigorous and efficient management, by promptness in inventing, as well as in adapting and perfecting improvements in processes and organization, will do more for progress than a public department.'[1]

Social progress presupposes economic progress; economic progress presupposes intellectual progress; intellectual progress presupposes individual freedom; and thus 'governmental intrusion into businesses which require ceaseless invention and fertility of resource is a danger to social progress'.[2] Governmental service is sterile when it comes to creativity, originality and initiative, and is for that very reason to be regarded as '*prima facie* anti-social', precisely because 'it retards the growth of that knowledge and those ideas which are incomparably the most important form of collective wealth': 'A Government could print a good edition of Shakespeare's works, but it could not get them written.'[3] Novelty and discovery, change and advance are simply not to be expected from large-scale bureaucracies: 'Very few inventions of any importance are made by them: and nearly all of those few are the work of men, like Sir W. H. Preece, who had been thoroughly trained in free enterprise before they entered Government service. Government creates scarce anything.'[4]

Sir W. H. Preece evidently was able to make a major contribution to accumulated knowledge and thence to economic growth *while* a civil servant; and what would appear to have made him abnormally efficient would seem to have been the character-building impact on motives and attitudes of his initial exposure to the hurly-burly of market capitalism, an impact which even the subsequent regimentation of the State bureaucracy could not obliterate. We are not told, of course, the nature of the firm in which Sir W. H. Preece had been employed, but Marshall's comments on the position of research and development in the large corporation make one wonder if 'the self-reliant and inventive faculties'[5] which accelerate the pace of progress could have been adequately nurtured in any but a small one: 'The chemist in his laboratory can make experiments on his own responsibility: if he had to ask leave from others at each step he would go but slowly, and though the officials of a company may have some freedom to make experiments in detail, yet even as regards these they seldom have a strong incentive to exertion; and in great matters the freedom of experimenting lies only with those who undertake the responsibility of a business.'[6] It is to be doubted if Sir W. H. Preece had been 'thoroughly trained' in the exercise of imagination by serving as a small cog in a big wheel operated by others; and Marshall's association of 'energy and inventiveness' with both 'freedom of initiative' and 'sufficient security of gain'[7] definitely leaves certain questions open in the work of an author who highly valued both economies of size *and* individual autonomy. Even if a corporate bureaucracy does deaden sensation, however, there is still no *a priori* reason to suppose that it is *as* repressive of novelty as would be an equivalent bureaucracy in the public sector. There seems in addition to be a widespread belief in Britain that the private sector is on balance significantly more friendly to novelty than is the State – a perception which is, as it happens, at the heart of the popular desire among Britons 'to keep Government management within narrow limits. They are most anxious to preserve the freedom of the individual to try new paths on his own responsibility. They regard this as the vital service which free competition renders to progress.'[8]

Novelty on the drawing-boards is not novelty in the shops; but market here again has the edge over State, in implementation as in invention. Marshall here again expressed grave doubts concerning the relative efficiency of the salaried bureaucrat and praised the individual entrepreneur for his superiority 'in energy and elasticity, in inventiveness and directness of purpose':[9]

> One of the chief elements of success in private business is the faculty of weighing the advantages and disadvantages of any proposed course, and of assigning to them their true relative importance. He who by practice and genius has acquired the power of attributing to each factor its right quantity, is already well on the way to fortune; and the increase in the efficiency of our productive forces is in a great measure due to the large number of able minds who are devoting themselves ceaselessly to acquiring these business instincts.[10]

The bureaucratic mentality, however, is significantly less friendly to such instincts (and to the 'incessant free initiative' which in industry after industry is 'needed for progress'[11]) than it is to habit, inertia, custom and that stagnation which is called tradition, and all of this constitutes a good reason for opposing, say, schemes for further nationalisation: 'We are bound to reflect that up to the present time nearly all of the innumerable inventions that have given us our command over nature have been made by independent workers; and the contributions from Government officials all the world over have been relatively small . . . . There is therefore strong *prima facie* cause for fearing that the collective ownership of the means of production would deaden the energies of mankind, and arrest economic progress.'[12] He who wants progress and prosperity, in other words, would be strongly advised to back the independent individual and not the organisation man: 'The advantages of economic freedom are never more strikingly manifest than when a business man endowed with genius is trying experiments, at his own risk, to see whether some new method, or combination of old methods, will be more efficient than the old.'[13] He who still thinks that good bureaucrats make good businessmen should be reminded of the less-than-successful experience of the mines: 'The history of the State management of mines is full of very dark shadows; for the business of mining depends too much on the probity of its managers and their energy and judgement in matters of detail as well as of general principle, to be well managed by State officials.'[14] The history of State tobacco monopolies is hardly more encouraging: 'Such monopolies have not been very successful; because their task is really more difficult than it seems: and Government officials have not the energy, the alertness, and the special faculties of fine discernment, which have enabled the managers of the American Tobacco Company to amass vast wealth, from a partial monopoly of tobacco obtained by able management and strategic marketing.'[15] Both industries yield, in sum, clear proof that bureaucratic judgements must 'always be inferior to those which an able business man forms, by the aid of instincts based on long experience with regard to his own business'.[16] Thus it is that Marshall, writing in 1907, was led to the following conclusion concerning the respective costs and benefits of bureaucratic methods on the one hand, free enterprise on the other: 'If Government control had supplanted that of private enterprise a hundred years ago, there is good reason to suppose that our methods of manufacture now would be about as effective as they were fifty years ago, instead of being perhaps four or even six times as efficient as they were then.'[17] Collective control, it would appear, has a strong tendency to impair the springs of material wealth; and that in itself is a good reason for preferring market to State.

The harm wrought by the bureaucratic mentality is not only material and current. The bureaucratic mentality is also prone deleteriously to affect character on a cumulative basis, and to impair in that way 'not only the springs of material wealth, but also many of those higher qualities of human nature, the strengthening of which should be the chief aim of social endeavour'.[18] Bureaucratic regimentation can only be likened to the military discipline which, in Rome as previously in Sparta, decisively crushed out 'strength of character and intellectual energy' – to such an extent, indeed, that it would be no exaggeration to say that it was the personality of the representative Roman, not the invasion of the foreign barbarian, which must bear the ultimate responsibility for the coming of the Dark Ages and the interruption of progress. In Rome, after all 'discipline conquered, and it conquered so thoroughly, as to dry up the sources of individual enterprise and self-reliant mental energy throughout the world, and therefore the civilised world, when it was once overthrown by the barbarians, had no power of recovery.'[19] The Romans would clearly have been more resilient if they had been trained by industrial rather than by militant institutions; for competitive capitalism teaches not conformity but 'freedom and vigour, elasticity and strength'[20] (to say nothing of frugality and rationality, creativity and assiduous alertness) and inculcates, by the very logic of the struggle for existence, not obsequious obedience and slavish followership but more appealing traits and characteristics such as 'a certain independence and habit of choosing one's own course for oneself, a self-reliance; a deliberation and yet a promptness of choice and judgement, and of forecasting the future and of shaping one's course with reference to distant aims'.[21] Such traits and characteristics (while undeniably the proper normative orientation with respect to advanced material well-being and maximal want-satisfaction) are, most significantly, highly-valued ends in their own right, precisely because they are fully compatible with man's nature as an active rather than a passive creature: 'The truth seems to be that as human nature is constituted, man rapidly degenerates unless he has some hard work to do, some difficulties to overcome; and that some strenuous exertion is necessary for physical and moral health. The fulness of life lies in the development and activity of as many and as high faculties as possible. There is intense pleasure in the ardent pursuit of any aim, whether it be success in business, the advancement of art and science, or the improvement of the condition of one's fellow-beings.'[22] An important reason for advocating policies that maximise individual freedom to take initiatives and to make decisions is thus quite simply the highly-subjective preference of individuals for wakefulness over lethargy, and this quite independently of the impact of behavioural upgrading on the subsequent *quid pro quo*: man 'delights in the use of his faculties for their own sake; sometimes using them nobly, whether with the abandon of the great Greek burst of life, or under the control of a deliberate and steadfast striving towards important ends; sometimes ignobly, as in the case of a morbid development of the taste for drink. The religious, the moral, the intellectual and the artistic faculties on which the progress of industry depends, are not acquired solely for the sake of the things that may be got by them; but are developed by exercise for the sake of the pleasure and the happiness which they themselves bring'.[23] It is necessary for the unfolding of my active essence that I be permitted 'hope, freedom and change' – that I be allowed, in other words, to be an entrepreneur and not compelled to be either a bureaucrat or the slave of bureaucrats. Other-directedness does not suit me; I happen to associate 'true inner freedom' (i.e. my freedom *to* become myself) with the full exercise of my 'faculties of self-reliance and self-determination'[24] (and therefore with my freedom *from* Governmental *diktat*); and this consideration is in itself an important reason for ranking market, *ceteris paribus*, well above State.

Even if the bureaucrat did possess 'those instincts with regard to public interests which able business men have with regard to their own affairs', yet there is another problem involved in the formulation and execution of sound public policies. That problem is the political constraint – as a result of which even the best bureaucrat 'is not very likely to be able to carry his plans with a free hand'.[25] The bureaucrat must answer to the politician, the politician has problems and objectives of his own, and there is no reason in consequence to expect that the resultant policy-mix will turn out to be the optimal one from the point of view of the community as a whole.

The simplest case of government failure caused by sub-optimality amongst political leaders is the case where certain politicians have a direct pecuniary interest in the adoption of certain policies. Thus Germany, on the eve of the First World War, was ruled by aristocratic officers who, being themselves great land-owners, successfully committed their nation to protectionism: 'Protection, nearly the whole of the pecuniary gains of which come to the class from which the officers are almost exclusively drawn . . . seems to me to indicate a narrower class-selfishness.'[26] And Britain, a century earlier, had consistently refused, despite repeated bad harvests, to repeal the Corn Laws, so great was the power and the pressure of 'the landlords who ruled in Parliament'[27] – a 'cruel abuse of political power by the classes that chiefly controlled the legislature' and one which 'spread its dark shadow far into the nineteenth century'.[28] Nowadays few legislatures are in the pocket of land-owners, but money still talks in debates on the tariff, such vested interest being one of the reasons that must be adduced to account for 'the bias in favour of cartels that is shown by a Government that is largely under the control of a wealthy minority': 'Cartel policy is greatly dependent on the aid of a Protective tariff, which tends to enrich many of those who are already rich; though it lowers the purchasing power of incomes generally, and especially those of the poorer classes.'[29] A similar point concerning the way in which money talks must be made about 'the class legislation which denied to trade unions privileges that were open to associations of employers';[30] about outright corruption (in the time of Adam Smith, Marshall reflected, 'experience gave little reason to anticipate that the leading statesmen of the country would cease to regard public affairs as a source of private booty',[31] and the phenomenon, while less prevalent, is not now extinct[32]); and about the 'cynical selfishness', in pre-Revolutionary France, 'with which the Court and its adherents sacrificed the wellbeing of the people for the sake of their own luxury and military glory'.[33] None of these instances of State intervention inspired by *turpe lucrum* is conspicuously in the social interest. All lend support to the proposition that where money talks it talks against the State.

Some politicians are no doubt deeply concerned with the maximisation of personal pecuniary rewards; but a more common case of government failure in a modern democratic country (Marshall defines this as 'a nation which governs its own Government',[34] presumably through a system of universal male suffrage) has to do with the vote-motive and the desire to win elections. Thus it comes about that a policy with much to recommend it (arguably, a sensible amount of protection being granted to infant industries until such a time as they have acquired adequate economies of large size to face unaided the bracing cold winds of international competition) is nonetheless 'apt to be wrenched from its proper uses, to the enrichment of particular interests' for the simple reason that, to continue with the example of the tariff, the protected senile are likely also to be the votogenic senile: 'Those industries which can send the greatest number of votes to the poll, are those which are already on so large a scale, that a further increase would bring very few new economies.'[35] Votes are at stake where tariffs introduced on a short-term basis come to be regarded by major interest-groups as something approaching a natural right – the reason why 'protective duties are easy to impose, and hard to remove'[36] – and yet the failure to remove such tariffs imposes a significant welfare loss on the community as a whole. The bribe is in votes, not cash, but the harm done to economic growth and ethical evolution via the intervention in question is not less because of the difference in the mode of remuneration. Where government aid is there for the plucking, of course, it is only rational that each of us should come to see himself more as a potential plucker than as a good citizen, and that in itself is an important danger inherent in any form of discretionary State assistance: 'The greatest evil of all is that it tends to undermine political, and through political, social morality. For if a voter thinks that a candidate for Parliament or for the town council seems likely to help him to a favourable contract, or to protection to his special industry, or to a higher salary than his work is worth to the community, then, human nature being what it is, he is likely not to regard his vote as a sacred duty, but to use it for his own pecuniary interests.'[37]

The vote-motive must inevitably play a significant part in helping to explain why democratic governments, like spendthrift individuals, normally 'mortgage their future resources in order to obtain the means of immediate expenditure'.[38] Normally 'a borrower rather than an accumulator of capital',[39] the modern government is compelled to look for loanable funds where it also looks for enterprise, growth and advance, in the private sector – as the experience of the First World War so vividly demonstrates: 'If the private capital at the disposal of Britain and America had not been available, German troops would have treated Britain as they did treat Belgium.'[40] Admittedly such borrowing by the government inevitably competes with borrowing by business men, and this means both some crowding-out of the latter sector by the former (thereby reducing *ceteris paribus* the potential availability of private saving out of new income at some date in the future) and some rise in interest-rates (thereby imposing a *de facto* tax on growth fuelled through borrowing and redistributing income from active manufacturers to passive rentiers), as in the Napoleonic Wars: 'The capital required by war could not have been obtained entirely by taxation without extreme measures, and in fact a very large part of it was obtained by loans. The loans could not be taken up abroad, so they came from the existing stock of capital: thus making capital scarce for industrial purposes, and securing high rates of interest and profits to capitalists and employers.'[41] High rates of interest are a major inconvenience to capitalists and employers. Not so to 'spendthrifts or governments', however, who, 'but little governed by cool calculation', tend frequently to borrow with 'but little reference to the price they will have to pay for the loan'.[42] The behaviour-patterns of democratic governments come in that way to resemble those of large sections (the less rational and less progressive sections) of the electorate which returns them. That, incidentally, is why oligarchy is capable of good husbandry whereas democracy is better at spending than it is at saving: 'Oligarchic governments have sometimes made great efforts to accumulate collective wealth; and it may be hoped that in the coming time, foresight and patience will become the common property of the main body of the working classes. But, as things are, too great a risk would be involved by entrusting to a pure democracy the accumulation of the resources needed for acquiring yet further command over nature.'[43] Adam Smith makes a similar point when he contrasts 'the orderly, vigilant, and parsimonious administration of such aristocracies as those of Venice and Amsterdam' with the mass-produced alternative, 'the thoughtless extravagance that democracies are apt to fall into'.[44]

The vote-motive, finally, is a source of considerable frustration to the bureaucrat in a Government department. For one thing, his efficiency is as a direct consequence of what Marshall describes as 'political immorality'[45] likely to be rendered lower *ceteris paribus* than that of his counterpart in a private sector joint stock corporation: 'Such a department is more liable to have the efficiency of the management interfered with for the purpose of enabling other persons to gain the votes of their constituents on questions in which it has no direct concern.'[46] Then, apart from the fact that his minister has political responsibilities such as easily create 'a grievous, if not a disastrous hindrance'[47] to the execution of his economic duties, the bureaucrat is likely to feel disheartened at 'wasteful duplication', 'clashing and overlapping', lack of over-all coordination, such as make it extremely difficult to predict in advance which Ministry will please which majority most: 'Governmental administration is apt to suffer from lack of concentration of authority.'[48] Looking at the matter from a more personal point of view, the civil servant, aware of the possible impact of political pressures on his own career structure, is likely to press for rules rather than authorities in that sphere in particular: 'The fear that political influence may distort the course of promotion, is one of the many causes that tend to make seniority dominant in public offices.'[49] No doubt such promotions are fully deserved but there remains much to be said nonetheless in favour of advancement based not on length of service but on straightforward efficiency. Civil servants fear this latter criterion not least because they of all people know what is encapsulated in the phrase 'political immorality' and are exceptionally hostile to the idea that vote-seekers should make selective judgements concerning the job prospects of those who serve the public interest in their Ministries.

To the vote-motive, to the maximisation of personal pecuniary reward, must be added a third case of government failure caused by sub-optimality amongst political leaders, namely the case where those political leaders are somewhat deficient in judgement: 'Human nature is, unfortunately, to be found in Government as elsewhere; and in consequence Government management even if perfectly virtuous, is very far from being infinitely wise.'[50] Politicians, hardly omniscient and often even rather ignorant, suffer like the rest of us from the fact that accurate information is a scarce commodity: 'The requisite facts come within the direct experience of only a very few persons, and even in the case of those few, only to a very limited extent and in a very imperfect way . . . Much of the failure and much of the injustice, in which the economic policies of governments have resulted, have been due to the want of statistical measurement.'[51] No matter how well-intentioned his desires (his wish, say, to defend consumers' surplus against monopolists' profits), no man can intentionally do what he does not rationally grasp.

Adequate information being a scarce commodity, politicians have often turned for enlightenment to the men in the trade; and in that way partial knowledge has produced partial policies, measures emanating from biased advice and 'perverted to the selfish and corrupt purposes of those who had the ear of Government'.[52] The great Adam Smith had said as much: 'Though he himself, like all his chief followers, was unselfishly devoted to the well-being of the people, experience had taught him to look with suspicion on those who invited the Government to new enterprises for the public weal: for their real motive was generally to increase their own gains, or to provide easy and well-paid posts for themselves or their relatives.'[53] In such a fluid environment the multiplied 'openings for fraud and corruption'[54] that tempt and lure the interested lobbyist and the pressure group constitute a genuine threat to the moral fibre of all concerned ('they lower character by diverting energy from creation to wirepulling'[55]) – and also cause economic policies to emerge such as are unlikely to represent any interest more general than that of a small but powerful minority. Witness the case of the protective tariff: 'I . . . regard Protection as socialistic, in that, especially in a democratic country, it gives a first place to those business men who are "expert" in hoodwinking officials, the legislature and the public as to the ability of their branch of industry to take care of itself.'[56]

Witness the case of industrial bounties and the danger that 'people would divert their energies from managing their own businesses to managing those persons who control the bounties'.[57]

Adequate intelligence being in short supply, interest groups, it would thus appear, come to enjoy considerable influence; and that influence, moreover, is hardly distributed equally throughout the community as a whole. As a matter of fact, the policies to which that influence leads are particularly likely to favour not consumers ('the unvocal many') but producers ('the vocal few who speak on behalf of the trade'): 'The pushing and clamorous few in an economic controversy are often a group of producers who can put their case well, and who show great energy and resource in making themselves heard.'[58] As a matter of logic, this distortion reflects not only unbalanced power but also – perhaps even more significantly – unbalanced concern: 'A few people who have been strongly interested on one side have raised their voices loudly, persistently and all together; while little has been heard from the great mass of people whose interests have lain in the opposite direction; for, even if their attention has been fairly called to the matter, few have cared to exert themselves much for a cause in which no one of them has more than a small stake. The few therefore get their way.'[59] Anthony Downs's famous conclusion – that 'men are more likely to exert political influence in their roles as income-receivers than in their roles as income-spenders, whether acting as private citizens or as members of a corporate entity'[60] – may thus be derived, in the work of Marshall as in that of Downs, from the interplay between two closely-connected variables: unequal endowments of background knowledge and an unequal vested interest in the outcome of the struggle.

The combination of incomplete information and political democracy leads to an odd policy-mix: 'At all events in a democratic country no great public undertaking is secure of being sustained on consistent lines of policy, unless its advantages can be made clear, not only to the few who have direct experience of high public affairs, but also to the many who have no such experience and have to form their judgement on the materials set before them by others.'[61] The very words 'made clear' are a cause for alarm, reminding us as they do of the extent to which demand-manipulation and want-creation are topics central to political as well as microeconomic theory. Thus it happens, for example, that 'a man of great administrative force, but not a fluent speaker' cannot automatically assume that he will 'get the better of a less able man who had a great faculty of persuasiveness, and had perhaps learnt a thing or two about the great machine which American politicians are perfecting';[62] and the danger of the demogogue becomes more acute, the more complex is the issue on which he is asked to pronounce. Foreign trade, for instance: 'The real nature of foreign trade is so much disguised by the monetary transactions in which it is enveloped, that a clever sophist has a hundred opportunities of throwing dust in the eyes of ordinary people, and especially the working classes.'[63] The cleverest sophist, needless to say, is he who seeks, in the field of trade policy, not merely to deceive the silent majority but also to join together in his crusade the representatives of more than one passionate minority: 'In earlier times, as now, unscrupulous politicians would boast that, by going from one constituency to another, and holding before each a protective duty which would give a visible bounty to a considerable portion of the constituency, they could work up an eager cry for a protective policy, and could thus shout down any arguments based on the general interest.'[64] It is, moreover, not only the general interest that is sacrificed by such devious strategies and interested exaggerations but also the partial interest of those industries whose contribution belongs not to the past but to the future: politicians, knowing full well who is too young to vote, have 'seldom ranged themselves on the side of movements which, though still weak, were yet destined to render great services to the country',[65] while not hesitating to act on the biased information supplied by the aged and the powerful. In this way protected groups which 'did excellent work in their youth' continue to command protection even after they have begun 'to outlive the strength and high purpose of their founders, and to become obstructive as well as incompetent in their old age'[66] but young and dynamic organisations remain invisible and unprotected, being small and new. A high profile and a good income are important assets to undertakings which wish to ensure that their advantages are 'made clear' to others. Potential social benefits and unexploited economies of size, sadly, speak somewhat less loudly.

Then there is the cost in terms of time. For one thing, legislative intervention typically means that numerous groups must first be consulted and alternative scenarios be mooted and remooted; and, frankly, 'the worst of several possible manoeuvres, if adopted promptly, will often turn out better than the best of them if delayed till its *pros* and *cons* have been well talked out'.[67] Also, an 'elaborate system of checks and counterchecks' must be set up lest the 'probity' of State officials should 'receive but little external support' – a system, as it turns out, 'so elaborate and cumbrous that many clerks are needed where one would suffice in private service'.[68] These and other time-consuming developments mean that when new laws are indeed ultimately introduced, they are also often already out of date, responses to a past age 'when the economic structure of England was entirely different'[69] and inelastic and inflexible brakes on progress in the altered economic conditions of the present day. Put in the simplest terms, the position is this: 'Though the enforcement of the law in economic matters occupies the time of a rapidly increasing number of people, and its administration is improving in every way, it fails to keep pace with the demands resulting from the growing complexity of economic organization.'[70]

Laws which lag when market leads are an invitation to evasion – as when, for example, the imposition of a local tax on the printing industry simply causes printers to pack up their presses and move beyond the boundaries of the locality,[71] or when smugglers and other free traders successfully defend the consumer interest against the diswelfares of protective tariffs and wartime blockades[72] – and the very ineffectiveness of such laws gives governmental intervention a bad name. All in all, governments should never neglect the momentum inherent in matter or ignore the ebb and flow of demand and supply; for 'when one person is willing to sell a thing at a price which another is willing to pay for it, the two manage to come together in spite of prohibitions of King or Parliament, or of the officials of a Trust or Trade-Union'.[73] All in all, governments, unable to police the vast network of by-paths by which economic arrangements seek to frustrate political institutions, should ensure that man-made regulations are also such as would 'confirm to Nature': 'That is, they must not set up by artificial means arrangements widely different from those which would have been naturally brought about. For if they do, their work will be in strong conflict with natural forces, and it will be destroyed.'[74] Since a law which conforms to Nature enforces itself while a law which does not conform to Nature is unenforceable at the best of times, there would even appear to be a strong case to be made out for Nature *in place of* law – precisely because our human foresight and vision are so desperately deficient when compared with the solid and basically-beneficent forces of gravity and evolution.

Evasion testifies to the initiative and inventiveness of the English character, which is favourable to energy, originality and daring and hostile to the 'vexatious meddlings' of 'an army of officials'[75] under the thumb of a strong State: 'Englishmen have no liking for things so controlled and drilled by a central government.'[76] Other countries, of course, may have different values. Thus 'the German people have a great faculty of obedience' and are notable for their 'steadfast docility'; and, accordingly, 'the control of industry by Government is seen in its best and most attractive forms in Germany'.[77] The 'natural adhesiveness of the Teutons'[78] is favourable to custom, regulation and regimentation, and geographical situation (by providing a stimulus to nationalism and patriotism) reinforces collectivist culture and contributes to an atmosphere of direction bordering on the autocratic: 'Surrounded by powerful and aggressive armies Germany can exist only by the aid of an ardent national feeling.'[79] The fact that Germany is largely an agricultural country reinforces her general climate of *stasis*. Yet England is an industrial and a commercial nation (and therefore a dynamic one), she is an island (and therefore better situated for defence than if she had common frontiers with potential enemies), and her people have a strong bias towards the protection of economic activity both '*by* the Government and *from* the Government':[80] 'We (for I would here include myself) believe that bureaucratic management is less suitable for Anglo-Saxons than for other races who are more patient and more easily contented, more submissive and less full of initiative, who like to take things easily and to spread their work out rather thinly over long hours.'[81] And therefore, precisely because those who are imbued with the 'Anglo-Saxon spirit' would rebel at controls and constraints which the Teutonic temperament would accept without question, the conclusion must be reached that, speaking of the English, 'the arrangements best suited for the German character are perhaps not quite the best for them'.[82]

This is Marshall at his most tolerant and least dogmatic. This is, however, the same man who, in his account of economic history, identified the process of individual liberation *from* State interference as uninterrupted even by Mercantilism (a system which, in his view, tended on balance to '*loosen* the fetters of trade'[83]), who insisted that no one had yet 'thought out a way of checking competition generally without lessening freedom'[84] – and who declared succinctly that 'in my view Freedom *is* life'.[85] It is not easy to believe that such a man genuinely regarded the interventionist Teutons as institutionally different from but morally equal to the liberating Britons. What is more likely is that he regarded them as yet another case of arrested development on the continuous road to progress, as he indeed ultimately concedes: 'There is reason for thinking that the advantages which some other countries, and especially Germany, have derived from a semi-military organization of industry are not in fact as great as may appear at first sight; and because immediate material gains, obtained at the expense of a diminution of the spirit of free enterprise, may prove to have been too dearly bought, even from a merely material point of view.'[86] Even in Germany, it would appear, market retains a certain edge over State where creative advancement is concerned: 'It seems to remain almost as true now, as in former times, that the heavy hand of Government tends to slacken progress in whatever matter it touches.'[87] The word 'almost' clouds the issue, however, for it suggests that the hand of government, while undeniably heavy 'now', is yet less heavy at the present than it was 'in former times'. Something is evidently in motion. Something is obviously taking its course.

4.3 STATE AND IMPROVEMENT

Marshall was not a static but a dynamic thinker, and his evolutionary perspective is as much in evidence in his political as in his economic thought. Circumstances alter cases, one moment's meat is another moment's poison, and our task in this section is accordingly to seek to identify those trends and development in economy and society which have significant causative implications for the position of the polity in a changing – and an improving – situation.

The first point to make concerns economies of large size and the managerial revolution. More specifically, the 'energy and judgement' of undertakers – the principal reason for the economic superiority *ceteris paribus* of private over public, the principal reason why 'the small mine or quarry may fairly be expected, other things being equal, to hold its own against the large one'[1] – is, precisely because other things are not equal, in some areas of economic life positively on the endangered species list. The explanation is to be found in the advantages of size: 'In some cases the cost of deep shafts, of machinery and of establishing means of communication, are too great to be borne by any but a very large business.'[2] Large business becomes bureaucratised business, however, and this may well be a cause for concern even in 'private establishments': 'Experience shows creative ideas and experiments in business technique, and in business organization, to be very rare in Governmental undertakings, and not very common in private enterprises which have drifted towards bureaucratic methods as the result of their great age and large size. A new danger is thus threatened by the narrowing of the field of industry which is open to the vigorous initiative of smaller businesses.'[3] The difference between 'very rare' and 'not very common' is modest, and this suggests a certain degree of organisational convergence – a phenomenon which Marshall must have found rather alarming, believing as he did that entrepreneurs bear risks and innovate while bureaucrats favour routine and administer: 'The carcase of municipal electric works belongs to the officials; the genius belongs to free enterprise.'[4] Matter is in motion, and when Marshall notes that civil servants do not 'do their work with as much energy and enterprise as is shown in private establishments',[5] what is implicit is that the 'private establishments' in question are the old-style smaller ones, not the new-style bureaucratised giants. These latter corporations, however, as Marshall was forced to concede at approximately the same time as he bade farewell to his trees-in-the-forest account of business rise and fall, 'have recently increased fast';[6] and the inference to be drawn is that organisational behaviour is increasingly similar in the two sectors. Such convergence does not significantly strengthen the case for State. It does, however, significantly weaken the case for market.

Marshall makes a further telling comparison between bureaucracies public and bureaucracies private and that involves the question of control. The shareholder-capitalist in the modern joint stock company is, he confesses, 'almost powerless', but he then hastens to add that the same is nowadays true of the voter-citizen in the modern State: 'The same may be said of the undertakings of Governments imperial and local: they also may have a great future before them, but up to the present time the tax-payer who undertakes the ultimate risks has not generally succeeded in exercising an efficient control over the businesses.'[7] The phrase 'up to the present time' is intriguing if also vague; but it does seem to lend support to the hypothesis that social evolution brings with it upgraded accountability of organisation men to concerned constituents. Such upgrading is true of the modern joint stock company as well as of the modern State. Such upgrading is true of the modern State – and this is the important point in the present context – as well as of the modern joint stock company. Given such upgrading – and this is the conclusion we wish to draw – State intervention where genuinely appropriate need less and less be eschewed on the grounds that intervention *per se* must inevitably render our servants ever more our masters. The fact is that social evolution *per se* is simultaneously rendering our servants ever more our servants, that 'the power of the nation to govern its Government is on the increase',[8] and that political leaders and their bureaucratic followers are today subject to the discipline of public opinion and the ballot-box to a greater extent than was previously the case: 'The people are now able to rule their rulers, and to check class abuse of power and privilege, in a way which was impossible before the days of general education and a general surplus of energy over that required for earning a living.'[9] In such an atmosphere of informed scrutiny the community can 'safely venture on many public undertakings'[19] which would formerly have been distorted by venal lobbies and corrupt leaders and which are nowadays kept continously on course by 'the growing sense of responsibility of public opinion'.[11] Because you and I increasingly watch, therefore he and she increasingly behave.

Nowadays, due to the spread of popular education (itself reflecting State intervention, as in the case of the 'great impetus'[12] to enlightenment represented by Forster's Education Act of 1870 – 'the first of a series, which have brought the education of the children of the working classes to a higher efficiency than was to be found in many middle class schools half a century ago'[13]), due to the substitution of capital for manual labour in the execution of unrewarding operations (a vote in itself for higher incomes and greater challenge, shortened hours and lessened fatigue[14]), due to 'the cheapening and improvement of literature'[15] and the extension of the telegraph and the railway ('By their aid a nation can now read in the morning what its leaders have said on the evening before; and, ere another day has passed, the judgement of the nation on it is pretty well known'[16]), the fact is that – for the first time – 'even a large country can . . . be ruled by its people'.[17] By *all* its people, moreover, due to the spectacular intellectual advancement even of the – newly enfranchised – lower income groups: already 'some leaders of the working classes are able to hold their own in discussions of grave problems of politics, as well as of industry, with the foremost men of the time',[18] soon 'the control of the working classes of Imperial and Local Government will cease to be nominal and become real',[19] and the nature of that control is bound to be both increasingly stringent and increasingly wise. Nowadays, in short, society has become more active and more inter-active, better informed and more careful, and all of this has had a significantly positive impact on the feasibility of responsible collective action taking the form of State intervention: 'By the aid of the telegraph and the printing press, of representative government and trade associations, it is possible for the people to think out for themselves the solution of their own problems. The growth of knowledge and self-reliance has given them that true self-controlling freedom, which enables them to impose of their own free will restraints on their own actions; and the problems of collective production, collective ownership and collective consumption are entering on a new phase.'[20] Adam Smith was 'a shrewd observer of human behaviour *in the eighteenth century*'[21] – but even he held that the future might be significantly different from the past: 'It is here argued that the conduct of public affairs in England in the middle of the eighteenth century was bad, and that the potential virtues of Governmental intervention in business were over-shadowed by its actual vices: but that Adam Smith's doctrine, carefully interpreted, supports its active intervention in many affairs in an age in which it has acquired the power and the will to govern the people wisely; and the people have acquired the power and the will to govern their Government with knowledge, discretion and restraint.'[22]

Economic growth brings with it 'progress towards government of the people by the people'[23] and therewith an increasing check on the ability of the corrupt, the selfish and the sordid to abuse the power with which they are entrusted. Given the new circumstances, for example, 'no political committee, however devoid of high sentiment, would be shortsighted enough to follow a recent example in choosing a candidate who had been proved judicially to owe much of his wealth to base means',[24] while no candidate, once elected, can afford to be seen to be guilty of mismanagement, negligence, immorality – or of insensitivity to 'expressions of public opinion, which may culminate in an agitation for the intervention of Government',[25] such as have, in both Britain and America, frequently been associated with alleged oppressive depredations on the part of natural monopolies. In America, for example, 'railways have been the chief mark of popular criticism, just and unjust' (including, on occasion, 'organized mob-violence'),[26] and popular pressures have not only led to State intervention in that industry but also significantly influenced the form that it has taken: 'A public authority, when intervening in the railway industry, will receive more assistance from the people themselves than would be possible in almost any other industry. For the people are the purchasers of the services rendered by railways; they can form a fairly good opinion as to whether those services are well performed, and they can set out their grievances simply and clearly. They cannot indeed generally form a direct judgement as to the inherent reasonableness of those charges: but they have fair opportunities for making comparisons with charges for similar services at home and abroad; and even for making some allowance for differences in the conditions under which the services are rendered.'[27] Public opinion is admittedly not always an unmixed blessing in such affairs; and Marshall appears to have a certain degree of sympathy with the views of Ackworth ('whose authority is perhaps greater than that of any other Englishman, who is not himself a great administrator of railways') to the effect that 'the rank and file will be able to bring such pressure to bear at the polls, that political considerations will be apt to weigh in matters, that ought to be decided on technical grounds'.[28] Public opinion evidently carries costs as well as conveying benefits, but the key point in the present context is simply that it *exists* and has made a significant contribution to the gradual 'increase in the power of the people to govern the Government that governed them' – 'and this power was destined to become so large and far-reaching, that many tasks may now reasonably be entrusted to Government in the twentieth century which would have been grossly mismanaged in the first half of the nineteenth, and would have been hot-beds of corruption in the eighteenth: thus a certain new tendency to a widening of the appropriate functions of Government gradually set in.'[29] In that sense greater accountability has actually been productive of greater intervention.

Economic growth means growing intellectuality (in the form of better education and improved communications) and therewith a closer and more continuous audit of our politicians and our bureaucrats. Economic growth also means improving character-patterns, however, and therewith a tendency on the part of those politicians and those bureaucrats to acquit themselves well for reasons entirely separable from rational calculations made in the glare of publicity: 'In Adam Smith's time Government was corrupt . . . Matters improved but slowly during the next fifty years. But honesty and true philanthropy grew apace during the earnest, if somewhat ungainly, beginning of the Victorian era.'[30] A general atmosphere of truthfulness and trustworthiness, altruism and chivalry, needless to say, is itself eminently favourable to an extension in the role of the State: 'Mill had seen a vast increase in the probity, the strength, the unselfishness, and the resources of Government during his life; and it seems that each succeeding decade has enlarged the scope of those interventions of Government for the promotion of general well-being which he thought likely to work well.'[31] Naturally the glare of publicity has had a considerable impact on standards of behaviour: 'Shorthand reporting, the electric telegraph, and the improved printing press have given strength to the general movement towards higher ethical standards, which has been steadily cleansing Parliament, and invigorating Governmental departments.'[32] Naturally policy changes have significantly contributed to the process of improvement, both in 'diminishing the money value of political power'[33] (notably through the elimination in England of the protective tariff) and in increasing the degree of public awareness – transparency of technique being one reason why subsidies to domestic producers are preferable to tariff walls: 'The whole costs to the nation of direct subsidies are definite and conspicuous: those who are favoured by them are brought immediately under the eye of the people, and their accounts are liable to public audit.'[34] But when all is said and done, something else has simultaneously occurred – something which can in no way be boiled down to a simple broth of carrots and sticks – and that something has been an autonomous increase in the 'moral integrity' of all our citizens – not least our politicians and our bureaucrats. It then follows from that welcome *deus ex machina* that 'the increased intelligence and probity of Government officials generally make us willing to take the risks of Government for intervention in many matters, in which Adam Smith Smith and his immediate followers would have truly asserted that such a remedy would probably be worse than the evil'.[35] Where leaders and administrators are corrupt and incapable, there is little to be gained by asking them to take on tasks at present performed (albeit imperfectly) by private enterprise and philanthropy. Once leaders and administrators have become reliable and punctilious, however, Adam Smith's strictures become little more than museum pieces of essentially historical interest: 'Adam Smith's criticisms on the Mercantilists of his own age may seem harsh. But it is to be remembered that he knew the weaknesses and the corruption of those who were posing as masters of economic statecraft. His condemnation of officious meddling by such men in the affairs of industry and trade is indeed not limited to the conditions of his own time. But he had no means of anticipating the vast increase in the resources of Government, and in the honesty of public officials which began in the nineteenth century. He could look backwards only.'[36]

Ethical standards have improved. So too has the provision of reliable information: 'Government has now many new large and subtle resources for finding out where it can do more harm than good'.[37] Such a development is entirely positive when seen from the perspective of beneficial intervention; for ignorance in the past has not only reduced the technical efficiency of governments but also made them the prisoners of vested interests for essential intelligence – which has led in turn to biased policies reflecting 'the special interest of . . . one section of the population'[38] and to that debasement of character which is normally associated with officials being 'bamboozled by individuals',[39] even where that bamboozlement is not also 'permeated by evil uses of money'.[40] Undeniably, in the past, 'much of the failure and much of the injustice, in which the economic policies of governments have resulted, have been due to the want of statistical measurement'.[41] Nowadays, of course, the State is increasingly coming to the conclusion that it and it alone has 'an imperative duty to inspect and to arbitrate' and is increasingly acknowledging the fact that (while independent outsiders, such as professional economists[42] and investigative journalists,[43] retain some role to play) 'the State alone can order an adequate inquiry where agents betray their trust, or where fraudulent producers or dealers can outwit the consumer'.[44] These are important steps in the right direction, but we need to go much further still in the generation of reliable data: 'The rapid growth of collective interests, and the increasing tendency towards collective action in economic affairs, make it every day more important that we should know what quantitative measures of public interests are most needed and what statistics are required for them, and that we should set ourselves to obtain these statistics.'[45]

Statistics are permissive, in the sense that they permit us to do things that we could not otherwise do. This would be the case, for instance, where we independently decided upon a system of taxes and bounties and then suddenly found ourselves up against 'the difficulty of securing that the burdens of the tax and the benefits of the bounty were equitably distributed'.[46] Statistics, however, are suggestive as well, in the sense that unbiased quantification often focuses our attention on new ways of increasing social welfare by political means – as is illustrated by the relationship between measurement of consumers' surplus and the demand for State intervention: 'It is perhaps not unreasonable to hope that as time goes on, the statistics of consumption will be so organized as to afford demand schedules sufficiently trustworthy to show in diagrams that will appeal to the eye, the quantities of consumers' surplus that will result from different courses of public and private action. By the study of these pictures the mind may be gradually trained to get juster notions of the relative magnitudes of the interests which the community has in various schemes of public and private enterprise; and so other doctrines may replace those traditions of an earlier generation, which had perhaps a wholesome influence in their time, but which damped social enthusiasm by throwing suspicion on all projects for undertakings by the public on its own behalf which would not show a balance of direct pecuniary profit.'[47] Statistics are, admittedly, all too frequently somewhat less than perfect – as where 'important causes relevant to the issues under discussion'[48] are either neglected or missed out altogether; or where data supplied is consciously or unconsciously 'distorted by personal bias';[49] or where time-lags are so complex that there is lack of agreement, say, 'as to the length of time which elapsed between a tariff change and the full development of any of its good or evil results';[50] or where data on objective facts give us no guidance as to the subjective meaning of those facts.[51] But imperfect or not, statistics are improving, we are every day learning more and more about the nature and workings of our economy and society, and such upgrading of information-flows without any doubt makes possible State activity on a scale that would previously have been ill-advised, over-ambitious and even foolhardy.

Nor should we forget the important contribution to potential State activity that is nowadays represented by a more streamlined and better organised administrative apparatus. Bureaucracies today, public and private, tend to eschew nepotism in favour of merit and to open wide the doors to talented individuals able to comprehend economic matters: 'They offer an attractive field to people who have good business abilities, but have not inherited any great business opportunities.'[52] The State today strives increasingly to monitor the activities of the various Ministries (succesfully so: 'It is perhaps true that the power of Government to control the administration of a great Departmental business is on the increase'[53]) and has ensured that the various members of the body politic have come to march in step – with the encouraging result that, 'partly through the co-ordination and mutual aid of the forces of central and of local authorities, it has a much increased power of putting into effectivve operation any decision at which it has arrived'.[53] Not only do we increasingly have the proper data, it would appear, we even have the proper men and the proper structure necessary to make State intervention in economic matters a more realistic proposition than ever before.

Intervention, it is true, distorts automaticity, and automaticity, it might be argued, is the precondition for adaptation. It might so be argued, but it was not so argued by Marshall, whose view on the survival of the fittest was in effect that the fittest are not always and everywhere necessarily the best specimens or those most deserving of survival. Those who *do* survive, in other words, are not always and everywhere necessarily those who *ought to* survive, and what is true of individual specimens is true as well of institutional arrangements: 'The struggle for survival tends to make those methods of organization prevail, which are best fitted to *thrive in* their environment; but not necessarily those best fitted to *benefit* their environment, unless it happens that they are duly rewarded for all the benefits which they confer, whether direct or indirect. And in fact this is not so.'[54]

Thus one mode of economic organisation triumphs over another 'when it offers a direct and immediate service at a lower price', but the introduction of the time variable nonetheless makes the complete picture somewhat less appealing: 'The indirect and ultimate services which either will render have, as a general rule, little or no weight in the balance; and as a result many businesses languish and die, which might in the long run have done good work for society if only they could have obtained a fair start. This is especially true of some forms of co-operative associations.'[55] Given adequate time, those economic institutions which benefit their environment will normally 'strengthen the foundations of their own strength, and thereby increase their chance of surviving and prospering',[56] but the problem in the here-and-now remains essentially a straightforward one – that without 'a helping hand',[57] an exogenous impetus of extra-economic origin, the economic benefits which infant industries and analogous modes of organisation could potentially confer upon the community would in the cruel environment of the survival of the fittest never become accessible. And, speaking more generally: 'The struggle for survival may fail to bring into existence organisms that would be highly beneficial: and in the economic world the demand for any industrial arrangement is not certain to call forth a supply, unless it is something more than a mere desire for the arrangement, or a need for it. It must be an efficient demand; that is, it must take effect by offering adequate payment or some other benefit to those who supply it. A mere desire on the part of employees for a share in the management and the profits of the factory in which they work, or the need on the part of clever youths for a good technical education, is not a demand in the sense in which the term is used when it is said that supply naturally and surely follows demand.'[58]

Market mechanism and social interest need not, it is clear, point in the same direction. Normally they do so, and it is this fact which makes the free enterprise system philosophically acceptable despite the second-best and self-centred incentive structure on which it so extensively depends for its successful performance: thus, and whatever the position in the animal kingdom, 'in the higher world of man's action, those plans which benefit the environment most are likely to have a moral strength which will enable them to prevail in the long run'.[59] Sometimes, however, they do not – as is illustrated by the parable of the builder who houses twenty rich people on an acre of good land while simultaneously relegating two hundred poor ones to a second acre of poor land: 'His private interest will lead him to put the denser population on the unhealthy ground. For well-to-do people will generally pay a higher percentage of increase in rental or purchasing price on account of a favourable soil than working classes will. But, from a social point of view, the health of two hundred of the working classes is of more value than that of twenty of the well-to-do persons; unless indeed some of them happen to be of exceptional mental quality.'[60] The builder acts on the basis of 'efficient demand' and 'private interest' and is accordingly led as if by an invisible hand to supply – *de gustibus non est disputandum*, he will presumably tell himself – magnificent palaces for the wealthy and the prodigal, wretched hovels for the impoverished and the humble. The economist, however, is somewhat less complacent about this state of things. Identifying here as he is likely to do a definite 'difference between money value and social value'[61] – 'Adam Smith's *Wealth of Nations*, interpreted by his *Theory of Moral Sentiments*, supplies a sound basis for the introduction of such considerations',[62] he will presumably tell anyone who is willing to listen – he sees without difficulty what the builder does not see at all, that it is economically unwise and ethically unjustifiable to house large numbers of our fellow-citizens in conditions that will stunt their growth merely because they are at present somewhat lacking in funds. The economist, who is normally without any doubt the friend of the natural order, is not ashamed to admit that economic biology is, let us say, six or seven per cent short of perfection or to declare openly that 'the fact that a thing is beneficial to its environment will not by itself secure its survival either in the physical or in the moral world'[63] – or to demand 'the constructive activity of the State in social matters'[64] where the alternative to collective action and the visible hand would be under-provision and under-development.

Effective demand might not be adequate with respect to the provision of certain commodities and activities truly in the social interest. It might by the same token be more than adequate with respect to some things which are 'injurious'.[65] In the animal kingdom we have the unambiguous instance of the parasite which thrives 'without giving any good return' or,[66] alternatively, that of the aggressive predator which makes no contribution to the environment off which it feeds: 'A race of wolves that has well organized plans for hunting in packs is likely to survive and spread; because those plans enable it to catch its prey, not because they confer a benefit on the world.'[67] In economic life we have instances no less unambiguous, both of unneeded commodities (such as drink and the casino[68]) and of spurious activities – and the misguided advocate of consumer sovereignty would therefore do well to remember this: 'The fact that there is an economic demand for the services of Jewish and Armenian money-dealers in Eastern Europe and Asia, or for Chinese labour in California, is not by itself a proof, nor even a very strong ground for believing, that such arrangements tend to raise the quality of human life as a whole.'[69] Evidently there are cases of social over-supply as well as of social under-supply; and here once again we are reminded that, while those organisms 'that utilize the environment most, often turn out to be those that benefit those around them most',[70] yet automatic is nonetheless not always and everywhere a synonym for optimal. In such cases scope clearly exists for collective action if the society is to proceed *despite* human freedom to human betterment.

A society which is poor is compelled by its economic situation 'to subordinate almost every other consideration to the need of increasing the total produce of industry'.[71] A society which is affluent is however enabled by its economic resources increasingly to support the burden of collective action: 'Increased prosperity has made us rich and strong enough to impose new restraints on free enterprise; some temporary material loss being submitted to for the sake of a higher and ultimate greater gain.'[72] Nor does growth merely generate the resources which are the precondition for intervention. It also generates altruism, chivalry, generosity, and therewith the *will* to move towards a society 'in which the common good overrules individual caprice'.[73] Witness our embryonic welfare state: 'The ever-growing outlay on popular education, old age pensions, insurance, etc., is an expression of the public conscience needed to palliate extreme inequalities of wealth.'[74] Witness our willingness 'to give expression and effect to the public conscience' in the form of progressivity in taxation: 'It used to be held that all persons should contribute to the system of onerous taxes in proportion to their net incomes. But now the opinion seems to be gaining ground that the poorer classes should contribute a smaller percentage of their revenues than the middle classes; and these, again, a smaller than the richer classes. This arrangement seems to me to be "equitable" in the broader sense of the word.'[75] Witness the impact of our 'obligations of duty' on the geographical distribution of local imposts, given 'the tendency of the well-to-do to move away from crowded districts to roomy and fashionable suburbs: thus leaving the working classes to bear an undue share of the national duties towards the very poor. But no sooner does this evil become conspicuous, than legislation is invoked to remedy it, by widening the areas of rating for some purposes, so as to include poor and rich districts under the same budget.'[76] All of these are instances where economic growth and moral advance have moved in step – and in the direction of institutionalised altruism as well as of individual activity.[77] Obviously the reforms which are made must be made gradually for the simple reason that human nature does not evolve overnight: 'Projects for great and sudden changes are now, as ever, foredoomed to fail, and to cause reaction; we cannot move safely, if we move so fast that our new plans of life altogether outrun our instincts.'[78] Obviously too the constraints of State intervention must be voluntarily embraced if individual autonomy is genuinely to be the progenitor rather than the slave of collective action, for unselfishness then and then only 'will be the offspring of deliberate will; and, though added by instinct, individual freedom will then develop itself in collective freedom'.[79] Given that changes must be gradual and that constraints are only legitimate if voluntarily embraced, however, it must be conceded that the social conscience of the representative citizen in an affluent society is fuller and larger than was that of the representative citizen on a lower rung of the economic ladder: 'It is true that human nature can be modified: new ideals, new opportunities and new methods of action may, as history shows, alter it very much even in a few generations; and this change in human nature has perhaps never covered so wide an area and moved so fast as in the present generation.'[80] Man *as he is* is every day blending, and at an ever-increasing rate, into man *as he is becoming* – with the clear consequence that the extreme *freedom from* of early market capitalism is more and more being complemented by the new-found *freedom to* which is so characteristic of our increasingly affluent, increasingly concerned society. Because I increasingly love my neighbour, therefore I increasingly believe that I possess responsibilities and duties towards my fellow-citizen; because I increasingly feel integrated by the ties of culture, consensus and conscience in a common moral community, therefore I increasingly feel prepared to permit the State to act as the agent for my activity; and the conclusion to be drawn is that it is increasingly Green and not Spencer who emerges as the prophet of the new social order.

Increasingly moral men, Marshall argued, generate as if in their own image an increasingly moral State: 'The imagination, which endowed the individual with heroic virtue, endowed the State with an equally heroic wisdom and activity in the service of all: and imagination, though vain, was logically consistent; for the State at any time and place is the chief emanation of the character of mankind then and there. Of course a despotic State may represent the aims of a military minority, but we are now concerned with a self-governing people. The State, which they evolve, will reflect whatever purity of aim and nobility of purpose are to be found in their lives, but no more.'[81] Increasingly moral men accordingly take the view that increasingly honest, increasingly rational politicians can now be entrusted with tasks which at an earlier stage of social evolution would have been too much for them: Adam Smith himself 'frequently stated or implied that it would be possible for an omniscient and omnipotent Government to direct the actions of merchants, and other people, in a course more conducive to public well-being than that in which they would be led by their own interests',[82] although he also contrasted the benefits which might conceptually be conferred on the nation by 'statesmen of superhuman knowledge, intelligence, activity, and probity' with something far less appealing, namely 'the concrete realities of the world in which he lived'.[83] His world is not our own and it is salutary to remember that his scepticism regarding the role of governments refers not to all governments, Marshall reflected, but simply to 'Governments, such as he knew them'.[84]

Even though a sceptic, Smith was also an eclectic: 'He discovered numerous and important exceptions to the "natural law of liberty", and these discoveries were seldom *a priori*; they were nearly all supported by inductive studies of the world around him.'[85] Smith believed that the State should abstain from action where private sector initiative and energy, aspiration and striving, would deliver a more satisfactory service – but that the State had a duty to become involved in the processes of social change where 'the private hand', in matters of fundamental social concern, was demonstrably not 'competent for action'.[86] Marshall's view on State versus market was essentially the same, that in a system of division of labour sectors as well as individuals would be well advised to concentrate and specialise on that which they do best: 'So I cry "*Laissez-faire*: – let the State be up and doing" . . . Let everyone work with all his might; and most of all let the Government arouse itself to do that work which is vital, and which none but Government can do efficiently.'[87]

Obviously, as compared with autonomous individuals, the State 'is likely to be much less efficient for its purposes than they are for theirs, because its tasks are much heavier than theirs. Nevertheless the State is the most precious of human possessions; and no care can be too great to be spent on enabling it to do its special work in the best way.'[88] Given, however, that 'a chief condition to that end is that it should not be set to work, for which it is not specially qualified, under the conditions of time and place',[89] it becomes of considerable importance to find general guidelines which would help us, at a particular time and in a particular place, to identify an appropriate subject for intervention.

The first and most fundamental consideration in a political democracy must be, naturally enough, the power of public opinion. Thus it is that the state should, sensitive to the social consensus, intervene in cases where what social actors unambiguously want they are unable independently to procure in adequate quantities or indeed at all. This would appear to be the case with redistribution of income or town and country planning schemes (where what all can do collectively, none can do in isolation), with the provision of State education and of a tabular standard of value (both public goods generating spillover benefits – general culture and economic stability, respectively – accessible even to the free rider), with legislation to combat restrictive practices (a valuable investment in the competitive system), with collective action to relieve poverty (action necessitated by the very fact that the amount of distress that you and I generously wish to relieve clearly exceeds the amount of poverty currently being relieved by the voluntary sector). In all of these cases – cases of perceived collective need but demonstrated market failure – State action follows social consensus. It serves and obeys and it does not independently initiate.

But there is more. The State, Marshall believed, should occasionally lead as well as normally follow, and should, at such times, keeping one step in advance of public opinion, promote 'the growth of our higher social nature by giving it always some new and higher work to do, some practical ideal towards which to strive'.[90] The politician here, admittedly, marches in advance of consensus and boldly draws it forward. Where, however, philosophers rule and leaders are wise, the man-made article may actually be morally superior to the natural alternative: 'there is no general economic principle which supports the notion that industry will necessarily flourish best, or that life will be the happiest and healthiest, when each man is allowed to manage his own concerns as he thinks best. No considerable thinker has ever denied that *if* the rulers of a people are immeasurably superior to their subjects in knowledge and insight, there are many directions in which the people may be forced against their will for their good.'[91] This is not, one suspects, an argument in favour of large-scale experiments in central economic planning, and Marshall, one feels sure, shared the strong bias towards freedom of enterprise which he identified in the work of Adam Smith: 'He held that, evven if a statesman is the ablest man in his country, he cannot divide out his mind among a great number of trades and businesses; and give to each of them a better judgement, than will be worked out by the combined mental activities of hundreds of more or less able merchants, who give much of their time and strength to that one thing.'[92] What this is, one presumes, is a reminder that wise and thinking leaders with the missionary's in-bred paternalistic streak have the power not only to compel hardened criminals and the underserving poor against their will to act in their own best interests but also to discourage those consumables and activities which retard our process of *collective becoming* while lending support to those which encourage it. Marshall goes so far as to advocate (in defiance of consumer sovereignty) a system of subsidies and taxes such as favours those industries which are growing more efficient and discriminates against those which are simply growing old. He could have gone further still by calling (in defiance of moral consensus) for legislation to enforce temperance and to outlaw gambling. It is a matter of record that he did not do so. Social facts, however, are in continuous upward motion; something is obviously taking its course; and his very incorporation of this second criterion would seem to suggest nothing so much as the rational activity of the future-oriented shopper who buys two sizes too large for his children in anticipation of growth.

4.4 CO-OPERATION

Marshall was an individualist who was fascinated by collective action and a believer in market exchanges who was also an advocate of the unreciprocated gift. These seemingly disparate strands in his thought constitute the background to his discussion of voluntary association and help to explain the warmth and enthusiasm which he demonstrated towards the co-operative movement of his own times: 'I regard it as the typical and most representative product of the age; because it combines high aspirations with calm and strenuous action, and because it sets itself to develop the spontaneous energies while training the member to collective action by the aid of collective resources, and for the attainment of collective ends.'[1] Marshall served as President of the Central Co-Operative Union in 1889 and delivered his Presidential Address – in which he praised the co-operatives for combining the 'high social aim' of harnessing ambition to duty with the no less important objective of developing a 'broad and strong business basis'[2] – at the very time when he was putting the final coat of paint on the first edition of his *Principles*.

Marshall, like Mill, welcomed the co-operative form, but this is not to deny that he also had serious reservations about this mode of doing business. For one thing, the administrators of the co-operatives are by no means untouched by that bureaucratisation of the spirit which all too often represses experimentation, innovation, initiative, enterprise and dynamism in non-entrepreneurial organisations: 'The managers of a co-operative society seldom have the alertness, the inventiveness and the ready versatility of the ablest of those men who have been selected by the struggle for survival, and who have been trained by the free and unfettered responsibility of private business.'[3] History teaches us that efficient and go-ahead managers are tempted in any case rather to start their own firm than to continue to put their talents at the disposal of a constraining collectivity (whether a co-operative or a joint stock corporation), and the problem of retention in co-operative enterprise is that much greater than in the non-State sector as a whole due to its sustained propensity to under-pay management – and its need in consequence to make do with other people's rejects who cause it to lag still further behind the genuine pace-setters of modern business life: 'No co-operative workshop has yet offered a sufficient salary to retain the services of a manager of first-rate ability, unless he is so much under the influence of the Co-operative Faith as to be willing to work for the Cause at a less salary than he could get in the open market.'[4] It is naturally open to the co-operative to offer to pay the going rate to men of unique creativity and flair. Such a course of action would, however, exacerbate existing discontent within the firm on the part of the unenlightened rank-and-file concerning what they perceive as excessive remuneration being paid to highly-skilled professionals: 'The hardest work of business management is generally that which makes the least outward show; those who work with their hands are apt to underrate the intensity of the strain involved in the highest work of engineering the business, and to grudge its being paid for at anything like as high a rate as it could earn elsewhere.'[5] Higher pay would in addition feed existing tensions and resentments associated with the functional distinction *per se* between captain and crew: 'Human nature being what it is, the employees themselves are not always the best possible masters of their own foremen and managers; jealousies and frettings at reproof are apt to act like sand, that has got mixed with the oil in the bearings of a great and complex machinery.'[6] Should the captain be made accountable to the crew, however, it is clear that the same danger might arise as in the democratic polity – that guile, manipulation 'and a glib tongue would be likely to give a man more prominence and influence than could often be attained by originality and energy'.[7] In the co-operative as in the nation, it must be emphasized, genuinely democratic control presupposes the ability of the operative-elector with reasonable accuracy to 'estimate the characters of those who bear large responsibilities': 'Unless and until he can do that, democratic control of industry will be full of hazards. For a people which endeavours to rule its rulers, without being able to enter into the difficulties of the work to be done, is apt to fall under the guidance of plausible speakers. In such a case, what appears as democratic control becomes in effect haphazard oligarchy.'[8] In the co-operative as in the nation, evidently, effective performance waits upon social progress, but the conclusion to be drawn is for that very reason an optimistic one: 'The world is only just beginning to be ready for the higher work of the co-operative movement . . . . Its many different forms may therefore be reasonably expected to attain a larger success in the future than in the past; and to offer excellent opportunities for working men to practise themselves in the work of business management, to grow into the trust and confidence of others, and gradually rise to posts in which their business abilities will find scope.'[9] Many of the problems belong to the present. Many of the advantages belong to the future. Chief among the advantages associated with the important co-operative mode of collective action are the following:

(1) Economic efficiency

Marshall believed that greater efficiency due to greater involvement inevitably results from a system wherein 'a part or the whole of those shareholders who undertake the risks of the business are themselves employed by it. The employees, whether they contribute towards the material capital of the business or not, have a share in its profits, and some power of voting at the general meetings at which the broad lines of its policy are laid down, and the officers appointed who are to carry that policy into effect. They are thus the employers and the masters of their own managers and foremen, they have fairly good means of judging whether the higher work of engineering the business is conducted honestly and efficiently, and they have the best possible means for detecting any laxity or incompetence in its detailed administration. And lastly they render unnecessary some of the minor work of superintendence that is required in other establishments; for their own pecuniary interests and the pride they take in the success of their own business make each of them averse to any shirking of work either by himself or his fellow-workmen.'[10]

What this means is best understood by examining carefully the four inter-related concepts which figure so prominently in Marshall's account of the relationship between involvement and efficiency.

First, at the level of *property*, the point is that there exists both conspicuous and intrinsic 'delight in ownership' and 'pleasure of possession',[11] and that 'many people derive from the mere feeling of ownership a stronger satisfaction than they derive from ordinary pleasures in the narrower sense of the term'.[12] Worker-shareholders, being givers as well as takers of employment, may thus be expected to take pride in their own property and to devote greater attention to its good husbandry than if the capitalist were one man, the labourer another. Of course this is a second-best solution when compared with the idealism of ethical absolutes such as altruism and obligation. The world itself, however, is second-best. Co-operators are evidently much to be praised for entertaining a more realistic notion than that of the socialists concerning the functionality of property-rights at our present stage of social evolution, as is illustrated by the following: 'The earlier co-operative societies had desired that all funds subscribed should at once become common property: but the Rochdale weavers recognized that human nature was not ready for that.'[13]

Second, at the level of *profits*, the point is that men have *ceteris paribus* a greater incentive to marginal exertion where they also have a direct share in marginal reward. This means that profit-sharing *per se* (in itself one of many 'partial applications of the co-operative principle'[14] irrespective of the locus of property-rights) is attractive to both sides of industry, it being hoped presumably 'that the firm will find a material as well as a moral reward in the diminution of friction, in the increased willingness of its employees to go out of their way to do little things that may be of great benefit comparatively to the firm, and lastly in attracting to itself workers of more than average ability and industry'.[15] Profit-sharing *per se* fosters a community of interest between workers and capitalists such that 'the relations between employers and employed are raised to a higher plane both economically and morally' (most of all where it is regarded 'as but a step towards the still higher but much more difficult level of *true* co-operation')[16] and it is in all respects a development warmly to be welcomed: Marshall made clear that he regarded 'the movement towards the direct participation by the employee in the profits of the business as one of the most important and hopeful events of modern times, and as one of the best and most valuable fruits of the co-operative spirit'.[17]

Third, at the level of *power*, the point is that few self-respecting Englishmen are likely to give of their best when they perceive themselves merely as passive agents, as objects to be manipulated by others. Historically speaking, 'the attitude of Anglo-Saxon workers differed from that of Germans and others, who rejoiced in the apparent vigour of autocratic Government, and cared little about freedom for its own sake';[18] and that is why, while foreigners accustomed obediently to follow the leader have been more attracted to Statist control from above when seeking reform ('The German socialists have been bitter foes of co-operation'[19]), Englishmen with a strong feeling for individual dignity and personal autonomy have had a preference instead for consultative and participative modes of decision-making such as were embodied in the Whiteley Report (when, in the atmosphere of solidarity and belonging born of the First World War, valuable proposals were made to the effect that 'everyone shall contribute, both as an individual and in association with his comrades, to the solution of such business problems as are of most direct interest to him and to them'[20]) and such as long have been the property of the best of the co-operators (the men of the Halifax Cooperative, for example, who 'retain the supreme control of the store in their hands'[21]). Where *morale* is concerned, nationalisation by itself is no solution: 'The postman is not made free by escaping from the control of an employer, who may be sympathetic; and coming under that of officials, who must obey orders, and have no power to indulge their sympathies.'[22] Where *morale* is concerned, some form of power-sharing is called for, and that in itself is a characteristic of co-operation: 'I incline to think that the real advantages of having employees on the committee are greater, and the disadvantages less, than they are likely to appear at first both to the shareholders and the manager. I think that in this matter the co-operative spirit has a high, though difficult duty, the brave performance of which would ultimately bring its own reward.'[23]

Fourth, at the level of *performance*, the point is that the firm which takes the trouble to consult the men in the field about 'work, with which they are familiar'[24] is able by means of that process of consultation to tap specialised knowledge and background information such as might point management in the direction of new initiatives that it might not otherwise have considered. A more co-operative, less traditional mode of organisation also enables the workers to play some part in monitoring the managers and, indeed, one another (a valuable constraint on free riders); and such disciplining of all by each thus helps to ensure higher productivity and higher standards of workmanship than would otherwise have obtained.

(2) Moral upgrading

Co-operation improves human character as well as contributing to the increase in material comfort and material well-being which has constituted the principal focus of our discussion thus far. It was with such considerations in mind that Marshall singled out co-operatives for particular praise when he came to speak of organisations in his paper to the Industrial Remuneration Conference: 'Among these associations the genuine co-operative societies have the noblest work. Besides his wages and interest on his capital, they are giving the workman high mental and moral aspirations; they afford him a real insight into the problems of business, and they help to diminish industrial strife.'[25]

First, as to *aspirations*, Marshall is saying that co-operatives give men a much-needed opportunity to manifest their emotive attachment to collectivities. Such attachment existed once, in the days when one craftsman laboured alongside another to produce a product in which both took pride. It subsequently decayed when industrial revolution caused many different tasks to be grouped together in the impersonal environment of the factory, for in such circumstances contiguity as perceived by the craftsman is in truth a world away from community: 'Loyalty to craft gave scope to some of his higher emotions: but the general interests of the business in which he was engaged did not appeal strongly to him.'[26] Co-operatives have the useful function of giving working men an opportunity to transcend differentiation, competitiveness and selfishness and of providing an outlet for other-regarding actions and a wider view of interest based upon 'brotherly trust and association'[27] within the organisation – without, of course, having simultaneously to sacrifice the benefits outside the organisation that are to be reaped not by mutual aid and cordial fraternalism but via the *quid pro quo* of the market mechanism and the sheer egocentricity of the market mentality. Marshall is well aware that the dual ethos he is propounding (while economically superior to the totally fraternalistic ethos that is so naively advocated by certain communistic thinkers) also involves the social actor in a definite conflict of orientations. Such a conflict is not, however, as serious a problem as might be imagined. For one thing, business life today is becoming itself increasingly cordial, and in that sense no longer really in harmony with that 'aggressive competition, which was frequently to be observed among the crude, though energetic men, who mastered English industry in the first half of (the nineteenth) century':[28] our era, unlike theirs, is as much characterised by the co-operative use of shared research facilities and the pooling of information on distant markets as it is by the cut-throat drive to beggar my neighbour, and it is to be expected that the former tendency will continue to wax while the latter tendency will continue to wane. More importantly, perhaps, men demonstrably able to manage the conflict (men, in other words, unambiguously both of unquestioned business capability and of unimpeachable moral tone) have not failed to step forward to serve as officers of the societies in response to a perceived need: 'Co-operation has a special charm for those in whose tempers the social element is stronger, and who desire not to separate themselves from their old comrades, but to work among them as their leaders. Its aspirations may in some respects be higher than its practice; but it undoubtedly does rest in a great measure on ethical motives. The true co-operator combines a keen business intellect with a spirit full of an earnest faith; and some co-operative societies have been served excellently by men of great genius both mentally and morally – men who for the sake of the co-operative faith that is in them, have worked with great ability and energy, and with perfect uprightness, being all the time content with lower pay than they could have got as business managers on their own account or for a private firm.'[29] Co-operation for its success presupposes the preexistence of men with such latent aspirations (to whom it offers the valued chance of unfolding what is in themselves); but it also has a dynamic of its own via the encouragement which it gives to 'the upright and brotherly instincts' of those who are active in the movement.[30] Co-operation is thus not simply the product of prior moral advance (although it is that, for it '*requires* habits of mutual trust and confidence'[31]) but an active cause of further advance as well.

Second, as to *insight*, Marshall believed that co-operatives have an educative function and provide stimulus to the intellectual faculties of their members. Taking the view that in modern society 'production is at fault, but it is the production of human beings',[32] Marshall welcomed the co-operative mode at least in part because of the manner in which it improves our national stock of creative citizens. Thus, he pointed out, the best men in the movement not only possess 'enthusiasm' and 'high aspiration' but also make use of 'terse, pointed, business-like arguments'[33] which cannot help but educate their followers in technical and commercial matters. The pioneers of the co-operative idea had expressed the hope that co-operative activity itself 'would gradually develop a set of working class leaders with wide business experience'; and while experience in Britain and abroad has 'partly moderated' this expectation, experience has also 'partly confirmed the bright hopes that were entertained in this and other countries'.[34] Besides that, the very process of learning by doing by co-operating and participating is itself a case of becoming a more thoughtful democrat as well as a more competent technocrat: 'It is an education in itself to any member of a local society to have to consider whether his representative on the Wholesale is to advocate a forward policy – whether, for instance, he is to support a policy for starting one more new line of ships of their own.'[35] Participation is the mother of self-respect and the father of well-considered judgements; but the precondition for the acquisition in this manner of the valuable transferable skill of acting as a good citizen is that decision-making in the organisation is sufficiently decentralised to ensure that the 'more independent parts are not crushed out'[36] by a concentration and a bureaucratisation of power such as would cause the movement to 'miss its highest aims'.[37] Marshall accordingly opposes centralisation within the co-operative movement on the grounds of the case for education in collective action: 'It is a better training in seamanship to sail a fishing-boat, than to watch a three-masted ship, the tops of whose masts alone appear above the horizon'.[38] While he could without any doubt usefully have said more than he did about the relevance of this principle to the proposal for devolution of political powers which he is presumably espousing when he calls, within the body of total State intervention, for 'an extension of local responsibilities wherever possible',[39] the point he is making is clear enough, that participation in democratic activity cannot but be regarded as a nursery and a school for democrats and thus a good thing in its own right.[40]

Third, as to *strife*, Marshall, distressed by the bitterness and market imperfections associated with the 'new unionism' of the 1880s, would seem to have been searching for some mode of worker involvement and self-help which would constitute a viable alternative to the progressively less moral and less chivalrous trades unions of his own times. In his Presidential Address of 1889 he would seem to have singled out the co-operative form as that alternative. He there praises the 'high social aim' of organisations such as the unions but then notes that the co-operatives (which share this aim) have a 'broad and strong business basis' as well[41] – the only movement to have both, making in that way a genuine contribution to Marshall's own personal crusade 'to get rid of the evils of competition while retaining its advantages'.[42] Co-operation and competition go together and reinforce one another, and it is important to remember, Marshall stressed in 1901, that co-operation is in fact 'a part of (the) ideal free system as J. S. Co's are: it is not as T. U.s a hostile correcting force'.[43] Unions unite, and that is moral and good – but, sadly, they are also becoming increasingly imbued with egocentricity and obsessed with redistribution to an extent that inflicts harm on their fellow-citizens, and that is immoral and bad: 'Every sort of association that enriches life by giving to the individual broader, and therefore presumably higher, interests than those which directly concern his own well-being, is to be cherished: but any tendency to curtail important activities unduly (*i.e.* before they have reached the point at which fatigue becomes a serious evil) in order to obtain an artificial advantage in bargaining, is to be condemned as antisocial.'[44] Unions are esentially redistributive, and in that sense sadly limited in their aspirations. Co-operatives, however, are essentially constructive, and in that sense on a superior plane to the zero-sum game: 'The co-operative faith is a belief in the beauty and the nobility, the strength and the efficiency, of collective action by the working classes, employing their own means, not indeed suddenly to revolutionize, but gradually to raise, their own material and moral condition.'[45] Macroeconomic redistribution may well occur in the nation where there is an expansion in the collective ownership of capital by those who supply labour in the firm. Reallocation of shares within a fixed and constant sum is, however, hardly the primary concern of the co-operative organisation. Its principal objective is material and moral *progress* and the transcendence of strife via the perception and activity of working together. Its true work is to teach that, even in a market economy based on individual freedom and private property, nonetheless every one of us in an atom fully a part of the whole and needing to manifest that integration, once perceived, by means of collective action in corporations large (the State), small (the family) and intermediate (the Charity Organization Society, the union – and the co-operative). Leviathan, it would appear, is a large association made up of many smaller ones, a 'common centre for help and advice' for its respective members but 'not controlling and directing them, not interferring with their freedom without absolute necessity'.[46] Such a corporate State is fully in keeping with our national character; for the truth is that 'broad-based, highly-organised freedom of action is characteristically English'.[47] Even more important, perhaps, it is fully consonant with a realistic view of human nature as it is and as it is becoming; for when all is said and done concerning individual and collective action, the fact remains that, looking about us in an ever-improving real world, 'whenever we get a glimpse of the economic man he is not selfish'.[48]

5 Microeconomic Policy

Marshall believed that the State could and should intervene to do work 'specifically its own' and in that way help to secure 'social ameliorations that are not fully within the range of private effort'.[1] Adam Smith before him had introduced a similar *caveat* into his theory of *laissez-faire* when assigning to the State (alongside the less controversial obligations of law and order and national defence) 'the duty of erecting and maintaining certain public works and certain public institutions, which it can never be for the interest of any individual, or small number of individuals, to erect and maintain'.[2] Milton Friedman after him, although undeniably a libertarian with a strong intellectual commitment to minimal State intervention, stated categorically that 'the consistent liberal is not an anarchist',[3] and assigned a number of positive functions to Government – while indicating clearly that these must be modest, limited, and above all complements to (not substitutes for) voluntary contracts made by rational individuals, 'within the range of private effort'.

Hutchison sees Marshall as a classical liberal who when all is said and done ultimately recommended that as little as possible be said and done where State-inspired social engineering is concerned: 'Though Marshall was keenly aware of the looming problem of the changing relative economic position of Britain, he had no major policy changes to propose. . . . In fact, though Marshall's interests extended across the whole range of feasible extensions of government intervention in the economy, for the most part he had no far-reaching proposals to make. . . . It seems, therefore, in some ways rather strange for Keynes (and especially Keynes) to have complained that "Marshall was too anxious to do good". It is not very apparent that the good was very extensive that Marshall was too anxious to do.'[4] Hutchison sees Marshall as a traditional liberal who, much prone to moralizing and preaching, was contented to exhort his fellow citizens to do good but was unprepared to institutionalise such benevolence in the form of a powerful, all-pervasive, reformist State. Hutchison, it would be fair to infer, finds more than a hint of Friedman in

Marshall, and would no doubt situate both without reservation in the mainstream of *freedom from*.

Liberal, as it happens, is a word with more than one connotation; and that is why Hutchison is able to treat Marshall as a traditional liberal (in the anti-Statist sense of Philosophic Radicalism) while simultaneously Jha is able to interpret Marshall as a modern liberal (in the pro-Statist sense of Asquith). Jha insists that 'the urgency of reform' – *not* the preeminence of unfettered markets and invisible hands – is the centrepiece of Marshall's political economy, and he reaches the following conclusion concerning the significance and thrust of Marshall's contribution: 'The period 1890–1915 in the history of British Economic Thought may aptly be described as the Age of Marshall. His influence as teacher, and his ideas as presented in the *Principles of Economics* (1890) and other writings, stimulated and often dominated the ideas and writings of most of the younger economists of the period. His ideas also provided a theoretical basis for increasing state intervention in economic life of the community in Britain, and thus helped the Liberal Government of Great Britain lay the foundations of a Welfare State.'[5] Jha's view of a busy, interfering Marshall helping to lay the foundations of a busy, interfering State is also that of Bernard Gerbier, who points out that economies of scale and the emergence of large corporations put paid to that defence of the market which relies on the automatic equilibration of highly competitive markets – and raise questions concerning the social interest which admit of one and only one answer: 'Il est évident que dans le capitalisme de monopoles, et Marshall devait s'en rendre compte puisqu'il justifiait *de cette manière* l'existence des cartels et autres ententes, *les adaptations ne peuvent plus provenir des seuls méchanismes automatiques du marché* . . . . La puissance des firmes empêchant le libre-jeu des adaptations, l'ampleur de leurs interventions conduisent à des modifications très importantes des divers équilibres d'industries, ne permettant plus en effet aux seules forces régulatrices de la distribution et de l'échange de parvenir à rétablir les déséquilibres. La seule concurrence n'apparaît plus être un moyen suffisant. L'Etat doit intervenir massivement et l'explication marshallienne ne peut plus servir à nous expliquer le fonctionnement réel du système à l'heure où la planification indicative est mise en place pour prévoir les adaptations et modifications du système, que l'on ne peut plus laisser agir librement. *L'Etat paraît alors venir en force sur la scène de l'économie alors qu'il n'en avait jamais été absent* . . . Marshall devait bien savoir tout ceci.'[6]

Both Jha and Gerbier regard Marshall as a thinker on and of the middle ground while Hutchison draws attention to the fact that Marshall's precise recommendations with respect to State intervention are strikingly limited. Here as elsewhere, it would appear, Marshall was far from clear. It is, however, useful nonetheless to try and make some sense of Marshall's views on the important choice between automaticity and policy, between hands visible and hands unseen; and that task of interpretation accordingly constitutes the subject-matter of both this Chapter and the next. In Chapter 6 we shall be concerned with macroeconomic issues. In the present chapter our concerns are microeconomic in nature and four in number: The Nature of Taxation, Collective Consumption, The Relief of Poverty, and Industry and Trade. Our impression is that an author who shuns controversy and who has a pragmatist's bias for considering each case on its own merits is likely also to be an author whose theoretical explanations for *what is* and for *what is evolving* will more often than not fail to win the attention which they deserve. Our conclusion is that, while in the case of Alfred Marshall hardly anything is ever certain, still one cannot help but suspect that it was Jha and Gerbier who best had the measure of the man even if they, like the rest of us, could see nothing but the shadow on the wall.

5.1 THE NATURE OF TAXATION

My earnings and my garden, like my blood and my kidneys, are my private property. Yet many of us are prepared to see some of our blood alienated through donorship schemes in order to help those in need of blood, and many of us are equally prepared to see some of our earnings alienated through democratically-imposed redistributive measures in order to help those in need of earnings. Many of us, similarly, are prepared to see our natural endowment of healthy organs increased by an external donation (as an alternative to meeting the Invisible Hand before we have optimally allocated our resources), and many of us are equally prepared to see our personal endowment of goods and services augmented by a free gift (the case of the hostess who is flattered rather than embarrassed when her dinner-guests bring her flowers). Life itself, it would appear, is an on-going drama of interpersonal transfers. What requires explanation therefore is not the drama *per se* but rather the employment of a stage-manager in the form of the State – and the size, nature and direction of the transfers to be effected.

Money plays a central part in Marshall's economics, and it is no surprise that he devoted so much of his attention to an analysis of State-managed transfers taking the pecuniary form.

(1) Taxes on income

Marshall was concerned about 'the evils arising from the unequal distribution of wealth'[1] and even includes in his initial enumeration, in the *Principles*, of 'some of the chief questions to which the economist addresses himself'[2] the following rather value-laden set of queries: 'Taking it for granted that a more equal distribution of wealth is to be desired, how far would this justify changes in the institutions of property, or limitations of free enterprise even when they would be likely to diminish the aggregate of wealth? . . . How ought the burdens of taxation to be distributed among the different classes of society?'[3]

The key point about the evil in question would seem to be the diminishing marginal utility of money. Clearly, if it is true that 'a shilling is the measure of less pleasure, or satisfaction of any kind, to a rich man than to a poor one',[4] then optimality in resource allocation without redistribution of income would not refer to the same equilibrium as maximum aggregate felicity consequent upon some optimal reallocation of effective demand. Where in other words, 'the total utility of increasing wealth increases less than in proportion to its amount',[5] the thoughts of the student of satisfaction must inevitably turn to sharing and a redistribution of that which the market has made: 'An increase by (say) a quarter of the wages of the poorer class of *bona fide* workers adds more to the sum total of happiness than an increase by a quarter of the incomes of an equal number of any other class . . . . It is the duty of society to carry yet further an increase of wellbeing which is to be obtained at so low a cost.'[6] The principle of equality of sacrifice thus directs us to reject proportional in favour of progressive income taxation; for the truth is that the 'hurt' caused by raising a national revenue of £1000 via a levy of £20 on each of 50 incomes of £200 is 'unquestionably far greater' than that caused by raising the sum in question via a single levy of £1000 on a single income of £10 000,[7] and no sound utilitarian with a genuine commitment to the greatest happiness of the greatest number would opt for more 'hurt' when he could equally well opt for less. Admittedly this argument presupposes the validity of interpersonal comparisons of utility – and utility, as is well known, is individual, subjective, and non-observable. But Marshall and his followers refused to allow what they obviously regarded as little more than trivial debating points to cloud their judgement when it came to results which they obviously regarded as buttressed by nothing less than solid common sense. As Pigou puts it, explaining how to increase total happiness even without increasing national wealth: '*Prima facie* all large inequalities of income entail social loss; for the ninth course of the plutocrat's dinner, despite the individual benefit that it may confer on his doctor, yields much less satisfaction on the whole than the milk which the cost of it might have secured for a poor man's child.'[8]

Tampering with market-determined incomes means tampering with property rights (which Marshall apparently viewed at the best of times as relative and functional, not absolute and eternal[9] and which must be seen against the background of the following dictum: 'Wealth exists only for the benefit of mankind. . . . Its true measure lies only in the contribution it makes to human well-being.'[10]); and perhaps also some 'lessening of national material wealth' (which Marshall evidently was prepared to countenance in the interests of 'maximum satisfaction'). Perhaps so, but not definitely so; for Marshall, aware of the need to preserve incentives and insistent that 'men are not equal by nature and cannot be made equal by art',[11] warned that a levelling process that went too far should be rejected precisely because it would only raise 'the fortunes of the masses . . . *for the time*',[12] and stressed the need for moderation in this as in other areas of social policy. An economy should eschew extremes of equalisation such as might reduce the supply of effort and/or drive enterprise abroad. An economy should, however, not hesitate to adopt measures leading to a modest amount of levelling, most notably where surplus earnings exist (the case with rents and quasi-rents) that are unambiguously over and above the minimum income needed to attract the right men into the right jobs and to induce them to 'exert themselves to the utmost' – and it is frankly 'untenable to assert, as some authors do, that "nothing less than the enormous fortunes which successful men now make and retain would suffice for that purpose"'.[13] Nor should one neglect the stimulatory effects of redistributed income on those who benefit from the expenditures which the taxes in question serve to finance (as where the health and strength of the lower classes are improved as a consequence of better education and fresher air) or forget that the supply of savings does not depend on the waiting of wealthy capitalists alone: 'Any change in the distribution of wealth which gives more to the wage receivers and less to the capitalists is likely, other things being equal, to hasten the increase of material production, and . . . will not perceptibly retard the storing-up of material wealth.'[14] So while happiness and well-being were in the last analysis more important to Marshall than were efficiency and prosperity, the fact is that both sets of considerations would seem in his view to have pointed in the same direction.

One advantage of income tax over private charity with respect to efficiency and prosperity is that the latter transfer is voluntary whereas the former transfer is compulsory – and, being compulsory, is able to tap great wealth in order to relieve great poverty while leaving relative positions *within* reference groups strictly unaffected. None of us spends all of his time in the ivory tower of the social vacuum; and, clearly, where our colleagues, our friends, our neighbours and our rivals are subject to a handicap similar to our own, there is no discouraging loss of 'social distinction' when taxation makes inroads on disposable income and thence on private expenditure. Because there is no loss of 'reputation', even the loss of income might not in the event 'sap the springs of free initiative and strength of character' or 'materially check the growth of the national dividend', and in such a case the redistributive measure 'would seem to be a clear social gain'[15] in the sense that the loss of income has no appreciable effect on the supply of effort. It is relativities, not absolutes, which so often matter, particularly to the more enterprising, intelligent and socially-sensitive member of the community, and it is indeed precisely because of the fact that so much of his consumption is conspicuous that such a man would not be excessively tax-averse: 'His energy would not be much affected by a tax which lowered his share, provided it did not put him at a disadvantage relatively to others. The zeal of a yachtsman in a race is not lessened when an unfavourable tide retards the progress of all.'[16] An altruistic man imbued with economic chivalry who is also a social actor fearful lest his peers become free riders on the coat-tails of his generosity and thereby usurp his place in the status-stakes might positively welcome the constraint of all upon each that is represented by the income tax. All in all, Marshall concluded, there would seem to be 'a margin of at least one or two hundred millions which might be diverted to social uses without causing any great distress to those from whom it was taken; provided their neighbours were in a like position, and not able to make disagreeable remarks on the absence of luxuries and of conventional "necessaries for social propriety".'[17] Needless to say, where 'enterprise may be maintained, even though those who are rich are required to make large contributions for national purposes',[18] there is a very real sense in which it would be true to say that it would be 'socially wasteful' not to demand such contributions, for this is a clear case where something is gained while nothing is lost – provided only that all members of one and the same reference group are subjected to one and the same handicap.

A further argument in favour of levelling has to do with the composition of consumption. Marshall took the view that 'the well-to-do spend largely on things that do not make life worth living; and the loss of which would involve no serious detriment to the progress of art and knowledge, or to general refinement.'[19] Much of their expenditure, he insisted, is not only not 'necessary for their *true* well-being'[20] but even 'tends to lower rather than to raise human character'[21] (both of the rich themselves and, presumably, also of those in 'employments that are subservient to luxury'[24]) – and all of this in a society where so many of our fellow citizens, in great need and suffering absolute deprivation, 'lack the material conditions of a healthy, clean, vigorous and effective family life'![23] Much good could be done if the rich would agree to be somewhat less rich that the poor might be somewhat less poor, and not least because so many of the consumables of the more affluent classes are – at least at our present stage of social evolution – upon closer inspection merely baubles and trinkets 'of little solid advantage':[24] 'A vast increase of happiness and elevation of life might be attained if those forms of expenditure which serve no high purpose could be curtailed, and the resources thus set free could be applied for the welfare of the less prosperous members of the working classes; the whole change being so made as not considerably to slacken the springs of productive energy.'[25] That you eat two dinners while I eat none is a good enough reason in itself for Marshall to attack your luxuries for crowding out my necessaries: 'As human nature is, the high consumption of the rich seems to me excessive and to necessitate in effect a meagre life on the part of others.'[26] That you eat cream cakes instead of soya beans only compounds your offence – since not only do you consume my dinner but you also order food which by its very nature reveals that you are wasteful as well as greedy.

As, of course, our society evolves, so you too evolve; and Marshall, as we saw in Chapter 2, was pleased to identify even now both an improvement in the nature of consumables demanded and a significant extension of altruism and of chivalry in economic affairs. The former development is indicative of a 'steadfast suppression of personal luxuries',[27] and is thus complementary to the second – which embraces among other things your acknowledgement of moral obligation inextricably linked to personal wealth: 'The rich have duties as well as rights in their individual and in their collective capacity.'[28] Part of your moral obligation will, one would expect, be directly discharged by means of individual charity towards the poor; and Marshall's proposals for an institutionalisation and a formalisation of the gift relationship build upon but do not seek to replace the more personalised transfer. Both the coordinated and the uncoordinated effort have their role to play, as Marshall explained in his Presidential Address to the Co-operative Congress in 1889: 'I myself certainly think, that the rich ought to be taxed much more heavily than they are, to provide for their poorer brethren the material means for a healthy physical and mental development; and .... that the rich are in private duty bound to contribute freely to public purposes far more than the taxgatherer ought by force to take from them, and to confine within narrow bounds their expenditure on their own personal enjoyment, and that of their families.'[29]

The academic economist is the friend of the poor: his training being utilitarian, 'he accepts the premises of the working classes that the well-being of the many is more important than that of the few.'[30] The academic economist accordingly finds himself drawn, as if by an invisible hand, to the 'broad proposition' that 'aggregate satisfaction can *prima facie* be increased by the distribution, whether voluntarily or compulsorily, of some of the property of the rich among the poor'.[31] The academic economist is therefore the friend of the rich – since, both through their voluntary transfers and through their chivalrous attitude to progressive taxation, the rich have shown themselves increasingly concerned with the needs and aspirations of such low-income groups as still remain.

(2) Taxes on wealth

Marshall (despite an infuriating linguistic propensity to treat 'income', 'wealth', 'capital' and 'property' in places as if the terms were synonymous) had a clear perception of the distinction between stocks and flows, lakes and rivers. In the foregoing discussion our focus was on flows. Our focus now shifts to stocks as we consider Marshall's attitude to the taxation of assets other than those represented by the refreshing stream of current earnings.

One obvious candidate for taxation is the estate when transferred at close of play. Marshall in 1897 was unable to deny the undoubted attractions of taxes levied on inheritance ('death duties seem less inequitable, and . . . press less hardly on anyone, than other taxes of equal intensity') but concluded that the well-worn objections nonetheless had 'great force still': 'On the whole I think no one generation should very much increase them; experience alone can show whether we have outgrown the stage in which the incidence of such taxes lies heavily on the springs of prosperity.'[32] Marshall in 1897 thus adopted a watching brief: 'Our duty at present is to experiment freely, but to move cautiously.'[33] Marshall by 1909, however, seems to have concluded his exercise in listening and learning, and to have reached the decision that death duties are indeed a valuable mode of public finance. As he wrote to Lord Reay in that year: 'For about fifteen years I taught somewhat eagerly that "Death Duties" were a grievous evil because they checked the growth of capital. For the next few years I hesitated. Now I think they are on the whole a good method of raising a rather large part of the national revenue; because they do not check accumulation as much as had been expected, and a small check does not seem to me now as great an evil as it did then.'[34] Marshall in 1880 had warned of the threat to accumulation: 'A tax on property has this objection: that it is a tax which can only be paid by those who save. A man who spends all his income as fast as he gets it, escapes this tax nearly altogether.'[35] Marshall in 1897 repeated his warning – that taxes on inheritance 'are paid out of capital, and that the heir is apt to live up to the full income which he has inherited'.[36] Marshall in 1917 was more radical with respect to death duties and less anxious with respect to the supply of savings: 'The annoyance which a man feels on reflecting that his heirs will inherit somewhat less than he has owned does not seem to affect conduct much'.[37] Besides that, even if the duties were to administer a 'small check' to savings, the fact is that we can now afford such a luxury: Britain is, after all, no longer a capital-poor country, but rather a nation whose capital daily 'grows fast relatively to her area'.[38] The ease of collection of a graduated tax on estates left behind at death is an additional point in favour of such a tax. Nor should we forget that the tax recommends itself to our increasingly chivalrous 'ethical conscience'[39] and is thus buttressed by the power of public opinion.[40] The philosopher in addition perceives a deleterious impact on character where great wealth derives from privilege and birth rather than from energy and enterprise: 'Though the earning of great wealth generally strengthens character, the spending of it by those who have not earned it, whether men or women, is not nearly an unmixed good.'[41] In the sense that inheritance itself stifles initiative, death-duties actually improve growth-performance by helping to negate a previous negation; and a moderate amount of creaming-off is hence to be welcomed as a source of both moral and material betterment.

Land is an asset which for purposes of taxation would seem to be an obvious target; and it is therefore striking how few recommendations Marshall in the event chose to make concerning a functionless surplus not linked to real cost or individual effort, a reward which could easily be reduced or even abolished without affecting the quantity supplied of the factor, a return which increases over time due principally to rising site-values in urban areas and which must inevitably be boosted as well by government policies (notably the convenience of roads and the proximity of parks). A letter of 1909 reveals not only Marshall's continuing opposition to the nationalisation of land but also his continuing state of confusion as to what to do about the injustices that land not mixed with effort represented to him: 'I have repeatedly stated my opinion that the owners of such land have not truly paid income tax. It is true that they have not "evaded" it. But the law has hitherto been a sustained social injustice in this respect: what they have been required to return as income is only a part of it. This injustice I regard as "predatory"; its redress I regard as anti-socialistic.'[42] Other statements show him in a moderately more decisive mood, as in the following comment, buried at the end of Appendix G of the *Principles*, concerning the taxation of site values: 'Rich private gains accrue, not merely through causes which are public rather than private in their character, but also at the expense of one of the chief forms of public wealth. Large expenditure is needed to secure air and light and playroom. And the most appropriate source from which that expense can be defrayed seems to be . . . extreme rights of private property in land.'[43] This is hardly the statement of a Henry George but it does show that Marshall somewhat more than flirted with the concept of 'taxes on immoveable property'.[44]

The problem of capital gains is 'similar in some respects' to that of land, but Marshall here again did not make any significant proposals for taxation. The administrative problems associated with an annual tax on accruals are so great as to make such a tax 'impracticable'. Besides that, asset-appreciation need not be in all cases afunctional: 'Few forms of intellectual effort are more important socially than forecasting the future and contriving so that the future may turn out well. The shareholder who directly or indirectly takes part in the management of a company is generally doing good service; and his rewards, like those of the able and courageous fisherman, come largely in the form of big hauls or "windfalls". I do not see how to tax the passive stock holder, without taxing the active one.'[45] When in doubt, Marshall concluded, the best course of action is simply not to levy the tax at all.

(3) Taxes on expenditure

Marshall much preferred direct to indirect taxation. Taxes on goods, where levied at different rates on different commodities, violate the natural liberty of sovereign consumers and hinder them 'in the selection of those routes for the satisfaction of their wants'[46] by making one route artificially more appealing, another relatively more repulsive. Taxes on goods, moreover, are deplorably regressive and 'likely to press with undue weight on the poorer classes of the community',[47] in flagrant contradiction to the definition of fairness currently adopted in Britain both by public opinion and by Parliament: 'The great glory of the fiscal policy of the latter two-thirds of the nineteenth century is, that it found the working classes paying a very much greater percentage of their income in taxes than the rich did, and that it left them paying a less percentage.'[48] Admittedly some countries (especially where sparsely populated) might have no administratively-feasible mode of public finance but indirect taxation – and not all countries are as concerned as we are about the regressive element inherent in all taxes on commodities. But those countries are foreign countries and 'England has no excuse for that injustice'.[49]

Marshall much preferred direct to indirect taxation, but he was far from unaware of the potential for social engineering which has so frequently attracted social reformers to taxes on expenditure. Thus, echoing Adam Smith's recommendation that higher turnpike tolls should be levied on the carriages of the wealthy than would be charged for ordinary freight (in consequence whereof 'the indolence and vanity of the rich is made to contribute in a very easy manner to the relief of the poor'[50]), Marshall declared: 'Assessed taxes on male servants, horses, carriages, and dogs were once "progressive" in England; perhaps they should be so now.'[51] Elsewhere, calling for discriminatory rating of luxury accommodation, he defended the disproportionate burden in effect because 'our age has reversed the old rule that the poor paid a larger percentage of their income in rates and taxes than the well-to-do'[52] but he also admitted that undesirable vestiges of the *ancien régime* nonetheless remain behind: 'Those who live in expensive houses are just those who now pay less than their fair share to the general expenses of the country.'[53] So clearly did he recognise the potential for social engineering which is so frequently a characteristic of indirect taxation that he might even have recommended punitive taxation for those commodities (alcohol, gambling, ostentatious but non-durable dress) which in his view yielded no genuine happiness – and it is indicative of the libertarian bias which caused him to rely on evolutionary upgrading and public opinion in preference to social order enforced by coercive law that only very occasionally, as in an uncompleted manuscript dating from 1873 or 1874, does Marshall consider such a possibility: 'On what might perhaps be called educational grounds a tax upon alcohol might be retained, even if economically the income tax were the sole basis of taxation.'[54] He is on balance somewhat more eloquent when it comes to attacking particular indirect taxes which engineer society in a manner which is positively unhealthy, as in the case of stamp duties which hamper and hinder market adjustments fully in the wider interests of the community: 'A heavy tax on the transfer of land and buildings assists the laws of entail in keeping property in the hands of landlords who cannot do their duty by their tenants.'[55]

Marshall early in life looked forward with eagerness to some future day when 'the whole revenue of the country could easily be collected by direct taxes on income' and when taxes on expenditure would ultimately wither away: 'Since great evils are inseparable from all taxes on particular commodities, every country should strive to prepare herself for a large increase of direct taxation levied equitably on the incomes of all classes.'[56] Marshall throughout his life retained a strong commitment to taxing the money that I earn but not the commodities on which I choose to spend such net rewards as are left to me: 'Income . . . seems, on the whole, the best basis of a system of taxation.'[57] Which is why his well-know arguments concerning State intervention via the tax system to improve the allocative efficiency of the economy as a whole are surprising, uncharacteristic, and strangely out of place – even if one takes great care never to forget his clearly-worded warning that his propositions 'do not by themselves afford a valid ground for government interference'.[58] It is to those well-known arguments that we must now turn.

Marshall was aware of the celebrated doctrine that 'the free pursuit by each individual of his own immediate interest, will lead producers to turn their capital and labour, and consumers to turn their expenditure into such courses as are most conducive to the general interest'.[59] Marshall was, of course, on balance friendly to this doctrine, but he also took the view that it was not of universal validity. One important reason for his caution in this respect was his perception of the wastage of resources that exists where an industry is subject to diminishing returns: 'Even without taking account of the evils arising from the unequal distribution of wealth, there is *prima facie* reason for believing that the aggregate satisfaction, so far from being already a maximum, could be much increased by collective action in promoting the production and consumption of things in regard to which the law of increasing return acts with especial force.'[60] In the case of industries experiencing increasing returns, expansion of output increases welfare 'because a largely increased production would add much more to consumers' surplus than to the aggregate expenses of production of the goods'.[61] Here a fall in price (which benefits the consumer) need not mean a net loss of profit to the producer (since average cost falls as well, perhaps considerably) and there is clearly some scope for the State to push private enterprise in a direction that unambigously confers an excess of welfare gain over welfare loss on the community as a whole: 'One simple plan would be the levying of a tax by the community on their own incomes, or on the production of goods which obey the law of diminishing return, and devoting the tax to a bounty on the production of those goods with regard to which the law of increasing return acts sharply.'[62] Where freedom of enterprise means loss of potential welfare, Marshall seems to be saying, a vote for extreme *laissez-faire* is also a vote for market failure and for living standards lower than we would have enjoyed had the State bravely separated the wasteful sheep from the economical goats.

Marshall found such intervention in industry by means of fiscal policy an interesting theoretical construct but he did not in the event call for the introduction of the scheme he explored. He drew attention in particular to the great administrative problems which the members of the community would have to bear in mind in seeking to make the system operate effectively: 'They would have to reckon up the direct and indirect costs of collecting a tax and administering a bounty; the difficulty of securing that the burdens of the tax and the benefits of the bounty were equitably distributed; the openings for fraud and corruption; and the danger that in the trade which had got a bounty and in other trades which hoped to get one, people would divert their energies from managing their own businesses to managing those persons who control the bounties.'[63] To this must be added a further problem which Marshall does not consider but which he would have had to face had his focus been on the firm rather than on the industry – namely, the need for the policy-maker to make a choice between the *many* trees of the *same* forest (some growing more economical, others growing less) and then to become involved in the perceived injustice of putting public money into the till of an efficient producer while simultaneously withdrawing private money from the till of his less efficient rival. To say that Marshall was able legitimately to ignore this problem because his concern was with the representative firm, his time-frame the stationary state, is no answer at all; for if Marshall did in fact reason in this way, then he was clearly confounding abstract theory with practical policy in a manner which, to be honest, would have been uncharacteristic as well as unrealistic.[64] A final difficulty is concerned with conflict of objectives, with elasticity of demand, and with Marshall's curious propensity in this somewhat unique case to consider one blade of the scissors without reference to the other. Specifically, your tax on my tea (a necessity, let us say, but produced subject to decreasing returns) only raises the cost of my tea without significantly reducing my consumption of tea – although I am a poor man (and like you no fan of regressive taxation) and although tea is a wholesome beverage (whereas gin is not, despite the fact that dramatic economies of scale in the gin-making industry attract to it your bounty). I, a thinking consumer with a fondness for bread, will no doubt listen with respect to your macroeconomic argument that my real income has risen in consequence of the bounty to and economies in the cake-making industry; and that my consumption of bread can now rise precisely because of your action with respect to my cake. Being too poor to eat cake, and finding cake unpalatable at the best of times, I, a thinking consumer, am likely to conclude that your argument takes into account an insufficient number of the relevant characteristics of the commodities that I consume.

Many objections can be raised to Marshall's hint concerning intervention in industry by means of fiscal policy. Far fewer objections can be raised concerning the important principle which underlies that hint: 'We have to admit that the manner in which a man spends his income is a matter of direct economic concern to the community. For in so far as he spends it on things which obey the law of diminishing return, he makes these things more difficult to be obtained by his neighbours, and thus lowers the real purchasing power of their incomes; while in so far as he spends it on things which obey the law of increasing return, he makes those things more easy of attainment to others, and thus increases the real purchasing power of their incomes.'[65] What Marshall is saying is that your individual purchase is to a significant extent not individual at all where it simultaneously imposes spillovers and externalities on me – neighbourhood effects analogous in virtually every respect to those which you would have imposed on your community had you situated a factory in our street or consumed alcohol in our office. Marshall accordingly declares that 'maximum satisfaction is *generally* to be attained by encouraging each individual to spend his own resources in that way which suits him best'[66] – but by use of the word '*generally*' conspicuously draws attention to the fact that in certain situations our decisions are both interdependent and potentially malign.

That being the case, there is perhaps something to be said for altruistic citizens (strengthened in their resolve, no doubt, by the power of public opinion) voluntarily opting for the product of the welfare-furthering industry even in the absence of the governmental policy to which Marshall alludes. Where the State does not cheapen our cake, we might reason, we can, acting as private citizens, ourselves nonetheless procure for all the important public good of cheapened cake by the simple expedient of substituting cake for bread in our budgets. Yet, as Whitaker points out, Marshall, who in so many other contexts made clear that other-regarding activity can as legitimately be individual as institutionalised, seems not to have extended his welfare duality to the field of industrial policy: 'Marshall fails, interestingly, to propose, or expect, that conscientious individuals direct their expenditure towards increasing return industries, thus conferring an indirect benefit on others. Such a proposal would certainly have been consistent with his other views, even if unworldly.'[67] The 'other views' with which such a proposal would have been consistent are any of a number of positions which Marshall took with respect to the extent to which moral pressures and informal sanctions ought to constrain and direct the choice of consumables even where formal State directives would do more harm than good. But, as Whitaker says, it is 'unworldly' to suppose that individuals will via exhortation alone abandon one industry and move to another merely because the former has diminishing and the latter has increasing returns. This in turn must raise the question of whether other aspects of Marshall's theory of collective discipline might be 'unworldly' as well. Be that as it may, Marshall did not seek to harness collective discipline to the plough of industrial reform, and with respect to his own hints on the use of fiscal policy in this area ultimately returned a verdict more nearly negative than cautious. As we have seen in this section, however, he was in other areas of economic life somewhat more adventurous in the proposals he chose to make concerning the nature of taxation.

5.2 COLLECTIVE CONSUMPTION

Our State cannot be 'up and doing' when it comes to prohibiting Winter, and there is no need for it to be 'up and doing' where the provision of newspapers, books, cabbages and clothing is concerned. The position is, however, somewhat different when we are speaking of factory inspection, punishment of fraud, drainage and sewage, 'an abundance of open-air recreation even in large towns',[1] and a wide range of other shared benefits and amenities which each citizen enjoys in 'common to him with his neighbours':[2] 'They include civil and military security, and the right and oportunity to make use of public property and institutions of all kinds, such as roads, gaslight, etc., and rights to justice or to a free education.'[3] In the case of such 'collective goods', such 'elements of collective wealth', there is simply no alternative to 'collective action for the purpose of securing common wellbeing',[4] and this more often than not means that the State has a positive duty to become involved: 'Everyone in health and strength can order his house well; the State alone can bring the beauties of nature and art within the reach of the ordinary citizen.'[5] It is significant that one of the fundamental questions which Marshall identified as being suitable for consideration by the economist is the following: 'Have we ... carried as far as we should the plan of collective ownership and use of open spaces, of works of art, of the means of instruction and amusement, as well as those material requisites of a civilized life, the supply of which requires united action, such as gas and water, and railways?'[6] His own personal answer was in the negative. Writing just after the outbreak of the First World War, Marshall made a declaration, in a letter to Louis Fry, which could easily have been penned by any one of those later British Fabians who, in the shadow of the Second shared trauma and the Spirit of Dunkirk, called in language reminiscent of the Prophets for welfare to be born of warfare: 'I think the time has come for the general principle: – Make towards a more steadfast suppression of personal luxuries and a larger devotion of resources to public ends. When the war is over, let the new seriousness which it has brought into life, endure. Let more of the resources of the nation go to keeping children longer at school, and at better schools; to clearing out all unwholesome dwellings; and to levelling up the incomes of the poorer classes by an extension of the general principle that all may use freely roads, bridges, etc. which are made at public expense.'[7] Marshall was a reformer as well as a moralist, and it is with his specific proposals for reform in the general area of collective consumption that we shall be concerned in the two parts of this section – the first to do with Health and Housing, the second with Education – which follow.

(1) Health and housing

Marshall points out that medical discoveries which 'increase our health and working power' are an 'aid to production',[8] and his reference to the 'ever-growing activity and wisdom of Government in all matters relating to health'[9] would seem to imply a conviction that the State has a legitimate role to play in this form of upgrading. Public policy here would seem, after all, to satisfy two important criteria – that involving spillovers (since your improved health is our faster rate of growth in productivity, as is the case with the benefits accruing to public money invested in recreational areas: 'If spent on fresh air, it would add so much to the industrial vigour of the population that it would go far towards arresting England's industrial (relative) decline; and might even turn the tide'[10]) and a second involving equality of opportunity ('Public aid and control in medical and sanitary matters will work . . . to lessen the weight that has hitherto pressed on the children of the poorer classes'[11]). What is in the circumstances surprising is not how far Marshall actually went in proposing State intervention but rather the fact that he did not go further still by coming down in favour of a full-blown health service, at least for the lower classes. What he does say on the subject of health is more directly concerned with prevention than with cure, and most frequently with the recommendation that public money should 'flow freely to provide fresh air and space for wholesome play for the children in all working class quarters':[12] 'There is no better use for public and private money than in providing public parks and playgrounds in large cities, in contracting with railways to increase the number of workmen's trains run by them, and in helping those of the working classes who are willing to leave the large towns to do so, and to take their industries with them.'[13] If the State does have a legitimate role to play with respect to 'that side of the wellbeing of the poorer working class which they cannot easily provide for themselves',[14] it would appear, a significant part of its activity, in Marshall's view, should lie in the field of environmental health. Writing in 1909 on the subject of the '"Fresh Air" rate' of that year (a case in point where 'a little money may do much towards raising the level of life of the people and increasing their happiness'), Marshall had nothing but praise for the undeniable distortion of the market-determined structure of effective demand that was represented by this form of social planning: 'I hold that the most important capital of a nation is that which is invested in the physical, mental, and moral nurture of its people. That is being recklessly wasted by the exclusion of, say, some ten millions of the population from reasonable access to green spaces, where the young may play and the old may rest. To remedy this evil is, in my opinion, even more urgent than the provision of old-age pensions; and I wished the first charge upon the rapidly-growing value of urban land to be a "Fresh Air" rate (or general tax) to be spent on breaking out small green spots in the midst of dense industrial districts, and on the preservation of large green areas between different towns and between different suburbs which are tending to coalesce. I thought that the gross amount of the Fresh Air rate or tax should be about ten millions a year, till we have cleared off the worst evils caused by many generations of cruel apathy and neglect.'[15]

A healthy environment is fostered by public planning as well as provision. Alfred Marshall accordingly recommended to property developers and profit-seeking business men 'that no row of high buildings be erected without adequate free space in front and behind'[16] and also sought to limit by law the individual freedom of unchivalrous votaries of the Invisible Hand: 'Unless our laws as regards buildings and open spaces are organically changed, the result must be the degeneration of the race.'[17] Both in the case of urban congestion (with an associated 'scarcity of fresh air and light and playroom so grievous as to lower the vigour and the joyousness of the rising generation'[18]) and in that of rural desecration (with an associated loss of 'many of Nature's best gifts to man', including 'a bright, clear sky and beautiful scenery' – things which, although free of charge and not therefore included in statistics on national wealth, 'are as real a source of enjoyment as . . . expensive furniture'[19]), State intervention is needed, private rights must be restrained by laws and by-laws, and legislation is the mother of utility where a high-quality environment is concerned. Thus, 'unless accompanied by energetic action on the part of urban authorities in planning out the lines on which towns should grow, it would result in hasty and inappropriate building; a mistake for which coming generations would pay a high price in the loss of beauty and perhaps of health'.[20] Here as elsewhere *benefit* and *thrive* can all too easily go their separate ways, the more extreme forms of *laissez-faire* evolutionism are demonstrably inferior to planned modification, and 'the argument that if such a change had been beneficial, it would have been already brought about by the struggle for survival, must be rejected as invalid'.[21]

It is, moreover, not only speculators and wheeler-dealers who want regulating, but parents as well. If children are to develop into healthy adults, then the adults who care for them while dependent must ensure that 'the inside of the houses be kept clean, and fit for those who will be needed in after years to act as strong and responsible citizens'.[22] Because we as a community will require good citizens and not decadent wrecks, therefore you as the parental influence acquire the duty to parent responsibly – and we, incidentally, acquire the right to compel you to do so: 'The most urgent among the first steps . . . is to insist on regular school attendance in decent clothing, and with bodies clean and fairly well fed. In case of failure the parents should be warned and advised: as a last resource the homes might be closed or regulated, with some limitation of the freedom of the parents.'[23] It is, of course, not middle class parents who are most likely to fail or default with respect to their duty, and this should perhaps be borne in mind when we reflect both on such State compulsion and on Donald Winch's comment concerning such compulsion: 'In their general attitude to state intervention and socialism, the economists of Marshall's generation shared the viewpoint of other enlightened members of the English middle classes. While they professed to dislike most forms of paternalist legislation, they were not free from paternalism in their attitude to those beneath them in the social and educational scale.'[24]

Bad housing is, needless to say, a great enemy of good parenting, and therewith a cause for public concern: 'It is undeniable that the housing of the very poorest classes in our towns now is destructive both of body and soul; and that with our present knowledge and resources we have neither cause nor excuse for allowing it to continue.'[25] Polluted air, darkness, filth and 'close packing' sap the energy and undermine the character of the lower classes and their children, and there is something singularly distressing about 'living in small apartments in crowded cities, where children are not easily accommodated; and where placid recreations, which build up strength of body and character, are supplanted by nervous excitements, which consume strength, and consume also a large part of the family income unprofitably'.[26] Yet healthy surroundings in huge urban agglomerations are simply not to be had at prices which the lower income groups can afford to pay: 'Ground rents, and therefore house rents, are so high, that poorly paid workers cannot afford decent lodgings: the poverty of the poor is their destruction. Their low earnings make them lodge badly, their unwholesome lodgings weaken them physically and morally, and render them more and more unable to get higher earnings.'[27] Given a slum atmosphere 'that is foul physically and morally', it is no surprise to learn that 'even the sober residents are as a rule weakly in body and devoid of self-respect'[28] – and still less to be told that by no means all the residents are in fact sober.

Bad housing is a cause for public concern and therewith an appropriate candidate for public action. But the answer is not provision: 'Municipal housing seems to me scarcely ever right and generally very wrong.'[29] The reason for Marshall's opposition to municipal housing schemes, it must be stressed, is not exclusively to do with the fact *per se* that they are collectively supplied and subsidised (ever the pragmatist, Marshall also expresses the conviction that 'municipal free baths seem to me nearly always right') and is indicative most of all of Marshall's general belief that the municipal areas – London most of all – have in effect reached saturation point. That being the case, subsidised housing would actually worsen the plight of the London poor. Cheap housing would yield its greatest benefits not to the workers but to 'owners of ground rents'[30] and to the capitalist class: 'Taxes levied on the community in general, including the working classes, would be used to enable the owners of London factories to get their labour artificially cheap.'[31] Besides that, 'a closely peopled district is impoverished by every one who adds a new building or raises an old one higher'[33] – and such an act of vandalism is no less an act of vandalism merely because the want of 'air and light', of 'peaceful repose out-of-doors for all ages', of 'healthy play for all ages', is the result of action taken by politicians and bureaucrats rather than speculators and companies. The problem in a nutshell is that large towns such as London suffer from 'much preventable chronic depression . . . owing to the presence of classes who would do better elsewhere', and in such circumstances municipal housing is positively counter-productive: not only does it 'bribe people to stay where their work is not wanted'[33] but its known availability actually attracts still more migrants into the towns, thus affording only a 'temporary respite' while ensuring that 'after a while all would be as before, except that there would be a larger population, suffering from want of healthy recreation and fresh air, which are on the whole the deadliest evils that are caused by the pressure of population on the means of subsistence'.[34] The supply of land for habitation in the towns being absolutely fixed, collective intervention to facilitate and cheapen the process of congestion would be foolish and misguided intervention; and no wise State – whatever the ideological proclivities of its leaders with respect to the optimal balance between public and private – will ever consciously opt for that which is foolish and misguided.

The State should not provide housing but it should regulate it. Specifically, the State should get involved in the inspection ('by a large staff of officers in a rigorous, uncompromising way'[35]) of rented accommodation in certain 'proclaimed' areas of London where overcrowding was so rampant as to represent a serious threat to health and morals. It would obviously be impossible to enforce laws prescribing minimum house-room per dweller on too global a scale (and 'it is a mistake to propound regulations that cannot be enforced') but selective enforcement – your house but not mine – via concentration on the worst-affected areas is another matter. The possibility of a surprise visit from an inspector to a five-to-a-room tenement would at least compel prudent landlords to minimise fines by exercising 'a due control over the sanitary habits of their tenants'.[36] Social costs and diswelfares such as cholera would no doubt be reduced in this way, but so too would congestion be – and because isolated individuals cannot unaided combat these externalities, therefore what is needed is the deliberate interference of the State with the freedom of 'individuals and corporations to conduct their own affairs as they please'.[37] Inspection limits overcrowding, minimum standards limit the mobility of the healthy into the slums, and it is precisely because the State knows better than the individual what is in his own best interest that the admittedly vexatious and expensive regulation which Marshall proposes ought in his view to be adopted: 'To hinder people from going where their presence helps to lower the average standard of human life, is no more contrary to economic principle than the rule that, when a steamer is full, admission should be refused to any more, even though they themselves are willing to take the risk of being drowned.'[38] Low pay and bad housing have demonstrably failed to exclude new entrants from miserable conditions; and where the market has failed, the State must act. Inspection is not a new Law of Settlement but it is certainly a step in that direction. It is a step which the childless Londoner welcomed for a reason which the childless Scotsman neglected, that the costs of urban life do not lie where they fall but are visited even upon by generations as yet unborn: 'The enjoyments of London life come to the parents and the chief ill results of it to the children. If there is any case for government interference it is when the interests of the coming generation are in the danger of being sacrificed by the mistakes of this.'[39]

The problem of housing in urban agglomerations is more complex still, for not only is there a need to adopt measures such as will discourage new migrants from re-settling in large towns but there is simultaneously a need to transfer some of our existing passengers to other vessels less perilously overloaded. Marshall's article 'Where to House the London Poor' appeared in *The Contemporary Review* of 1884 and sought to provide a solution in the form of new towns. It was, according to Pigou, 'written before the Garden City movement started and probably gave an impetus to that movement';[40] and it is interesting in that it seeks to solve a major social problem without direct *State* action. Marshall's view in this early but important essay is that the urban poor should be assisted by an *ad hoc* committee to re-locate: 'The general plan would probably be for a committtee, whether formed specially for the purpose or not, to interest themselves in the formation of a colony in some place well beyond the range of London smoke. After seeing their way to building or buying suitable cottages there, they would enter into communication with some of the employers of low-waged labour . . . They would find an employer – and there must be many such – who really cares for the misery of his employees. Acting with him and by his advice, they would make themselves the friends of people employed, or fit to be employed, in his trade; they would show them the advantages of moving, and help them to move both with counsel and money.'[41] Even greater benefits would be reaped if complementary businesses were to be set up in the same area (which would in that way turn into 'a prosperous industrial district'[42] with each industry generating external economies for its customer industries and markets for its local suppliers). Such de-urbanisation of industry is favoured by improvements in transport and communications and confers exceptional benefits on those who, abandoning the squalor of the slums, now find that 'they can get house-room cheaply, and fresh air for nothing':[43] 'Most families can have separate houses, many can have gardens, and nearly all children can play freely in the open air.'[44] Meanwhile, the reduction in the supplies of unskilled labour left behind in the large towns such as London will mean less congestion (and *ceteris paribus* lower rents) and also more competition for the increasingly scarce input (and *ceteris paribus* higher pay): 'The only cure for the misery of large towns is to have no one there who cannot earn a great deal. Highly-skilled workmen can pay their way well enough, and those unskilled workers who are really necessary for the work of the towns would get high enough wages to compensate them for the dearness of house-room, if only their labour were scarce.'[45] Lower rents and higher pay constitute rising real wages; rising real wages lead both to improved health and heightened self-respect; and the net result is *as if* a minimum wage law had been introduced in an attempt to assist the urban poor.

Eventually the committee which through its 'liberal and vigorous action' did so much to help those who were not wanted in the towns and whose work 'could be done more healthily and more to the advantage of the community elsewhere'[46] would disestablish itself; for the child colony, 'after being once started ... ought to be self-supporting'.[47] But initially its services are indispensable. On the one hand the bulk of the potential beneficiaries are, being 'weak and poorly paid', too 'feeble and timid' to make the move: 'their spirit crushed out of them', their nerves 'overwrought', they are of 'poor physique and a feeble will', men with 'no enterprise, no courage, no hope, and scarcely any self-respect'[48] who are simply incapable unaided of breaking out of the vicious circle of urban poverty. On the other hand the State itself 'could not safely do the work – there would be too much room for jobbery and imposture'.[49] So if there is to be pump-priming and a rise in average standards of living caused by de-urbanisation of industry and population, then the coordination and the impetus must come from some third force – and, while not wishing to minimise the contribution made by profit-seeking entrepreneurs such as Mr Pullman and Mr Salt to the development of new towns,[50] Marshall ultimately reached the conclusion that the key initiative can only come from private and independent committees, 'properly chosen' (we are not told how), and dependent on the bare minimum of public money.

Whether Marshall as he grew older ever became more optimistic about the competence of politicians and civil servants to undertake some or all of the functions which he in 1884 delegated to economic chivalry and individual altruism is a matter for debate. What is clear is that he by 1903 was more prepared than he had previously been to throw public money at the problem. Writing in that year to Mrs Bosanquet on the subject of housing, he declared: 'I should *like* an expenditure comparable with that required for the South African war to be devoted to the removal of this source of degradation for a good many years to come.'[51] Naturally enough the State should not get involved in the provision of municipal housing, and there is still no explicit recommendation that the State should take a leading role in the drama of de-urbanisation. Nor is there any hint that the State should take corrective action to deal with existing medical problems born of life in unheated, damp and unhygenic environments – tuberculosis, bronchitis, lice, rheumatic complaints, the uncorrected squint (none of these necessarily symptomatic of individual weakness in the sense that drunkenness might be, and all of them genuine obstacles to meaningful integration in the mainstream of economic activity). Marshall's recommendation in 1903 may have been for larger sums of money to be spent on a healthy environment, but his favoured candidates remained unchanged and remained essentially two in number. First, the State should 'provide opportunities of healthy play for all children' and 'bring fresh air and light more generously into all urban homes':[52] 'If the Government can afford to buy land for the working-classes, let it make more playgrounds and breathing-spaces. Every pound so spent now will yield an income of national health and happiness for ever.'[53] Second, the State should plan for green belts in the countryside very near the towns and should simultaneously take full responsibility for 'mapping out in advance the ground plans on which cities should expand – a task more vital to the health and happiness of coming generations than any other which can be accomplished by authority with so little trouble, while private effort is powerless for it'.[54] Parks and playgrounds accompanied by town and country planning do not, of course, by themselves constitute a much mixed economy, and no doubt the absolutely deprived and their champions will find Marshall's proposals on health and housing somewhat less satisfying than those of eminent social democrats such as Tawney and Titmuss. While not wishing for a moment to deny the limitations of Marshall's obsession with the 'free sky' and the 'open air' (categories which include, as we all know, 'playgrounds where noisy, healthy play, even with a little energy, is allowed: where cricket may be played with hard balls, and where the joyous young creatures need not keep one eye always on the policeman'[55]), it is nonetheless not with the modesty of Marshall's proposals that we wish to terminate our discussion of his views on health and housing but rather with the open-endedness of his principles. Marshall's proposals are so restricted as positively to invite a moderate degree of limited ridicule: 'The State could so care for the amenities of life outside of the house that fresh air and variety of colour and of scene might await the citizen and his children very soon after they start on a holiday walk.'[56] Marshall's principles, on the other hand, are so explosive as inevitably to put the reader in mind of celebrated reformers such as John Kenneth Galbraith, who, and not Alfred Marshall, could well have been the author of the following defence of an enthusiastic government that is 'up and doing': 'Every one in health and strength can order his house well; the State alone can bring the beauties of nature and art within the reach of the ordinary citizen.'[57] The proposals are modest. The principles are not.

(2) Education

Education is an end in its own right, 'inferior to none of those which the production of material wealth can be made to subserve':[58] 'If the growth of a man's mind, if his spiritual cultivation be the end of life; and material wealth, houses and horses, carpets and French cookery merely means; what temporary pecuniary loss can we set against the education of the nation?'[59] Education has a positive effect on consumption-patterns and on the use of leisure; for without it an ignorant man such as a poor labourer 'may live and die without ever realizing what a joy there is in knowledge, or what delight in art'.[60] Education has an improving impact on character-patterns and on conduct, as is illustrated by the extent to which orderly meetings replace violent uprisings once education for the masses has become widespread: 'By the aid of education, their moral strength is gaining new life. Look at the grand conduct of the Lancashire artisans during the cotton famine. In old times of ignorance they would have struggled violently against the inevitable; but now their knowledge restrained them, and they suffered with quiet constancy.'[61] Education, finally, is an important means to the valued end of economic growth, since 'industrial efficiency' as well as 'elevation of life'[62] is the result where scarce skills are formed through formal schooling: 'Increasingly during the last hundred years national well-being has depended on the progress and dissemination of sound education.'[63] Education, clearly, is a good thing.

Parents, as we have seen, increasingly recognise the significance of education, for they, increasingly future-orientated, increasingly save in order to plunge resources in their children's life-chances; and employers too, increasingly altruistic, it would appear, are increasingly prepared to make a free gift of transferable skills. Evidently, therefore, the fact that education is so clearly a good thing does not mean that the funding of education is in any sense exclusively a topic in public finance. Far from it: 'There are few practical problems in which the economist has a more direct interest than those relating to the principles on which the expense of the education of children should be divided between the State and the parents.'[64] Marshall never says precisely what those principles are which govern and determine the optimal balance between public and private, but he does say that 'popular education . . . ought to have been accepted two centuries ago as a chief duty of the State'[65] and that 'a great part of the funds for this purpose must be supplied by the State'[66] – and that the State without any doubt ought for two reasons to be 'up and doing' with respect to the supplying of education even though there is a strong case for abstention and neutrality with respect, let us say, to the supplying of pins. Those two reasons – the same criteria as we previously encountered in our analysis of health and housing – are the following:

First, spillovers. We all know that there is a private rate of return on investment made by parents in the human capital of their children.[67] We all know as well that a little investment goes a long way: 'The difference between the value of the labour of the educated man and that of the uneducated is, as a rule, many times greater than the difference between the costs of their education.'[68] What we do not all know, and therefore need to be told, is that the private rate of return is less than the social rate, and that private investment in education is likely to be sub-optimal: precisely because 'no individual reaps the full gains derived from educating a child',[69] there is therefore *ceteris paribus* a tendency on the part of parents and employers to under-fund and for the private sector to under-supply. Other nations saw long before Britain did that 'a niggardly policy of education was a mistake even from a purely commercial point of view'[70] and Britain in consequence fell behind until we elected to rectify our mistake: 'English business men were slow to recognize a chief cause of decline in their industrial leadership. But about 1904 they began to see clearly that they must follow other nations in promoting industrial efficiency by improved education.'[71] About 1904 English businessmen began to see what English economists had known for some time, that good education is good business.

Education can be general (in the sense of 'causing a man to form an intelligent opinion with regard to the ordinary matters of life, and to be full of resources for meeting new emergencies') or it can be technical (in the sense of 'enabling him to understand the processes and the machinery of the special work in which he is engaged').[72] Both types make a considerable contribution to the increase of national wealth – a contribution so great that the heightened tax revenues thereby occasioned would actually 'be sufficient to repay with interest any outlay that Government may make on that general and technical education, which is required to enable Englishmen to hold their own in competition with those who have been taught in the admirable schools, that are to be found in some foreign countries'.[73] That which adds to economic efficiency is not a negative-sum game which retards growth by redistributing wealth but rather a positive-sum game which – by ensuring that human faculties are 'turned to their best account'[74] – is analogous to the seed-corn which is ploughed back today in the interests of a bounteous harvest tomorrow: 'If taxes are levied so as to impair enterprise they *pro tanto* lessen employment at good wages: but if they are so spent as to increase vitality, they increase employment at good wages; because they increase earning power.'[75] A State which taxes and wastes is as much the enemy of economic growth as a miser who hides and hoards – but we are concerned here with a State which taxes and invests and which, through its expenditure on both general and technical education, makes a genuine and worthwhile contribution to the wealth of nations.

General education involves general information and imparts background knowledge both of the sciences and of the arts. Such facts and figures, details and dates give the child a valuable insight into the human and the natural order, and that insight is both good in itself and an external economy to some future employer. Marshall stressed, however, that crammed knowledge is more often than not knowledge which the child 'will forget as soon as he is grown up'[76] (much as you and I have long since forgotten our genitive cases and irregular verbs, our endless if arid lists of kings and queens) and that in any case, once the schoolmaster has taught the child to read, 'a few shillings will buy more printed knowledge than a man's brain can hold'.[77] Information and knowledge are no doubt very fine, Marshall believed, but it is nonetheless in the area of the 'hidden curriculum' that the principal contribution of general education is to be made: 'The chief function of education is to "educate" faculties, that is to bring them out and develop them.'[78] It is character and activity, not information and knowledge,which are the chief products of the general education industry, and thence follow the inevitable guidelines. First, general education should instill scientific habits of thought, lest our children grow up unable to solve new problems because they lack the proper intellectual methodology: 'The study of the relation between cause and effect should be begun early: large use being made of verifications by experiment, such as are afforded by elementary hydrostatics, even without the aid of mathematics. History should also be treated in some degree as a study of cause and effect: though here verification is seldom possible.'[79] Second, it should encourage the characteristics of order, regularity and assiduity (as where the quasi-military nature of the German school both reflects and reproduces the quasi-bureaucratic nature of the German character: 'The disciplined life of the German schoolboy is indeed a good preparation for subordinate work in factory or counting-house'[80]) but, even more significantly, the characteristics of spontaneity ('the chief creator of original work, and especially of that which makes epochs in thought'[81]), self-reliant innovativeness (an essential cause and effect of rapid social change: 'Our needs are so different from those of our forefathers that if we are filled with their best spirit, we shall not follow in their tracks'[82]), and, last but not least, a 'powerful exercise of the imagination' (such breadth of vision and overall alertness of mind being indispensable where economic variables are interdependent and many of them are 'far off'[83]) – characteristics (both of conformity and of initiative) which are, as it happens, bred and formed abnormally well when a boy is confronted at an impressionable age with the multiple challenges represented by the Latin language: 'Demands are made on his general intelligence, his judgement, his sense of proportion, his logical acumen, his perceptive sensibility and his taste; and in a greater or less degree he can rise to these demands. He is architect, engineer, and skilled artisan all at once.'[84] Third, general education should take into account the fact that 'the development of the artistic faculties of the people is in itself an aim of the very highest importance, and is becoming a chief factor of industrial efficiency'[85] and it should pay particular attention to the artistic needs of deprived classes situated in the dulling, deadening conditions of modern conurbations, not least because of considerations involving countervailing power exercised in the social interest: 'The growth of towns makes it doubly urgent to supply wholesome thoughts and suggestions, lest unwholesome should prevail: and to turn music and painting and other fine arts to account in filling the void in man's life caused by the want of the free light and freshness and beauties of nature... It is therefore imperatively necessary, if the child is to grow up in any fulness of life, that he should see and hear and read of the brightest ideals that have come to mankind.'[86] Fourth, general education should foster sympathy, empathy, and understanding – through a study of literature (which 'gives a man knowledge of human nature'[87]), through team sports ('On the river and in the football field the student learns to bear and to forbear; to obey and to command'[88]), and simply through the informal social training represented by learning and living with others: 'The comradeship of generous youth, unless marred by extravagance or vice, tends to develop the sympathies, which separate man by an impassable gulf from the most powerful machine.'[89]

None of the four guidelines which Marshall provides with respect to general education is of sector-specific vocational relevance, although each of the four is of undeniable economic significance when seen in a broader context. The case of technical education is therefore different in that we are speaking here quite explicitly not of general knowledge and predispositions (implicitly, of course, these are in a very real sense the indispensable foundation for what is to come) but rather of useful skills and important how-tos, narrowly defined: 'While much general education may be advantageously given to all youth, there is also a need for specialized education adapted to the needs of agriculture, and every other industry, as well as to the learned professions. This matter is of vital importance.'[90] Your dentist may have developed strength of reasoning through early exposure to mathematics and sense of proportion through early exposure to the visual arts, but his constructive faculties will still not be fully harnessed to his trade until he has been instructed in the boring of molars and the extraction of canines. Your research chemist may have benefited greatly from the *cameraderie* and the initiative that is bred 'by life in a residentiary university of the Anglo-Saxon type',[91] but he also needs hands-on experience in the laboratory if his work is to place you, his employer, in the vanguard of technological advance: 'Mother-wit counts for much, but only on condition that it is equipped with thorough training and high-class laboratories.'[92] Your turner or presser may have learned at school those character-patterns which cause you to regard him as responsible while turning, hard-working and trustworthy when pressing, but he also needs to be shown how to operate his tools and made 'to feel at home in the workshop'.[93] It is in sum clear that we as a nation require trade-specific technical training as well as more general learning if the education imparted to the child is genuinely to be of use to him in the outside world of non-academic work: 'It should help him to understand the reason of everything that goes on in his trade, and thus enable him to accommodate himself to new machinery or new modes of production. And it should train him in the use of his fingers.'[94]

Our nation requires that your child be trained in the use of his fingers if he is to play his part in our shared drama of growth and improvement. Our nation recognises, however, that work itself can make a significant contribution to the production of workers, that learning-by-doing can be a valuable mode of acquiring trade-specific *how-tos* (on the principle that 'an hour's rowing behind a first-class oar teaches more than much verbal exhortation'[95]), and that the opportunity cost of on-the-job training foregone must be borne in mind when we assess the case for and against an extension of formal schooling. Your child is, after all, only young and impressionable once – and 'for great good on the balance, but for evil in some degree, the boy now remains at school till his susceptibility to the supreme educational influence of imitation has been somewhat dulled'.[96] Besides that, perhaps because those who can, do, suitable role-models are thin on the ground in the classroom: 'Since those, whose example is to be followed, are relatively few in a school, though they are numerous in workshops, imitation in it has to yield the first place to formal instruction.'[97] So while no one would wish to deny that 'the boy's general faculties are now more highly developed when he comes into the workshop',[98] and while scarcely anyone would wish to deny that 'technical education should be begun at school',[99] all must inevitably concede that, just as home environment alongside that of the school has an important part to play in the process of general education (as where, for example, 'a thoughtful mother does not repress, but encourages that childish curiosity which is the raw material of scientific habits of thought'[100]), so the work environment may enjoy an analogous position with respect to technical education: after all, 'a great deal of the education that is wanted in many trades can only be got in workshops'.[101]

The analogy is an interesting one but should not perhaps be carried too far. For one thing, a mother will probably behave somewhat more altruistically towards her child than will even the most chivalrous of modern employers: the decay of the apprenticeship system has meant that property-rights in transferable skills lie with the man, not with the master, and the employer can in consequence never entirely free himself from the fearful spectre that the return on any investment he chooses to make in a worker could at any time cross the road to his competitor's shop. Furthermore, the growth of the large corporation has meant that the identification of talent and the inculcation of skill are functions which a busy entrepreneur nowadays tends to delegate to overseers, supervisors and assorted subordinates – to men of limited vision, in other words, who might inadvertently undertrain due to that very inability to distinguish the high-flying sheep from the low-flying goats which accounts for their own lack of success; and who might even deliberately turn a blind eye to potential due to the well-know jealousies born of insecurity combined with the acquired indolence of the man on the salary.[102] In such circumstances your child might well be better off learning his technical skills in the classroom and not in the workshop. And there is a final point (one which in itself is an important reason why the apprenticeship and similar systems are 'not exactly suited to modern conditions'[103]), that our modern economic system is a highly dynamic system, a rapidly changing and constantly evolving system, a system in which the Maginot man is at a positive disadvantage when compared with his more flexible, more elastic, more adaptable counterpart: 'That general ability which is easily transferable from one trade to another, is every year rising in importance relatively to that manual skill and technical knowledge which are specialized to one branch of industry. . . . Economic progress brings with it . . . a constantly increasing changefulness in the methods of industry, and therefore a constantly increasing difficulty in predicting the demand for labour of any kind a generation ahead.'[104] What is increasingly in demand is the man open to new impressions and able to assimilate new skills, not yesterday's man locked in to a *status quo* which has meanwhile moved on; and your child should perhaps keep such considerations in mind before accepting an offer from King Priam to learn chariot-making in his workshop. Chariot-making, your child should reflect, might not be for all seasons, and the same might have one day to be said about King Priam himself. Given that change is the ultimate Achilles-heel of the localised expertise that is imparted through technical education provided in the workshop, your child might rationally express a preference for technical education being provided, perhaps not exclusively but certainly significantly, in the classroom: such technical education, he might reason, will at least be more general than that provided by a specific employer in a specific workshop and will therefore make him a more attractive property on the more general labour market.

Your child wants technical education, but he also wants it to be general technical education. Marshall went further by indicating that general education *per se* is in a sense technical education broadly defined, since general education *per se* teaches what are nowadays the most valuable of all *how-tos* – how to perform well and how to learn quickly: 'The chief need of the large majority of modern industries is for alert intelligence, good judgement, promptness and trustworthiness in conduct on the part of the more responsible employees. Where this need has been met, resolute and capable men and women can generally be found who will quickly acquire adequate familiarity with the materials, the plant, and the operations of the industry.'[105] Nowhere more, it would appear, is general education *per se* also technical education broadly defined than in the crucial case of breeding business leaders and forming captains of industry, and that is why Marshall was so hostile to the very suggestion that extensive instruction in the detailed applications of accountancy should become part of his beloved new Tripos in Economics: 'They fill the mind, without enlarging it and strengthening it. And the ablest business men tell us that it is faculty rather than knowledge which the business man of to-day needs. It is a powerful and capacious mind, rather than one already crammed with dead matter, that a University should send out to the work of the world.'[106] Techniques are not enough: 'For truth we need judgement.'[107] The return on that judgement accrues to the community as a whole (in the form of faster economic growth and consequent social progress) as well as to the individual business man (in the form of higher pecuniary income and associated social status); and this brings us back, as if guided by an invisible hand, to our initial point of departure – that the State, because of the significant spillover benefit, ought without any doubt to be 'up and doing' with respect to the provision of education.

Second, equality of opportunity. Need, even where it is perceived need (say, 'the need on the part of clever youths for a good technical education'[108]) is by itself not enough. It must be backed up by funds if it is to be translated into effective demand; and since many parents possess neither adequate resources for proper skill-formation nor the self-control and foresight necessary to accumulate such resources, the result is that 'many first-rate abilities go for ever uncultivated'.[109] This is deeply to be regretted: 'Every system, which allows the higher faculties of the lower grades of industry to go to waste, is open to grave suspicion.'[110]

It is clearly a monstrous waste of potential productivity and would-be efficiency to deny to 'those who are born in a humble station of life' the opportunity to make the most of their 'latent mental faculties'.[111] Such persons are, like the rest of us, unambiguously ends in their own right. But they are also means; and this instrumentality Marshall the economist can hardly be accused of neglecting in his discussion of equality of educational opportunity. On the contrary, since in calling for State intervention in the field of education he refers repeatedly to the specifically *economic* need to reduce the wastage of natural talent that would, in a system of genuinely free enterprise, 'have died unknown':[112] 'There is no extravagance more prejudicial to the growth of national wealth than that wasteful negligence which allows genius which happens to be born of lowly parentage to expend itself in lowly work. No change would conduce so much to a rapid increase of material wealth as an improvement in our schools.'[113] Our nation is rich in clever sons of working men, and it is in your interest and mine as well as in their own that public money should be forthcoming where private is not in an attempt to maximise the juice and minimise the lemons: 'The wisdom of expending public and private funds on education is not to be measured by its direct fruits alone. It will be profitable as a mere investment, to give the masses of the people much greater opportunities than they can generally avail themselves of. . . . All that is spent during many years in opening the means of higher education to the masses would be well paid for if it called out one more Newton or Darwin, Shakespeare of Beethoven.'[114] Equality of opportunity in the field of education is evidently a sound business proposition: 'from the national point of view', it would appear, 'the investment of wealth in the child of the working man is as productive as its investment in horses or machinery',[115] and it is therefore entirely correct, economically speaking, that 'a State, which has with success invested capital in telegraphs, should now venture to invest capital in men'.[116] Because you and I want growth and progress, therefore we are reluctant to see potential high-flyers relive the poverty of their parents and then bequeath it to their own offspring. Because, in other words, you and I want the social gains which we correctly identify as being inextricably bound up with equality of opportunity, therefore we are happy to see our government become involved in activities which we might in other circumstances be tempted to condemn as distortions both of the capital and of the labour market: 'A Government which can borrow money, as ours can, at a little over three per cent. interest, may make a good investment by spending money on education.'[1117] Human faculties 'are as important a means of production as any other kind of capital'; and where the poor man does not put up his stake, either because he will not (sadly, the 'habit of distinctly realizing the future' is 'as yet not very common'[118]) or because he cannot (as when 'the poor man has no means of borrowing at any tolerable rate of interest'[119]), then there is much to be said for you and me, as his co-partners in our national economy, to ask the Government to put up his stake on his behalf. From a purely monetary point of view the investment thereby made in the formation of skills and the upgrading of faculties is, for the nation as well as the individual, unambiguously good business.

Equality of opportunity can be legitimated in terms of the furtherance of positive externalities. It can also be legitimated in terms of the avoidance of negative ones, as Marshall pointed out in 1873. Then, writing in the shadow of the Education Act of 1870, he declared that society as a whole 'is bound to see that no child grows up in ignorance, able only to be a producing machine, unable to be a man', and gave as one reason for this assertion the simple fact that neither you nor I would want otherwise to live next door to him: 'low and limited in his thoughts, his tastes, his feelings, his interests and his aims, to some extent probably low and limited in his virtues', he is likely if not exposed to the civilising influence of schoolmaster-missionaries (men who make a real contribution to society by helping 'to form a sound public opinion in those parts of the country in which they settle'[120]) to be involved 'in every way' in lowering and limiting his neighbours'.[121] For your sake and mine, therefore, as well as for his own, that child and others like him must be given every opportunity to become enlightened and upgraded.

Not only given every opportunity but also compelled to take advantage of it: 'It is abundantly clear that, unless we can compel children into the schools, we cannot enable multitudes of them to escape from a life of ignorance so complete that they cannot fail to be brutish and degraded.'[122] Compulsion to attend school, needless to say, is also compulsion not to attend work, and the Factory Acts are therefore much to be praised for restricting those manifestations of industrial labour which were 'needlessly unhealthy and oppressive for all, and especially for young children'.[123] The State itself acts under compulsion in the sense that we as a nation have an absolute duty to compel the brutish and the degraded to demand that which they would unassisted have failed to identify as lying within the domain of their own best interests: society as a whole 'is bound to compel children, and to help them, to take the first step upwards; and it is bound to help them to make, if they will, many steps upwards'.[124] The brutish and the degraded, it would appear, have the duty to demand and we as a community have the duty to supply the means of liberation, and any mention of duty inevitably raises the moral tone of a case for paternalism couched thus far in terms of the utilitarian need to maximise positive and minimise negative externalities. But undeniably the main thrust of Marshall's appeal for external compulsion is Benthamite rather than Kantian and has to do with the underprovision of skills and attitudes in an atmosphere of freedom of choice. Both the individual and his community will benefit in the long-run, but paternalistic coercion is nonetheless the indispensable pump-priming stimulus which ensures 'that the children even of those parents who are not thoughtful themselves, may have a better chance of being trained up to become thoughtful parents of the next generation. To this end public money must flow freely.'[125]

Naturally, as public policy contributes to economic growth via induced and accelerated social upgrading, so it at the same time reduces the numbers of those poor fish left behind in the pool of unskilled labour – a considerable boon to those unfortunates who fall through the net of progress and remain outside the mainstream of improvement, as is the case with the marginal employed by the marginal that is so well illustrated by the following example: 'Those domestic servants who have no specialized skill, and who hire themselves to persons with very narrow means, have not been able to make even tolerably good terms for themselves: they work very hard for very low wages.'[126] Such unskilled workers are hardly in a strong bargaining position at the moment due to the existence of a market glutted with what they have to sell; they are frequently employed in industries 'in which the workers are scattered, not able easily to organize themselves, and most at the mercy of the unscrupulous employer';[127] and they are themselves, in consequence of low pay, poor food and bad housing, typically 'weak and broken-spirited'.[128] Such persons are likely to benefit considerably from an education policy linked to the *carrière ouverte aux talents*, and the benefit will arise, moreover, even if their *talents* are few and their *carrière* basically the one they are already enjoying, since others will rise and those only suited to hewing and drawing will in consequence acquire scarcity value. Thus, Marshall calculated, those unfortunates only capable, in terms of 'moral and physical stamina', of straightforward unskilled manual labour represented in his own time something approaching one quarter of the population – whereas a century earlier they had represented upwards of one half.[129] The reason for the change was, on the side of demand, an increasing requirement for men able to 'act wisely and promptly in responsible positions'[130] and perhaps in a position as well to exercise a specific skill. On the side of supply, however, the reason was not so much market as State; for a century earlier 'the education of the people was not then recognized as a national duty and a national economy'[131] and by Marshall's time it was. The process of inducing scarcity at the bottom by shifting supplies towards the top has admittedly not yet had the desired effect of producing very good pay for very nasty work, but matter is in motion and the ultimate objective is clear: 'There is no more urgent social need than that labour of this kind should be made scarce and therefore dear.'[132] In a situation of induced scarcity, employers 'with very narrow means' would have either to offer good wages to their domestic servants or else learn to do their own cleaning; and the net result, as with de-urbanisation of industry, is *as if* a minimum wage law had been introduced in an attempt to assist those who *ceteris paribus* 'are not worth much to any employer'.[133]

Equality of opportunity thus favours both those who run like the wind in life's race and those who are just as quickly left behind. As these benefits then become cumulative and absolute poverty becomes as a result less prevalent, as the altruism of parents and employers expands simultaneously with the increase in their resources, so one is, of course, tempted to ask if the need for *State*-sponsored education will not at that stage become somewhat less acute; but if Marshall did hold a view on the potentially transitional nature of the intervention in question, he carefully kept it to himself.

Underinvestment, brutishness, degradation, deprivation and suffering are serious matters, and the very success of the State in promoting 'the well-being of the people at large'[134] in the fields which we have examined in this section – those of health, housing and education – must inevitably fuel speculation as to whether there might not be still other strands in the social fabric which are equally in a position to benefit from collective reinforcement. Obviously 'foolish ostentatious expenditure by the State . . . is, no doubt, an enemy to good employment'.[135] Yet the same is true of similar expenditure made by private persons; and, besides that, spending on health and housing or on education simply cannot realistically be regarded as 'foolish' or 'ostentatious'. On the contrary: 'The notion that the investment of funds in the education of the workers, in sanitation, in providing open air play for all children etc. tends to diminish 'capital' is abhorrent to me. Dead capital exists for man: and live capital that adds to his efficiency is every way as good as dead capital.'[136] Social overheads which make us a more efficient nation are evidently worthwhile expenditures; and one feels strongly that Marshall, in opting for State spending not only on the social services considered in this section but also on 'other requisites of a wholesome life'[137] such as he never fully enumerated, was in the last analysis enunciating principles far more ambitious than those which might be inferred from the modest nature of the precise proposals which he chose to make.

5.3 THE RELIEF OF POVERTY

Marshall used to tell how, at about the same time as he began to study economics, he saw in a shop-window a painting of a 'down-and-out' which he bought 'for a few shillings': 'I set it up above the chimney-piece in my room in college and thenceforward called it my patron saint, and devoted myself to trying how to fit men like that for heaven. Meanwhile I got a good deal interested in the semi-mathematical side of pure Economics, and was afraid of becoming a mere thinker. But a glance at my patron saint seemed to call me back to the right path.'[1] The celebrated concluding words of his Inaugural Lecture at Cambridge in 1885 remind us how value-laden Marshall's perception of economics continued to be, and what position was occupied in it by 'dirt and squalor and misery', 'haggard faces and stunted minds': 'It will be my most cherished ambition, my highest endeavour, to do what with my poor ability and my limited strength I may, to increase the numbers of those, whom Cambridge, the great mother of strong men, sends out into the world with cool heads but warm hearts, willing to give some at least of their best powers to grappling with the social suffering around them; resolved not to rest content till they have done what in them lies to discover how far it is possible to open up to all the material means of a refined and noble life.'[2] Looking back in 1893, in his evidence to the Royal Commission on the Aged Poor, Marshall indicated just how much he personally had sought to utilise his own influence and trained intelligence in the on-going struggle against deprivation and degradation: 'I have devoted myself for the last twenty-five years to the problem of poverty, and very little of my work has been devoted to any inquiry which does not bear on that.'[3]

Marshall had in effect two approaches to the problem, two sets of solutions – one dynamic, the other static – and it is the former which is by far the senior partner. The key concepts (and it is hardly surprising that we have already met them so frequently) are the following: additional training, up-skilling, rising productivity, parsimony and prudence, the cumulative impact on housing, health, nutrition and character-patterns of good pay combined with a moderate amount of State provision, regulation and environmental planning. This mix may be expected over time to produce a society of gentlemen in which the weak, the exhausted, the ignorant and the oppressed will have benefited from the opportunity to 'work out their own social salvation by their own efforts'[4] and will successfully have themselves upgraded themselves through hard work and the adoption of responsible attitudes.

That is the dynamic solution. But there is, sadly, a static problem as well, a major problem desperately in need of a static solution, and that is the dilemma represented by that 'Residuum' which is left behind once the rest of us have moved upwards on the escalator of growth and progress. Those unfortunates are trapped in a vicious circle of self-perpetuating absolute deprivation, and the principal reason is not so much nature (i.e. a singular lack of innate mental and physical capabilities) as it is nurture (i.e. a social failing in the form of a dead-end conditions such as inhibit and stifle genuine natural selection): 'The poverty of the poor is the chief cause of that weakness and inefficiency which are the causes of their poverty.'[5]

The Residuum is in a double-bind situation for it, conscious of its misery, would appear to have lost the will to substitute success for misfortune: 'For instance, the normal condition of many of the very poorest inhabitants of a large town is to be devoid of enterprise, and unwilling to avail themselves of the opportunities that may offer for a healthier and less squalid life elsewhere; they have not the strength, physical, mental and moral, required for working their way out of their miserable surroundings.'[6] They are deeply to be pitied, for they are 'physically, mentally, or morally incapable of doing a good day's work with which to earn a good day's wage.... The system of economic freedom is probably the best from both a moral and material point of view for those who are in fairly good health of mind and body. But the Residuum cannot turn it to good account.'[7] Humanitarian and economic considerations alike speak in favour of a *deus ex machina*, and that to Marshall meant interventionist action to help the unfortunates and upgrade the degraded. Interventionist action, specifically, taking the form of the minimum wage and income maintenance.

(1) The minimum wage

The very poor are very poor in essence *because* they are very poor: 'No doubt their physical, mental, and moral ill-health is partly due to other causes than poverty; but this is the chief cause.'[8] And that is why those private individuals who voluntarily offer their low-paid employees a supra-competitive wage are likely to be surprised by the extent to which their altruistic gesture engenders an unexpected *quid pro quo*. As Marshall explained in 1900 in a letter to Bishop Westcott: 'We can find out people who, because they are old, or broken, or perhaps a little stupid, would be avoided by the money-making employer, even if he could get them a good deal below the "standard" wage: and we can pay them a good deal more than the market value of their labour; and help them up. After a while they will often find themselves worth good wages and steady employment; and will leave the rest where they have been sheltered, making room for others.'[9] High pay can evidently *lead to* as well as *result from* high productivity; but for this to happen, obviously, what is required is some exogenous shock to break the inertia, some outside force to prime the pump.

Private philanthropy which takes the form of pay in excess of marginal productivity in preference to cash hand-outs not the concomitant of any service rendered itself constitutes just such an exogenous shock, just such an outside force: 'It was never more important than now to insist on the futility of philanthropy which cares only for increasing happiness and diminishing misery, and pays little regard to the effect of its action on character. . . . But while reckless philanthropy is as rampant as ever, there is a great modern growth of wide and far-seeing effort to help people to strengthen themselves and thus permanently to raise themselves.'[10] So valuable indeed is that private philanthropy which is dispensed by an employer to a worker who is only worth wages that are 'too low to support a healthy life'[11] that there might even be a case for the institutionalisation of such generosity on a collective basis, along the lines of the prediction that 'economic chivalry on the part of the individual would stimulate and be stimulated by a similar chivalry on the part of the community as a whole'[12] – and in view of the sound economic benefits which a chivalrous attitude to pay would clearly seem to confer *ex post facto*. Marshall, however, demonstrates in the event a degree of hesitation in recommending a compulsory minimum wage which, frankly, is not easy to grasp save in terms of his habitual aversion to controversy. Thus he notes certain 'central difficulties'[13] in the scheme (such as the need to relate the minimum, if it is to be meaningful, to family rather than individual earnings, and also to correct for local and regional factors which would not be picked up by national scales[14]); he points out that he knows of no major country which has adopted such a minimum with success (or, for that matter, at all); and he stresses that the implementation of the scheme would require better statistics than we at present have if some measure were to be obtained of 'the numbers of those who under it would be forced to seek the aid of the State'[15] (since Marshall nowhere denies the possibility of induced unemployment, as in the case, say, of a needle-woman whose work is simply not worth a living wage[16]). Marshall also seems to have entertained fears that militant dockers and other powerful groups in society would, presumably through their new-style unions, press for legislation guaranteeing a very high minimum wage indeed – a wage that would 'cause to working men as a whole a loss greater than the benefit' and even 'impoverish all'.[17] So there is at best a penumbra of doubt surrounding Marshall's views on the compulsory minimum wage. His clearest statement on the subject, in fact, conveys nothing more clearly than his hesitation: 'If it could be made effective, its benefits would be so great that it might be gladly accepted, in spite of the fear that it would lead to malingering and some other abuses; and that it would be used as a leverage for pressing for a rigid artificial standard of wages.'[18] The voluntary minimum wage, fortunately, presents no similar problems.

A minimum wage is by definition a non-competitive, non-market norm, imposed (whatever its ultimate consequences) upon a given set of supply and demand curves; and an obvious alternative is for policy to ignore the norm but to shift the curves – the demand curve to the right via a dissemination of economic intelligence and popular education such as raises the average efficiency (and therefore average remuneration) of the labour-force; the supply curve to the left via industrial relocation and slum clearance schemes such as reduce the quantity of low-value labour in metropolitan markets (and boost its pay in consequence). Such shifting of curves can only be described as an incomes policy by the back door. Whatever his views on a legislated mimimum wage, Marshall was very much in favour of governmental action of this kind – policy which aims to raise the average wage of the low-paid classes via the indirect route of prior structural change.

(2) Income maintenance

Marshall, unlike Malthus, was optimistic, not pessimistic, when reflecting on poverty and on the future: 'With greater wealth, knowledge and social activity a hope is arising that not only paupers but all the very poor may be improved away.'[19] The problem being transitory, not permanent, he reasoned, schemes to assist the deprived 'contain in themselves, the seeds of their own disappearance' and must be designed in such a way as to vanish from the scene once they have attained their intended objective: 'I regard all this problem of poverty as a mere passing evil in the progress of man upwards; and I should not like any institution started which did not contain in itself the causes which would make it shrivel up, as the causes of poverty itself shrivelled up.'[20] The fact that the vast bulk of poverty will one day wither away, however, does not, he insisted, absolve us, a caring community, from the moral duty of providing a safety net for those unfortunates who in the here-and-now tumble into states of genuine destitution – since poverty, quite simply, is a bad thing: 'A man ought not to be allowed to live in a bad home . . . . Extreme poverty ought to be regarded, not indeed as a crime, but as a thing so detrimental to the State that it should not be endured.'[21] Extreme poverty is detrimental to the welfare of all of us, and all of us must in consequence resolve to take some share in the pecuniary relief of the starving man on our doorstep.

Marshall was an advocate of income maintenance (the most static of all static solutions to the problems of the poor), but he also emphasised the protective alongside the affirmative purpose of any system involving benefits in cash (namely, 'relieving misery *without* making pauperism'[22]) – and he warned strongly that handouts, however well-intentioned, can all too easily prove counter-productive. That perverse result, he indicated, was precisely what had emerged in Britain in the Napoleonic wars:

> The sufferings of the working classes caused by a series of famines and by the French War made some measure of relief necessary; and the need of large bodies of recruits for the army and the navy was an additional inducement to tender-hearted people to be somewhat liberal in their allowances to a large family, with the practical effect of making the father of many children often able to procure more indulgences for himself without working than he could have got by hard work if he had been unmarried or had only a small family. Those who availed themselves most of this bounty were naturally the laziest and meanest of the people, those with least self-respect and enterprise.[23]

The net outcome of such a policy was to be expected, that it 'undermined the independence and vigour of the people',[24] and thereby retarded the highly-desirable process of adaptation to a changing environment: 'The kindly meant recklessness of the poor law did even more to lower the moral and physical energy of Englishmen than the hard-headed recklessness of the manufacturing discipline: for by depriving the people of those qualities which would fit them for the new order of things, it increased the evil and diminished the good caused by the advent of free enterprise.'[25]

On the surface benefits in cash appear 'sheer gain': 'If people do not get help when they really need it, they and their children are apt to become weak in body and character, and unable to contribute much to the production of material wealth.'[26] Looking beneath the surface, however, we cannot fail to notice 'the harm to strength of character and to family life that comes from ill-considered aid to the thriftless'[27] or to observe that the degraded 'are sure to become even more degraded if they frequently get help when they do not need it, and so drift into the habit of laying themselves out to get it'.[28] It is in addition positively insulting to the worthier of the recipients themselves that relief 'should take account only of destitution and not at all of merit': where assistance is distributed among beneficiaries on the basis of need alone it is in effect 'distributed among them in inverse proportion to their industry and thrift and foresight', and the result (the habitual fellow-traveller with moral hazard) is that the greatest rewards in bad times end up in the hands of those who in good times 'thought it foolish to make provision for the future'.[29] Not only does this pattern corrupt still further the character of 'rogues and vagabonds'[30] but it also imposes stigma by association on the deserving poor – hardly the proper reward for a conscientious man who, despite having limited his family, developed 'strength and manliness of character',[31] shown forethought and parsimony, eschewed the demon drink,[32] nonetheless finds himself bracketed in the public mind with indolent scroungers and destitute profligates should he fall upon hard times.

Such a system of income maintenance breeds inefficiencies and multiplies injustices; and Marshall (declaring firmly that he was 'opposed to lax administration of relief of every kind'[33]) accordingly chose to identify himself with that 'enlightened view' which assigns a considerable importance to discrimination in matters of welfare. Specifically, he argued that support to the poor should in future be channelled more and more to 'those who are weak and ailing through no fault of their own'[34] and to 'those who have helped themselves and endeavoured to provide for their own future',[35] less and less to 'the idle and the thoughtless'[36] and to those who 'will not work'.[37] We should not, Marshall maintained, be hard 'where hardness is unmerited', but nor should we be tender 'where tenderness is the parent of crime'; and this suggests that 'being without the means of livelihood must be treated, not as a crime, but as a cause for uncompromising inspection and inquiry. So long as we shrink from the little pain that this would give, we are forced to be too kind to the undeserving, and too unkind to the unfortunate.'[38] Besides that, a man who has nothing to hide has nothing to fear from an examination of his past conduct accompanying an analysis of his present need: 'Public inquiry does not necessarily involve disgrace. A University examination is disgraceful to those who are plucked, but it confers honour on those who acquit themselves well.'[39] Such a man, like the naval or military officer who vociferously demands a court martial in order to clear his honour in the face of some slight, might positively welcome the selective system of relief subject to inspection and inquiry for the simple reason that it decisively exonerates him from the suspicion that he had been guilty of 'any grave crime or persistent evil living': 'If he passed this examination successfully, if he proved that he had made all efforts that could be reasonably expected of him, and that the misfortunes by which he had been borne down were more than he could be reasonably expected to have provided against, then he might receive relief without disgrace.'[40] It is the scallywag and the wastrel who need tremble at the thought of inspection and inquiry; and that in itself is no bad thing.

Inspection and inquiry are, however, not free goods, and reform of relief therefore presupposes that more money will be spent on more men: 'Our national income is four times as great as in 1834, but our expenditure on Poor-relief is rather less. To double the number of Relieving Officers would have been a serious burden then, it would be a light one now.'[41] On more men and on better men as well: 'To find a sufficient number of educated, judicious men was almost impossible then; with a little care it could be easily done now.'[42] But the contribution of the voluntary sector and of private charity simply cannot be underestimated. The 'growing spirit of the age'[43] is eminently favourable to the Charity Organisation Societies, which are a first-rate illustration of economic chivalry in operation:

> I think it would be difficult to conceive a body of people to whom the country is under greater obligations than the leaders of the chief societies, and of the London society in particular: I think that the self-devotion with which they have pursued the higher interests of the people, without fear and without caring for favour, doing what they thought to be right, with steady persistence and resolve, showing great versatility and an immense deal of the higher wisdom of kindliness, will make them a landmark in English history. I think that the things of which England may be proud are not her wealth, but her trades unions, her Friendly Societies, her co-operative societies, and her Charity Organisation Societies.[44]

It is no surprise that, in designing the ideal welfare system of the future, Marshall strongly recommended the adoption of the mixed model: 'The strength of public authority should be combined with the versatility, sympathy and delicacy of volunteer agencies'.[45] The voluntary sector can show flexibility where the Poor Law Guardians must apply rules rigidly; private charity is able to deal imaginatively with 'exceptional cases – cases which cannot be adequately relieved from public funds without making dangerous precedents';[46] and the State and non-State sectors complement one another to an all but symbiotic extent in the important process of discriminatory treatment based upon antecedent inspection and inquiry.

In that important process three separate activities are embodied. First, information must be collected on the specific case in question and on the background of the person or family in distress. Second, a recommendation must be made concerning the mode of relief that might be appropriate in the circumstances. Third, the advice must be translated into actuality and the assistance made available. Marshall said: 'I wish that no relief should be given at all, except interim relief, until the case has been examined by the Charity Organisation Society.'[47] Marshall so much admired the voluntary sector that he was evidently keen to give it ultimate responsibility with respect both to initial intelligence-collection and to subsequent diagnosis-formulation. To be more specific, he suggested in his evidence to the Royal Commission on the Aged Poor that the COS should assign each case to one of three categories or classes – A, B and C. Different categories would then receive different treatment (some of it at the hands of the private sector, some of it at the hands of the public). Assistance, in other words, was not to be indiscriminate ('I think the State ought not to shovel money, so to speak, upon anybody',[48] Marshall commented pointedly) but rather linked to prior classification by the invaluable voluntary sector within the framework of a tailor-made relief system condemned by its very nature to be far more complex than the mass-produced alternative: 'I want relief to be very often very complex; the centre of relief, I think, should be the aim of raising a man out of the position of being a pauper; and that means, I think, a great variety of methods of treatment of individual cases. I would like it to be as quick as it can be, but I do not think I want to make it simple.'[49]

The allocation of assistance presupposes prior classification, and the three categories or classes which Marshall envisaged are the following:

First, class A. Class A poverty involves 'the simple good cases'[50] of men who had not bred recklessly, had made every effort to save (say, by subscribing to a provident society), and had genuinely exerted themselves to find honest labour despite accumulated misfortunes not brought on by personal malfeasance. Such men constitute the 'deserving poor' and must be recommended by the COS to the Poor Law Guardians 'for good treatment',[51] for relief that is provided 'in a way as little painful to the applicant as possible'.[52] Such men simply cannot be asked to endure the cruelty and hardship of custodial care ('The deserving poor feel, and ought to feel, great anguish when they are forced into the workhouse',[53] not least because of the coarse manners and 'gross and obscene talk'[54] of the 'vicious poor' with whom they have to consort in that environment of shame and failure): such modes of treatment 'cost more pain than they are worth for the purposes of education'.[55] The State, while recognising that private charity will do its part as well, should accordingly allow good men who have fallen upon bad times to claim outdoor relief in cash while remaining in the dignity of their own homes: 'It would be a very great mistake to attempt to abolish outdoor relief before private charity is ready to take its place in cases in which relief ought to be given.'[56]

Even where private charity does not provide pecuniary assistance to all those who genuinely deserve such help, it is important to stress the exceptional value of voluntary helpers with respect to class A poverty.[57] Positively speaking, they have the time and the human qualities required 'for getting to the bottom of the sad tale which is unwillingly and shrinkingly told by those who have nobly struggled against misfortune':[58] they play the role of amateur social workers who, having 'gone into the applicant's history', having 'drawn forth by sympathy whatever good there was in him',[59] then open wide to him the gates of a welfare world in which no stigma is inflicted nor punishment implied. Negatively speaking, they make the system of cash-benefits to the needy a viable one by seeing through the guiles of the unworthy, by reporting truthfully on scoundrels claiming from several sources, and in general by excluding from the high-grade system of outdoor relief those who are only out to use and abuse the system: 'Outdoor relief is often the booty of the idle, the dissipated, the crafty and the hypocritical; for the Guardians, and Relieving officers employed by them, have not the time for investigating properly the merits of each case; and they have not as yet entered into systematic alliance with private distributors of charity. Thus while the honest poor suffer great hardships, those who are dishonest often receive Outdoor relief at the same time that their wants are abundantly provided for by private charity.'[60] If the butter of welfare is spread too widely it will be spread too thinly; and since paid officials would appear to be poor judges, each and every friend of 'the thrifty, the provident and the upright, when struck with adversity'[61] will also welcome the commitment to the welfare of the deserving poor that is shown by the individual volunteer.

The process of careful vetting does at least reduce the danger of welfare-addiction and that debasement of character which results from long-term dependency (whereas without vetting 'it has been found that wherever Outdoor relief has been given freely, a large part of the population has become idle, thriftless, and base, in short "pauperised" '[62]). But even vetting does not prevent one unfortunate side-effect associated with grants of money from arising: outdoor relief, if given to the poor in work, 'does tend almost invariably to lower wages'[63] and thus makes it impossible for the recipients subsequently to 'live without support from the rates'.[64] Even if the character of such recipients does not become so debased in this manner that they are ultimately vetted altogether out of class A, it must be confessed that the prospect of permanent low pay linked to permanent cash grants is not an attractive one.

Second, class B. Class B poverty involves 'the doubtful or difficult cases',[65] where relief without the workhouse is appropriate but where more flexibility and discretion in welfare is called for than would be possible were the funds for assistance to be public rather than private. It is obviously with respect to Class B poverty that the Charity Organisation Societies most forcefully come into their own: 'Class B would be all those people whom a Charity Organisation Society (supplemented by a few people who look at poverty not very much from above) thought it not undesirable in the public interest, and consistent with charity, to relieve without disgrace, but whom yet they could not put into Class A without establishing a dangerous precedent. Those I would have relieved out of Charity Organisation money, and not out of public money.'[66]

The difficulty with Class B cases as far as the State sector is concerned is that 'you must, more or less, follow rule when you are acting in a public capacity'.[67] Rules and guidelines are important and valuable but the very rigidity which they impose and must impose does on many occasions mean that the State sector is unable to do what is in the best interests of society. The private sector is not similarly constrained when it comes to acting *ad hoc* and *ad hominem*: 'For instance, there are many things that the Charity Organisation Societies do which the guardians do not do, and perhaps could not safely do; taking tools out of pawn, sending a person to the seaside, paying rent, and all sorts of exceptional things of that kind.'[68] The private sector can send one individual to the seaside without then being compelled by precedent to do likewise for all similar individuals; the State sector does not have the same freedom to make such qualitative distinctions as between different degrees of distress of different individuals requiring relief. So long as private charities have adequate funds for discretionary action, there is thus evidently much to be said for the intermediate case of Class B.

Third, class C. Class C poverty involves 'the bad cases' – the 'undeserving', the 'vicious', the 'unworthy', the 'habitually idle and profligate', the 'reckless', 'the man who can work and will not', 'the resolute tramp'.[69] These people too have a right to welfare; but that does not mean that they can reasonably expect the same treatment as those innocent persons who shelter under the umbrella of class A from a tempest not of their own brewing. In the case of class C poverty we are dealing not with men of good character but with 'unstable excitable blood';[70] and while the freedom of choice associated with outdoor relief might be appropriate for the class A claimant, the class C pauper requires something more than merely spendable resources, namely re-moulding and re-shaping if he is ever to escape from the unfortunate conditions of poverty and degradation which drove him to welfare. What he requires, in other words, is correction and education by means of discipline – including 'the kindly but severe discipline of those who are bringing up children under physical and moral conditions which will make them recruits to the great army of the habitually unemployed'.[71] Such 'paternal discipline' has worked well in Germany in dealing with unemployables and barely employables[72] and it is entirely appropriate for the treatment of class C poverty in Britain.

Paternal discipline is a future-orientated concept which is concerned with the dynamics alongside the statics of deprivation: 'I have always held that poverty and pain, disease and death are evils of much less importance than they appear, except in so far as they lead to weakness of life and character; and that true philanthropy aims at increasing strength more than at diminishing poverty.'[73] Discipline is particularly important where the parents of young children are involved lest the state of helplessness become a cumulative intergenerational transfer, and this explains the distinction which Marshall drew between paupers situated at different ends of the life-cycle: 'Elderly people might be helped with a chief regard to economy and to their personal inclinations. But the case of those, who are responsible for young children, would call for a greater expenditure of public funds, and a more strict subordination of personal freedom to public necessity.'[74] The right to relief of immediate distress, it would appear, carries with it a duty on the part of the recipient to reform himself, to overcome his feebleness, and to abandon the vicious circle in favour of the upward spiral: 'Everybody who, whether through his own fault or not, was incapable of keeping together a home that contributed to the well-being of the State, that person should, under the authority of the State, pass into a new life.'[75] As naturally, more and more of the class C poor pass into a new life, as more and more of them are trained to live 'braver and stronger lives'[76] than before they became charges on the community, so the need for and cost of paternal discipline will shrivel up: 'It would remove the great canker that infects the whole body of the nation: and when the work was done the resources that had been absorbed by it would be free for some more pleasant but less pressing social duty.'[77] Money spent on paternal discipline is clearly money cost-effectively spent, the very objective of the expenditure being to render itself self-liquidating.

Paternal discipline is the responsibility not of the Charity Organisation Societies but of the State sector and the Poor Law guardians, and if the treatment is to be successful it must be severe. For the very worst elements in category C there is no point in denying that this means workhouses that are positively more 'deterrent' and more 'educational'. The prisons as well:

> I think it is a very great trouble at present that there are many persons who prefer to go to prison to going into the workhouse, and yet those are the very people for whom I want more discipline. The difficulty is a great one, and I cannot see that there is any way out of it except to start with the prisons. I think the discipline in the prisons ought to be made, generally speaking, the severer. If you do not want to give a man a harder punishment you may reduce the time, but I think it is unendurable that a person should feel that the best way of getting lodged as he likes is to go to a prison. The workhouse at present has for many people all the deterrence of a prison, and for some more, and yet they are the very people whom I want to deter more still. I want the workhouse discipline to be made rather more severe for them, and I think that account must be taken, therefore, of the over-gentle treatment in many of our prisons.[78]

For the less evil elements in category C the workhouse remains the solution, but the inference is that less pain and suffering is called for in the attempt to inculcate the qualities of independence and self-reliance that are so necessary for life on the outside.[79] Marshall does not discuss other modes of paternal discipline within the State sector, but a number of scenarios involving strict social workers could be elaborated which would fit in well with his approach of being cruel in order to be kind. One would certainly expect that the care of well-intentioned volunteers and visitors from the private agencies would prove of use where the man of the family alone enters the workhouse: 'I assume . . . that able-bodied men would not receive outdoor relief under ordinary circumstances; though the plan of giving temporary outdoor relief to their families on condition that they themselves came into the workhouse might be extended.'[80]

Our discussion of Marshall's views on income maintenance has thus far drawn attention to differentiated treatment of different categories: 'As between lax and rigid administration of the poor law, he was on the side of rigid. But he thought the question for the future was between discriminating and indiscriminating poor relief; and he was on the side of discrimination.'[81] Our discussion has in addition drawn attention to the importance of division of labour between State and private sectors, and therewith too the division of finance between compulsory burdens and voluntary subscriptions: 'He did not think that the burden of providing for the deserving poor should fall entirely on charity organisation societies. Other rich people besides the subscribers to these societies should be made to pay their share. We all owed the greatest gratitude to the officers of those societies for their splendid work; but they had undertaken more than they could manage, because they did much that ought to be paid for by taxes and rates which fell upon the whole of the wealthier classes, both those who were and those who were not selfish.'[82] Our discussion of Marshall's views on income maintenance must now range more widely and take into account two final topics that inescapably figure in Marshall's general theory of material poverty and its relief. The first of these topics is the role of the working classes. The second is the problem of unemployment.

First, the role of the working classes. Marshall undeniably writes in places as if he believed that the relief of the poor is the responsibility of the privileged – and that, just as landholding in England 'has never been divorced from special obligations to the poor, with the consent of those immediately concerned, and the approval of economists generally',[83] so our long tradition of *noblesse oblige* helps to account for the spread of charitable activity among that 'large and increasing number of people' who have not only the will but also 'the leisure, the means, the education'[84] to get involved in such work: 'I think that there is a very great tendency on the part of the rising generation to care about these things. Oxford and Cambridge represent, as it has been often said, what cultured England is going to be twenty years hence; and the difference in the tone and sentiment of the undergraduates now from what it was twenty years ago is something astonishing. The number of movements that there are by both Universities for working with the poor is very remarkable; and one of the best developments of the higher education of women has been the very great interest which many of the students at the women's colleges have taken in social problems. I believe that a considerable number of the best workers for the London Charity Organisation Society are young people from those colleges, who have taken the question of poverty seriously to heart, in a way in which people of that age did not often do twenty years ago.'[85] Yet Marshall's language, which speaks of increase and changes, is indicative of a position which is more nearly trickle-up than lord-of-the-manor: as more and more of us become upgraded and improved, he seems to be saying, so we too will want to – and be able to – manifest our altruism in the manner pioneered for us by the vanguard which has gone before. As time goes by and progress goes on, Marshall seems to believe, even the independent member of the working classes will want to invest cash and energy in the relief of the dependent and the needy precisely as Lady Bountiful did and does – and with respect to the elderly at least the future is nowadays all but the present: 'A growing feeling of duty is making the working classes willing to sacrifice themselves in some respects, though not in all, more for the old than they used to.'[86]

The working classes can do what the *noblesses obligées* are already attempting – and they can do more. For one thing, 'the conscience of the best of the working classes'[87] is better placed to provide information 'from below' on what it feels to be poor than can those 'experts in the art of raising the poor' whose lives have been comfortable and whose reliance on charities and guardians has been minimal: they who 'know where the shoe pinches' may be expected to 'have the knowledge that we want, and which I find I do not get from reading Blue Books, and the publications of the Charity Organisation Society.'[88] Again, 'the far-seeing prudence of the best leaders of the working classes'[89] is a great asset in the actual operation and on-going administration of societies in the voluntary sector – a benefit in terms of democratic involvement which is in every sense a child of our times: 'In 1834 there was not the trained working-class intelligence which could have been utilised for the purpose. The working class intelligence that we want to utilise is almost entirely a creation of the last sixty years, and in a great measure of the last twenty years.'[90] Furthermore, 'the honest working man'[91] is likely to spend more of his time with the wilfully idle, the profligate and the drunken than is the civil servant, and he is therefore well situated to harness informal social sanctions and peer group pressures to the plough of self-respect purchased through hard work: 'The working classes alone can rightly guide and discipline the weak and erring of their own number.'[92] In all of these ways the working classes themselves can contribute to the relief of the poor along jungle tracks which he who surveys the bush from above will fail to spot and to exploit.

There is a final point concerning working class involvement in relief, and it concerns self-help schemes – not least those set up by trades unions: 'Unions get a powerful hold on those working men who dread nothing so much as becoming dependent on the parish.'[93] The union is naturally in an ideal position to assess claims for unemployment benefit: 'It can promise to maintain a man comfortably whenever he is out of work. But any provident society which did not consist of men in the same trade with himself, would fail if it attempted to do this: for it could not test the truth of his statement when he said that he could not get work at a reasonable wage.'[94] All self-help schemes take advantage of the increasing prudence and increasing parsimony which so clearly characterise our era of rising incomes and improving behaviour-patterns; and they in that way provide an alternative source of funds to that represented by the *quo sine quid* of charity, public and private. Self-help schemes set up by unions would seem to have particular value where inquiry and inspection of men out of work is concerned precisely because those of us in the trade are by our very situation compelled to be experts in our own market conditions – and just as we will recognise the errant skiver and refuse to subsidise him for swinging the lead rather than the pick, so will identify the honest good man who can only get work by undercutting his former mates and will by giving him welfare be investing in effect in the important public good for all of us in the trade of the 'going rate'. Be that as it may, self-help schemes are a final illustration of the manner in which, in Marshall's view, the working classes themselves could and should become actively involved in the complex structure of welfares.

Second, the problem of unemployment. The oldest form of welfare is that which is extended by a worker to himself and his family when he is in work and bringing home good wages; and it must be remembered that underlying Marshall's discussion of the relief of poverty is his conviction that we can all find work if we are willing to be flexible about pay. Obviously if I refuse to accept a wage-cut when the level of demand for output (and therefore of derived demand for input) falls in the downswing of the cycle, then either I will lose my job or you will fail to secure one; but increasing rationality on my part concerning market conditions (accompanied perhaps by a State-sponsored index of prices to assist me in separating real from nominal values) will presumably make me more willing to accept early adjustments in my money-wages, while increasing rationality accompanied by increasing altruism (both being characteristic of our age of improvement) will presumably make me less unwilling to act chivalrously towards you once I come to share in what is nowadays 'a more general and clear appreciation of the fact that high wages, gained by means that hinder production in any branch of industry, necessarily increase unemployment in other branches.'[95]

Rationality and altruism, pay-plasticity and Say's Law, all add up to the general prediction that there will be minimal involuntary unemployment in the modern economy. Minimal does not, however, mean zero; and there are in practice two important processes endogenous to the modern economy which can, if only for a limited period, seriously disrupt the workings of the oldest form of welfare. One of these is the contraction phase of the trade cycle – a case to which we shall return in the next chapter as the topic to which it refers essentially macroeconomic in nature. The other is new inventions, temporary dislocations, and therewith the diswelfares which some of our citizens bravely suffer that the rest of us might enjoy the full benefits of a dynamic and a changing economy: 'Almost every invention does some partial harm; and as the rate of invention increases so this harm increases. But as there is a large net surplus of good, all that is to be wished is that those who reap the great good should bestow some of it to shield those on whom the harm falls. This is already done to some extent voluntarily; it might be profitable to inquire whether it could not be made compulsory in some cases.'[96] Marshall was evidently concerned with the need to relieve those individuals who bear the vicissitudes of progress on our behalf from the evil consequences of the 'discontinuity of labour' with which such technological and economic upheavals are normally associated; and he was also in favour of some relief being granted to those unfortunates temporarily forced into involuntary unemployment by the contraction phase of the trade cycle. It is no surprise that Marshall was taken to task not only by socialists (who in the discussion following his paper to the Industrial Remuneration Conference appear to have called him a 'bookworm' whose attitude was 'timid' and whose proposals were 'paltry'[97]) – for being too hard – but also by market-orientated liberals, who seem to have thought he was too soft. The Reverend J. Llewellyn Davies (very much resembling on this issue yet another 'kind-hearted clergyman'[98] with a propensity to blame the poor for the crime of poverty) was only one among many who found the Cambridge professor's recommendations unrealistic, sentimental and counter-productive: 'I am quite convinced, the testimony to this effect being abundant and unquestionable, that there is less of painful poverty where there is little hope of obtaining relief from the rates than where the poor are tempted to expect it and count upon it. Prudence is stimulated by self-dependence; and sons and daughters and other relatives are induced to fulfill their obligations when the public does not take over the discharge of them.'[99]

Marshall would not have accepted that he was a soft touch, but he did believe in relief of poverty, and not least in the relief of that poverty which is caused by lack of jobs – as in 1885: 'There is certainly a want of employment now.'[100] In such circumstances the unemployed should be given access to public and private hand-outs by means of the complex system of discriminatory evaluation outlined above, and the State should in addition – when the out-of-work cannot find employment because the requisite openings quite genuinely do not exist – itself become a temporary employer of the slack, always provided that it does so sensibly and that it bows back out immediately private employers bow back in: 'Political economy does, I think, prove that if relief works at full wages are started to employ ten thousand men, and kept going for a few years, the result will be that ten thousand extra families will drift into London. This will mean further overcrowding, more children brought up without healthy play, more race deterioration, and in the long run larger crowds of people out of work .... Works that are not in themselves necessary, but are undertaken to give employment, should be such as can be suspended at any time. The pay should be enough to afford the necessaries of life, but so far below the ordinary wages of unskilled labour in ordinary trades that people will not be contented to take it for long, but will always be on the look-out for work elsewhere. I for one can see no economic objection to letting public money flow freely for relief works on this plan.'[101] Such relief works are to be short-run and contra-cyclical; the pay is to be below that in the outside market for the same reasons that conditions in the workhouse are to be less attractive than those in the outside world; and in no circumstances should policy involve a 'make-work' element such as would bolster up a declining industry which clearly has no long-run future.[102] Subject to those safeguards, however, there would appear to be a reasonable case for the short-run deployment of the weapon in a period of widespread unemployment by a government sincerely committed to the relief of poverty.

For Marshall himself was sincerely committed to the relief of poverty – so much so that he was opposed neither to State intervention in evolutionary processes nor to the expenditure of public as well as private money in the pursuit of so eminently justifiable an objective: 'We ought not to be afraid of very large expenditure of public and private funds in removing or lessening the causes of the disease.'[103] A disease poverty certainly is, and one which a society committed to the dignity of man simply cannot allow to survive:

> The conditions which surround extreme poverty, especially in densely crowded places, tend to deaden the higher faculties. Those who have been called the Residuum of our large towns have little opportunity for friendship; they know nothing of the decencies and the quiet, and very little even of the unity of family life; and religion often fails to reach them . . . . Overworked and under-taught, weary and careworn, without quiet and without leisure, they have no chance of making the best of their mental faculties . . . . The study of the causes of poverty is the study of the causes of the degradation of a large part of mankind.[104]

It was a study which Marshall made his own with an earnestness seldom found in economics: 'I care about it', he said, 'more than about all other political questions put together',[105] and the sheer mass and intensity of his work on the subject suggests that he is indeed very much to be believed.

5.4 INDUSTRY AND TRADE

Economic growth and social improvement are intimately linked; and it is in the circumstances not altogether surprising that Marshall had so few proposals to make concerning State intervention in the processes of industry and trade. It is, after all, the very success of free enterprise and market capitalism which is chiefly responsible for the economic growth and social improvement that so greatly characterise our modern era of progress. At the same time, however, there remain even in a healthy atmosphere of market freedom certain policy-options which an intelligent government ought to explore with a view to improving still further the performance of enterprise and capitalism. Four of those policy-options are the following.

(1) Control of monopoly

Marshall was concerned – increasingly so as he grew older – about the increase in the 'number and importance' of what we would call natural monopolies and what he calls 'indivisible industries': 'Such are the industries that supply gas or water in any given area, for only one such company in any district can be given leave to pull up the streets. Almost on the same footing are railways, tramways, electricity supply companies, and many others.'[1] Sometimes the existence of such power is positively beneficent: 'In industries which obey the Law of Increasing Return, as very many of these indivisible industries do, a reduction of price or an improvement of quality will confer on the consumer a benefit out of all proportion to the extra cost involved.'[2] Sometimes, however, the power is malign and liable to abuse – as where, in Pittsburgh, no sooner had manufacturers installed costly plant at their own expense in order to make use of cheap gas rather than dear coal but the 'partial monopolist' in the gas-supply industry saw to it that the price of gas was 'suddenly doubled';[3] or where 'predatory pricing' is deliberately employed in an effort to keep out competitors;[4] or where, should firms form associations such as cartels which take as their marginal cost for purposes of pricing the marginal cost of the least efficient member, the result is that 'the public pay more than is necessary for their goods';[5] or where employees and employers in a particular trade do not conflict but collude via a compact in restraint of trade that in truth constitutes nothing less than a 'grievous danger to the public in those trades in which there is little effective competition from foreign producers'.[6] While the community can no doubt turn a blind eye to cases where the suspension of competitive conditions brings clear benefits to the consumer (where prices fall in consequence of economies of large size being exploited, for example, or where quality improves as a result of research projects collaboratively undertaken by businesses nominally rivals), and while progress is undeniably more favourable to Us than to Them (as witness the increasing moral pressures exercised by better-informed public opinion, or modern developments in transportation such as accelerate market-penetration on the part of interlopers), and while constant change means constant fall as well as constant rise (whatever doubts Marshall may have entertained in later years concerning the life-cycle of the trees in the economic forest in an age of corporate capitalism),[7] one thing is clear: where businesses act in a manner that is 'exceptionally cruel and malign',[8] and where no endogenous forces emerge such as are demonstrably capable of stemming the tide, there is simply no alternative to the State's making itself the champion of the public interest and intervening actively in defence of the community's welfare. What is somewhat less clear is what form that intervention should ideally take, and it must be said that Marshall is here not really at his most decisive. Nor, however, is he content to remain the passive spectator of a drama which clearly caused him a moderate degree of anxiety.

The *first* step, Marshall believed, is for the State to find out the facts: 'The chief successes of the medical treatment of bodily ailments have been achieved by measures which tend to give free play to the remedial forces of nature. The chief of the remedial forces of nature in regard to human action is knowledge: and nearly all beneficial intervention of authority in social troubles begins with the acquirement and publication, voluntarily or under compulsion, of information, which some of those interested in the conflict are not likely to offer spontaneously.'[9] The prominent and powerful businessman has a pecuniary vested interest in secrecy, distortions and half-truths, and will strive to argue that his anti-social raising of the price of the necessity was in reality only a conscious attempt to generate resources for research and development such as would lead to a lower price for a better product at some time in the future: 'A great trust starts with expert knowledge of its own business; it can hire the most expensive expert witnesses to support the arguments of its highly paid counsel – themselves in some measure experts – on technical points. Against so strongly fortified a defence little can be done by a relatively small and impecunious business, which thinks itself aggrieved; and still less by the inarticulate public, which may be the chief sufferer in the long run.'[10] Aggrieved parties will no doubt present countervailing evidence of their own – but much of what they say is bound to be as 'exaggerated',[11] as partial, as confused as one would expect from men who 'seldom have the time, the faculties or the knowledge required for the work. They are apt to lay undue stress on matters which specially concern them, and to pass by the larger issues which are of national concern: and they are often afraid to attack powerful interests, whose hostility might destroy them.'[12] There is clearly a need in a situation of this description for the appointment of a Commission of Inquiry prepared to listen to the testimony of both sides; willing itself paternalistically 'to take some initiative in regard to the interests of the non-vocal multitude, in order that it may present a well-balanced picture of the whole position';[13] and competent ultimately to draft a careful and authoritative report of which the educational and publicity value is bound to be substantial even where the recommendations are never actually made binding. More generally, the State should on a continuous basis compel any 'Corporation of semi-monopolistic scope . . . to make returns to the Government for publication of a kind which it would not be well to demand from an ordinary Company'[14] – and it should not hesitate to compare the statistics on costs and prices disgorged by a firm suspected of making a 'bad abuse' of its power with the data provided by other corporations in the same industry. The railways, for example: 'Some of these railways are sure to be managed efficiently and honestly: and they will serve as a touchstone for the rest.'[15] Such State intervention on a continuous basis has worked well in the United States, where since its establishment in 1903 the Bureau of Corporations has had a signal success 'in checking abuses of monopolistic power by merely publishing the results of its investigation of them'.[16] The first step, Marshall believed, is for the State to find out the facts; and such a Bureau, if the idea were to be adopted here, undeniably has a valuable role to play in helping to undermine trade secrecy.

The *second* step, logically speaking, is for the State to act where action is appropriate. As it has done in Germany, where the government, while recognising how frequently big is beautiful should great efficiency dictate great overheads, is also prepared to intervene should business policy contravene the public interest by artificially and unscrupulously raising prices to the consumer:

> Prussia's deposits of potash constitute an important partial monopoly. If they were owned by a single company, with sole regard to its own profit, the price would probably be set so much above cost of production as to yield a huge monopoly revenue, at the expense of stinting German agriculture's supply of a much needed fertilizer. Private owners tend to exercise their influence in the cartel in that direction: but, partly by legislation, and partly by means of its large holdings of the deposit, the Government compels the price of domestic sales to be kept rather low; while leaving the cartel free to put the price for exportation where it will.[17]

As it has done in America, where the government, while accepting that consolidation and expansion are often the preconditions for effective production and marketing, is also quick to become involved via restrictive practices legislation should competitive strategies in consequence of size become destructive rather than constructive in nature: 'One runner may outdo his rivals by greater energy as much as he can: but, if he puts his hand on another's shoulder to pull him back, while pulling himself forward, that is the unfair competition against which the Anti-Trust Act is directed.'[18]

Both the Germans and the Americans are, of course, foreigners with cartels, trusts and protective tariffs such as create abuses which in the more competitive British economic environment are far less likely to arise: 'Special circumstances in America, and still more in Germany, have put great power into the hands of monopolistic sellers or combinations of sellers. But buyers in England seldom suffer more than a trifling inconvenience from the refusal of a seller to supply them at a fair cost price: for the sources of supply are generally numerous, and they are very rarely combined under one control.'[19] But the fact that the British see less of the dark side of the market than do foreigners, the fact that 'the conditions of British industries seldom call for strong authoritative intervention in such matters',[20] does not mean that the British see nothing of the dark side of the market (of which an example near at home is the giant firm of Coats, which has blocked the highway of commerce to potential new entrants by refusing to supply any dealer who trades with any rival[21]) or that British economic conditions never call for intervention over and above the protection afforded by the Common Law. Thus government should take an interest in the regulation of railway charges where it identifies an attempt to drive rivals out of business: 'Railway competition with water-routes should . . . be subject to the ordinary rules against monopolistic underselling: any lowering of railway charges should be stayed by administrative authority, when the evidence indicates that its aim was to destroy competition.'[22] And government should remember that the rent of land is the longest-established demand-determined reward for the services of a natural monopoly and not hesitate where appropriate to impose administered maxima in place of free market equilibria: 'The command of all convenient routes of access to the shore, where it offers sites for deep-water berths, might be a source of great monopolistic power, were not the charges of docks controlled by public authority. Again, owners of land surrounding a rich mine might charge way-leaves, which would absorb nearly the whole net profits of the mine, if the law had not provided against it.'[23] Such modes of intervention on the part of government only bend the bent rod and distort the distortions of the distorters. They are fully in keeping with our national traditions of fair play and 'ordered freedom':[24] 'British traditions call on Government to concentrate its chief energies on guarding the public against oppressive action or inaction, on the part of private individuals or corporations.'[25] Because the objective is safeguarding the public interest, however, government should not be afraid to create a giant as well as to regulate it where it is demonstrably the case that *we* benefit when *they* collaborate:

> Abuses of monopolistic power on the part of railways demand now but little attention from the Railways and Canal Commission and its constitution might perhaps advantageously be altered, so as to fit it better for the work of constructive statesmanship: its semi-legal functions are still important, but the new age calls for work of a wider scope. It might devote special attention to opportunities for such constructive cooperation among railways as would increase the economy or efficiency of railway work; while taking care that a fair share of the gains, thus arising, accrue to the public.[26]

Sometimes taking the form of the slap on the wrist and at other times having much of the character of the orchestral conductor, it is clear that appropriate action to Marshall was, with respect to the control of monopoly, never less than pragmatic in nature.[27]

(2) Public ownership

The State is a lion, not a fox, and no lion is likely to score a great success in industries where what is needed is 'ceaseless creation and initiative'.[28] Not all industries fall into this category, however. In some industries operations are routine and can be 'reduced to rule', not much entrepreneurial flair is called for as not much change and development take place, and the consumer is so familiarised with the product that he is able immediately to detect laxity. In such industries the fox is likely to complain of boredom – but the lion stands a chance:

> The industries in which Government Departments and Local Authorities have succeeded are few in number, but important. They are mainly concerned with 'things that sell themselves'; that is, things which are in large demand, and more or less standardized by natural causes. The chief of them are connected with facilities for transport, and the distribution (by aid of way-leaves) of water, light and power: they all meet elementary needs; call for little or no adaptation to changing habits, or varying tastes; and make use of plant, the central ideas of which have been worked out by private enterprise and gradually become common property.[29]

These conditions are not fulfilled by the mining industry, which should therefore remain private.[30] These conditions 'are fulfilled in an eminent degree by the postal business'.[31] So much so that Marshall's conclusions concerning that business come as a surprise: 'We secure, so far as the influence of the Post Office reaches, most of the evils of Socialism with but few of its benefits.'[32]

Marshall observed that 'the greater part of the postal system is an absolute Governmental monopoly almost everywhere'[33] and made it clear that the evils had arisen not because of State provision *per se* but because of *monopolistic* provision: 'So long as the net revenue of the Post Office is reaped, not solely by rendering services to the public, but in part by prohibiting other people from rendering similar services, it must, I think, be entered in a general list of taxes.'[34] The tax in question is the monopoly profit pure and simple: 'It is probable that that part of the Post Office revenue which depends on its having a monopoly is not very great; (but) that so far as it goes it is very nearly the worst form of tax ever invented.'[35] In writing in such strong terms about the tax levied via monopolistic provision (public or private), the English eclectic was not only making a point of his own but also, delicately and discreetly, administering a gentle rebuke to perhaps his greatest hero, the Scottish eclectic, who had praised State provision of postal services precisely because the *quo* of public provision is normally linked to the *quid* of public finance: 'The post-office . . . over and above defraying its own expence, affords in almost all countries a very considerable revenue to the sovereign.'[36] The English eclectic did not deny the existence of the revenue that had been identified and eulogised by the Scotsman, but he did warn that a monopoly need not be in the consumer interest merely because it is a State monopoly. The truth is, Marshall declared, that 'evils' arise within the postal system despite the fact that the routine nature of the operations involved renders its business 'just that one which a Government department cannot fail to manage tolerably well',[37] and that the *onus probandi* therefore lies with those who believe that the State monopoly must be retained. The fact that the lion *stands a chance* in industries such as the postal services does not mean that the fox *should therefore be denied* equality of opportunity. The fact that the lion *can provide* postal services does not mean that the lion *ought therefore to provide* postal services. Each case must be judged on its own merits, and with reference to the specific case of the postal services Marshall, after deep reflection on the relevant costs and benefits in the clear light of the long shadow cast by the Scottish eclectic, ultimately made two recommendations concerning the future of that nationalised industry in which we at present reap 'most of the evils of Socialism with but few of its benefits'. Neither recommendation involves privatisation or putting back the clock on public ownership: that, like the long shadow of the Scottish eclectic, is something that is here to stay. Nor is either recommendation concerning the future of the postal services entirely free from a moderate degree of ambiguity – and it would be wrong to suppose that, in the supply of intellectual evasiveness and hidden assumptions, the Scottish eclectic held an absolute monopoly.

Marshall's first recommendation involves competition. Recognising that there is a need for 'the vivifying forces of private enterprise and origination within that region which has hitherto stagnated under the deadly shades of official monopoly', but recognising also that there exist even now potentially able and energetic men of 'bold enterprise and public spirit' in the Post Office itself, Marshall suggested that active rivalry between suppliers public and suppliers private would unfetter and liberate efficacy deriving from both sectors simultaneously. Such competition would increase consumers' surplus (as where charges are reduced), it would boost quality of the service rendered (Marshall speaks of 'twenty deliveries a day' in the towns), and it would even compel the Post Office to shake itself free of its bureaucratic habits – a change of attitude from which that organisation is bound in due course to derive great benefit: 'Though it would find the work very hard at first for its stiff joints, yet they would soon become more supple; and after a time it would be doing many times its present local business, and without any loss of net revenue.'[38] For the free market to work its wonders, of course, the State-run corporation must not enjoy 'any artificial advantages in competition with private enterprise',[39] and this brings us to the moderate degree of ambiguity which dwelt with the English eclectic and so frequently accompanied him on his intellectual travels: Why then should the public sector of the postal services not be made fully private? Why then should a significant proportion of other regimented activities not be taken into public ownership? Marshall leaves his first recommendation tantalisingly vague – perhaps deliberately so, should he have felt that there was no simple criterion to be enunciated and that each individual case must be subjected to individual scrutiny.

Marshall's second recommendation involves monopoly – for the very same man who on 24 March 1891 sought to pin on the Post Office 'most of the evils of Socialism with but few of its benefits' wrote as follows on 6 April of the same year: 'I not only think that a State Post Office is an absolute necessity, but I further think it ought to have a virtual monopoly of many kinds of postal business.'[40] No contradiction is involved and it was indeed the very same man. Marshall's concept is a simple one: competition in areas suitable for competition will reduce the evils of socialism while monopoly in areas not suitable for competition will do those things which only monopoly can do. Marshall's defence of monopolistic provision under public ownership would appear to be couched in terms of three arguments, and these arguments are central to his general view on the appropriate role which State-run operations should play in the modern mixed economy.

The *first* argument in defence of monopolistic provision under public ownership is natural monopoly and analogous market imperfections approximating thereto. Thus, Marshall notes, whatever the future of the postal services in the towns, the position on a national scale is different and leads to different recommendations: 'Much of the collection and distribution of large and small parcels over a very wide area, though open to everyone, falls necessarily into the hands of one or more powerful organizations: it is in fact of a scope too large to be perfectly managed by any force less than that of the universal State post.'[41] Economies of size, it would appear, are not always and everywhere the allies of the consumer interest; and where the problem of concentrated economic power can be resolved in no other way there would appear to be a presumptive case for State activity. Marshall knew that 'railways and tramways are constantly increasing in size, and the capital required to work them is increasing at an even greater rate', he reflected that the same processes are already at work in the shipping industry, and he reached a tentative conclusion concerning concentration which is not entirely what one would expect from so staunch a believer *ceteris paribus* in private enterprise: 'As a consequence the arguments in favour of the State's undertaking business are stronger in some branches of the carrying trade than in any other, except the allied undertakings of carrying away refuse, and bringing in water, gas, etc.'[42]

All things considered, Marshall declared, '*inevitable* monopoly' belongs 'in public hands'.[43] His actual arguments, however, do not entirely support so strong a statement. For one thing, Marshall himself does in the body of his work suggest various policy instruments which impose public control without necessitating public ownership (while leaving intact, in other words, 'the elastic energies of private enterprise' which he saw as the motor of advancement) – as where he recommends that the State fix charges for standard units of electricity and then leave the process of supply in private hands;[44] or where he notes that would-be monopolists could, conceptually speaking, be made to tender competitively for their rights and privileges and exercise them on a strictly short-term basis subject to continued satisfactory performance.[45] Again, Marshall is less than clear on the sheer technicalities relating to efficiency and novelty in a system of public ownership. He does say that, whatever the situation on the Continent with respect to 'public management of indivisible undertakings' (a topic which, in 1890, Marshall chose to pass over 'without . . . expressing any opinion'[46]), it is clear that in Britain and America managerial autonomy must be respected regardless of the locus of property-rights in undertakings where concentrated economic power has been identified: 'Such undertakings, though always under public control, and sometimes even in public ownership, should wherever possible be worked and managed by private corporations.'[47] What he does not say is what objectives they are to pursue (as in the case of unprofitable cross-subsidisation of postal services in 'sparsely peopled districts'[48]) or in what way their economic power is to be made to subserve the public interest (although he does make allusion in passing to social forces such as press, Parliament and public opinion[49]). But an eclectic, to be fair, has the right to let the facts speak for themselves, and Marshall, comparing size and power public with size and power private, does just that. In connection with the delivery of parcels, for example: 'A comparison of the practice of the Governments of Western Europe in this matter with that of American Express Companies in regard to the collection and delivery of parcels is not favourable to private capitalistic organization.'[50] Organisations in the private sector, of course, are subject to organic rise-and-fall associated with new entrants anxious to tap monopoly profits, whereas organisations in public hands continue to exercise their legally-protected power forever. In view of the potentially large number of activities besides the long-haul side of the Post Office business which are ripe for take-over by the Government under the highly-restrictive-practices criterion, the threat of potential stagnation would appear so great that Marshall's very failure not to make much of it in itself once again builds a moderate degree of ambiguity into his recommendations.

The *second* argument in defence of monopolistic provision under public ownership has to do with coordination and planning – with 'the suggestion that the provision of a system of main roads, open freely to all, and extending over the whole country, must be regarded as a single transport business, so immense that the nation as a whole is more fully qualified to undertake it'.[51] Needless to say, 'somewhat similar remarks are applicable to the great transport and communication industries of the Post Office, Telegraph and Telephone',[52] where the need for coordinated national provision (accompanied by the subsidiary consideration of great cost) once again militates in favour of State action. As in the obvious case of defence: 'The most costly business of all, that of national defence, is of necessity unified.'[53]

The problem of inadequate coordination among private suppliers in an anarchic free enterprise environment is well illustrated by confusion on the canals: 'As things were, the numerous companies, that were responsible for individual canals, seemed perversely to ignore one another's practice: and the strong Royal Commission on Canals and Waterways, 1906–9, found that some companies had made provision for boats of moderate size by long narrow locks, and others by broad short locks; so that many journeys were possible only for boats that were both short and narrow, and therefore very wasteful of the labour of man and horse.'[54] Nor were things much better in the electricity supply industry – where in 1918 some 600 separate organisations were generating electricity, but with so many different frequencies as to render cooperation impossible.[55] Yet the solution in the case of the latter industry could take the form of coordination without ownership should the State make it its business simply to fix standards for the whole country;[56] the same medicine could have been applied to the canals if applied at the initial planning stage; and even the railways could where appropriate even without State ownership be made subject to unified State mobilisation (as when the railways, 'if not owned by Government, are necessarily taken *under its control* in war time'[57]). In such cases public control is apparently a valid alternative to public ownership for purposes of coordination; and there is therefore a moderate degree of ambiguity surrounding Marshall's tendency in places to associate coordinated provision with public ownership. Or perhaps not – since the examples which Marshall cites (roads and certain postal services, for example) refer explicitly to activities which have already been identified as obvious candidates for nationalisation by virtue of the concentrated-power argument. Whether coordinated provision is a cause or a result of nationalisation, however, one thing at least is clear, namely that monopolistic provision under public ownership may reasonably be legitimated in these terms.[58]

The *third* argument in defence of monopolistic provision under public ownership is the *faute de mieux* argument, the argument that was so eloquently formulated by the Scottish eclectic when he assigned to 'the sovereign or commonwealth' the duty, noted above, 'of erecting and maintaining those public institutions and those public works, which, though they may be in the highest degree advantageous to a great society, are, however, of such a nature, that the profit could never repay the expence to any individual or small number of individuals, and which it therefore cannot be expected that any individual or small number of individuals should erect or maintain'.[59] Our people need good roads and navigable canals, the Scotsman reasoned; the invisible hand is in these important areas invisible quite simply because it is not there; and the alternative to State provision may confidently be said to be the unfortunate prospect of no provision at all.

The English eclectic was here much in sympathy with the Scotsman. On the subject of roads, for instance, his conclusion is unhesitating and forthright – 'The State has constructive duties in the matter.'[60] – and his argument (a compact bundle of separable points) is as follows: 'The abolition of tolls on highways is now universally recognized as good policy; because the revenue yielded by them would be small in comparison with the excess value of the services rendered by a free road over those rendered by a tolled road: the country would be in a poor way if no roads were made save those, the tolls on which would cover the expense of making them and keeping them in repair.'[61] There are at least three strands bound together in this complex web. The first is 'universally regarded': while public authority *could* regulate tolls on privately-owned turnpikes (since otherwise 'tolls at any one link might be so heavy as choke through traffic, and thus in effect to be taxes on all the neighbouring links'[62]), what Marshall is saying is that we as a community have in the event evolved a consensus of a different colour. The second is 'excess value': social spillovers and economic externalities are generated by the road such as are reaped by parties other than those who actually pay the toll, with the implication that market-provided means under-provided. The third is 'now': a more enlightened public opinion is more favourable to State enterprise in the field of roads than is a less enlightened public opinion such as was more common in the bad old days when our nation was less wealthy.

With respect to canals Marshall is more cautious. When the canal network was in its infancy, he says with evident regret, 'the time had not yet arrived for the general recognition of the fact that canals, being in effect public highways, need to be organized by Government, and perhaps financed by it',[63] and the result is that our present-day canal system is inadequate for our needs: in France and Germany 'the goods traffic by inland waterways is increasing much faster than that by railways',[64] in Britain it is declining, and we have only ourselves to blame. The lack of subsidisation from the State meant that high-spillover but low-toll routes were neglected; 'the financial aid, which the shipping industry has derived from public outlays on the improvement of harbours and of the channels which connect them with the sea, was not forthcoming to English canals',[65] which meant that they were left, metaphorically speaking, high and dry with respect to essential complementary services; and the absence of coordination previously examined meant that the discrete links in the chain of canals were not of equal (to say nothing of adequate) depth and length. In the early days a 'far-seeing strong Government' could have planned and paid (perhaps 'in return for a deferred claim on the income that might ultimately be earned'[66]) but the fact is that it did not. Nowadays our Government is more dynamic and less ignorant as to what is to be done. Marshall nonetheless remains conspicuously more cautious than the Scotsman. State ownership is not advocated in the case of canals despite the fact that it had been advocated in the case of roads, and Marshall limits himself to two proposals. One is coordination of enlargement – since few canals were 'so far self-contained as to be able to derive much benefit from such an enlargement, unless similar improvements were made by its neighbours'.[67] The other is finance and funding – since 'the revival of canals can be effected only by the State', and 'much capital will be needed for it'.[68] By State Marshall means Whitehall rather than Town Hall, and the reason, here as in analogous cases, is the fact that 'local interests cannot be isolated'.[69] Such is the price we pay for increasing interdependence and organic integration.

Marshall does not mention the Post Office in formulating what we have asserted is the third of his three arguments in defence of monopolistic provision under public ownership – the *faute de mieux* or residual supplier argument. The omission is no doubt deliberate and is almost certainly to be taken as indicative of a belief that there could and would be private sector provision of postal services even if the State sector were to abstain totally from this activity. The two other arguments – that concerning concentrated power and that referring to coordinated supply – remain of relevance, however, and remind us just how much Marshall actually had to say in favour of collective ownership.

(3) The provision of intelligence

Knowledge being one of the most important of all the inputs in the production function as he conceivd it, it is no surprise to learn that Marshall, in his discussion of industry and trade, chose to assign to the State the duty of generating and diffusing essential information: 'The function of Government is to govern as little as possible; but not to do as little as possible. . . . A Government to succeed, must be ceaseless in learning and diffusing knowledge, in stimulating and co-operating.'[70] Consider the case of 'the careless treatment of milk', where supervision and enforcement of sanitary regulations should be complemented by the maxim of '*laissez-faire*; let the Government arouse itself to do energetically its proper work of educating British farmers up to the Danish standard, if not beyond.'[71] Consider the case of 'the secret policies of American trusts', where the Americans even now appoint Commissions, hold public inquiries, publish detailed reports based on 'the prolonged, systematic study by trained experts, armed with compulsory powers of interrogation and inspection of documents',[72] and in all of these ways make their Government, via the powerful weapon of 'full publicity', an important moulder and shaper of public opinion with respect to restrictive practices: 'It can turn the balance in its favour by organizing the knowledge, that is necessary to present the case of the nation on fairly even terms with the case of a private interest: and by making public the knowledge it thus acquires, it can bring public opinion along with it.'[73] Consider the case of 'a proper standard of purchasing power', where the State ought to prepare and publish statistics on fluctuations in nominal values lest the rest of us trade on erroneous and obsolete information: 'In proposing this remedy I want Government to help business, though not to do business. It should publish tables showing as closely as may be the changes in the purchasing power of gold, and should facilitate contracts for payments to be made in terms of units of fixed purchasing power.'[73] These examples demonstrate clearly the extent to which Marshall identified the provision of intelligence as a legitimate function of the State.

The generation and diffusion of essential information in the crucial area of science and technology is an interesting case from the point of view of economic policy in that it, like the relief of poverty, is an instance of the mixed economy at work. Some research and development is in-house, conducted by 'a single giant business which is pioneering new developments of a subtle industry' and which therefore 'may reasonably set up a great laboratory for the conception and testing of improvements on current usage'[75] – but such laboratories are costly to establish and maintain (a barrier to active new entry) and they are not unfavourable to monopolistic abuses (since information privately generated is unlikely to become information publicly disseminated). Some research and development is collaborative, conducted by firms nominally competitors in the same branch of industry which opt despite their rivalries to pool their expenditures via 'cooperative Research Associations'[76] – but such constructive sharing of know-how is all too likely to turn into a destructive sharing-out of markets, with the result that the consumer pays a higher price for the (admittedly improved and altered) product. Thus it is that the State becomes involved in the advancement of science and technology – proceeding, here as always, with the exemplary pragmatism of the bridge player who knows that no two games are exactly the same.

Horses for courses in research and development need mean nothing more ambitious than a grant to a private-sector laboratory operated collaboratively by an association of firms in an industry, a grant which not only helps to pay for the advancement of science but which also allows the State to maintain a watching brief within the walls of secrecy: 'It may perhaps be to the public interest that some limited contribution should be made from public funds to the support of such associations; partly to facilitate the intervention of public authority in case an association should develop anti-social tendencies.'[77] Needless to say, if public assistance is given to private sector corporations that they might acquire 'special knowledge, which has a high pecuniary value', then 'some provision must be made for securing that all, who desire it, shall obtain access to that knowledge on reasonable conditions'[78] – a valuable spillover benefit to all who wish to apply a particular advance to a particular industry, whether or not they have paid their share of the contributions to its cost. Marshall does not say that 'some provision' must be made as well for the consumer interest. Presumably this because he believed that rivals who become collaborators for the purposes of product development will return to being aggressive competitors when the time comes to market and sell, and will be forced in that way to pass on to the rest of us some or all of the gain in productivity that they have made.

Horses for courses in research and development can mean a grant to a private sector laboratory. It can also mean the funding of a public sector institution – an alternative particularly to be recommended where the spillovers are far-reaching and the free riders in consequence exceptionally difficult to identify and charge: 'There are a few subjects, such as that of Fuel Research, which are of direct value to so many industries, that the simplest form of cooperation for their study is that of the nation as a whole: and public opinion has concurred in national expenditure on their account.'[79] Nor should the economic value of university-based research be underestimated: 'History shows that almost every scientific discovery, which has ultimately revolutionised methods of industry, has been made in the pursuit of knowledge for its own sake, without direct aim at the attainment of any particular practical advantage: Universities are the proper places for the pursuit of such "pure" science.'[80] Even 'pure' science, it would appear, is 'useful', in the narrower technicoindustrial sense. It can also usefully become even more 'useful': 'Though the eagerness of an academic student should increase with every prospect of establishing a new truth, independently of any practical gain which it may promise; yet his studies will lose nothing, and the world may gain much, from his keeping in touch with some of those industries, whose methods might be improved by increased knowledge of the properties of the products which he is studying.'[81] Of course knowledge is an end in its own right, and a highly-valued one: 'National funds are rightly given liberally to the advancement of knowledge for its own sake.'[82] But that which is an end when seen from one perspective is frequently a means to some other end when seen from some other perspective; and Marshall, desiring both knowledge and growth and aware of the extent to which they are interdependent, felt there was much to be said for a moderate degree of communication and contact between organisations as disparate as Cambridge University, Imperial College, the National Physical Laboratory and the British Dyestuffs Corporation. He also felt that appropriate public funding should be made available for these and other institutions which are directly involved in the generation and diffusion of new knowledge – a further illustration of his belief that the State must take an appropriate interest where the provision of intelligence is concerned.

(4) Trade policy

One of the greatest checks to abuse of power on the part of domestic monopolists is 'effective competition from foreign producers',[83] and in that sense the freedom of trade from tariffs and subsidies, together with the improvements in transport that are the precondition for converting the *de jure* into the *de facto* in this important area of economic policy, has unquestionably conferred great benefits on the consumer. Once, when distances were short, life was nasty and brutish: 'In Adam Smith's time England was full of trade combinations, chiefly of an informal kind, indeed, and confined to very narrow areas: but very powerful within those areas, and very cruel.'[84] Nowadays, however, trade has become genuinely international, and the British consumer is no longer at the mercy of the cossetted bully-boy: 'England's Free Trade has prevented the Law of Increasing Return from strengthening combinations of wealthy manufacturers against the general weal here to the same extent as it has in countries in which Protection has prevailed.'[85] All in all, Free Trade has brought 'unmixed blessings'[86] to this country and Marshall consistently opposed any attempt to deprive our consumers of those benefits.[87]

Admittedly costs would seem to be involved alongside the benefits, for the large firm in a country like the United States which did adopt protectionist policies is undeniably put thereby in a position where it is capable of reaping economies of size such as are less easily accessible to the smaller firm in a country like Great Britain which provides no captive domestic market: 'It is obvious that an industry which offers large scope for the economies of massive production stands to gain much from Protective duties, if they can be so arranged as to insure it the almost undisturbed possession of the home market, while keeping open for it opportunities for large sales abroad.'[88] Even so, however, the case for size through protection should perhaps not be pressed too strongly.

For one thing, trade being a two-way process, if Britain shuts out imported goods produced in foreign countries, she also reduces the effective demand from those countries for the goods produced in Britain which she should very much like to export: '*Other things being equal*, a diminution by £10 000 of the imports, which any merchant finds it advantageous to make into Britain, diminishes the demand for bills on other countries to the amount of about £10 000. That is to say, it tends to cause British producers for exportation, together with the shipowning and other mercantile houses associated with them, to curtail operations to the extent of about £10 000.'[89] The dynamic effects of a tariff being imposed are even greater since, where foreigners cannot afford to buy from Britain precisely because Britain refuses to buy from them, they will make strenuous efforts to produce in their own countries that which the British otherwise would have been able to sell to them (witness the perverse effects of Britain's Corn Laws on her would-be trading partners: 'The more she refuses to take from them the wheat and other things which they are able to supply to her, the more will they yearn for manufactures that will make them independent of her: it may be that by restrictive taxes and regulations she delays their progress for a while: but she thereby puts an artificial premium on their efforts to rival her'[90]) or, at the very least, will seek out and find alternative sources of supply (witness what happened in 1862 when King Cotton from the Deep South was deposed due to Civil War, new suppliers were found in India and Egypt, and 'the practical monopoly of raw cotton which America once had (was) broken'[91]). Clearly, a policy which shuts out imports but simultaneously cuts down exports is not automatically to be recommended to a trading nation anxious to reap economies of size by means of an extension of its markets.

Besides that, 'many of the advantages which a single industry derives from a Protective duty in its favour, involve loss and hindrance to other industries' and 'may perhaps injure the nation at large'.[92] The protective tariff, by inducing the domestic consumer to buy the expensive home product in preference to the imported alternative, retards growth in living standards: 'The general purchasing power of money is low in countries with a high protective tariff.'[93] Such a destruction of potential effective demand is no way to expand domestic sales while, looking at world markets, the effect of such trade diversion on our exports is to make them dearer (and thus *ceteris paribus* less in demand) where domestic firms, like domestic consumers, are compelled by bad policies to pay more for worse. Nor should the monetary implications of exclusionist policies be neglected. The free gift of extensive protection is an influx of gold instead of goods; the free gift of gold (as Hume knew and the Mercantilists did not) is inflation; and the free gift of inflation, given an international gold standard, is an automatic correction to our balance of payments position such as wipes out the surplus and restores the equilibrium.[94] An extensive use of the protective tariff thus threatens to raise our domestic price-levels because of macroeconomic as well as microeconomic causes – a poor way to attract paying customers into our shop.

A final reason for opposing protection is both the most obvious and the most important: the tariff is only needed by those industries which are unable to generate their own protection via the competitive route of selling a quality product at a reasonable price, and it is not intuitively obvious that we as a nation ought to sacrifice economic welfare in this way in order to absolve 'the plague spots'[95] from the consequences of their own complacency and incompetence. French experience lends strong support to the hypothesis that protected industries are not normally those which have flourished most ('Their progress has been sufficiently slow to give some support to the notion that Governmental aid to old industries tends to check enterprise'[96]), and even a freely trading nation such as Britain has in the past made serious errors with respect to exposure to importation – errors which in truth 'checked that growth of the vitality of the masses of her people which ought to have resulted from her new command over the forces of nature' and which therefore actually 'hastened the day in which she would cease to hold the unchallenged leadership in industry'.[97] The fact is that even the most viable industry tends to become sleepy and inefficient when insulated from the stimulus to 'constructive ability and initiative'[98] that is the normal concomitant of rivalry, and rivalry with foreigners has the additional advantage that it permits us to examine their innovations and developments at close quarters: 'It is not merely expedient – it is absolutely essential – for England's hopes of retaining a high place in the world, that she should neglect no opportunity of increasing the alertness of her industrial population in general, and her manufacturers in particular; and for this purpose there is no device to be compared in efficiency with the plan of keeping her markets open to the new products of other nations, and especially to those of American inventive genius and of German systematic thought and scientific training.'[99] Competitive activity teaches us to compete actively; and that educational function of freedom is a vital point in its defence.

The case against protective tariffs, Marshall believed, was a strong one, but he was acquainted with the infant industries argument – with the concept, in other words, that some institutions need 'a helping hand' to enable them 'to prevail early, or at all events to secure that their career is not cut so short that they have no "long run" in which to prevail'.[100] Just as time must pass before your child becomes your dentist, so time must pass before your new industry feels strong enough to compete with its more mature fellows abroad; and in the interim, proponents of the infant industries argument would maintain, our home-grown delicate plant needs to be sheltered from the blighting frosts of unequal competition if the nascent is indeed ever to become the fully developed.

Marshall did not deny that the infant industries argument had a certain appeal. Britain's own industrialisation, he was aware, had been founded on a healthy domestic market in which (for a variety of reasons including an early start and the costs of transport alongside the force of statute) her own producers enjoyed a privileged position: 'The growing richness of her home markets lowered the cost of production of those of her exports which conformed to the law of Increasing Return, and therefore enabled her to sell more of them abroad.'[101] And German industrialisation in the last third of the nineteenth century, he pointed out, had been remarkably rapid not least because of 'the defence which the German protective tariffs gave to weak nascent industries against the invasion of the more mature and stronger industries of some other countries, and especially England'.[102] Children, however, normally grow up, England past must not be confused with England present, and what Marshall did deny is that the infant industries argument retained any particular appeal to the impartial spectator of economic life in the Britain of his own times. As he put it in 1903, in a letter to the Secretary of the Unionist Free Food League:

> About 30 years ago I became convinced that a protective system, if it could be worked honestly as well as wisely, might on the whole benefit countries in a certain stage of industrial development, and that set me on the inquiry whether a free-trade policy was wholly right for England. I have pursued that inquiry ever since, and have gradually settled down to the conclusion that the changes of the last two generations have much increased the harm which would be done to England by even a moderate protective policy, and that free trade is of more vital necessity to England now than when it was first adopted.[103]

For England, Marshall stressed, a return to the protective system 'would, I believe, be an unmixed and grievous evil'[104] – since, like it or not, the truth is that we have grown up and are now an advanced and developed nation: 'The industries in a country so long familiar with machinery as England is, have generally passed the stage at which they can derive much real help from such Protection.'[105] England, Marshall concluded, 'is the oldest of all industrial countries. She has no industries which need protection on the ground of youth . . . . In her case, therefore, import duties, levied otherwise than with a direct view to revenue, seem to me to have no economic justification.'[106] Such an argument, it must be said, is uncharacteristically static and unimaginative for a thinker who wrote so extensively of new departures and continuous change: even a developed nation, after all, can possess within its territory a new and less-developed industry. That individual industry might, even in an advanced nation, be *not yet* 'strong enough'[107] to dispense with protection in its struggle with the Germans, and one can well imagine a selective defence of such a Lilliputian amongst the Gullivers being formulated on the basis of precisely the same logic as Marshall employed when he declared that 'the Colonies will not and ought not to allow the competition of English manufactures to strangle their rising industries'.[108] What is important to remember is that Marshall did not formulate such a defence and that, faced with the acknowledged threat of *Made in Germany*, he chose to point, as if with an invisible hand, to 'the increasing need which British business has of that fluidity, that freedom from artificial restrictions, by which it has held its own in spite of some disadvantages . . . It has long been manifest that England is threatened by a cloud very much bigger than a man's hand. But the greater the chance of rough weather, the more rash are they, who would impetuously cut away a support of our prosperity.'[109] Latent economies of size may where appropriate be encouraged by means of a subsidy granted to an industry experiencing increasing returns or by means of government-sponsored research and development and analogous external economies. A protective duty, however, should be used exclusively as a last resort when 'no other help is possible', for it is no less than 'a clumsy, wasteful, demoralizing method' of rendering assistance: the industry in question 'wants to be waked: and a Protective duty would be a mere sleeping draught'.[110]

At least in the case of an adult industrial nation such as Britain, Marshall believed, there is simply no valid alternative to freedom of international trade, precisely because such a device 'is *not* a device, but the absence of any device. A device contrived to deal with any set of conditions must become obsolete when they change. The simplicity and naturalness of Free Trade – that is, the absence of any device – may continue to outweigh the series of different small gains which could be obtained by any manipulation of tariffs, however scientific and astute.'[111] Internationally as well as intra-nationally, Marshall believed, freedom of trade is an eminently desirable negation of the negation, representing as it does the liberating abolition of 'artificial hindrances to the "simple" and "natural" tendency of each man to deal with those persons who are best able to meet his wants in return for his meeting theirs'.[112] Your deer becomes my beaver, my beaver becomes your deer, and this magic is worked by market, not by plan. Protection would reduce both your economic welfare and mine. Protection should accordingly be avoided by an adult industrial nation such as we are.

Trade, as it happens, involves the beaver I wish to sell as well as the deer I wish to buy; and Marshall, as he grew older in a nation less and less the workshop of the world, was forced to accept that not all adult industrial nations were as concerned with the furtherance of the international division of labour as Britain – in consequence whereof the goods which Britain wished to buy entered tariff-free while the goods which Britain wished to sell were more and more being hammered by 'the blows of foreign tariffs'.[113] This obviously constituted a retrograde development when seen from the point of view of allocation of resources. No less significant, however, are the implications for a social philosophy which linked altruism inextricably to exchange. Whatever happens in home markets, Marshall seems to be saying, the international market would appear to be a world away: 'The time seems far off at which each country will deliberately abstain from any action, which would bring benefit to her, on the ground that it would cause somewhat greater detriment to others.'[114] But if the others, behaving like pigs, rebarbarise their usages, there is still a strong case for Englishmen, behaving like gentlemen, to continue along the path blazed by the Scottish eclectic and by the Parlementarians of the 1840s. Thus it is that our Chapter on microeconomic policy concludes on a note of *laissez-faire*. It is not, however, *laissez-faire* but rather case-by-case pragmatism which best characterises the views which we have encountered; for the views, when all is said and done, were not those of a party hack but rather those of a pensive philosopher who was anxious to do good.

6 Macroeconomic Policy

Keynes expressed his regret in 1925 at 'Marshall's postponement of the publication of his *Theory of Money* until extreme old age, when time had deprived his ideas of freshness and his exposition of sting and strength. There is no part of Economics where Marshall's originality and priority of thought are more marked than here, or where his superiority of insight and knowledge over his contemporaries was greater. There is hardly any leading feature in the modern Theory of Money which was not known to Marshall forty years ago.'[1] *Forty years*: for it was in 1885, 1886, 1887 and 1887–8 respectively that Marshall made important public contributions to national debates on money and macroeconomics (at a time, it must be recorded, of considerable unemployment, depression and distress) by means of his paper to the Industrial Remuneration Conference, his evidence to the Royal Commission on Trade and Industry, his essay on 'Remedies for Fluctuations of General Prices' in *The Contemporary Review* and his testimony to the Gold and Silver Commission. *Less than forty years*: for the first (and, in the event, the only) volume of the *Principles* in the 1890 and in subsequent editions contained brief but tantalisingly stimulating suggestions such as led Wicksell among others to declare that 'the second volume of Marshall's *Principles*, in which he intends to publish a full discussion of monetary questions, will be awaited with the greatest interest';[2] since Marshall addressed these questions in some detail in his evidence to the Indian Currency Committee of 1899 (making in that way a significant early contribution to the application of macroeconomic theories to the problems of developing countries); and because Marshall was, of course, the author of *Money Credit and Commerce* (his only attempt at a complete synthesis of his thinking on the subject – and by 1923, in Keynes' words, 'nearly all his main ideas had found expression in the works of others'[3]). *More than forty years*: for 'The Pure Theory of Domestic Values' and the *Economics of Industry* (both 1879) contain long sections on macroeconomic issues (occasionally incorporated *verbatim* in later writings), and there are also uncompleted papers from an early date which Marshall never subsequently prepared for publication and which demonstrate a considerable grasp of monetary theory. Thus Keynes writes: 'The earliest extant manuscript of Marshall's, written about 1871, deals with his treatment of the Quantity Theory. It is a remarkable example of the continuity of his thought from its first beginnings between 1867 and 1877, that the whole of the substance of Book I, chapter iv of his *Money Credit and Commerce* is to be found here.'[4]

Marshall's thought on monetary and macroeconomic matters displays sophistication as well as continuity; and before we reach his precise policy recommendations – in the concluding section of this Chapter – we must first seek clearly to understand his specific hypotheses with respect to those variables which influence the stability of aggregate demand. The first section of this Chapter deals, accordingly, with the quantity of money, the second with the transmission mechanism, and the third with credit and fluctuations.

6.1 THE QUANTITY THEORY OF MONEY

There have, in the history of economic thought, been authors who described the quantity theory in terms so dehumanised and mechanistic that it might well have been taken to refer, like the second law of thermodynamics, to an automatic process bereft of human decision-making, volition and deliberation. Such was not, however, the approach of a subjectivist such as Alfred Marshall who – long before Hicks's 'suggestion'[1] – extended supply, demand and the marginal revolution even to the theory of money itself. Marshall's usual position was that, the more I have of a thing, the less I value it; and in his famous Appendix F to the *Principles* he applied this result to the case of A (who has apples but wants nuts) and of B (who has no apples and wants to spend nuts in order to acquire them). A and B are rationally induced to exchange and barter, for each wishes to maximise his utility and minimise his disutility. As they trade,

> every apple that A loses will increase the marginal utility of apples to him and make him more unwilling to part with any more: while every additional nut that he gets will lower the marginal utility of nuts to him and diminish his eagerness for more: and *vice versa* with B. At last A's eagerness for nuts relatively to apples, will no longer exceed B's; and exchange will cease because any terms that

> the one is willing to propose would be disadvantageous to the other. Up to this point exchange has increased the satisfaction on both sides, but it can do so no further.[2]

In the barter instance the marginal utility of both that which is given up and that which is acquired varies in the course of exchange as the parties gravitate inexorably towards general equilibrium. The same theoretical result holds in monetary economics as well when instead of apples we speak of the effective money supply and instead of nuts we speak of all commodities (goods, services and financial assets) which serve as alternatives to the holding of money in the form of idle balances. The laws which determine the value of money are evidently no different from the laws which determine the value of any other item in a market economy, and unambiguously bound up with 'that balancing of advantages which in the ultimate analysis must be found to determine the magnitude of every quantity which rests upon the will of man'.[3]

The total amount of monetary demand in a nation that can be spent on goods, services and financial assets depends upon two variables – the quantity of money and the velocity of circulation. Each of these much now be considered in turn if we are subsequently to be in a position to make statements of a general nature concerning money, velocity and prices.

(1) The quantity of money

Money, said Marshall, 'is not desired mainly for its own sake, but because its possession gives a ready command of general purchasing power, in a convenient form' – analogous therefore to a railway ticket save in the sense that the latter medium commands one and only one commodity ('A railway ticket is desired for the sake of the journey over which it gives control') while the former (representing as it does purchasing power that is general and not specific) has the ability to command any and all commodities.[4] If, therefore, you as an economist should be asked to indicate 'what is the nature of the advantage which each individual obtains from keeping on hand a large stock of money', you will no doubt think immediately of general acceptability in exchange and reply that 'he thereby retains in his hands what may be called a large ready command over commodities in general'.[5] Such instantaneous liquidity with respect to transactions of all kinds is not something of which that individual could so readily boast should he have on hand not a stock of money but instead, let us say, a horse:

> If a man has a horse he may be said to have potentially the command over any other commodities which he might possibly be able to obtain in exchange for the horse but he could not in general obtain for it nearly its full value in those particular commodities which he might happen to want readily, that is (he could not) by direct exchange. If instead of the horse he has the money which is its equivalent he is able to obtain readily the full amount of its value in any kind of commodities which are offered for sale in the markets accessible to him. It is therefore with the object of being able readily to satisfy such of his wants as he cannot easily make provision for a long time beforehand that a person desires to retain in his possession a supply of money.[6]

A man who holds cash has 'the advantage of being able to buy little things when he wants to' while a man who holds sheep must not only defer satisfying his wants at the best of times but is vulnerable in addition to the uncertain, the unknowable and the unknown: 'If he happens to want money unexpectedly he must wait till he has sold his sheep: thereby incurring inconvenience and possibly making a bad bargain owing to his being pressed for time.'[7] A man who is rational enough to appreciate that he cannot spend sheep in an Oxford Street emporium and who is able correctly to perceive that no one can forecast the future with complete accuracy will therefore be quick to value 'the advantage that the possession of cash gives of buying exactly what he wants'[8] – and will demand some money.

The principal function of money is 'to facilitate business transactions'[9] and to help the community break free of the inconveniences and delays associated with the barter system. Money is a 'flux' which 'makes real capital fluid, and enables it to get at its work'.[10] Its authority can come from law or custom or even from intrinsic value, and that is why any or all of quite a large number of assets might with perfect propriety be appointed to serve as money: 'Money needs only to be a clearly defined, easily handled, and generally acceptable medium of exchange.'[11] The test of whether a particular asset is up to the task assigned to it is evidently no more than whether it is up to the task assigned to it – whether, in other words, it is popularly accepted 'without doubt or special inquiry'[12] in transactions involving goods, services and debt. Money is used in 'bargains that are completed almost as soon as they are begun' and is attractive 'because its value can be read at a glance'.[13] It is also widely used as a standard of value with respect not only to current but also to deferred payments and contracts involving time – and here, it must be confessed, definite problems can arise where the general price level is not stable and the real value of money in consequence not constant.

Turning now to specific assets, it is clear that coins with an intrinsic value (say, in gold or silver) are money, and so too is convertible paper 'issued by Government or other competent authority':[14] these assets, after all, represent 'media of exchange, which pass freely from hand to hand, even among persons who are strangers to one another; and thus transfer the command of amounts of general purchasing power, which are set out in clear type on their faces'.[15] The advantage of a metallic currency supported by paper known to be convertible on demand into specie is clearly that it 'passes from hand to hand as a means of purchasing, without requiring any special or trade knowledge on the part of those who handle it'.[16] Britain remained on the Gold Standard from 1821 to 1914 – a period which embraced Marshall's formative years and virtually the whole of his active academic life – and convertibility was to him an important reason why the "flux" of paper was indeed "generally accepted" in his own times.

Important certainly, but not always adequate. In Marshall's time, after all, and despite the gradualist but centralising provisions of the Bank Charter Act of 1844, some private banks other than the Bank of England still retained the right of note-issue. These non-Bank notes were as much a part of the money-supply as were Bank notes and coins, but they were also more vulnerable insofar as they only circulated so long as the issuer remained 'in good repute'.[17] Obviously, where rumours were about that a particular private bank had 'got into trouble'[18] and might, approaching insolvency, be unable *tomorrow* to convert its paper into Bank notes or specie, that paper was likely rapidly to become unacceptable for the purposes of exchanges made *today*. Convertibility, it is evident, is by itself insufficient without the expectation of *continued* convertibility. Expectations, needless to say, reside in the mind, not in the asset – and they are also notorious for their volatility.

Paper and coin in any case are, as Marshall noted in 1899, 'but a small part of the means of payment used in England; and under most, though not all, conditions, bank money is the main means of payment; and that is elastic.'[19] Nowadays, Marshall is saying, there exist 'artificial substitutes for the currency as means of payment',[20] and one of the most popular of these is the cheque, an instrument which, in England, has already 'displaced both coin and bank notes in nearly all wholesale and in many retail transactions'.[21] Clearly, a cheque is not as readily acceptable in the shops as, for instance, a gold coin would be: 'A cheque requires the receiver to have formed some opinion for himself as to the individual from whom he receives it. If a stranger offers me a 5*l*.note, I am willing to give him five sovereigns for it, if I feel sure it is a genuine note; but if he offers me a cheque, I will not give him anything for that, because I have no special knowledge of him.'[22] Where, however, I do have the requisite 'special knowledge' – both of him and of his bank – then I am quite happy to treat his cheque *as if* gold coin; and in such a case that cheque has an impact on quantities and prices identical to that of the coin of which it takes the place. We all know how frequently cheques are used in this way: 'In England a large purchase is generally effected, not by transfer of currency itself, but by transfer of a cheque (or other document) that gives command over currency.'[23] So great, indeed, is the amount of business today transacted by means of the cheque that currency is coming to appear positively old-fashioned: 'The total value of currency needed by the business of England is relatively small. For her middle and upper classes discharge most of their considerable obligations by cheques; and but few of these cheques are presented for payment in cash: most of them merely transfer command over currency from one banking account to another.'[24] Not all classes, of course, are so firmly ensconced in the cashless society, and Marshall takes pains to point out the significant class bias which aggregative data on the demand for currency function would tend to conceal. Thus, speaking of currency, he says: 'In England, all but the very poor keep a good deal; the lower middle classes keep a relatively very large quantity; while the very rich who pay all their tradesmen by cheques use relatively little.'[25] And, indicating that the tendency at the moment 'is for all well-to-do people to keep less cash about them', he immediately stresses that our nation is hardly made up exclusively of the well-to-do: 'The common people have no bank accounts, and we must recollect that with regard to numbers, it is the common people that count and not the well-to-do people.'[26] Our nation is, however, continuing to evolve, and there is in consequence every reason to expect that today's common people will tomorrow repeat the experience of today's well-to-do in moving from cash to cheques. Institutional change is itself likely to reinforce the trend: 'I think that it would be quite possible for changes in the methods of business to diminish the total amount of purchasing power that people require to keep with them; that, for instance, the growth of the use of small cheques, the extension of banking accounts generally, might diminish the amount of currency.'[27]

Cheques by themselves, it must be emphasized, are no more synonymous with 'bank money' than the coin I spend on a cup of tea is synonymous with my total stock of coins. Some of my coined money may be unspent and lying idle in my pocket even as I drink the tea I have purchased and, similarly, some of my 'bank money' may take the form of a positive balance in my bank-account which I am not just about to liquidate by means of cheques. Marshall, clearly aware that deposits *per se* represent purchasing power in precisely the same manner as do idle coins asleep in the pocket, occasionally conflates the two categories, as where he speaks of a man with 'a large amount of ready purchasing power under his immediate control, either in his own keeping; or in his current account with a bank',[28] or where he declares baldly that gold is held by individuals 'either in their own custody or in their banks'.[29] Bank deposits *per se*, and not merely cheques drawn upon those bank deposits, are, in Marshall's view, unhesitatingly to be taken into account in assessing the national stock of spendable assets. In the expansion of such deposits, moreover, the banks play an active role, the reason being that banks hold fractional reserves and are able as a result to pyramid derivative deposits in 'a geometrical progression' – 'the effect being that if each bank could lend two-thirds of its deposits, the total amount of loaning power got by the banks would amount to three times what it otherwise would be. If it could lend four-fifths, it will then be five times; and so on'.[30] Banks, in other words, not only hold deposits but also create them. The money-multiplier and 'the relation which the amount of bankers' money bears to the amount of currency' is, sadly, a complex problem which 'has never been worked out in public' and which 'has not yet been thoroughly investigated by economists in any country', but 'the most pregnant hints on it are, I think, those given by Mr. Giffen in his *Stock Exchange Securities*'[31] – not least in passages such as the following: 'Say a banker has to keep half the amount of his liabilities in cash, the limit to the credit he can give is measured by this necessity. The moment his deposits are twice the amount of his cash, the amount of his lending must cease. In actual fact, then, the process of extending credit, which seems at first sight indefinite, because the loan which is made to A. is re-deposited directly or indirectly, and then re-lent to B., is not really indefinite.'[32] Marshall the mathematician must have found Giffen's 1877 *tâtonnement* towards 1/n rather primitive, but Marshall the economist was deeply impressed: 'I do not think that his solution is complete, but he seems to have pointed towards the right solution', Marshall told the Gold and Silver Commission in 1887, and the relevant passage in Marshall's personal copy of Giffen's book attracted a note in the margin to the effect that 'this is important, and perhaps not so well brought out elsewhere'.[33]

Banks create derivative deposits by means of redeposited loans and overdrafts; and this reminds us that the expansion of 'bank money' presupposes not only that your banker is willing to supply you with money but also that you are willing to demand that money at a non-zero rate of interest. It takes two to tango, it is easier to pull on a string than to push on a string, and confidence of expectations inevitably plays as important a role in the credit-mechanism as does the quantity of reserves and specification of the ratio. As Marshall puts it, criticising the mechanistic approach to deposit-creation, 'I think it important to insist that the supply of the precious metals is only one of many causes that affect the expansion of credit'.[34] At the same time, the supply of the precious metals is an important part of deposit-creation; and when, say, a favourable balance of trade brings gold into the country, undeniably 'the influx of gold inclines bankers to enlarge their loans'.[35] Those loans do not in themselves generate derivative deposits, and borrowers have a perfect right to carry off their money in the form of currency. If, however, they are confident and optimistic, then borrowers are likely to develop 'habits and temperaments' such as induce them to employ 'surrogates'[36] including current accounts, seeing as they will do that such 'surrogates' are 'commonly accepted';[37] and in such a case 'perhaps little or none of the new gold may go at once into currency: but the substitutes for currency are increased: and prices will be restrained from falling, even if they are not set on a rise'.[38] Borrowers will, of course, be less keen to hold 'surrogates' when the economy is disturbed and fears abound concerning default. Hence the unfortunate result that 'the effective stock of the means of discharging monetary obligations are in danger of being curtailed at those times, at which the amount of work set for them is greatest'.[39] The mind creates the moneyness of money which lubricates the wheels of trade; and sometimes the mind destroys all or part of its own creation.

Cheques and bank-accounts do not by any means constitute the only monetary instruments to which the precious metals and convertible notes can 'delegate their functions',[40] and bills of exchange in particular have been among the leading 'surrogates' for currency. Henry Thornton himself, by whom Marshall was much influenced, said in 1802 that 'bills and notes constitute what is called the circulating medium, or paper currency, of the country'.[41] Marshall adds to this in 1923 the historical fact that 'the chief means of payment (sometimes even spoken of as "currency") in English manufacturing districts early in last century, consisted of bills of exchange'.[42] Obviously bills of exchange were not then and are not now gold coins, but they could and can nonetheless, so long as confidence is maintained, serve as close substitutes – closer indeed than cheques in cases where local banks were not trusted and people 'often felt themselves able to judge the security given by the names on the back of a bill, better than that offered by a neighbouring bank'.[43] In terms of near-money, bills and current accounts are the 'chief of these substitutes'[44] for currency. They are also remarkably similar in origin and function: 'The modern system of credit enables a man who has neither money nor anything that immediately represents money, to obtain from a banker or other money dealer the means of purchasing goods. He can do this not only on his own credit (as when a bank allows him a "Book credit"), but on the credit of others who have undertaken to pay him money at a future date (as when he "discounts a Bill").'[45] Which is not, of course, to deny that a bill is qualitatively different from a cheque. On the minus side, a bill is typically (but not always) less liquid because of the information problem: 'Since a bill of exchange cannot pass freely from hand to hand, unless everyone to whom it is tendered, knows at least one of the signatures on it; and since there is no easy means of ascertaining whether this condition is satisfied in any particular case, even such bills of exchange are better described as substitutes for currency than as money or currency.'[46] On the plus side, a bill yields an income to the holder (the creditor) which induces him to retain the asset rather than to exchange it for another (whether an investment or a consumable): 'In this respect it is even less properly to be classed as pure money than is a good cheque; for there is no similar gain to be got from holding a cheque.'[47] Differences apart, however, the fact remains that if I lack notes and coin and want goods I have the option of discounting a bill as well as writing a cheque (perhaps on a borrowed deposit), and he who neglects the wide spectrum of spendable assets at my disposal does so at the risk of underestimating just how much shopping I am in reality capable of doing.

No less distinguished a quantity theorist than Knut Wicksell criticised the naive formulations of the quantity theory for assuming either that all exchanges or that a constant proportion of exchanges were transacted through the medium of money, 'in the sense of coin or notes': 'In actual fact the border line between money in this sense and true instruments of credit (ordinary book credit, bills, cheques, etc.) is extremely vague; and over a wide range one can be substituted for the other – and on occasion is so substituted.'[48] No less imaginative a quantity theorist than Henry Thornton undermined the static formulations of the quantity theory by underlining the extent to which new forms of quasi-liquidity are constantly evolving, including 'the custom of transacting payments by means of entries in books, and of other expedients': 'In proportion as contrivances of this sort prevail; and they must abound more and more as commercial knowledge advances in the world; the demand for bullion will be diminished.'[49] Both the point concerning a wide range of substitutes and the point concerning the dynamic development of instruments are central to the monetary thought of Alfred Marshall, as the following will serve to demonstrate:

> As commerce advances, cheques, book credits, promissory bills, bills of exchange real and fictitious, exchequer bills, circular notes and lastly clearing houses are established. The effect of these contrivances is to cause other modes of exchange to be substituted for those into which money enters. They render many kinds of transactions possible which would otherwise have been impossible, they accelerate others; and, being employed only where they are more convenient than payment by cash, they increase the convenience of all transactions into which they enter. They cause the amount of commodities over which persons choose to keep a command in the form of money to diminish.[50]

We began by substituting notes for coins (learning as we did so that 'they pass freely from hand to hand, and exert nearly the same influence over prices as an equivalent amount of coined money does'[51]) and are now showing considerable ingenuity in dreaming up ever more near-money assets: 'Changes in the methods of business are certainly diminishing the amount of currency we require to do a given amount of business.'[52] The more backward Indians, on the other hand, are now at a stage in their economic evolution where they are actually making an ever greater use of currency: 'It seems to me that, as India is passing from what we may call a medieval condition to a modern Western condition, it is using a great deal more currency as a specific medium of exchange on modern methods in lieu of the old-fashioned barter and payment of dues in kind.'[53] It is therefore tautologous to say that 'the volume of the business in each country, which requires the use of coin, is determined by her wealth and habits'[54] – and vital to remember that the 'wealth and habits' of all countries are not constant but variable. Matter is in motion as the clock ticks on, and the precise specification as well as the absolute amount of spendable assets in an economy is in truth relative and transitory, the product both of place and of time. Besides that, different horses are suited to different courses and/or to different riders, and this in itself is a good enough reason for a loose constructionist to recommend elasticity and flexibility in the definition of the term 'money': 'There are some inquiries in which it may with advantage be used narrowly, and others in which a broad use of it is appropriate.'[55] Marshall may have been vague and woolly but he was also undogmatic and open; and in definitions as in life, he seems to be saying, there is much truth in the proposition that you pays your assets and you takes your choice.

(2) The velocity of money

Even if we know precisely what money is, we still have no conception of the magnitude of total demand as expressed in monetary terms – since each unit of money may be employed more than once in a given time period. In order to ascertain the magnitude of total demand as expressed in monetary terms, we need to take into account 'the rapidity of circulation'[56] ('the average number of times that each coin or each element of the currency changes hands during the year'[57]) and the causes that govern it.

The fact is that 'in every state of society there is some fraction of their income which people find it worth while to keep in the form of currency'.[58] Whatever that fraction ('it may be a fifth or a tenth or a twentieth'), it is determined by the work which, it is expected, money will have to do, and by the preferred form of purchasing power with respect to the performance of that expected work. Thus it is that 'the amount of coins which a person cares to keep in his pocket is determined by the amount of business he has to do, and by the proportion which that part of his payments which he finds it most convenient to make in currency bears to the whole'.[59]

Some trades are more currency-intensive than others ('A shop-keeper with an income of 1000 *l.* a year would be likely to use a great deal more gold than an architect with the same income'[60]) and sectoral shifts in the economy can therefore exert an influence on the demand for currency. So can an alteration in overall wealth, either real ('The amount of coin which a person finds it convenient to carry about, taking one with another, depends upon his general wealth'[61]) or nominal ('I think that, the habits of business being unchanged, a rise of prices requires an increase of the coin in people's pockets to sustain it'[62]). Nor should one neglect the extent to which improvements in the methods of business permit of greater use of currency-economising financial instruments (bank-drafts and telegraphic transfers, for example); while an atmosphere of confidence and general *embourgeoisement* is, as we have seen, favourable to the use of the cheque and the bill on occasions where in less fortunate times the coin (and perhaps the convertible note) would have been employed.

Currency is convenient. It is not, however, a free good, in the sense that if money-holders are plunging their resources in idle balances, then they are by definition not purchasing the services of those consumables and investments to which it constitutes a genuine alternative: 'A large command of resources in the form of currency renders their business easy and smooth, and puts them at an advantage in bargaining; but, on the other hand, it locks up in a barren form resources that might yield an income of gratification if invested, say, in extra furniture; or a money income, if invested in extra machinery or cattle.'[63] Because, in other words, of positive opportunity-cost, the demand curve for money balances is not infinitely elastic and money-holders may be expected rationally to relate their real balances to the marginal utility of the liquidity thereby acquired: 'Currency held in the hand yields no income: therefore everyone balances (more or less automatically and instinctively) the benefits, which he would get by enlarging his stock of currency in the hand, against those which he would get by investing some of it either in a commodity – say a coat or a piano – from which he would derive a direct benefit; or in some business plant or stock exchange security, which would yield him a money income.'[64] The money-holder is nobody's fool and quite sensibly weighs, acting as usual on the basis of 'instinct and experience'[65] but hardly the prisoner of the past for that, the costs of holding money against the benefits to be expected therefrom: 'He knows that, if he keeps too little purchasing power at his command, he will be frequently brought into straits; and that if he keeps an inordinate quantity, he will diminish the material sources of his income, and yet may find but few occasions on which he can turn the whole of his ready purchasing power to any great advantage.'[66] The money-holder's lot is not a happy one, but one thing in an uncertain world is certain: he is a natural and a continuous maximiser (of utility if a consumer, of return if an investor) even with respect to the inventories of cash which he holds at the ready. Such a picture of the money-holder as an economiser and a decision-maker definitively renders redundant the concept of constant velocity and fixed coefficients as between money and commodities. The 'rapidity of circulation' is not a thing to be regarded as exogenous and to be taken for granted. On the contrary, it is in every sense a part of the drama of general equilibration and a thing to be explained.

The money-holder is sensitive not only to current values but also to expected future values, and these too must be incorporated into an account of his motives and attitudes with respect to his portfolio. If, for instance, he loses confidence in an inconvertible currency, then he will seek to run down his stocks before they lose their value: in such a case a reckless expansion in the money-supply tends to 'incline everyone to hold a rather smaller share of his resources in that form than he otherwise would', a reaction which obviously is likely to 'lower the value of each unit more than in proportion to the increase'.[67] If, again, he experiences general apprehension concerning the state of his nation, then he will seek to stockpile precious metals in which he retains faith: thus hoarding 'is always greatest after a collapse . . . of commercial undertakings in which the country people have been lured on to invest their savings'.[68] If, finally, he observes fluctuations in the price-index of commodities, then he will seek to make a speculative gain (or avoid a loss) by varying in the appropriate manner the stock of cash that he holds: 'The demand for a metal for the purposes of hoarding is increased by a continued rise in its value and diminished by a continued fall, because those people who hoard believe that what has been rising in value for some time is likely to go on rising and *vice versa*. Thus the law of demand for a metal for the purpose of hoarding is the opposite of the law of demand for a commodity for the purpose of using it.'[69] The position here is in effect nothing but the macroeconomic analogue of the speculative holding of stocks of a non-perishable commodity in the microeconomic market-period, where expected future price-levels acquire the status of an independent causal variable in the theoretical explanation of the supply-curve.[70] It would be reasonable to infer that Marshall extended this approach to embrace expected future interest-rates as well; and that he, like Keynes, was able to conceive of a speculative motive for holding money (even at a non-zero interest rate) in anticipation of a coming rise.[71] It is interesting to note that Keynes himself regarded the older idea of 'hoarding' (particularly if read as 'propensity to hoard') as a 'first approximation'[72] to his own theory of liquidity preference.

(3) Money, velocity and prices

It is obvious that if we double demand as expressed in monetary terms (the product of money supply times velocity of money) we will ultimately double supply as expressed in monetary terms (the product of average price per transaction times number of transactions): 'Gold prices in England and rouble prices in Russia', Marshall declared, 'are determined by the work which the currency has to do in either country on the one hand and the volume of that currency on the other',[73] and he said that 'if the currency in gold countries is large relatively to the business which it has to do, prices then will be high'.[74] Prices in England, Marshall told the Gold and Silver Commission, 'are determined by the relation in which the amount of business done in England stands to the volume of the currency, *account being taken of the methods of business*'.[75] Once, however, the methods of business are to be taken into account, then it would be unfair not to take a multiplicity of other independent variables into account; and at that point the beautiful simplicity of the pure quantity theory ('the now familiar doctrine that the value of a unit of currency varies ... inversely with the number of units and their average rapidity of circulation'[76]) is revealed to be vulnerable to its own explicit assumption of *ceteris paribus*: 'I hold that prices vary directly with the volume of currency, if other things are equal; but other things are constantly changing.'[77] Ricardo was a strict constructionist on the question of proportionality: 'If the mines cease to supply the annual consumption of the precious metals, money will become more valuable, and a smaller quantity will be employed as a circulating medium. The diminution in the quantity will be proportioned to the increase of its value.'[78] Compared with Ricardo, Marshall appears a sizeable sceptic indeed: 'I accept the common doctrine that prices generally rise, other things being equal, in proportion to the volume of the metals which are used as currency', he confirmed to the Gold and Silver Commission, but then immediately added 'I think that changes in the other things which are taken as equal are very often, perhaps generally, more important than the changes in the volumes of the precious metals'.[79] With friends such as Marshall, one reflects, the quantity theory did not need enemies.

Marshall was not a strict constructionist with respect to the quantity approach. Nor, however, was he a complete atheist who denied that money matters. Far from it, in fact, and Marshall was able indeed to adduce real-world evidence which pointed to the important influence of demand as expressed in monetary terms on other economic variables, including nominal values. Thus he reported that, in the early 1840s, 'the world's stock of gold had been shrinking relatively to the work it had to do; and, in consequence, general prices had been falling: but the new supplies of gold, coming suddenly from California and Australia, upset men's cool judgement and forced general prices up to a temporarily inflated level'.[80] And, speaking of India in the 1890s, Marshall, reasoning that it was only common sense to infer that 'the general conditions of the country' impose 'a certain amount of work on her currency',[81] had this to say about demand-pull inflation caused quite clearly by an expansion in that currency relative to that work: 'I think the level of prices is higher than it would have been had there not been so much importation of silver for currency purposes. Had silver not been imported for those purposes, then I think prices could not have risen and would probably have fallen, because there was an increased demand for currency owing to the adoption of Western methods of business.'[82] Marshall did not deny the importance of demand as expressed in monetary terms on other economic variables. Simply, with his belief in the potential elasticity of the spendable asset supply, his emphasis on a variable 'rapidity of circulation', his concern with the volatility of expectations – to say nothing of supply-side changes over time in real variables such as population and output, industrial integration (which reduces the percentage of business transactions effected directly via money)[83] and market-imperfections (as where unions and cartels make nominal values sticky when they should be flexible and responsive) – Marshall was not a confident man who loudly proclaimed that $M\overline{V} = P\overline{Q}$[84] but rather a cautious man who feared that there might be many an unforeseen slip twixt cup and lip in monetary as in all branches of economics.

Such caution Marshall shares with a number of other eminent theorists who have considered the proportionality rule. With Thornton: 'An exact correspondence between the quantity of paper and the price of commodities can by no means be expected always to subsist.'[85] With Giffen: 'The rule is correct of course only with certain conditions. To give it validity, it must be assumed that a scarcity of money produces no expedients for economising money, and that an abundance of money does not lead to want of economy, which can hardly ever be the actual conditions of life.'[86] With Wicksell: "The Quantity Theory is *theoretically* valid so long as the assumption of *ceteris paribus* is firmly adhered to. But among the "things" that have to be supposed to remain "equal" are some of the flimsiest and most intangible factors in the whole of economics – in particular the velocity of circulation of money, to which in fact all the others can be more or less directly referred back. It is consequently impossible to decide *a priori* whether the Quantity Theory is *in actual fact* true – in other words, whether prices and the quantity of money move together in practice'.[87] With Fisher: 'Since periods of transition are the rule and those of equilibrium the exception, the mechanism of exchange is almost always in a dynamic rather than a static condition. . . . As to the periods of transition . . . an increase in M produces effects not only on the p's, but on all the magnitudes in the equation of exchange . . . . Therefore the "quantity theory" will not hold true strictly and absolutely during transition periods.'[88] Marshall was clearly not the only monetary economist to adopt a position of considerable caution with respect to the quantity theory. But when all the requisite modifications have been made, Marshall said, the quantity theory then becomes 'almost a truism',[89] and he was not one for leaning against the prevailing winds in the case of a proposition of such exceptional veracity – as in the following: 'Whatever the state of society, there is a certain volume of their resources which people of different classes taken one with another care to keep in the form of currency; and, if everything else remains the same, then there is this direct relation between the volume of currency and the level of prices, that, if one is increased by 10 per cent, the other also will be increased by 10 per cent.'[90] Cautious quantity theorist though he was, Marshall was – despite his caution – a quantity theorist nonetheless.

6.2 THE TRANSMISSION MECHANISM

Suppose, starting from a position of equilibrium, that there were to be an influx of bullion into Britain and into the City of London. Britain as a nation is in the first instance economically indifferent; for money (whatever form it takes) is sterile, and the increased quantity of it in a country does not *per se* mean that the country is better off or worse off than before. A greater quantity of money *per se* 'does not increase the amount of capital, in the strictest sense of the word; it does not increase the amount of building materials, machinery, etc.'[1] Money may be called capital by careless people, but the economist knows better, aware as he is that 'it is, of course, real capital alone that can provide the substantial force needed to make business prosperous'.[2] Once, therefore, the extra command via extra money caused by the influx of bullion has worked its way through the system, once we have all settled in to a new position of equilibrium then we are all likely to grasp that money in comparative statics is nothing but a veil: 'A mere permanent increase of currency does not make capital more fluid; it simply depreciates the currency.'[3] No one wants the shadow when he can have the substance; and that is why we are all likely ultimately to say with Marshall 'I do not think that any change in the counters which are used will have any effect whatever upon the general course of trade.'[4] Comparing one position of equilibrium with another, the fact is that real variables determine real variables, nominal variables determine nominal variables, and the two kinds of variables are – *ceteris paribus* – strictly dichotomised one from the other. As Patinkin puts it, speaking of their irrelevance of the money supply for the determination of exchange ratios and relative real values:

> To say that these values are independent of the nominal quantity of money is to say that they can be determined even without knowing this quantity. This permits us to conceive of the pricing process of our exchange economy as being divided into two successive stages: In the first one, specification of the real framework determines the equilibrium values of the real variables of the system. In the second, specification of the monetary framework then determines the equilibrium value of the monetary variable – for this value is simply the ratio between the specified nominal quantity of money and the equilibrium real quantity.[5]

All of economics is not, as it happens, captured by comparative statics; and money, however irrelevant when we juxtapose one position of equilibrium with another, is far from neutral in the disequilibrium states that constitute the adjustment process – and which indeed are more the rule than the exception in a dynamic economy which not only changes but goes on changing. Two impact-variables – the rate of interest and the level of prices – are of particular importance in demonstrating that money can and does influence real variables and the general course of trade. It is with these two impact-variables that we shall be concerned in this section.

(1) The rate of interest

When new bullion flows into Britain (or when, alternatively, existing currency is dishoarded), its effect, as soon as it reaches the money-merchants of Lombard Street, is clearly to 'make people inclined to lend more':[6] 'It does increase the amount of command over capital which is in the hands of those whose business it is to lend to speculative enterprise. Having this extra supply, lenders lower still more the rate which they charge for loans, and they keep on lowering it till a point is reached at which the demand will carry off the larger supply.'[7] Thus it is that an influx of bullion, leading as it does to an expansion of bank-loans made to households and firms, has the same effect as that expansion in the credit-base which is brought about in the work of Keynes by central bank purchases of government securities – namely, a fall in the rate of interest due to an increase in the money-supply.

The influx of gold swells deposits and encourages lenders to reduce interest-rates in an effort to attract borrowers into their shop, and much of that which is borrowed is spent on capital goods: 'While credit is expanding, the extra purchasing power which credit gains goes chiefly to traders and trading companies, who, whether they want it to begin or to extend their business, are sure to spend a great part of it on machinery, buildings, ships, railway material, and other forms of Fixed Capital.'[8] An increase in the supply of money in such a case clearly has a significant dynamic effect on the economy; for it stimulates investment by capitalists in the marginal machine which previously did not attract them but which, at the lowered rate of interest, becomes 'just worth their while to employ'.[9] In the short-run disequilibrium situation, Marshall is saying, the classical dichotomy does not hold and an explicitly monetary rate of interest can without doubt induce expanded output in the real sector of the economy.

The long-run equilibrium case is somewhat different, however: 'The supply of gold exercises no permanent influence over the rate of discount. . . . All that the influx of gold does is to make a sort of ripple on the surface of the water.'[10] Whatever may happen in the short run, in other words, money is strictly neutral in the long run with respect to the rate of interest – and in practice as well as in theory: 'I conceive that the average rate of discount during the last ten years has had nothing to do with the supply of precious metals . . . . If the supply of the precious metals had been twice larger, then the average rate of discount would not have been affected considerably.'[11] Ignoring 'ripples' and looking instead at 'permanent' influences and 'average' values, what we find basically is that 'the permanent rate of discount has no connection with the amount of currency'[12] ('gold and silver merely acting as counters with regard to it'[13]), that the rate of interest is determined not by the money supply but by the relationship between the supply of savings and the relevant demand – between 'the amount of capital seeking investment' (which reflects 'parsimony' and 'prospectiveness', themselves proxies for cultural and societal variables such as commitment to children[14]) and 'the extent and the richness of the field for the investment of capital'[15] (which reflects 'profitableness' and 'productivity' on the part of the representative business – the word representative converts partial into general equilibrium analysis – combined with the consumption demand of 'thriftless borrowers who desire to anticipate future incomes'[16]): 'Interest, being the price paid for the use of capital in any market, tends towards an equilibrium level such that the aggregate demand for capital in that market, at that rate of interest, is equal to the aggregate stock forthcoming there at that rate.'[17] Money does not enter into it – as Ricardo had said ('The rate of interest for money is totally independent of the nominal amount of the circulating medium. It is regulated solely by the competition of capital, not consisting of money.'[18]), and Mill: 'The rate of interest . . . depends essentially and permanently on the comparative amount of real capital offered and demanded in the way of loan.'[19] Marshall was truly being fully 'classical', in the sense of Keynes,[20] when he reached the following conclusion concerning the two blades of the scissors of funds: 'The rate of interest for long loans is governed on the one side by the needs of businesses for capital to carry them through the undertakings which they have in hand, or in view; and, on the other side by the amount of capital which is not as yet specialized or 'fixed' in any particular use. This amount is in effect the excess of recent aggregate production over the corresponding consumption of wealth; together with the amount of new wealth, which has already been given over to productive uses, but is not yet distinctly specialized to any one.'[21]

Money to Marshall is potent in the short run and impotent in the long run insofar as its impact on the rate of interest is concerned. Before, however, we are able to turn to the level of prices (the second element in our discussion of the transmission mechanism), it is necessary to clarify several complexities in Marshall's interpretation and application of the classical theory of interest.

First, all that is commonly called interest is not in the event interest as Marshall uses the term. Interest to Marshall means exclusively the return to free, non-embodied loanable resources – to funds on the loose and in search of an investment. Interest therefore is not the return to investible funds already invested – to resources not on the loose but tied up in projects where a sudden change of mind is not possible: 'The income derived from capital already invested in particular things, such as factories or ships, is properly a quasi-rent.... The phrase "the general rate of interest" applies in strictness only to the anticipated net earnings from new investments of free capital.'[22] Thence the paradox of interest, that, because here as elsewhere bygones are forever bygone, interest *per se* only exists in the mind and can never *per se* actually be earned: 'It cannot be repeated too often that the phrase "the rate of interest" is applicable to old investments of capital only in a very limited sense.'[23] Interest *per se* refers, in other words, always to new flows and never to old stocks.

Second, the 'profitableness of business' as well as the rate of interest dwells exclusively in the mind at that moment when the investment decision is being made, for it is expected and future returns – not current (which is to say past or historic) returns – which most crucially influence the demand for loans. If, for example, the business community entertains expectations ('whether well founded or not') that 'general prosperity is likely to be high', then they will, other things being equal, increase their borrowing and expand their plant; and this is why 'the rate of interest often rises rather high, under the influence of hope, in an ascending phase of industrial and commercial activity and prosperity'.[24] If, on the other hand, the business community foresees bad times ahead (due, let us say, to an anticipated outflow of bullion and the consequent contraction in currency), then they will, other things being equal, decrease their borrowing; for 'people are unwilling to borrow if they think that prices will fall',[25] let alone become involved in 'new enterprises'.[26] All interest rates fluctuate in accordance with the volatility of beliefs – short rates, however, most of all: 'The rates of interest for short periods, and of discount, are of course often changed at short intervals, in accordance with fluctuations in the general activity of the markets and their confidence as to the prosperity of the near future.'[27] The long rate would seem to be more stable and even to possess a 'natural' or a 'normal' level around which market rates are seen to oscillate and towards which they are seen from both sides to gravitate: 'When the economic conditions of a country have been nearly uniform for a long period of time, the supply of capital is such, that the rate of interest which can be obtained for it is that which has been required to cause this supply to be forthcoming; and the rate thus determined is the Normal rate. The rate is in equilibrium when it is just that at which the whole supply of capital can find employment.'[28]

Third, while it is conceptually possible that 'economic conditions' could be 'nearly uniform' over long periods, it is highly unlikely in practice that this will be the case in the *very* long run. Reality in truth is dynamic, not static, and it is therefore extremely improbable in a progressive economy such as that of modern Britain that today's 'normal' levels will survive long enough to be regarded as permanently 'normal' levels. Equilibrium is moving and moving on, and that is why an evolutionary thinker such as Marshall was able both to identify today's normal value ('about four per cent. a year on good security'[29]) and to predict its self-transcendence due to forces already operative within the system: 'I do not see any necessity at all why interest should be more than 2 per cent. a century hence.'[30] Specifically, the principal cause of this secular trend downward in the rate of interest is an increasingly abundant supply of savings relative to the demand for such loanable capital: 'It seems to me that the great economic feature of this age, more important than every other fact put together, is that the amount of capital is increasing many times as fast as that of population . . . . In spite of all the inventions which are continually making new uses for capital in the form of machinery and in other ways, this vast increase forces down the interest that can be got in business.'[31] Such savings is real in nature and not monetary: 'I do not mean the growth of credit, I mean the growth of things, the actual excess of production over consumption.'[32] It is above all else a function of income: 'The power to save depends on an excess of income over necessary expenditure; and this is greatest among the wealthy.'[33] Admittedly saving is also a function of the rate of interest: 'A strong balance of evidence seems to rest with the opinion that a rise in the rate of interest, or demand-price for saving, tends to increase the volume of saving'.[34] Yet the fall in the rate of interest, as we noted in Chapter 3, would not appear to exercise a significant check on the quantity supplied – family affection and habitual frugality are such powerful incentives to action that more rather than less might actually be saved at low rates in an attempt to keep total returns from funds saved at a stable level[35] – and the most one can say about the interest-elasticity of the supply of savings schedule is that it is not likely to be great. Thus it has happened that, while one suspects that 'the higher the rate of interest the greater the saving as a rule',[36] one also knows that the impact of income on saving is far more powerful: 'The amount of capital has been increasing so fast that, in spite of a great widening of the field of investment, it has forced down the rate of discount.'[37] The existence of a trend does not, of course, rule out the incidence of fluctuations – far from it, in fact, as where Marshall speaks as follows about the elasticity of supply of plant: 'An extensive increase in the demand for capital in general will . . . be met for a time not so much by an increase in supply, as by a rise in the rate of interest.'[38] What the existence of a trend does indicate, however, is that even if we net out short-run fluctuations, we have even then not arrived at the permanent normal equilibrium value – since the equilibrium itself is on the move and the value in question therefore not unique. Such a conclusion seems to have come as something of a surprise to the Keynes of the *General Theory*:

> In my *Treatise on Money* I defined what purported to be a unique rate of interest, which I called the *natural rate* of interest – namely, the rate of interest which, in the terminology of my *Treatise*, preserved equality between the rate of saving (as there defined) and the rate of investment . . . I had, however, overlooked the fact that in any given society there is, in this definition, a *different* natural rate of interest for each hypothetical level of employment. And, similarly, for every rate of interest there is a level of employment for which that rate is the "natural" rate, in the sense that the system will be in equilibrium with that rate of interest and that level of employment.[39]

The perception that normal values can prove variable values need not have come as such a surprise; for it is in truth an important part of Alfred Marshall's account of the dynamic properties of interest as time passes and the clock ticks on.

(2) The level of prices

One of the things that most people most like to do with money is to spend it. Obviously the households and firms which borrow money in order to purchase consumables or expand plant may be expected to spend their newly-acquired resources – and while ultimately the expanded plant will lead to an expanded flow of output, what happens in the initial stages is that prices rise as more demand chases fixed or inelastic supply: 'The immediate effect of the starting of new companies is to add to the demand for commodities much more than to the production of commodities.'[40] New bullion (as the source of new loans made at a lowered rate of interest) means more spendable assets in circulation, and those assets if spent on plant will – say, in a year – lead to an increased quantity supplied of commodities; 'but a year is a long time when we are talking of the action of a rate of discount upon speculation and prices'.[41]

The reference to speculation is important and reminds us that it is not only investors in plant who leap at the chance of borrowing at lower rates of interest. Money-merchants lend not only to investors in plant but also to 'speculative investors, who come on the market for goods as buyers, and so raise prices'.[42] Speculators employ borrowed funds, increase the demand for commodities, and – as is so often the case with speculation on the expectation of rising price-levels – help to bring about the very eventuality which they predict: 'People rush to borrow money and buy goods, and thus help prices to rise.'[43] While inflation can be caused by exceptional circumstances (the impact of a harvest failure on India, for example), it is normally changes in the money-supply – via such speculation, together with the demand for funds for the purposes of real investment and households' consumption – that are the chief cause of an overall rise in prices: 'Especially in the West, a sudden rise of prices is generally the result of either currency inflation or improvement in credit.'[44]

Life with inflation is, as it happens, qualitatively different from life without inflation; and once the general price index is perceived to be rising, then that price index ceases to be a passive or dependent variable and becomes itself active and independent, the cause of further and future changes in the economy as well as the effect of past. If therefore you tell me that to double the quantity of money is to double the level of prices, I am likely to reply that your story is incomplete; that you have not fully accounted for the reflux or feedback effect of rising prices on other economic magnitudes; and that you have in particular failed to clarify certain complexities in Marshall's interpretation and application of the classical theory of prices. Those complexities, which have major implications with respect to the validity of the proportionality hypothesis, are three in number.

First, a change in the velocity of money. 'An increase in the volume of a country's currency, other things being equal, will lower proportionately the value of each unit. In fact, if that increase threatens to be repeated, the value of each unit may fall *more than in proportion* to the increase already made.'[45] Once, in other words, a man comes to anticipate a continuing rise in prices, then he tends *ceteris paribus* to run down his stocks of the depreciating asset, lest he subsequently suffer regret at having 'failed to take advantage of a good bargain which came within his reach'.[46] Thus it is that expectations of on-going price rises tend to 'lower the credit of the currency; and incline everyone to hold a rather smaller share of his resources in that form than he otherwise would'.[47] Such a loss of confidence in the currency is productive of apprehension concerning the deferred purchasing-power of money. That apprehension in turn is productive of still more inflation: 'The lower is the credit of the currency, the lower will be the share of their resources which people care to keep in the form of currency; the more, therefore, the currency will be depreciated, and the higher prices will rise.'[48] The optimum quantity of currency is clearly not a mechanistic thing alone but deeply subjective in nature, reflecting as it does popular perceptions concerning the future stability of its value. The less the national currency is believed to be 'firmly set on a sound foundation', the more it is 'distrusted', the more it is linked in the popular imagination to 'disturbances arising from uncertainties as to its quantity or quality',[49] the more people will flee from it – the more the Indians, to take one example, will 'avoid rupees and seek gold and silver bars for their hoards'.[50]

To be fair, however, the rise in velocity in a period of inflation is only *ceteris paribus* – since as prices rise, so does the demand for currency to hold for transactions purposes. Assuming 'methods of business' to be constant (and these at least Marshall does not seem to regard as inflation-sensitive),[51] then 'prices having risen, a person who had found it answer his purpose to have on the average 17*l*. in currency in his pocket, would now require 18*l*. or 19*l*.'[52] Higher prices (quantity of transactions being constant) necessitate larger amounts of cash on hand if they are to be sustainable; and it is worth making the point that 'the volume of things on sale'[53] is itself capable of expansion (due to the taking-in of previously spare or unemployed resources where appropriate and/or to rising average productivity in the usage of existing inputs). When, therefore, an increase in the supply of money increases prices, it is likely to impel me – my social habits and individual peculiarities being constant – in two directions at once: to run down my money balances and to increase my money balances. My decision is neither automatic nor easy where the increased quantity supplied of the asset causes me simultaneously both to demand less and to demand more of the thing, and here as usual I will be guided in my difficult decision by my tentative expectations concerning an unforeseeable future. A money-holder's lot is not a happy one.

Second, a rise in interest rates: 'The general rate of interest will be raised by a gradual and anticipated fall in the value of currency relatively to commodities, and . . . it will be lowered by a rise in that value, even when there is no change in the conditions of general demand and supply. The high rate of interest on permanent investments in India seems to be attributable partly to a relative scarcity of real capital, and partly to the continuous fall in the value of the rupee relatively to the currencies of the West.'[54] So 'high rates do go with high prices'[55] – in part, no doubt, because speculative borrowers are heavily in the market for loans when prices are rising (a demand-side phenomenon), but due too in no small measure to rationality on the supply side and to the desire of the lender to exact compensation for anticipated inflation.

Anticipation is crucial and frequently the horizon is long. If, for example, gold is known to be flowing into the country, then speculators, by the very nature of their calling and temperament prone to be quick off the mark, will borrow on the strength of that rise, but, being clever, well in advance of its occurrence: 'When gold comes to the country it is known and people expect that prices will rise. Now if a person doubting whether to borrow for speculative purposes has reason to believe that prices will rise, he is willing to take a loan at 3 per cent., which before he would not have taken at 2½ per cent., and consequently the influx of gold into the country by making people believe that prices will rise increases the demand for capital and raises therefore, in my opinion, the rate of discount.'[56] If, indeed, the gold-mining industry itself – the chicken and not even the golden egg – is known to be expanding or contracting supplies, experiencing increasing or decreasing costs, then these developments (which are 'canvassed far and wide' due to the obvious premium on accurate intelligence in such a key area of economic life) will have an immediate effect in advance of the gold actually being mined. One does not encounter such splendid reflexes in many areas of economic life – not in the pin-making industry, one would have guessed, and certainly not in construction: 'A fall in the cost of building does not act much on house rents till it has had time to increase considerably the supply of houses.'[57] Money, one is bound to confess, not only matters but is widely perceived to matter. The concerns of the construction industry are somewhat more parochial.

Anticipation is crucial but not always operative; and very often it is the case that economic behaviour is not anticipative but rather reactive with respect to price. In such a situation the lender who keeps his nominal rate of interest constant in the short run is likely to experience a surprise, for as the purchasing power of money falls, so too does his real rate of return: 'Assuming the arts of production to remain stationary and that there is no change in the pressure of population on the means of subsistence, a rise in prices will enable the borrower to pay interest at less outlay and to pay back capital at less outlay than would otherwise be the case.'[58] The problem is a straightforward Wicksellian one – where, in Wicksell's formulation, the expansion in the money-supply leads to an initial reduction in nominal interest rates, thus to price-inflation, therefore to a further fall in (real) interest rates. The problem, fortunately, generates its own solution, basically because borrowers increasingly compete for the possession of that which has, for them, become increasingly cheap. Their competition pulls up nominal interest-rates as a mechanism for allocating credit: 'A high rate of interest always indicates strong demand for the loan of capital. This demand may be the result of lasting general distress; but it is more often the result of expectations, whether well founded or not, that general prosperity is likely to be high.'[59] Lenders too form such expectations, and their shrewd alertness in insuring themselves against a further fall in the value of the currency serves to reinforce the upward pressure on the rate of interest: 'Creditors and lessors can often defend themselves against injury in this matter; for creditors are often quite as able to foresee changes in the purchasing power of money as borrowers are; and they can accommodate the interest which they charge to coming events.'[60] Rationality of expectations with respect to an unknown future is something which clearly differentiates lenders from labourers: 'Those who lend capital are not in so bad a position as those who supply labour. . . . History seems to show that they are able to anticipate changes in the purchasing power of money very much, and to accommodate the rate of interest which they charge to those changes.'[61] Because, however, expectations are unlikely to be fully rational (because foresight is likely in the real world to be less perfect than it would have been, let us say, in the permanent equilibrium of a hypothetical stationary state), because, moreover, reality is dynamic and beliefs once altered are likely to alter again (as, of course, they do in the course of the psychological credit cycle which we examine in the next section), one is bound to be curious as to whether a genuine rate of interest purified of monetary distortions will ever actually emerge. Ricardo, of course, believed that it would, and issued the following declaration on the subject of long-run proportionality: 'It is only during the interval of the issues of the Bank, and their effect on prices, that we should be sensible of an abundance of money; interest would, during that interval, be under its natural level; but as soon as the additional sum of notes or of money became absorbed in the general circulation, the rate of interest would be as high and new loans would be demanded with as much eagerness as before the additional issues.'[62] Marshall, although like Ricardo a quantity theorist, was more cautious, and would probably have taken the view that uncertainty and upheaval in the real world in some measure call into question the mechanical automaticity of $M\bar{V} = P\bar{T}$ and similar models. As Shackle puts it: 'A statistical investigation of the interest-rate, to be effective, valid and meaningful, would have to look into people's thoughts and not merely into their bank statements.'[63] And that, needless to say, no statistical investigation can do.

Third, redistribution of the national income: 'When prices are rising, the rise in the price of the finished commodity is generally more rapid than that in the price of the raw material, always more rapid than that in the price of labour.'[64] All values in a period of monetary expansion are evidently not pulled up at the same time and by the same amount, and this can cause injury and injustice to those left behind when the escalator of inflation commences its climb.

Thus, 'when wages were in great measure fixed by custom or authority in terms of money, operatives generally were likely to be seriously injured by a fall in the real value of the currency, however caused'.[65] In India, for example, money wages are sticky upwards, and that means the unpleasant burden of falling real wages in a period of inflation: 'Indian employés, particularly as they would not be likely to possess an energetic trades union leader who could prompt them as to the right time to strike, would receive wages at the old rate in a currency which was worth less; and they would suffer.'[66]

People in Britain are less-custom-ridden than are the Indians and have the additional benefit of energetic trades union leaders who are deeply concerned with rising wages, nominal and real. Even so, however, prices in Britain seem to rise before wages do, and the lag is the source of forced savings. A steady upward trend in prices thus 'keeps industry somewhat better employed'[67] than does a downward trend – and for this reason Marshall is being uncharacteristically simplistic when he treats money as a veil, as in passages such as the following: 'A supply of currency is but the flux that makes real capital fluid, and enables it to get at its work.'[68] Money is not capital in equilibrium – only command over capital. By the same token, however, money is not neutral in disequilibrium – where monetary expansion creates jobs and stimulates growth in output by virtue of the redistribution of the national income in favour of capital. An increase in spendable assets can clearly have an impact on real (and not merely on nominal) variables where, as Thornton puts it, 'antecedently idle persons' are set to work and 'fresh industry' is called into life: 'It must be . . . admitted, that, provided we assume an excessive issue of paper to lift up, as it may for a time, the cost of goods though not the price of labour, some augmentation of stock will be the consequence; for the labourer, according to this supposition, may be forced by his necessity to consume fewer articles, though he may exercise the same industry.'[69] Needless to say – needless, one hastens to add, because no reader of Hume on inflation could be ignorant of this point – it is, as Hume states, 'only in this interval or intermediate situation, between the acquisition of money and rise of prices, that the encreasing quantity of gold and silver is favourable to industry.'[70] But until 'workmen become scarce', Hume reflected, a rise in prices caused by an 'encrease of gold and silver' can indeed have an impact on employment and output; and it would appear that Marshall took a similar view with respect to the short-run benefits consequent upon the taking-up of slack.

In concluding our discussion of the transmission mechanism and the proportionality hypothesis, we must say this: Marshall stated that 'the purchasing power of a unit of currency varies, other things being equal, inversely with the number of the units'[71] and gave the impression thereby that a change in the money-supply influences nominal but not real variables; but he also demonstrated as clearly as is possible in the field of economics that that impression conceals as much as it reveals. Quantity theorist though he was, Marshall was – despite his quantity theorising – a man of caution nonetheless.

6.3 UPSWINGS AND DOWNSWINGS

Growth, in Marshall's perception of that process, is closely linked with cycles. Cycles, in turn, are closely linked with money and credit. Money and credit, finally, are closely linked with expectations relating to the future course of nominal and real variables. These relationships form the subject of this section.

(i) The boom

The story begins with something new: 'Inflations and contractions of credit and prices will always be caused by wars and rumours of wars, by good and bad harvests, and by the alternative opening out of promising new enterprises, and the collapse of many of the hopes founded on them.'[1] The *deus ex machina* might be nominal (say, the discovery of new supplies of gold in California and Australia) or it might be nothing more sophisticated than a simple recovery of confidence as memories fade of the distrust associated with the antecedent slump. Whatever the nature of the something new, it constitutes the impulse which breeds the boom.

The *deus ex machina* is frequently agricultural in nature, and Marshall's incorporation of the income effect and the falling marginal utility of money are of particular interest: 'The beginning of a period of rising credit is often a series of good harvests. Less having to be spent on food, there is a better demand for other commodities.'[2] A change originating in the real sector – in this case, an expanded quantity supplied of an absolute necessity of which the price in consequence falls – here triggers off a demand-led period of expansion: 'Producers find that the demand for their goods is increasing; they expect to sell at a profit, and are willing to pay good prices for the prompt delivery of what they want.'[3] Where demand for their goods is expanding, they will reason, so therefore should their output produced.

One of the things that they want as they expand is the key input of labour, and what happens then is not difficult to predict: 'Employers compete with one another for labour; wages rise; and the employed in spending their wages increase the demand for all kinds of commodities.'[4] Even at this early stage in the cycle, it would appear, the labour market is already so tight that an increase in the demand for men is already being accompanied by an increase in the price of men. Not exclusively, of course – since some persons previously not in paid employment (men shaken out in some earlier downturn, women who find that the opportunity cost of being housewives has become intolerably high, genuine beginners such as school-leavers and immigrants) will now be taken on. Not proportionately, – since wages and salaries tend initially to have sticky nominal values on balance in the face of fluctuations in supply and demand: 'They can seldom be changed without much friction and worry and loss of time.'[5] But despite modifications and inflexibilities such as these the basic point remains that more demand leads to more income, more income to more demand, and such spending and earning and spending cannot but feed and nourish the upswing: 'Prices, wages and profits go on rising: there is a general rise in the incomes of those engaged in trade: they spend freely, increase the demand for goods and raise prices still higher.'[6] Expectations are as buoyant as incomes, and the result is an encouraging one to the friend of good times: 'The desire to buy and the willingness to pay increased prices grow together.'[7]

Where expectations are buoyant, there speculators are confident and trade confidently on credit: 'Many speculators seeing the rise, and thinking it will continue buy goods with the expectation of selling them at a profit. At such a time a man, who has only a few hundred pounds, can often borrow from bankers and others the means of buying many thousand pounds' worth of goods; and every one who thus enters into the market as a buyer, adds to the upward tendency of prices, whether he buys with his own or with borrowed money.'[8] Here as usual, it would appear, the speculator who rushes to borrow money in order to buy goods actually helps to bring about the very rise in prices the expectation of which had led to his original initiative in the field of borrowing and buying. Meanwhile, the signal number of 'promising openings which shew themselves among the general activity' causes new companies to be founded, old ones to be expanded, and stimulates lenders to be nothing less than 'jubilant' when presented with requests for funds; and 'this movement goes on for some time till at last an enormous amount is being carried on by credit and with borrowed money.'[9] Demand cumulatively breeds demand, workers have well-paid jobs while capitalists enjoy good profits and speculators confidently dream of capital gains. It is all great fun. Sadly, however, it can't last forever; for such a boom in truth carries within it the seeds of its own destruction.

One reason for this is an over-expanded quantity demanded of labour due to the fact that, wages and salaries being fixed in the short-run in money terms, the real value of labour – initially – 'varies in the wrong direction' in the period of demand-led upswing: 'It falls when prices are rising, and the purchasing power of money is falling; so that the employer pays smaller real salaries and wages than usual, at the very time when his profits are largest in other ways, and is thus prompted to over-estimate his strength, and engage in ventures which he will not be able to pull through after the tide begins to turn.'[10] The problem with lagged adjustment would seem to arise because of stickiness of nominal values, on the one hand, and failure to predict their eventual rise on the other: 'When an increase in the demand for a commodity raises its price, the gain at first goes almost entirely into the hands of the manufacturers. But soon their eagerness to extend their business leads them to compete with one another for the hire of labour, and gradually wages rise till a large part of the gain is transferred from the employers to the employed.'[11] A 'large part' is, of course, not the whole part: 'The upward movement in wages is scarcely ever so great in proportion as the upward movement of prices, and therefore scarcely ever so great as the upward movement of the Earnings of Management.'[12] In addition, expectations in wage-bargaining being explicitly non-rational and the prerequisite recognition on the part of the wage-earners being undeniably lagged, the passage of time confers a definite benefit on the employer of labour: 'It may be noticed here that movements in wages almost always follow, and scarcely ever occasion, movements in prices. A rise in price is occasioned by an increased demand: after a time wages rise; still the demand increases, and still the price rises; but the further rise in price is occasioned as the first rise was by the fact that demand has increased more rapidly than supply.'[13] Even the employer of labour, however, would appear inadequately to have grasped that his rise in profits caused by a rise in prices will in due course be nibbled away by a rise in wages. His failure to perceive and anticipate leads to an over-expanded quantity demanded of labour, and this in turn constitutes a real threat to stability should prices rise less rapidly or even not rise at all.

A further threat to stability in the boom is that wastefulness and carelessness which inevitably accompanies a buoyant economy:

> Inflation causes lenders to be careless; all business men seem to be having a large margin of profits; speculative buyers can borrow and become rich by selling for many counters what they have bought for few counters, and their gains, which add nothing to the common stock, are merely the result of successful raids on the common stock; and these gains give to a business a fictitious appearance of prosperity. In such times . . . there is relatively little improvement in machinery and general plant. The seeds of progress are not sown in those times of apparent prosperity.[14]

Admittedly some investment in plant takes place. Admittedly some antecedently idle persons are set to work. But there is a negative side to this as well – 'the launching of frail enterprises by fraudulent or incompetent people who have floated into prosperity at the cost of others on the top of the wave of rising prices'.[15] In the short run it is 'morbid inflation' which keeps such frail craft afloat. Yet they are condemned by their nature eventually to sink.

The greatest threat to stability in the boom has to do with credit. In a highly buoyant economy old firms, new firms, old and new speculators all rush to borrow – and lenders are keen to oblige: 'In the ascending phase, credit has been given somewhat boldly, and even to men whose business capacity has not been proved. For, at such times a man may gain a profit on nearly every transaction, even though he has brought no special knowledge or ability to it; and his success may probably tempt others, of like capacity with himself, to buy speculatively.'[16] Notes and deposits are created via loans and overdrafts, bills of exchange multiply, and the resultant acceleration in inflation, precisely because it pushes down the real rate of interest, stimulates still more borrowing in the anticipation of still further price rises. The expansion in demand is cumulative and multiplicative and is bound to exert some upward pressure on interest rates: 'The loans to one man make him a good customer for others at good prices, and make them therefore eager to borrow, and that makes them good customers; and so the movement grows. Thus, a fall in the purchasing power of money tends after a while, to raise the rate of discount as well as the rate of interest on long investments.'[17] Even at higher rates of interest, however, would-be debtors in a confident mood need not be discouraged and are indeed likely to remain 'impatient to start ill-considered enterprises in order to gain by the expected rise in general prices'.[18] Expected inflation by means of active borrowing in good times is easily translated into realised inflation, and the result is a fall once again in the real rate of interest – and therewith a further stimulus to active borrowing.[19]

In such an environment, it must be conceded, 'trade is in a dangerous condition', and lenders – whose willingness to lend so generously in the upswing is central to the drama of pyramided credit, low interest and rising prices – at last come to see that the time has come to substitute caution for covetousness: 'Those whose business it is to lend money are among the first to read the signs of the times; and they begin to think about contracting their loans. But they cannot do this without much disturbing trade. If they had been more chary of lending at an earlier stage, they would simply have prevented some new business from being undertaken; but when it is once undertaken, it cannot be abandoned without a loss of much of the capital that has been invested in it.'[20] Creditors would appear not only to have over-expanded their loans to a dangerous degree in the upswing but also to show no compunctions, once 'distrust increases', about suddenly rendering scarce and expensive that which only a short time before had been abundant and cheap: 'Those who have lent become eager to secure themselves; and refuse to renew their loans on easy or even on any terms.'[21] This, needless to say, causes great distress among those firms which had borrowed heavily in order to install fixed capital (in iron-works, factories, docks, railways, for example), which had suffered badly due to inflation ('prices being high they do not get much building done for their outlay'[22]), and which urgently need to borrow still more simply in order to complete their investment-projects and begin to reap their hoped-for profits. Some firms are particularly vulnerable where lenders (never absolutely certain whether or not even the most plausible business man has 'a strict sense of honour') have taken the precaution of making a series of short-term renewable loans rather than extending a single long-term credit – for such firms not only do not get more but are in grave danger of having to make do with less:

> A man who is much dependent on such short loans labours under great disadvantages. For if any misfortune should injure his credit, or if a disturbance of the money market should cause a temporary scarcity of loanable capital, he may be quickly brought into great straits. He may not be able to obtain a renewal of the loans on moderate terms, or even on any terms, and may thus be cut short in his most hopeful enterprises. One of the chief symptoms of an impending commercial crisis is a rapid succession of forced sales at a loss by those who have been trading with capital borrowed for short periods.[23]

Meanwhile, certain speculators, noting with horror the forced sales and under pressure in any case to repay their own debts, decide to liquidate stocks before prices fall; 'and by so doing they check the rise of prices. This check makes all other speculators anxious, and many rush in to sell. For a speculator who has borrowed money at interest to buy goods may be ruined if he holds them a long time even while their price remains stationary; he is almost sure to be ruined if he hold them while their price falls.'[24] More and more speculative holders dump stocks – each trying to get out before prices fall still further – and the accelerating collapse of business confidence bears something more than silent witness to the chaos which ensues when the fittest make a determined effort to survive. We all know that 'the fall of a lighted match on some thing that smoulders has often started a disastrous panic in a crowded theatre';[25] we should all remember that speculators too are prone to the house-of-cards reflex and the *sauve qui peut* reaction; and we must all inevitably conclude that herd instincts can be a major cause of massive instability where they provoke men with imperfect foresight to move quickly and to move together. Your pessimism becomes my pessimism, my optimism produces your optimism, and we who as businessmen know at first hand the real feel of crises and fluctuations are on balance likely, eschewing the more mechanistic explanations of cycles (over-investment, under-consumption, indivisibilities within the capital stock, epoch-making technological innovations, intersectoral dispro-portionalities, uneven rates of depreciation, bunched replacements and similar theories), to express considerable sympathy with those approaches which assign pride of place to anticipation, expectation and little else. Individual and mass psychology have much to answer for, as John Mills argued in his important paper of 1867 to the Manchester Statistical Society: 'The malady of commercial crises is not in essence a matter of the purse but of the mind. . . . Broadly defined, panic is the destruction in the mind of a bundle of beliefs.'[26]

As their beliefs are destroyed, so speculators stampede to sell; and that stampede, occurring as it does at a time of contracting credit, distrust of paper currency, hoarding of metallic money, contributes significantly to the incipient deflation. Clearly, it is only a matter of time until a major house fails. That failure, by inducing creditors to demand immediate payment, then brings other failures in its wake:

> When a large speculator fails, his failure generally causes that of others who have lent their credit to him; and their failure again that of others. Many of those who fail may be really 'sound', that is their assets may exceed their debts. But though a man is sound, some untoward event, such as the failure of others who are known to be indebted to him, may make his creditors suspect him. They may be able to demand immediate payment from him, while he cannot collect quickly what is owing to him; and the market being disturbed he is distrusted; he cannot borrow, and he fails.[27]

One failure thus leads to another once the bubble of credit has burst: 'As credit by growing makes itself grow, so when distrust has taken the place of confidence, failure and panic breed panic and failure. The commercial storm leaves its path strewn with ruin.'[28] The downswing has replaced the upswing, recession has replaced buoyancy, and what has happened at the upper turning point is nothing more – nor less – than a loss of nerve.[29]

(2) The slump

In the upswing one business constitutes a market for another and both expand together. The same interdependence may be observed in the downswing – with the sad difference that suppliers and demanders are at that stage not expanding but contracting. Spencer in 1876 had warned what would be the fate of Middlesex if not organically integrated with the rest of England: 'We cannot cut a mammal in two without causing immediate death. Twisting off the head of a fowl is fatal. Not even a reptile, though it may survive the loss of its tail, can live when its body is divided. . . . If in high societies the effect of mutilation is less than in high animals, still it is great.'[30] Bagehot in 1873 had placed precisely such organic integration at the centre of his explanation of 'Why Lombard Street is Often Very Dull and Sometimes Extremely Excited': 'There is a partnership in industries. No single large industry can be depressed without injury to other industries.... Under a system in which every one is dependent on the labour of every one else, the loss of one spreads and multiplies through all, and spreads and multiplies the faster the higher the previous perfection of the system of divided labour.'[31] Marshall, an admirer both of Spencer[32] and of Bagehot,[33] was evidently only standing on the shoulders of giants when he drew his picture of cumulative contraction – a picture which depicts in essence a situation in which one hand used to wash the other but now is unwilling and unable to do so.

What happens in the downswing is that, because of falling prices, some firms fail while others (forecasting and fearing that prices will have fallen still further between the time when they purchase their inputs and the time when they market their finished product) decide voluntarily to cease production altogether – their objective being, of course, not to maximise profits but rather to minimise losses. Still other firms opt for a partial diminution in quantity supplied, hoping by means of such a contained curtailment to improve market-conditions for the particular commodity in question – a vain hope, as it happens, since all trades are interdependent and your ability to sell depends on my ability to buy. Firms tend to forget, in other words, that 'every stoppage of work in any one trade diminishes the demand for the work of others; and that, if all trades tried to improve the market by stopping their work together, the only result would be that every one would have less of everything to consume.'[34] Stoppage feeds on stoppage, paper promises are (because of the want of confidence) presented for payment, stocks of gold are (because of the rise in their value consequent upon the fall in other values) held in speculative hoards, and the ripples born of demand-deficiency at home quickly spread abroad to embrace other countries and to damp down market demand there as well: 'Credit is already in great measure international: a large and severe shock to business anywhere is likely to cause tremors of credit in almost every part of the Western world.'[35] International transmissibility of fluctuations from country to country 'over the whole of the industrial world' is closely linked to world division of labour (the phenomenon of organic interdependence once again) and is, as is well known, much facilitated by improvements in the technology of communications: 'The telegraph causes the pulses of one country to synchronize with those of another, as do the beats of a group of clocks that are connected electrically.'[36] While we would all welcome such specialisation and contact as on balance contributory to growth and progress, we must nonetheless recognise that they are simultaneously contributory to parallel fluctuations in the economies of separate nations. Nowadays, in other words, we increasingly sway in the same direction at the same time, and are therefore less able to lend one another support than if each were buffetted by a different wind.

Demand being scarce in the downswing, it would clearly be beneficial both to employees and to employers if money wages could be cut in line with the fall in prices. Just as wages are sticky upwards in the upswing, however, so they are sticky downwards in the downswing:

> At such times it would often be well for both sides and for the community at large that the employees should take rather less real wages than in times of prosperity. But, in fact, since wages and salaries are reckoned in money which is rising in value, the employer pays higher real wages than usual at such a time unless he can get money wages reduced. This is a difficult task, partly because the employees, not altogether unreasonably, fear that when nominal wages are once let down they will not be easily raised. So they are inclined to stop work rather than accept a nominal reduction even though it would not be a real one.[37]

What Marshall is saying is that workers with an eye to the future might voluntarily quit their jobs today rather than set a precedent by means of a wage-cut which they will live to regret tomorrow; and that in such a case it is the employee's decision that the burden of the diminution in demand should fall on real rather than on nominal variables. Such inflexibility is no doubt reinforced by institutions such as unions – and it must be recognised by even the most market-orientated economist that wage-bargaining is 'a great deal influenced in England at the present time by trade combinations'.[38] Stickiness in money wages means a rise in real wages in a period of falling prices; and while a sentimental philosopher such as Marshall was able to describe 'the difficulty which the employer finds in getting wages to follow prices' as 'a difficulty at which I rejoice, on the whole',[39] a clear-headed economist's economist such as Marshall was bound to acknowledge that this redistribution of purchasing power in favour of the workers was likely to be at the cost of employers who could not be expected for an indefinite period to suffer the tax of forced dissavings. Those employers might in the short run keep wages constant, employment constant, and pray for natural wastage, but sooner or later they will have to take more decisive action simply in order to survive. The nature of that action is well-known and the outcome not particularly beautiful: 'Forced interruption to labour is a terrible evil. Those, whose livelihood is secure, gain physical and mental health from happy and well-spent holidays. But want of work, with long continued anxiety, consumes a man's best strength without any return. His wife gets thin, his children get, as it were, a nasty notch in their lives, which is perhaps never quite outgrown.'[40] Unemployment is a dreadful thing from a human point of view (quite apart from representing as it does a loss of output and a wastage of productive potential) and the only optimistic thing to be said about it concerns not the cycle but the trend:

> I have very little to go by except general impressions, and general impressions on a matter of this sort are not worth much; but, on the other hand, I do not know that anybody else has anything else but general impressions, and I have been studying for many years the question whether the tendency of our modern forms of industry is not to increase the irregularity of employment. I believe that it is not, and I believe that the statistical evidence brought forward to prove that it is, is invalid.[41]

When prices are falling, the fall in the price of the finished product is 'always more rapid than that in the price of labour' – and is in addition 'generally more rapid than that in the price of the raw material'.[42] This additional rigidity represents an additional burden on the entrepreneur. It squeezes his profits and makes it more difficult for him to keep up his outlays on inputs, let alone pay himself a satisfactory rate of return for his own personal toil and trouble embodied. Besides that, deflation always enriches creditors at the expense of debtors, and manufacturers (as opposed, say, to *rentiers* and financiers) are more likely to be the victims than the recipients of rising real interest associated with fixed money payments in a period of falling prices: 'Many industries, especially those of a capitalistic form, have fixed money charges, the burden of which is increased by a fall of prices.'[43] Lenders are not displeased with redistribution consequent upon such downward rigidities in interest-rates (Marshall was somewhat less pleased at the thought of the social injustice and economic burden involved: 'No doubt some rich lenders of money in the form of debentures and other ways get their incomes increased at the expense of the public, which I regret'[44]), not least because lenders in bad times are not eager in any case to expand business: where my expectations of the future are gloomy and pessimistic, I experience no particular desire to attract into my shop still more owners of ships which I suspect may be sinking. I therefore lend little and lend dear, and in that way make clear that no more from finance than from labour or from materials can the hard-pressed employer anticipate significant short-run relief on the side of cost.

Not every ship sinks in the storm of failure and loss of confidence but that fact in itself is unlikely to yield much comfort to the friend of booms and buoyancy, for in the 'dull heavy calm' which succeeds the storm 'those who have saved themselves are in no mood to venture again': 'Iron works and ships are for sale, but there are no buyers at any moderate price.'[45] Businessmen are simply not motivated to found new companies or expand old ones in a period of commercial depression and economic disorganisation: 'After a crisis the warehouses are overstocked with goods in almost every important trade; scarcely any trade can continue undiminished production so as to afford a good rate of profits to capital and a good rate of wages to labour.'[46] The crisis is not particular (as would be the case with an unintended oversupply of, say, cloth, furniture or cutlery). It is general: all trades experience low sales and are hence poor customers for one another. It is also a crisis far more of mind than of matter: 'The chief cause of the evil is a want of confidence. The greater part of it could be removed almost in an instant if confidence could return, touch all industries with her magic wand, and make them continue their production and their demand for the wares of others.'[47] It is a crisis nonetheless – since while the recovery indubitably waits upon a revival of confidence, the sad truth in the trough is that confidence has not revived and that mind is as depressed as matter.

Whatever goes down must, however, come up, and just as prosperity was followed by quiescence at the upper turning point, so quiescence is bound to be followed by prosperity at the lower. A runner having stumbled and fallen is likely at first to feel depressed, but he is also likely eventually to pick himself up and continue to run. As with runners, so with businessmen, who may be expected to 'strike' at first but then to drift back to work: 'I admit that when a fall of prices sets in, many business men strike. . . . But after they have struck for a little while it occurs to them that there is no great use in striking, that although they may lose money by working their mills, they would lose more money by not working them.'[48] A few admittedly do not drift back to work and 'positively refuse to go on with their business. Some great works have been completely closed, and never reopened; but these are exceptional cases, due to exceptional causes'.[49] Besides that, even where the fighter does in the event chuck in his towel, it is normally the case that a younger, fitter man (a new tree in the forest, as it were) takes his place and acquires for purposes of exploitation his businesses and enterprises: 'As a rule when closed they are sold to new men, who, purchasing them at a comparatively low rate, have all the benefit of the past fall of prices, and are able to go on, and make profits.'[50] The misfortune of the fighter who chucks in his towel is great, but it must not, clearly, be scaled upwards and made indicative of the misfortune of the nation.

Initially it would seem to be the consumer-goods industries which take the lead in generating new demand and which launch anew the multiplier process of expansion, but the capital goods industries are unlikely to lag too far behind: 'If all trades which make goods for direct consumption agreed to work on and to buy each other's goods as in ordinary times, they would supply one another with the means of earning a moderate rate of profits and of wages. The trades which make Fixed capital might have to wait a little longer, but they too would get employment when confidence had revived so far that those who had capital to invest had made up their minds how to invest it.'[51] This is not to say that investment in plant does not take place in a slump – rather the opposite in fact, since businessmen are by definition *future*-oriented: 'In some periods of commercial depression almost the only demand for Fixed capital comes from manufacturers who do not like to close their works for alterations while trade is brisk; but who, when trade is slack, and the prices of building and machinery are low, take the opportunity of making such extensions and repairs as may enable them to profit by the revival of trade when it comes.'[52] Inelasticity of expectations evidently impels the more rational among businessmen to re-stock and re-tool in times of slump so as to be in a position fully to exploit their opportunities in times of boom; and this factor and others causes some investment to take place in a period of depression. Simply, it is not enough: 'This demand is not nearly sufficient to make up the deficiency that arises from the general contraction of credit, from the failure of old firms and public companies, and from the absence of new companies.'[53] Firms with excess capacity are reluctant to invest in more (an important reason why 'the demand for Fixed capital is liable to more extreme fluctuations than the demand for commodities that are wanted for immediate consumption, and the trades which make Fixed capital are more affected than any others by alternations of commercial prosperity and adversity'[54]), and there is also the disincentive effect of falling prices: 'Where credit is contracting many find their means of purchasing altogether cut off, while those whose means are not straitened do not care to invest in Fixed capital until they think prices have nearly reached their turning point.'[55] Derived demand only picks up when firms 'think' that demand overall is picking up; and that is why the contribution of investment to the revival of confidence should not be exaggerated. Once, however, firms 'think' that demand overall is picking up, then they invest, and that in itself helps to validate their expectations *ex post*, representing as it does a genuine and significant contribution to additional total demand.

The key to revival, it must be stressed, is to be sought for in mind and not in matter:

> Confidence by growing would cause itself to grow; credit would give increased means of purchase, and thus prices would recover. Those in trade already would make good profits, new companies would be started, old businesses would be extended; and soon there would be a good demand even for the work of those who make Fixed capital. There is of course no formal agreement between the different trades to begin again to work full times and so make a market for each other's wares. But the revival of industry comes about through the gradual and often simultaneous growth of confidence among many various trades; it begins as soon as traders think that prices will not continue to fall; and with a revival of industry prices rise.[56]

A rise in prices causes businessmen to expect a further rise, memories fade of 'old causes of distrust, which had had their origin in some previous misfortune or mismanagement',[57] and the economy rapidly finds itself returned, as if guided by an invisible hand, to the upswing once again.

(3) Say's law

The slump is caused by a crisis of confidence, accompanied or not by an exogenous shock such as a harvest-failure. The slump is not caused by a deficiency of total demand: 'There is no such thing as general overproduction.'[58] For, as Adam Smith had clearly understood (and Malthus and Lauderdale had not), that portion of income which is initially saved is as much a part of total demand as that portion of income which is initially spent:

> The whole of a man's income is expended in the purchase of services and of commodities. It is indeed commonly said that a man spends some portion of his income and saves another. But it is a familiar economic axion that a man purchases labour and commodities with that portion of his income which he saves just as much as he does with that portion which he is said to spend. He is said to spend when he seeks to obtain present enjoyment from the services and the commodities which he purchases. He is said to save when he causes the labour and the commodities which he purchases to be devoted to the production of wealth from which he expects to derive the means of enjoyment in the future.[59]

Consuming is spending, saving (via lending) is spending, and to argue otherwise – in a money as in a barter economy – is to render oneself guilty of nothing short of a 'monstrous fallacy':[60] 'It is true that some wealth is hoarded; and that while being hoarded it is not being used; but hoarding has gone out of fashion in civilized countries. An Englishman, when he saves capital, intends either to use it himself, or to lend it out to be used by others; and capital when it is used is almost always spent.'[61] Consuming is spending, saving (once the savings have been lent on to would-be consumers and investors) is spending, and 'general over-production' is therefore 'a malady which I contend we cannot suffer from'.[62]

This is not, of course, to deny the possibility of partial over-production; and it would obviously be wrong, confusing macroeconomics with microeconomics, to ignore the involuntary unemployment experienced in the short-run by a particular trade which is experiencing a sector-specific period of adaptation and readaptation. This is the case, to take one example from many, with small shops, which are increasingly being deserted by consumers in favour of large ones. The larger shops have substantial economies of size and convey unquestioned benefits to shoppers: 'But the change will of course diminish the number of shopkeepers whose work is required; and the process of thinning out must be painful; the suffering need not however be great if shopkeepers adapt themselves quickly to the requirements of the new age, and urge all young men who have not special reasons for becoming shopkeepers to choose some other occupation.'[63] Such involuntary unemployment is of a short-run structural followed by frictional nature – the inevitable accompaniment to change in a dynamic economy and in no way indicative of a deficiency in aggregate demand. Such involuntary unemployment is welcome, to be expected, and normal.

In a slump, it must be admitted, the level of unemployment is much more than normal and firms complain both of excess capacity and of excessive output. In the downswing, clearly, the phenomenon is general and not partial. Even then, however, the cause of the problem is not to be sought in deficiency of total demand but rather in commercial disorganisation, loss of confidence and exceptional unwillingness to part with that wealth which one undeniably possesses: 'Though men have the power to purchase they may not choose to use it, for when confidence has been shaken by failures, capital cannot be got to start new companies or extend old ones. Projects for new railways meet with no favour, ships lie idle, and there are no orders for new ships.'[64] Trade A is a poor market for trade B; trade B by contracting is then a poor market for trade C; and 'thus commercial disorganization spreads: the disorganization of one trade throws others out of gear, and they react on it and increase its disorganization'.[65] All of this looks suspiciously like too much supply chasing too little demand. That, however, is not the case: 'There cannot be general over-production, though there is sometimes a disorganization of industry which looks very like it.'[66] What has happened is a lack of the will, not a lack of the way: 'The chief cause of the evil is a want of confidence. The greater part of it could be removed almost in an instant if confidence could return'.[67] The remedy is no more sophisticated than that pessimists should recover their former optimism and resume their normal role as buyers, as sellers – and as employers of labour.

Marshall's confidence in confidence is an important part of his approach to applied macroeconomics. Curiously enough, however, there are two underdeveloped insights in his work which to some extent undermine the reader's confidence in that confidence.

The *first* problem involves the equation of desired prospectiveness with desired parsimony. We know that the entrepreneurs' demand function for incremental capital slopes upwards to the left ('A rise in the rate of interest would diminish their use of machinery'[68]) while the households' supply function for savings slopes upwards to the right ('The higher the rate of interest the greater the saving as a rule'[69]) – but we still have no guarantee that the two functions will intersect at some positive rate of interest, so dependent is the former on non-rational variables such as attitudes and expectations, so dependent is the latter on family affection and the search for security. The rate of interest might accordingly not be able unaided to equilibrate desired savings and desired investment. The relationship is complicated still further by the redistribution of income over the cycle and/or in the course of economic growth (although Marshall does maintain that all classes have a high propensity to save), and by the secular upward trend in the average propensity to save which in Marshall's view is to be expected in an economy as it grows richer (since more desired savings presupposes more desired investment if stagnation and over-saving are to be avoided). Marshall presumably believed that the interest-rate was in some sense powerful enough to deal with structural changes in the economy such as those associated with redistribution of income and the skewing of the national product away from consumption.

The *second* problem involves liquidity preference and the utility of cash balances. Logically speaking, if money is deliberately held idle (in anticipation, let us say, of a fall in commodity prices or of a rise in interest rates) then by definition some goods produced for sale are not being bought. Marshall seems not to have grasped the relevance of liquidity preference for his wider theory of total demand. Yet if the medium or intermediary is being held as an asset in its own right, then it would be reasonable to expect there simultaneously to develop a glut of those things on which the medium or intermediary would otherwise have been spent. If a deer exchanges not for two beaver but for two shillings, and if those two shillings are held rather than spent, then the question inevitably arises of who will purchase the two beaver which are also seeking an entry into the circular flow of transactions. Marshall discussed both the utility of liquidity and the doctrine that crises do not result from a failure of total demand. It is unfortunate that he did not, in his discussion, seek to combine these two topics; for that combination would in itself seem to cast some doubt on the confidence in confidence which is so important a part of Marshall's approach to applied macroeconomics.

6.4 STABILISATION POLICY

A 'steady upward tendency in general prices' contributes more to the 'general well-being' than does an equivalent impulse in the downward direction in so far as it 'keeps industry somewhat better employed'[1] – but it also breeds great distress among the wage-earning classes (the matter of forced savings), it enriches debtors at the expense of creditors (such redistribution in turn feeding the inflation by making loanable funds abnormally cheap), and it stimulates speculation to an extent that is potentially destabilising to confidence (since the paper profits born of inflation are to be earned only so long as speculators expect a continued rise in prices). Again, there is much to be said for a 'tendency downwards', which puts wealth into the hands of the poorer classes (typically on fixed or sticky incomes) and which weeds out the weak and the wasteful (who then benefit their community by ceasing to borrow and trade, thereby making way for the strong and the fit) – but it also produces disruptions, dismissals, bankruptcies, contractionary spirals and multipliers: 'Even if the prices of labour and raw material fall as rapidly as those of finished good, the manufacturer may lose by continuing production if the fall has not come to an end. He may pay for raw material and labour at a time when prices generally have fallen by one-sixth; but if, by the time he comes to sell, prices have fallen by another sixth, his receipts may be less than is sufficient to cover his outlay.'[2] All in all, therefore, 'I think there is much less difference than is generally supposed between the net benefits of periods of rising and falling prices'; 'I think it is not clearly established that a rise of prices is on the whole to be preferred to a fall'; and – the crucial conclusion – 'I think that the general interests of the country are best promoted by stationary prices'.[3] Stable prices are evidently preferable to any fluctuation, up or down: the alleged benefits of price-changes lack statistical confirmation, the potential costs are liable to serious distortion by pressure groups with vested interest to defend,[4] and in any case even the most moderate fluctuation is likely eventually to become violent, self-magnifying and thus 'injurous both physically and morally to the community at large'.[5] No sensible man would want to inflict such moral and physical harm on his community. No sensible man would, accordingly, want to play with matches when the consequence might be a forest-fire: it is 'the rapid fluctuations of general prices from year to year' (especially where due to the reckless expansion and contraction of credit, 'the chief cause of all economic malaise'[6]) which are mainly to blame for the 'uncertainties of business', for the 'discontinuity of industry', and for a considerable part of the 'human suffering and degradation'[7] which characterise our age.

Progress, fortunately, smiles on price-stability. Admittedly change does bring into the industry new men who, oblivious to the 'odium'[8] with which neighbours reward anti-social price-cutters, are not afraid to spoil the common market in the interests of their own pecuniary advantage. Admittedly change is associated with rapidity of invention and innovation (which renders that much more risky the difficult task of long-term forecasting and of investing on the basis of such predictions) – and also, it would appear, with 'the spread of fickle habits in matters of fashion among all classes of society'[9] (regrettable in itself and a cause, moreover, of fluctuations, of 'bursts of feverish activity alternating with deadening idleness'[10]). On balance, however, progress smiles on price-stability. For one thing, improvements in knowledge and rationality reduce the number of self-amplifying errors likely to be made by manufacturers, traders and lenders: 'Later stages of (industrial) progress may be expected to increase the power of thoughtful men so to anticipate the future that means may be fitly adapted to coming needs and business credit may develop more steadily and surely.'[11] The specialist press, the telegraph and other improvements in the communication of 'prompt, thorough and exact trade news'[12] permit of arbitrage as between dearer and cheaper markets, while improvements in transport allow a glut in one country quickly to relieve a dearth in another without those sudden price-rises which bad harvests would otherwise occasion. Some contingencies remain, of course, unknown and unknowable (contingencies ranging from future harvest-failures to the outbreak of the next war); but other contingencies capable of engendering macroeconomic instability (the case of wild swings in fashion, for example) are likely to wither away in the course of social evolution and the upgrading of character. The conclusion to be reached is unambiguous: while business life is by its very nature fraught with uncertainty, there are nonetheless powerful forces endogenous to the economic system which are progressively favourable to confidence and to calm.

Progress smiles upon price-stability and this is just as well; for the truth is that psychological dispositions (including moods, attitudes, expectations, and anticipations), an open-ended definition of spendable assets (ranging from coins to notes, cheques, bills, and trade credit in a system in which, to be frank, 'paper means of purchase can be manufactured to an unlimited extent'[13]), a velocity variable which fluctuates with the state of confidence, all make life next to impossible for a well-intentioned Chancellor who foolishly sets out to fine-tune the macroeconomy, as the example of high interest-rates will serve to illustrate. The Chancellor, let us assume, observes high interest-rates and experiences a generous desire to make more abundant that for which men are competing so intensively. He would be well advised to resist the temptation, for here as usual he can see the bank-statements but not the thoughts and the perceptions:

> Stringencies and crises which arise from unexpected deficiencies of currency relatively to the demand for it are not to be avoided by a mere increase in the volume of the currency. They are just as likely to occur with a large stock of currency as with a small; indeed they may be caused by an inflation of currency leading to distrust, not only of currency, but of all other agents and instruments of credit. For instance, in 1893 it was not a scarcity of currency, but a belief that the currency had been unduly increased, and might be increased even more, which led to a crisis in the United States; 50 per cent. was the common rate of discount for a considerable time.[14]

If the Chancellor were able to increase the money-supply in such an environment, he might succeed thereby in reducing interest-rates (through the usual supply and demand mechanism), but, alternatively, he might actually make interest-rates higher still (by feeding expectations of a further fall in the purchasing power of money). Radical ignorance means general impotence in a situation where an actively interventionist stabilisation policy presupposes for its success that the authorities are able to predict not only the future course of matter but the future course of mind as well; and the wise Chancellor is he who accepts that there is not a great deal that the State can usefully do in the field of demand-management.

Demand-management is not, however, the whole of stabilisation policy; and while Marshall stressed that ignorance and volatility severely circumscribe the scope for discretionary intervention, he also took the view that the State had an important background role to play in the area of macroeconomic policy. His specific proposals for State action are in essence three in number.

(1) The tabular standard

Money is both a medium of exchange (save in a barter economy where apples are exchanged directly for deer) and a standard of value (which is to say, time being absolutely continuous, a standard for deferred payments as well). Money is not suited to the simultaneous execution of both tasks; and that is why the medium of exchange should be relieved 'of the duty, which it is not fitted to perform, of acting as a standard of value' and should be replaced in that regard, 'in accordance with a plan which has long been familiar to economists', by 'an authoritative standard of purchasing power independent of the currency'.[15] The money-supply would then continue to fluctuate in value, as it does now, based on the relationship between the demand for and the supply of its services; but it would be possible nonetheless for agreements and contracts to be concluded explicitly in terms of real values, of constant purchasing power, of a stable and predictable *quantum* of 'command over the necessaries, comforts and luxuries of life'.[16] Real values, by means of indexation and the use of a table, would thus become divorced from nominal values and relative exchange ratios would in consequence be unaffected by a fall or a rise in absolute values.

There are obvious gains to be reaped from such a scheme in terms of social justice – for much of modern business life involves 'contracts to make definite payments at distant times' (with respect, say, to interest or rents) and while the nominal rate is fixed the inequity arises because of the fact that 'the real rate is constantly fluctuating with every change in the purchasing power of money'.[17] Besides that, the amplitude of cycles is significantly reduced where real values (such as employment and production) can be cut loose from nominal values (such as wages and prices): since a producer experiencing what the table tells him is general (not firm-specific or even product-specific) price-cuts benefits at the same time from index-linked wage-cuts, interest-cuts and other cost-cuts (thereby avoiding the instabilities born of unexpected redistribution), he instantaneously perceives, quite correctly, that the trade is 'as profitable to him as before the fall'[18] and takes no further action. He receives, it is true, less pound notes for his product. Each pound note, however, purchases precisely as much of other commodities as it previously did, and he sees clearly that he is no better (and no worse) off than before. Should that producer, of course, experience a fall in the price of his own product such as exceeds the fall registered by the index, he would then have to accept the existence of a specific as well as a general fall – use of a table reduces uncertainty by rendering such a state of affairs fully transparent – and would in such a case have no alternative but to take action of a real nature.[19] Use of a table undeniably makes possible the apperception of such a situation to an extent that would not have been possible in the absence of such an index.

A tabular standard makes a real contribution to macroeconomic stabilisation policy. The compilation and publication of the relevant statistics (monthly or annual), moreover, is properly the task not of private enterprise but of a governmental department or agency: 'In proposing this remedy I want Government to help business, though not to do business.'[20] One reason for State intervention here is market failure, that private enterprise would not find the production of such intelligence sufficiently profitable to get involved in an activity which it accepts (like Smith's canals and roads) is nonetheless eminently in the social interest. A second reason why the task of preparing the index 'cannot, I think, be performed properly except by a permanent Government department' has to do with exclusive access to data: 'Government alone can command the machinery requisite to secure properly tested figures for the purpose.'[21] A third reason is the spillover effect and the externalities argument, for each individual trader must make 'fairly accurate forecasts'[22] if he is to survive (and greatly fears the distortions that are introduced by macroeconomic instabilities), all traders taken together regret the extent to which 'changes in the purchasing power of money . . . put difficulties in the way of agreements between different sections'[23] (and deplore the confusion in the balance of payments position which those changes bring about), and we as a community acknowledge that ignorance costs jobs: 'A great cause of the discontinuity of industry is the want of certain knowledge as to what a pound is going to be worth a short time hence.'[24]

Not only is there a strong case to be made in favour of State intervention with respect to the tabular standard but the proposal is in addition conspicuously 'free from the evils which generally surround the interference of Government in business'[25] – basically because the proposal involves the dissemination of information by means of published tables but in no way compels households and firms to make use of the new knowledge in the contracts which they conclude. Once statistics on the value of a unit of purchasing power had been made available, Marshall argued, households and firms would have the option of making contracts in terms of constant units, but the decision to do so or not would remain their own: the use of the index, Marshall stressed, was to be voluntary rather than a matter for State compulsion. His use of the externalities argument is therefore oddly one-sided: the State has a duty to publish tables (so as *inter alia* to restore the dichotomy and reduce the amplitude of real fluctuations) but you evidently have no analogous duty to make use of it. The State, it would appear, has a duty to facilitate but still you, retaining the right of 'free choice',[26] have no particular duty to conform. That having been said, however, Marshall had faith in common sense and was able confidently to predict that rational men would be increasingly attracted by the scheme: 'The plan would have to win its way into general use; but when once it had become familiar, none but gamblers would lend or borrow on any other terms, at all events for long periods.'[27] And Marshall was prepared to see the State set a good example by expressing rates and taxes in terms of constant real values rather than fluctuating price-tags. Such indexation, he said, might be extended from State credits to State debits (to the wages, salaries and pensions of civil servants, for example, or to interest on Consols) – a good thing in its own right and a convenient way of demonstrating to the private sector the considerable benefits of contracts made in units of fixed purchasing power.

Few of us, of course, have budgets identical to that of the 'average' or 'representative' consumer; and it is obvious that 'the effectual purchasing power of money to each individual depends partly on the nature of his wants'.[28] Different people (and different classes of people) consume different things, and in such a situation a meaningful index is by no means easy to construct:

> A perfectly exact measure of purchasing power is not only unattainable but even unthinkable. The same change of prices affects the purchasing power of money to different persons in different ways. For one who can seldom afford to have meat, a rise of one-fourth in the price of bread accompanied by a fall of one-fourth in that of meat means a fall in the purchasing power of money: his wages will not go as far as before. While to his richer neighbour, who spends twice as much on meat as on bread, the change acts the other way. The Government would of course take account only of the total consumption of the whole nation.[29]

What emerges in this way is a numerical average: 'What we must mean by a unit of purchasing power for, say, the United Kingdom, is merely that which will give an approximately uniform means of satisfying his wants to the average consumer.'[30] Obviously the 'average' is just a number, and there is considerable variation in the size and composition of household budgets (as where a well-to-do bachelor, to take one example, spends more on luxuries than, say, a married man with the same income and a large family). But Marshall does suggest that there could be more than one index (a mining unit or a 'working-man's budget' or some other weighted standard targeted specifically at a particular group or trade); and in any case, he argues, while admittedly 'a theoretically perfect standard of purchasing power is unattainable',[31] still the sliding scale which he proposes would reduce uncertainty and increase security to a greater extent than would any known alternative policy instrument.

There is a further technicality to be mentioned, and it concerns the nature of the commodities which Marshall indicates ought to be included in his index: 'It would probably be best to follow the ordinary method of taking very little account of any but raw commodities. Manufactured commodities and personal services are always changing their character, and are not easily priced.'[32] Primary products, Marshall reasoned, tend to be relatively standardised and do not change significantly in nature over time whereas finished goods are simply too various and varying to be suitable for comparison and grouping; and concentration on the wholesale (as opposed to the retail) prices of the former is particularly to be recommended in order to benefit from the not inconsiderable advantages of 'simplicity and definiteness' (these being, at least in this case, 'far more important than theoretic accuracy'[33]). Besides that, 'manufactured commodities tend to fall in value relatively to raw commodities, and at present, at all events, personal services tend to rise; so that the errors made by omitting both probably nearly neutralise one another'.[34]

Marshall did not say that the unit was perfect. What he did say is that no one can take the second step who has not taken the first, and that the momentum of progress itself favours the future betterment of this mode of State intervention. As Marshall put it in a letter to *The Economist* in 1887 concerning their unfavourable comments on his proposals ('the proposed standard is an impossibility', they had said, adding that it was in any case no novelty but 'merely the revival of an oft-mooted project'[35]): 'You are . . . mistaken in supposing that I propose to substitute for Jevons' simple kind of unit a very complicated one, I propose to take the simplest kind of unit, with only such improvements as we can see our way to introducing safely at once, and to let it gradually develop itself with the progress of statistical science and practice.'[36] *The Economist*, he argued, had simply not grasped that the real refinement of the scheme was yet to come and could not reasonably be expected until *after* a Government department responsible for administering the standard had actually been set up – precisely the sort of misunderstanding one would expect from careless journalists who had not even perceived that the tabular standard was neither cash nor intended to be used as such: 'You prove that a man buying tea or drawing a cheque on his bankers would have to deal in terms of the currency, and not in terms of the unit. No one, so far as I know, has ever proposed that the unit should be used except for deferred payment: current business would be left to the currency.'[37]

Marshall did not say that the unit was perfect. What he did say is that it is a significant improvement on the present system. Under the present system, Marshall argued, prices and quantities (the latter frequently because of the former) tend to fluctuate over the cycle. Under the new system, however, nominal values would acquire the freedom to fluctuate without having an unintended feedback effect on output and employment. Improved intelligence would in addition reduce the amplitude of multiplier swings in confidence and credit: 'Better and more widely diffused knowledge is a remedy for that excessive confidence which causes a violent expansion of credit and rise of prices; and it is also a remedy for that excessive distrust that follows.'[38] Artificial manipulation of the level of total demand on the part of the State is doomed to radical impotence as far as the objective of stability is concerned. Nor is bimetallism the sought-after panacea; and its adherents should be reminded that our present-day problems associated with the fluctuating standard for deferred payments 'would be but very slightly diminished by the adoption of gold and silver instead of gold alone as the basis of our currency'.[39] Gold and silver ('separately or conjointly') can perhaps provide a stable standard of value 'in regard to obligations and business transactions, which do not range over more than a few years' – but 'obligations, which range over long periods, call for standards that are not dependent on the hazards of mining':[40] 'As the arts of life progress (and indeed as a condition of that progress) man must demand a constantly increasing precision from the instruments which he uses, and from money among others: and he is beginning to doubt whether either gold or silver, or even gold and silver combined, give him a sufficiently stable standard of value for the ever widening range of space and time over which his undertakings and contracts extend.'[41] So while Marshall did not say that the unit was perfect, what he did say is that it is more scientific and more exact than the next best mode of stabilisation which he examined: even a 'rough-and-ready' unit, he concluded, 'would give a far better standard for deferred payments than even a stable bi-metallic currency'.[42] Where stabilisation policy is concerned, it would appear, there is much to be said for the man-made article and the consciously designed schema – for the visible hand, in short, as opposed to the spontaneous flow. But that does not mean that Marshall rejected the spontaneous flow of the second-best solution, simply that he genuinely regarded it as second-best with respect to the specific objective of a stable standard.

(2) Bimetallism

Marshall told the Committee on Indian Currency that he had a strong bias towards automaticity in the determination of the money supply: 'The function of a legislator as regards currency is to do as little as possible. Almost any currency of which the position is certain will do its work fairly well. Frequent changes in its basics disturb expectations, upset reasonable calculations, and infuse a spirit of unrest into business. They may all aim at increased certainty, but their effect must on the balance be increased uncertainty. They resemble the frequent wakings of a patient in order to administer sleeping draughts.'[43] There is, in other words, a strong case for political *laissez-faire* in this as in so many other areas.

We live, of course, in a dynamic economy, and no rational man would therefore call for a money supply that is absolutely fixed in its dimensions. On the contrary: 'What is wanted is a currency which expands when business expands, and thus enables real capital to become fluid when it is wanted to become fluid; and which shrinks when business shrinks, and thus preserves itself from becoming superfluous and falling in value. By this means only can the currency retain its full power; and be ready by expanding again to supply the needful flux for business, when it again becomes exceptionally active.'[44] What is wanted, clearly, is a money supply that not only varies without continuous State direction but which demonstrates elasticity of dimension as well – for without such elasticity of dimension there can be no overall stability of values. We live, after all, in a dynamic economy; and if our national output of goods and services grows while our national money supply does not, then we are bound to face unwanted, destabilising and self-aggravating fluctuations in price-levels and in real variables as well. These fluctuations are bad, and 'they would certainly be much mitigated if each decade's supply of the metallic basis of our currency could be made uniform – *i.e.*, to grow proportionately to our commercial wants'.[45] Thence the argument for bimetallism, for a system anchored by two precious metals instead of by only one in the interests of economic stability: 'Some tendency in this direction would be exercised by the addition of silver to gold as the basis of currency.'[46]

Money is not to be compared to a machine but rather 'to oil used to enable a machine to run smoothly'.[47] As we in the nation come to employ more machines, so it is only natural that we will need more oil. Certainly there were a large number of observers of the economic scene in the depressed years of the 1880s who believed that 'the recent fall of prices is caused by a check to the available supply of gold' and who,[48] fearful of crucifying mankind upon a cross of gold, maintained that an additional monetary metal was indispensable if our economic system were to have the lubricants it required for its smooth operation. Marshall fully understood the arguments of those observers and himself said in 1887 that 'I have a bimetallic hobby of my own . . . I have had it by me now for more than ten years.'[49] Thought is not, however, to be confused with action, and Marshall – always a man of caution – also said: 'I contend that we ought not to alter our currency in a hurry, but take a little more time to look round us.'[50] For such caution concerning bimetallism three reasons may be adduced.

First, as we have already noted, even if adequate supplies of monetary gold are indeed not forthcoming and the nation is thereby compelled ultimately to restrict (the amount, or the rate of growth in the amount of) its currency, the resultant price-cuts need nonetheless not have a significantly deleterious impact on real variables in a country which has wisely adopted a tabular standard: 'The index-numbers with which we are already familiar would give a ten times better standard of value for optional use within the country in long-standing contracts than even a true bimetallic currency.'[51] Those advocates of bimetallism who are in truth closet inflationists (who want more currency precisely because it leads to rising prices and therewith to economic growth financed out of forced savings) will have little time for a scheme orientated towards the maintenance of a fixed and constant value of purchasing power. Marshall, however, was no inflationist; and when he does flirt with bimetallism he indicates clearly that its attraction to him is 'only as a means of diminishing fluctuations'.[52] That being the case, anything that bimetallism can do, a tabular standard can do better: though admittedly 'strange at first sight', the tabular standard upon closer acquaintance 'would really be much simpler than bimetallism, while its influence in steadying industry would be incomparably greater'.[53] Besides that, there is something singularly arbitrary and therefore repellent because unscientific in a stabilisation policy which finds one metal a bad standard and accordingly opts for two: 'Even a true bimetallism would afford only a little better standard of value than monometallism. Monometallism may be compared to a standard of length got from the measure of the senior judge's foot at the assizes; while bimetallism corresponds to that got by taking the mean of the lengths of the feet of both judges.'[54] Of course the tabular standard is not perfect; but it is even so more accurate than that.

Second, 'there is no security that the yield of the silver mines will be great when that of the gold mines is small': 'History indeed indicates that the probability is the other way, for, when a new country is prospected, silver mines are often found in one part and gold in another, while some mines produce both gold and silver.'[55] In such circumstances the stabilisation of the economy and the elimination of fluctuations in values will not be facilitated by a move from the monometallic to the bimetallic system; for, it would seem, the quantities supplied of the two metals have, at least in the past, typically moved in step.

Third, Marshall said, and while accepting that there exists a link between price-levels and the supply of gold, 'it is beyond question that changes in this supply are not accountable for more than a very small part of the total fluctuations in the general purchasing power of money'.[56] The wide range of spendable assets, the mutability of velocity, the presence in the model of confidence as an additional causal variable, all have the potential to insulate the economy (completely or partially) from major exogenous shocks including sudden specie outflows, and it must in addition be remembered that the central bank, in Marshall's view, should and does hold excess reserves so as not to be obliged to contract the note-issue immediately there is a drain (international or internal): 'The Directors of the Bank of England, aided by Lombard Street generally, have earned the gratitude of the country by increasing that ultimate reserve. The combined strength and elasticity which the currency of a country requires as provision against external and internal drains is most efficiently provided by a large reserve stock of bullion and coin.'[57] Wise central bankers evidently wait to discover whether the outflow is a self-correcting fluctuation or a long-run trend before they begin to contract the money supply in response – a degree of discretion more reminiscent of Thornton and Bagehot than of Ricardo and one which permits fiduciary paper to be substituted for monetary metal to an extent that would have been anathema to, let us say, the Currency School. Such discretion reinforced by reserves (a topic to which we shall return later in this Chapter) makes the money supply more flexible and more elastic than it would have been if linked to treasure alone; but the success of such a policy is not guaranteed, being dependent as it is on the ability of the authorities to 'make the public absolutely certain that genuine notes will not be issued in excess'.[58] Provided that such confidence is maintained, however, then the fiduciary issue can expand even where the supply of monetary metal does not, and the problem to which bimetallism is envisaged as the solution becomes that much less acute.

These considerations led Marshall to the general conclusion that, while there were undoubtedly definite gains to be had from the mintage of both gold and silver (as opposed to the mintage of gold alone), yet the arguments were not on balance adequate demonstration that the adoption of the bimetallic standard was important enough to warrant urgent attention: 'On the contrary, I think the time has not yet come for changing our currency. I regard both the immediate effects of such a change and its indirect and distant effects as likely to involve very serious evils. I am not convinced that it would be worth while to go through these evils even for the sake of a true bimetallism.'[59] Marshall, it must be stressed, was in favour of bimetallism: 'I regard true bimetallism as the best basis of an international currency.'[60] Marshall, simply, was not in favour of bimetallism now: 'I do not myself consider that the experiment ought to be ventured on until more time has been allowed for considering the problem of international currency from many points of view.'[61]

From many points of view not least because there are many types of bimetallism – and because certain types of bimetallism are doomed to auto-destruction, as is the case with fixed-ratio mintage: 'If the future history of the development of gold and silver monies should be similar to that of recent years, fixed-ratio-mintage would be likely to land us in silver monometallism, that is a paper currency on a silver basis.'[62] It hardly helps significantly to expand the money supply if we join B to A only to find that B (all too obedient in this respect to the dictates of Gresham's Law) then completely drives A out of circulation.

The danger in fixed-ratio mintage lies in the fact that the ratio of the values of the two metals is specified as constant. So long as the two values genuinely remain constant, there is no problem or threat. If, however, the relative values should happen to alter, then at that moment the system becomes unstable. Suppose, for example, that the cost of mining silver should fall relative to that of gold. Then 'the result of fixing the ratio of the values between the two metals would be to stop gold mining' and therewith to dry up the flow of new gold destined for monetary purposes.[63] Meanwhile, existing stocks of old gold would come to be hoarded as an investment by households, by firms and by governments – all of them willing to bear the opportunity-cost in terms of interest foregone because of their confident expectation that the convention was likely to snap and the value of an ounce of gold thereupon be increased: 'They would be unwilling to give an ounce of gold for 15½ ozs. of silver, when there was a considerable chance that before long it might be worth 20 or 30 ozs.'[64] Reduced production on the side of supply, increased speculation on the side of demand, both generate disturbances in credit, but apart from that – and this is the key point in the present context – they tend, where gold is widely believed to be undervalued, to cause gold and silver bimetallism to degenerate into silver monometallism: the gold sovereign would be 'very shortly as obsolete as the dodo',[65] one metal alone would be in circulation, and 'the value of the currency would then fluctuate with every variation in the value of silver'.[66] Such an outcome is not indicative of bimetallism but rather of alternative monometallism; since at the end of the day the currency is not convertible into *either* gold *or* silver (as was the intention) but into silver *instead of* gold (which re-names the problem but does not resolve it).

Marshall, aware of changes in the relative productivity of mines (and aware too of the destabilising rumours about such relativities which so frequently acquire a momentum of their own, not least due to the presence in the market of major speculators with a vested pecuniary interest in future values), saw clearly that 'fixed-ratio mintage is not what it claims to be, a stable bi-metallism'.[67] Such bimetallism (even if reinforced by international agreements such as that made by the 'Latin Union' group of countries) is bad bimetallism, bimetallism which does not take into account the impact on values of changes in supply and demand and which therefore is not likely – 'as human nature is constituted' – to 'endure very long after changes in the conditions of mining had made the relative costs of production of the two metals differ widely from their relative ratings in the agreement'.[68] Which is not to say that bimetallism *per se* is unstable, simply that the fixed-ratio mintage system works better when a realistic ratio is adopted than when the values are unreasonable ('It probably would be strong enough to maintain itself for a long time, if the ratio adopted were 20 or 22 to one; but not if it were 15½ to one'[69]) – and that 'symmetallism' ('a plan . . . which would make the two metals work together'[70]) is in any case infinitely preferable to any fixed-ratio system whatsoever: 'I think that if we do want bimetallism we should have to make sure that we get it, that is to say, we should make a rule that every debt should be discharged by the payment of a certain amount of gold *and* silver instead of a certain amount of gold *or* silver.'[71] Paper should, in other words, be made convertible not into *either* of the two metals but rather into *both*.

Both, indeed, at once. Ricardo had recommended that paper currency be made convertible into stamped gold *bars* (as opposed to gold *coins*). Marshall's scheme builds, with modifications, on his: 'My alternative scheme is to be got from his simply by wedding a bar of silver of, say, 2000 grammes to a bar of gold of, say, 100 grammes; the Government undertaking to be always ready to buy or sell a wedded pair of bars for a fixed amount of currency. (It would be somewhere about 29*l*.) This would be true bimetallism. The value of the currency would be fixed absolutely by the means of the values of a gramme of gold and, say, 20 grammes of silver. It would have no chance of deteriorating into a silver monometallism.'[72] The combination and proportions would be arbitrary. Far more important is the fact that they would be (and would be known to be) permanently fixed. This means that if, say, the quantity of silver were to expand due to the productivity of the silver mines, the market value of the mix would vary (due to supply and demand) but not in such a way as to cause one metal to push out its partner (due to the employment of the fixed-coefficient system).[73] Marshall, on this as on so many other issues a man of caution, said: 'I do not urge this . . . proposal of mine for immediate adoption.'[74] But when all is said and done it would be unfair to regard him as anything but a bimetallist with a distinctive twist of his own.

(3) Reserves and exchanges

Marshall, like Ricardo, looked forward to a day when paper (not coin) would be the domestic medium of circulation, thereby releasing monetary metals for use in international trade. As Ricardo had put it, speaking of a note-issuing bank in a country which needs specie for purposes of foreign commerce and sees no reason to waste it in High Street exchanges where something equally convenient can take its place: 'The bank substitutes a currency of no value for one most costly, and enables us to turn the precious metals (which, though a very necessary part of our capital, yield no revenue), into a capital which will yield one.'[75] Ricardo, like Smith, wanted our currency to resemble a highway through the air such as permits highways on earth to be redeployed more productively as pastures and cornfields; and he took the view that for genuine conversion from notes into metal to be at its minimum, confidence in the possibility of that conversion must be at its maximum. Ricardo and Smith thought of gold as the relevant standard while Marshall had a bias for paired bimetallic bars ('it would be better to base our currency on two metals than on one',[76] he said, without specifying a precise date for the switch from the real to the ideal); but when all is said and done Ricardo and Smith wanted paper to be convertible into metal and so did Marshall.

Convertibility need not, of course, mean a one-to-one correspondence between metal and notes. Some ratio between metal and notes should exist and it should be definite, but in 1923 Marshall declared that paper could legitimately be 'twice'[77] backing and in 1887 he was even more generous in the illustration he then provided of the proper relationship in the normal situation: 'To ensure convertibility the currency would not be allowed to exceed, say, three times the bullion reserve.'[78] But that is not the end of the story. Over and above the bullion reserve required to back the paper pound at the prescribed metal-to-paper ratio, Marshall urged, the central bank should hold an *additional* reserve, an *extra* hoard of bullion. The excess was to be large (Marshall cites the impressive figure of £20m.[79]) and was to be regarded as a buffer stock held in the interests of stability in order to ensure that a short-run drain should not immediately be accompanied by a reduction in the money supply. Such a contraction in the currency in response to each and every loss of bullion would unnecessarily disrupt domestic industry and might even, as Henry Thornton had warned, 'so exceedingly distress trade and discourage manufactures as to impair . . . those sources of our returning wealth to which we must chiefly trust for the restoration of our balance of trade, and for bringing back the tide of gold into Great Britain'.[80] In the long-run, Thornton had said, paper must contract if gold abandons us – but in the short-run the position is somewhat different:

> There may be an error on the side of too much diminishing bank notes, as well as on the side of too much increasing them . . . . There must, in short, then, be some point at which the bank must stop in respect to the reduction of its notes, however progressive may be the drain upon it for guineas . . . . If there has been any fault in the conduct of the Bank of England, the fault, as I conceive, has rather been . . . on the side of too much restricting its notes in the late seasons of alarm, than on that of too much enlarging them.[81]

Thornton's recommendation – rules and automaticity in the long-run, authorities and discretion in the short – was that of Alfred Marshall, who advocated the mobilisation within the Bank of England of what Thornton had called 'a considerable fund of gold'[82] so as thereby to insulate and protect our permanent from the vicissitudes and misapplications of our temporary. Of course the Bank of England should contract where contraction is inescapable. But it should nonetheless strive to maintain stability so long as stability remains possible; and it should in particular attempt 'to prevent a small exportation of bullion from causing a stringency in the discount market'[83] by means of managed money and leaning against the prevailing winds. Speaking of India, for example, Marshall is quite decisive about the need not to magnify 'occasional disorders of modern business and credit' through too hasty and too violent a use being made of the rate of discount: it is 'the bounden duty of the Government' to preserve stability, he said, and 'the Government is not morally free to give the go-by to this question'.[84]

The Bank of England, in Marshall's view, would seem to be exceptionally wise; for it would seem to be able to make quite difficult decisions with respect both to the price of money (as where, say, it elects to put up interest-rates in an attempt to check the 'unreasonable expansions of credit; which might otherwise grow, after the manner of a fall of snow on a steep mountainside'[85]) and to the quantity of money (the case of ignoring an internal drain linked to a seasonal fluctuation while allowing the money-supply to shrink should a long-run trend be involved). The Bank of England would in addition seem to be exceptionally generous; for, and despite the fact that it was in Marshall's time a private corporation rather than a national monument, it would seem unambiguously to have acknowledged its responsibility to the public interest by agreeing to hold the nation's reserves. The Directors of the Bank, Marshall was pleased to report, have at all times remembered that they are Englishmen first and the servants of their shareholders a poor second: 'No suggestion is made that they have sacrificed general to particular interests. In fact, they act with that full sense of responsibility which belongs to public ministers.'[86] That they are not public ministers at all but rather private businessmen is beside the point: when all is said and done Thornton and Bagehot had wanted the Bank to recognise the public duties associated with its peculiar position and Marshall shared their view.

Excess reserves should be held so as in the short-run to be able to ride out 'occasional pressure'[87] without 'shock to credit' or 'violent fluctuations of discount'.[88] Discretion, however, extends to the short-run and to the short-run alone, and in the long-run a country on the gold standard is compelled by the logic of its situation to adopt the hands-off policy of *laissez-faire* with respect to the quantity of money and to put its faith in the automatic specie-flow mechanism which, via gold movements and price-level adjustments, ensures balance in the international position. Consider two countries on the gold standard: 'Trade tends so to adjust the supplies of gold relatively to the demands for gold in the two countries as to bring gold prices at the seaboards of the two countries to equality, allowance being made for carriage.'[89] Relative prices adjust, purchasing power parity is established, and equilibrium comes about as if guided by an invisible hand. The brutal truth is that ultimately 'our imports have to be paid for by our exports'[90] (Marshall in saying this conspicuously neglects capital flows[91]) and that our business men – however favourable they might be in the short-run to 'a limited and automatic elasticity of fiduciary paper currency'[92] – will not thank a central bank which delays excessively a contraction of currency and a fall in prices that is genuinely indispensable for the recovery of our foreign trade.

What is true of the gold standard is no less true of paired-bars bimetallism – most of all in the case, it must be said, where the new scheme is adopted not by one country alone (although this is technically possible) but rather on a multi-national basis: 'If adopted by several nations it would constitute at once a perfect international basis of currency and prices.'[93] Given such a *de facto* world currency it is clear that if you experience a net influx of bars your prices will tend to rise, if you suffer a net outflow your prices will tend to fall, and the long-run equilibrium situation will be in all but the nature of the metals which balanced the trade the same as under the pure gold standard system:

> The precious metals are then so distributed throughout the world, that, independently of the demand for them for the purposes of hoarding and of the arts, each country has just that aggregate amount of the two metals which corresponds in value to the volume of that part of her business which the habits of her people cause her to transact by payments in coin, account being taken of the rapidity of circulation of coin, and of the absorption of some quantity of the precious metals to act as the basis of a paper currency.[94]

Interestingly, a rather similar outcome is to be expected even where the countries involved are not on gold, not on paired bars, but on entirely different metals. Thus India is on a silver standard, Britain is on a gold standard, and the equilibrium condition is as follows: 'The value of each metal is determined by the relation in which the supply of it stands to the demand for it. The ratio between the two values thus determined is the gold price of silver. According to this old, and I had thought well-established, doctrine, the gold price of silver is determined by the ratio between the prices of commodities in gold and in silver countries.'[95] Should this condition not hold, then, via a change in the quantity of exports relative to that of imports, specie will flow from the country of which the currency is relatively overvalued to the country of which the currency is relatively undervalued and the purchasing power parity equilibrium will, via a change in relative prices as between the two nations, automatically be established. The Indians may be on silver while we are on gold but their exporters nonetheless cannot expect to benefit for any length of time from an under-valuation of the rupee. Sooner or later the invisible hand will come to adjust prices and balance trade – and this despite the fact that their metallic standard and ours are as different as chalk and cheese.

The invisible hand is powerful indeed. The Indians are at least on silver. The Russians, however, are on nothing but the rouble. The Russians issue an inconvertible paper currency and might be assumed to have in that way cut themselves off from balance of payments adjustments via price-level changes. That is not the case: 'Gold prices in England and rouble prices in Russia are determined by the work which the currency has to do in either country on the one hand and the volume of that currency on the other. And when trade is in equilibrium, the gold price of the rouble will be fixed just at the ratio which gold prices in England bear to rouble prices in Russia.'[96] The result obtains exclusively in long-run equilibrium states (Marshall, much under the influence of Ricardo, Mill and Goschen[97] and surprisingly indifferent to short-run disequilibria, declared: 'I am speaking only of permanent, not of the temporary effects'[98]) and the adjustment takes place entirely through inflation and deflation (as opposed to changes in physical quantities, contraction being easy enough at any time and expansion being a real alternative where there is excess capacity[99]), but the implications are clear: even the Russians, despite their fully fiduciary currency, are subject to price-variations caused by differences in 'comparative costs',[100] variations which continue up to that point at which I cannot buy a furry hat more cheaply in Moscow than I can in London (not, indeed, more cheaply in London than you can in Moscow). The 'gold price of roubles cannot be in equilibrium'[101] save at this unique point; while at that unique point there is no further pressure on imports and exports such as might generate further price-variations and therewith any challenge to balance of trade. Russian price-levels would seem to behave very much as our own in response to variations in international supply and international demand. Yet our paper pound is convertible into metallic gold while their paper rouble is only convertible into their paper rouble. The invisible hand is powerful indeed.

Because, indeed, the invisible hand is powerful, the question must inevitably be asked if we really need a proper metallic standard at all. There is a real sense in which a believer in the market-mechanism can legitimately put his faith in paper, and Marshall recognised that an inconvertible pound was a genuine and a valid option: 'In spite of the severe criticism to which this suggestion has been subjected, there seems no good ground for regarding it as wholly impracticable.'[102] In the long-run international supply and international demand coordinate the price levels of all trading countries. In the short-run the central bank holds large reserves and, as Walter Bagehot had insisted, 'must lend that reserve most freely in time of apprehension'[103] – even though a significant increase in the money-supply at a time when the nation is losing specie is hardly in keeping with the gold standard rules of the game. Both in the long-run and in the short, it would appear, the metallic standard in Marshall's monetary economics has something of the character of a fifth wheel. As Marshall was fully prepared to admit: 'If an inconvertible currency is controlled by a strong Government, its amount can be so regulated that the value of a unit of it is maintained at a fixed level.'[104] Yet Marshall unambiguously opted for metal rather than men – presumably because of the following considerations.

First, Marshall was by nature a man of caution. In the case of the proposal for an all-fiduciary currency, this caution led him to postpone outright acceptance or dismissal in favour of a call for further investigation: 'Many long and tedious studies, stretching perhaps over several generations; and many tentative experiments moving cautiously towards the ideal goal, would need to be taken before any venture in this direction could properly be made.'[105] One day we will know more about the implications of the proposal; and the simple principle of risk aversion causes the wise man to defer his final decision until then.

Second, Marshall believed that a 'strong Government' could and would limit fiduciary issues in the interests of price-stability – but that a weak Government might behave irresponsibly in the absence of the metallic constraint. Inconvertibility, in other words, was only acceptable to him where it was not accompanied by government failure. A nation which is on the moral standard has a diminished need for a gold standard; and it may be that Marshall anticipated a withering-away of convertibility consequent upon the upgrading of human character that is brought about through economic growth – but reasoned nonetheless that, 'while human nature remains as it is', convertibility into (a limited supply of) gold remains the best mode of limiting the currency available to us at the moment.

Third, Marshall predicted the emergence of an international currency. Writing in 1887 about the evolution of something for which he was convinced that there existed a genuine social need he said: 'Before very long our foreign trade will, I hope, be simplified by the adoption of some kind of international currency.'[106] Marshall therefore opposed unilateral action in Britain, fearing that one country's premature conversion to paper would hinder rather than help the adoption of an international currency and thereby retard the course of progress.

Fourth, Marshall closely associated the adoption of a tabular standard with the adoption of a non-metallic currency. Speaking of open-market operations, for example, he states that such policy would be conducted by an 'automatic government department' empowered to 'buy Consols for currency whenever £1 was worth more than a unit, and . . . sell Consols for currency whenever it was worth less'[107] – which indicates clearly that the use of discretionary monetary policy and an evolutionary shift from rules to authorities presupposes the prior availability of reliable data on the general price-index. And elsewhere, turning to the international scene, Marshall declared that, if a good index of purchasing power were to be introduced, the world would 'be prepared in say twenty years for an international "fixed standard" paper currency'.[108] Twenty years. Those words were written in 1911.

7 Progress, Politics and Economics

Alfred Marshall believed that the economy matters and that economic growth matters most of all. Economic growth means human betterment – since, and allowing for the element of chaff which inevitably accompanies even the finest of wheat, growth on balance yields a rich harvest of improvements in consumption, conduct and character. Human betterment means good politics – since, and allowing for the fact that the bureaucrat by definition lacks the alertness, flair and initiative of the entrepreneur, a more enlightened and more responsible environment upgrades the ship of State and renders it capable of sailing into waters previously inaccessible to it. Good politics means human betterment – by correcting an undesirable if market-determined distribution of income and by providing a safety-net of care for those in states of dependency. Good politics means economic growth – by plugging potential leaks in the circular flow (the case of the tabular standard of value as a means of obviating the destabilising crisis) and by supplying better fuel for an upgraded vessel (the case of the provision of public goods such as education which we as a nation need and we as individuals do not adequately purchase). Human betterment means economic growth – by generating the tastes and preferences, traits and aptitudes, necessary to render steady advance self-sustaining. Economic growth means human betterment and good politics. Alfred Marshall believed that the economy matters and that economic growth matters most of all – and that economics was therefore an eminently suitable subject of study for a moralist and a missionary who was anxious to do good: 'The dominant aim of economics in the present generation', he insisted, 'is to contribute to a solution of social problems.'[1]

It is with Marshall's perception of the nature and function of that which economists do that we shall be concerned in the four sections of this Chapter – four sections entitled, respectively, The Definition of Economics, Induction and Deduction, Organicism and Economics, and The Mission of the Economist. We shall conclude that there is much truth in Pigou's assessment that Marshall was 'a mixture of philanthropist and scientist, with the philanthropist always struggling, not always struggling successfully, to keep the scientist in order'.[2] Each of us will, however, no doubt reflect that the same might in some measure be said of himself – since a man would be peculiar indeed who devoted his life to the production of poisons without seeking to predict and evaluate the uses that would subsequently be made of his discoveries. As Marshall put it, very early on in his long career, 'a chemist's balance takes no account of the medical properties of an ounce of arsenic, but the chemist does'.[3] What the chemist does in the field of chemistry, the economist does in the field of economics. Does and must do, since no man with self-respect and a sense of responsibility will wish on the Day of Judgement to announce that he was merely following orders.

7.1 THE DEFINITION OF ECONOMICS

Marshall says: 'Economics is a study of men as they live and move and think in the ordinary business of life'.[1] The phrase 'ordinary business of life' is misleading in view of the fact that Marshall so obviously has in mind the 'ordinary life of business': 'Political Economy or Economics is a study of mankind in the ordinary business of life; it examines that part of individual and social action which is most closely connected with the attainment and with the use of the material requisites of wellbeing.'[2] Economics would appear to be particularly concerned in addition with the attainment of those 'material requisites' by means of exchanges involving a *quid pro quo*: ' "Business" is taken here broadly to include all provision for the wants of others which is made in the expectation of payment direct or indirect from those who are to be benefited. It is thus contrasted with the provision for his wants which each one makes for himself, and with those kindly services which are prompted by friendship and family affection.'[3] People do not normally get involved in such exchanges if every hunger is already stilled and every thirst already slaked; and to that extent Lionel Robbins's definition is implicit, that 'economics is the science which studies human behaviour as a relationship between ends and scarce means which have alternative uses'.[4] Implicit it may be, but what is explicit is the narrower, less ambitious, more traditional approach of the classical economists – that economics is, in the words of Senior, 'the Science which treats of the Nature, the Production and the Distribution of Wealth';[5] in the words of McCulloch, the 'science of the laws which regulate the production, distribution, and consumption of those articles or products which have exchangeable value, and are either necessary, useful, or agreeable to man';[6] in the words of Say, a science which 'montre comment se forment, se distribuent et se consomment les richesses';[7] in the words of Mill, a science concerned with 'the nature of Wealth, and the laws of its production and distribution: including, directly or remotely, the operation of all the causes by which the condition of mankind . . . is made prosperous or the reverse'.[8] None of these definitions denies the existence of scarcity but each – perhaps in recognition of the fact that making choices between alternatives is the stuff of human action *in toto* and not simply of economic actions *per se* – chooses to limit the range of specifically *economic* activity to something less than the whole of human life. Marshall's definition is in keeping with the modesty of his classical forebears.

Economics, Marshall believed, is as a science concerned in practice not so much with some physical *quantum* of 'material wealth' as with the subjective meaning and valuation of that wealth; and he reflected that much of the appeal of his subject is indeed due to its ability to estimate perception in terms of money ('so much the best measure of motives that no other can compete with it'[9]). Economics cannot, obviously, examine the contents of the human mind at first hand; but what it can do is to capture a non-observable mental state by means of an outward manifestation, namely 'its motor-force or the incentive which it affords to action'[10] and of which money is 'a fairly good measure'.[11] In this way money comes to serve as quite a reasonable proxy for psychological variables such as intent, desire, pleasure, exertion, and allows the economist to quantify that which, to the student of, say, ethics, never goes beyond the level of impressions and intuitions: 'It is this definite and exact money measurement of the steadiest motives in business life, which has enabled economics far to outrun every other branch of the study of man.'[12] Ordinary people have, relying on common sense, long used the same proxy and acted as if market value in some way measures mental state. Adam Smith was the man chiefly responsible for introducing the measuring rod into economics and for making it the centrepiece of the theory of supply and demand: 'The best economic work which came after the

Wealth of Nations is distinguished from that which went before, by a clearer insight into the balancing and weighing, by means of money, of the desire for the possession of a thing on the one hand, and on the other of all the various efforts and self-denials which directly and indirectly contribute towards making it.'[13] Economics is concerned with the pecuniary trade-off between benefits and costs, wants and sacrifices; and it proceeds by means of 'exact definition and measurement'[14] to an extent unknown to primitive man and evidently one aspect of progress in its own right.

The pecuniary proxy is useful for purposes of comparisons as between alternative commodities, each yielding utility to the consumer: 'If we find a man in doubt whether to spend a few pence on a cigar, or a cup of tea, or on riding home instead of walking home, then we may follow ordinary usage, and say that he expects from them equal pleasures.'[15] The proxy is also useful for purposes of comparisons as between discrete purchasers – provided that we limit the range of such inter-personal comparison to individuals with similar levels of income and for whom the marginal utility of money is in consequence approximately the same: 'If the desires to secure either of two pleasures will induce people in similar circumstances each to do just an hour's extra work, or will induce men in the same rank of life and with the same means each to pay a shilling for it, we then may say that those pleasures are equal for our purposes, because the desires for them are equally strong incentives to action for persons under similar conditions.'[16] Such comparisons are to be made with increased confidence where the sample is large and we, recognising that 'the same surgical operation causes different amounts of pain to different people',[17] therefore opt for 'averages sufficiently broad to cause the personal peculiarities of individuals to counterbalance one another'.[18] Here as elsewhere, it would appear, the proper concern of the economist is with the normal value, as in the following example:

> If there are a thousand persons living in Sheffield, and another thousand in Leeds, each with about £100 a-year, and a tax of £1 is levied on all of them; we may be sure that the loss of pleasure or other injury which the tax will cause in Sheffield is of about equal importance with that which it will cause in Leeds . . . . This probability becomes greater still if all of them are adult males engaged in the same trade; and therefore presumably somewhat similar in sensibility and temperament, in taste and education.[19]

Obviously 'the pleasures which two persons derive from smoking cannot be directly compared', but a careful use of the pecuniary proxy does at least permit us to measure mental states of others 'indirectly and conjecturally by their effects'.[20] Such a second-best solution is far from perfect but it is also far from useless.

Whether or not we may 'be sure' that a valid comparison of subjective sacrifice can be made as between individuals with similar levels of income, the problem cannot be avoided that the aggregate demand for a commodity normally reflects the effective demand of individuals with quite different levels of income. An umbrella costing £1 is, after all, likely to be purchased not only by cutlers and weavers on £100 in Sheffield and Leeds but also by barristers on £500 in London and dustmen on £50 in Exeter, and these persons, so different in reference group and (marginal utility of) income, help to establish, in markets based on supply and demand, a price the subjective meaning of which in terms of satisfaction is not easy to interpret. Marshall was aware of this difficulty but saw no reason for it to detract from the validity of the comparisons which he wished to draw – since he was, he felt, in possession of a vital piece of information which constituted the missing link in the logic of his argument: 'On the whole . . . it happens that by far the greater number of the events with which economics deals, affect in about equal proportions all the different classes of society; so that if the money measures of the happiness caused by the two events are equal, there is not in general any very great difference between the amounts of the happiness in the two cases.'[21] In a letter to Pigou, he made his position on aggregation and inter-personal comparisons clearer still: 'I have always insisted that the demand price of a group is not any approximate measure of satisfaction, save on the assumption that people of different incomes and also of different sensibilities are evenly distributed throughout the group.'[22] Given that assumption however, then even in highly aggregative situations money measures may still be taken as 'rough approximations'[23] of the relative utilities of different commodities for purposes of comparison. Thus, 'if it be given that a bottle of wine and a pound of tea can be disposed of for the same price in the same open market at a given period, the gratifications of the purchasers in this market at this time due to the bottle of wine and the pound of tea, have this price as their common exchange measure'.[24]

The image of man rationally proportioning marginal expenditure to marginal utility would seem to suggest that economic action presupposes a calculative, maximising orientation. Insofar as economic science is concerned with reality, of course, it cannot presuppose anything of this kind; for 'in this, as in every other respect, economics takes man just as he is in ordinary life: and in ordinary life people do not weigh beforehand the results of every action'.[25] That having been said, however, there remain good reasons nonetheless for presupposing a rational orientation in economic theory. There is, for one thing, a straightforward empirical observation to be reported: 'The side of life with which economics is specially concerned is that in which man's conduct is most deliberate, and in which he most often reckons up the advantages and disadvantages of any particular action before he enters on it.'[26] Then there is a behavioural explanation in terms of the momentum inherent in matter – since survival itself in a competitive business environment requires a disposition significantly more practical than that which relies heavily on reflexes and instincts 'similar to those that lead a beaver in confinement to build himself a dam': 'In business matters in the modern world such habits quickly die away'[27] as if they did not the businesses themselves soon would. And there is, finally, an important general point to be made about social evolution and about the extent to which the norm of rationality is on the increase in increasingly affluent societies: after allowing for persons of 'wayward temperament', Marshall reflected, one cannot fail to notice that more and more people nowadays are taking the trouble to look before they leap. Clearly, 'if a man is steadfast and thoughtful, even his impulses are the products of habits which he has adopted more or less deliberately'.[28] If therefore such a person were on a particular occasion to act without current calculation and on the basis of habits and customs, yet still 'the habits and customs themselves are most nearly sure to have arisen from a close and careful watching the advantages and disadvantages of different courses of conduct'.[29] Deliberateness nowadays is in the air; and for that reason it is entirely correct to expect not only a high degree of rationality in economic affairs but, indeed, a 'Principle of Continuity' in the economising temperament, a 'continuous gradation from the actions of "city men", which are based on deliberate and far-reaching calculations, and are executed with vigour and ability, to those of ordinary people who have neither the power nor the will to conduct their affairs in a business-like way'.[30] Different peer-groups have different behaviour-patterns even in an era in which means-ends thinking is becoming increasingly prevalent; but, 'when that is once understood, the theory of normal value is applicable to the actions of the unbusiness-like classes in the same way, though not with the same precision of detail, as to those of the merchant or banker'.[31] The rational orientation being increasingly characteristic of social action as a whole, the economist can with increasing legitimacy seize upon it and use it as the basis for the special theories which he formulates to explain and predict human behaviour in the special area of social action which is uniquely his own – and to which, it must be added, the rational orientation would seem to be particularly appropriate.

Rational actions lend themselves to quantification and precision. Non-rational actions do not; 'and it is for this reason, and not because they are not based on self-interest, that the machinery of economics cannot be brought to bear on them'.[32] Perhaps it cannot, but the fact remains that human problems do not divide themselves neatly along the lines which divide the various academic disciplines; and we in economics accordingly have no choice but to 'deal with the whole of man's nature, though we lay chief stress on certain special aspects of it'.[33] Our task in this respect is difficult. It is not, however, as difficult as it would appear to an outside observer who did not grasp that presupposing a rational orientation in economic theory is in no way tantamount to presupposing a material or monetary *quid pro quo* in economic action: 'The only conditions required in a measure for economic purposes are that it should be something definite and transferable. Its taking a material form is practically convenient, but is not essential.'[34] Public honours, for example, can and do in certain circumstances 'serve to measure the strength of motives almost as conveniently and exactly as money does with us',[35] and a similar observation might be made concerning the exchange of extra achievement for extra approbation which is so often to be found within a closed community of professionals, scientists or artisans: 'The desire to earn the approval, to avoid the contempt of those around one is a stimulus to action which often works with some sort of uniformity in any class of persons at a given time and place.'[36] In such cases the machinery of economics can be brought to bear on the measurement of motives ('the chief task of economic science'), and this without any need to assume 'an exclusive regard for material wealth, to the neglect of other and higher objects of desire'.[37] Other cases present greater difficulties, however, for reasons which would appear in essence to fall into two categories.

The first category involves actions emanating from absolutes. Marshall, as we have seen, laid great stress on the extent to which ethical forces constrain the pursuit of economic objectives: 'Everyone who is worth anything carries his higher nature with him into business; and, there as elsewhere, he is influenced by his personal affections, by his conceptions of duty and his reverence for high ideals.'[38] Such a man will 'delight in doing his work well for its own sake, or in sacrificing himself for the good of his family, his neighbours, or his country';[39] and to the extent that underlying absolutes render his response a constant irrespective of the immediate stimulus, the economist will be compelled to confess that there is no good measure of his immediate motivation. The requisite schedule could, of course, be constructed were we to learn that the man in question were willing to 'look mean'[40] to others – or appear unfair in his own eyes – in exchange for compensation of some form at the margin; and the fact that egoism is so frequently mixed in with altruism would seem to suggest that such trade-offs are not inconceivable. Thus Marshall says that, 'as there may be a taint of selfishness in a man's desire to do what seems likely to benefit his fellow-workers, so there may be an element of personal pride in his desire that his family should prosper during his life and after it'[41] – and where motivation is thus mixed, the economist will reason, elasticity of substitution and variability of response are likely then to restore to his discipline its *raison d'être*. The economist's logic is entirely correct save in one respect, that actions involving such trade-offs are by definition not actions emanating from absolutes; and thus by definition have no place in the present category.

The second category involves actions the incidence of which is spasmodic, unpredictable and irregular. Clearly, 'those manifestations of nature which occur most frequently, and are so orderly that they can be closely watched and narrowly studied, are the basis of economic as of most other scientific work'.[42] The search for such real-world regularities would indeed seem to suggest the need rather to include than to exclude the many-sidedness of the human experience: 'Nature's action is complex: and nothing is gained in the long run by pretending that it is simple, and trying to describe it in a series of elementary propositions.'[43] Thus it is that scholars, increasingly unhappy with 'Ricardo's tacit assumption that no motive of action except the desire for wealth need be much considered by the economist',[44] have sought to improve the real-world relevance of eonomic science by incorporating in it an increasingly wide range of human action, including the philanthropic: 'They welcome the fact that some kinds of philanthropic action can be described in statistical returns, and can to a certain extent be reduced to law, if sufficiently broad averages are taken.'[45] All this is well and good – except for one thing: 'It will however probably be always true that the greater part of those actions, which are due to a feeling of duty and love of one's neighbour, cannot be classed, reduced to law and measured.'[46] The economist ought to be concerned not with some abstract 'economic man' but with 'man as he is . . . a man of flesh and blood'.[47] Sadly, the facts let us down the more widely that we range; and, given that we want theories which 'can be verified by results',[48] we are (purely as statisticians and not at all as theoreticians) condemned to reject observations relating to motives refractory to systematisation.

Marshall said that 'the economist studies mental states rather through their manifestations than in themselves';[49] and he defined 'economic laws' quite specifically as 'those social laws which relate to branches of conduct in which the strength of the motives chiefly concerned can be measured by a money price'.[50] Marshall's discussion, however, extending as it does from pecuniary compensation to remuneration via honour and approbation and thence to moral absolutes and psychological unpredictabilities, would seem itself to range beyond the narrow confines of the subject as he delimits it. Marshall had no fear of such voyages of discovery, arguing as normally he did that there is no 'hard and sharp line of division between those social laws which are, and those which are not, to be regarded also as economic laws' but rather 'a continuous gradation from social laws concerned almost exclusively with motives that can be measured by price, to social laws in which such motives have little place'.[51] Clearly, where the lines of division which man draws are in essence artificial ones, rigid demarcation can lead to radical error should the economist fail to grasp that the boundaries of his republic are mere abstractions, drawn for the convenience of the occasion and little else: 'The more simple and absolute an economic doctrine is, the greater will be the confusion which it brings into attempts to apply economic doctrines to practice, if the dividing lines . . . cannot be found in real life.'[52] There is evidently much to be said for 'greater breadth of outlook',[53] and the economist ought at the very least to take an interest in the related human sciences: 'It is the duty of those who are giving their chief work to a limited field, to keep up close and constant correspondence with those who are engaged in neighbouring fields. Specialists who never look beyond their own domain are apt to see things out of true proportion.'[54]

Which is not to say, however, that the boundaries between those domains and fields should be ignored, or that the discipline of economics *per se* ought to be swallowed up by the Comtean interdisciplinarity of unified social science. Such an approach would have the advantage of underlining 'how complex social phenomena are, how intricately interwoven with one another, and withal how changeful',[55] but the disadvantage of being 'too wide and too various' to be of much practical utility: 'Doubtless there is a unity underlying all the forces of nature; but whatever progress has been made towards discovering it, has depended on knowledge obtained by persistent specialized study, no less than on occasional broad surveys of the field of nature as a whole.'[56] So while Marshall obviously shared with Comte the desire to correct the bias caused by isolation from the other human sciences that has characterised much of English economic thought, he also saw the advantages of division of labour and the case for breaking up the complex problem into its component parts, each then to be treated 'by a special scientific organon'.[57] There is a need, in other words, for depth as well as breadth, and much accordingly to be said for the precision that can only come from 'patient detailed work'[58] concentrating on one aspect of social action at a time. Besides that, and as a purely factual matter, the unified social science so highly praised by the Comteans 'does not exist; it shows no signs of coming into existence. There is no use in waiting idly for it; we must do what we can with our present resources.'[59] Economics as a separate study of one and only one part of the human condition has in effect, at least at the present stage of intellectual evolution, no choice but to retain its separate identity.

Within that separate identity the economist may legitimately schematise and organise but he has no right to mystify. An economist who wishes to be useful must also be intelligible; and where he does allow himself to become incomprehensible, he not only 'confuses business men' but is in addition 'in some danger of committing himself to untenable positions'.[60] Normally, therefore, 'the economist must forego the aid of a complete set of technical terms. He must make the terms in common use serve his purpose in the expression of precise thought.'[61] Normally but not always, as in the case of 'consumers' surplus', a new concept and a new term which Marshall defends as follows: 'In this, as in other cases, the apparent simplicity of popular phrases veils a real complexity, and it is the duty of science to bring out that latent complexity; to face it; and to reduce it as far as possible: so that, in later stages we may handle firmly difficulties that could not be grasped with a good grip by the vague thought and language of ordinary life.'[62] The use of technical terminology may be defended on similar grounds in instances such as 'elasticity of demand', 'quasi-rent', 'internal and external economies', 'the representative firm', where the use of household words would tend to veil the essential complexity and uniqueness of the phenomena in question. When dealing with such phenomena, Marshall reflected, it would be unwise to adopt the unjustifiably careless usages of numerous distinguished authors. He mentioned John Stuart Mill, for example, who 'feared to weight the science, which was not then popular, with the burden of technical terms' and whose style, accordingly, is 'so easeful as to incite his readers to overmuch rapidity';[63] and W. S. Jevons, whose apparent lucidity 'serves to render darkness visible; to make us conscious of the absence of a specialised economic vocabulary, perhaps, on the whole, the severest penalty that the science has paid for its popularity'.[64] Such authors courted popularity at the cost of precision. Normally, it is true, 'the economist must accommodate himself to the practice of the market-place',[65] and must ensure (as, quite properly, did Mill and Jevons) that technical terms are 'kept within very narrow limits'.[66] Normally but not always; and where precision is called for even at the cost of popularity, then the economic scientist has no option but to 'escape ambiguity by the adoption of a great number of technical terms; each of which is defined sharply, and has no variations of meaning'.[67]

Evidently cases do exist where jargon is acceptable and technical terms should be employed. In such cases, 'the use of technical terms at starting adds nothing to knowledge: but it puts familiar knowledge in a firm compact shape, ready to serve as the basis for further study'.[68] The phrase 'adds nothing to knowledge' is here highly significant and reminds us of the extent to which Marshall, a man of considerable personal humility, consistently abstained from making exaggerated claims for his profession. Economic science, Marshall concluded, 'is but the working of common sense aided by appliances of organized analysis and general reasoning, which facilitate the task of collecting, arranging, and drawing inferences from particular facts';[69] and the economist himself 'merely brings to light difficulties that are latent in the common discourse of life, so that by being frankly faced they may be thoroughly overcome'.[70] Even in as abstruse an area as the theory of capital, Marshall noted, economic science has in truth made 'no startling discoveries': 'Everything of importance which is now known to economists has long been acted upon by able business men, though they may not have been able to express their knowledge clearly, or even accurately.'[71] Economists may in the circumstances legitimately schematise and organise, and even where appropriate employ technical terms, but they should never forget how many of their facts are already in the public domain nor that common sense must remain 'the ultimate arbiter in every practical problem':[72] 'The only resources we have for dealing with social problems as a whole lie in the judgement of common sense. For the present, and for a long time to come, that must be the final arbiter.'[73]

If the task of the economist is to so great an extent that of sensing and making sense of what is 'in the air', then he needs to be sensitive as well as intelligent: 'The economist needs the three great intellectual faculties, perception, imagination and reason: and most of all he needs imagination.'[74] Imagination, so as to grasp the multiplicity of potential future consequences of present-day causes that lie buried and hidden beneath the surface of things. Imagination, in addition, so as to enter into and share the wealth of perceptions, norms, orientations and ideas of his fellow men; for economics to Marshall was first and foremost about *thinking* people, about social actors whose mental states as well as concrete behaviour-patterns were to figure prominently in the economist's investigations. All of this presupposes an ability to empathise which, indeed, the study of economics helps us to develop. In a defence of emotive identification and *Verstehen* which could have come straight from the pages of Max Weber and is strongly reminiscent of Adam Smith on the *Moral Sentiments*, Marshall writes as follows concerning the capacity to change places in the mind via an act of empathetic imagination: 'Economic studies call for and develop the faculty of sympathy, and especially that rare sympathy which enables people to put themselves in the place, not only of their comrades, but also of other classes.'[75] One way in which economic investigation develops this latent capacity for fellowship is, incidentally, through the very use of the empirical method itself, as in the case of 'inquiries ... of the reciprocal influences which character and earnings, methods of employment and habits of expenditure exert on one another'.[76] The study of economics (particularly where use is made of everyday language and excessive abstraction is eschewed) thus exercises a humanising influence on the economist by making him more open to the feelings of others. His own character is upgraded through economic activity. He too benefits fully from the on-going process of economic growth and human betterment.

7.2 INDUCTION AND DEDUCTION

Marshall, on methodology as on most topics, studiously avoided controversy and was generous in his praise for all schools. As Pigou puts it, 'All economists for him were fellow-workers.... Co-operation, not rivalry, was the way to advance science': 'Marshall's view was that economics is a field needing the co-operative work of many men with many different bents of mind. He would have nothing to do with controversies between deductive schools, inductive schools, historical schools and so on. There was work for all, and he welcomed all. Constructive work was what he wanted.'[1]

Here as usual Marshall contrived to have the best of both worlds. On the one hand he believed strongly that the economist must be 'greedy ... for facts':[2] 'Facts are the bricks out of which reason builds the edifice of knowledge.'[3] On the other hand he argued consistently that 'facts by themselves are silent':[4] 'We can seldom infer particulars from other particulars without passing in effect through generals, however simple be the subject-matter of our study; and we can never do so in the complex problems of social life.'[5] Here as usual Marshall sought to occupy the middle ground, in this case between the extreme inductivists such as Schmoller and Ashley and the extreme deductivism of Ricardo's *Principles* and Cournot's *Recherches* – quite deliberately so, as in the following declaration concerning the economist and his task: 'He needs to make careful use of analysis and deduction, because only by their aid can he select the right facts, group them rightly, and make them serviceable for suggestions in thought and guidance in practice.... Or to put the same thing in another way the explanation of the past and the prediction of the future are not different operations, but the same worked in opposite directions, the one worked from effect to cause, the other from cause to effect.'[6] It was for postulating a false dichotomy rather than continuity and synthesis that Marshall took J.N. Keynes to task in correspondence about the latter's *Scope and Method of Political Economy* of 1891:

> You make all your contrasts rather too sharply for me. You talk of the inductive & deductive methods: whereas I contend that each involves the other, & that historians are always deducing, & that even the most deductive writers are always implicitly at least basing themselves on observed facts.... I think the right order is *first* to emphasize the mutual dependence of induction & deduction, &

> *afterwards* to show in what kinds of inquiry the economist has to spend the greater part of his time in collecting arranging & narrating facts, & in what kinds he is chiefly occupied in reasoning about them & trying to evolve general processes of analysis & general theories which shall show the Many in the One & The One in the Many.[7]

Here as usual it was Marshall's study to have one foot in each camp precisely because each, like the two blades of the scissors of supply and demand, was bereft of real world relevance save in combination with the other. It is to those two camps – the fact-gatherers and the theorizers, respectively – that we now turn our attention.

(1) Induction

Marshall identified that aspect of economic methodology which proceeds from 'experience' as being 'the search for and arrangement of facts with a view to discovering the ideas, some temporary and local, others universal and eternal, which underlie them'.[8] A statement, as it happens, which is in effect a bundle of three separate elements.

The *first* element in this formulation is the empirical emphasis on collection and tabulation of data, something, Marshall maintains, which is very much part of the English economic tradition. The classical economists themselves 'wrote economic histories that are in their way at least equal to anything that has been done since'; 'most of them were practical men with a wide and direct personal knowledge of business affairs'; and 'they brought about the collection of statistics by public and private agencies and that admirable series of parliamentary inquiries, which have been a model for all countries, and have inspired the modern German historic school with many of their best thoughts'.[9] We today must follow in their footsteps: 'Our first duty as economists is to make a reasoned catalogue of the world as it is.'[10] Scholarship 'thrown back on general impressions'[11] cannot expect to make significant advances; 'the progress of economic science depends largely on the stock of trustworthy and appropriate statistics at its command';[12] and even the 'constructive faculty' of the modern business genius benefits considerably from the assistance of 'the printed figure' and 'cumulative progressive knowledge based on organized records of observed facts'.[13] Both economics and the economy, it would appear, require a sound foundation in factual evidence, in observation and investigation. Looking forward in 1897, Marshall reflected that the full development of quantitative economics remained on the agenda as a task for the century to come,[14] but he also noted with approbation just how much research in that area had already been done: 'It is one of the great achievements of our age; and an important addition to our real wealth. It has done more than almost anything else to broaden our ideas, to increase our knowledge of ourselves, and to help us to understand the evolution of man's moral and social life, and of the Divine Principle of which it is an embodiment.'[15]

The *second* element in Marshall's formulation of the inductive approach is the positivist stress on repetition of sequences and with it the ability to predict. It is this capacity to say not only what people *now* want or have in the *past* wanted but also what they will in the *future* want that makes the extrapolative or inferential method in economics particularly useful for policy purposes: 'The action of the statesman and the advice of the economist must be based upon as exact an estimate as may be got of the relative importance of different sets of advantages.'[16] It is this utility of 'wide knowledge' that above all else renders socially legitimate the accumulation of 'a vast mass of facts';[17] since it is those facts which then give us some power to generalise, to formulate 'general statements or laws'[18] based on a careful observation of habitual association. It is therefore only logical that the economist, like any other rational person, should be greedy for facts, for facts in truth 'are the bricks out of which reason builds the edifice of knowledge'[19] – and thence action the edifice of the economy.

The *third* element in Marshall's conceptualisation of the inductive approach is the analytical predisposition and the preexistence of intellectual baggage carried over into today's experience from yesterday's discovery. It is the preexistence of such schemata which guides the observer in his selection and classification of phenomena, and which in addition assists him in his struggle to distinguish the temporary from the eternal, the local from the universal. The inductive method almost by definition cannot be simply the careful processing of 'the facts which have been . . . brought together and arranged by the historian and the observer of contemporary life'[20] precisely because a choice must be made as to *which* facts to collect and *which* mode of arrangement to adopt – and that choice (the precondition for the drawing out of social laws from the inspection of raw data) presupposes the preexistence of a map to direct and guide. Such a map is by its very nature antecedent to today's learning process and represents therefore an essential *deus ex machina* without which the inductive method would be condemned to radical impotence when confronted with data. As Adam Smith himself was fully aware: 'Adam Smith saw clearly that while economic science must be based on a study of facts, the facts are so complex, that they generally can teach nothing directly; they must be interpreted by careful reasoning and analysis.'[21] Even the Historical School, despite its boast that it merely stockpiled evidence without drawing inferences, played in truth an active rather than a passive role via the execution of the indispensable tasks of selection and grouping: 'The human mind abhors a vacuum in its notions of the causal relations between the events that are presented vividly to it. By merely placing things together in a certain order, and consciously or unconsciously suggesting *post hoc ergo propter hoc*, the historian takes on himself some responsibility as a guide.'[22]

The inductive approach, as Marshall explained it, was one which employed theories derived from past experience in order to spin new theories capable of explaining present-day observations and of predicting future occurrences. Marshall had, however, no illusions concerning the limitations of the method, and drew attention in particular to three of these.

The *first* limitation has to do with the deficiencies of the data: 'Economists know that nearly all their "statistics" are mere aggregates of guesses; even such relatively definite figures as those relating to exports and imports are made up largely of conjectural items. Consequently when a mathematical outsider . . . incessantly upbraids them for setting mere opinions against the statistical "facts" which he has culled in a hurry, they are apt to observe that if he knew more he would know that he knew less.'[23] Such deficiencies are endemic to all empirically-orientated modes of investigation, but are a particular problem in the study of man: 'Even sciences, which deal with concrete facts and conditions as definite and immutable as those of physics appear to be, cannot claim certainty over the whole of their area. In biological sciences the area over which certainty extends is relatively very small; and in the social sciences it is less than in those which deal with the lower forms of life.'[24] The information available to the scientist is all too frequently either incomplete or inexact (or, worst of all, both), and in such circumstances he has no choice but to acknowledge the tentative nature of his knowledge: 'A navigator who has for some time been unable to take good observations, and is in waters where the currents are uncertain, must be content with probability... The function of economic analysis is to render a service within its sphere similar to, though less thorough than, that which the science of navigation renders within its sphere.'[25] As any science (physical or social) matures, so it acquires not only more knowledge but also a growing awareness of the vastness of the area which lies beyond its knowledge. Thus, via patience and perseverence, 'the certainties of physics increase in number, but its uncertainties increase much faster'.[26] And in economics: 'Adam Smith cleared up many obscurities and uncertainties: but the area of his conscious uncertainty was far greater than that of his predecessors.'[27] Such an apprehension of the major constraint on accurate explanation and prediction that is represented by deficiencies of the data is indeed an important reason for his superiority over Ricardo: 'Ricardo's bias was towards making his ground certain, so far as he went, rather than towards broadening his outlook: and his vigorous narrow certainties had such sway that men rested on them, with the result that little truly constructive work was done for a long while; though in consequence of that very stagnation, the science appeared to increase in certainty.'[28] Since Ricardo's times, fortunately, perceived uncertainty in economics has increased in 'larger proportions'[29] than has perceived certainty, and this is all to the good: 'Great... is the usefulness of Ricardo's method. But even greater are the evils which may arise from a crude application of its suggestions to real problems. For that simplicity which makes it helpful, makes it also deficient and even treacherous.'[30] Marshall himself, fond as he was of quoting statistics or reporting factual information gleaned from technical monographs, industrial visits, conversations with union leaders, parliamentary reports (*Industry and Trade* is a veritable encyclopedia of such information), demonstrated in the last analysis a profoundly Smithian modesty when it came to recognising the limitations imposed by imperfect understanding. Marshall can be infuriatingly vague and tantalisingly obscure; and Terence Hutchison is hardly alone in pointing to the reluctant agnostic's 'steady refusal to sacrifice more of the variety of reality to rigid definition and logical precision than is absolutely necessary for the analysis in hand'.[31] Marshall's comment would presumably have been that reality itself is viscous and difficult to schematise and that he, the sculptor, was only being faithful to the nature and limitations of his medium.

The *second* limitation has to do with the fallacy of misplaced *ceteris paribus*. A fire tends *ceteris paribus* to make a room warmer – but 'when a warm day is being followed by a frosty night, a room with an open window may become colder as the newly-lighted fire in it obtains strength'.[32] A strong wind tends *ceteris paribus* to cause apples to drop – but 'no one denies that a gust of wind will bring down apples that are ready to fall',[33] and in such a case it is not the wind but the ripeness that is the principal cause of the observed phenomenon. A restriction on new entry into a trade tends *ceteris paribus* to raise wages in that trade – but 'if the supply of one factor is disturbed, the supply of others is likely to be disturbed also'[34] and higher pay might in addition lead to lower pay where men in consequence are replaced by machines. An expansion of sales on the part of a perfect competitor tends *ceteris paribus* to increase revenues – but what one can do, all cannot: 'This fact is analogous to the fact that, though a shipwrecked man will increase his chance of reaching the shore, if he is able to rest one hand on the shoulder of another of the crew, yet the general adoption of this practice would greatly increase the chance that they would all be drowned.'[35] A tariff newly imposed tends *ceteris paribus* to have a short-run impact on imports – but also any number of 'deferred effects'[36] complicated by 'many side issues'[37] arising none the less surely for arising subject to a certain 'retardation':[38] 'If reckoning is made with them, the main issues are obscured: the particular trees close at hand prevent us from seeing the wood: and, if they are ignored provisionally, a partial solution is apt to be mistaken for the complete.'[39] All of which serves to demonstrate the problems and pitfalls associated with the fallacy of misplaced *ceteris paribus* and to underline why Marshall, writing to Louis Fry in 1914, was able to declare: 'My favourite *dictum* is: – Every statement in regard to economic affairs which is short is a misleading fragment, a fallacy or a truism.'[40] This is not to say that the economist should make no use of 'tendency laws' (an approach, after all, which has a long and distinguished history in his discipline, as is illustrated by the Malthusian theory of population or the Marxian theory of profit), only that he should take great care not to fall victim to his own propaganda. A straightforward comparison of concomitant variations in two variables is a tempting exercise but also in some measure a meaningless one – since the progress of knowledge *per se* 'is throwing increasing doubt on the possibility of attributing any event to a single cause. The more an event is studied, the larger is generally the number of causes, by which it is seen to have been influenced; and there is seldom an easy and decisive means of isolating the influence of any one cause.'[41] The economist should accordingly approach 'tendency laws' with some caution and recognise the complexities and kaleidoscopic interdependencies inherent in the nature of the phenomena with which he is concerned: 'A selection of relevant items is a difficult task. An untrained student is likely to overlook some of the influences which bear strongly, though indirectly, on the matter at issue: and an unscrupulous partisan can often so select his data and so group them as to suggest false conclusions; even though every statement on which he bases them is true, as far as it goes.'[42] In the area of inference from evidence as in so many others, it is clear, 'sharp tools cut inexpert fingers';[43] while even experts acknowledge that complexities and kaleidoscopic interdependencies severely restrict their ability to explain and predict with the confidence that would have been theirs had they remained the prisoners of the fallacy of misplaced *ceteris paribus*.

The *third* limitation has to do with time ('the centre of the chief difficulty of almost every economic problem'[44]), with dynamic adaptation, with continuous change so great that in area after area 'history does not repeat itself'[45] and 'the experience of the past does not foretell the future':[46] 'We of this generation, being hurried along in a whirl of change, cannot measure accurately the forces at work, and it is probable that the best guesses we can make will move the smiles of future generations'.[47] Matter is in motion and even the guarded inference based on precedent might in the circumstances be somewhat wide of the mark. New facts are constantly emerging, old facts are constantly combining and re-combining in new mixes; and the impression one has is of a future that is genuinely 'complex and uncertain': 'The forces of which economics has to take account are more numerous, less definite, less well known, and more diverse in character than those of mechanics; while the material on which they act is more uncertain and less homogeneous.'[48] The human sciences are concerned, save for the purposes of elementary exposition exclusively, not with physical equilibrium and comparative statics but with organic evolution and perpetual dynamics; and thus not with 'the immutable basis of human nature' but with the 'ever-shifting arrangements of society' and the 'constant changes in human nature'.[49] Intellectual obsolescence in such an environment is more likely than immortality: 'Our present economic conditions are quite unlike any that have existed before', even 'habits and institutions which had been assumed to be inherent in human nature are comparatively of modern growth',[50] and forecasts in a world which is 'constantly changing'[51] are bound to be 'falsified by new developments, such as that of aviation, which are already becoming prominent; and by others of which we have as yet no inkling'.[52] Obviously, 'if the subject-matter of a science passes through different stages of development, the laws which apply to one stage will seldom apply without modification to others',[53] and Marshall for his own part was fully aware of the implications of such change for the longevity of his treatise: 'I think it will make my poor *Principles*, with a lot of poor comrades, into waste paper. The more I think of it, the less I can guess what the world will be like fifty years hence.'[54] Where time passes and changes take place, in other words, any prediction of the future on the basis of the present is bound to be eminently problematic. As Marshall put it in a fragment dating from 1922: 'Prediction in economics must be hypothetical. Show an interrupted game at chess to an expert and he will be bold indeed if he prophesies its future stages. If either side makes one move ever so little different from what he has expected, all the following moves will be altered; and after two or three moves more the whole face of the game will have become different.'[55] In such a situation sustained ignorance would seem to be the inescapable travelling-companion of sustained upheaval; and explanation and prediction based on careful induction from out-of-date information reveal themselves as subject to very considerable limitations indeed.

Which is not to say that forecasts should not be made of history-to-come. On the contrary, they can and must be made – despite the undeniable fact that they situate the scholar 'on dangerous ground' – since, when all is said and done, 'greater risks are taken where no attempt is made to forecast the future, while considering methods of action or inaction that will largely affect the future, than by straining inadequate eyes in reading such faint indications of the future as can be discerned by them'.[56] Our grasp of history-to-come is imperfect but our curiosity is great, and it is entirely appropriate for us in the circumstances to 'allow ourselves to venture a little on untried ground, and speculate as to the future; not being deterred by the reflection that the fond fancies of one age as to noble possibilities of social development have not very often evoked as much approval as mirth in later generations'.[57] Marshall himself ventured more than a little on 'untried ground', but he was fully aware of the essential incompatibility of his anxieties concerning forecasting and his hopes with respect to progress.

(2) Deduction

Marshall identified a second strand in economic methodology, namely the analytical input, and stressed that economic theory is 'essential': 'No one gets any real grip of economic problems unless he will work at it.'[58] Marshall had a great deal of respect for the historical school ('The more I knew of the work of Sir W. J. Ashley and the late Professor Schmoller, the warmer became my regard for them'[59]) and for antecedent historicists such as Richard Jones (an author whose 'great services to English economics have been insufficiently recognized'[60] and which, indeed, 'gave a direction to a good deal of my subsequent reading'[61]); but he also criticised extreme empiricists for seeking to argue directly from facts to facts 'without the intervention of any formal theory'.[62] Without theory, Marshall maintained, the scholar simply does not know which facts to select, how to organise and group his data, how to interpret his results – and, most important of all, perhaps – how to explain the causes of the phenomena he investigates; since 'observation discovers nothing directly of the actions of causes, but only of sequences in time'[63] and some purchase on causality can accordingly be acquired not through the facts *in vacuo* but 'only by reason acting on the facts'.[64] The economist of the future, Marshall emphasized, must 'work in the light of facts, but the light will not be thrown directly, it will be reflected and concentrated by science'.[65] Without the power yielded by theory – and, specifically, the 'power to order and arrange knowledge'[66] – the economist of the future would be bewildered by the multiplicity of facts at his fingertips and unable to make constructive use of those facts in order to elucidate and improve the human condition. The facts by themselves, it must at all times be remembered, are quintessentially silent in the absence of the 'systematic and organised methods of reasoning'[67] that go by the name of theoretical economics: 'The economist . . . must be suspicious of any direct light that the past is said to throw on problems of the present. He must stand fast by the more laborious plan of interrogating facts in order to learn the manner of action of causes singly and in combination.'[68]

Economic theory, Marshall said, is 'essential', but he also warned that its claims should not be exaggerated and that it is, for all intents and purposes, 'but a very small part of economics proper': 'Economic theory is, in my opinion, as mischievous an imposter when it claims to be economics *proper* as is mere crude unanalysed history.'[69] Such, sadly, was the claim of some of the classical economists who, overconfident about their axioms and their logic, had an unjustifiable tendency 'to indulge in excessively abstract reasonings'[70] and to neglect 'a large group of facts'[71] – and to produce in consequence a series of propositions which were all too frequently narrow, inelastic and unrealistic. Even if Ricardo's economic theories actually 'corresponded very closely to the actual facts of his time'[72] (and this would appear to have been the case), there is still no reason to expect them to be 'universally true'[73] (as certain naive deductivists amongst his followers maintained); and the extent to which those theories led to misleading generalisations 'under conditions of time and place different from those in which they had their origin'[74] was bound to discredit economic theory *per se*. The reputation of economic theory would have been higher if, eschewing analysis in the abstract and adopting a healthy scepticism towards 'universality' in 'economic dogmas',[75] the theoretician had avoided 'a few long chains of reasoning'[76] and opted instead for short chains based on 'specific experience', 'new facts' and careful observation of the 'forces of the real world':[77] 'Even in mechanics long chains of deductive reasoning are directly applicable only to the occurrences of the laboratory'[78] and the scientist who wishes to be useful has as a result no choice but to acknowledge 'the importance of supplementing and guiding deduction by induction'.[79] Just as the inductive approach requires analytical schemata in order to make sense of raw data, so, it is clear, the deductive approach must remain in continuous dialogue with raw data if its analytical schemata are not to become bogus, arid and out-of-date. It would thus be fair to conclude that Marshall regarded the inductive and the deductive approaches as complements rather than substitutes, differences in emphasis rather than radical alternatives: just as 'every one must both eat and drink', so, it is apparent, 'every genuine student of economics sometimes uses the inductive method and sometimes the analytical, and nearly always both of them together'.[80] Conceptually speaking, however, the two approaches are distinct and separate, and the attractiveness of cutting through complexities (institutional obstacles to factor mobility, for example) so as thereby to arrive at essentials (with respect, say, to the market mechanism) cannot be denied. The economist must, of course, never lose sight of the restrictive assumptions which he is making in the course of formulating his hypotheses; but, while taking care, here as elsewhere, not to take himself too seriously, still 'as a preparation for dealing approximately with complex conditions of equilibrium he first practises himself in the "pure" theory of economics – in the exact solution of problems that treat of simple conditions'.[81] The restrictive assumptions in question can subsequently be relaxed in order, at a later stage of the work, to secure a closer correspondence between analytical conclusions on the one hand, factual conditions on the other. Naturally, there is a trade-off, in the sense that 'the greater the simplicity of the hypotheses the less close can be this correspondence; but the greater can be the exactness of the conclusions deduced from them'.[82] Even so, the very exactness of the conclusions, however provisional, has considerable appeal to an economist keen to come to the point; and that, no doubt, helps to explain the not inconsiderable popularity of the deductive method in economic science.

One manifestation of the deductive method is the employment of mathematical symbols to express economic doctrines – an approach to which Marshall himself, whose own First was secured in mathematics, in truth made a lasting contribution through the elaborate Mathematical Appendix to his *Principles* and through the frequently reiterated assertion that the 'terse, compact, precise language of Mathematics'[83] is a valuable form of shorthand which permits of 'precision of expression' ('the special property of mathematical language'):[84] 'A training in mathematics is helpful by giving command over a marvellously terse and exact language for expressing clearly some general relations and some short processes of economic reasoning; which can indeed be expressed in ordinary language, but not with equal sharpness of outline.'[85] Because the language is terse, it 'enables us to express general statements . . . with the utmost brevity'.[86] Because the language is exact, it is an aid to logical thought which compels economists to 'state distinctly the premises on which they reason': 'It is indeed doubtful whether much has been gained by the use of complex mathematical formulae. But the application of mathematical habits of thought has been of great service.'[87]

Some men can evidently develop into rigorous analytical economists without ever passing through the brook of fire of formal discipline in mathematical techniques: 'Ricardo himself had no mathematical training. But his instincts were unique; and very few trained mathematicians could tread as safely as he over the most perilous courses of reasoning.'[88] Alas, for 'anyone of less genius than Ricardo', there exist a wide range of economic problems which would better be treated with the intellectual crutch of mathematics than without. The benefits associated with the apparatus are apparently reaped by the thinker himself and the need normally arises less from the intractability of the subject-matter than from the mediocrity of the normal theoretician: 'The chief use of pure mathematics in economic questions seems to be in helping a person to write down quickly, shortly and exactly, some of his thoughts for his own use . . . When a great many symbols have to be used, they become very laborious to any one but the writer himself . . . It seems doubtful whether any one spends his time well in reading lengthy translations of economic doctrines into mathematics, that have not been made by himself.'[89] As with mathematics, so with diagrams, and Marshall encouraged the reader of his *Principles* to look for them principally in the footnotes and to regard them normally as no more than 'supplementary': 'The argument in the text is never dependent on them; and they may be omitted.'[90]

Marshall's most famous statement on the use in economics of mathematical symbols is to be found in a letter to Bowley dated 27 February 1906. There, speaking of his own development, he wrote as follows: 'A good mathematical theorem dealing with economic hypotheses was very unlikely to be good economics: and I went more and more on the rules – (1) Use mathematics as a shorthand language, rather than as an engine of inquiry. (2) Keep them till you have done. (3) Translate into English. (4) Then illustrate by examples that are important in real life. (5) Burn the mathematics. (6) If you can't succeed in 4, burn 3. This last I did often.'[91] Mathematical virtuosity is no substitute for *social* science, Marshall is saying; but he is nonetheless fully aware of the constructive role that mathematics might come to play in economic analysis. Marshall does not in the event have a great deal to say about the precise problems to the clarification of which mathematics has the greatest contribution to make, but the following would appear paticularly significant.

First, with respect to partial equilibrium, Marshall praises the 'terse language of the differential calculus'[92] and implies that even Ricardo's exposition (say, of diminishing returns, agricultural improvements, incidence of taxation) would have been improved had Ricardo been exposed to a set of techniques unambiguously 'helpful to clear thought'.[93] Certainly much of the excellence in the work of Cournot, Dupuit and Gossen must be attributed to the use of 'semi-mathematical language for expressing the relation between small increments of a commodity on the one hand, and on the other hand small increments in the aggregate price that will be paid for it'.[94] Continuity, moreover, suggests not only calculus but also curves; and Marshall's diagrams (even if principally in the footnotes rather than in the text) are very much there and very much part of the story – as where Marshall, speaking of the relationship of demand curves with differences in elasticity to supply curves with differences in returns to scale, declares: 'All this can be most clearly seen by the aid of diagrams, and indeed there are some parts of the problem which cannot be satisfactorily treated without their aid.'[95]

Second, with respect to general equilibrium, Marshall states: 'Experience in handling physical problems by mathematical methods gives a grasp, that cannot be obtained equally well in any other way, of the mutual interaction of economic changes.'[96] This is demonstrated clearly by Note XXI of the Mathematical Appendix, which Marshall identified as his 'general survey of the problem of distribution and exchange',[97] and which is in effect a Walrasian system of *n* interdependent equations with *n* interdependent variables. In 1908 Marshall was to write as follows concerning that Note: 'My whole life has been and will be given to presenting in realistic form as much as I can of my Note XXI.'[98]

Mathematics clearly has a direct contribution to make to economic theory, and one which includes – but also goes beyond – the inculcation of 'sound instinctive habits (like the practising of scales on the piano)'.[99] Mathematics, however, although sometimes useful, is also sometimes unnecessary, and even sometimes dangerous. Mathematics evidently is a tool which must be used with caution. For the exercise of such caution four reasons in particular may be adduced.

The *first* reason is the threat of omission of the inconvenient, the danger that the use of mathematics in economics will cause economists to skew their studies towards problems which are susceptible of mathematical treatment and away from those which are not: 'Many important considerations, especially those connected with the manifold influences of the element of time, do not lend themselves easily to mathematical expression: they must either be omitted altogether, or clipped and pruned till they resemble the conventional birds and animals of decorative art. And hence arises a tendency towards assigning wrong proportions to economic forces; those elements being most emphasized which lend themselves most easily to analytical methods.'[100] To avoid analytical methods merely because not all problems are susceptible of mathematical treatment would, needless to say, be to throw out the baby with the bathwater, to 'abandon the chief means of scientific progress'.[101] But the economist should certainly keep in mind the danger of bias and take special care not to sacrifice reality to elegance.

The *second* reason involves not omission but commission and refers to the case where the scholar, often simply for the sake of 'mathematical diversions', employs mathematical techniques and automatically assumes that 'material *appropriate* to their use had been supplied by economic study': 'He takes no technical responsibility for the material, and is often unaware how inadequate the material is to bear the strains of his powerful machinery.'[102] Where the material is in the event *not appropriate*, the use of mathematical symbols is likely to confuse rather than clarify.

Such is the case with kaleidoscopic change, where the variables fluctuate rapidly and in a seemingly random fashion. There is no point in setting up an equation or system of equations if it is so deficient in robustness that its predictions barely attain the status of tendencies: 'The causes which prevent those tendencies from being applied in prediction resemble those which prevent mathematical reasonings from being applied to the course of a ball on the deck of a ship that is rolling and pitching in cross seas. If the ship would but stay at one inclination, the movement of the ball could be calculated. But before any one tendency has had time to produce much result it will have ceased to exist, and its successor cannot be predicted.'[103] This is in essence the *ceteris paribus* problem of many variables varying simultaneously in ways not easy to anticipate even where careful and imaginative use is made of the best-known theoretical constructs and established inter-relationships. Marshall argued that in such real world situations, 'every economic force is constantly changing its action', 'no two influences move at equal pace', and facile explanations are to be regarded with radical mistrust: 'In this world . . . every plain and simple doctrine as to the relations between cost of production, demand and value is necessarily false: and the greater the appearance of lucidity which is given to it by skilful exposition, the more mischievous it is.'[104] Thus, to take a concrete instance, it would serve no useful purpose save to demonstrate the futility of mathematics imperialism to try and capture, in a series of equations, the essence of the whole of a complex problem such as that of 'commodities of which the expenses of production diminish rapidly with every increase in the amount produced': 'Here the causes that govern the limits of production are so complex that it seems hardly worth while to attempt to translate them into mathematical language.'[105] It was with such complexities in mind that Marshall cautioned Edgeworth in 1902 against confusing '*abstract* economics' with '*real* economics': 'You know I never apply curves or mathematics to market values. For I don't think they help much. And market values are, I think, either absolutely abstract or terribly concrete and full of ever-varying (though individually vital) side issues.'[106]

The sheer dynamism inherent in economic phenomena raises problems of institutional change (notably those of contingency, relativity and evolution) with which mathematics is not really equipped to cope. There is the snowball or knock-on effect ('It has been remarked, that in economics every event causes permanent alterations in the conditions under which future events can occur'[107]), the qualitative factors involved in the life-cycle of the firm, the unpredictable nature of invention, innovation, technological advance, the variable and varying lags associated with the coming fully into operation of internal and external economies; and human nature itself, of course, is subject to a developmental process which can hardly be captured with any degree of accuracy by the techniques of the 'mathematico-physical group of sciences'.[108] In such circumstances the errors of commission involved in using a tool to perform a task for which it is unsuited are such as to militate strongly against its employment. As Pigou puts it, commenting on Marshall's reservations with respect to mathematics: 'Marshall was essentially and emphatically *pro-realism*. So far as he was against mathematical elaborations in economics, it was only because he feared that realism might suffer. Convince him that any particular line of mathematical attack would indirectly help realism and he would have been its enthusiastic friend.'[109] Even in the field of mathematical economics, it is clear, Marshall believed that the economist should not proceed mechanically but rather be governed by an eminently intellective and pragmatic standard.

The *third* reason for the exercise of caution in the employment of the logico-symbolic tool has to do with the interaction between deduction and induction, between analysis and evidence, between mathematics and statistics. Specifically, if everything depends on everything else (the interdependence property which is inherent in Marshall's functionalist perception of the economic system) but if not everything is in practice quantifiable and measurable (as in the case of the instances previously encountered in connection with errors of omission and of commission), then the use of mathematics might actually shunt the car of economic science on to a wrong line leading directly down a blind alley: 'In my view every economic fact, whether or not it is of such a nature as to be expressed in numbers, stands in relation as cause and effect to many other facts: and since it *never* happens that all of them can be expressed in numbers, the application of exact mathematical methods to those which can is nearly always a waste of time, while in the large majority of cases it is positively misleading; and the world would have been further on its way forward if the work had never been done at all.'[110] Yet this warning offers an element of consolation nonetheless to the mathematical economist, for it suggests that the real failure lies in the data, not in the economist's treatment of the data. As Marshall explains it in his essay on 'The Graphic Method of Statistics', the problem is in effect this: 'The results obtained by statistics generally, and in particular the economic branch of statistics, are seldom sufficiently definite and trustworthy to afford much useful material for mathematical *theory* to work on.'[111] Consolation – and hope, since some progress may legitimately be expected in the future towards the '*quantitative* determination of the relative strength of different economic forces': 'That higher and more difficult task must wait upon the slow growth of thorough realistic statistics.'[112] Whatever the future may bring, however, the experience of the past is clear, that the progress of economics has been less on the quantitative than on the qualitative side (the study, for example, of 'the characters and directions of the changes which various economic forces tend to produce')[113]; and the result is that mathematical economists today are starved of empirical evidence on the basis of which to weight and quantify their parameters. Like the rest of us when in a state of ignorance, scholars who wish to be 'not pure mathematicians but realistic economists,'[114] ought accordingly – at least until our statistics have been improved and our lack of knowledge correspondingly reduced – to adopt an agnostic posture and to 'leave mathematics for a little on one side':[115] 'Surely *the* thing to do is to build the basis of our economic structure soundly and not put a varnish of mathematical accuracy to many places of decimals on results the premises of which are not established within 20 or 50 per cent.: many not even so far as to put beyond dispute the question whether A is the cause of B, or B the cause of A, or A and B are the result of a+b+c+d. . .'[116]

The *fourth* and last reason concerns intelligibility. Marshall was conscious of the fact that mathematics 'is not intelligible to all readers'[117] (including, needless to say, most of the business men whom he wanted so much to reach), and that formal exposition was likely for that reason to limit the accessibility of economic argumentation. Thus Fouraker, stressing that Marshall was aiming at a wider readership than that of the economics profession alone, suggests that it was the desire for intelligibility and accessibility which more than anything else accounts for Marshall's own deceptively simple mode of expression: 'There is, after all, ample evidence in the history of economics that one can bury his ideas for a generation or more by mathematical treatment: the works of Gossen and Slutsky are examples.'[118] Fouraker then expresses his personal doubts concerning the wisdom of adopting that elliptical method so much beloved of Cambridge authors (Keynes as well as Marshall) which conceals – without eliminating – the more difficult parts of the theory: 'The price of the method is a high one. Although the novice can quickly grasp the concept of consumer demand or the propensity to consume, the professional frequently is confused about the precise meaning of those indispensable analytical tools.'[119]

Confused perhaps; but the real question is how much less or more he would have been confused if Marshall had used more mathematical and less verbal symbols. Pigou, referring the reader to a particular argument, seems to agree with Fouraker that the analysis would have been tighter if the mathematics (a 'dragon in the path'[120] certain to frighten off the timid) had not been concealed: 'A smooth platitudinous argument it seems at first: later on one discovers with a shock that the central part of it is a translation into ordinary language of a close mathematical argument, not perhaps to be grasped completely until it has been translated back again into the symbolic form in which it must first have been built up.'[121]

That Marshall made such translations has long been appreciated by authors ranging from Edgeworth (who said that Marshall bore 'under the garb of literature the armour of mathematics'[122]) to Schumpeter (who, reflecting that Marshall was a trained mathematician to whom 'the concept of limits and hence the formal part of the marginal principle would be as familiar as would be his breakfast bacon',[123] commented that Marshall nonetheless 'never gave full credit to the faithful ally' but rather 'hid the tool that had done the work'[124]). What is more controversial is whether Marshall genuinely and deliberately sacrificed precision in an attempt to purchase intelligibility or whether, alternatively, he chose to hide the tool that had done the work for the simple reason that its work was done. What is clear is his conviction that, while 'skilled mathematicians' obviously have the right to play with toys if they so wish, the fact remains that 'all that has been important in their reasonings and results has, with scarcely an exception, been capable of being described in ordinary language.'[125] Hence the invocation to Bowley: 'I think you should do all you can to prevent people from using Mathematics in cases in which the English Language is as short as the Mathematical.'[126] Where the English language is not sufficient, moreover, the economist should not forget that 'the language of diagrams' can often express the relevant ideas 'as tersely and as clearly as that of the mathematics':[127] 'There are many problems of pure theory, which no one who has once learnt to use diagrams will willingly handle in any other way.'[128] Writing of *The Theory of Political Economy*, Marshall complained that Jevons had overlooked key relationships not least 'as a result of not thinking in English'[129] but managed to praise Jevons for his 'graphic representation' of 'reasonings and results': 'The book before us would be improved if the mathematics were omitted, but the diagrams retained.'[130] Most of all, however, what must be retained is a clear apperception of the confused and confusing character of external reality: 'Nature's action is complex: and nothing is gained in the long run by pretending that it is simple, and trying to describe it in a series of elementary propositions.'[131] Scientific methods (whether inductive or deductive, statistical or mathematical, empirical or analytical) are all very well in their place, and each of us should naturally do his best to get to know the causes of the things; but when all is said and done, the economist has need most of all 'of a shrewd mother-wit, of a sound sense of proportion, and of a large experience of life'.[132] And of humility in the face of the intractable but fascinating: 'A man is likely to be a better economist if he trusts to his common sense, and practical instincts, than if he professes to study the theory of value and is resolved to find it easy.'[133]

7.3 ORGANICISM AND ECONOMICS

Marshall believed strongly that matter is in motion and that the economist must accordingly take great care to capture in his models the essence of continuous evolutionary development: 'The main concern of economics is . . . with human beings who are impelled, for good and evil, to change and progress . . . . The central idea of economics, even when its Foundations alone are under discussion, must be that of living force and movement.'[1] Marshall also emphasized that everything depends on everything else and that the economist who couches his theories in terms of the discrete actions of isolated individuals in effect misleads and mystifies by concealing the vital importance for any understanding of economic issues of mutual causality and systemic interdependence: 'Just as the motion of every body in the solar system affects and is affected by the motion of every other, so it is with the elements of the problem of political economy.'[2] It was because of his belief in gradual upgrading combined with his emphasis on synthetic integration that Marshall was attracted to organic rather than physical analogies and was motivated to declare that 'the Mecca of the economist lies in economic biology rather than in economic dynamics'.[3] Kenneth Boulding, in many ways the natural successor to Marshall's evolutionary perspective in his well-known declaration that 'economics has rested too long in an essentially Newtonian paradigm of mechanical equilibrium and mechanical dynamics',[4] has expressed his regret that Marshall's Mecca exercised significantly less influence on the subsequent development of economic science than so important a thesis of so important a thinker in fact merited: 'In his day biological theory had not really advanced to the point where it would be integrated into economic models. The implicit evolutionary model in Marshall, however, is very strong. His equilibrium mechanical models of supply and demand he always regards as mere stepping stones toward a richer Dynamic evolutionary theory . . . . Unfortunately, the twentieth-century mainline of economics followed Walras a good deal more than it did Marshall, with concentration on the equilibrium concept almost to the exclusion of evolutionary change.'[5] Boulding at least correctly identifies Marshall as an organic thinker. It is one of the numerous *curiosa* in the history of institutional economics that Thorstein Veblen did not and saw Marshall's *Principles* as nothing but

> an inquiry directed to the determination of the conditions of an equilibrium of activities and a quiescent normal situation. It is not in any eminent degree an inquiry into cultural or institutional development as affected by economic exigencies or by the economic interest of the men whose activities are analysed and portrayed. Any sympathetic reader of Professor Marshall's great work – and that must mean every reader – comes away with a sense of swift and smooth movement and interaction of parts; but it is the movement of a consummately conceived and self-balanced mechanism, not that of a cumulatively unfolding process or an institutional adaptation to cumulatively unfolding exigencies.[6]

Much may be excused a non-institutional economist such as J. M. Keynes for returning a similar verdict, as in his rather dismissive statement that Marshall 'was a little disposed sometimes to camouflage the essentially static nature of his equilibrium theory with many wise and penetrating *obiter dicta* on dynamical problems'.[7] Veblen, however, is another matter; and it is exceptionally difficult to understand how Marshall's analysis of conspicuous consumption, the instinct of workmanship, the position of women, the mutability of motivation, adaptation to environment (to say nothing of Marshall's latent asceticism, commitment to industrialism and optimism concerning the future), could have entirely escaped his notice. Perhaps it did not. Perhaps Veblen's conspicuous failure to treat Marshall as an organic thinker and an evolutionary economist was just another of his practical jokes.

It is with Marshall as an organic thinker and an evolutionary theorist that we shall be concerned in this section. Marshall's belief in continuous evolutionary development is encapsulated by the motto which appears on the title-page of his *Principles of Economics*, while his emphasis on mutual causality and systemic interdependence is embodied in the equivalent motto in his *Industry and Trade*. Our examination of Marshall's approach will therefore be divided into two parts – the first examining the implications of *Natura non facit saltum*, the second dealing with *The Many in the One, the One in the Many*.

(1) Natura non facit saltum

Nature is in a permanent process of change, Marshall said, and there is no point, save for purposes of deliberate simplification or first-approximation illustration, in pretending that it is not: 'Economic problems are imperfectly presented when they are treated as problems of statical equilibrium, and not of organic growth. For though the statical treatment alone can give us definiteness and precision of thought, and is therefore a necessary introduction to a more philosophic treatment of society as an organism, it is yet only an introduction.'[8] The economist must for that reason handle with great care the 'statical analogy'[9] and the concept of 'equilibrium', suggesting as they do timelessness and inertia; since the fact is that the keynote of economic science is 'dynamics, rather than statics'.[10] Marshall knew that he was giving a 'relatively large place to mechanical analogies' in his *Principles*, but he also warned the reader that such analogies are merely 'preliminary devices' of an expositional nature that should not be prominent 'in the later stages of our work': 'Consider, for instance, the balancing of demand and supply. The words "balance" and "equilibrium" belong originally to the older science, physics; whence they have been taken over by biology. In the earlier stages of economics, we think of demand and supply as crude forces pressing against one another, and tending towards a mechanical equilibrium, but in the later stages the balance or equilibrium is conceived not as between crude mechanical forces, but as between the organic forces of life and decay.'[11] It is in the circumstances not entirely fair to accuse Marshall, as Mark Blaug does, of adopting a 'schizoid' attitude to partial equilibrium analysis (and *a fortiori* to the general equilibrium approach): 'Ostensibly, the *Principles* is a study of static microeconomic theory, but time after time the reader is told that the conclusions of static analysis are unreliable and that microeconomics fails to come to grips with the vital issues of economic policy. . . . And yet Marshall's efforts throughout his life were devoted to teaching, expounding, and refining the very kind of theory that he deprecated repeatedly in his book.'[12] Marshall, after all, consistently made clear that it was his procedure to move sequentially from the perspective of the lower sciences to that of the higher – as when, presenting his life-cycle approach to the rise and fall of the firm, he quickly added: 'But to prepare the way for this advanced study we want first to look at a simpler balancing of forces which corresponds rather to the mechanical equilibrium of a stone hanging by an elastic string, or of a number of balls resting against one another in a basin.'[13] Marshall's approach is sequential rather than 'schizoid' and therefore entirely evolutionary in itself. It cannot, however, be denied that far more of Marshall's time was spent on theories of price determination than on models of never-stationary states, or that the architect used up so much of his scarcest resource on the foundations that he was left with little more than an invisible hand with which to complete his edifice. Marshall's intentions, even so, are as clear as his conviction that nature is in a permanent process of change: 'The main importance of the particular facts of nature lies in the light which they throw upon the processes of nature; or, in other words, that from what *is* we have to learn what *is becoming*; from *das Sein* we have to learn *das Werden*.'[14]

Das Werden is *wichtig* and *interessant* but also *langsam*, *kriechend* and *schneckenartig*; and economic science, when incorporating continuous change into its models, should accordingly concentrate on on-going processes and gradual developments rather than sudden upheavals and dramatic leaps which are so uncharacteristic of nature as to be of limited value to the student of nature. As Marshall puts it, speaking of smooth adjustments: 'Economics is concerned mainly with general conditions and tendencies: and these as a rule change but slowly, and by small steps . . . Thus the maxim that 'nature does not willingly make a jump' (*Natura abhorret saltum*) is specially applicable to economic developments.'[15] Matter is in motion, it would appear, but that motion is slow: 'Economic evolution is gradual. Its progress is sometimes arrested or reversed by political catastrophes: but its forward movements are never sudden; for even in the Western world and in Japan it is based on habit, partly conscious, partly unconscious.'[16] Gradual steps upwards obviously lack 'the rapid pace of a revolution: but a revolution sometimes rushes backwards faster and further than it had moved forwards; and steps such as these move steadily onwards'.[17] Besides that, historically speaking, 'violent change was uncongenial to the English temper',[18] and such a conservative predisposition Marshall himself shared with his fellow Englishmen: 'I am not an advocate of hurried change.'[19] In the circumstances Marshall must have been pleased to identify evolutionary but not revolutionary tendencies in the Britain of his own times. Speaking of the *Principles* as a whole and clearly having in mind the temporal alongside the spatial dimension, Marshall declared: 'If the book has any special character of its own, that may perhaps be said to lie in the prominence which it gives to . . . applications of the Principle of Continuity.'[20] The spatial dimension of continuity may be illustrated by the substitution of factors at the margin or the mobility of inputs in response to stimulus. The temporal dimension may be illustrated by the following two cases of change so steady but so gradual that one colour in truth shades imperceptibly into the next without a clear break or interruption in the spectrum.

The *first* case is that of economics itself. The first line of the first edition of the *Principles* reads as follows: 'Economic conditions are constantly changing, and each generation looks at its own problems in its own way.'[21] Matter being in motion, the laws of a science 'must have a development corresponding to that of the things of which they treat'[22] and the scholar's interpretations reveal themselves to be as contingent as the observations upon which they are based: 'Those propositions which are the most important in one stage of economic development, are not unlikely to be among the least important in another, if indeed they apply at all.'[23] The very term 'normal' refers to that which is normal 'relative to the members of a particular class at a given time and place',[24] and thus has a precise content which is no more constant than the external reality to which it refers. Since, of course, that external reality changes but gradually, it is clear that economic science 'is and must be of slow and continuous growth',[25] each generation relying perforce 'on the powerful machinery of thought and knowledge that has been gradually built up by past generations'[26] and no generation pretending to mount a revolution which would be out of keeping with the evolutionary nature of the phenomena which it studies – as in the theory of value, where the modern doctrines of Jevons and others involve in truth 'no real breach of continuity in the development of the science': they have 'supplemented the older, have extended, developed, and sometimes corrected them . . . but very seldom have subverted them'.[27] It is no surprise in the circumstances that the mathematical marginalist has been so much attracted by the continuity of calculus; for the fact is that 'our observations of nature, in the moral as in the physical world, relate not so much to aggregate quantities, as to increments of quantities'[28] and the differential medium is undeniably appropriate to the incremental message.

Economics itself has experienced steady but gradual mutation: 'In economics, as in physics, changes are generally continuous.'[29] Such changes have been triggered off by antecedent changes in economic conditions. They are also indicative of what can only be described as an evolution towards evolution. To be specific, the progress in the social sciences that has been observed in recent times has, Marshall believed, involved a movement away from the Newtonian approach (whereby phenomena are treated as invariant and universal) and in favour of the Darwinian paradigm (whereby phenomena are regarded as experiencing organic adaptation and purposive betterment). Citing with approval the names of teleological, functionalist and organicist thinkers such as Goethe, Hegel and Comte, Marshall then reflected with satisfaction on recent developments in the human sciences: 'In sociology as well as in biology we are learning to watch the accumulated effects of forces which, though weak at first, get greater strength from the growth of their own effects.'[30] The biological perspective of gradual evolutionary change had, needless to say, particular appeal to an economist such as Marshall whose own theories of economic efficiency and improvement rely so heavily on the concept of survival of the fittest in a competitive environment (and whose comparison of the life-cycle of a firm to that of a tree in the forest introduces a secondary organic dimension in its own right: 'A business firm grows and attains great strength, and afterwards perhaps stagnates and decays; and at the turning point there is a balancing or equilibrium of the forces of life and decay'[31]). Furthermore, the concepts of organic adaptation and survival of the fittest were themselves pioneered by an economist – Malthus – whose work then served as the inspiration for natural scientists such as Darwin. Since that time, of course, 'biology has more than repaid her debt; and economists have in their turn owed much to the many profound analogies which have been discovered between social and especially industrial organization on the one side and the physical organization of the higher animals on the other'.[32] The evolution towards evolution in economic science would thus appear to represent not only significant betterment in the discipline itself but also further evidence of continuity – since it increasingly leads us to follow Spencer in postulating a 'fundamental unity of action between the laws of nature in the physical and in the moral world'.[33]

The *second* case of change steady but change gradual is that of 'the ever changing and subtle forces of human nature'.[34] The change is gradual, and social science must come to recognise this fact: 'It will expect no sudden improvement in man's conditions of life, because he forms them as much as they form him, and he himself cannot change fast.'[35] The change is steady; and social scientists are to be congratulated on themselves steadily 'getting to pay every year a greater attention to the pliability of human nature'.[36] The change is above all important; since economic growth and human betterment are linked together in a relationship fundamentally symbiotic, each both feeding and feeding off the other in a manner which can hardly be described as unknown.[37]

In a traditionalised, conventionalised, routinised society there is little change, economic or social: 'There is a sense in which it is true that custom dominates early forms of civilization; for in them status and methods of work, utensils and implements are all ruled by custom: and, though even in such matters, custom is found on investigation to be much more plastic than it appears to those who live under its sway; yet conscious, deliberate, direct breaches of custom were undoubtedly very rare.'[38] There is little social change, moreover, *because* there is little economic change – and the proposition is not reversible: 'Human nature is never absolutely rigid; and custom never holds its own in opposition to a strong active economic force working for many generations persistently in the same direction.'[39] Custom is, it would appear, very often indeed 'the gradual result of economic conditions; even where it appears at first sight to be their governing cause, rather than their effect':[40] 'I believe that very many economic customs could be traced, if we only had knowledge enough, to the slow equilibration of measurable motives: that even in such a country as India no custom retains its hold long after the relative positions of the motives of demand and supply have so changed that the values, which would bring them into stable equilibrium, are far removed from those which the custom sanctions.'[41] Custom may, in short, be compared to a glacier which – unless it be so frozen in its stationary state as to be completely immobile – has no option but to adapt its shape to that dictated by the contours of the terrain through which it passes,[42] where the motor-force that steadily but gradually shifts the glacier of culture is the cumulative advance of the 'business point of view': 'That phrase could not have been understood in a primitive society: and there is a sense in which it may be argued that business operations are merely one drift of a tendency to adapt means to ends, which is universal throughout all forms of life.'[43] As therefore the glacier of culture moves from the terrain of self-replication time out of mind (terrain that breeds and forms a traditionalised, routinised, conventionalised society) to the terrain of innovative upgrading and freedom of enterprise (terrain that breeds and forms welcome improvements in want-satisfaction and conduct and character), so each of us ought to be grateful for the conscious adaptation of means to ends which, via the economic impulsion to social progress, is the proximate cause of the evolutionary advance. Adaptation of means to ends is 'universal throughout all forms of life': 'Biology is indeed discovering numerous ways in which inheritance and natural selection – supplemented by the imitation of the successful actions of parents and other older individuals, and by other post-natal influences – have enabled even low grade animals so to adjust their structure and their operations to their environment, that they may be able to utilize it for their own benefit with ever increasing ease, efficiency and certainty.'[44] *Conscious* adaptation of means to ends is somewhat less universal. It is uniquely human. It is also significantly economic.

It is also gradual, since with respect to economic growth as with respect to the changes in human nature which it generates, the rule remains *natura non facit saltum*. Even the most dramatic of epoch-making inventions (of the printing-press, for example) typically take several generations for their full impact to become manifest, while the famous Industrial Revolution of the eighteenth century reveals itself upon closer inspection to be nothing more than one link in an unbroken chain of steady development: 'In fact what then happened was not a Revolution; it was merely one stage of Evolution which had proceeded almost without interruption for several hundred years.'[45] There is, it must be conceded, some evidence of acceleration in the pace of change, in that 'the present generation is the first that has seen the whole rise of several great inventions from nothing to dominating positions'.[46] Nowadays, in fact, the rate of progress is such as to be altering our 'conditions of work and life . . . perceptibly in each decade',[47] and the truth is that the 'Industrial Revolution of the present generation . . . has far outdone the changes of a century ago, in both rapidity and breadth of movement'.[48] Such acceleration is indeed a characteristic feature of the cumulative nature of science, where each generation in effect sees better because it stands on the shoulders of its predecessors and each new piece of knowledge is both 'the offspring of others that went before, and the parent of many that follow'.[49] But accelerated change does not imply sudden change; and the conclusion that must be drawn is that the nature of change remains gradual, organic evolution rather than mechanical reconstruction.

Marshall's account of change has overtones of the unilinear growth path, where the idea of 'backward countries'[50] would seem to mean just that (i.e. an arrested stage of human development) and where, as Parsons suggests, 'even socialism is not a step *away* from his line of progress, but one *backward* along it, into sluggishness and stagnation'.[51] It was indeed his belief in developmental uniformities which was among the more significant factors that attracted Marshall in 1875 to visit America: 'I wanted to see the history of the future in America . . . It appears that many of the changes that are being worked out in England, America has with more rapid steps gone through before us, and that by a study of the present of America we may learn much directly about the future of England . . . I returned on the whole more sanguine with regard to the future of the world than I had set out.'[52] Similarly, it was, in a slightly different period, the industrial leadership of England that led Germany to examine carefully the practices of a nation which had contributed so greatly to 'pioneering the way for the rest of the world':[53] 'She has been able to profit by England's experience and to avoid many of her mistakes.'[54] England could not have served as the model for Germany nor America for England if there were no important similarities in the evolutionary experience of the diverse nations; and it must also be stressed that Marshall's optimistic account of the progress of human nature in the direction of honesty, respect for persons, pursuit of excellence, generosity and deliberateness is clearly intended by its author as something of wider applicability than would be a mere *histoire raisonnée* of British economic and social development. As Marshall told the Cambridge Moral Science Club, 'I do not wish to underrate the influence which is exercised on a man by his ideals of excellence – religious ideals, moral ideals, art ideals, ideals of action, ideals of power, ideals of affection . . . . But the influence exerted by ideals of excellence does not come into competition with that exerted by a man's daily occupation: rather does this contribute much to the forming of these ideals.'[55] If the argument in Chapter 2 proves anything at all, it must prove that Marshall throughout his life continued to stress the causal significance of occupation and economy for consumption, conduct and character; and the inference must be that, in his view, similar causes in similar conditions would have a tendency to produce broadly similar effects (just as dissimilar causes and/or dissimilar conditions would tend to produce 'more or less divergent effects'[56]). Since Marshall saw the growth process as involving broadly similar structural characteristics (notably free market exchanges and the atmosphere of alertness which such exchanges presuppose and inculcate), one is bound to reaffirm that his optimistic account of the progress of human nature was intended as a cautious prediction of broadly similar developments in consumption, conduct and character.

Broadly similar but not identical, since – without meaning to deprecate the primacy of occupation and economy – the truth is that these are by no means the only causal variables which impact upon the formation of human nature. Climate, race, geographical location, national character and natural resources are, as we saw in Chapter 3, five exogeneities which help to explain the different experiences of the different economies; and which suggest that even within the same *genus* there can be considerable heterogeneity as between the different *species* (a point which Englishmen should keep in mind should they wish, say, to emulate recent German successes: 'The arrangements best suited for the German character are perhaps not quite the best for them'[57]). Opinions too can influence the precise direction of a nation's adaptation to its material environment, in a manner that would be unthinkable in an anthill or a beehive: so much does the use which man makes of his resources depend on 'his ideals of life' that the ideational and ideological constraint cannot be neglected nor the conclusion avoided that 'inextricably therefore the religious, political and economic threads of the world's history are interwoven'.[58] Great preachers, needless to say, administer a random shock to the course of history by transforming those opinions and those ideals; and similar shocks result from time to time (in flagrant if perhaps not frequent violation of *natura non facit saltum*) from the impact of 'great political events' and the influence of 'the strong personalities of individuals'.[59] Should great preachers and other great men win us round to plan rather than market, acceptance rather than growth, the course of matter would in the event follow mind rather than lead it and habits and customs would emerge for reasons entirely extra-economic – and entirely unexpected. The unexpected is indeed precisely what is to be expected from a kaleidoscopic thinker who even in his economic theories narrowly-defined spoke of 'endless complexities' and 'reciprocal influences'[60] and who said: 'Economic events react upon the conditions by which they were produced; so that future events cannot happen under exactly the same conditions as they did.'[61] As a kaleidoscopic thinker Marshall was compelled to declare: 'When a force moves the thing on which it acts, it thereby changes the force which that thing afterwards exercises.'[62] As, however, a teleologist and an organicist, Marshall, much influenced by the biologists and the evolutionists, was obliged to announce: 'If we look at the broad facts of human history, we find progress.'[63] Radical uncertainty and incorrigible optimism are unusual bedfellows; and taken together they would seem to explain why Marshall evidently saw the exceptions as well as the rule when analysing the developmental trajectory of the social organism.

Marshall spoke preponderantly about growth and progress, but the use of the organic analogy commits us to the reflection that those variables might enjoy a negative sign. Certainly in his discussion of the life-cycle of the firm Marshall did not hesitate to end his account with decay and death even though it had begun so hopefully with birth and infancy and continued so vigorously through youth and prime of life; and it is interesting to note that Marshall applied the concepts of youth and old age to whole nations as well. Thus, comparing Britain to her newer rivals, America and Germany, he said: 'Old and young are alike inclined to thing more of their own strengths than of their weaknesses: and it is specially incumbent on Britain to strive against that stiffness of the joints that is almost inevitable in each old country, and in the general relations of industries and trades in each old country. Above all is an old business in an old country in danger of underrating the advantages of that which is new.'[64] Marshall is here exhorting the cells consciously to strive to rejuvenate the organism; and such is, frankly, not the ultimate solution one would logically have expected from a socio-biological thinker, let alone one whose personal correspondence betrays an almost obsessive concern with his own mortality. Just as a businessman substitutes the good input for the bad one, Marshall might reasonably have argued, just as 'in a somewhat similar way society substitutes one undertaker for another who is less efficient in proportion to his charges',[65] so the international conflict for survival and dominance (a conflict emanating from 'the combative instincts, implanted in man's nature by countless centuries of fierce struggle for existence',[66] obviously not stilled by friendly fraternal interdependence based on 'the mutual knowledge which results from close trade intercourse',[67] up to now not held in check by a '*Pax Cosmopolitana*, enforced by an international police'[68]) could well lead to a decline-and-fall situation in which impoverished ancient Britons expend what is left of their national energies in displaying shards of a glorious past to hoards of bored tourists. Such a line of argumentation is fully in keeping with the life-cycle approach and the organic analogy; but it is in spite of that not Marshall's own, which concludes not with national demise but with national pulling-yourself-togetherness, as if guided by a stiff upper lip. With respect to nations, economies and societies, therefore, even if not to individuals and firms, the rule is normally *natura non facit saltum* – and the sign on the steady but gradual rate of change is normally positive.

(2) The many in the one, the one in the many

Organicism in economics suggests mutual causality and systemic interdependence as well as continuous evolutionary development; and therewith the concepts captured by Marshall's second motto, which appears to have been taken from Plato's *Philebus*. The first part of the second motto refers to the organic unity of the social whole, to the multiplicity of disparate units which have somehow grown together. The second part of the second motto refers to the distinguishable identity of the separate organs, to the quintessential differentiation that exists as between the individual cells. The motto may have been taken from Plato, but the real debt is to Herbert Spencer, whose entire theory of social evolution is in effect reducible to the explanation of two basic processes – concentration, consolidation and unification on the one hand ('In every more or less separate part of every aggregate, integration has been, or is, in progress'[69]), divergence, specialisation and multiformity on the other ('The change from the homogeneous to the heterogeneous, is displayed equally in the progress of civilization as a whole, and in the progress of every tribe or nation; and is still going on with increasing rapidity'[70]). It is precisely those two basic processes characteristic of continuous evolutionary development that Marshall clearly has in mind when analysing mutual causality and systemic interdependence.

Interconnections and interrelationships abound in economic life, and it is to the credit of economics as a discipline that it is becoming more and more holistic in its aspirations, more and more concerned with the wider picture as well as the isolated atom: 'Perhaps the earlier English economists confined their attention too much to the motives of individual action. But in fact economists, like all other students of social science, are concerned with individuals chiefly as members of the social organism. As a cathedral is something more than the stones of which it is made, as a person is something more than a series of thoughts and feelings, so the life of society is something more than the sum of the lives of its individual members.'[71] Society being an entity *sui generis*, everything being dependent on everything else, it is highly desirable that social scientists themselves should come to recognise that there is 'continuous gradation'[72] without radical break between the traditional confines of their differentiated disciplines – and not hesitate to adopt a multi-disciplinary approach where such breadth of scope in investigation is needed to capture the essence of a phenomenon: 'The less we trouble ourselves with scholastic inquiries as to whether a certain consideration comes within the scope of economics, the better. If the matter is important let us take acount of it as far as we can.'[73] The domain of the economist is, of course, economic; but the fact remains that the economic strand of a phenomenon is seldom observable in its pure form, and that the economist who wants his results to be relevant and useful should accordingly take into account the need for bridges to be built between the diverse approaches to the study of man. On the very last page of the *Principles* Marshall seems actually to be apologising for his own deficiencies in this respect: 'We have reached very few practical conclusions; because it is generally necessary to look at the whole of the economic, to say nothing of the moral and other aspects of a practical problem before attempting to deal with it at all.'[74]

Interconnections and interrelationships abound in economic life – ignored, perhaps, in 'rapid and popular discussions of the business affairs of the world', but nonetheless not to be ignored in any study that 'makes any claim to thoroughness': 'This requires many things to be borne in mind at the same time: and for that reason economics can never become a simple science.'[75] The interdependence may be that of the various firms sharing a common geographical setting (as where a tax on printing has an effect not only on authors and publishers concentrated in an area – Spencer had given the example of Paternoster Row[76] – but also on 'local bakers, grocers, etc.'[77] who operate there); or it might be illustrated by the manner in which 'increased efficiency in any trade tends to raise real wages in others'.[78] Alternatively, we might wish to conceive of interdependence, in an even more grandiose and imaginative manner, as a convection of forces operative at the international level – as where improved transport and modern means of communication render economic events parallel to an unprecedented extent despite national frontiers ('The whole civilised world is more closely bound together for many purposes than the different parts of England were some time ago'[79]) and 'are preparing the way for true self-government and united action by the whole people, not merely of a town such as Athens, Florence or Bruges, but a broad country, and even in some respects of the whole civilized world'.[80] The political dimension is well illustrated by 'the recent growth of a strong sentiment in favour of a League of Nations',[81] while in economic affairs, in an epoch of world growth and world division of labour, it is undeniably the case that 'the international element is becoming increasingly prominent in the history of all trade': 'It is easy to remember that one's own country is ever growing and changing: but it sometimes requires effort to consider how many of the changes near at hand are partly due to the expansion of life far away.'[82] That effort once made reveals something of great importance, that not only are the local carpenters and local publicans united in their diversity within the confines of a 'compact industrial district', but, increasingly, 'in one sense the whole world, in so far as it is in touch with western trade, is a single workshop'.[83] Internationally as well as domestically, it is clear, the basic law of evolution is that 'the development of the organism, whether social or physical, involves an increasing subdivvision of functions between its separate parts on the one hand, and on the other a more intimate connection between them': 'Increased subdivision of functions, or "differentiation", as it is called, manifests itself with regard to industry in such forms as the division of labour, and the development of specialized skill, knowledge and machinery: while "integration", that is, a growing intimacy and firmness of the connections between the separate parts of the industrial organism, shows itself in such forms as the increase of security of commercial credit, and of the means and habits of communication by sea and road, by railway and telegraph, by post and printing-press.'[84] Speaking of the authors who had had the greatest influence on his *Principles*, Marshall singled out the approaches typified by the work of Hegel and Spencer and said that they had 'affected, more than any other, the substance of the views expressed in the present book'.[85] No one who considers carefully Marshall's account of organic adaptation via differentiation and integration will find this statement as surprising as would, no doubt, virtually every later Marshallian.

Interconnections and interrelationships abound in economic life, and that is why arguments of the 'A caused B' type are inferior to those which make much of 'manifold mutual action': 'In popular discussions on economics one event is represented as determining a second, which determines a third, which determines a fourth, and so on. Reasoning of this kind can be followed without effort by anyone; but it does not correspond to the facts of nature and has been the source of much confusion. In human conduct one condition does not control another, but altogether they mutually determine one another.'[86] Even where writing partial analysis Marshall is thinking general, and he takes his much-respected Ricardo to task for not doing likewise: 'He does not state clearly, and in some cases he perhaps did not fully and clearly perceive how, in the problem of normal value, the various elements govern one another *mutually*, and not *successively* in a long chain of causation.'[87] Not that Jevons's practice was any better: 'The greatest objection of all to his formal statement of his central doctrine is that it does not represent supply price, demand price and amount produced as mutually determining one another ... but as determined one by another in a series.'[88] Both Ricardo and Jevons, it would appear, fell victim to their own abstractions in the theory of value and lost sight of the fact that, in the world of reality (in contrast to the world of the textbook), the truth is that 'no one part of the problem can be isolated from the rest':[89]

> In Nature changes generally react on one another. For instance, it is not true that the state of a man's lungs is determined by that of his heart, or *vice versa*; but subject to external influences, the conditions of his heart, lungs and other parts of his body determine one another. So when two unequal balls are put into a smooth basin, it is not right to regard A's position as determining the position of B. For though it is true that if we know exactly where A is, we can tell at once where B is, it is equally true that if we know where B is, we can tell where A is. The positions of A and B are determined simultaneously by the action of the Law of Gravitation.[90]

As a first approximation, of course, in the 'earlier stages of economic reasoning', the economist might choose consciously to impound potential complexities via a deliberate assumption of *ceteris paribus*. Here, 'the existence of other tendencies is not denied, but their disturbing influence is neglected for a time. The more the issue is thus narrowed, the more exactly can it be handled; but also the less closely does it correspond to real life.'[91] That being the case, and while recognising that 'man's powers are limited' whereas 'almost every one of nature's riddles is complex', the economist with a genuine interest in 'real life' will want not simply to employ the reductionist approach to a problem (whereby he 'breaks it up, studies one bit at a time') but ultimately the more ambitious synthetic method as well (whereby he at last 'combines his partial solutions with a supreme effort of his whole small strength into some sort of an attempt at a solution of the whole riddle').[92] The truth in a world of organic interdependence, after all, can never be less than the whole truth: 'Many tendencies have gone to the making of each industry and each economic institution: therefore a thorough realistic study of any part of the economic field, calls for some reference to the interaction of many diverse tendencies, and gives occasion for some care in analysis. And, conversely, almost every important tendency is so far modified by the conditions under which it operates, that an exhaustive study of it may need to range over many fields of work.'[92] Applied to the theory of value, what this means in practice is that the economist with a genuine interest in 'real life' will ultimately eschew simplistic explanations that assign causal primacy to *either* demand *or* supply when the truth is that *neither* by itself 'has a claim to predominance':[94] 'We might as reasonably dispute whether it is the upper or the under blade of a pair of scissors that cuts a piece of paper, as whether value is governed by utility or cost of production.'[95] The economist with a genuine interest in 'real life' will, in other words, eschew arguments of the 'A caused B' type in favour of theories of mutual and simultaneous causality – as between so many variables, moreover, that Schumpeter, after noting Marshall's important contribution to partial equilibrium economics, added that it is right 'to list Marshall also among the builders of the general-equilibrium system as well as of the marginal utility analysis per se'.[96] General *equilibrium* is perhaps not the most felicitous phrase to use in connection with an evolutionary economist who believed that 'economics, like biology, deals with a matter, of which the inner nature and constitution, as well as the outer form, are constantly changing',[97] but the essence of Schumpeter's point is as clear as it is valid: a shift outward in your demand curve for my product (reflecting the success of my aggressive salesmanship in a market-structure typified by perceived rivalry) causes my supply price to fall (reflecting the fact that the extent of my increasing returns is a function of your willingness to buy), a fall in the price of tea not only stimulates the consumption of sugar (a complement) but releases real income for the purchase of clothing (the income effect), a reduction in the supply of masons leads to a reduction in the demand for glass (the two being complementary inputs in the production of houses) and thence to redundancies and/or wage-cuts and price cuts in the glass industry (which may trigger off a multiplier contraction in the economy as a whole), and the inescapable conclusion to be drawn is that arguments of the 'A caused B' type are somewhat unrealistic in a world of 'manifold mutual action'.

Interconnections and interrelationships abound in economic life, and with them unifying relationships and common properties capable of bringing together the most diverse of phenomena. Spencer had stressed the universality of his two basic developmental processes (processes which, in his view, served as meta-laws that unlocked the mysteries of the solar system, language and painting as well as of human society) while Adam Smith (much influenced by what he called the 'superior genius and sagacity of Sir Isaac Newton'[98]) had sought to integrate the differentiated through an appeal to the shared principle of gravity. Marshall shows the influence of both – as where, in his Preface to the first edition of his *Principles*, he states initially that 'in spite of the great differences in form between birds and quadrupeds, there is one Fundamental Idea running through their frames' and then adds 'so the general theory of the equilibrium of demand and supply is a Fundamental Idea running through the frames of all the various parts of the central problem of Distribution and Exchange'.[99] Marshall, indeed, shows the influence of Spencer and Smith precisely by virtue of the fact that he consciously seeks out such Fundamental Ideas where less-ambitious scientists would have settled for adumbration as if guided by a simple list of names. Thus, not content with merely recording the importance of interdependent causality (as in his statement that 'all the elements of the great central problem of distribution and exchange mutually govern one another'[100]), he makes the further point that the interdependent elements may in fact be explained by a skilful use of a single body of theory: 'The theories of Distribution and Exchange are so intimately connected as to be little more than two sides of the same problem.'[101] Another illustration of this propensity to search out similarities would be Marshall's account of the theoretical continuities between human capital and machines[102] (where machines are 'themselves . . . the result of human efforts and sacrifices'[103] and thus not all that different in the first place from the human input narrowly defined). Yet another illustration would be his explanation of rent accruing to scarce human skills as well as to plots of land: 'The rent of land is no unique fact, but simply the chief species of a large genus of economic phenomena.'[104] And even great economists themselves, Marshall observed, are best regarded not as one-offs and freaks but as the children of their times, unified by the common parentage of the *Zeitgeist* to a large number of *Zeitgenossen* and *Zeitgefährten*: 'The substance of economic thought cannot well be to any great extent the work of any one man: it is the product of an age. Perhaps an exception should be made for Ricardo: but everything of importance that was said in the five generations 1740–65, 1765–90, 1815–40, 1840–65, 1865–90, seems to me to have been thought out concurrently more or less by many people.'[105] Each economist differentiated by the novelty of his contribution is an instance of The One in the Many. Every economist integrated by common ground and common purpose is an instance of The Many in the One. The steady but gradual progress in economics itself is an instance of *natura non facit saltum*. Organicism in economics, one is bound to conclude, would appear to be, like the air, ubiquitious, everywhere, and all around.

Without an understanding of organicism in economics and of the evolutionary paradigm, much of Marshall's theorising does in truth appear over-simplified, over-abstract, lifeless and timeless – the famous fiction of the Stationary State, the frequent references to 'normal' values, the idea of a 'representative' firm,[106] to cite but three of the many static constructs which Rogin clearly had in mind when he wrote that the *Principles* 'provide, in the main, a technique of analysis adapted merely to the investigation of the consequences of what happens when nothing of much consequence happens'.[107] Yet no one understands Marshall who understands only the statics, and Clark Kerr was nearer the mark when, introducing his Marshall Lectures at Cambridge in 1968, he said that 'they deal with the changing institutional context of economic activity rather than with economics proper'.[108] That context, he admitted, was 'of more interest to Marx and also to Marshall than it is to the economist of today',[109] whose concerns are likely to be somewhat less far-reaching than were those of the Grand Tradition. Scott Gordon in particular has argued that the Grand Tradition was not especially successful in its attempt to 'unravel the skein of history' and that non-evolutionary economists (whose ambitions are undeniably 'mean and petty' when compared with the aspirations of the institutional approach) have in the event made the more useful contribution: 'It was their efforts to analyze the mechanics of markets that produced the problem-solving economics we now possess. Modern economics can say very little about the laws of historical evolution – Marshall's 'Mecca' was more of a mirage than an insight – but it can say a great deal that is relevant to immediate issues that are focal points of social concern and public policy. In the pragmatic test, it is the latter that deserves man's gratitude.'[110] It is worth pointing out, however, that just as Rogin neglects the dynamic element in Marshall's economics, so Gordon neglects the problem-solving dimension; and that there is in truth more in Marshall than is likely to be found by an observer who focuses on a single element or identifies a single dimension as *the* key rather than *a* key. Marshall was an intellectual millipede with a foot in every camp. A foot in every camp – but they were all his own feet; all carried him in the direction in which he wanted to go; and such, it must be conceded, is in itself the *ne plus ultra* of organicism in economics.

7.4 THE MISSION OF THE ECONOMIST

Marshall believed that the economist has an absolute duty to help the world 'turn its growing resources to the best account for social well-being'[1] and argued that this very conviction had indeed given the discipline its primary sense of purpose ever since the days of the Physiocrats: 'The chief motive of their study was not, as it had been with most of their predecessors, to increase the riches of merchants and fill the exchequers of kings; it was to diminish the suffering and degradation which was caused by extreme poverty. They thus gave to economics its modern aim of seeking after such knowledge as may help to raise the quality of human life.'[2] This is admittedly 'an aim to which economics can do no more than contribute some important elements'[3] – given the urgency of the proposition that 'with £150 the family has, with £30 it has not, the material conditions of a complete life',[4] the man who *studies* wealth will inevitably have a sense of second-best when he compares himself with the man who *creates* it – but it is an objective nonetheless which renders the work of the economist legitimate and worthwhile: 'The growth of mankind in numbers, in health and strength, in knowledge, ability, and in richness of character is the end of all our studies.'[5] Economising leads to prosperity, prosperity is the antithesis of poverty, and this explains why, despite the fact that 'material wealth has ever had but slight charms for the Academic mind',[6] yet scholars of refinement and cultivation have even so forced themselves to study topics which out of context might seem dry and dull, to say nothing of sordid and selfish: 'Nearly all the founders of modern economics were men of gentle and sympathetic temper, touched with the enthusiasm of humanity. They cared little for wealth for themselves; they cared much for its wide diffusion among the masses of the people.'[7] Increasing wealth is the essential means to material upgrading. Material upgrading is of social utility. Economics too, therefore, is of social utility, concerned as it is with increasing wealth.

Economics is of social utility because it is concerned with the production of things. Yet the production of things is also by its very nature the production of the people who supply and demand those things. As Marshall puts it:

> Man's character has been moulded by his every-day work, and the material resources which he thereby procures, more than by any other influence unless it be that of his religious ideals; and the two great forming agencies of the world's history have been the religious and the economic. . . . Religious motives are more intense than economic, but their direct action seldom extends over so large a part of life. For the business by which a person earns his

> livelihood generally fills his thoughts during by far the greater part of those hours in which his mind is at its best; during them his character is being formed by the way in which he uses his faculties in his work, by the thoughts and the feelings which it suggests, and by his relations to his associates in work, his employers or his employees.[8]

As you work, so to a significant extent you are; and the economist, alert as he must be to the important causal impact of economic activity on human nature, thus comes willy nilly to take an interest in variables such as society and culture which cannot realistically be regarded as things apart, of no interest whatsoever to his discipline. Because, moreover, economic activity involves change, the economist comes willy nilly to take an interest in questions of development and decay, improvement and retrogression, the passage of time and the manner in which we all become different as a direct consequence of economic evolution and occupational mutation. The economist would therefore, simply by virtue of the fact that he is an economist, become anxious about the social utility of his discipline should he come to believe that increasing wealth of nations brings with it not desirable character-traits such as honesty, respect for persons, pursuit of excellence, generosity and deliberateness, but rather abominations of affluence such as mental mutilation and mean rapacity. The economist need not, fortunately, harbour such anxieties or fear that mind will sink as matter rises, and this the fraternity is coming increasingly to perceive: 'Economists have . . . now learnt to take a larger and more hopeful view of the possibilities of human progress. They have learnt to trust that the human will, guided by careful thought, can so modify circumstances as largely to modify character.'[9] Economics is thus of social utility because 'the end of all production' is in effect to 'raise the tone of human life'[10] – and because improvements in character-patterns as well as rising standards of material affluence are so demonstrably a feature of the modern industrial economy.

The modern industrial economy requires more and more economic intelligence, more and more economists, more and more 'University men' who have studied carefully 'the subject-matter of the age in which they live'.[11] Writing in 1907, Marshall pointed to 'many recent indications that economic questions are to play a greater part in the life and thought of the present century than they did in that of the past'.[12] Clearly, as economic questions come to play a 'greater part' in our 'life and thought', so the duties and opportunities of the economist become *pro tanto* greater; and the growth of State intervention reinforces the need for reliable economic intelligence – with respect to the incidence of taxes and rates, for example, or the costs and benefits of collective consumption (including the furtherance of a healthy environment: the economist 'has no higher duty than to examine the principles and the limits appropriate to it'[13]), or the extent and alleviation of poverty, or the policy-issues raised by giant corporations and protective tariffs, or the appropriate means to regulate the money-supply and stabilise prices, or the precise measurement of aggregate value added (Pigou, in his review of the fifth edition of the *Principles*, stresses that, here too, to Marshall, social purpose transcends the game for graduates: 'The conception of the National Dividend is not an academic toy, but a practical instrument of great power designed for service in the concrete solution of social problems'[14]). In all of these areas reliable economic intelligence is high-powered in the solution of important contemporary problems and accordingly of undeniable social utility. Nor should the beneficial impact on public opinion be forgotten of the economist's 'laborious study of actual conditions'.[15] Time after time we encounter in Marshall phrases like 'the ordinary observer neglects the fact . . .',[16] with the implication that ordinary people would act differently if only they were better informed – the case of trades unionists, say, who would be more likely to act less irresponsibly if they came to see 'the grave evils they are inflicting on others',[17] or of employers who would not confuse real and nominal values in the course of the cycle if only economists presented them with sound and up-to-date price-indices and deflators.[18] The fact that our knowledge is never perfect is in no way a major obstacle to the employment of the by no means unsatisfactory data which economists even now generate: 'The function of economic analysis is to render a service within its sphere similar to, though less thorough than, that which the service of navigation renders within its sphere: the value of such services is seldom very much diminished by a little uncertainty as to some of the data.'[19] If, of course, economists are to continue to produce work of high social utility, then they must continue consciously to ferret out research-topics of genuine social relevance. Clearly, not all possible pieces of knowledge help equally to raise the quality of human life: while we all know that 'intellectual thoroughness and sincerity is its own reward',[20] nonetheless so long as so many of our fellow-countrymen remain brutalised and in need there must inevitably be a premium on investigation which bears 'a direct relation to practical issues'.[21] The choice of problems for careful and impartial examination is obviously a task of paramount importance. Ricardo 'did not make a very good selection'.[22] The Physiocrats did.

Economists select their own problems for study and thus, deciding autonomously as they must on the precise specification of social relevance, evidently do much more than simply speak when spoken to. It is in the circumstances only to be expected that they will take the obvious next step of the educated man and situate themselves in the vanguard of social reform. Thus they will come to demonstrate and laud the vital function of economic chivalry: 'Economists cannot do it alone. Perhaps it may be found that their share in it will not be large, but I myself believe it will be very large. I submit, then, that a most pressing immediate call on us is to associate in our own minds and those of others economic studies and chivalrous effort.'[23] Economists, moreover, have a professional duty to exercise countervailing power in society, 'taking an attitude of reserve towards movements that are already popular'[24] (with respect to the minimum wage, for example), speaking loudly in defence of the consumer interest where the producer speaks loudly in defence of his own,[25] reinforcing with sound arguments where appropriate 'the new force of public opinion as a means of eliminating much of the evil effects of competition, while retaining its good effects'.[26] Economists, finally, convinced as they are that consumption must be turned away from 'silly show'[27] into 'paths that strengthen the consumer'[28] and aware of the valuable support that can be lent to this effort by *virtuosi* and *cognoscenti* ('we need to foster fine work and fresh initiative by the warming breath of the sympathy and appreciation of those who truly understand it'[29]), have a duty to protest against immoralities and perversions even where these result, as if guided by an invisible hand, directly from supply and demand – as in the case of an oriental tapestry which is expensive because so many persons had lost their eyesight or been in other ways seriously injured while working on it and of which Marshall says: 'The whim or the artistic lust of the rich consumer had outweighed the welfare of the producers in this instance . . . . Such instances of social discord are facts which the economist must admit: they are the result of natural laws which it is his business to help to counteract.'[30] Naturally, the economist should make haste very slowly indeed in his role of preacher. We must, for one thing, recognise more fully than was done by previous generations 'how little we know of the causes by which progress is being fashioned, and how little we can forecast the ultimate destiny of the industrial organism',[31] and we must for that reason proceed cautiously in the promulgation of ethical norms: 'The economist needs imagination especially in order that he may develop his ideals. But most of all he needs caution and reserve in order that his advocacy of ideals may not outrun his grasp of the future.'[32] And economists must, needless to say, recognise more fully than is done by any number of well-meaning enthusiasts, that 'change in human nature ... is a growth, and therefore gradual; and changes of our social organization must wait on it, and therefore they must be gradual too'.[33] Even so, however, 'though they wait on it, they may always keep a little in advance of it, promoting the growth of our higher social nature by giving it always some new and higher work to do, some practical ideal towards which to strive';[34] and in the process of leading and shaping public opinion so as to render acceptable such learning by doing in the field of human nature the economist has an active role to play in influencing the development of his society. Given such scope for the sculptor as well as the photographer, it is clear why Marshall believed so strongly of economics that 'there are very few fields which offer so important and rich a harvest to scientific enterprise'.[35]

The economist, Marshall believed, legitimately approaches his studies 'fortified by the consciousness of his own rectitude'[36] and aware of his high calling – to advance well-being, welfare and happiness. It is with this missionary zeal in mind that Keynes describes Marshall the economist as 'not less ordained in spirit than if he had fulfilled his father's desire'[37] and become a clergyman. Quoting a review of the *Principles* which emphasised just how much of Marshall's economics is moralistic and humanising rather than mechanistic and dismal ('It is a great thing to have a Professor at one of our old Universities devoting the work of his life to recasting the Science of Political Economy as the Science of Social Perfectibility'[38]), Keynes speculates on whether Marshall might not in the event have gone too far in his concern with human betterment:

> Marshall was too anxious to do good. He had an inclination to undervalue those intellectual parts of the subject which were not *directly* connected with human well-being or the condition of the working classes or the like, although *indirectly* they might be of the utmost importance, and to feel that when he was pursuing them he was not occupying himself with the Highest. It came out of the

> conflict . . . between an intellect, which was hard, dry, critical, as unsentimental as you could find, with emotions and aspirations, generally unspoken, of quite a different type. When his intellect chased diagrams and Foreign Trade and Money, there was an evangelical moraliser of an imp somewhere inside him, that was so ill-advised as to disapprove. Near the end of his life, when the intellect grew dimmer and the preaching imp could rise nearer to the surface to protest against its lifelong servitude, he once said: 'If I had to live my life over again I should have devoted it to psychology. Economics has too little to do with ideals. If I said much about them I should not be read by business men.'[39]

Pigou also stresses Marshall's concern with ideals, Marshall's desire to be of genuine service to his fellow men. Marshall, Pigou says, started out 'with the firm view that economic science is chiefly valuable, neither as an intellectual gymnastic nor even as a means of winning truth for its own sake, but as a handmaid of ethics and a servant of practice':

> It was through ethics that he came to economics: because, when you have decided what things, or, if you will, what states of consciousness are ultimately good, it becomes your duty to try and bring about these things, and, in order to bring them about, you need, above all, ability to trace the interworking of causes and effects in the economic sphere. So economics for him was a handmaid to this, not an end in itself, but a means to a further end: an instrument, by the perfecting of which it might be possible to better the conditions of human life. Things, organisation, technique were incidents: what mattered was the quality of man.[40]

It is this concern with right conduct and the tone of life which sharply differentiates Cambridge rationalists such as Sidgwick and Marshall from 'the sensation – psychology and the atomist sociology of traditional utilitarianism'[41] while unambiguously aligning them with Oxford idealists such as Toynbee and especially Green, of whom Richter writes: 'A recurrent image in Green's thought was the social reformer, a type he esteemed as of higher value than the saint . . . . No other mode of life seemed to him more worthy. It is not at all difficult to understand his admiration for Wilberforce and Shaftesbury, Chadwick and Florence Nightingale.'[42] Green's secular missionary is Marshall's political economist, aware as he is that the question of 'the pains of poverty and the stagnating influences of excessive mechanical toil' urgently demands an answer – and 'the answer depends in a great measure upon facts and inferences, which are within the province of economics': 'This it is which gives to economic studies their chief and their highest interest.'[43] Marshall's favourite student and his successor to the Cambridge Chair was in that sense no less an idealist and a missionary, for Pigou's own inaugural address, like Marshall's twenty-three years earlier, contains an open invitation to the economist to pyramid actions on ideals and commitment on conviction: 'I shall be glad if a man comes to Economics because he has been interested by Professor Edgeworth's *Mathematical Psychics* or Dr. Fisher's *Appreciation and Interest*: just as I shall be glad if he comes to it because he is looking forward to business and wishes to learn something of the broader aspects of his future career; but I shall be far more glad if he comes because he has walked through the slums of London and is stirred to make some effort to help his fellow men. Wonder, Carlyle said, is the beginning of philosophy: social enthusiasm one might add, is the beginning of economic science.'[44] The economy *matters*, economics *matters* – and so does the economist.

And yet Marshall was fond of saying that the economist *qua* economist should distinguish between 'sentiment' and 'reason' and make clear when he is speaking 'as a citizen rather than specially as an economist'.[45] Thus an economist who gives his own personal opinion 'as to the relative claims of different social aims'[46] does not, and must not be assumed to, 'speak with the voice of his science' in the way that he would be doing if speaking with authority on a straightforward matter of technique analogous to the manner in which 'an engineer might say with authority that a certain kind of canal lock is unsuitable for its purpose': 'An economist as such cannot say which is the best course to pursue, any more than an engineer as such can decide what is the best route for the Panama canal.'[47] The economist *qua* economist, in other words, must eschew individual value-judgements and 'expressions of sentiment or desire in the optative mood'[48] and confine himself to the analysis of facts and regularities: 'The Laws of Economics are statements of tendencies expressed in the indicative mood, and not ethical precepts in the imperative.'[49] It is a matter of record that Marshall only very infrequently became directly involved in the practical politics of his own day (even when the debates touched on matters of some concern to him such as the ugly face of trade unionism) and it would be charitable to say that the reason was not his well-known fear of controversy so much as a conviction that the economist *qua* economist ought to keep his individual attitudes and preferences to himself. As he wrote to the Bishop of Durham: 'I think that, when the academic student takes on himself the role of preacher, he is generally less effective than when he treats the problems of life objectively.'[50]

Marshall felt compelled to put in a *plaidoyer* for scientific detachment. It is advice which he himself consistently ignored whenever it suited his purposes and objectives to do so. A missionary, a philosopher, a critic first and foremost, Marshall's moralising is not *obiter dictum* but rather part and parcel of the system. As Theodore Levitt has so accurately pointed out, it is simply not possible to distinguish Marshall the compulsive investigator from Marshall the obsessive sermoniser: 'Even when speaking strictly qua economist, Marshall unhesitatingly intruded normative and moral prescripts into his discussion, and these his readers learned to ignore almost toally; and if not ignore, treat as either solecistic quaintness or irrelevant mush. Yet they show again that Marshall, each time he faced an impasse in the use of economics to solve problems of general social well-being, was forced, and had no hesitation in returning, to strictly personal judgements of moral rightness and social oughtness.'[51]

No hesitation but also no choice – for to look at the economy, as Marshall did, in the broader context of evolutionary upgrading and collective intervention, of progress and politics, must inevitably force even the economist to reflect on the nature of the new society which his investigations and the actors whom he investigates are helping to bring about. The inspection of data may be value-free, Marshall seems to be saying, but the selection, significance and dynamic consequences of that data are not and can never be; and for that reason no socially responsible economist has the right to distance himself too far from ethical speculation and a concern with *ought-to-bes*. As Marshall puts it, speaking of a drug which has the potential to do evil as well as good: 'A chemist's balance takes no account of the medical properties of an ounce of arsenic, but the chemist does.'[52] Economic growth is precisely such a drug. The economist must be precisely such a chemist.

Notes and References

All works cited are by Alfred Marshall unless otherwise indicated.

ABBREVIATIONS

EAM	D. A. Reisman, *The Economics of Alfred Marshall* (London: Macmillan, 1986).
EI	*The Economics of Industry*, 2nd ed. (London: Macmillan, 1881) (with Mary Paley Marshall).
EEI	*Elements of Economics of Industry*, 2nd ed. (London: Macmillan 1896).
Guillebaud II	A. Marshall, *Principles of Economics*, 9th (Variorum) ed. with annotations by C. W. Guillebaud (London: Macmillan, 1961), Vol. II: Notes.
IRC	Paper to the Industrial Remuneration Conference (1885) in *Industrial Remuneration Conference: The Report of the Proceedings and Papers*, (London: Cassell, 1885).
IT	*Industry and Trade*, 4th ed. (London: Macmillan, 1923).
Marshall Papers	Papers of A. Marshall, in the Marshall Library of Economics, Sidgwick Avenue, Cambridge. Quoted by permission of the Marshall Librarian and the Faculty Board of Economics and Politics, University of Cambridge.
Memorials	A. C. Pigou, ed., *Memorials of Alfred Marshall* (London: Macmillan, 1925).
MCC	*Money Credit and Commerce* (London: Macmillan, 1923).
OP	*Official Papers by Alfred Marshall* (London: Macmillan, (1926). These are: Answers to Questions on the Subject of Currency and Prices circulated by the Royal Commission on the Depression of Trade and Industry (1886);

	Memoranda and Evidence before the Gold and Silver Commission (1887); Preliminary Statement and Evidence before the Royal Commission on the Aged Poor (1893); Evidence before the Indian Currency Committee (1899); Memorandum on the Classification and Incidence of Imperial and Local Taxes (1897); and Memorandum on the Fiscal Policy of International Trade (1903).
PE	*Principles of Economics*, 8th ed. (1920) (London: Macmillan, 1949).
Whitaker	J. K. Whitaker, ed., *The Early Economic Writings of Alfred Marshall, 1867–1890* (London: Macmillan, 1975), Vols. I, II.
Wood	J. C. Wood, *Alfred Marshall: Critical Assessments* (London: Croom Helm, 1982), Vols. I–IV.

1. INTRODUCTION

1. Preface to the fifth (1907) edition of the *Principles*, in Guillebaud II, p. 45.
2. J. M. Keynes, 'Alfred Marshall, 1842–1924', in *Memorials*, p. 65.

2. HUMAN BETTERMENT

1. *PE*, p. 600.
2. *PE*, p. 601.
3. *PE*, p. 6.
4. J.A. Schumpeter, 'Alfred Marshall's *Principles*: A Semi-Centennial Appraisal', *American Economic Review*, Vol. 31, 1941. In Wood II, p. 109.
5. J. Viner, 'Marshall's Economics in Relation to the Man and to his Times', *American Economic Review*, Vol. 31, 1941. In Wood I, p. 254.
6. Cited in R. Coase, 'Marshall on Method', *Journal of Law and Economics*, Vol. 18, 1975. In Wood I, p.409.
7. Cited in R.F. Harrod, *The Life of John Maynard Keynes* (London: Macmillan, 1951), p. 117n.

2.1 Want Satisfaction

1. *IRC*, p. 182.
2. 'The Future of the Working Classes' (1873), in *Memorials*, p. 111.
3. *PE*, p. 450.

4. *PE*, p. 450.
5. Discussion on F. Schuster's paper 'Foreign Trade and the Money Market', Institute of Bankers, 16 December 1903. In *Journal of the Institute of Bankers*, Vol. xxv, 1904, p. 96.
6. *IRC*, p. 182.
7. *PE*, p. 567.
8. *PE*, p. 567.
9. *IRC*, p. 182.
10. *IRC*, p. 182. A fall in the rate of interest consequent upon prudence and accumulation does not by itself, of course, mean a fall in the share of the national income that accrues to capital-owners: shares reflect quantity of units (which has increased) as well as price per unit (which has fallen). Nor is it entirely clear why an increase in quantity supplied is associated with diminished remuneration: demand for as well as supply of the input must surely be a relevant consideration in such a context. For a further discussion of these ambiguities, see *EAM*, Chapter 10.3.
11. *PE*, p. 571. The small investor might take some comfort from Marshall's *dictum* 'the risks of trade are on the whole diminishing rather than increasing' (*PE*, p. 516), although it is far from clear what Marshall means by this.
12. See *EAM*, Chapter 8. There is a temptation to assert that Marshall, like Ricardo, believed that economic growth favours labour and land to the detriment of capital. It would be more honest to say, however, that Marshall makes no clear statement as to precisely what happens to relative income-shares as between the various factors in the course of development.
13. *PE*, p. 571. Marshall's final verdict on the statistics he cites is not, as it happens, unambiguous, and passages such as the following betray a not inconsiderable hesitancy: 'The aggregate income of the very rich is perhaps not a larger part of the whole in England now than in earlier times.' (*PE*, pp. 571–2).
14. *PE*, p. 571.
15. *PE*, p. 592.
16. *PE*, p. 519.
17. *PE*, p. 563.
18. *PE*, p. 563. In fact, a modern house is qualitatively so different from an older one that it is in effect all but a totally different consumable. For example: 'An average ten-roomed house is, perhaps, twice as large in volume as it used to be; and a great part of its cost goes for water, gas, and other appliances which were not in the older house.' (*MCC*, p. 33).
19. *PE*, p. 563n.
20. 'Where to House the London Poor' (1884), in *Memorials*, p. 142n. The statement in question was made circa 1923, and despite its overall optimism, does betray a certain degree of apprehension concerning the possibility that there had since 1884 been a 'great increase in the number of children who rarely see a green field'. Inevitably, where nature does fail, man must intervene – a topic to which we shall return in later Chapters of the present book.

21. *PE*, p. 362. Elsewhere, speaking of the consumption of meat by the lower classes, Marshall says: 'No doubt much of the meat is of kinds which no one would be proud to say that he had bought. But it is wholesome, and probably much better on the average than meat which the same classes used to buy, in earlier times, if they bought fresh meat at all.' (*MCC*, p. 31n).
22. Speech at the meeting of what was to become the Royal Economic Society held on 14 June 1893, as reported in the *Economic Journal*, Vol. III, 1893, p. 390.
23. *MCC*, p. 35.
24. *MCC*, p. 33.
25. *PE*, p. 574.
26. *PE*, p. 144.
27. *PE*, p. 440.
28. *PE*, p. 170. Artificial in this context does not, of course, mean producer-induced, as in the Galbraithian 'revised sequence'. It means a want not subservient to an activity which contributes to the unfolding of man's higher nature.
29. *PE*, p. 441.
30. P. H. Wicksteed, *Getting and Spending* (London: Essex Hall, 1888), p. 15. Wicksteed admits that he is being intolerant in rejecting the theory of consumer sovereignty and the doctrine of *de gustibus non est disputandum*, but he is adamant that effective demand and utility provide no tenable measure of real worth: 'Do not tell me that all things are alike useful that are alike wanted, that it is equally honourable to minister to vice or folly and to minister to decency and comfort. Do not tell me that any man can escape from his responsibility before God and man for what he makes by saying that as long as it is *money* – which purges all commodities, and obliterates all history – it is what men want, and, therefore, what they ought to have,' (*Ibid*, p. 16). Negative freedom with respect to spending money, Wicksteed maintained, is both a great and 'a most pernicious and disastrous error, and one against which moral and religious men should protest by word and deed, in season and out of season, till no man dares to maintain it any more. . . . The way in which we spend our money is the deliberate and emphatic setting forth and preaching of our ideal' (*Ibid*, p. 27). Wicksteed is similarly dismissive of effective demand in his *Is Christianity Practical*? (London: William Reeves, 1884). I am grateful to Ian Steedman for these references, which demonstrate that Marshall was hardly alone among nineteenth century economists in speculating on the moral significance of needs and wants.
31. Cited in M. Richter, *The Politics of Conscience: T. H. Green and His Age* (London: Weidenfeld and Nicholson, 1964), p. 324.
32. Letter to *The Times* of June 2, 1885, p. 3.
33. *PE*, p. 76.
34. 'The Future of the Working Classes' (1873), in *Memorials*, p. 107.
35. 'The Future of the Working Classes' (1873), in *Memorials*, p. 107.
36. 'Where to House the London Poor' (1884), in *Memorials*, pp. 146–7.
37. 'Where to House the London Poor' (1884), in *Memorials*, p. 149.

38. Letter to T. C. Horsfall dated 8 March 1900, in *Memorials*, p. 409.
39. *PE*, p. 113.
40. *PE*, p. 75n.
41. *PE*, p. 441.
42. *IRC*, p. 214.
43. *IRC*, p. 214. On that occasion he seems to have broken with his usual propensity to select the materialistic in preference to the mentalistic solution since he added that education 'did stop drunkenness'.
44. 'The Future of the Working Classes' (1873), in *Memorials*, p. 102.
45. *PE*, p. 74.
46. *PE*, p. 74n.
47. *PE*, p. 74n.
48. 'The Present Position of Economics' (1885), in *Memorials*, p. 173.
49. *EI*, pp. 17–18.
50. Lecture delivered in Bristol on 5 March 1883. Quoted in G. J. Stigler, 'Alfred Marshall's Lectures on Progress and Poverty', *Journal of Law and Economics*, Vol. 12, 1969. In Wood IV, p. 173.
51. 'The Old Generation of Economists and the New' (1897), in *Memorials*, p. 310.
52. *PE*, p. 76.
53. T. Parsons, 'Wants and Activities in Marshall', *The Quarterly Journal of Economics*, Vol. 46, 1931, and in his *The Structure of Social Action* (1937) (New York: The Free Press, 1968). In Wood I, p. 182. The concluding four words were added in 1937 and are not to be found in the 1931 text.
54. F. Knight, 'Ethics and the Economic Interpretation', *The Quarterly Journal of Economics*, Vol. 36, 1922, in his *The Ethics of Competition and Other Essays* (1935) (Freeport, New York: Books for Libraries Press, 1969), p. 21. The extent to which Knight was influenced on this and other issues by Marshall deserves to be more widely known.
55. *PE*, p. 566. See also *IT*, p. 637.
56. *PE*, p. 599.
57. *PE*, p. 566.
58. *PE*, p. 566.
59. *IT*, p. 637.
60. *PE*, p. 578.
61. *PE*, p. 578.
62. *PE*, p. 462.
63. *PE*, p. 599.
64. Letter to *The Times* of 10 November 1898, p. 10.
65. *PE*, p. 599.
66. *PE*, p. 599.
67. *PE*, p. 599.
68. *PE*, p. 76.
69. *PE*, p. 600.
70. *PE*, p. 75.
71. *IT*, p. 663. Speaking of his 'new society', Marshall says that overtime and overwork would diminish and 'a man would not in general perform manual work for more than six hours a day' – which points to a more

extensive reliance on shift-working: 'In our society the hours of labour are to be very short, but it does not follow that the hours of work of the machinery would be short too' ("The Future of the Working Classes" (1873), in *Memorials*, p. 113). See also *PE*, pp. 578–80.
72. *IT*, p. 637.
73. *IT*, p. 637.
74. *PE*, p. 564.

2.2 Conduct and Character

1. 'The Present Position of Economics' (1885), in *Memorials*, p. 153.
2. 'The Present Position of Economics' (1885), in *Memorials*, p. 169.
3. *PE*, p. 196.
4. *PE*, p. 194.
5. *PE*, p. 631.
6. 'The Present Position of Economics' (1885), in *Memorials*, p. 154.
7. *PE*, pp. 631–2.
8. *PE*, p. 1.
9. 'The Present Position of Economics' (1885), in *Memorials*, p. 154.
10. 'The Present Position of Economics' (1885), in *Memorials*, p. 155.
11. *PE*, p. 631. In his paper to the *IRC* (pp. 173–4) fifty years is reduced to thirty: 'Economic institutions are the products of human nature, and cannot change much faster than human nature changes. Education, the raising of our moral and religious ideals, and the growths of printing press and the telegraph have so changed English human nature that many things which economists rightly considered impossible thirty years ago are possible now. And the rate of change is increasing constantly and rapidly. But we have not now to speculate boldly for the future; and we have to act for the present, taking human nature not as it may be, but as it is.'
12. 'The Present Position of Economics' (1885), in *Memorials*, p. 155.
13. 'The Old Generation of Economists and the New' (1897), in *Memorials*, p. 299.
14. *PE*, p. 631.
15. *PE*, p. 116.
16. 'Distribution and Exchange' (1898), in Guillebaud II, p. 63.
17. 'Distribution and Exchange' (1898), in Guillebaud II, p. 75.
18. *PE*, p. 574.
19. *PE*, p. 76. Unlike Jevons, in other words, who had seen economics in more static terms as a science concerned essentially with the adaptation of scarce means to exogenously-determined wants, and who was far from assigning pride of place to the active unfolding of potential.
20. *PE*, p. 5.
21. *PE*, p. 253.
22. *PE*, p. 6.
23. *PE*, p. 6.
24. *PE*, p. 253.
25. *PE*, p. 253. Emphasis added to bring out Marshall's conviction that

probity is the *precondition* for the joint stock form – not an aid to its full flowering but the *sine qua non* of its very existence. See also *IT*, pp. 164–6.

26. *PE*, p. 552.
27. *PE*, p. 253.
28. *PE*, p. 29.
29. *PE*, p. 19.
30. *PE*, p. 6.
31. *PE*, p. 6.
32. 'A Fair Rate of Wages' (1887), in *Memorials*, p. 213.
33. Manuscript footnote dating from circa 1923. See 'The Future of the Working Classes' (1873), in *Memorials*, p. 101n.
34. 'The Future of the Working Classes' (1873), in *Memorials*, p. 102.
35. 'The Future of the Working Classes' (1873), in *Memorials*, p. 103. The distinction between the individual and the general, the exception and the rule, in this passage is an early instance of Marshall's propensity to focus on *normal* values.
36. 'The Future of the Working Classes' (1873), in *Memorials*, pp. 103, 104.
37. 'The Future of the Working Classes' (1873), in *Memorials*, pp. 103–4.
38. 'The Future of the Working Classes' (1873), in *Memorials*, p. 104.
39. 'The Future of the Working Classes' (1873), in *Memorials*, p. 105.
40. 'The Future of the Working Classes' (1873), in *Memorials*, p. 115.
41. 'The Future of the Working Classes' (1873), in *Memorials*, p. 113.
42. 'The Future of the Working Classes' (1873), in *Memorials*, p. 107.
43. 'The Future of the Working Classes' (1873), in *Memorials* p. 106.
44. 'The Future of the Working Classes' (1873), in *Memorials*, p. 115.
45. 'The Future of the Working Classes' (1873), in *Memorials*, p. 105.
46. 'The Future of the Working Classes' (1873), in *Memorials*, p. 106.
47. 'The Future of the Working Classes' (1873), in *Memorials*, p. 105.
48. 'The Future of the Working Classes' (1873), in *Memorials*, p. 110.
49. 'The Old Generation of Economists and the New' (1897), in *Memorials*, p. 311
50. 'Some Features of American Industry' (1875), in Whitaker II, p. 369.
51. 'Some Features of American Industry' (1875), in Whitaker II, p. 373.
52. F. Hirsch, *Social Limits to Growth* (London: Routledge & Kegan Paul Ltd., 1977), p. 5.
53. A. Smith, *The Wealth of Nations* (1776), ed. by E. Cannan (London: Methuen, 1961), Vol. II, p. 308.
54. Smith, *Wealth of Nations*, Vol. I, p. 433.
55. A. Smith, *Lectures on Justice, Police, Revenue and Arms* (circa 1763), ed. by E. Cannan (Oxford: Clarendon Press, 1896), p. 256.
56. Smith, *Wealth of Nations*, Vol. II, p. 303.
57. R. H. Tawney, *Equality* (1931) (London: George Allen & Unwin Ltd., 1964), p. 108.
58. *EI*, p. 9.
59. *PE*, p. 218. And in other branches as well since nowadays 'there is scarcely any work which does not need some mental effort. Even in agriculture machinery is being introduced, the management of which requires much skill and intelligence.' (*EI*, p. 10).

60. *PE*, p. 214.
61. Undated fragment, in *Memorials*, p. 365.
62. *PE*, p. 1.
63. 'The Future of the Working Classes' (1873), in *Memorials*, p. 115.
64. *OP*, (1887), p. 95.
65. 'The Future of the Working Classes' (1873), in *Memorials*, pp. 110–11.
66. 'The Future of the Working Classes' (1873), in *Memorials*, p. 111.
67. *MCC*, p. 101.
68. *MCC*, p. 139.
69. *OP*, (1903), p. 381.
70. 'The Theory of Foreign Trade' (1873–7), in Whitaker II, p. 15.
71. 'The Theory of Foreign Trade' (1873–7), in Whitaker II, p. 15.
72. *MCC*, p. 64. Elsewhere, in *OP*, (1887), p. 135, he writes: 'I think that there is a real, though very slow-moving, tendency for national interests to overrule provincial interests, and international interests to overrule national, and I think the time will come at which it will be thought as unreasonable for any country to regulate its currency without reference to other countries as it will be to have signalling codes at sea which took no account of the signalling codes at sea of other countries'.
73. Discussion on F. Schuster's paper 'Foreign Trade and the Money Market', Institute of Bankers, 16 December 1903. In *Journal of the Institute of Bankers*, Vol. xxv, 1904, pp. 97–8.
74. Discussion on F. Schuster's paper 'Foreign Trade and the Money Market', Institute of Bankers, 16 December 1903. In *Journal of the Institute of Bankers*, Vol. xxv, 1904, p. 98.
75. Letter to *The Times* of August 22, 1914, p. 7.
76. *PE*, p. 75.
77. *PE*, p. 75. The discussion of wants and activities does not appear in the first edition of the *Principles* and was inserted in the second edition of 1891. This is surprising in view of the whole tenor of Marshall's economics, in which creativity at all stages plays a far more significant role than does absorption.
78. *PE*, p. 72.
79. 'The Future of the Working Classes' (1873), in *Memorials*, p. 111.
80. 'The Future of the Working Classes' (1873), in *Memorials*, p. 112.
81. *PE*, p. 75.
82. 'The Future of the Working Classes' (1873), in *Memorials*, p. 116.
83. Letter to the Bishop of Durham dated 20 January 1901, in *Memorials*, p. 391.
84. *PE*, p. 220.
85. A term which Marshall actually employs in some fragmentary lecture-notes dated 26 April 1884 and headed 'On Utilitarianism: A Summum Bonum'. There he considers various aspects of happiness in the tradition of Bentham and Edgeworth and concludes that 'maximum happiness' might not point in the same direction as the development of 'the highest ideal of humanity' where 'the highest ideal may be taken to mean the highest capabilities of action, "highest" being taken as defined according to the "evolver" theory'. Marshall comments that this evolutionary process might indeed 'bring with it happiness so much

more intense than can be got in any other way' that the 'maximum happiness' and 'highest ideal' theories ultimately coincide, but he quickly adds concerning such convergence that 'it is not probable'. That being the case, a clear choice must be made between happiness and development. In Whitaker II, p. 317.

86. 'The Old Generation of Economists and the New' (1897), in *Memorials*, p. 310.
87. 'The Future of the Working Classes' (1873), in *Memorials*, p. 115. And almost half a century later, in an unpublished note dated 6 March 1922 bearing the heading 'Ideals': 'Work is not a punishment for fault: it is a necessity for the formation of character; and, therefore, for progress.' In Marshall Papers, Red Box 1 (3).
88. *PE*, p. 597.
89. See *EAM*, Chapters 3.1 and 7.2 for a further discussion of this point.
90. Parsons is not being entirely fair to Marshall, who did in fact see clearly – even if not resolve – the tension between 'activities' and 'efforts and sacrifices', as in the following passage concerning the formation of human capital in particular: 'The problem is as much philosophical as economic; it is complicated by the fact that man's activities are ends in themselves as well as means of production, and also by the difficulty of dividing clearly the immediate and direct (or prime) cost of human effort from its total cost; and it must be left imperfectly solved' (*PE*, p. 684). Marshall's implicit reminder in this passage that the disutility theory refers specifically to the *marginal* cost is of particular interest. See also *EAM*, Chapter 3.1.
91. Parsons, 'Wants and Activities in Marshall', (Chapter 2.1, note 53), p. 193.
92. Parsons, 'Wants and Activities in Marshall', (Chapter 2.1, note 53), p. 188.
93. 'The Future of the Working Classes' (1873), in *Memorials*, p. 105.
94. *PE*, p. 596.
95. 'The Old Generation of Economists and the New' (1897), in *Memorials*, p. 308.
96. 'Some Aspects of Competition' (1890), in *Memorials*, p. 281.
97. *IT*, p. 180.
98. *IT*, p. 633.
99. *IT*, p. 156.
100. *PE*, p. 467.
101. Letter to John Hilton dated 14 April 1919, in Marshall Papers, Letters 3 (62). Note, however, that in describing competition as 'a chief factor of progress', he specifies that it is 'chivalrous competition' to which he is referring – and that he is 'therefore a little troubled by any suggestion that competition must be greedy'.
102. *PE*, p. 202.
103. *PE*, pp. 202–3.
104. *PE*, p. 202.
105. 'Social Possibilities of Economic Chivalry' (1907), in *Memorials*, p. 327. p. 327.
106. *PE*, p. 599. See also *PE*, p. 566 and 'Social Possibilities of Economic

Chivalry' (1907), in *Memorials*, pp. 323–46. The topic was first broached in *IRC*, pp. 182–3.

107. Hirsch, *Social Limits to Growth*, p. 137.
108. Hirsch, *Social Limits to Growth*, p. 143.
109. R. C. O. Matthews, 'Morality, Competition and Efficiency', *The Manchester School*, Vol. 49, 1981, p. 293. Matthews gives a second example of the functionality of morality, the case of long-term contracts (explicit or implicit). These clearly economise on the costs associated with search for information, negotiation and sequential re-contracting but they may also impose costs of their own simply by virtue of the fact that they increase the vulnerability of each party to the potential depredations of the other: 'During the duration of these contracts, each party enjoys a degree of monopoly, since his services cannot be replaced by competition without expense, inconvenience and delay. Furthermore, the relationship between the parties in such contracts typically has some complexity and leaves some room for discretion in implementation, since it is too difficult to draft a contract that spells out every conceivable contingency in advance, let alone enforce it in a court of law . . . . It is necessary for efficiency that the parties to a contract or an implicit contract should feel, and be trusted to feel, an obligation to observe its spirit as well as its letter. If everyone is expected to exploit ruthlessly every short-run monopoly position when it is in his interest to do so, the division of labour will be seriously impaired.' Self-interest does not normally lead to theft and murder not least because it is constrained by ethics, Matthews argues, and there is, similarly, no reason why it should normally lead to immoral business practices such as the seizing of short-term monopoly gains in the manner described above. In stressing the functionality of moral norms and the sanction of guilt, Matthews situates himself decidedly in the Cambridge tradition of ethics in economics to which Alfred Marshall made so significant a contribution.
110. *PE*, p. 632.
111. *PE*, p. 621.
112. *PE*, pp. 5–6.
113. A. Smith, *The Theory of Moral Sentiments* (1759) (New York: Augustus M. Kelley, 1966), p. 297.
114. *PE*, p. 621.
115. *PE*, p. 5.
116. 'Social Possibilities of Economic Chivalry' (1907), in *Memorials*, p. 328.
117. 'Social Possibilities of Economic Chivalry' (1907), in *Memorials*, p. 327.
118. 'Social Possibilities of Economic Chivalry' (1907), in *Memorials*, p. 327.
119. 'Social Possibilities of Economic Chivalry' (1907), in *Memorials*, p. 345.
120. 'Social Possibilities of Economic Chivalry' (1907), in *Memorials*, p. 330.
121. *PE*, p. 5.
122. *PE*, p. 202.
123. *PE*, p. 5.
124. *PE*, p. 566.
125. *PE*, p. 468.
126. See, for example, *PE*, pp. 470–1.

127. *PE*, p. 470. The employers' motive in providing the training naturally has something of the pecuniary in it (i.e. 'it pays them to do so'). The point being made is that their motive, at least in the case of genuine business leaders, is not *exclusively* pecuniary. Nonetheless, since not all employers are genuine business leaders and since the investment in human capital is of 'uncertain tenure' (with 'no security of compensation' should the worker go elsewhere, perhaps to a competitor), the inference must be that training is likely *ceteris paribus* to be undersupplied if left to the private sector. See on this *EAM*, Chapter 10.4.
128. *PE*, p. 470.
129. *PE*, p. 621.
130. *PE*, p. 621.
131. 'Social Possibilities of Economic Chivalry' (1907), in *Memorials*, p. 331.
132. *PE*, p. 470.
133. *IT*, p. viii. Emphasis added.
134. 'Where to House the London Poor' (1884), in *Memorials*, pp. 142n, 150.
135. Smith, *Theory of Moral Sentiments*, p. 194.
136. F. Y. Edgeworth, *Mathematical Psychics* (London: C. Kegan Paul & Co., 1881), p. 16.
137. *EI*, p. vi. Marshall's observation that we can have 'no theory of Normal values' in a situation of complete bilaterial altruism is an important one. The rather absurd conclusion of indeterminacy of outcome is illustrated as follows by Matthews: 'I am selling you a house. Your utility ranks equally with mine, both in my eyes and in yours. So the price is a matter of indifference to both of us. £10 000 more to me, £10 000 more to you – there is nothing in it. As a result, no market signals emerge.' Matthews, (note 109, above), p. 291.
138. See, for example, *PE*, pp. 581–3.
139. Undated fragment, in *Memorials*, p. 362.
140. *PE*, p. 21.
141. 'Social Possibilities of Economic Chivalry' (1907), in *Memorials*, p. 343.
142. *IT*, p. 681n.
143. *PE*, p. 566.
144. *PE*, p. 202.
145. *PE*, p. 202.
146. See *PE*, pp. 167–8.
147. *PE*, p. 600.
148. *IRC*, p. 173.
149. Knight, 'The Ethics of Competition', (Chapter 2.1, note 54), p. 72.
150. R. H. Tawney, 'A Note on Christianity and the Social Order' (1937), in his *The Attack and Other Papers* (London: George Allen & Unwin Ltd., 1953), p. 170.
151. *PE*, p. 202.
152. *PE*, p. 161.
153. *PE*, p. 162.
154. *PE*, p. v.
155. *PE*, p. 8.
156. *IT*, p. 163.

157. *PE*, p. 5.
158. Quoted in A. C. Pigou, 'In Memoriam: Alfred Marshall', in *Memorials,* p. 83.
159. *PE*, p. 607.
160. *PE*, p. 602.
161. *EI*, pp. 62–3. Emphasis added. The Irish cottier is, in Marshall's view, a good example of a man who, *de facto* an intellectual child, urgently needs temporary protection from himself – in the form of rent-fixing by outside authority, security of tenure against eviction, and other paternalistic measures.
162. *EI*, p. 64.
163. *PE*, p. 73.
164. *PE*, p. 604.
165. *PE*, p. 177n.
166. *PE*, p. 531.
167. *PE*, p. 177.
168. *IT*, p. 195.
169. Letter to *The Times* dated 24 March 1891, p. 11.
170. 'Social Possibilities of Economic Chivalry' (1907), in *Memorials*, p. 334.
171. *PE*, p. 7.
172. *EI*, p. 115.
173. *PE*, p. 40.
174. 'The Old Generation of Economists and the New' (1897), in *Memorials*, p. 311.
175. *PE*, p. 576.
176. 'The Old Generation of Economists and the New' (1897), in *Memorials*, p. 311.
177. *PE*, p. 164n.
178. *PE*, p. 164n.
179. *PE*, p. 165n.
180. *PE*, p. 164n.
181. *PE*, p. 615.
182. *PE*, p. 614.
183. See for these and other examples Appendix A of the *Principles*. Marshall's account of mankind's march from habit and custom to calculation and rationality constituted the opening pages of the 1890 edition but attracted considerable adverse comment from specialist economic historians such as William Cunningham, who suggested delicately that Marshall had not been entirely unbiased in his choice of illustrations and had in effect concentrated on those which confirmed his personal *a prioris*. The controversy is carefully analyzed in J. Maloney, 'Marshall, Cunningham, and the Emerging Economics Profession', *Economic History Review*, Vol. 29, 1976. In Wood IV. See also, by the same author, *Marshall, Orthodoxy and the Professionalisation of Economics* (Cambridge: The University Press, 1985), esp. Chapter 3.
184. *PE*, p. 606.
185. *PE*, p. 608.
186. *PE*, p. 610.

187. *PE*, p. 177n.
188. *IT*, p. viii.

2.3 Change – The Negative Side

1. 'The Future of the Working Classes' (1873), in *Memorials*, pp. 115–6. The words 'partial retrogression'are important and remind us that not *all* change is to be regarded as moral and desirable: 'When we speak of progress . . . we do not mean every change that comes with the progress of time, e.g. not the destruction of the arts of Rome by the Goths; or of those of the Moors & the Mexicans by the Spaniards: at least this is progress backwards.' See 'Lecture notes on Mill Book IV' (*circa* early 1870s), in Marshall Papers, Box 5 (2). *Most* change is improvement but *some* is not; and it would appear the duty of the social philospher to guide his readers in the separation of the wheat from the chaff.
2. *PE*, p. 207. See, for an interesting examination of observations such as this, R. C. O. Matthews, 'Darwinism and Economic Change', in D. A. Collard *et al.*, *Economic Theory and Hicksian Themes* (Oxford: Clarendon Press, 1984), pp. 97–8n.
3. *PE*, p. 113.
4. *PE*, p. 113.
5. See *PE*, p. 111 and *EAM*, Chapter 2.4.
6. 'The Future of the Working Classes' (1873), in *Memorials*, p. 116.
7. *PE*, p. 206.
8. 'Social Possibilities of Economic Chivalry' (1907), in *Memorials*, p. 329.
9. *PE*, p. 204.
10. *IT*, p. 809.
11. *IT*, p. 809n.
12. *IRC*, p. 176.
13. *IRC*, p. 176. This is not to say that there should be *no* changes in fashion, only that changes, here as in other spheres of social life, should be gradual and not sudden.
14. *IT*, p. 809. This defence of 'ancient custom' and the force of tradition is in a sense somewhat out of place in the work of an author who wrote so extensively about economic dynamics. That he did enter such a plea for 'time out of mind' is not, however, in question. Thus, declaring that 'modern conditions have given some solid foundation for the common statement that utility and beauty are hostile to one another', Marshall is quick to make the point that a breach with the normal and the conventional is likely to have occurred: 'For when a thing is marked out for description as useful, it is almost sure to be a device for attaining some utility, old or new, by a new method; that is to say, it has not had time to be gently moulded by innumerable light touches of successive makers, who have tried to bring it more into harmony with their sense of fitness. But in the ages of patient custom time was abundant. Perhaps
43. Lecture delivered in Bristol on 5 March 1883. Quoted in Stigler, 'Alfred

those which were bad, passed away; while those which the people approved, were almost unconsciously incorporated in hallowed usage; and they became material for further moulding by the delicate breathings of the spirit of the race.' The carpet, the axe, the sword in the course of their evolution thus came to 'combine grace with efficiency in high degrees': 'So far as we can tell, men had then generally less quick, subtle, and fine instincts than now; and if each generation had moulded its own implements with little guidance from the past, the effects might probably have been crude; but, working on the plastic standard received from the past, each made its own step towards the Ideal' (*IT*, p. 198). There is evidently much to be said for remembering, in this as in other contexts, that *natura non facit saltum*. Even so, the reader may well wonder if Marshall does not ultimately prove more than he would want to prove with respect to making haste slowly, so powerful is his defence of convention. Thus, while conceding that 'a few ceremonial costumes which have come down from early times are ugly as well as inconvenient' (*IT*, p. 198n), nonetheless, he concludes, 'it seems that with comparatively few exceptions those parts of the local costume, which are worn in every-day life, are convenient and in good taste' (*IT*, p. 199n). Such durability, such lasting excellence, must be contrasted with the mediocrity and the built-in obsolescence of a cheap-and-nasty culture such as our own where all is flux – with the result, to cite only one example, that 'a great deal of excellent talent is insensibly diverted from high aims by the ready pay to be got by hastily writing half-thoughts for periodical literature' (*PE*, p. 179n).

15. *IT*, p. 809.
16. *IT*, p. 810.
17. *PE*, p. 113.
18. See on this *EAM*, Chapters 4–6 inclusive.
19. *IT*, p. 306.
20. 'Some Aspects of Competition' (1890), in *Memorials*, p. 278.
21. *IT*, p. 307. The exclusion of competitors (existing and potential) reinforces market-power, and all monopolistic positions *ceteris paribus* involve yet another kind of waste.
22. *IT*, p. 509.
23. 'The Future of the Working Classes' (1873), in *Memorials*, p. 116.
24. *PE*, p. 113.
25. 'Social Possibilities of Economic Chivalry' (1907), in *Memorials*, p. 344.
26. 'Social Possibilities of Economic Chivalry' (1907), in *Memorials*, p. 344. If such a desirable consensus could reasonably be expected to develop spontaneously it would not need to be 'worked up'. Marshall's argument is that a sense of duty can be enforced by public opinion but that public opinion might have to be shaped and mobilized by opinion-leaders (not least by economists). The implications of this argument both for evolutionary theory and for the position of the economist in society will be considered further in Chapter 7.
27. *PE*, p. 165n. See also *IT*, pp. 149–50.
28. 'Some Features of American Industry' (1875), in Whitaker II, p. 364.

29. 'Social Possibilities of Economic Chivalry' (1907), in *Memorials*, p. 326.
30. 'Social Possibilities of Economic Chivalry' (1907), in *Memorials*, p. 326. The sixth edition of the *Principles* which appeared in 1910 also displays a concern with population growth and diminishing returns to land. See Guillebaud II, p. 59.
31. *PE*, p. 318.
32. *PE*, p. 139.
33. See *IT*, p. 162, 788–90; 'Water as an Element of National Wealth' (1879), in *Memorials*, pp. 134–41; undated fragment, in *Memorials*, p. 364.
34. *IT*, p. 628n. And in an undated fragment (in *Memorials*, p. 364) he makes the point that a country lacking in mineral oil 'must always jealously guard her supplies of coal for use at sea'. His criticism of freedom of trade in the case of this crucial commodity stops short, however, of a recommendation for State intervention along the lines of the export prohibitions that were in force in the Mercantilist period.
35. Letter of Louis Dumur dated 2 July 1909, in *Memorials*, p. 468. Emphasis added.
36. Letter to Sir Horace Plunkett dated 17 May 1910, in *Memorials*, p. 468. Emphasis added.
37. *PE*, p. 469n.
38. *PE*, p. 469.
39. 'The Future of the Working Classes' (1873), in *Memorials*, p. 106.
40. Letter to Louis Dumur dated 2 July 1909, in *Memorials*, pp. 459–60.
41. *PE*, p. 165.
42. *EI*, p. 12.
43. Lecture delivered in Bristol on 5 March 1883. Quoted in Stigler, 'Alfred Marshall's Lectures on Progress and Poverty', (Chapter 2.1, note 50), p. 173.
44. *PE*, p. 469.
45. *EI*, p. 102.
46. *PE*, p. 67.
47. *PE*, p. 165.
48. *PE*, p. 570.
49. *PE*, p. 469.
50. *PE*, p. 9.
51. *PE*, p. 58.
52. 'The Future of the Working Classes' (1873), in *Memorials*, p. 115.
53. *PE*, p. 163.
54. *IT*, p. 117.
55. *PE*, p. 599.
56. Report of the discussion at the Royal Statistical Society on Henry Higgs' paper 'Workmen's Budgets', 16 May 1893. In *Journal of the Royal Statistical Society*, Vol. LVI, 1893, p. 288.
57. *PE*, p. 616.
58. *PE*, p. 20.
59. *PE*, p. 5.
60. *PE*, p. 616.
61. *PE*, p. 600.

62. *PE*, p. 600.
63. *PE*, p. 578.
64. *PE*, p. 589n.
65. *PE*, p. 570.
66. Keynes, 'Alfred Marshall, 1842–1924', in *Memorials*, p. 58.
67. *PE*, p. 277.
68. *PE*, p. 297.
69. *PE*, p. 359n.
70. *PE*, p. 598.
71. *PE*, p. 502.
72. *IT*, p. 331, 332.
73. *IT*, p. 262n.
74. *IT*, p. 319.
75. *IT*, p. 262.
76. *IT*, p. 263n.
77. *IRC*, p. 214.
78. *PE*, p. 494.
79. *PE*, p. 490.
80. *IT*, pp. 56–7.
81. *MCC*, p. 259.
82. *IRC*, p. 177. He adds that 'Government might do a little; it might begin by publishing income-tax returns in local newspapers; a tax on honesty does harm in many ways'. Marshall never seems to have grasped the utility of *some* secrecy (as opposed, admittedly, to *excessive* secrecy) as a legitimate component in business strategy.
83. See Chapter 3.1 of the present volume and *EAM*, Chapters 4 and 6.
84. *IRC*, p. 181.
85. This matter is discussed further in Chapter 6.4 of the present volume.
86. *MCC*, p. 259.
87. *IRC*, p. 177.
88. *IRC*, p. 176.
89. *IT*, p. 265.
90. *IT*, p. 331.
91. *IT*, p. 337.
92. *PE*, p. 502.
93. *PE*, p. 559.
94. *IT*, p. 332.
95. *IRC*, p. 177.
96. *IRC*, p. 178.
97. IRC, p. 178. He makes a similar use of exhortation when he encourages individuals to act in the social interest (i.e. not to cause wastage of resources at the microeconomic level nor interruption of trade at the macroeconomic) by voluntarily electing not to follow 'all the vagaries of fashion' (*IRC*, p. 176). He never makes clear why he thinks people would be receptive to advice of this nature.
98. Letter to *The Times* of 17 November 1919, p. 8.
99. *PE*, p. 552.
100. *PE*, p. 487.
101. *PE*, p. 571.

102. *PE*, p. 571–2.
103. *PE*, p. 598.
104. *PE*, p. 572.
105. *IT*, p. 344.
106. *IT*, p. 345.
107. *PE*, pp. 598–9.
108. Letter to Bishop Westcott dated 20 January 1901, in *Memorials*, p. 394.
109. Undated fragment, in *Memorials*, p. 367.
110. *PE*,p. 7.
111. *PE*, p. 9. Such a period of over-rapid change is characterised by shoddy workmanship and the ugliness of the uncompleted – and by much else besides that is nothing less than 'vicious': 'A vicious age is always the beginning of a long period in which excitement is substituted for happiness, and the alternate fever and despondency of ill regulated passions takes the place of the tranquil and peaceful bliss of honest earnest domestic life.' The problem is not one of change but of *accelerated* change, not one of competition but of *too much competition*: 'We have lost through our hurry. It is the hurry of competition more than its definiteness and deliberateness of purpose that is injurious to art and to social life.' Note dated 20 February (no year, but could be *circa* 1920–1), in Marshall Papers, Red Box 1 (3).
112. *IT*, p. 179.
113. *PE*, p. 190.
114. *IT*, p. 179.
115. One interpretation of the observed phenomenon (see, for example, *PE*, p. 300) that labour is frequently treated as a fixed overhead.
116. *PE*, p. 380.
117. 'Some Aspects of Competition' (1890), in *Memorials*, p. 290.
118. *PE*, p. 10.
119. *PE*, p. 466n.
120. *IT*, p. 655.
121. *PE*, p. 7.
122. Unpublished note dated 18 August 1901, in Marshall Papers, miscellaneous Box 2. The qualification 'in some trades' appears to have been an afterthought. See also EAM, Chapter 9.3.
123. Letter to Edward Caird dated 5 December 1897, in *Memorials*, p. 401.
124. 'The Future of the Working Classes' (1873), in *Memorials*, p. 113.
125. *IT*, p. 639.
126. *IT*, p. 381.
127. *IT*, p. 103.
128. *IT*, p. 225.
129. *IT*, p. 638. See also his letter to Bishop Westcott dated 26 October 1899, in *Memorials*, p. 385, where he speaks of 'cruel apprenticeship regulations' and expresses regret at such anti-social restrictions on new entry – imposed, he says, so that the small group of workers in the trade can boost their pay by means of limiting supply. Such workers are evidently not showing that altruistic self-restraint which we considered in the previous section of this Chapter.
130. *IT*, p. 641n.

131. *IT*, p. 640.
132. *IT*, pp. 640–1.
133. *IT*, p. 391.
134. Letter to Edward Caird dated 22 October 1897, in *Memorials*, p. 398.
135. *PE*, p. 589. This also has macroeconomic implications in that money-wages are rendered sticky downwards in a recession (as Marshall points out on p. 590).
136. C. Kerr, *Marshall, Marx and Modern Times* (Cambridge: The University Press, 1969), p. 51.
137. For an extended discussion of imperfect competition, see *EAM*, Chapter 6.
138. *IT*, p. 325.
139. *EI*, p. 137.
140. J. Schumpeter, *Capitalism, Socialism and Democracy* (1942) (London: George Allen & Unwin Ltd., 1976), p. 84.
141. See on this *EAM*, Chapter 5.
142. *IT*, p. 557
143. *EI*, p. 138.
144. *IT*, p. 557. See also *EAM*, Chapters 5.2 and 11.
145. *IT*, p. 655.
146. 'A Plea for the Creation of a Curriculum in Economics and Associated Branches of Political Science' (1902), in Guillebaud II, p. 166.
147. Letter to Bishop Westcott dated 20 January 1901, in *Memorials*, p. 392.
148. Letter to Bishop Westcott dated 20 January 1901, in *Memorials*, pp. 392, 393.
149. *IT*, p. 132.
150. *IT*, p. 103.

3 GROWTH AND BETTERMENT

1. *PE*, p. 289.
2. *PE*, p. vii,
3. *PE*, p. 185.
4. *PE*, p. vii.
5. D. P. O'Brien, 'A. Marshall, 1842–1924', in D. P. O'Brien and J. R. Presley, eds, *Pioneers of Modern Economics in Britain* (London: Macmillan, 1981), p. 51.
6. G. J. Stigler, *Production and Distribution Theories* (1941) (New York: Agathon Press, 1968), p. 62.

3.1 From Growth to Betterment

1. The nearest he came to formulating an actual *model* of the growth process would appear to be the notes and equations which he jotted down in the early 1880s and never subsequently wrote up. See 'Notes on

the Theory of Economic Growth' (circa 1881–2). In Whitaker II, pp. 305–16.
2. *PE*, p. 603. A further discussion of climate, race, geographical location and national character will be found in *EAM*, Chapter 7.3.
3. *EI*, p. 10.
4. *PE*, p. 606.
5. *MCC*, p. 100.
6. *EI*, p. 44.
7. *EI*, p. 10.
8. 'The Present Position of Economics' (1885), in *Memorials*, p. 153.
9. *IT*, p. 700.
10. *PE*, pp. 613–4.
11. *EI*, p. 48.
12. *IT*, p. 60.
13. *EI*, p. 10.
14. *EI*, p. 10.
15. 'Water as an Element of National Wealth' (1879), in *Memorials*, p. 140.
16. *EI*, p. 48.
17. *EI*, p. 48.
18. *IT*, p. 656.
19. *IT*, p. 35.
20. *PE*, p. 579.
21. *IT*, p. 656.
22. *IT*, p. 447.
23. *MCC*, p. 99.
24. Discussion on F. Schuster's paper 'Foreign Trade and the Money Market', Institute of Bankers, December 16, 1903. In *Journal of the Institute of Bankers*, Vol. xxv, 1904, p. 95.
25. *IT*, pp. 34, 35.
26. *MCC*, p. 100.
27. *EI*, p. 9.
28. *EI*, p. 9. See also *IT*, p. 557, where he says that the rapid rise of Germany has been due in part to 'rich stores of iron ore' – whereas 'British supplies of ore have been rapidly dwindling and becoming more difficult of access'. His concern with explicitly domestic supplies in an age of extensive international trade is somewhat mystifying. Not much clearer is a similar statement in a different context where he explains (citing Petty) that Britain's early start in modern economic life was based on the utilisation of domestically-produced inputs, notably wool (*IT*, p. 33). This reliance on native products, he should perhaps have added, was only relevant at a very early stage of Britain's development, and one which antedated the transportation revolution. He must have known of Britain's dependence even in the eighteenth century on imported raw cotton for her textiles industries.
29. *EI*, p. 48.
30. *EI*, p. 48.
31. *PE*, p. 553.
32. *PE*, p. 122.
33. *PE*, p. 247. It would be wrong to assume *ceteris paribus* in such a case or

to speak as if we are merely unplugging one source of energy in order to plug in its successor. The truth is that the ripples spread out and can spread quite far. One unintended outcome of the new sources, for example, was to reduce the initial capital cost relative to that which was associated with, say, the steam-engine; a second was to ensure greater freedom of choice with respect to location than had obtained, say, when power was generated by the water-wheel. Here as elsewhere in Marshall's economics we are reminded of the essential interdependence of phenomena.

34. *EI*, pp. 38–9.
35. *PE*, p. 187.
36. *PE*, p. 443.
37. *EI*, p. 39.
38. 'A Plea for the Creation of a Curriculum in Economics and Associated Branches of Political Science' (1902), in Guillebaud II, p. 165.
39. *MCC*, p. 7.
40. *MCC*, p. 298.
41. *MCC*, p. 302n.
42. *EI*, p. 39.
43. 'Water as an Element of National Wealth' (1879), in *Memorials*, p. 141. Much of the military power was no doubt orientated towards foreign and not domestic enemies – the reason, presumably, why it coexisted so peacefully with civil liberties at home. In the absence of a world government and/or a *Pax Cosmopolitana*, Marshall reasoned, our security abroad depends in no small measure on 'the strength of the British navy and army' (IT, p. 53).
44. *IT*, p. 693.
45. *IT*, p. 695.
46. *IT*, p. 664.
47. *PE*, p. 339n.
48. *PE*, p. 587. Workers compete for the most attractive jobs (where attractiveness involves the subjective valuation of a number of discrete characteristics combined in different bundles for different modes of employment), employers compete for the most attractive labourers (where attractiveness to a survival-conscious and rational profit-maximiser probably is synonymous with efficiency), and proportionality at the margin may therefore be expected to result in the market equilibrium state.
49. *IT*, p. 688.
50. *IT*, p. 689.
51. *PE*, p. 627n.
52. *PE*, p. 7.
53. *IT*, p. 683. These highways, it would appear, were, in earlier times, frequently constructed by strong rulers in order to undermine local particularism (and thereby to foster national unity), to link regional centres with the national capital, to improve access to frontiers liable to attack – and yet the explicit pursuit of one objective (essentially, political security) gave an unintended boost to the pursuit of another (an increase in the wealth of nations) that was no part of the monarch's

original design in launching a transportation revolution. The invisible hand works in ways that are at times inscrutable. The point made in the text is that the friend of national defence who is also an enemy of economic growth and change would do well to draw the king's attention to the latent function, the unexpected spin-off, of the measures adopted.

54. *IT*, p. 197.
55. *IT*, pp. 197–8. Thus (*IT*, p. 198n, emphasis added), 'whenever a man of genius arose, he would leave ballads or melodies *a little* altered for the good'.
56. *PE*, p. 605.
57. Lecture delivered in Bristol on 26 February 1883. Quoted in Stigler, 'Alfred Marshall's Lectures on Progress and Poverty', (Chapter 2.1, note 50), p. 160. But Marshall's conclusion, there as elsewhere, was basically optimistic: 'A century ago we took off the last shackles from the fierce monster-competition. That was necessary for our own freedom. Without it there have been free aristocracies, but there has never been, and cannot ever be, a free nation. The unshackled monster was terrible to deal with; but we are learning fast how to manage him . . . Scarcely ever, if ever, has the moral and mental strength of the great mass of a nation risen so fast as has that of England or Scotland during the last thirty years; and it is, I believe, rising today faster than ever.'
58. For example: 'Traditions indeed are to-day little better than fetters in some branches of business: but they are supports rather than fetters in banking; where the welfare of all requires imperatively that the enterprise of each should take account of considerations other than those enforced by the letter of the law, and his own immediate profit.' (*IT*, p. 344). Here public opinion and conformity to convention would appear to be advocated as a means of preventing an incipient market failure – an incipient market failure, one hastens to add, due exclusively to rational profit-maximisation within limits set by statute.
59. *PE*, p. 561.
60. *PE*, p. 560.
61. *IT*, p. 804.
62. *IT*, p. 275.
63. *PE*, p. 560. Germany, however, apparently had sufficient markets 'within her own borders' (*OP* (1903), p. 399) – rather a surprising thing for Marshall to say in view of the fact that effective demand in the British market cannot have been so far inferior to that of Germany that Britain had no choice but to rely on world markets in order that her industries might secure adequate economies of size.
64. *MCC*, p. 111.
65. *EI*, p. 15.
66. *IT*, p. 284.
67. *IT*, p. 817.
68. *PE*, p. 115.
69. *PE*, p. 448.
70. *OP* (1887), p. 127.

71. *IT*, p. 799.
72. *MCC*, p. 143.
73. *MCC*, p. 235.
74. *IT*, p. 799.
75. *PE*, p. 3.
76. *PE*, p. 237.
77. *IRC*, p. 177.
78. 'The Old Generation of Economists and the New' (1897), in *Memorials*, p. 308.
79. *IT*, p. 159.
80. *OP* (1903), p. 378.
81. *IT*, pp. 697, 698.
82. *MCC*, p. 219.
83. *OP* (1903), pp. 398, 397.
84. *MCC*, p. 173.
85. An interesting problem which Marshall describes as follows in his early and uncompleted manuscript on 'The Theory of Foreign Trade' (circa 1873–7), in Whitaker II, pp. 23–4: 'Experience has shown that countries which suffer others to pioneer the way for them, will often get into work each successive improvement just at the time at which it is being abandoned in favour of its successor in the countries in which mechanical genius has its home . . . . The latter class of countries have the same advantage over the former that the Greek of old had over the barbarian boxer who guarded ever the place which he had last been struck.'
86. *MCC*, p. 173.
87. *IRC*, p. 198.
88. Letter to Louis Dumur dated 2 July 1909, in *Memorials*, p. 461.
89. Letter to Louis Dumur dated 2 July 1909, in *Memorials*, p. 459.
90. Letter to Louis Dumur dated 2 July 1909, in *Memorials*, p. 459. Writing to a French correspondent at a time when the French population was declining, Marshall was thus able to offer words both of comfort and of caution on the interesting phenomenon of Malthusianism in reverse. His words of comfort took the form of a reminder that a modest fall in population is not in itself an intolerable evil, but he then sounded a note of caution by saying that it might be indicative of such an evil, a proxy-variable which picks up the same causes as those of more general and more serious national decadence: 'These are, I think, often associated with the growth of wealth and the cessation of the need for incessant energy and self-devotion in the overcoming of difficulties.'
91. *PE*, p. 573.
92. *PE*, p. 572.
93. *PE*, p. 229.
94. *PE*, p. 230.
95. *PE*, p. 230. What Marshall is saying is that it is difficult to increase productivity in the area of services. If, therefore, 'the wants for which they make provision increase in proportion to our general wealth, it is only to be expected that they should absorb a constantly growing proportion of the industrial population' – and the reader is tempted to

conclude that this means that the rate of growth will for that reason tend to be slower in the more advanced stages of economic growth, as compared with the earlier. Marshall apparently does not draw such an inference.

96. *EI*, pp. 10–11.
97. *PE*, p. 517. See also *PE*, p. 514 and *EAM*, Chapter 10.4.
98. *MCC*, p. 171.
99. *PE*, p. 1911.
100. *IT*, p. 663.
101. *PE*, p. 598.
102. *IT*, p. 663. Needless to say, Marshall did not see the supply of attractive jobs as strictly limited, a positional good which some can have and all cannot. On the contrary: 'There is plenty of room in the upper ranks of the artisans; and there is abundant room for new comers in the upper ranks of the middle class' (*PE*, p. 598).
103. *IT*, p. 5. Marshall describes his meritocratic ideal in more detail as follows: 'A nation as a whole may be regarded as composed of irregularly shaped *horizontal* strata, arranged in pyramidical form, those most poorly endowed being at its base; and each successive stratum consisting of people better endowed than the last. The endowment may be measured in terms of money or of faculty: and the problem is to bring these two measurements as nearly as may be into accord; while narrowing the lower and broadening the upper strata' (*IT*, p. 8).
104. *IT*, pp. 694–5.
105. *IT*, p. 388.
106. *IT*, p. 354.
107. *PE*, p. 35.
108. *IT*, p. 340n.
109. *IT*, p. 699.
110. *IT*, p. 808n.
111. *IT*, p. 808n, where Marshall concludes the story as follows: 'An inquiry as to such a load evoked the answer – "Before our father died, he taught us to make horses like this, and we cannot venture on anything new". The horses' necks were all bent in the same impossible and ugly curve.'
112. *PE*, p. 204.
113. *IT*, p. 340n.
114. *IT*, p. 774.
115. *IT*, p. 698.
116. *PE*, pp. 212–3.
117. *PE*, p. 205.
118. *OP* (1887), p. 96.
119. *PE*, p. 214.
120. *PE*, p. 200.
121. *PE*, p. 216.
122. *EI*, p. 56.
123. *EI*, p. 56.
124. *EI*, p. 111–12. But despite the fact that transferable skills now represent

an increasing *proportion* of the total stock of skills, it is worth remembering that there continues to exist 'much technical trade knowledge with regard to processes and the quality of materials, which is of little use save in the trade in which it was acquired; and the progress of industry tends to increase the amount of the specialised knowledge which is needed by the better class of workmen in almost every trade.' (*EI*, p. 112).

125. *IT*, p. 104. There is, of course, the concomitant loss to the old country of much of the best of its human resources: but Marshall (despite the high level of emigration in his own times) apparently did not regard this as a significant brake on British economic growth. His focus at any rate is on the benefits from new blood as opposed to the loss of the old – as where he explains how the revocation of the Edict of Nantes in 1685 conferred a 'bounteous gift' (*IT*, p. 110) on the British people in the form of the skilled and energetic Huguenots. Immigrant labour is an external economy to the nation as a whole (most notably so where the expense of forming human capital was incurred abroad by others); and the foreign-born worker is thus 'likely to produce more than he consumes in the country of his adoption' precisely because the 'cost of rearing in his early years was defrayed elsewhere' (*PE*, p. 469n). Most of all, of course, immigrants are a stimulus to growth because they are by nature restless, ambitious and enterprising; and because, not tied to local customs and traditions, they are not afraid to challenge existing habits of thought and action in their relentless pursuit of something better. The members of a settled community are more willing to acquiesce in the reproduction of the done thing and to treat convention as something akin to the law of nature. Thus it happens that initiative is so frequently linked with mobility and the change of scene: 'The stability and quiet of settled life affect character for evil as well as for good. Few men are prophets in their own land: neighbours and relations are generally the last to pardon the faults, and to recognise the merits, of men who differ from themselves by being less docile and more enterprising. It is doubtless chiefly for this reason that in almost every part of England a disproportionately large share of the best energy and enterprise is to be found among those who were born elsewhere' (*IT*, p. 143). In apparent contradiction to what happens at the level of production, however, the migrant and especially the immigrant would appear at the level of consumption to be abnormally keen to fit in and to be accepted; and such conformity, by reinforcing existing tendencies in the direction of standardisation and mass production, makes a further contribution to economic growth by virtue of the fact that it is so conducive to economies of large size.

126. *EI*, p. 52. Marshall, not least because of his interest in economic growth, much sympathised with the objective of the talented labourer of one day moving upward to become a capitalist: 'The prosperity of the nation depends greatly upon how far the upper classes are recruited by the best strength and ability that is born among the lower classes. And one of the easiest and healthiest routes upwards which a working man can follow is that of first saving a little money while working as foreman

or overlooker, and then starting a small establishment in that branch of his business of which he is a master' (*EI*, p. 52). Economies of large size, Marshall then reflects, might have the regrettable effect of impeding such mobility, with negative consequences for the rate of economic growth.

127. *PE*, p. 164n.
128. *PE*, p. 447.
129. *PE*, p. 165n, Excessive mobility is presumably the reason why economic growth in America has not invariably been associated with the pursuit of excellence. As Marshall puts it in 'Some Features of American Industry' (1875) (in Whitaker II, p. 361), 'I do not believe that the American is less capable of thorough work than the Englishman or the German. When he thinks it worth his while to do thorough work he does it: but he seldom does think it worth his while.' One reason for this is excessive *occupational* mobility; since where a man is likely frequently to change his job, 'he will not expend his energies in acquiring a minute technical proficiency that he may soon cease to require' (with the obvious consequence that such proficiency is likely to be under-supplied, at least without reliance on immigrant labour trained in less dynamic environments). A second reason is excessive *geographical* mobility – since 'all migration tends to foster isolated action and individualistic aims: separated from old associates, each one is apt to care mainly for his own interest, and those of any friends and relatives who may be with him' (*IT*, pp. 149–50). Once again, too much is too much, just as too little is too little; and Marshall's recommendation is for a middle way.
130. *PE*, p. 476.
131. *PE*, p. 648.
132. *PE*, p. 60.
133. *PE*, p. 68.
134. *PE*, p. 69n.
135. *PE*, p. 553. The fall in the rate of interest is unambiguously *caused by* an increase in the supply of savings greater than the increase in demand for those funds. In such a case the increasing supply of savings will 'prevent it from obtaining employment at as high a rate of interest as before. That is, the rate of interest will constantly fall' (*PE*, p. 450). It is not clear what Marshall understands by 'constantly' or precisely why he believes that the rate of change of supply exceeds the rate of change of demand. What is clear is that a capital glut is more likely than a capital famine – but that an appeal to Say's Law is sufficient to obviate even that threat.
136. *PE*, p. 553.
137. *PE*, p. 190.
138. *PE*, p. 191.
139. *MCC*, p. 199.
140. *PE*, p. 186
141. *PE*, p. 180.
142. *PE*, p. 180.
143. *PE*, p. 483.

144. *PE*, p. 189.
145. *EI*, p. 41.
146. *MCC*, p. 71.
147. *IRC*, p. 195. Marshall continues in a manner reminiscent of Malthus by noting that 'population is not quite doubling itself in fifty years, while capital is doubling itself in less than twenty-five'.
148. *PE*, p. 257.
149. *PE*, p. 196.
150. *OP* (1887), p. 49. Even at such low rates of interest, however, there is no suggestion that foreign investment will be preferred to domestic to an extent which is threatening or malign.
151. *PE*, p. 450.
152. *PE*, p. 185.
153. 'The Theory of Foreign Trade' (circa 1873–7), in Whitaker II, p. 47.
154. *MCC*, p. 126.
155. *IT*, p. 799.
156. *MCC*, p. 202. Clearly, the fact that the surplus has been passed from nations where it is not wanted to nations where it is scarce indicates – quite literally – that the transfer of capital 'has been of great use to the world' (*EI*, p. 46). To the extent that the capital transferred to the poorer countries takes not a monetary but a real form (where what is transferred, in other words, is not cash but plant), this will presumably stimulate internal economies of size in the machine-making industries which then become external economies to our own domestic producers.
157. *MCC*, p. 150. This is a good illustration of the familiar Spencerian condition that increased division of labour goes hand in hand with greater economic integration and interdependence. This matter is considered further in Chapter 7.3.
158. *EI*, p. 38.
159. *IT*, p. 320. This provides a new outlet for savings in general – and not least for the savings of the increasingly educated and affluent members of the working classes.
160. *IT*, p. 735.
161. *PE*, p. 179.
162. 'Social Possibilities of Economic Chivalry' (1907), in *Memorials*, p. 338.
163. *IT*, p. 466.
164. *PE*, p. 170.
165. *PE*, p. 510.
166. *PE*, p. 237.
167. 'Social Possibilities of Economic Chivalry' (1907), in *Memorials*, p. 333. Marshall does not seem to appreciate that a climate of experimentation in which research is performed not for profit but because of the approbation-motive might generate *more* knowledge than is functionally necessary for sustained economic growth – a surprising omission when one reflects on the extent to which he normally castigates wastefulness with respect to scarce resources.
168. *PE*, p. 237. The communications revolution (in forms ranging from trade-journals to conferences and congresses) thus reinforces the approbation-motive in disturbing the complacency of organisation-men

on a salary and in retarding tendencies towards institutional ossification.

169. *OP* (1903), p. 387. These inventions, Marshall reflects elsewhere, then become 'accessible to all, at any rate on the payment of a royalty for patent right' (*PE*, p. 233) – a valuable external benefit from the machine-makers to industry as a whole, and yet another instance of division of labour leading to improved efficiency through specialisation and inter-dependence.
170. *IT*, p. 694.
171. *PE*, pp. 238–9. Economies of size are a supply-side construct and obviously no more than potential so long as adequate demand is not forthcoming. Whether the demand constraint will continue in the future to impede the full exploitation of these economies is not clear. Standardisation of home demand due to widening reference groups (the American experience and, arguably, likely also to characterise Marshall's ideal society in which 'every man is a gentleman') together with a world mass-market created *inter alia* by the transportation revolution could well favour the falling average cost curve. Whether the large organisations that benefit would want to share the gains in efficiency with the rest of the economy is in Marshall's view of the future even less clear.
172. Letter to Louis Dumur dated 2 July 1909, in *Memorials*, p. 460.
173. *MCC*, p. 246.
174. *PE*, p. 508. The capitalist-undertakers in the modern world are the men who take the risks and make the profits – or the losses. They are thus the buffer or shock-absorber of change in an uncertain world where losses as well as gains can be made.
175. *PE*, p. 513.
176. Letter to Manohar Lal dated 22 February 1911, in *Memorials*, p. 458.
177. See, for instance, 'Social Possibilities of Economic Chivalry' (1907), in *Memorials*, p. 339.
178. *IT*, p. 173.
179. *PE*, p. 550. Coefficients in Marshall's economics are seldom fixed and bottlenecks seldom a problem. It is because of ease of substitutability, to take an example, that 'on the margin of indifference between hand-power and horse-power their prices must be proportionate to their efficiency' (PE, p. 336). Factor proportions do not adjust themselves, however, and the importance of the conscious and rational action of the undertaker in this area cannot be underestimated. The theories of derived demand and marginal productivity, in other words, cannot be divorced from a consideration of the social and psychological characteristics of the entrepreneur himself.
180. *IT*, p. 309. Including work for which they might in time *become* fit.
181. *IT*, p. 355.
182. *IT*, p. 351.
183. *IT*, p. 173.
184. *EI*, p. 116.
185. *IT*, p. 358.
186. *PE*, p. 503.

3.2 From Betterment to Growth

1. *OP* (1903), p. 407.
2. *PE*, p. 568n.
3. *PE*, p. 564.
4. *PE*, p. 583. Note that wages rise both for the same job (as where constant labour is complemented by increased capital) and for different jobs (as where the worker earns additional money in consequence of education and upgrading).
5. *PE*, p. 583.
6. *PE*, p. 537.
7. *PE*, p. 58.
8. 'The Present Position of Economics' (1885), in *Memorials*, p. 155.
9. *PE*, p. 574.
10. 'The Present Position of Economics' (1885), in *Memorials*, p. 172.
11. *PE*, pp. 441–2. The emphasis on 'the coming generation' is, of course, characteristic of Marshall's approach, and he takes great care whenever possible to draw attention to 'the effects that high wages have in increasing the efficiency not only of those who receive them, but also of their children and grand-children' (*PE*, p. 423). The worse fed are the children of this generation, the less efficient they will be, the less they will earn, the less they will be able to develop the faculties of their children; and so the vicious circle of low pay and low productivity proceeds. Efficient labour by contrast is well-paid labour – and produces further labourers who are likely in turn to be efficient and well-paid.
12. *PE*, p. 168. An increase in wages contributes to the health and strength of this generation and of the generation to come. It may in addition influence the rate of economic growth, as in the theories of Smith and Malthus, through its effect on the quantity supplied of labourers. Marshall was acquainted with the numbers argument but evidently did not consider it a particularly strong one: 'The total numbers of the people change under the action of many causes. Of these causes only some are economic; but among them the average earnings of labour take a prominent place; though their influence on the growth of numbers is fitful and irregular' (*PE*, p. 119).
13. *IT*, p. 672.
14. Public lecture delivered in Bristol on 9 October 1877 on 'The Aims and Methods of Economic Study', cited in J. K. Whitaker, 'Alfred Marshall: The Years 1877 to 1885', *History of Political Economy*, Vol. 4, 1972. In Wood I, p. 138.
15. *PE*, p. 574. Emphasis added.
16. *PE*, p. 574.
17. *PE*, p. 75n.
18. *EI*, p. 38.
19. *PE*, p. 164.
20. Letter to *The Times* of 18 January 1877, p. 6.
21. In saying that Marshall took the view that a rise in the 'standard of life' and an improvement in economic efficiency go hand in hand, it is

important to remember that the efficiency to which we are referring is long-run efficiency (as opposed to short-run maximisation given a fixed endowment of resources) and that the dynamic variation in the 'standard of life' renders wants endogenous rather than exogenous (and, specifically, a source of productivity as well as utility). Marshall believed in individual freedom of choice, in morality of choices made, in economic efficiency and in economic growth. He also believed that these four considerations pointed in the same direction and reinforced one another. Were the modern consumer to have revealed himself not as a paragon of virtue but as a greedy glutton obsessed with the harmful indulgence of wasteful appetites, it is unlikely that Marshall – hardly a typical nineteenth century utilitarian in his approach to consumer sovereignty and the 'best-judge' principle – would have been as friendly as he was to individual autonomy. Evolution, to Marshall, was more important than freedom; but the two in the event turned out to be complements and not substitutes.

22. *PE*, p. 409.
23. *PE*, p. 112.
24. *PE*, p. 441.
25. *PE*, p. 439.
26. *PE*, p. 185.
27. *PE*, p. 185.
28. *PE*, p. 55.
29. *PE*, p. 74n.
30. *PE*, p. 12.
31. *PE*, p. 21.
32. *PE*, p. 165. Note the reference to occupation and work, not social class.
33. *PE*, p. 144.
34. *IT*, p. viii. In other words, in Marshall's own working life.
35. H. Spencer, *The Principles of Ethics* (London and Edinburgh: Williams & Norgate, 1900), Vol. II, p. 251. Although the statesman should keep this end 'in view', he should also remember, Spencer stresses, that *freedom from* is the best way, in an industrial society, to promote it: 'It is impossible for artificial moulding to do that which natural moulding does. For the very essence of the process as spontaneously carried on, is that each faculty acquires fitness for its function by performing its function; and if the function is performed for it by a substituted agency, none of the required adjustment of nature takes place' (*ibid.*, p. 259).
36. *EI*, p. 11.
37. *IT*, p. 324.
38. 'The Old Generation of Economists and the New' (1897), in *Memorials*, p. 307.
39. *EI*, pp. 135–6. As far as the unpaid supplier or the unemployed worker is concerned, the cause of market failure in this case would appear to be lack of personal morality on the part of an irresponsible entrepreneur.
40. *IT*, pp. 165-6.
41. *EI*, p. 182.
42. *IT*, p. 580.
43. *IT*, p. 580.

44. 'Co-operation' (1889), in *Memorials*, p. 229.
45. 'Co-operation' (1889), in *Memorials*, p. 253.
46. *IT*, p. 94n.
47. *PE*, p. 439.
48. *PE*, p. 206.
49. Quoted in Pigou, 'In Memoriam: Alfred Marshall', in *Memorials*, p. 82.
50. 'Social Possibilities of Economic Chivalry' (1907), in *Memorials*, p. 331.
51. 'Social Possibilities of Economic Chivalry' (1907), in *Memorials*, p. 332.
52. 'The Future of the Working Classes' (1873), in *Memorials*, p. 115.
53. *PE*, p. 12.
54. 'Some Aspects of Competition' (1890), in *Memorials*, p. 281.
55. 'The Old Generation of Economists and the New' (1897), in *Memorials*, p. 310.
56. 'The Old Generation of Economists and the New' (1897), in *Memorials*, p. 309.
57. 'The Present Position of Economics' (1885), in *Memorials*, p. 160.
58. See *PE*, p. 470.
59. *IT*, p. 327.
60. *EI*, p. 198.
61. 'Social Possibilities of Economic Chivalry' (1907), in *Memorials*, p. 330.
62. *PE*, p. 520.
63. *PE*, p. 520n.
64. *PE*, p. 521.
65. *IT*, p. 325. What Marshall is saying is that the care for employees to which he refers was prompted 'mainly' by altruistic motives and that the commercial profitability which that care engendered was principally an unintended outcome – as when a kindly boss varies the tasks of his workers because of a generous desire to 'let in fresh air past the barriers of monotony' and then discovers that he has unknowingly also stimulated their intelligence and boosted their efficiency as a result. Marshall's position is, however, characteristically vague, as is illustrated by his use of the word 'mainly' in the passage cited in the text and by his use of 'still' in the following: 'The large majority of employers and their officers are still apt to keep philanthropy and business in different compartments of their mind.' (*IT*, p. 354). The obscurity arises because, terminologically speaking, philanthropy by definition ceases to be philanthropy the moment that generosity of intent is replaced by the rational search for profits – and because Marshall believes that nobility of character *per se* enjoys a high income elasticity of demand as a nation grows from rags to riches. What Marshall can logically assert is that the businessman regards virture *as its own reward* and then earns a *supplementary reward* due to the fact that a reputation for 'fairness and generosity in dealing' (*IT*, p. 270) bears an economic return in the form of customer loyalty, good-will, a stable clientele, a saving of the costs that would be incurred in attracting new trade: such a man, obviously, 'has a valuable property. He does not generally expect to get better prices from his clients than from others. But he expects to sell easily to them because they know and trust him' (*IT*, p. 182). What Marshall does assert is, however, somewhat less clear, since he in places seems to

suggest that a rational businessman might want to treat virtue as a means and an investment. In the passage cited above, for example, the word 'still' would appear to imply that business men are likely one day to integrate philanthropy with business in the *same* compartment of their mind – which may be true, rational and even desirable, but philanthropy then is no longer the appropriate term, altruism no longer the relevant concept. A similar problem is presented by Marshall's discussion of the joint stock company in America, where 'a full control at meetings of shareholders is generally exercised by a few wealthy and able business men, who do not grasp crudely at small savings, but support a far-seeing policy' (*IT*, p. 327). Thus it happens that the corporation in America does not hesitate to spend money on 'improving the condition of its employees' – 'due partly to a certain generosity of spirit, which has always accompanied the keen pursuit of wealth by her people; partly to the clearness with which her employers recognize the economy of attracting those workers who will get the greatest amount of good work out of the expensive plant which is committed to their charge' (*IT*, p. 327). Such employers appear to be partly soulful, partly interested; and the precise position of absolute values in the theory of social evolution is hardly clarified by such a plethora of partlies (in unspecified proportions) – or by the fact that both generosity and deliberateness would seem to prescribe the same basic course of action.

66. *EI*, p. 212.
67. *EI*, p. vi. But obviously such unselfishness towards one's children is reinforced by the perception of one's duty (since no one wants to suffer from a guilty conscience) and by the desire to avoid disapprobation (since no one wants to be seen to look mean).
68. *PE*, p. 144. Although, writing to Louis Dumur on 2 July 1909, Marshall did complain that it was 'a selfish devotion to "sports" and other amusements' that accounted for the fact that – in Anglo-Saxon nations as well as in France – 'men delay marriage till their best strength has gone'. In *Memorials*, pp. 459–60.
69. *PE*, p. 469.
70. *PE*, p. 190. Presumably there is no ceiling to the quantity of educated manpower that the economy can absorb.
71. *PE*, p. 585.
72. *IRC*, p. 198.
73. *PE*, p. 585.
74. B. Webb, *My Apprenticeship* (London: Longmans, Green & Co., 1945), p. 154.
75. Welfare *society* – as distinct from Welfare *State*.
76. 'Co-operation' (1889), in *Memorials*, p. 228. One of the reasons why Marshall approved so strongly of co-operatives is that they provided an outlet and a focus for altruistic sentiments.
77. *PE*, p. 586.
78. *PE*, p. 585.
79. *IT*, p. 392.
80. *EEI*, p. 391. Admittedly the leaders themselves might adopt anti-social postures; but the rank and file, increasingly enlightened and increasing-

ly responsible, may increasingly be relied upon to exercise a democratic check on potential abuse of power. Improved communications makes grassroots opinion that much more effective: 'By their aid the council of a large trades union can at a trifling cost submit a difficult question to the judgement of their members in every part of the country and get their decisions within a few days.' (*PE*, p. 510)

81. 'Some Features of American Industry' (1875), in Whitaker II, p. 365.
82. *MCC*, p. 233.
83. *MCC*, p. 7.
84. *MCC*, p. 203.
85. 'Social Possibilities of Economic Chivalry' (1907), in *Memorials*, p. 345.
86. *PE*, p. 180.
87. *PE*, p. 566.
88. *PE*, p. 566.
89. *EI*, p. 202.
90. *EI*, p. 37.
91. *EI*, p. 107. The same unwillingness to save and invest that one finds among savages, children and the very poor, incidentally, was also characteristic of the rich landowners of the Middle Ages, men who 'had no inclination to use their resources for any other purpose than the promotion of their own pleasure, power and prestige' (*IT*, p. 710). Saving, it must be stressed, is not automatically a function of income. It is also a function of the desire to save – a complex of cultural and sub-cultural considerations.
92. *PE*, p. 544.
93. *PE*, p. 533.
94. *PE*, p. 369.
95. *IT*, p. 51.
96. *IT*, p. 751. Besides that, at least in the short-run, 'when things go badly, the landlord, partly from sympathy and partly as a matter of business makes temporary remissions of rent, and bears the expense of repairs, etc. which he would otherwise have left for the farmer' (*OP* (1897), p. 355): yet another case where an exchange value is influenced at least 'partly' by considerations other than pure rationality.
97. *PE*, p. 471.
98. *PE*, p. 656.
99. *EI*, p. 173.
100. *PE*, p. 656.
101. 'The Pure Theory of Foreign Trade' (1879), in Whitaker II, p. 122.
102. *IT*, p. 20.
103. *PE*, p. 656.
104. *IT*, p. 400.
105. 'The Future of the Working Classes' (1873), in *Memorials*, p. 116.
106. 'Some Aspects of Competition' (1890), in *Memorials*, p. 278.
107. Letter to *The Economist* of December 30, 1916, p. 1228.
108. *EI*, p. 110. The reference to 'a man' is not accidental as it is Marshall's normal practice to refer to 'sons' rather than to 'children'.
109. *EI*, p. 176.
110. *EI*, p. 102. As was the case with the domestic system in England.

111. *IT*, p. 132. All that is missing from *Küche*, *Kinder*, *Kirche* is the *Kirche*. Marshall does say elsewhere, of course, that economic growth strengthens religious feelings.
112. *IT*, p. 76.
113. *IT*, p. 253. Such speculation must count as 'truly constructive work' despite Marshall's disparaging remarks about the 'great fortunes' that are often amassed in this way. See on this Chapter 2.3.
114. *IT*, p. 74. Such instability of incomes, it might be added, tends to foster not those patterns of conduct and character which are favourable to sustained economic growth but rather those – including 'debauch and sloth' – which are more suited than is, say, deliberateness to an up-and-down environment of radical uncertainty in which men live for today: 'Almost every trade in which high wages have been systematically misapplied is one in which employment is fickle and unsteady.' ('The Theory of Foreign Trade' (1873–7), in Whitaker II, p. 36). Work to a significant extent makes men. Unstable work to a significant extent makes unstable men: 'The employee of a manufacturer who works for an uncertain market, is apt to have frequent harvest-like orgies of work and high pay, following by long intervals of low-paid work or idleness: and, if it happens that his wife and children are in relatively steady work, he is likely to squander his high wages. Thus families in the manufacturing districts, whose aggregate earnings were twice as high as those of families at work on farms, often lived in greater squalor,' (*IT*, p. 75). Such secondary poverty is a social disease which society inflicts on itself – and which it should combat not so much through a multiplication of social workers as through a damping-down of instability. The government can help in this respect (via the introduction of a tabular standard of value, for example), but it is also the responsibility of the private sector to play its part – in the present context, by eschewing destructive speculation; in a previous context, by refusing to follow fashion. Secondary poverty caused by instability is in a sense worse than primary poverty, since the former is self-perpetuating whereas the latter is self-correcting – as is illustrated by the 'singular self-control' shown by the Dutch in the seventeenth century: 'Holland seemed poor in physical resources: but her poverty was a part of her strength: for it led her to give her whole energies to developing those resources which she possessed.' (*IT*, p. 692).
115. *IT*, p. 313. Emphasis added.
116. Letter to Bishop Westcott dated 20 January 1901, in *Memorials*, p. 394.
117. *IT*, p. 396.
118. *IT*, p. 474. Such cheating does, of course, benefit the consumer and may to that extent be favourable to economic growth. Besides that, if oligopoly does indeed demonstrate 'the most malignant features of unscrupulous competition, which recent research has brought to light' (*IT*, p. 180), then in a sense the oligopolist who destroys his cartel by refusing to behave honourably towards his fellow thieves is also a public benefactor. Even lack of morality, it would appear, can, at least in some circumstances, serve the public interest.
119. 'Co-operation' (1889), in *Memorials*, p. 238.

120. *PE*, p. 329.
121. *PE*, p. 263. This observation was first introduced in the sixth edition of 1910.
122. *PE*, p. 324n.
123. *OP* (1903), p. 413.
124. Letter to Bishop Westcott dated 23 July 1898, in *Memorials*, p. 384.
125. Letter to Bishop Westcott dated 26 October 1899, in *Memorials*, p. 385.
126. *PE*, p. 582. Including resistance to shift-working.
127. *IT*, p. 642.
128. *IT*, p. 850.
129. *IT*, p. 137.
130. *OP* (1903), pp. 407, 408.
131. Letter to Bishop Westcott dated 20 January 1901, in *Memorials*, p. 393.

4 COLLECTIVE ACTION

1. H. Spencer, *Social Statics* (London and Edinburgh: Williams & Norgate, 1868), p. 483.
2. Richter, *The Politics of Conscience*, p. 13. Marshall, like Green, assigned pride of place to ideals – as where, in a note on 'Progress' dated 27 February 1908 disparaging that approach to economics which sees the science merely as an apparatus orientated towards an increase in the supply of 'sugarplums' for young and old, he wrote: 'The aim of all is self-respect. Life: freedom = work for ideals.' In Marshall Papers, Red Box 1 (3). It must be remembered, however, that even authors more unambiguously in the economic tradition that was Green had long written on ethics in the marketplace. Adam Smith, for instance: 'Adam Smith: "kept his Moral Sentiments for Sunday", they say. No he did not. But he laid dominant stress on wealth of nations'. See unpublished fragment dated 17 October 1902, in Marshall Papers, Red Box 1 (3). And John Stuart Mill: 'Even when I differ from him, he seems to keep my mind in a higher plane of thought than ordinary writers on economics.' Letter to H. Foxwell dated 14 April 1897. In Marshall Papers, letters 3 (32). Marshall, in short, was no stranger to ideals in economics even before he discovered Green.
3. *Ibid*, pp. 12, 19.
4. *Ibid*, p. 13.
5. *Ibid*, pp. 134, 135.

4.1 Socialism

1. *IT*, p. vii.
2. IT, p. vii.
3. Letter to Lord Reay dated 12 November 1909, in *Memorials*, p. 462.
4. Letter to Lord Reay dated 12 November 1909, in *Memorials*, p. 462.

5. Letter to Lord Reay dated 12 November 1909, in *Memorials*, p. 462.
6. 'Social Possibilities of Economic Chivalry' (1907), in *Memorials*, p. 334.
7. 'Social Possibilities of Economic Chivalry' (1907), in *Memorials*, p. 334.
8. 'Social Possibilities of Economic Chivalry' (1907), in *Memorials*, p. 346.
9. *PE*, p. 7.
10. *PE*, p. 7.
11. PE, p. 7.
12. Letter to Lord Reay dated 12 November 1909, in *Memorials*, p. 462.
13. Letter to Mrs. Bosanquet dated 28 September 1902, in *Memorials*, p. 444.
14. *IT*, p. vii.
15. *IT*, p. vii. See Marshall Papers, Box 5 (1e), for further discussion of the precise authors in question (notably Louis Blanc, Saint-Simon, Owen, Marx and Lassalle).
16. Lecture delivered in Bristol on 29 September 1881. Quoted in Keynes, 'Alfred Marshall, 1842–1924', in *Memorials*, p. 16.
17. 'The Future of the Working Classes' (1873), in *Memorials*, p. 109.
18. 'Some Aspects of Competition' (1890), in *Memorials*, p.257.
19. 'The Present Position of Economics' (1885), in *Memorials*, p. 173.
20. *PE*, p. 635.
21. 'Some Aspects of Competition' (1890), in *Memorials*, p. 109.
22. 'The Future of the Working Classes' (1873), in *Memorials*, p. 109.
23. *PE*, p. 7.
24. *PE*, p. 7.
25. 'Social Possibilities of Economic Chivalry' (1907), in *Memorials*, p. 346.
26. 'Social Possibilities of Economic Chivalry' (1907), in *Memorials*, p. 341.
27. *IT*, p. 660n.
28. Lecture notes on taxation (1880), in Whitaker II, p. 380.
29. Lecture notes on taxation (1880), in Whitaker II, pp. 380–1.
30. *IT*, p. 176.
31. Letter to *The Times* of March 24, 1891, p. 11.
32. *IT*, p. 651.
33. 'Some Aspects of Competition' (1890), in *Memorials*, p. 283.
34. 'Some Aspects of Competition' (1890), in *Memorials*, p. 284.
35. *IT*, p. viii. Marshall's defence of private property is thus in no small measure not an individualistic but rather a collective, organicist and functionalist one, that if *we*, are to advance, then *you* must be free. Marshall himself appears to have retained serious misgivings about the moral status of private property throughout his life. In a note dated 7 May 1919, for example, he was still able to write that 'economic rights are economic wrongs justifiable only in order to prevent greater wrong', and concluded that property-rights are 'necessary' not on absolute grounds but because they provide an incentive to experimentation and risk-taking: were it not so, he said, 'it would be true that "property is theft" & the rich man would deserve only less condemnation than the society which tolerated his existence.' In Marshall Papers, Red Box 1 (3). A further note in the same box, dated 4 November 1920 and headed 'The future of mankind', makes the same point no less forcefully. There, after discussing various socialist alternatives, Mar-

shall the economist had ultimately to warn – with emphasis – that '*The time for all this is not yet.*' Property is functional, growth means progress, and this the student of injustice should never forget.

36. 'The Future of the Working Classes' (1873), in *Memorials*, p. 109.
37. *IRC*, p. 173.
38. 'The possible democratic control of industry in the Future', unpublished note dated 27 October 1921, in Marshall Papers, Red Box 1 (3). See also the Lectures on Socialism and the Functions of Government (1886), in Marshall Papers, Box 5 (1e).
39. 'The Present Position of Economics' (1885), in *Memorials*, p. 136.
40. *IT*, p. viii.
41. *IT*, pp. 650, 651.
42. *IT*, pp. 650–1.
47. 'Social Possibilities of Economic Chivalry' (1907), in *Memorials*, p. 334.
44. K. Marx, *A Contribution to the Critique of Political Economy* (1859) (London: Lawrence & Wishart, 1971), p. 21.
45. 'Social Possibilities of Economic Chivalry' (1907), in *Memorials*, p. 342. Note the express inclusion of the word 'until'. It is not clear why Marshall uses the term 'collectivism' when the context suggests that 'socialism' would suffice for his argument.
46. 'A Fair Rate of Wages' (1887), in *Memorials*, p. 212.
47. 'Social Possibilities of Economic Chivalry' (1907), in *Memorials*, p. 334.
48. 'A Fair Rate of Wages' (1887), in *Memorials*, p. 212.
49. 'The Present Position of Economics' (1885), in *Memorials*, p. 173.
50. Letter to Lord Reay dated 12 November 1909, in *Memorials*, p. 464.
51. *IRC*, p. 173. Elsewhere on the same page (emphasis added) he writes as follows: 'I admit that even now every right-minded man must regard himself rather as the steward than the owner of what the law calls his property. But there are very few directions in which I think it would be safe *at present* to curtail his legal rights. I admit that Utopian schemes for renovating society do good by raising our ideals, so long as they are only theories. But I think that they do harm when put *prematurely* into practice.'
52. 'Some Aspects of Competition' (1890), in *Memorials*, p. 285.
53. As when, in the *Principles*, after presenting the familiar objections to redistribution, he then adds that 'this cautious attitude does not imply acquiescence in the present inequalities of wealth' (*PE*, p. 594). The topic is considered further in Chapter 5.1 and 5.3.
54. Undated fragment, in *Memorials*, p. 366.
55. *IRC*, pp. 173–4.

4.2 Market and State

1. 'Some Aspects of Competition' (1890), in *Memorials*, p. 275.
2. 'Social Possibilities of Economic Chivalry' (1907), in *Memorials*, p. 338.
3. 'Social Possibilities of Economic Chivalry' (1907), in *Memorials*, p. 339.
4. 'Social Possibilities of Economic Chivalry' (1907), in *Memorials*, p. 338.

5. *IRC*, p. 174.
6. 'Some Aspects of Competition' (1890), in *Memorials*, p. 280.
7. 'Some Aspects of Competition' (1890), in *Memorials*, p. 276.
8. 'Some Aspects of Competition' (1890), in *Memorials*, p. 290.
9. *PE*, p. 416.
10. *PE*, p. 406.
11. 'Social Possibilities of Economic Chivalry' (1907), in *Memorials*, p. 346.
12. *PE*, p. 593.
13. *PE*, p. 336.
14. *PE*, p. 242.
15. *IT*, p. 534.
16. *PE*, p. 407.
17. 'Social Possibilities of Economic Chivalry' (1907), in *Memorials*, p. 338.
18. 'Social Possibilities of Economic Chivalry' (1907), in *Memorials*, p. 334.
19. 'Water as an Element of National Wealth' (1879), in *Memorials*, p. 140.
20. *PE*, p. 529.
21. *PE*, p. 4.
22. *PE*, p. 112.
23. *PE*, p. 206.
24. *PE*, p. 612.
25. *PE*, p. 407.
26. Letter to F. Y. Taussig dated March 1915, in *Memorials*, p. 491.
27. *PE*, p. 620. See also *MCC*, p. 237.
28. *MCC*, p. 6.
29. *IT*, p. 851.
30. *PE*, p. 39.
31. *IT*, p. 45.
32. As is illustrated by the following: 'The greatest calamity that has ever happened to the United States is the political corruption which has grown up through money's being allowed to influence politics. This has not injured the wealthy, who can take care of themselves, so much as the working classes. They have lost a pound for every shilling that Government interference has given them' (*IRC*, pp. 174–5).
33. *PE*, p. 146. Alas, Marshall adds, the 'humane sympathies of the Physiocrats' were in the event simply not adequate to overcome the 'frivolity and harshness of the privileged classes of France', and the result was 'tumult and bloodshed'.
34. *IT*, p. 666.
35. *PE*, p. 385.
36. *OP* (1903), p. 410. In a letter dated 28 January 1909 to Manohar Lal, Marshall, discussing protection to Indian cotton manufactures, comments pointedly that 'an industry that employs a quarter of a million people cannot be described as "an infant"'. (In *Memorials*, p. 457). This is obviously an important economic argument in favour of freedom of trade. Where each of the quarter of a million people has a vote, however, it is not impossible that the pecuniary interest of those voters and the party-political interest of elected politicians will cause the tariff to be retained despite the sound economic considerations which militate in favour of its removal.

37. *IRC*, p. 174.
38. *PE*, p. 432.
39. *IT*, p. 651.
40. *IT*, p. 649.
41. *IT*, p. 78. Marshall's analysis refers explicitly to defence spending but the argument applies equally to any other vote-catching public expenditure financed out of borrowing – support to the arts, for example, or the Welfare State.
42. *PE*, p. 432.
43. *PE*, p. 593. The qualifications 'in the coming time' and 'as things are' would appear to be highly significant in the light of Marshall's general theory of social progress.
44. Smith, *Wealth of Nations*, Vol. II, p. 342.
45. 'Some Aspects of Competition' (1890), in *Memorials*, p. 276.
46. 'Some Aspects of Competition' (1890), in *Memorials*, p. 275.
47. *IT*, p. 666.
48. *IT*, pp. 669n, 669. Ironically, the point about improvement in coordination and reduction in wasteful duplication is one frequently made in defence of State control, as we shall see in Chapter 5.4.
49. *IT*, p. 496.
50. *IRC*, p. 174. See also *IT*, pp. 43, 647, 651, 744 and *MCC*, pp. 212–4.
51. *PE* p. 407.
52. 'Social Possibilities of Economic Chivalry' (1907), in *Memorials*, pp. 336.
53. 'Social Possibilities of Economic Chivalry' (1907), in *Memorials*, p. 462.
54. *PE*, p. 392.
55. Letter to Lord Reay dated 12 November 1909, in *Memorials*, p. 462.
56. Letter to Lord Reay dated 12 November 1909, in *Memorials*, p. 462.
57. *PE*, p. 392. This passage closely resembles Smith's dictum on the fisheries in *The Wealth of Nations*, Vol. II, p. 25.
58. 'The Old Generation of Economists and the New' (1897), in *Memorials*, p. 303.
59. *PE*, p. 407.
60. A. Downs, *An Economic Theory of Democracy* (New York: Harper & Row, 1957), p. 255. Marshall is not cited in Downs's text or bibliography, however.
61. *PE*, p. 407.
62. 'Co-operation' (1889), in *Memorials*, p. 242.
63. 'Some Aspects of Competition' (1890), in *Memorials*, p. 264.
64. *OP* (1903), p. 390.
65. *IT*, p. 737.
66. *IT*, p. 568. In fact, the privileged organisations may be 'inert, effete and even corrupt' and still not lose their privileges for the simple reason that they are vocal, recognised, powerful – and therefore likely to be consulted on the nature of the benefits which they are bound to allege they render to the community. Clearly, in such circumstances, 'there is a danger that, when relying on private advice, a Department or the Cabinet may be influenced by biased opinion in deciding what industries should be aided on account of their exceptional importance

as "key" or "pivotal" industries' (*IT*, p. 671). The very opportunity to give advice is in itself a not insignificant economy of large size.

67. 'Co-operation' (1889), in *Memorials*, p. 243.
68. 'Social Possibilities of Economic Chivalry' (1907), in *Memorials*, p. 337.
69. 'Some Aspects of Competition' (1890), in *Memorials*, p. 285. The problem is the well-known tendency for changes in laws to lag behind changes in institutions despite the fact that 'old details are nearly always inappropriate' (*IT*, p. 739). Government regulations (like other regulations, of course, including those which craft guilds have at certain times in the past sought to impose) have no built-in stabilising mechanism such as would enable them to escape from statutory rigidities and inflexibilities and 'accommodate themselves to the changing methods of industry' (*IT*, p. 736) – which is why, to cite a particular instance, the 'chaos' which followed the withering away of Mercantilist restrictions as between England and her colonies 'may even have possibly been the best thing under the circumstances. For the economic and political conditions of the colonies, and the means of communication between them and the mother country changed so rapidly, that any complete system adapted to one generation might have caused friction in the next' (*IT*, p. 735).
70. 'Some Aspects of Competition' (1890), in *Memorials*, p. 285.
71. *PE*, p. 655.
72. *IT*, p. 66. Wise statesmen have accordingly been known deliberately to ignore the evasion of bad laws. Walpole, for example, who, 'with masterly inactivity, had shut his eyes to the enterprise of smugglers; and thus prevented the monopolies from irritating the American Colonies' (*IT*, p. 734). Such behaviour is admittedly incompatible with that truthfulness which, as we saw in Chapter 2.2, is a characteristic of progress and evolution, but it is also fully compatible with the imperative of respecting the natural momentum inherent in matter without which economic advance would be slow and progress and evolution severely retarded. To avoid this conflict of objectives, Marshall seems to be saying, Walpole would have done well to repeal the bad laws in question rather than merely turning a blind eye to their being evaded.
73. 'The Old Generation of Economists and the New' (1897), in *Memorials*, p. 306.
74. *EI* p. 215. He gives the examples of wage-rates which are set without regard to time or place.
75. *OP* (1897), p. 339. One cause of vexation is 'surprises' such as the levying of taxes which are not 'definite and certain'. The point being made is that business men suffer from considerable uncertainty at the best of times and do not look to their government for the generation of still more.
76. 'Co-operation' (1889), in *Memorials*, p. 249.
77. *PE*, p. 623. Talking of nothing more ambitious than restrictive practices legislation and protective tariffs, Marshall says: 'It must not be forgotten that Germany's strong, though harsh, military-bureaucratic organization has enabled her Government to intervene with a firm

strength and security, that are not to be found in the interventions of a democratic country.' (*IT*, p. 579). The Germanic culture breeds the Germanic State and permits it to become involved in interventionist policies to an extent that would be unthinkable here: 'An autocratic Government can exert certain kinds of discipline, which are not congenial to the temper of a self-governing people; and would, partly for that reason, involve lengthy discussions, and obstruct the proceedings of Parliament, if attempted in Britain' (*IT*, p. 851).

78. *PE*, p. 624.
79. *PE*, p. 634.
80. *EI*, p. 12.
81. 'Some Aspects of Competition' (1890), in *Memorials*, p. 275.
82. *PE*, p. 623.
83. *PE*, p. 625. Emphasis added.
84. Letter to Bishop Westcott dated 20 January 1901, in *Memorials*, p. 395.
85. Letter to Bishop Westoctt dated 20 January 1901, in *Memorials*, p. 394.
86. *IT*, p. 582. Central direction is apparently better suited to the task of administration than it is to invention and enterprise, as a comparison of British and French experience in the eighteenth century will serve to illustrate: 'The centralized administration of France, while admirably adapted for turning existing knowledge to a speedy account, proved itself inferior to England's enterprise in the power of adapting itself to new wants and of devising new methods for overcoming new difficulties' (*IT*, p. 741).
87. *IT*, p. 672.

4.3 State and Improvement

1. *PE*, p. 242.
2. *PE*, p. 242. See also *EAM*, Chapters 4 and 5.
3. *PE*, p. 254.
4. 'Social Possibilities of Economic Chivalry' (1907), in *Memorials*, p. 339.
5. *PE*, pp. 253–4.
6. *PE*, p. 254.
7. *PE*, p. 253.
8. *IT*, p. 672.
9. 'Social Possibilities of Economic Chivalry' (1907), in *Memorials*, pp. 335–6.
10. 'Social Possibilities of Economic Chivalry' (1907), in *Memorials*, p. 336.
11. 'Some Aspects of Competition' (1890), in *Memorials*, p. 285.
12. *IT*, p. 630.
13. *MCC*, p. 7n. More generally, 'school education . . . makes the mind elastic, ready to take in new ideas, and able to communicate freely with others' (*IRC*, p. 182), and that in itself conveys a spillover benefit to the health of political democracy.
14. See Chapter 2.1 of the present volume.
15. 'Social Possibilities of Economic Chivalry' (1907), in *Memorials*, p. 335.
16. *PE*, p. 610. Marshall makes much of the social benefits which are

conveyed by a cheap popular press capable of diffusing key information and widening perspectives, as when he says: 'To-day an important utterance on any large issue is made available through the press to the whole of the working classes: it is likely to be read carefully by perhaps a million of those who think for themselves, and influence the opinions of others' (*MCC*, p. 6).

17. *PE*, p. 610.
18. *IT*, p. 637. For example: 'It appears that they put the cases of their clients before Commissions of Inquiry at least as effectively as do the representatives of employers' (*IT*, p. 637n). Marshall cites the Royal Commission on Labour of 1891–4, of which he was a member, as bearing out this contention.
19. Letter to the Rev. J. Llewellyn Davies dated February 1886, in *Memorials*, p. 373.
20. *PE*, p. 622.
21. *IT*, p. 747. Emphasis added.
22. *IT*, p. 719. And in an unpublished note dated 27 October 1921 and headed 'The possible democratic control of industry in the Future', Marshall actually went so far as to state that the argument that unfettered private enterprise is essential if risks are to be taken 'is of less cogency now than it was two centuries or even one century ago. The State has as good right to exploit the inventions and other ideas of past times as a private person or company has. The control of the State is passing out of the hands of the well-born & the wealthy; and therefore its business is in but little danger of being exploited in the interests of a small part of the population.' In Marshall Papers, Red Box 1 (3). That political democracy facilitates and legitimates political intervention in the market economy would, of course, be hotly disputed by present-day libertarians such as Milton Friedman, who would make the point that the continuance of genuine political democracy *presupposes* the survival of a market economy in which political intervention is kept to an absolute minimum.
23. *IT*, p. 655.
24. 'Social Possibilities of Economic Chivalry' (1907), in *Memorials*, p. 343.
25. *IT*, p. 435.
26. *IT*, p. 446. In a footnote on that page Marshall adds: 'I attended a "Granger" (*i.e.* farmer-in-revolt) meeting in San Francisco in 1875.'
27. *IT*, pp. 492–3. A second example which Marshall gives of popular pressures generating a governmental response refers to the United States in the 1880s, the epoch of Rockefeller's trusts in oil and related products: 'Public opinion was strongly moved by the danger that the Trusts might become powerful monopolies. And the attempt to exercise the privileges, while evading the legal responsibilities of corporations, evoked the 'Sherman Anti-trust Act' of 1890.' (*IT*, p. 513). Yet another example refers to the German experience at a slightly later date: 'The stronger the cartels became, the louder and more eager were the complaints of those who were injured by them, or even feared that they might be injured. So, early in this century, the German Government took the matter in hand' (*IT*, p. 546). Curiously, the most striking

instance which Marshall cites where this principle was *not* operative – where the creaking wheel did *not* get the oil – relates not to the private sector abroad but to the public sector at home: 'The character of Post Office business is such that we might expect *a priori* that there, at least, Socialism would not perceptibly tend towards lethargy. But experience has shown otherwise. In most other kinds of business the producer anticipates the wants of the consumer, and invents new ways of satisfying them; in postal affairs alone the consumer has to clamour long before he gets the most simple and obvious reforms; and . . . he often does not get them at all' (Letter to *The Times* of March 24, 1891, p. 11).

28. *IT*, p. 494.
29. *IT*, pp. 42–3.
30. 'Social Possibilities of Economic Chivalry' (1907), in *Memorials*, pp. 334–5.
31. 'Social Possibilities of Economic Chivalry' (1907), in *Memorials*, p. 335.
32. *OP* (1903), p. 395.
33. *OP* (1903), p. 395.
34. *IT*, p. 671.
35. *OP* (1903), pp. 396–7.
36. *IT*, pp. 44–5.
37. 'Social Possibilities of Economic Chivalry' (1907), in *Memorials*, p. 335.
38. *IT*, p. 494.
39. 'The Theory of Foreign Trade' (1873–7), in Whitaker II, p. 97.
40. *IT*, p. 43.
41. *PE*, p. 407.
42. Public opinion is admittedly capable of being swayed by 'clever sophists', but educational upgrading is reducing this danger – as is the countervailing power exercised by those already educated: 'Hence has arisen the tradition that the economist is generally on the side of the consumer as against the producer: he aims at protecting the unvocal many who consume the products of a particular trade, against the vocal few who speak on behalf of the trade.' ('The Old Generation of Economists and the New' (1897), in *Memorials*, p. 303). The fact (and Marshall treats this observation not as a recommendation but as a part of his 'reasoned catalogue of the world as it is') that the economist is willing to assist those who most need his services to the detriment of those who are best placed to pay his consultancy-fees is yet another instance of increasing altruism in economic affairs.
43. Marshall knew that public opinion is, whether acting directly on the Government to enforce existing regulations or by creating an atmosphere of reform and thus 'by first altering the law', a powerful force in society ('Some Aspects of Competition' (1890), in *Memorials*, pp. 285, 286). He was therefore interested in the press, and in his Lecture Notes on Taxation (1880) (in Whitaker II, pp. 382–3) he observes, not without anxiety, that 'Government used to rule the land: now the Press rules the land through the Government'. In the circumstances it is important to know if the press (like the economists) has a bias. Certainly this is a topic which it would have been fruitful for him to pursue further than he did. His occasional musings on the theme

are, however, instructive, as in the case of his uncompleted Fragments on Trade Unions (circa 1874–5) (in Whitaker II, pp. 349, 348), where he concludes (in a summimg-up 'intended to be impartial') that union action in restraint of trade is actually more limited than it would be thought to be 'by those whose information is mainly derived from journals and other writings intended to be read mainly by the well-to-do classes': 'The Unions have few friends and many foes among newspapers: thus every injury that Unions inflict on the community is widely published and is exaggerated.' This bias – and that of the economists, previously cited – reinforces the case for the collection by the State of statistics as impartially as is humanly possible.

44. 'Social Possibilities of Economic Chivalry' (1907), in *Memorials*, p. 337.
45. *PE*, p. 408. See also *IRC*, pp. 176–7.
46. *PE*, p. 392. Another example which might be cited concerning the manner in which knowledge is an input in the decision-making process is that of railways and their regulation: 'Questions relating to absolute and relative costs continually arise, very often on the initiative of the railways themselves: and organized knowledge, based on systematic studies, is rendering it ever more possible to make fairly confident, though carefully limited, statements in regard to them.' (*IT*, p. 480).
47. *PE*, p. 408.
48. *IT*, p. 784n.
49. *IT*, p. 783. The danger of bias is an argument in favour of open government. As Marshall puts it, speaking of the tabular standard of value: 'Those who make the returns should work in the open day, so that they could not, if they would, be subject to many influences' (*IRC*, p. 186).
50. p. 783. Marshall points out, referring specifically to the tariff question in the United States in the early part of the nineteenth century, that debates relying on statistical evidence can prove sterile beyond a point: 'The facts are too complex, and the interweaving of the results of different causes is too intricate for such a treatment; and therefore each side has been able to find in the facts that conclusion which it desired' (*IT*, p. 779). Certainly in the case of the tariff question the facts do not speak for themselves – 'for the moment, though probably not for ever' (*IT*, p. 784). The afterthought reminds us that Marshall was an optimist as well as a sceptic with respect to human knowledge, the two characteristics only being rescued from potential inconsistency by the reference to the passage of time.
51. As where £1 of income represents greater subjective satisfaction to a poorer man than it does to a richer one – a consideration which would reinforce the chivalrous desire of the latter to help the former if the latter were to perceive the way in which pleasure varies in a manner not fully captured by the objective magnitude *per se*. The doctrine of marginal utility of income, as Joan Robinson puts it, therefore 'points to egalitarian principles, justifies Trade Unions, progressive taxation, and the Welfare State, if not more radical means to interfere with an economic system that allows so much of the good juice of *utility* to evaporate out of commodities by distributing them unequally'. (J.

Robinson, *Economic Philosophy* (Harmondsworth: Penguin Books, 1964, p. 53). This inference, needless to say, simply could not be drawn by an observer who relied on objective data without regard to subjective meaning.

52. *PE*, p. 249.
53. *IT*, p. 672. Marshall seems to have written this in a mood of considerable optimism concerning the State since he immediately (and, arguably, uncharacteristically) extends his point to embrace industry as well: 'The number of giant undertakings which have the apparent (though perhaps not the real) maturity of standardized routine methods, needed to make them in some measure suitable for Governmental ownership, is on the increase.' The question of Governmental ownership is discussed further in Chapter 5.4.
54. *PE*, p. 495.
55. *PE*, pp. 495–6.
56. *IT*, p. 176.
57. 'Co-operation' (1889), in *Memorials*, p. 243.
58. *PE*, pp. 202–2.
59. 'Co-operation' (1889), in *Memorials*, p. 243.
60. *IT*, pp. 45–6.
61. *IT*, p. 46.
62. *IT*, p. 46.
63. *PE*, p. 201.
64. *IT*, p. 46.
65. *PE*, p. 201.
66. *PE*, p. 203.
67. *IT*, p. 175.
68. Marshall's evaluatory schemata with respect to wants are discussed in *EAM*, Chapter 2.4. His views on the evolution of wants over time are discussed in Chapter 2.1 of the present volume.
69. PE, p. 203.
70. *PE*, p. 201.
71. *PE*, p. 621.
72. *PE*, pp. 621–2. Elsewhere, speaking of the manner in which economic growth generates the resources which are the necessary – but not the sufficient – condition for expanded collective expenditure, Marshall says: 'It is becoming clear that this and every other western country *can now afford* to make increased sacrifices of material wealth for the purpose of raising the quality of life throughout their whole populations' (*IT*, p. 5, emphasis added). The will to act is, of course, a separate point.
73. *PE*, p. 622.
74. 'The Equitable Distribution of Taxation' (1917), in *Memorials*, p. 348.
75. *OP* (1897) p. 336, 337. 'Equitable' in this context means that the measure in question confers benefits other than in proportion to tax burdens borne – benefits perhaps so widely diffused that some or all are received even by members of the community who make no contribution whatsoever by means of the particular tax.
76. *PE*, p. 658.

77. Affluence makes us more chivalrous – but increasing altruism by itself, it must be stressed, is not a sufficient (although a necessary) condition for an interventionist State. Given 'the purpose of defending the weak, and especially children and the mothers of children, in matters in which they are not able to use the forces of competition in their own defence' (*PE*, p. 622), after all, that humanitarian and economic objective could be attained by voluntary individual as well as by compulsory collective action. Where the Charity Organisation Societies are expanding by leaps and bounds, the State welfare system could conceptually even contract, and the same phenomenon could be observed in the case of open spaces: 'The chivalrous rich man could aid municipalities in such vastly expensive schemes as that of Miss Octavia Hall for gradually opening out several broad bands of verdure at different distances in and about every large town' ('Social Possibilities of Economic Chivalry' (1907), in *Memorials*, p. 345). Pigou, making much of Marshall's conception of increasing altruism (of parents and employers with respect to the education of children, of unions and other self-help collectivities with respect to income maintenance in states of dependency), gives the further instance of the Factory Acts – which, he reminds us, were regarded by Marshall as 'a standing disgrace to the country' not because they were instruments of State intervention but rather because they were lamentably indicative of private sector inaction and dereliction of duty: 'The disgrace, in Dr. Marshall's view, lay, not in the character of the Factory Acts, but in their existence. The source of it was the fact that some employers in England neglected their clear duty towards their workpeople to such a degree as to render these Acts necessary. The object of Dr. Marshall's phrase was not to condemn any existing law, but to hold up and to emphasize a binding obligation of personal honour, which some business men have so far failed to recognise.' A. C. Pigou, 'Employers and Economic Chivalry', in his *Essays in Applied Economics* (London: Frank Cass & Co. Ltd., 1923), p. 12. The point is that market failure in such cases results from moral failure and that moral rectitude renders corrective action unnecessary.
78. *PE*, p. 622.
79. *PE*, p. 622.
80. *PE*, p. 622.
81. *IT*, p. 647. Moral consensus being the precondition for State action, of course, it is not clear on what grounds the State in a democracy can legitimately intervene to correct the instances of market failure due to moral failure to which we refer in note 77, *supra*. The implication, to some extent at least, would appear to be that we most *need* the State at precisely those times when we least *want* it and, conversely, that we are most willing to pay taxes to finance public libraries and model dwellings at the very stage of social evolution when employers and other members of a caring community are themselves already actively engaged, spontaneously and voluntarily, in supplying such items of general utility.
82. *IT*, p. 744.
83. *IT*, p. 745

84. *IT*, p. 744.
85. *IT*, p. 747.
86. 'Social Possibilities of Economic Chivalry' (1907), in *Memorials*, p. 337.
87. 'Social Possibilities of Economic Chivalry' (1907), in *Memorials*, p. 336.
88. *IT*, p. 647.
89. *IT*, pp. 647–8.
90. *PE*, p. 622.
91. *IT*, p. 736.
92. *IT*, p. 744.

4.4 Co-operation

1. 'Co-operation' (1889), in *Memorials*, p. 227.
2. 'Co-operation' (1889), in *Memorials*, p. 240.
3. *PE*, p. 255.
4. *EI*, p. 221.
5. *PE*, p. 255.
6. *PE*, p. 255.
7. *IT*, p. 177.
8. *IT*, p. 393. The problem here, as in all cases of democratic election, would appear to be at least in part one of deficient information: 'Unfortunately the faculties needed for the higher work of business can be judged only by those who have those faculties. Under election from below several incompetent managers are likely to work havoc before one is found, who is capable of taking rightly those risks which are needed for progress' (*IT*, p. 642). Such a trial and error method of appointment weds inefficiency to democracy. Nor should it be forgotten that the less-moral of subordinates are unlikely to vote for managers who will seek to raise standards or make skills obsolete or in other ways push the organisation to the very frontiers of economic advance. Over time men become upgraded both in educated intelligence and in moral character, however, and there is accordingly some reason to suspect that evolution is on the side of rational choice in political as in economic markets.
9. *PE*, pp. 256–7.
10. *PE*, pp. 254–5.
11. *PE*, p. 101.
12. *PE*, p. 101. See also *PE*, p. 7.
13. *IT*, p. 290.
14. *PE*, p. 256.
15. *PE*, p. 256.
16. *PE*, p. 521. Emphasis added.
17. 'Co-operation' (1889), in *Memorials*, p. 252–3. Profit-sharing, he says there, 'certainly tends to award to the worker a better and juster share of his work than he would otherwise still get' – but he makes clear that it pales into insignificance when compared with the ultimate goal of 'a better organisation of industry'. Here as elsewhere his argument is developmental and evolutionary.

18. *IT*, p. 658. Marshall, in other words, is speaking explicitly of the personality traits of a specified sub-set of total humanity (basically, Englishmen and their descendants living overseas) when he says that co-operation is consonant with character. The importance of national character in his thought is discussed in *EAM*, Chapter 7.3.
19. 'Some Aspects of Competition' (1890), in *Memorials*, p. 284.
20. *IT*, p. 644. Marshall's description of the common culture and atmosphere of planning associated with the collective action of the First World War is strongly reminiscent of the Fabian account of warfare and welfare that one finds in the work of authors such as Tawney and Titmuss. For example: 'The world-war brought together men of all social ranks in the trenches, and thus helped them to know one another. It also enforced rapid changes in organization within industries and between industries: and it increased the need for explaining to all the urgency of new developments, and for enlisting their co-operation in overcoming the difficulties in the way' (*IT*, p. 643). See also *IT*, p. 179.
21. 'Some Features of American Industry' (1875), in Whitaker II, p. 367.
22. *IT*, p. 658.
23. 'Co-operation' (1889), in *Memorials*, p. 247.
24. *IT*, p. 319.
25. *IRC*, p. 199.
26. *IT*, p. 657.
27. *EI*, p. 218.
28. *IT*, p. 179.
29. *PE*, pp. 255–6. Obviously, an organisation which is dependent on such unusual individuals cannot count on their being replaced by persons of similar calibre when retirement or death removes them from the scene.
30. 'Some Features of American Industry' (1875), in Whitaker II, p. 368.
31. *PE*, p. 545. Emphasis added. Marshall then utilises this result to explain why, although agricultural co-operatives do exist (in Denmark, Italy, Germany, Ireland and even – in embryo – in Britain), 'the movement is however of limited scope: it scarcely touches work in the field itself'. On the one hand the material conditions are right: 'Co-operation might seem likely to flourish in agriculture and to combine the economies of production on a large scale with many of the joys and the social gains of small properties.' On the other hand, however, the requisite moral faculties are simply not to be found in agricultural areas such as would give co-operation there any real chance of success: 'It requires habits of mutual trust and confidence; and unfortunately the bravest and the boldest, and therefore the most trustful, of the countrymen have always moved to the towns, and agriculturalists are a suspicious race.'
32. 'A Fair Rate of Wages' (1887), in *Memorials*, p. 225.
33. 'Some Features of American Industry' (1875), in Whitaker II, p. 369.
34. *IT*, p. 854.
35. 'Co-operation' (1889), in *Memorials*, p. 235.
36. 'Co-operation' (1889), in *Memorials*, p. 237.
37. 'Co-operation' (1889), in *Memorials*, p. 240.
38. 'Co-operation' (1889), in *Memorials*, p. 241. Interest as well as opportunity figures in the discussion of such decentralisation. In the

case of elections and votes within the co-operativve movement, Marshall reflects, and despite the potentially educative and creative functions of such involvement, yet not every man 'knows well what the issues are' or takes the trouble to acquire information on matters which are unlikely to affect his daily life: 'If the issues are so remote that he does not attempt properly to grapple with them, the volume of his education is but slight.'

39. Undated fragment, in *Memorials*, p. 363. The passage continues by stating that devolution must extend to initiation as well as to administration of policy: 'Devolution under rigid superior control is in danger of becoming mechanical and formal. The devolution that makes for organic evolution must not be limited to responsibility for carrying out details of schemes devised by the central authority: it must extend to the thinking out and the carrying out of appropriate constructive schemes in which the central ideas of the national scheme are adjusted to particular local conditions and requirements.' In the circumstances it is genuinely surprising that Marshall had so little to say about more extensive mobilisation of civic duty at the grass roots level (even T. H. Green, and despite the Wholeness of his Hegelianism, went so far as to favour temperance legislation on a *local* basis and demonstrated his own active commitment to local democracy by serving as an elected member of the Oxford Town Council). Marshall's fullest discussion of devolution is to be found in the evidence he presented to the Royal Commission on Local Taxation (1897). His argument there is in effect that, given that the nation needs public services such as poor relief, asylums, education and a police force, there is nonetheless a case for devolution of provision where possible from Whitehall to Town Hall – accompanied where appropriate by Exchequer grants for specific local services and by central inspection to ensure that the duties were indeed being performed 'with vigour and intelligence' and 'efficiency' (*OP* (1897), p. 359). Devolution of powers gives local politicians and bureaucrats the opportunity to 'pioneer new paths, which the whole country is not yet ready to tread' and takes advantage of the fact that first-rate local authorities 'will have more initiative, more invention, more willingness to take trouble for the public good than is always found in the officials of a large central department' (*OP* (1897), p. 358). Besides that, variety and competition are good things in their own right, between authorities as between firms: 'The prospects of progress are increased by the multiplicity of parallel experiments, and the inter-communion of ideas between many people, each of whom has some opportunity of testing practically the value of his own suggestions' (*OP* (1897), p. 359). Admittedly, second-rate authorities will without the occasional threat that their grant might be cut or the occasional hint on how to raise standards tend to lag behind. Thus, 'the chief work of the central authority should perhaps be, on the one hand, to help the most enlightened local authorities in comparing, criticising, and profiting by the experiences of one another; and, on the other hand, to put pressure on the more backward to work up to a high level' (*OP* (1897), p. 358). Despite the disadvantages, however, the case for devolution would

seem to be so strong – and so consistent with Marshall's overall support for active participation in corporate collective action – that his failure to say more about this subject is a tantalising omission from his writings on political economy.

40. A good thing, incidentally, which, Marshall stressed, waits upon some antecedent education and some prior upgrading, in the sense that learning democracy by doing democracy is only genuinely possible in a society of 'gentlemen' and not in a society of louts. That is why experiments with co-operation in the past cannot be regarded as indicative of the nature of co-operatives in the future. Authentic co-operation has, simply, not yet been tried: 'What have been tried are associations among, comparatively speaking, uneducated men, men who are unable to follow even the financial calculations that are required for an extensive and complicated business. What have to be tried are associations among men as highly educated as are manufacturers now. Such associations could not but succeed.' ('The Future of the Working Classes' (1873), in *Memorials*, p. 114). Formal education, the occupational upgrading of unskilled to skilled, learning by participating itself – all of these tendencies in the modern economy create a populus with greater knowledge and with a greater capacity to share intelligently in democratic decision-making. So even if the co-operative mode has not yet shown 'conspicuous success', even if the requisite managers with high principles (although, of course, 'more common among officers of co-operative societies than in other occupations') are not yet 'very common', nonetheless tendencies exist in the modern economy which favour the further expansion of participatory production: 'It may be hoped that the diffusion of a better knowledge of the true principles of co-operation, and the increase of general education, are every day fitting a larger number of co-operators for the complex problems of business management.' (*PE*, p. 256).
41. 'Co-operation' (1889), in *Memorials*, p. 240.
42. Address delivered in Bristol on 29 September, 1881. Quoted in Keynes, 'Alfred Marshall, 1842–1924', in *Memorials*, p. 16.
43. Unpublished note dated 18 August 1901, in Marshall Papers, Miscellaneous Box 2. Similar ideas may be found in the 'Lectures to Women' (1873), in Marshall Library.
44. *IT*, pp. 654–5.
45. 'Co-operation' (1889), in *Memorials*, p. 229. The manner in which this is phrased reminds us that activities to Marshall were over time increasingly to be ranked above wants.
46. 'Co-operation' (1889), in *Memorials*, p. 249.
47. 'Co-operation' (1889), in *Memorials*, p. 249.
48. 'The Present Position of Economics' (1885), in *Memorials*, p. 160.

5 MICROECONOMIC POLICY

1. 'Social Possibilities of Economic Chivalry' (1907), in *Memorials*, p. 333, 336.

2. Smith, *Wealth of Nations*, Vol. II, p. 209.
3. M. Friedman, *Capitalism and Freedom* (Chicago: The University of Chicago Press, 1962), p. 34.
4. T. W. Hutchison, 'Economists and Economic Policy in Britain after 1870', *History of Political Economy*, Vol. 1, 1969, p. 255.
5. N. Jha, *The Age of Marshall*, (Patna: Novelty and Co., 1963), p. ix.
6. B. Gerbier, *Alfred Marshall: Théoricien de l'action efficace et critique radical de l'économie pure* (Grenoble: Université des Sciences Sociales de Grenoble, 1976), pp. 396–7. Elsewhere (p. 129) Gerbier says that 'Marshall était un bourgeois progressiste de son époque ... un représentant du nouveau libéralisme entendant dépasser le statu quo.' As the passage cited in the text would seem to indicate, Marshall's 'élan réformateur', in the view of Gerbier, pointed to an increased role for the State. A similar conclusion is drawn by Chasse, who writes: 'Marshall's response to weaknesses in the system was ... one of looking for a precise intervention suited to the historical moment. His suggestions, taken individually, seem minor: considered together, however, they constitute a significant intervention. In addition to public education and the fostering of 'economic chivalry', there were suggestions for caring for the 'Residuum' and providing old-age pensions. He proposed industry-wide research consortia, with government participation to prevent collusion. He wanted to move large groups of people together with footloose industries out of London. All this reflects a non-Spencerian belief that rational intervention can improve the system.' (J. D. Chasse, 'Marshall, the Human Agent and Economic Growth: Wants and Activities Revisited', *History of Political Economy*, Vol. 16, 1984, p. 402).

5.1 The Nature of Taxation

1. *PE*, p. 416.
2. *PE*, p. 33. Questions such as these, Marshall reflects (*PE*, p. 34), 'though lying for the greater part outside the range of economic science, yet supply a chief motive in the background to the work of the economist'.
3. *PE*, p. 34.
4. *PE*, p. 16.
5. *PE*, p. 330.
6. *PE*, p. 597.
7. 'The Equitable Distribution of Taxation' (1917), in *Memorials*, p. 348.
8. A. C. Pigou, *Economics in Practice* (London: Macmillan, 1935), p. 121.
9. See 'The Equitable Distribution of Taxation' (1917), in *Memorials*, p. 347.
10. Undated fragment, in *Memorials*, p. 366.
11. 'The Old Generation of Economists and the New' (1897), in *Memorials*, p. 311.
12. *PE*, pp. 593–4.
13. 'Some Aspects of Competition' (1890), in *Memorials*, p. 282.

14. *PE*, p. 191. Earning and spending, needless to say, are two separate activities, and an economist interested in fostering growth by encouraging saving might legitimately wish to do so by shifting the burden of taxation from the former flow to the latter. Marshall does not make such a proposal but he was clearly aware of the problem: 'Income . . . seems, on the whole, the best basis of a system of taxation; but it has many deficiencies. It presses unduly on those who do not spend the whole of their income, but save some of it: they are taxed on their savings, and they are taxed again on the revenue derived from their savings.' (*OP* (1897), p. 338). Because he wished to encourage corporate savings, Marshall made the following pointed observation concerning corporate taxation: 'All taxes on profits would tend to check the growth of capital and to increase its emigration; some of them would tend perceptibly to increase the emigration of persons and so on.' (*OP* (1897), p. 356). With respect to personal savings, however, Marshall was more reticent, and was clearly no more prepared to utilise differential taxes on expenditure to discriminate in favour of the choice of saving than he was prepared to utilise excise duties as part of a campaign to root out wasteful ostentation in fashionable dress.
15. *PE*, p. 594, which must be read in conjunction with the references cited in the next two notes.
16 'The Equitable Distribution of Taxation' (1917), in *Memorials*, p. 351.
17. 'Social Possibilities of Economic Chivalry' (1907), in *Memorials*, p. 325.
18. *IT*, p. 664. The influence of emulation may be *measured* in money but money, it must be stressed, is far from being the only *motive* which the student of economic behaviour must take into account. See on this *EAM*, Chapter 7.2.
19. Letter to Mrs Bosanquet dated 2 October 1902, in *Memorials*, p. 444.
20. Letter to Mrs Bosanquet dated 28 October 1903, in *Memorials*, pp. 445–6.
21. Letter to Lord Reay dated 12 November 1909, in *Memorials*, p. 463.
22. Letter to Louis Fry dated 7 November 1914, in *Memorials*, p. 485.
23. Undated fragment, in *Memorials*, p. 366.
24. 'Social Possibilities of Economic Chivalry' (1907), in *Memorials*, p. 325.
25. 'Social Possibilities of Economic Chivalry' (1907), in *Memorials*, p. 329.
26. Letter to Mrs Bosanquet dated 28 September 1902, in *Memorials*, p. 443. Apart from the 'meagre life' of the poor, the very low marginal utility of the extra tranche of income to the rich man must also be borne in mind: 'When wealth is very unevenly distributed, some have more of it than they can turn to any very great account in promoting their own well-being.' (Undated fragment, in *Memorials*, p. 366). That twice as much money does not *ceteris paribus* mean twice as much happiness is a standard result in Marshall's economics: 'The happiness of the rich does not exceed that of the poor nearly in proportion to the difference in their commands of material wealth' ('The Equitable Distribution of Taxation' (1917), in *Memorials*, p. 347). That twice as much money means *very much less* than twice as much happiness is a separate and an additional observation, and one which augurs well for the successful adoption of the redistributive measures which Marshall has in mind.

27. Letter to Louis Fry dated 7 November 1914, in *Memorials*, p. 485.
28. *PE*, p. 621.
29. 'Co-operation' (1889), in *Memorials*, pp. 228–9.
30. 'The Old Generation of Economists and the New' (1897), in *Memorials*, p. 305.
31. *PE*, p. 391. Marshall adds that, while the matter should not be forgotten, 'it is reasonable that the bearings of this proposition should be set aside during the first stages of an inquiry into existing economic conditions'; and this is presumably why he does not probe more deeply and carefully into the *minutiae* of income taxation. For present purposes he is content to contend that free exchange leads automatically to maximum satisfaction only if initial endowments of spendable resources are assumed optimal; that such endowments are neither optimal nor for that matter natural (the iron law of distribution based on the Malthusian population mechanism, the wages fund and diminishing returns to land having been replaced in his work by a marginal productivity theory subject to a considerable penumbra of discretion); and that State intervention can well do more to foster justice and harmony in the field of income distribution than would unthinking reliance on self-seeking behaviour and market forces.
32. *OP* (1897), p. 357.
33. *OP* (1897), p. 357.
34. Letter to Lord Reay dated 12 November 1909, in *Memorials*, p. 463.
35. Lecture Notes on Taxation (1880), in Whitaker II, p. 383.
36. *OP* (1897), p. 357.
37. 'The Equitable Distribution of Taxation' (1917), in *Memorials*, p. 352. It is not uncommon in Marshall's economics for him thus to posit a supply curve of an input (whether labour or capital) with respect to net remuneration which is inelastic over some range.
38. Letter to Lord Reay dated 12 November 1909, in *Memorials*, p. 463.
39. 'The Equitable Distribution of Taxation' (1917), in *Memorials*, p. 352.
40. 'Social Possibilities of Economic Chivalry' (1907), in *Memorials*, p. 345.
41. Letter to Lord Reay dated 12 November 1909, in *Memorials*, pp. 462–3.
42. Letter to Lord Reay dated 12 November 1909, in *Memorials*, p. 463.
43. *PE*, p. 662. An even more dramatic statement may be found in a letter to *The Times* of 16 November 1909, p. 10, where Marshall, discussing the 'Social Welfare Budget' of that year, expresses his support for a levy on accretions in land-values which come about in consequence of State-sponsored schemes and socially-funded amenities: 'Those Socialistic aims, which tend towards the supersession of the responsibility of the individual for his own career, seem to me the gravest of all the dangers that loom on the social horizon. But in so far as the Budget proposes to check the appropriation of what is really public property by private persons, and in so far as it proposes to bring under taxation some real income, which has escaped taxation merely because it does not appear above the surface in a money form, I regard it as sound finance.'
44. Letter to Theodore Llewellyn Davies dated 30 October 1909, in *Memorials*, p. 431.
45. Letter to Lord Reay dated 12 November 1909, in *Memorials*, pp. 463–4.

46. *OP* (1897), p. 339.
47. *OP* (1903), p. 409.
48. *OP* (1903), p. 410. See also 'The Equitable Distribution of Taxation' (1917), in *Memorials*, p. 350, where he expresses the hope that 'the various advances towards graduation made before (the war) will be sustained and developed after it'.
49. *OP* (1903), p. 410.
50. Smith, *Wealth of Nations*, Vol. II, p. 246.
51. *OP* (1897), p. 338.
52. 'Social Possibilities of Economic Chivalry' (1907), in *Memorials*, p. 327.
53. *OP* (1897), p. 362.
54. 'Abstract Theory of a General Uniform Tax' (circa 1873 or 1874), in Whitaker II, p. 296. Elsewhere in the same unpublished manuscript (pp. 299, 301) Marshall returns to the topic of discrimination via taxation. His discussion is muddled (he appears, for example, to be confusing the consumption-repressing and the revenue-raising functions of public finance) but it does provide an interesting insight into the mind of the born moraliser when confronted with the tempting banquet of the tax system: 'It might appear that necessaries should be taxed: and though on other grounds this is to be condemned, it appears that the fittest subjects for taxation are those luxuries which are almost necessaries. Whatever share of taxation the poor man is to bear is as well levied on his tobacco, alcohol and sugar as on anything else: tea comes early on this count but is a preventative of drunkenness: house room again when too cramped leads to immorality. Houses and tea are as regards all other classes good subjects of taxation. One of the great advantages of tobacco is that nothing (unless it be opium, which ought indeed to be heavily taxed) is a substitute for it.' Elsewhere, on the subject of discrimination and high duties, he wrote: 'Anti-social excess in the consumption of alcohol by any class is rightly subject to heavy taxation.' ('The Equitable Distribution of Taxation' (1917), in *Memorials*, p. 348). And is an unpublished fragment on 'The Future' dated 14 November 1920: 'Expenditure, which serves no considerable service other than a display of wealth, is to be discouraged by public opinion, by special taxation; or, in rare cases, by edict.' In Marshall Papers, Red Box 1 (3). It may therefore be the case that his general reticence on the subject of punitive taxation in this area merely indicates a tacit acceptance of the *status quo*. This argument is, however, not very convincing, and one would in all honesty have expected a man of his temperament to be an advocate of purchase tax levied at different rates on different commodities because of their different characteristics. Purchase tax is, of course, regressive, while progressive income tax by definition is not; and that is presumably why Marshall's proposals for public finance more frequently involve discrimination between persons than discrimination between things.
55. *OP* (1897), p. 356.
56. 'The Theory of Foreign Trade' (1873–7), in Whitaker II, pp. 81, 82.
57. *OP* (1897), p. 338.
58. *PE*, p. 394.

59. *PE*, p. 416.
60. *PE*, p. 416.
61. *PE*, p. 416. A believer in both blades of the scissors, it is curious that he has so much to say about consumers' surplus created but so little about producers' surplus destroyed.
62. *PE*, p. 392. Where the law of increasing return acts 'sharply', Marshall notes, the welfare gain might actually exceed the cost of the bounties.
63. *PE*, p. 392.
64. In some respects the stationary state positively confuses the issue in the present context, for economies of size are by their very nature a dynamic rather than a static concept. Interestingly, Marshall himself criticises Pigou's welfare economics for too great a reliance on *ceteris paribus* and for paying insufficient attention to time. See on this K. Bharadwaj, 'Marshall on Pigou's *Wealth and Welfare*', *Economica*, Vol. 39, 1972. In Wood IV, pp.216–7.
65. *PE*, p. 393.
66. *PE*, p. 393. Emphasis in original.
67. J. K. Whitaker, 'Some Neglected Aspects of Alfred Marshall's Economic and Social Thought', *History of Political Economy*, Vol. 9, 1977. In Wood I, p. 459.

5.2 Collective Consumption

1. 'Some Aspects of Competition' (1890), in *Memorials*, p. 282.
2. *PE*, p. 48.
3. *PE*, p. 49.
4. *PE*, p. 111.
5. 'Social Possibilities of Economic Chivalry' (1907), in *Memorials*, pp. 344–5.
6. *PE*, p. 35.
7. Letter to Louis Fry dated 7 November 1914, in *Memorials*, p. 485. Elsewhere (*IT*, p. 5) he even looks beyond the welfare society towards the welfare world: 'A time may come when such matters will be treated as of cosmopolitan rather than national obligation: but that time is not in sight.'
8. *PE*, p. 179.
9. *PE*, p. 169.
10. Letter to F. Y. Edgeworth dated 28 August 1902, in *Memorials*, pp. 436–7.
11. *PE*, p. 598.
12. *PE*, p. 597.
13. *PE*, p. 167. The words 'public and private money' remind us of the symbiotic relationship between the two sectors in matters of welfare.
14. *PE*, p. 597.
15. Letter to *The Times* of 16 November 1909, p. 10. Note the reference to taxation of land-appreciation, a topic considered in the previous section.
16. *PE*, pp. 597–8.

17. Letter to Theodore Llewellyn Davies dated 30 October 1901, in *Memorials*, p. 431.
18. *PE*, pp. 661–2.
19. 'Water as an Element of National Wealth' (1879), in *Memorials*, p. 134.
20. *PE*, p. 659. It is the State and not private enterprise which is the guardian of the social interest in such matters, as every would-be proprietor of a high-rise structure on a valuable plot will confirm: 'If the site is very valuable and the law does not limit the height of his house in the interest of his neighbours, he may build very high. . . . But in England bylaws restrain an individual from building so high as to deprive his near neighbours of air and light. In the course of time those who build high will be forced to have a good deal of free space about their buildings; and this will render very high buildings unprofitable.' (*PE*, p. 371n). As with ancient lights in the towns, so with horrendous sights in the countryside: 'Perhaps', Marshall reflected, 'we are too careless about letting private persons spoil, or what is nearly as bad, exclude the public from the enjoyment of our most beautiful scenery' ('Water as an Element of National Wealth' (1879), in *Memorials*, p. 136). Private enterprise, it would appear, often represents a threat to amenity and convenience, beauty and health, which then calls into being countervailing power in the form of State intervention.
21. *PE*, pp. 206–7.
22. *PE*, p. 597.
23. *PE*, p. 595n. Marshall is referring specifically to the Residuum and speaking about causing it "to cease from the land".
24. D. Winch, *Economics and Policy: A Historical Study* (London: Hodder & Stoughton, 1969), p. 34.
25. *PE*, p. 563.
26. Letter to Louis Dumur dated 2 July 1909, in *Memorials*, p. 460. The feedback effect from bad living conditions to wasteful consumption patterns is, of course, an important part of Marshall's system, as we indicated in Chapter 2.1.
27. *IRC*, p. 183.
28. Letter to *The Times* of 7 July 1910, p. 12.
29. Letter to Mrs Bosanquet dated 2 October 1902, in *Memorials*, p. 445
30. 'The Pressure of Population on the Means of Subsistence' (1885), in Whitaker II, p. 392.
31. *IRC*, p. 183.
32. *PE*, p. 547.
33. *IRC*, p. 183.
34. 'The Pressure of Population on the Means of Subsistence' (1885), in Whitaker II, p. 392. The population pressure in question is not *general* to the nation but *specific* to certain large towns.
35. 'Where to House the London Poor' (1884), in *Memorials*, p. 147.
36. 'Where to House the London Poor' (1884), in *Memorials*, p. 148.
37. *PE*, p. 35. Marshall thus indicates that the study of freedom – and of the limits to freedom – is a fundamental task for the economist as well as for the political scientist.
38. 'Where to House the London Poor' (1884), in *Memorials*, p. 148.

39. The Pressure of Population on the Means of Subsistence' (1885), in Whitaker II, p. 392. The mention of children is in an important sense an indirect reference to the vital economic variable of time. For one thing, the right of children as yet unborn to exercise their freedom of choice must be safeguarded, not least against shiftless parents dwelling in soul-destroying conditions. More significantly, perhaps, we as a community are stakeholders in the health of our population, and are aware of 'the action of causes which are constantly at work, and tend in the course of a few generations to enfeeble the physical, if not also the moral, constitution of the inhabitants of very large towns' (*IRC*, p. 184). We as a community know that the Mecca of the economist lies in economic biology and therefore devote considerable attention to measures such as might generate organic upgrading and produce a better endowment of citizens. It is precisely such evolutionary processes that, alongside alleviation of present-day distress, inspire us to make an investment in the quality of the environment – for 'adequate provision of fresh air and of healthy play for our town populations, could hardly fail to cause the strength and vigour of the race to improve' (*PE*, p. 169). Thus it happens that we as a community, wanting economic growth as a means to social progress, will fix our eyes firmly on your children's children and on their children in legislating today against urban over-building: 'By allowing vacant spaces to be built on recklessly we are committing a great blunder from a business point of view. For the sake of a little material wealth we are wasting those energies which are the factors of production of all wealth: we are sacrificing those ends towards which material wealth is only a means' (*PE*, p. 548). Whether we focus on the freedom of choice of the unborn or whether we regard them as a future input the quality of which we would like to see improved, one thing is clear: paternalism in its most literal sense is endemic to the world-vision of an author who sees his community as a continuously-evolving organism and who believes that our duty is to future as well as to present cohorts of fellow citizens.
40. A. C. Pigou, footnote in *Memorials*, p. 142n.
41. 'Where to House the London Poor' (1884), in *Memorials*, p. 149.
42. 'Where to House the London Poor' (1884), in *Memorials*, p. 150.
43. *IRC*, p. 184.
44. Letter to Louis Dumur dated 2 July 1909, in *Memorials*, p. 460.
45. *IRC*, p. 183.
46. *IRC*, p. 183, 184.
47. 'Where to House the London Poor' (1884), in *Memorials*, p. 149.
48. 'Where to House the London Poor' (1884), in *Memorials*, pp. 143–6, *passim*. You and I know that it is highly desirable for the workers to escape from 'densely populated districts' to 'industrial villages' where children can get involved in 'invigorating play' and where young and old alike derive healthy and constructive satisfaction from 'the opportunities which abundance of open space offers for invigorating exercise and refreshing repose' (*IT*, p. 502). Yet our quarry might not share our enthusiasm for diminished concentration of activity and might, precisely because of the baseness of character which slum life

engenders, prove difficult to shift. Fortunately, however, here once again the *deus ex machina* of on-going social improvement comes to our aid. Once upon a time 'some classes of operatives used to spend high wages somewhat crudely; and they were not easily attracted into the country' – but since then progress has happily put paid to such execrescences, false choices and distortions of philosopher's sovereignty: 'The working classes have become better educated, less addicted to coarser enjoyments, and more appreciative of the quiet of a many-roomed house with a garden' (*IT*, p. 229). It would be an embarrassment to organise a suburb only to find that no one came; but, happily, Henry Dubb is becoming every day more and more *pantouflard*.

49. 'Where to House the London Poor' (1884), in *Memorials*, p. 150.
50. See *PE*, p. 367–8 and *EAM*, Chapter 8.2.
51. Letter to Mrs Bosanquet dated 2 October 1902, in *Memorials*, p. 445.
52. Letter to Mrs Bosanquet dated 28 October 1903, in *Memorials*, p. 445.
53. *IRC*, p. 183.
54. 'Social Possibilities of Economic Chivalry' (1907), in *Memorials*, p. 336.
55. 'The Pressure of Population on the Means of Subsistence' (1885), in Whitaker II, p. 392.
56. 'Social Possibilities of Economic Chivalry' (1907), in *Memorials*, p. 344.
57. 'Social Possibilities of Economic Chivalry' (1907), in *Memorials*, pp. 344–5.
58. *PE*, p. 176.
59. 'The Future of the Working Classes' (1873), in *Memorials*, p. 117.
60. 'The Future of the Working Classes' (1873), in *Memorials*, p. 106. Marshall, for whom consumer sovereignty is not absolute, does not entertain the possibility that you or I might not share his 'joy' in knowledge or his 'delight' in art.
61. 'The Future of the Working Classes' (1873), in *Memorials*, p. 115. This passage would appear to show the influence of Adam Smith's defence of popular education and Smith's suggestion that such education is of value not least because it makes the operative 'less apt to be misled into any wanton or unnecessary opposition to the measures of government' (*Wealth of Nations*, Vol. II, p. 309).
62. *IT*, p. 377.
63. *IT*, p. 672.
64. *PE*, p. 180.
65. *IT*, p. 97.
66. *IT*, p. 672.
67. An extended discussion of this topic may be found in *EAM*, Chapter 10.4.
68. 'The Future of the Working Classes' (1873), in *Memorials*, p. 118.
69. 'The Future of the Working Classes' (1873), in *Memorials*, p. 118.
70. *IT*, p. 98. As the Germans seem to know: 'British education has lagged behind that of Germany in some respects by more than a generation' (*IT*, p. 97).
71. *IT*, p. 95. Economists were somewhat quicker off the mark: as early as the early nineteenth century, Marshall reflected, 'those who were giving

their main energies to the study of economics, much as they might differ on other matters, were to a man convinced that parsimony in popular education is uneconomical and even wasteful'. (*IT*, p. 765).

72. *EI*, p. 11.
73. *EI*, p. 113.
74. 'Some Aspects of Competition' (1890), in *Memorials*, p. 282.
75. Letter to Lord Reay dated 12 November 1909, in *Memorials*, p. 464.
76. Lecture delivered in Bristol on 9 October 1877. Quoted in Whitaker, 'Alfred Marshall: The Years 1877 to 1885' (Chapter 3.2, note 14), p. 145.
77. *PE*, p. 597.
78. *IT*, p. 356.
79. *IT*, p. 820.
80. *IT*, p. 129. The key words are 'subordinate work' – since, precisely because too much discipline breeds too little spontaneity, the Germans are not strong on initiative and creativity: 'Though German original work is of prodigious volume, it often is somewhat lacking in penetrative power.' (*IT*, p. 130). This propensity to substitute organisation of detail for genuine advance is in a sense surprising for, 'though German Schools have a severer discipline than the English, yet in German Universities both students and teachers have great freedom' (*IT*, p. 129). But one reason would appear to be the long arm of the secondary sector: 'It seems doubtful whether the discipline of German school life is a good preparation for making use of the unlimited opportunities for spontaneity which are offered at the University' (*IT*, p. 130). This in turn is reinforced by compulsory military service: 'Again, the military drill, which is imposed on all citizens of full physical strength, gives some firmness to very weak characters, and helps to prevent the growth of a class of professional paupers. But perhaps it does some injury to many fine and sensitive characters, and even checks the development of the subtler forms of manual skill; as well as of the highest genius that might find vent in literature, art, and science' (*IT*, p. 130). And, as if this were not enough, the German national character is hardly favourable to mould-breaking such as might necessitate a new filing system and a revised organisational chart: 'The character of the German people differs from that of Americans and Britons. It has more patience and steady assiduity; so that methodical, orderly procedure in school and college has peculiar attractions for them' (*IT*, p. 357). At the same time, it cannot be denied that the Germans, although apparently suited for a plethora of reasons only to 'subordinate work', do seem to be capable of making vast strides in fields such as applied chemistry and applied biology – and in the application of science to industry with 'a breadth and system which establish a claim to industrial leadership of a special kind' (*IT*, p. 131). They are lions with 'elaborate mental training' whereas we are foxes with 'a ready wit and sound judgement' (*IT*, p. 133), but even if they are stronger on plodding than on pioneering, they are obviously a force, economically speaking, to be reckoned with.
81. *IT*, p. 129.
82. Lecture delivered in Bristol on 9 October 1877. Quoted in Whitaker, 'Alfred Marshall': The Years 1877 to 1885' (see note 76, *supra*), p. 145.

83. *IT*, p. 822.
84. *IT*, p. 819. Greek apparently has a less beneficial effect, presumably because so much time is wasted in learning the proper intonation whereas a correct valuation of time (a scarce commodity) ought to form part of every boy's education: 'It injures character, by suggesting a low appreciation of the value of time; while the study of constructive science has the opposite effect, for its ever-growing ambitions are greedy of time' (*IT*, p. 820n).
85. *PE*, p. 177. He is speaking explicitly of the visual arts: literature and music, he notes, add much to the 'fulness of life' but not much impact upon the business life.
86. Letter to T. C. Horsfall dated 8 March 1900, in *Memorials*, pp. 409–10.
87. Lecture delivered in Bristol on October 9, 1877. Quoted in Whitaker, 'Alfred Marshall: The Years 1877 to 1885' (see note 76, *supra*), p. 145.
88. *IT*, p. 822.
89. *IT*, p. 823. The Germans, Marshall notes, are 'somewhat deficient' in affection and 'quick intuitive sympathy' (*IT*, p. 129), which inevitably has a negative effect on the sensitivity of the German manager to the feelings of the German worker. The English and the American manager seem better able to 'read the minds of the employees' (*IT*, p. 823), although it is not entirely clear why this should be so – particularly since the future manager in Britain is not educated in a comprehensive school and 'lives among his own class' while at university.
90. *IT*, p. 96.
91. *IT*, p. 822.
92. *IT*, p. 133.
93. *IT*, p. 99.
94. *EI*, p. 11.
95. *IT*, p. 351.
96. *IT*, p. 351. The passage continues 'and meanwhile the scope for boy labour in those occupations, which used to afford the most excellent training, has greatly diminished, for the work is done now mainly by machines' – which would seem to suggest that on-the-job training is most suited to the performance of precisely those tasks which are less and less required as an economy becomes more and more advanced.
97. *IT*, p. 351.
98. *IT*, p. 351.
99. *EI*, p. 11.
100. *PE*, p. 172n.
101. *EI*, p. 11.
102. See *EAM*, Chapters 5.2 and 10.4.
103. *PE*, p. 174.
104. *PE*, p. 476. The market will do its best to rectify anomalies and equalise net advantages, but the education industry should do its best to avoid the erection of artificial barriers such as impede mobility and therewith retard growth.
105. *IT*, p. 168.
106. Letter to *The Times* of 29 December 1905, p. 5.
107. Letter to *The Times* of 29 December 1905, p. 5. And elsewhere: 'It is

indeed true that a man is likely to be more efficient in business who has braced his mind to hard work in subjects that have no connection with it, than if he had occupied himself with an ennervating form of technical instruction, however directly that might bear on his after work.' As Marshall happens to be arguing here for greater State interest in Britain (as is already the case in Germany and America) in higher education for businessmen, he quickly adds that a man is more likely to work assiduously at the requisite mental gymnastics if he perceives them to be of specific vocational utility: 'Provided the studies be themselves of a truly liberal character, the closer their relation to his after work, the more active is his interest in them likely to be.' (*IT*, p. 821). Obviously no economist wishes to alienate the consumer and no teacher wants to bore the student, but Marshall's personal view is clear: the businessman needs some background information (on credit markets and trade, for example) and he needs some *how-tos*, (if he is, say, to make sense of a balance-sheet), but most of all he requires disciplined intelligence, sensitivity, imagination, and other character-traits which academic training can help to shape but which to a significant extent are independent of the precise subject-matter of the actual lessons attended. This suggests in turn that the method of instruction is itself of great importance. A bad teacher 'tends to hinder the movements of faculty by clogging it with inert matter': 'Continuous description and explanation tend to deaden the minds of the hearers.' A good teacher, on the other hand, free from intellectual stagnation himself and unprepared to let it develop in others, seeks to spread 'vitality and initiative', 'observation and reasoning', wherever he goes: 'Constructive genius of the highest kind seldom owes much to education: but, with that exception, all orders of business ability may be fostered by appropriate preparation in early years.' (*IT*, p. 356). See also *PE*, p. 597.

108. *PE*, p. 202.
109. *PE*, p. 550.
110. *PE*, p. 207.
111. *PE*, pp. 552, 206.
112. *PE*, p. 179.
113. *PE*, p. 176.
114. *PE*, pp. 179–80. See also: 'The economic value of one great industrial genius is sufficient to cover the expenses of the education of a whole town; for one new idea, such as Bessemer's chief invention, adds as much to England's productive power as the labour of a hundred thousand men.' (*PE*, p. 179).
115. *PE*, p. 196.
116. 'The Future of the Working Classes' (1873), in *Memorials*, p. 118.
117. *EI*, p. 113.
118. *PE*, p. 180. The words 'as yet' remind us of the self-liquidating nature of this diagnosis in the course of social evolution.
119. *EI*, p. 113.
120. Letter to E. C. K. Gonner dated 9 May 1894, in *Memorials*, p. 381.
121. 'The Future of the Working Classes' (1873), in *Memorials*, p. 117.
122. 'The Future of the Working Classes' (1873), in *Memorials*, p. 117.

123. *PE*, p. 165. Marshall evidently had strong views on hours of work – as when, for instance, arguing that the family must be kept functional, he said that 'society as a whole has a direct interest in the curtailment of extravagantly long hours of duty away from home' (*PE*, p. 600), or when he declared to the Master of Balliol 'I am very much of an 8 hours man' (Letter to Edward Caird dated 22 October 1897, in *Memorials*, p. 398). If he does not say more about factory conditions and hours of work, it is presumably because he wanted such matters to be settled voluntarily in the private sector, not because he was indifferent to their significance.
124. 'The Future of the Working Classes' (1873), in *Memorials*, p. 117.
125. *PE*, p. 597.
126. *PE*, p. 472.
127. 'Where to House the London Poor' (1884), in *Memorials*, p. 145.
128. 'Where to House the London Poor' (1884), in *Memorials*, p. 145.
129. *PE*, p. 596.
130. *PE*, p. 596.
131. *PE*, p. 596.
132. *PE*, p. 464.
133. *PE*, p. 464.
134. 'The Equitable Distribution of Taxation' (1917), in *Memorials*, p. 347.
135. Letter to Lord Reay dated 12 November 1909, in *Memorials*, pp. 464–5.
136. Letter to Lord Reay dated 12 November 1909, in *Memorials*, p. 464.
137. 'Some Aspects of Competition' (1890), in *Memorials*, p. 282. Examples which Marshall does not cite but which fit without insuperable difficulty in this category include libraries, museums, consumer protection, subsidies to the arts, and various other steps which a paternalistic State might take in an attempt to make life larger for its citizens.

5.3 The Relief of Poverty

1. Quoted in Keynes, 'Alfred Marshall, 1842–1924', in *Memorials*, pp. 37–8. The painting in question now hangs in the Marshall Library, Cambridge.
2. 'The Present Position of Economics' (1885), in *Memorials*, p. 174.
3. *OP* (1893), p. 205.
4. 'The Present Position of Economics' (1885), in *Memorials*, p. 152.
5. *PE*, p. 631.
6. *PE*, p. 29.
7. *PE*, p. 594.
8. *PE*, p. 2.
9. Letter to Bishop Westcott dated 24 January 1900, in *Memorials*, p. 387.
10. Letter to *The Times* of 2 June 1885, p. 3.
11. 'A Fair Rate of Wages (1887), in *Memorials*, p. 213.
12. 'Social Possibilities of Economic Chivalry.' (1907), in *Memorials*, p. 344.
13. *PE*, p. 595.
14. Marshall seems to have had in mind some sort of poverty line and in at

least one place (*PE*, p. 594) formulates his criterion in terms of relative (as opposed to absolute) deprivation: 'Though arithmetic warns us that it is impossible to raise all earnings beyond the level already reached by specially well-to-do artisan families, it is certainly desirable that those who are below that level should be raised, even at the expense of lowering in some degree those who are above it.' Absolute deprivation is the relevant concept from an economic point of view (as where more pay leads to better food, better food to greater efficiency) and also from the humanitarian perspective of assisting those in need, but relative deprivation has its importance too in the work of an author who wanted a more integrated society in which every man would be a gentleman. All things considered, however, Marshall, where he does talk about a minimum wage at all, is normally concerned with absolutes and not with relatives.

15. *PE*, p. 595.
16. Suppose that the seamstress in question is employed by a 'sweater' who, 'as some sweaters do, works hard himself, earns but a moderate income, and pays promptly and ungrudgingly the highest wages that his trade will bear'. ('A Fair Rate of Wages' (1887), in *Memorials*, p. 225). That sweater 'cannot be said to act unfairly' and *ceteris paribus* he will have to dismiss the labourer. Were he to keep her on, however, better food and accommodation, Marshall argued, would eventually be validated by improved health and strength. Indeed, Marshall might usefully have added, he, the sweater, might, compelled by the minimum wage to break out of the cocoon of inertia, make a real effort himself to improve the productivity of his work-force. So the prediction of unemployment is an eminently *ceteris paribus* one and thus at least partially out of keeping with the dynamic nature of Marshall's economics. Only partially, however, as Marshall does refer explicitly, as we have seen, to the phenomenon of induced unemployment.
17. 'The Old Generation of Economists and the New' (1897), in *Memorials*, p. 305.
18. *PE*, p. 595.
19. *OP* (1893), p. 199.
20. *OP* (1893), p. 244.
21. *OP* (1893), p. 245.
22. 'The Present Position of Economics' (1885), in *Memorials*, p. 173. Emphasis added.
23. *PE*, pp. 156–7.
24. *PE*, p. 619.
25. *PE*, p. 9.
26. 'The Poor Law in Relation to State-Aided Pensions', *Economic Journal*, Vol. II, 1892, p. 186.
27. *PE*, p. 37.
28. 'The Poor Law in Relation to State-Aided Pensions', *Economic Journal*, Vol. II, 1892, p. 186.
29. *PE*, p. 188. Elsewhere, returning once again to the topic of relief based on need without regard to merit, he comments as follows on the perverse effects of non-discriminatory policies: 'The dark shadow of the

French Revolution has enlisted the fears of the well-to-do classes on the side of their human sympathies, in arranging a system of poor-relief, which inverted the law of nature: for it made life least uncomfortable for those of the labouring classes who were least deserving: and it caused those, who had the least nobility of character, to marry early and to leave the largest number of descendants; and they in many cases lived to become degraded helots in manufacturing districts' (*IT*, p. 78). The mischief was not done by the relief *per se* 'but by its being given in the wrong way and to the wrong persons, so as to cause the survival of the worst in place of the best. Probably half of all the lives of extreme misery and want in the country are due to this cause' (*IRC*, p. 188).

30. 'The Poor Law in Relation to State-Aided Pensions', *Economic Journal*, Vol. II, 1892, p. 189.
31. *EI*, p. 29.
32. For just as physical or personal weakness can keep an inferior man in a low grade of work, so alcohol can shoot down the high-flyer and reduce even the superior man to such a grade: 'The strong drunkard probably came down to that low grade of work merely because he was a drunkard, while the sober man probably came there because he had not sufficient force of character and physique to earn a comfortable livelihood anywhere.' (Letter to *The Times* of July 7, 1910, p. 12).
33. *OP* (1893), p. 206.
34. 'Social Possibilities of Economic Chivalry' (1907), in *Memorials*, p. 345.
35. *PE*, p. 188.
36. *PE*, p. 188.
37. 'Where to House the London Poor' (1884), in *Memorials*, p. 150.
38. 'Where to House the London Poor' (1884), in *Memorials*, pp. 150–1.
39. 'The Poor Law in Relation to State-Aided Pensions', *Economic Journal*, Vol. II, 1892, p. 188.
40. 'The Poor Law in Relation to State-Aided Pensions', *Economic Journal*, Vol. II, 1892, p. 188.
41. 'Poor Law Reform', *Economic Journal*, Vol. II, 1892, p. 376. Marshall, it must be stressed, favoured discrimination in the administration of welfare (as opposed to the leniency, laxity and lavishness for which he took the system of his own time to task) but he was strongly opposed to cuts in total expenditure. On the contrary: 'I think we are wrong in allowing the amount spent in poor relief to become a continually and rapidly diminishing portion of the total income of the country.' Applied to the specific problem of personnel, what this suggests is clear, that if existing staff are so overworked that they have no choice but to allow supply of welfare to be in effect determined by the demand for welfare, then 'the remedy is to take some of that money which is now going into the pockets of the rich, and which by tradition was the property of the poor, and to apply it for this purpose – the increase of the number of relieving officers' (*OP* (1893), pp. 249–50). See also *OP* (1893), p. 239.
42. 'Poor Law Reform', *Economic Journal*, Vol. II, 1892, p. 376. Evolution and education thus generate the valuable external economy for the welfare sector of officials both better trained and of better character. See also *OP* (1893), p. 239.

43. *OP* (1893), p. 253. Marshall is predicting the spread of the COS to villages which at present have no voluntary sector.
44. *OP* (1893), p. 262.
45. *OP* (1893), p. 204.
46. 'The Poor Law in Relation to State-Aided Pensions', *Economic Journal*, Vol. II, 1892, p. 189.
47. *OP* (1893), p. 210. In the interim, of course, emergency grants or 'doles' (*OP* (1893), p. 252) will have to be handed out in advance of a recommendation being made. Such relief will naturally come from the Poor Law authorities, i.e. the public sector.
48. *OP* (1893), p. 239.
49. *OP* (1893), pp. 239–40.
50. *OP* (1893), p. 219.
51. *OP* (1893), p. 211.
52. *OP* (1893), p. 221.
53. *EI*, p. 34.
54. 'The Poor Law in Relation to State-Aided Pensions', *Economic Journal*, Vol. II, 1892, p. 189.
55. *OP* (1893), p. 203. It is clearly important to ensure, via careful investigation of each and every case, that no good man should be exposed to such discomfort and indignity; and this remind us of Marshall's general view that he who has no blemish or short-coming to hide cannot but welcome the questions of the COS visitor. Just as the visitor wishes to make sure that the bad man enters the workhouse, so, it is important to remember, the visitor wants to make sure that the good man is spared such severe medicine even though the complaint – poverty – is the same.
56. *OP* (1893), p. 206.
57. Despite their limited funds and oligarchic structure, Marshall said, 'it is difficult to overrate the debt that the nation owes to the Charity Organisation Societies' (*OP* (1893), p. 203). In view of the central role which the case-by-case approach plays in his recommendations, it is obvious that without the COS discrimination as he envisaged it would be all but impossible.
58. *EI*, p. 34.
59. *EI*, p. 35.
60. *EI*, p. 33.
61. 'Poor Law Reform', *Economic Journal*, Vol. II, 1892, p. 375.
62. *EI*, p. 33.
63. *OP* (1893), p. 224. Note that such lowering of wages appears to be specific to the trades in which the persons in receipt of relief are concentrated, and is not an across-the-board or general phenomenon. (*OP* (1893), p. 261).
64. *EI*, p. 32–3.
65. *OP* (1893), p. 219.
66. *OP* (1893), p. 218. Obviously, should private charities ever lack resources, then some persons who would have been relieved as B will have to be reclassified as A or C so as to become a charge on rates and taxes.

67. *OP* (1893), p. 218.
68. *OP* (1893), p. 252.
69. *OP* (1893), p. 233.
70. *OP* (1893), p. 244.
71. Letter to Percy Alden dated 28 January 1903, in *Memorials*, p. 447.
72. *PE*, p. 594.
73. Letter to Mrs Bosanquet dated 28 September 1902, in *Memorials*, pp. 443–4.
74. *PE*, p. 595n. The State is evidently to concern itself not only with destitution (due, say, to illness or old age) but also, and more significantly, with progress – which is why it must devote especial attention to the sanitary, educational and other requirements of children. Yet there are children and there are children, and in a letter to S. D. Fuller dated 21 November 1897 (in *Memorials*, p. 403) Marshall reminded his correspondent that, the genes of the fathers being visited upon the children, therefore 'to be overkind to the children of the pauper class, relatively to those of the self-respecting poor, would directly frustrate nature's rule that the better strains of population shall have a better chance of moving upwards and multiplying than the inferior strains have'. A similar observation may be found in an unpublished note (undated, but from the handwriting probably composed later rather than earlier in Marshall's life) on 'Ethico-economic problems', where Marshall reflected as follows on equality of opportunity with special reference to pollution through procreation: 'Is it right to diminish the death rate among the children of improvident and worthless parents, while leaving those children to be educated in vice; account being taken of the extent to which it may be necessary to levy for this purpose taxes which retard the age of marriages and otherwise diminish the birth-rate among those classes whose children are likely to become good citizens'. In Marshall Papers, Red Box 1 (3). This is Marshall at his harshest and most deterministic, and shows that he had not entirely left behind the taint-of-vice and inbred-weakness arguments with which he, in the shadow of Darwin and Spencer, had flirted decades earlier. Then he had written that 'the descendants of the dissolute are naturally weak, and especially those of the dissolute in large towns. It is appalling to think how many of the poor in London are descendants of the dissolute' ("Where to House the London Poor" (1884), in *Memorials*, p. 144). Upon inspection, however, it becomes clear that the inherited disability is a situational rather than a biological one; and that the physical and moral weakness that is handed on is no more than the vicious circle of nurture, not nature, which Marshall, as we saw in the previous section of this Chapter, was so keen to break by means of outside intervention (public and private). For that reason, the biological elements in the letter cited above – and with them the implication that not all children are equally deserving – would seem to be out of keeping with Marshall's more usual approach, which envisaged the potential perfectability of all.
75. *OP* (1893), p. 245.
76. *OP* (1893), p. 203.

77. *PE*, p. 595n.
78. *OP* (1893), p. 223. Marshall was angered by the irresponsible attitudes of, say, the man on a pension who discharges himself from the workhouse, spends his pension on drink, and then strives to 'come back scarcely like a man, and go on living in the workhouse' (*OP* (1893), p. 244). No one should be denied relief in the workhouse, Marshall believed, but the improvident and the lazy should nonetheless not be permitted to treat the system as if it were a string of luxury hotels.
79. See *OP* (1893), p. 255.
80. 'The Poor Law in Relation to State-Aided Pensions', *Economic Journal*, Vol. II, 1892, p. 189.
81. Discussion on Mr. Booth's Paper: Enumeration and Classification of Paupers and State Pensions for the Aged, *Jounal of the Royal Statistical Society*, Vol. LV, 1892, p. 61. The words are those of the *rapporteur*.
82. Discussion on Mr. Booth's Paper: Enumeration and Classification of Paupers and State Pensions for the Aged, *Journal of the Royal Statistical Society*, Vol. LV, 1892, p. 63. The reference to "*taxes* and rates" is important. The British system of relief had traditionally had a strong local bias. Marshall saw, however, that in modern economic conditions the concept of parish responsibility did not have the natural appeal that it had once enjoyed precisely because of the high degree of concentration of the needy: 'A place which has a large pauper population and offers no great attractions for industry or residence has a prospect of long-continued high poor relief rates; and such cases are considerable, even when allowance has been made for future widening of rating areas so as to make rich districts bear a larger share of the burden of the neighbouring poor'. (*OP* (1897), p. 347). Modern modes of transportation are likely to make the geographical separation of rich and poor 'even more marked'; it may therefore 'become even more true than now that local rates are sometimes least productive where they are most wanted'; and the need is accordingly ever greater *either* for fiscal regions to be defined in such a way as to 'include rich and poor in fair proportions' (the solution implicit in the previous quotation) *or* for additional funds to be made available from central government. (*OP* (1897), p. 364).
83. *OP* (1897), p. 361.
84. *EI*, p. 34.
85. *OP* (1893), p. 237. Mary Paley Marshall was a member of the COS, both in Oxford and then in Cambridge. Alfred Marshall was therefore speaking with a certain amount of personal knowledge, even if at second hand.
86. *OP* (1893), p. 246
87. 'The Poor Law in Relation to State-Aided Pensions', *Economic Journal*, Vol. II, 1892, p. 190.
88. *OP* (1893), pp. 257–8.
89. 'Poor Law Reform', *Economic Journal*, Vol. II, 1892, p. 376.
90. *OP* (1893), p. 245. Now that the requisite intelligence exists, it must be harnessed. This means convincing working class representatives that unnecessary hardship will not be imposed on the deserving; and also

reforming and democratising the COS structure in such a way as to make outsiders (workers with Friendly Society experience, for example) feel more welcome. About 80 per cent of the members of the COS should be elected by subscribers but one-fifth of the members should come from the outside – and include a liberal number of responsible members of the working classes. See *OP* (1893), pp. 212, 219.

91. Letter to *The Times* of 15 February 1886, p. 13.
92. Letter to the Rev. J. Llewellyn Davies dated February 1886, in *Memorials*, p. 373. The best leaders of the working classes are opposed to aid being given recklessly to the idle and the profligate and their cooperation must be enlisted in convincing others that the reforms which Marshall proposes will not be 'needlessly harsh, offensive, and patronising'. It is good that, 'in spite of occasional setbacks, their influence is increasing', for the truth is that they are now 'the mainstay of our hopes' – since 'to the foresight, moderation, and public spirit of the working classes themselves we must trust for much of the sympathy and the force needed to assist and to discipline the Residuum out of existence' ('Poor Law Reform', *Economic Journal*, Vol. II, 1892, pp. 375, 376, 377). No decent man wants to pamper the most worthless, and that in itself is an important cause of social change so long as the most worthless have any sensitivity at all to the informal judgements of others. See also the letter cited in the previous footnote.
93. *EI*, p. 193.
94. *EI*, p. 193.
95. *PE*, p. 591.
96. *IRC*, p. 176. The suggestion that innocent parties need to be protected against technological improvement, the fickleness of fashion and other 'social facts' is an interesting variant of the spillovers argument, where the spillovers from the majority to the minority are negative in nature and where, because the collectivity derives the ultimate benefit, it would be morally wrong to let the diswelfares lie where they fall. Institutionalised altruism on the part of the beneficiaries in favour of the victims figures prominently in the work of theoreticians of the welfare state such as Richard Titmuss.
97. See the comments in *IRC* and also the report of the discussion by George Bernard Shaw in *Commonweal*, March 1885, p. 15.
98. *EI*, p. 30.
99. Letter from the Reverend J. Llewellyn Davies to *The Times* of 19 February 1886, p. 14.
100. *IRC*, p. 175.
101. Letter to *The Times* of 15 February 1886, p. 13. Note there is no reference to the pump-priming impact of such fiscal policies.
102. If there is a long-term falling-off in demand for a commodity, then, Marshall believed, those who make it will have sooner or later to drift into alternative employment. It is economically inefficient – and not even particularly kindly to the beneficiaries – to employ artificial means to postpone the inevitable. It will be recalled that Marshall was also critical of trades-unions for their wasteful 'make-work' policies. See, for

example, his letter to Edward Caird dated 5 December 1897, in *Memorials*, p. 399.
103. Letter to Percy Alden dated 28 January 1903, in *Memorials*, p. 447.
104. *PE*, p. 2.
105. Letter to the Reverend J. Llewellyn Davies dated February 1886, in *Memorials*, p. 373.

5.4 Industry and Trade

1. 'Some Aspects of Competition' (1890), in *Memorials*, p. 274.
2. 'Some Aspects of Competition' (1890), in *Memorials*, p. 277.
3. *PE*, p. 376.
4. See on this *EAM*, esp. Chapter 6.4.
5. *IT*, p. 627.
6. 'Some Aspects of Competition' (1890), in *Memorials*, p. 289. He goes on to say that collusive arrangements of this nature might even 'have to be broken up by public force' – a topic to which he, perhaps wisely, does not return.
7. See *EAM*, Chapter 5.2.
8. *IT*, p. 527.
9. *IT*, p. 442.
10. *IT*, pp. 516–7. Final consumers can seldom be consulted – since they 'seldom have the special knowledge required for ascertaining exactly where their interests lie in the matter under discussion; or the organization required for setting out their case' (*IT*, p. 443). Indeed, should final consumers alone (and not other producers) suffer from, say, high prices brought about by high railway charges, there is a good chance that the abuse would not translate itself into actual complaint at all: 'The public would suffer: but they are not vocal, unless strongly aroused; and probably they would not be' (*IT*, p. 472).
11. *IT*, p. 442.
12. *IT*, p. 543.
13. *IT*, p. 443. Ignorance here leads to a paternalism – a distinction between 'needs' and 'wants' – which is more usual in Marshall's theory of the status of consumption (see on this *EAM*, Chapter 2.4) than in his theory of State intervention (which relies heavily on legitimation of action by means of consensus and public opinion). Perhaps the point Marshall is making is that 'able men' with specialist knowledge of a question but no vested interest in a particular solution represent the consumer and seek to speak as he would have spoken if in full possession of the requisite facts and theories. In a sense the eclectic test of 'good performance' is no more than this.
14. *OP* (1903), p. 413.
15. *IT*, p. 844.
16. *IT*, p. 517.
17. *IT*, pp. 574–5.
18. *IT*, p. 518. But he was not suggesting that Britain adopt similar

legislation – and when all is said and done, we are left in the dark as to whether destructive combinations should be broken up.

19. *IT*, p. 272.
20. *IT*, p. 536.
21. *IT*, p. 597.
22. *IT*, p. 479.
23. *IT*, p. 787.
24. *IT*, p. 656. National character, like public opinion, is actively involved in the campaign to combat restrictive practices; and underlying national character is the fundamental biological absolute of race (see *EAM*, Chapter 7.3). As good fortune would have it, the Anglo-Saxon shows traits of 'self-restraint' and 'resolute persistence' and thus develops a national character which is hostile to the more anti-social manifestations of the market turned malign – 'and as an indirect, but perhaps necessary, consequence of this character, both competition and combination in Anglo-Saxon countries generally have been more inclined to construction than to destruction' (*IT*, p. 656). In fact, race and national character would seem to have done much to keep even the Americans in line, occasional 'violent ebullitions of competition, chiefly in pursuit of monopolistic combination' notwithstanding: 'America has attracted the most eager and excitable strains of the Anglo-Saxon, the Celtic, and Slavonic races: and yet Anglo-Saxon moderation and stability have enabled competitive and monopolistic abuses to be kept within relatively narrow limits, with but little direct intervention of authority' (*IT*, p. 656). The inclusion of such arguments in a theory of the control of monopoly is by no means a commonplace in economics.
25. *IT*, p. 491.
26. *IT*, p. 491.
27. As Marshall puts it in 'Some Aspects of Competition' (1890) (in *Memorials*, p. 289): 'It is clear that combinations and partial monopolies will play a great part in future economic history; that their effects contain much good as well as much evil; and that to denounce them without discrimination would be to repeat the error which our forefathers made with regard to Protection .... It is ... a matter of pressing urgency that public opinion should accustom itself to deal with such questions.'
28. 'Social Possibilities of Economic Chivalry' (1907), in *Memorials*, p. 339.
29. *IT*, p. 668.
30. See *IT*, pp. 668–9.
31. *IT*, p. 668.
32. Letter to *The Times* of 24 March 1891, p. 11.
33. *IT*, p. 398.
34. *OP* (1897), p. 336.
35. Letter to *The Times* of 24 March 1891, p. 11.
36. Smith, *Wealth of Nations*, Vol. II, p. 246.
37. Letter to *The Times* of 6 April 1891, p. 13.
38. Letter to *The Times* of 6 April 1891, p. 13.
39. Letter to *The Times* of 24 March 1891, p. 11.
40. Letter to *The Times* of 6 April 1891, p. 13.

41. *IT*, p. 428.
42. *PE*, pp. 241–2.
43. 'Social Possibilities of Economic Chivalry' (1907), in *Memorials*, p. 339. Emphasis added. The debate naturally hinges on the word 'inevitable'. In view of the length of Marshall's explicit shopping-list, one wishes he had said more about the relationship between *inevitable* monopoly and State ownership.
44. Undated fragment, in *Memorials*, p. 364.
45. 'Some Aspects of Competition' (1890), in *Memorials*, p. 277.
46. 'Some Aspects of Competition' (1890), in *Memorials*, p. 275.
47. 'Some Aspects of Competition' (1890), in *Memorials*, p. 275. Pigou, apparently unaware that Marshall had made this suggestion, infers, interestingly, that it would have been much to his liking. Thus, Pigou writes, Marshall was hostile to State-run industry (in the sense of management by public department) – but there is 'one modern development of which he had had practically no experience and which, had he been able to reckon with it, might perhaps have made him less unbending.' That modern development involves the rise of autonomous State corporations (the BBC, for example) which are, 'in their day-to-day working, independent bodies for whose operations ministers can disclaim responsibility. They are thus in some degree outside politics. Further, they are not operated by those Civil Service methods which it is generally agreed are unsuitable for, and deadening in, industry.' Pigou adds that, while Marshall would have preferred public-sector corporations to civil service departments, he would nonetheless 'have put the burden of proof' firmly on those who wanted private enterprise to be superseded by what is unambiguously a second-best alternative. See A. C. Pigou. *Alfred Marshall and Current Thought* (London: Macmillan, 1953), pp. 61, 62.
48. Letter to *The Times* of 6 April 1891, p. 13.
49. In his letter to *The Times* of 24 April 1891, p. 11, Marshall writes as follows on the vexed question of accountability, in this case of the Post Office: 'It may be conceded that postal business suffers less from being under a Government monopoly than any other, except some affairs of local concern, such as water supply. For every negligence of the common postman is as patent to the persons injured by it, and therefore to their representatives in Parliament and the Press, as the sluggishness of dockyard officials is concealed from all critical eyes.' The crucial scarce input, here as elsewhere, would seem to be information – since press, Parliament and public opinion can only be expected to spring to the defence of the injured party where that injured party actually perceives himself to be injured. The willingness of press and Parliament to champion injured parties is, of course, open to question – as is the desirability of such outside intervention (an important topic which we consider in more detail in Chapter 4.2).
50. *IT*, p. 428n.
51. *IT*, p. 787.
52. *IT*, p. 787.
53. *IT*, p. 787.

54. *IT*, p. 498.
55. *IT*, p. 502.
56. *IT*, p. 502.
57. *IT*, p. 787. Emphasis added. Despite the success of central control and direction of railways in wartime, however, it is vital to keep two points in mind. First, the administrators and the techniques being unchanged in the industry despite the extension of overall State authority, 'nearly the whole of the brains, by which it has been directed, had been developed under the stimulating influences of free enterprise' (*IT*, p. 492). Second, in the wartime period of coordinated control trains were long and wagons full (i.e. plant was used economically and with minimal wastage or excess capacity) – but there were also 'delays', 'discomforts' and 'restrictions' (*IT*, p. 492) such as would have been singularly unpopular in peacetime with a singularly vocal class of consumer. At least centralised control and direction of the railways does not appear to have led to managerial slack or induced x-inefficiency. A similar result is recorded for the munitions industries, although accompanied by a reminder that the generally patriotic and altruistic atmosphere of the First World War had an important role to play in repressing what would otherwise have been the normal mode of behaviour: 'The centralized control of the munitions' industries has been aided by so much unselfish energy, that it seems to have been but little affected by the comatose slackness which frequently hinders Governmental industries from reaping the full fruits of their advantages of position' (*IT*, p. 226). Neither the railways nor the munitions industries, one must conclude, represents a particularly convincing argument for the retention of centralised control and direction once the national emergency has receded.
58. This is a further similarity between Marshall and Tawney.
59. Smith, *Wealth of Nations*, Vol. II, p. 244.
60. *IT*, p. 506.
61. *IT*, p. 506.
62. *IT*, p. 785.
63. *IT*, p. 831.
64. *IT*, p. 831.
65. *IT*, p. 498.
66. *IT*, p. 498.
67. *IT*, p. 831.
68. *IT*, p. 505.
69. *OP* (1897), p. 360. The passage cited refers specifically to water and reads in full as follows: 'As regards the supply of water, local interests cannot be isolated. The chief sources of water supply should therefore be declared national property; and, after compensation to private owners, they should be leased, subject to conditions, to local authorities.'
70. Undated fragment, in *Memorials*, p. 363.
71. 'Social Possibilities of Economic Chivalry' (1907), in *Memorials*, p. 337.
72. *IT*, p. 547. The lesson emerging from the US experience is clear – that systematic study is essential, and that decisions concerning allegedly

anti-social practices of trusts 'can be efficiently made only by a strong staff of men who give their whole time to the work' (*IT*, p. 543).

73. *IT*, p. 634. The State itself thus becomes a manipulator, if only through 'full publicity' and Commissions of Inquiry 'sitting with open doors'. Marshall's concern with public opinion is important and shows that he believed strongly in the need for democratic legitimation even of quite *micro*-economic policy decisions. It is reassuring in these circumstances to see that the manipulation he has in mind is of the full-publicity rather than the selective-revelation mode.
74. *OP* (1886), p. 10. But what is true for macroeconomics is apparently not true for microeconomics since Marshall makes no proposal for the dissemination by the State of sector-specific economic statistics. On the contrary: in a note in the margin of his personal copy of Pigou's *Wealth and Welfare*, at the point where Pigou states that the volatility of business expectations could be modulated were the government to publish monthly data on building, Marshall expresses his adverse reaction by commenting 'But it is already done by trade journals better than it could be by government'. See Bharadwaj, 'Marshall on Pigou's *Wealth and Welfare*' (Chapter 5.1, note 64). In Wood IV, p. 212.
75. *IT*, p. 100.
76. *IT*, p. 180.
77. *IT*, p. 101. A modern analogy might be the purchase by the State of a minority shareholding in a private corporation so as to enable itself in that way to keep a meaningful watching brief.
78. *IT*, pp. 608–9.
79. *IT*, p. 180.
80. *IT*, p. 100.
81. *IT*, p. 100.
82. *IT*, p. 99.
83. 'Some Aspects of Competition' (1890), in *Memorials*, p. 289.
84. 'Some Aspects of Competition' (1890), in *Memorials*, p. 267.
85. 'Some Aspects of Competition' (1890), in *Memorials*, p. 266.
86. *IT*, p. 85.
87. As is demonstrated by the fact that, despite his habitual fear of controversy, he was ultimately persuaded to sign the letter in defence of free trade – the 'manifesto' of the 'fourteen professors' – which appeared in *The Times* of 15 August 1903. See on this A. W Coats, 'Political Economy and the Tariff Reform Campaign of 1903', *Journal of Law and Economics*, Vol. 2, 1968.
88. *IT*, p. 138.
89. *MCC*, p. 212.
90. *MCC*, p. 212.
91. 'The Theory of Foreign Trade' (1873–7), in Whitaker II, p. 69.
92. *IT*, p. 139.
93. *OP* (1903), p. 378.
94. See *OP* (1899), p. 315 and the discussion of the Gold Standard in the following Chapter of the present volume.
95. 'The Theory of Foreign Trade' (1873–7), in Whitaker II, p. 96.
96. *IT*, p. 120. Marshall does admit that even in France protective

intervention can have a stimulatory rather than a depressant effect, provided that those business men who receive the support 'are exceptionally full of energy and encouraged by openings for great work' – but the operative word is 'exceptionally', and that is precisely why such support does not *normally* lead to such a positive outcome.

97. *OP* (1903), p. 376.
98. *IT*, p. 16.
99. *OP* (1903), pp. 408–9.
100. 'Co-operation' (1889), in *Memorials*, p. 243.
101. *IT*, p. 65. The doctrine that large-scale production for home consumption normally precedes penetration of world markets is an important one and is stated by Marshall in several places – most fully, perhaps, in the following passage: 'No country has ever attained leadership in manufacture for export, without previously developing manufacture on a rather large scale for domestic consumption: but the export trade affords exceptional opportunities for dealing on a large scale; and this, in its turn, tends to promote manufacture on a large scale' (*MCC*, p. 351). The world market undeniably allows us to reap economies of size and to keep in touch with new developments – but in order to be competitive internationally, Marshall seems to be saying, we must first have reached a minimum scale of output at home. Thus it is that the *international* division of labour comes to be a function of the size of the market. Time and evolution are, here as elsewhere, central to the argument which Marshall presents.
102. *OP* (1903), p. 379.
103. Letter to *The Times* of 23 November 1903, p. 10.
104. 'Some Aspects of Competition' (1890), in *Memorials*, p. 263.
105. *PE*, p. 385.
106. *OP* (1903), pp. 418, 419.
107. *OP* (1903), p. 394.
108. Discussion on F. Schuster's paper 'Foreign Trade and the Money Market', Institute of Bankers, 16 December 1903. In *Journal of the Institute of Bankers*, Vol. xxv, 1904, p. 97.
109. Discussion on F. Schuster's paper 'Foreign Trade and the Money Market', Institute of Bankers, 16 December 1903. In *Journal of the Institute of Bankers*, Vol. xxv, 1904, pp. 94–5.
110. Letter to B. Mukherjee dated 12 April 1911, in *Memorials*, p. 474.
111. *OP* (1903), p. 394.
112. *OP* (1903), p. 399.
113. Letter to Lord Reay dated 12 November 1909, in *Memorials*, p. 463.
114. *IT*, p. 653. Moral tone and considerations of justice are prominent in this passage – as one would have expected.

6 MACROECONOMIC POLICY

1. Keynes, 'Alfred Marshall, 1842–1924', in *Memorials*, p. 27. Eshag is

less confident about the pathbreaking nature of Marshall's contribution and points to the influence on his work of authors such as Thornton, Ricardo, Mill, Bagehot, Overstone, Giffen, Goschen and others: 'It is very difficult indeed to discover any important original ideas in the work of Marshall on money in relation to the works of his predecessors and contemporaries. Similarly, it is not easy to find many significant new notions in the writings of Marshall's pupils which were not known either to Marshall himself or to some other earlier writers.' See E. Eshag, *From Marshall to Keynes* (Oxford: Basil Blackwell, 1963), p. xiii.

2. K. Wicksell, *Interest and Prices* (1898), translated by R. F. Kahn (London: Macmillan, 1936), p. 77. Marshall, it must be stressed, was fully aware that the microeconomic maximising with which Volume I is predominantly concerned is in no sense to be regarded as the whole of economics. Thus he says that, for the sake of simplicity, 'we may throughout this volume neglect changes in the general purchasing power of money' (*PE*, p. 51), but he also confesses that on such a level of abstraction singularly few 'practical conclusions' can in the real world usefully be reached: 'In real life nearly every economic issue depends, more or less directly, on some complex actions and reactions of credit' (*PE*, p. 601), along with other influences similarly neglected in the first volume of what was to be a two-volume treatise. Marshall made clear what he was consciously omitting from his Volume I, but there is still some truth in Blaug's statement on Marshall's book, that 'his total neglect of monetary forces in a work on the principles of economics, however much he warned his readers of this failing, did much to persuade economists that monetary theory belonged to the periphery of the science.' See M. Blaug, *Economic Theory in Retrospect*, 4th edn (Cambridge: The University Press, 1985), p. 421.
3. Keynes, 'Alfred Marshall, 1842–1924', in *Memorials*, p. 28. It must be recorded, however, that most of the main works of the authors most unambiguously to be regarded as Marshall's 'pupils' – men like Pigou, Hawtrey, Lavington, Keynes himself and Robertson – appeared after rather than before 1923.
4. Keynes, 'Alfred Marshall, 18421–1924', in *Memorials*, p. 28. The manuscript to which Keynes refers, now in the Marshall Library, has subsequently been published as the 'Essay on Money' (circa 1871), in Whitaker I, pp. 165–76. The continuity which it demonstrates in Marshall's monetary thought is particularly interesting in view of the fact that Marshall was from an early age fond of lecturing to his Cambridge students on monetary and macroeconomic topics, and of discussing such themes with his colleagues. If many of his principal ideas were known before 1923, the reason is thus likely to have been Marshall's habit of making a free gift of his latest concepts through the intermediary of the Cambridge oral tradition. Forty or fifty years of lectures and discussions are bound to have an impact. Much of Marshall's influence on monetary thought is surely to be explained not so much in terms of originality *per se* as in terms of didactic effort (formal and informal) over an extended period of time.

6.1 The Quantity Theory of Money

1. See J. R. Hicks, 'A Suggestion for Simplifying the Theory of Money', Economica, Vol.II, 1935, esp. p. 2.
2. *PE*, p. 652.
3. 'Essay on Money' (circa 1871), in Whitaker I, p. 166.
4. *MCC*, p. 38.
5. 'Essay on Money' (circa 1871), in Whitaker I, pp. 166–7.
6. 'Essay on Money' (circa 1871), in Whitaker I, p. 167.
7. 'Essay on Money' (circa 1871), in Whitaker I, p. 174.
8. 'Essay on Money' (circa 1871), in Whitaker I, p. 176.
9. *MCC*, p. 49.
10. *OP* (1899), p. 323.
11. *MCC*, p. 15.
12. *MCC*, p. 13.
13. *MCC*, p. 16.
14. *MCC*, p. 12.
15. *MCC*, p. 12.
16. *OP* (1887), p. 35.
17. *MCC*, p. 12.
18. *MCC*, p. 14.
19. *OP* (1899), p. 282.
20. *OP* (1887), p. 180.
21. *EI*, p. 151.
22. *OP* (1887), pp. 35–6.
23. *MCC*, p. 43. And elsewhere (*MCC*, p. 46): 'The large trader holds relatively little currency in a modern country in which nearly all considerable payments are made by cheques.'
24. *MCC*, p. 46.
25. *OP* (1899), p. 268.
26. *OP* (1887), p. 44.
27. *OP* (1887), p. 140.
28. *MCC*, p. 228.
29. *MCC*, p. 39.
30. *OP* (1887), p. 37.
31. *OP* (1887), p. 37.
32. R. Giffen, *Stock Exchange Securities* (London: George Bell & Sons, 1877), p. 31.
33. Quoted in Eshag, *From Marshall to Keynes*, p. 16.
34. *OP* (1887), p. 23.
35. *MCC*, p. 149.
36. *MCC*, p. 57.
37. *MCC*, p. 12.
38. *MCC*, p. 149.
39. *MCC*, pp. 12–13.
40. *MCC*, p. 19.
41. H. Thornton, *The Paper Credit of Great Britain* (1802) (London: Frank Cass & Co. Ltd, 1962), p. 85. Marshall refers directly to Thornton in

MCC, pp. 83n, 304, 307. His own annotated copy of the *Paper Credit* is kept in the University Library, Cambridge.

42. *MCC*, p. 14.
43. *MCC*, pp. 14–5.
44. *MCC*, p. 43.
45. *EI*, p. 151.
46. *MCC*, p. 15.
47. *MCC*, p. 15.
48. Wicksell, *Interest and Prices*, pp. 41–2.
49. Thornton, *The Paper Credit of Great Britain*, p. 267. Elsewhere (p. 101) Thornton writes as follows concerning man's inventiveness with respect to spendable assets: 'If bills and bank notes were extinguished, other substitutes than gold would unquestionably be found.'
50. 'Essay on Money' (circa 1871), in Whitaker I, p. 173.
51. *EI*, p. 151.
52. *OP* (1887), p. 39.
53. *OP* (1899), p. 306.
54. *MCC*, p. 230.
55. *MCC*, p. 13.
56. *MCC*, p. 43.
57. *OP* (1887), p. 35.
58. *MCC*, p. 45.
59. *OP* (1887), p. 36.
60. *OP* (1887), p. 43.
61. *OP* (1887), p. 43. In *MCC* (p. 44) he says that the amount of money demanded depends on both 'annual income' and 'property', He does not, however, develop this distinction further, thus leaving unanswered the question of whether the demand for money depends more on the stock or on the flow.
62. *OP* (1887), p. 45.
63. *MCC*, p. 45.
64. *MCC*, pp. 38–9.
65. *MCC*, p. 46.
66. *MCC*, p. 47.
67. *MCC*, pp. 47–8. And elsewhere, in *OP* (1899), p. 269: 'The lower is the credit of the currency, the lower will be the share of their resources which people care to keep in the form of currency . . . . If the credit of a currency falls, its value falls relatively to commodities, even when there is no change in its volume.' The reason for the fall in value to which Marshall refers is the rise in prices consequent upon the unexpected dumping of unwanted cash. It is worth mentioning, at the risk of anticipating arguments to be examined later in this Chapter, that the rise in effective demand is likely to have an impact on other variables besides prices alone (employment, interest and output, for example) and that further adjustments in the economic system will then occur.
68. *OP* (1886), p. 6. Henry Thornton makes a similar point when discussing the causes 'which lead to a variation in the rapidity of the circulation of bank notes' – one of them being, of course, the 'state of confidence': 'A

high state of confidence contributes to make men provide less amply against contingencies... When, on the contrary, a season of distrust arises, prudence suggests, that the loss of interest arising from a detention of notes for a few additional days should not be regarded.' (Thornton, *The Paper Credit of Great Britain*, pp. 96–7). Unless, of course, the distrust relates specifically to the notes themselves, as was the case with the *assignats*: their value reflected 'their credit' as well as 'their quantity', and over-issue of the latter 'operated on' the former to its extreme detriment' (*ibid.*, p. 233). Otherwise, however, distrust militates in favour of hoarding, to Thornton as to Marshall. Neither author seems to have recognised that by attributing utility to money *per se* he was simultaneously refuting that naive version of Say's Law which states that I supply a deer in order to demand a beaver. Once I am entitled to demand cash in preference to beaver, an important question of a macroeconomic nature must be asked and neither author explicitly did so.

69. *OP* (1886), p. 6.
70. For an extended discussion of this problem see *EAM*, Chapter 3.2.
71. Thornton, in the passage quoted in note 68, treats the rate of interest as the relevant opportunity cost with respect to cash balances, and elsewhere (p. 76) clearly propounds the doctrine that the 'expence' of keeping stocks of money is 'an expence consisting chiefly in the loss of interest'. Marshall regarded consumption as well as investment (financial or real) as a genuine alternative to holding cash, but the presence of the former variable should not cause us to forget the presence of the latter. Marshall indeed refers specifically to the 'stock exchange security' – a term which can without difficulty encompass the Consols which figure so prominently in the Keynesian approach and which in addition recalls *Stock Exchange Securities*, in which (p. 154) Giffen writes as follows: 'It must also be recognised that for ordinary investors a practical choice must often be made between buying at a high price or foregoing an income for the time. It does not always answer to wait, for there is a loss of interest in waiting.' Marshall, familiar with the work of both Thornton and Giffen and capable himself of treating investments as a substitute for cash, could have said more about the interest-related speculative motive but had a lucid appreciation of it nonetheless.
72. J. M. Keynes, *The General Theory of Employment, Interest and Money* (1936) (London: Macmillan, 1961), p. 174.
73. *OP* (1887), p. 172.
74. *OP* (1887), p. 179.
75. *OP* (1887), p. 176. Emphasis added.
76. *MCC*, p. 48.
77. *OP* (1899), p. 267.
78. D. Ricardo, *The High Price of Bullion* (1810–11), in *The Works and Correspondence of David Ricardo*, ed. by P. Sraffa (Cambridge: The University Press, 1962), Vol. III, p. 90.
79. *OP* (1887), p. 34. Earlier in his evidence, comparing statistics on annual production of gold with statistics on movements of general prices, he

had declared (p. 21) that 'we find that there is no intimate connection between them. While accepting the doctrine that, "*other things being equal*, prices rise or fall proportionately to every increase or diminution in the metal or metals which are used as the standard of value", I consider that the conditioning clause "other things being equal", is of overwhelming importance and requires careful attention.' Later in his evidence (p. 54) he was to make his point even more decisively: 'I do not consider that the main causes of fluctuations of prices have been fluctuations in the supplies of the precious metals. I believe that changes in the methods of business and the amounts of the commodities, or, as we may say, changes in the commercial environment, have much greater effects in disturbing prices than changes in these supplies of the precious metals.'

80. *IT*, p. 756. See also *EI*, pp. 150–1, for a further discussion of money and prices in the early nineteenth century: 'No important fresh supplies of metals came from the mines till 1850. During that time the stock of precious metals was being diminished by their use in the industrial arts and by wear and tear; and meanwhile population and wealth were increasing rapidly. So the purchasing power of gold rose; and prices fell.' Why credit or some other 'permanent substitute for the precious metals' did not simply replace one medium with another is not explained.
81. *MCC*, p. 41.
82. *OP* (1899), pp. 306–7. The situation in India is reminiscent of the position in Europe at the time of the 'price revolution' of the sixteenth century. Both illustrations tend to support Marshall's underlying theoretical hypothesis, which is in effect that, if money 'increases very fast', then 'there will be more than is wanted to carry on the business of the country at the old prices, and prices will rise' (*EI*, p. 150). Marshall's confidence in the evidence he cites is surprising in the light of the statements quoted above concerning the relative importance of variables other than money. His confidence is surprising in addition in view of his own reservations concerning the limitations of our knowledge – as, for instance, in *OP* (1887), p. 34: 'I think that we have not the statistics, and that we shall not, in this generation, be able to get the statistics which would enable us to trace any statistical connection between the amount of the precious metals, or, as I would prefer to say, between the amount of currency and the average level of prices.' And elsewhere, in *OP* (1887), p. 57, he gives the following illustration of spurious correlation by way of warning against excessive reliance on the inductive approach of letting the facts speak for themselves: 'For about fifty years from 1820 the mean price of wheat in terms of gold remained almost stationary; and if we applied the method of concomitant variations hastily, we might say that that showed that there was a connection between the two. But the real explanation of the stationariness of the gold price of wheat is that until 1850 there was a continually growing scarcity of wheat accompanied by a growing scarcity of gold.' The most favourable comment one can make is that Marshall must have selected the statistics he cites from data which he

regarded as 'trustworthy' and that he took care to apply the test of theory before reporting his evidence.

83. See, for example, the 'Essay on Money' (circa 1871), in Whitaker I, p. 131, where Marshall writes as follows concerning the transactions demand for currency: 'If carriage makers bought the wheels of their carriages instead of making them themselves, the number of transactions involved in making a carriage would be increased and the change would disturb our calculations.'
84. Marshall does not, of course, make use of any algebraic formulation of this kind – not even the so-called Cambridge cash balance equation of M = kPY. The principal reason is that Marshall feared that such a proposition could all too easily acquire the status of a tautology. As he explains in *OP* (1887), p. 159: 'If the only change is a change in the supply of gold; if the real wealth of the country is just the same as it was before, and the habits which people have of paying certain shop bills by cheques and certain shop bills by cash remain the same as before, then it follows it is an identical proposition, merely saying the same thing in other words, that they get the same purchasing power in their pockets as before, and if prices have fallen 10 per cent. they therefore have 10 per cent. less coin in their pockets.' To a loose constructionist with respect to spendable assets who believed in addition that velocity is determined by a continuous balancing of advantages and disadvantages at the margin, both M and k are fully endogenous to the model, and the equation accordingly loses much of its predictive power.
85. Thornton, *The Paper Credit of Great Britain*, p. 197.
86. Giffen, *Stock Exchange Securities*, p. 6.
87. Wicksell, *Interest and Prices*, p. 42. Like Marshall, Wicksell was concerned lest the quantity theorist fall victim to his own propaganda and come to confuse the simplified abstraction with the genuine prediction: 'The Theory provides a real explanation of its subject matter, and in a manner that is logically incontestable; but only on assumptions that unfortunately have little relation to practice.... It assumes that everybody maintains, or at least strives to maintain, his balance at an average level that is constant (relatively to the extent of his business or his payments). Or, what really comes to the same thing, that the *velocity of circulation* of money is, as it were, a fixed, inflexible magnitude, fluctuating about a constant average level; whereas in practice it expands and contracts quite automatically and at the same time is capable, particularly as a result of economic progress, of almost any desired increase, while in theory its elasticity is unlimited' (*ibid.*, p. 41). Wicksell was clearly not a theorist who treated the velocity of money in a legalistic, mechanistic manner, as a fixed accounting magnitude and nothing else. But when all is said and done, even a subjectivist can conclude – on the basis of contingent empirical information and without prejudice to the viscosity of his theoretical structure – that velocity is *relatively* stable, and such was the case (*ibid.*, pp. 61–2) with Wicksell: 'The velocity of circulation of money is now seen to be a somewhat elastic quantity, but it still possesses sufficient powers of resistance against expansion or contraction for the conclu-

sions of the Quantity Theory to retain the appearance of substantial validity.' It is likely that Marshall would have had considerable sympathy with this conclusion. Whether the continuous maximisation of utility which is at the centre of his model gives sufficient grounds for such sympathy is, however, another matter.

88. I. Fisher, *The Purchasing Power of Money* (1911) (New York: Augustus M. Kelley, 1963), pp. 71, 159, 161.
89. *MCC*, p. 48.
90. *OP* (1899), p. 268.

6.2 The Transmission Mechanism

1. *OP* (1887), pp. 51–2.
2. *OP* (1899), p. 323.
3. *OP* (1899), p. 323.
4. *OP* (1887), p. 65.
5. D. Patinkin, *Money, Interest, and Prices*, 2nd edn (New York: Harper & Row, Ltd., 1965), p. 173. The dichotomy means that absolute prices are determined by the money-supply and its velocity while relative prices are determined by (microeconomic) utility at the margin. At least (once the cost of production approach to value had been abandoned) the nature of valuation in both sectors was based on the same principle, namely that of subjective estimation.
6. *OP* (1887), p. 38.
7. *OP* (1887), p. 52. This account is similar to that of Thornton, who writes as follows in *Paper Credit* (p. 235) about a banker who acquires the ability to issue extra paper currency: 'He will make haste to part with the whole superfluous quantity; he will offer to lend it to any safe merchants, and even at a reduced rate of interest, in case he shall find that borrowers cannot otherwise be invited.' And even Ricardo acknowledges the short-run impact of money on interest: 'I do not dispute, that if the Bank were to bring a large additional sum of notes into the market, and offer them on loan, but that they would *for a time* affect the rate of interest.' (*The High Price of Bullion*, p. 91, emphasis added). It would evidently be incorrect to maintain that the classical quantity theory neglected the non-neutrality of money, despite the undeniable propensity of classical authors (notably Ricardo) to theorise in terms of long-run equilibrium states.
8. *EI*, p. 163.
9. *EI*, p. 122.
10. *OP* (1887), p. 41.
11. *OP* (1887), p. 45.
12. *OP* (1887), p. 51.
13. *OP* (1887), p. 41.
14. See *EAM*, Chapter 10.2
15. *OP* (1887), p. 51.
16. *OP* (1899), p. 270.

17. *PE*, p. 443.
18. D. Ricardo. Letter to the Editor of the *Morning Chronicle*, 18 September 1810, in *Works*, Vol. III, p. 143.
19. J. S. Mill, *Principles of Political Economy* (1848), ed. W. J. Ashley (New York: Augustus M. Kelley, 1965), p. 647.
20. Keynes, in the *General Theory* (p. 3n) defines 'the classical school' as 'the followers of Ricardo, those, that is to say, who adopted and perfected the theory of Ricardian economics, including (for example) J. S. Mill, Marshall, Edgeworth and Prof. Pigou'.
21. *MCC*, p. 255.
22. *PE*, p. 443.
23. *PE*, p. 492.
24. *MCC*, p. 254.
25. *OP* (1887), p. 130.
26. *OP* (1887), p. 45.
27. *MCC*, p. 255.
28. *EI*, p. 126.
29. *EI*, p. 126.
30. *OP* (1887), p. 49.
31. *OP* (1887), p. 49.
32. *OP* (1887), p. 49.
33. *PE*, p. 190.
34. *PE*, p. 443. In the market period, needless to say, interest is not a functional reward but – like the price of fresh fish in such a situation – a demand-determined surplus: 'The annual addition to the capital of a country is not any considerable part of the whole, so that if we consider only short periods of time we may, without any great error, regard the supply as fixed during that time. On this supposition, the Law of the rate of interest becomes similar to that of the value of a commodity, the amount of which cannot be increased: Demand is the sole regulator of value' (*EI*, p. 124). The passage of time, however, permits of genuine (if lagged) responsiveness in the supply schedule of savings in response to (perhaps a change in) anticipated reward, and at that stage interest does become an authentic decision-variable with respect to the supply of toil and trouble: 'We are justified in speaking of the interest on capital as the reward of the sacrifice involved in the waiting for the enjoyment of material resources, because few people would save much without reward; just as we speak of wages as the reward of labour, because few people would work hard without reward' (*PE*, p. 193). At the same time, the reward need not be pecuniary. Marshall's belief that people would want to save something at a zero or even at a negative rate of interest reminds us that, while the supply schedule in question might accurately describe the relationship between extra interest and extra savings, the total picture is somewhat more complicated.
35. *PE*, p. 195.
36. *PE*, p. 195.
37. *OP* (1887), p. 51.
38. *PE*, pp. 443–4. The words 'for a time' are important but also ambiguous: on one interpretation the time-lag in question might be no

more than that perfectly normal period of time that must always elapse when something not supplied off the peg must be made to measure, while on another interpretation the lag might be due to full employment of men and machines in the capital goods industries (reflecting a similar absence of excess capacity in the economy as a whole). Related to this is a second ambiguity, that even if more capital goods genuinely cannot be produced and the existing stocks of plant must in consequence be rationed, it is still not clear why rationing caused by excess demand should take the form of rationing by a rise in the rate of interest. As Keynes grumbles in the *General Theory* (p. 187n), 'why not by a rise in the supply price of capital-goods?' Such a rise in the price of an input pulls down profit-rates (as an alternative to pushing up interest rates) and thereby restores equilibrium in the market for funds. The quotation we are examining, however, states explicitly that interest-rates rise – which suggests implicitly that the price of real capital (at least in the short-run) does not. But demand for finance does normally precede demand for goods then bought with that finance, and perhaps such process-analysis is what Marshall had in mind.

39. Keynes, *General Theory*, p. 242. Keynes's approach turns out to be somewhat less dynamic than that of Marshall, however, since he then explains (pp. 242–3) that the reason why there can exist more than one equilibrium level of the rate of interest in an economy is that there can exist more than one equilibrium level of employment (and therefore of national income): 'It was a mistake to speak of *the* natural rate of interest or to suggest that the above definition would yield a unique value for the rate of interest irrespective of the level of employment. I had not then understood that, in certain conditions, the system could be in equilibrium with less than full employment.'
40. *OP* (1887), p. 168.
41. *OP* (1887), p. 168.
42. *OP* (1887), p. 52.
43. 'Remedies for Fluctuations of General Prices' (1887), in *Memorials*, p. 190. The implication in passages such as this is that there is an implicit price-index and that it is this index of the general level of prices which rises. An explicit index did not, of course, exist in Marshall's time.
44. *OP* (1899), p. 285.
45. *MCC*, p. 38. Emphasis added.
46. *MCC*, p. 44.
47. *MCC*, pp. 47–8.
48. *OP* (1899), p. 269.
49. *MCC*, p. 225.
50. *OP* (1899), p. 297.
51. This is reassuring in view of the well-known phenomenon that institutional arrangements such as payments-periods tend to alter as inflation gives way to hyper-inflation – and, obviously, 'a sufficient change in the methods of business would enable prices to be ten times as they are with the same amount of gold and silver'. See *OP* (1887), p. 39.
52. *OP* (1887), p. 38.

53. *OP* (1887), p. 35. Not only is it relevant to know the change in the volume of things for sale ('with regard to that no doubt we have fairly good statistics') but we need also to know something of the 'increase or diminution in the average number of times each of these things changes hands during the year' ('and with regard to that we have no statistics whatever'). The point being made is the important one that I can spend my money on an old painting as well as on a new car – even though the former case relates to a simple transfer of assets and only the latter case involves net value added.
54. *OP* (1899), p. 271. Note the mix of real and monetary influences on the rate of interest.
55. *OP* (1899), p. 271. Since high interest-rates and high prices go together, the investor would appear to have not one reason but two for running down his cash balances, thereby boosting their 'rapidity of circulation' and presumably fueling the flames of inflation as a consequence.
56. *OP* (1887), p. 131.
57. *OP* (1887), p. 22.
58. *OP* (1899), p. 270.
59. *MCC*, p. 254.
60. *OP* (1899), p. 284.
61. *OP* (1899), p. 322.
62. Ricardo, *The High Price of Bullion*, p. 91. Note the proportionality indicated by 'as high' and 'as much' and therewith the idea that money, being neutral, cannot 'permanently' (*i.e.* in the next static equilibrium state) lower the rate of interest.
63. G. L. S. Shackle, *The Years of High Theory* (Cambridge: The University Press, 1967), p. 157.
64. *EI*, p. 156.
65. *MCC*, p. 237. Emphasis deleted.
66. *OP* (1899), p. 321.
67. *OP* (1886), p. 9.
68. *OP* (1899), p. 323.
69. Thornton, *The Paper Credit of Great Britain*, p. 239. Thornton does say, however, that the opportunities for 'additional industry' are 'limited in number' and that there exist 'some bounds' to the benefits to be derived. Once full employment is reached, he stressed, an augmentation of money will not lead to the generation of extra output, but will lead instead to a proportionate 'rise in the cost of articles' – a rise, in other words, such that, after the increase in the money-supply, 'the existing paper will then bear only the same proportion to the existing quantity of goods, when sold at the existing prices, which the former paper bore to the former quantity of goods, when sold at the former prices; the power of purchasing will, therefore, be the same.' (*Ibid.*, pp. 255–6).
70. D. Hume, 'Of Money' (1752), in *Writings on Economics*, ed. by E. Rotwein (London: Nelson, 1955), p. 38. Initially the workmen 'never dream of demanding higher wages, but are glad of employment from such good paymasters'; and thus it happens that in the disequilibrium state before *all* nominal values rise (of inputs as well as outputs) rising

production and rising employment accompany rising prices and rising profits. Once all values are in equilibrium, of course, once all prices reach 'a just proportion with the new quantity of specie which is in the kingdom', then at that point money is once again neutral. Whether the full employment which is produced by the injection of new money is neutral as well is more problematical: 'If workmen become scarce, the manufacturer gives higher wages, but at first requires an increase of labour; and this is willingly submitted to by the artisan, who can now eat and drink better, to compensate his additional toil and fatigue.'

71. *MCC*, p. 47.

6.3 Upswings and Downswings

1. 'Remedies for Fluctuations of General Prices' (1887), in *Memorials*, p. 194. In *MCC*, p. 249, he alludes once again to exogenous shocks and accidental disturbances such as 'the opening out of foreign markets after a war', a 'good harvest' or 'some other definite change' leading to an 'improvement of credit'.
2. *EI*, p. 152.
3. *EI*, p. 152. Giffen, two years before Marshall, had in his *Stock Exchange Securities* (1877), pp. 105–6, written in very similar terms concerning good harvests, low grain prices, and the consequent increase in real incomes: 'Probably this element has for many years in England been less important than it used to be in the commencement of a cycle of prosperity, because the masses of our workmen have usually a much larger margin than formerly for other articles than food, and the changes in the price of wheat, since the free-trade period began, have been much less extreme than they were when the dependence of commercial prosperity on cheap food was noticed. Still there is no doubt that a cycle of prosperity does seem to arise out of a period of generally low prices.' Giffen acknowledges his debt to Bagehot for this insight concerning the relationship between agriculture and fluctuations, Bagehot having written as follows four years earlier: 'The most common, and by far the most important, case where the depression in one trade causes depression in all others, is that of depressed agriculture. When the agriculture of the world is ill off, food is dear. And as the amount of absolute necessaries which a people consumes cannot be much diminished, the additional amount which has to be spent on them is so much subtracted from what used to be spent on other things. All the industries, A, B, C, D, up to Z, are somewhat affected by an augmentation in the price of corn . . . . Every one by becoming poorer, makes every other poorer too. All trades are slack from diminished custom, and the consequence is a vast stagnant capital, much idle labour, and a greatly retarded production . . . . If (however) corn should long be cheap, the labouring classes have much to spend on what they like besides. The producers of those things become prosperous, and have a greater purchasing power. They exercise it, and that creates in the class they deal with another purchasing power, and so

all through society. The whole machine of industry is stimulated to its maximum of energy, just as before much of it was slackened almost to a minimum.' See W. Bagehot, *Lombard Street* (1873) (London: John Murray, 1931), pp. 123–4. Not only does *Stock Exchange Securities* appear to contain the long-lost reference to 'Giffen's Paradox' (see *PE*, pp. 109–10) but *Lombard Street* as well offers an – earlier – analytical account of the phenomenon.

4. *EI*, p. 152. Bagehot, reflecting that budgets vary as between classes and that not all groups benefit proportionately in the succeeding stages of the cycle, preferred to disaggregate and to distinguish between kinds of industry: 'The most affected are the large ones, which produce the objects in ordinary times most consumed by the working classes. The clothing trades feel the difference at once.' (Bagehot, *Lombard Street*, p. 123). Marshall, as we have seen in the text, speaks simply of 'all kinds of commodities'.
5. *MCC*, p. 18.
6. *EI*, p. 152. Hyperinflation would seem to be a genuine possibility should credit and confidence indeed be maintained.
7. *EI*, p. 152.
8. *EI*, p. 152.
9. *EI*, p. 152.
10. 'Remedies for Fluctuations of General Prices' (1887), in *Memorials*, p. 191.
11. *EI*, p. 165.
12. *EI*, p. 166. Note the implicit denial of wage-push inflation.
13. *EI*, pp. 165–6.
14. *OP* (1899), p. 285.
15. *OP* (1899), p. 286.
16. *MCC*, p. 247.
17. *OP* (1899), p. 274.
18. 'Remedies for Fluctuations of General Prices' (1887), in *Memorials*, p. 198.
19. Inflation evidently causes nominal rates to lag behind real ones in the upswing – but only, presumably, because lenders' expectations concerning the future behaviour of prices and interest-rates are less than perfect, since otherwise they would have taken care to inflation-proof their contracts. This phenomenon of imperfect foresight reminds us that the rate of inflation is not constant in the upswing but rather accelerates.
20. *EI*, pp. 152–3.
21. *EI*, p. 153.
22. *EI*, p. 153.
23. *EI*, p. 136.
24. *EI*, p. 153.
25. *MCC*, p. 247.
26. J. Mills, 'Credit Cycles and the Origins of Commercial Panics', *Transactions of the Manchester Statistical Society*, 1867. Cited in T. W. Hutchison, *A Review of Economic Doctrines 1870–1929* (Oxford: Clarendon Press, 1953), p. 367.

27. *EI*, p. 153.
28. *EI*, p. 153.
29. This is not to deny, of course, that the upper turning point might be the product of an exogenous shock such as that represented by a bad harvest or the outbreak of war. Marshall mentions a number of exogenous influences on the cycle, a number of outside factors capable of generating the *malaise* of crises and violent fluctuations. But when all is said and done, the explanation of turning points which he most frequently adopts is the psychological one which focuses on endogenous changes in attitudes and expectations. For that reason, incidentally, Marshall's theory of cycles is not able to explain the rhythm of their periodicity or to account for the fact that confidence seems to fail in a surprisingly regular pattern.
30. H. Spencer, *The Principles of Sociology*, 3rd ed. (London: Williams & Norgate, 1906), Vol. I, p. 474.
31. Bagehot, *Lombard Street*, p. 121. Marshall cites a part of this passage in *IRC*, pp. 184–5.
32. 'There is probably no one who gave as strong a stimulus to the thoughts of the younger Cambridge graduates thirty years or forty years ago as he. He opened out a new world of promise; he set men on high enterprise in many diverse directions; and though he may have regulated English intellectual work less than Mill did, I believe he did much more towards increasing its utility. He has, perhaps, been more largely read and exercised a greater influence on the Continent than any other recent English thinker except Darwin.' 'On a National Memorial to Herbert Spencer', *Daily Chronicle*, November 23, 1904.
33. Bagehot had died in 1877 without completing his work on *The Postulates of English Political Economy*. The book appeared posthumously in 1885 and Marshall contributed a Preface. There, after paying tribute to the exceptional 'sagacity and suggestiveness' of the author's insights, he provided the following appreciation of Bagehot and his work: 'He was excellently qualified for the task he undertook. He had a well-trained scientific mind, and a large experience of City life. He was an independent thinker, and perfectly free in his criticisms; but he reverenced the great men who had gone before him, and knew nothing of the temptation to try and raise himself by disparaging them. Though he has shown more clearly than perhaps anyone else the danger of a careless application of theory, he saw with great distinctness the need of its aid in dealing with complex economic problems. . . . Perhaps there never was anyone better fitted to show the real bearing of Ricardian modes of reasoning on the practical problems of life, or to bring out the fundamental unity which, in spite of minor differences, connects all the true work of the present with that of the earlier generation of economists.' Preface to W. Bagehot, *The Postulates of English Political Economy* (London: Longmans, Green & Co., 1885), p. vi.
34. 'Remedies for Fluctuations of General Prices' (1887), in *Memorials*, pp. 191–2.
35. *MCC*, p. 235.
36. *MCC*, p. 313.

37. 'Remedies for Fluctuations of General Prices' (1887), in *Memorials*, p. 191. Note that the productivity of the employee is here apparently being treated as constant over the cycle (a questionable practice in the work of an author who wrote so extensively of the manner in which cost varies with output) and that there is no explicit mention of any feedback effect on total demand and on production of the transfer via forced dissavings of income from savers to consumers (as opposed to the impact of falling prices on profit-margins, which Marshall does incorporate).
38. *EI*, p. 165.
39. *OP* (1887), p. 75. Deflation of prices in advance of wages means that 'the employer has to suffer, and I pity him as an individual' (*OP* (1887), p. 77), but the overall effect of a fall in prices has in truth 'been no great disadvantage to the country' (*OP* (1887), p. 74): 'During such a fall a powerful friction tends to prevent money wages in most trades from falling as fast as prices; and this tends almost imperceptibly to establish a higher standard of living among the working classes, and to diminish the inequalities of wealth. These benefits are often ignored' (*OP* (1887), p. 19). Related to this is the curious phenomenon of wage-illusion and its beneficial implications for good husbandry: 'People of all classes, and especially of the working classes, spend their incomes more wisely when prices and money-wages are falling, and they think themselves worse off than they are, than when a rise of prices and money-wages leads them to exaggerate their real incomes and to be careless about their expenditure.' (*OP* (1886), p. 9). Ignorance and error in such a case is the cause of efficiency and economy, and the reason is that people mistakenly think their real incomes are falling when in fact their real incomes are rising. One is tempted to ask whether a better-informed citizenry might not come to show a similar concern with good husbandry in the upswing – when the living standards of those on inelastic wages are quite genuinely under threat.
40. *IRC*, p. 175.
41. *OP* (1887), p. 92. Impressions concerning 'inconstancy of employment' (what Keynesians would call involuntary unemployment) are misleading not least because of improvements in communications: 'When a large factory goes on half time, rumour bruits the news over the whole neighbourhood, and perhaps the newspapers spread it all over the country. But few people know when an independent workman, or even a small employer, gets only a few days' work in a month; and in consequence, whatever suspensions of industry there are in modern times, are apt to seem more important than they are relatively to those of earlier times' (*PE*, p. 572). Marshall accepted that the phenomenon of unemployment is more visible in modern conditions than was the case, say, in the days of cottage industry, but he nonetheless denied that there was an upward trend (despite new inventions, the replacement of long-term by short-term contracts, the spread of 'migratory habits', and the growth in specialised, sector-specific, non-transferable skills). Nor, indeed, he maintained, need there be a significant rise in the downswing of the trade cycle. Speaking in the 1880s, for example, he expressed the

view that the current depression was in essence no more than 'a severe depression of profits and of prices': 'I cannot see any reason for believing that there is any considerable depression in any other respect. There is, of course, great misery among the poor; but I do not believe it is greater than it used to be . . . . My belief is that there have not been a larger number of people unemployed during the last ten years than during any other consecutive ten years.' (*OP* (1887), pp. 98, 99). Of course a *sudden* deflation could have an adverse effect on jobs and output – but, Marshall said, 'I doubt whether the influence exerted in this direction by a slow and gradual fall is very great' (*OP* (1887), p. 19). Of course there is *some* rise in enforced idleness in the slump, if only due to the bankruptcies and closures which occur. On balance, however, Marshall appears not to have regarded prolonged inconstancy of employment as a serious threat. He would no doubt have had more to say about unemployment in general if he had regarded it as a genuine problem.

42. *EI*, p. 156.
43. *OP* (1887), p. 193.
44. *OP* (1887), p. 91.
45. *EI*, p. 153.
46. *EI*, p. 154.
47. *EI*, pp. 154–5.
48. *OP* (1887), pp. 90, 91.
49. *OP* (1887), p. 91.
50. *OP* (1887), p. 91. There is clearly benefit to be drawn even from the occasional crisis of credit and confidence, occurring as it does when the atmosphere of business becomes 'increasingly sultry until it breaks in a storm': 'Overcharged hopes are then quenched: and the businesses, which survive, gradually resume their activities under conditions more favourable than before; because weak credits have succumbed, and the strong have been strengthened by being freed from entanglements in dubious schemes' (*MCC*, p. 90). The crisis drives to the wall the incompetent entrepreneur and the over-speculative wheeler-dealer; but that in itself need be no more a cause for regret than is the fact that surviving manufacturers are forced to 'exert themselves to the utmost', lenders to be 'much more careful about their loans' (*OP* (1887), p. 92). Good men in bad times are compelled by their situation to invent and innovate, to cut back on waste, to boost efficiency, to consider new projects carefully; and in all of these ways bad times would seem actually to make good men better. Since the downswing is a spur to productivity while the upswing redistributes towards profits, the conclusion to be reached would seem to be that each phase of the cycle makes some contribution to economic growth.
51. *EI*, p. 155.
52. *EI*, p. 163.
53. *EI*, p. 163.
54. *EI*, p. 163.
55. *EI*, p. 163.
56. *EI*, p. 155. The key word is 'think' for the key variable is expectation:

'The belief that prices will rise often makes prices rise, because it expands credit.' (*OP* (1887), p. 27). The odd exogenous shock – such as a good harvest – may contribute to buoyancy and optimism but it is not to be confused with buoyancy and optimism any more than mind is to be confused with matter. Nor, as the text of this Chapter makes clear, is an exogenous shock necessary if buoyancy and optimism are to be restored to an economy currently enjoying a slump.

57. *MCC*, p. 249.
58. *EI*, p. 196.
59. 'The Pure Theory of Domestic Values' (1879), in Whitaker II, p. 233. Keynes, in the *General Theory* (pp. 19–20), cites this passage in full (clearly regarding it as a prime specimen of the Classical position) and then says: 'It is true that it would not be easy to quote comparable passages from Marshall's later work or from Edgeworth or Professor Pigou. The doctrine is never stated to-day in this crude form. Nevertheless it still underlies the whole classical theory, which would collapse without it . . . . Contemporary thought is still deeply steeped in the notion that if people do not spend their money in one way they will spend it in another.' Since Keynes states – quite correctly, in our view – that the 'whole classical theory' would collapse without the notion that supply creates its own demand, it is likely that he over-estimates the difference between the younger and the older Marshall, as in the following passage (*General Theory*, p. 20n): 'The Marshall of the *Principles* had become sufficiently doubtful to be very cautious and evasive. But the old ideas were never repudiated or rooted out of the basic assumptions of his thought.' There is simply no reason to believe that Marshall became 'doubtful'; and much reason to believe that he did not (see *PE*, pp. 591–2 for proof that the older Marshall not only continued to believe in Say's Law but chose to describe its workings in language taken *verbatim* from Book III of the *Economics of Industry* of 1879). Keynes himself ultimately concedes (*General Theory*, pp. 177–8) that Marshall, although here as elsewhere rather vague, was in essence a classical economist where injections and withdrawals were concerned: 'Marshall . . . surely believed, although he did not expressly say so, that aggregate saving and aggregate investment are necessarily equal.'
60. 'Remedies for Fluctuations of General Prices' (1887), in *Memorials*, p. 192.
61. *EI*, p. 15.
62. *OP* (1887), p. 91.
63. *EI*, p. 227.
64. *PE*, p. 591.
65. *PE*, p. 592.
66. *EI*, p. 212.
67. *PE*, p. 592.
68. *PE*, p. 431.
69. *PE*, p. 195.

6.4 Stabilisation Policy

1. *OP* (1886), p. 9.
2. *EI*, p. 156. Not that while here as elsewhere Marshall refers explicitly to fluctuations in prices, the context clearly implies fluctuations in output and employment as well – in real alongside nominal variables.
3. *OP* (1880), p. 9, *OP* (1887), p. 19. In his evidence to the Indian Currency Commission (*OP* (1899), p. 286), Marshall stated that he had once been an inflationist: 'I will confess that, for ten or fifteen years after I began to study political economy, I held the common doctrine, that a rise of prices was generally beneficial to business men directly, and indirectly to the working classes. But, after that time, I changed my views.' There is no evidence of his ever having flirted with deflation. His mature position, as indicated in the text, was that of the advocate of stable prices.
4. Marshall notes that 'general opinion with regard to the prosperity of the country is much influenced by the authority of manufacturers and merchants' (*EI*, p. 157) – and that such (vocal, articulate and frequently powerful) men prefer rising to falling prices for the simple reason that they have many sunk costs and fixed money payments to cover. Their opinion must be taken seriously, and in early passages such as the following (*OP* (1886), p. 9) Marshall demonstrated that he had fallen to some extent under its spell: 'I agree with the general opinion that a steady upward tendency in general prices conduces a little more to the general well-being than does a tendency downwards, because it keeps industry somewhat better employed.' His initial support soon turned to scepticism, particularly as he came to see that businessmen are not the whole nation and that their arguments are bound to be partial. For example: 'One wants a very much stronger statistical evidence than one yet has to prove that a fall of prices diminishes perceptibly and in the long run the total productiveness of industry' (*OP* (1887), p. 91).
5. *OP* (1887), p. 20.
6. *PE*, p. 591.
7. 'Remedies for Fluctuations of General Prices' (1887), in *Memorials*, p. 193.
8. 'The Theory of Foreign Trade' (1873–7), in Whitaker II, p. 46. See also *PE*, p. 310–11 and *EAM*, Chapter 6.1 The new entrant is a problem to the rest of us precisely because he is new: he is not a member of our tacit or open combination, he has an incentive to cut his prices in order to attract existing customers away from existing suppliers, and he (not knowing the rest of us personally) is not as sensitive to the informal snub as are the rest of us (and our wives). The new entrant is also likely to be more adventurous than existing firms; and that very lack of conservatism can be a further cause of instability.
9. 'The Theory of Foreign Trade' (1873–7), in Whitaker II, p. 49.
10. *IRC*, p. 176. The recent history of 'the alpaca trade, the lace trade, the straw hat trade, the ribbon trade, and a multitude of others' confirms the hypothesis that he or she who slavishly follows fashion 'adds to the

wreck of human lives that is caused by hungry pining for work'.

11. *MCC*, pp. 244–5.
12. 'The Theory of Foreign Trade' (1873–7), in Whitaker II, p. 51.
13. Quoted in Whitaker, 'Alfred Marshall: The Years 1877 to 1885' (Chapter 5.2, note 76), p. 143.
14. *OP* (1899), p. 281.
15. 'Remedies for Fluctuations of General Prices' (1887), in *Memorials*, p. 188.
16. 'Remedies for Fluctuations of General Prices' (1887), in *Memorials*, p. 198.
17. 'Remedies for Fluctuations of General Prices' (1887), in *Memorials*, p. 189. Once, Marshall says, long-term contracts were 'rare and unimportant'. That, he continues, is simply not the case in present-day business conditions, where the problem of deferred command and distant valuation can in consequence simply not be ignored.
18. *EI*, p. 156.
19. Marshall throughout his discussion of the tabular standard neglects the feedback effect of cuts in nominal values (whether general or specific) on the level of total demand. Yet it is clear that such cuts, the consequence of a previous fall in total demand, themselves lead to a further fall in total demand – a fall which necessitates yet another round of wage and price cuts. It is odd that Marshall who had so much in other places to say about the multiplier should have neglected this effect when discussing the tabular standard.
20. *OP* (1886), p. 10.
21. *OP* (1886), p. 11.
22. *PE*, p. 591.
23. *IT*, p. 9. The words missed out are the qualification 'though not as important as appears at first sight'. They do not materially affect the general drift of Marshall's argument.
24. *IRC*, p. 178.
25. *OP* (1886), p. 12.
26. *OP* (1886), p. 11.
27. *IRC*, p. 185. Marshall made his first reference to the optional tabular standard in this essay.
28. 'Remedies for Fluctuations of General Prices' (1887), in *Memorials*, p. 207.
29. *IRC*, p. 185.
30. *MCC*, p. 28.
31. *OP* (1887), p. 31.
32. *IRC*, p. 186.
33. *IRC*, p. 186.
34. *IRC*, p. 186.
35. *The Economist*, Vol. XLV, 5 March 1887, p. 303. On p. 304 the unsigned article concludes as follows: 'The standard which Professor Marshall proposes is, thus, it seems to us, impossible and impracticable, and to say more of it would be superfluous . . . It is not a little surprising to find it advocated by men of such unquestioned ability as Professor Marshall.' In the face of such strong language concerning his article in

The Contemporary Review, it is perhaps no surprise that the over-sensitive Marshall felt he had no choice but to engage in much-dreaded controversy.

36. Letter to *The Economist*, Vol. LXV, 12 March 1887, p. 339. To this defence of variability *The Economist* (p. 334) replied wiltingly as follows: 'The very feature of his plan which he regards its special merit is, in fact, a fatal defect. It is all very well to talk about "developing" the unit, but this translated into plain language means that the tabular standard is to be made to undergo a constant process of change. It is to be made to represent one thing this year, and another the next, its transformation being subject, not to any fixed rules, but to the changing ideas of a few Government officials. And how such a fluctuating quantity can be accepted as a reliable standard we fail to see.' *The Economist* in its earlier article had objected that the quality of a product tends to alter over time even where its name remains the same (it had instanced the changes that occur in the ratio of solid food to water in a pound of meat or the size of each room in a ten-roomed house); and had added that no two 'imaginative statisticians' will ever reach consensus on the appropriate weighting-scheme (as it says on p. 304: 'You know perfectly well that their imposing tables are the sheerest guess work'). The second article thus reinforces its earlier criticism that Marshall's standard is so variable as to be positively unreliable.
37. Letter to *The Economist*, Vol. LXV, 12 March 1887, p. 339. *The Economist* was not happy with this statement, pointing out that while some of Marshall's examples do refer to long-term contracts (e.g. leases, mortgages and bonds), others quite clearly refer to current payments (e.g. salaries and wages, rates and taxes). So even if the unit is not to be used as currency, some short-run transactions would seem to be likely to come under its influence nonetheless.
38. *IRC*, pp. 177–8.
39. Letter to *The Economist*, Vol. LXV, 12 March 1887, p. 339.
40. *MCC*, p. 52.
41. *MCC*, pp. 53–4.
42. Letter to *The Economist*, Vol. LXV, 12 March 1887, p. 339.
43. *OP* (1899), p. 292.
44. *OP* (1899), p. 323.
45. *MCC*, p. 19.
46. *MCC*, p. 19.
47. *MCC*, p. 38.
48. *OP* (1886), p. 12.
49. *OP* (1887), p. 101.
50. Letter to *The Economist*, Vol. LXV, 12 March 1887, p. 339.
51. *OP* (1887), p. 31.
52. *OP* (1899), p. 286.
53. *IRC*, p. 186.
54. *OP* (1887), pp. 30–1.
55. *MCC*, pp. 19–20.
56. *OP* (1886), p. 12.
57. *OP* (1899), pp. 323–4.

58. *MCC*, p. 49.
59. *OP* (1886), pp. 14–5.
60. *OP* (1887), p. 28.
61. *OP* (1887), pp. 26–7.
62. *OP* (1887), p. 102.
63. *OP* (1886), p. 13.
64. *OP* (1887), p. 25.
65. Letter to *The Times* of 25 January 1889, p. 13. The stock of monetary gold is, of course, very large relative to the flow, which is why the speculative scramble for gold to hold is a more immediate cause of the sudden scarcity of the metal than is a diminution in new production (a phenomenon which 'might, perhaps, do no very great harm for some years').
66. *OP* (1886), p. 13.
67. Letter to *The Economist*, Vol. LXV, 12 March 1887, p. 339.
68. *MCC*, p. 63.
69. Letter to *The Times* of 25 January 1889, p. 13. Marshall favoured synmetallism as a long-term objective but was evidently prepared to assign some role in the short run to the fixed-ratio system, provided that the ratio selected was a realistic one: 'Though I myself have a hankering for a true bimetallism, instead of that "final-ratio-mintage" or "alternative monometallism", which has usurped the name, I have no objection to the experiment being tried of fixed-ratio-mintage at 20 or 22 to one.' Such a system was a viable one, Marshall believed, and might even usefully be regarded as a step in the direction of something better: 'It would be almost sure to last long, and might last very long. When it fell through, public opinion might be ready for some more truly scientific scheme.' It is odd that a man with such an evolutionary perspective should have taken such pains to deny that he was among those who had 'substantially approved the bimetallic theory'.
70. *MCC*, p. 64.
71. *OP* (1887), p. 102. Emphasis added.
72. *OP* (1886), p. 14.
73. The value of each composite ingot is related to the 'means of the values' (*MCC*, p. 66) of each individual metal, and for that reason the absolute value of a bar can and does vary with variations in the absolute value of either or both metals. What does not vary is the mix of the metals. That remains constant, which is why changes in the relative value of one metal compared with the other does not have the disastrous impact on the working of the system that the great Ricardo had predicted when he wrote: 'No permanent measure of value can be said to exist in any great nation while the circulating medium consists of two metals, because they are constantly subject to vary in value with respect to each other. However exact the conductors of the mint may be, in proportioning the relative value of gold to silver in the coins, at the time when they fix the ratio, they cannot prevent one of these metals from rising, while the other remains stationary, or falls in value.' Ricardo, *The High Price of Bullion*, p. 65.
74. *OP* (1886), p. 14. One reason for his caution, needless to say, was

his belief that change *per se* breeds uncertainty and undermines confidence, and in that way constitutes a new evil in its own right: 'Almost any currency of which the position is certain will do its work fairly well' (*OP* (1899), p. 292), he said, indicating that every operation involves risks and that curing the disease might therefore prove less desirable on balance than continuing to suffer its effects.

75. Ricardo, *The High Price of Bullion*, p. 55. This shows the influence of a number of observations made by Smith, despite the well-known differences between the two authors on monetary matters. See in particular the *Wealth of Nations* I, p. 309.
76. 'Remedies for Fluctuations of General Prices' (1887), in *Memorials*, p. 188.
77. *MCC*, p. 66.
78. *OP* (1887), p. 29.
79. *OP* (1887), p. 112.
80. Thornton, *The Paper Credit of Great Britain*, p. 152.
81. Thornton, *The Paper Credit of Great Britain*, pp. 124, 127.
82. Thornton, *The Paper Credit of Great Britain*, p. 111. See also Bagehot, *Lombard Street*, pp. 48, 53, 63, 152, 175, 303, 314.
83. *OP* (1887), p. 110.
84. *OP* (1899), p. 324. Thus he said that paper was in normal times to be a given multiple of the Bank's gold reserves but also recommended that the Directors be permitted to exceed that quantity of notes issued once the interest-rate had reached a specified level: 'The directors should have the right to neglect that restriction in times of great pressure: they might, for instance, be empowered to issue notes in excess of twice the value of their metallic stores when the minimum rate of discount had risen to 10 per cent.' See *OP* (1887), pp. 111–2. Such a recommendation is closer to the needs-of-trade argument of the Anti-Bullionists and the Banking School than it is to the theories which lay behind the Bank Charter Act of 1844.
85. *MCC*, p. 258.
86. *MCC*, p. 84.
87. *OP* (1887), p. 163.
88. *OP* (1899), pp. 322, 323. Internationally speaking, a country on a metallic standard must take care to prevent external drains from generating domestic strains – a real danger in contemporary business conditions: 'The developments of modern business have caused a country to be liable, under severer penalties than before, to pay up many millions' worth of capital at short notice.' (*OP* (1899), pp. 303–4). Similarly, in the case of internal drains there is a strong case for cushioning the economy by means of buffer stocks – particularly where the drains are caused by foreseeable factors such as seasons and crops. The more predictable the reflux, needless to say, the more moderate the excess reserves that the country must hold for precautionary purposes (a result which is likely to be welcomed in agrarian-type poorer countries such as India which are stronger on prediction of harvests than they are on disposable wealth to be held idle as surplus monetary metal).

89. *OP* (1887), p. 170. Eshag (*From Marshall to Keynes*, p. 33) points to an important ambiguity in Marshall's presentation of the purchasing power parity doctrine: 'He does not make it clear whether he has in mind only the prices of goods which enter into international trade or the general price-levels. It can, for instance, be inferred from some parts of his work, where he refers to the equality of prices at the "seaboards" or "ports", that he has in mind only the commodities which enter into foreign trade. Yet in other sections of his work he talks of the equality of the "gold prices in England" with the "rouble prices in Russia" and the "silver prices in India", from which one may reasonably deduce that he is considering general price-levels as the relevant bases for the determination of the purchasing power parity.' Eshag says that the chief reason for 'this lack of precision and clarity on his part' was 'an implied assumption that the prices of all commodities change, more or less, in the same proportion' (*idem*) and cites as evidence the passage (*MCC*, pp. 231–2) in which Marshall explains that the prices of a nation's exports 'are governed by their money cost of production, which bears fairly settled relations to the money costs of production of the things she makes for herself: because the fluidity of labour within a country tends to equalize the earnings of efforts that are similar in kind and equal in quantity in different occupations'. The passage does, of course, continue with an explicit admission that the prices of exports and the prices of other commodities can and do diverge: 'The general level of prices in a country will not necessarily rise and fall in the same proportions as do those of her exports; if the industries which produce those exports are not representative of the general body of her work . . .; or if the movement of labour . . . is not easy and rapid; or if many kinds of her agricultural and other bulky produce are raised at so great a distance from her frontier, that their prices at the frontier exceed very much the average prices at which they are supplied to her own people.' But evidently Marshall did not view these qualifications as particularly significant in view of the fact that he did not modify his theory in accordance with them.
90. *OP* (1887), p. 72.
91. Which is not to say that Marshall consistently neglected the capital account of the balance of payments, as the following passage will serve to demonstrate: 'Even when the exchanges are at par, the trade bills on the one side need not exactly balance those on the other, for those on either side are likely to be supplemented by paper documents or telegrams representing (i) the transfer of newly borrowed capital, (ii) the repayment of business outlays and the payment of interest or profits on previous investments of capital, (iii) the drawings by absentees . . . and (iv) the drawings of a government which expends in one country part of the income which it derives from another.' (*OP* (1887), p. 171). Trade is not the only component of the balance of payments, which is why a nation with a surplus on trade account might nonetheless suffer an overall deficit because of adverse capital movements – as where, say, 'political discredit', 'political apprehensions', 'distrust' in a nation's future (*OP* (1887), pp. 171, 173, 175) cause speculators (domestic and

foreign) to 'avoid' one currency and hold another (*OP* (1899), pp. 296–7). In such a case the exchanges could turn against a nation due entirely to the withdrawal of speculative balances consequent upon a loss of confidence in its currency. Again, and turning from mind to matter, the rate of interest is a variable which can exercise a short-term influence on capital flows and foreign lending (after allowing for the actual cost of physically transporting the precious metals - a considerable one where they are in India) (*OP* (1899), pp. 309–11). Marshall mentions the capital account role of the rate of interest but does not discuss it in detail. Nor does he comment on the feedback effect (on domestic output and employment) of the change in the rate of interest – an odd omission in the case of an author interested in interdependencies and aware of the income-creating/income-destroying properties of a change in the quantity of *ex post* investment undertaken in response to a change in the rate of interest. Be that as it may, the inclusion of the capital account significantly alters the argument concerning purchasing power parity and the restoration of balance of payments equilibrium via price adjustments alone; and one regrets that Marshall contented himself with a partial explanation when what was called for was a more extended discussion.

92. *OP* (1899), p. 324.
93. *MCC*, p. 66.
94. *OP* (1887), p. 177. A similar statement may be found in *MCC*, p. 19, where Marshall, commenting on price-changes, states that they are 'chiefly caused by changes in the amounts of the precious metals relatively to the business which has to be transacted by them, allowance being of course made for changes in the extent to which the precious metals are able at any time to delegate their functions to bank-notes, cheques, bills of exchange, and other substitutes'.
95. *OP* (1887), p. 177.
96. *OP* (1887), p. 172.
97. See *OP* (1887), p. 170.
98. *OP* (1887), p. 116.
99. As, for example, at the trough of the cycle, when involuntary unemployment and idle resources unambiguously exist, even if for a limited period of time.
100. See *OP* (1887), pp. 76, 115, 151, 174, 194.
101. *OP* (1887), p. 173.
102. *MCC*, p. 20.
103. Bagehot, *Lombard Street*, p. 63.
104. *MCC*, p. 50. Seeing that Marshall knew how much of spendable assets are bank-created current accounts, it is surprising that he was able to make statements of this kind without any reference to the regulation of assets other than currency. He does not suggest, for example, that the fractional reserve ratio be fixed by statute, and he says little about the use of the interest-rate as a means of establishing stability of prices via its effect on the money-multiplier.
105. *MCC*, p. 20.

106. 'Remedies for Fluctuations of General Prices' (1887), in *Memorials*, p. 203.
107. 'Remedies for Fluctuations of General Prices' (1887), in *Memorials*, p. 206n.
108. Letter to I. Fisher dated 16 September 1911, in *Memorials*, p. 477.

7 PROGRESS, POLITICS AND ECONOMICS

1. *PE*, p. 35. The *dominant* aim is clearly 'to obtain guidance in the practical conduct of life, and especially of social life', but this is not to deny the existence and validity of another aim, 'to gain knowledge for its own sake'. Marshall, as will by now have become clear, was actively involved on both fronts, both as a private citizen offering his opinion and as a positive economist ferreting out facts.
2. Pigou, *Alfred Marshall and Current Thought*, p. 65.
3. 'Mr Mill's Theory of Value' (1876), in *Memorials*, p. 125.

7.1 The Definition of Economics

1. *PE*, p. 12.
2. *PE*, p. 1. Marshall speaks here of 'Political Economy or Economics'. As is well known, however, he favoured the latter term over the former and was instrumental in bringing about the change in usage – not least through the title itself of his major work. His reasons are two in number. The *first* may be found on the second page of the *Economics of Industry* of 1879, where he writes: 'The nation used to be called "the Body Politic". So long as the phrase was in common use, men thought of the interests of the whole nation when they used the word "Political" and then "Political Economy" served well enough as a name for the science. But now "political interests" generally mean the interests of only some part or parts of the nation; so that it seems best to drop the name "Political Economy", and to speak simply of Economic Science, or more shortly, Economics.' He makes a related observation in *Money Credit and Commerce* (p. 107): 'Political economy is sometimes described in Germany and elsewhere as "National economy": and, in its early stages, it was much concerned with the material interests of individual nations; especially in regard to the importation and exportation of the precious metals.' What Marshall is saying is that 'Political Economy' is by tradition concerned with the *national* interest (as, for example, in the Mercantilist theory of exchange, which treats the country as a whole as in some sense an entity *sui generis*, distinct from the parts which constitute it); that 'Economics' is concerned with human well-being and the perceived interests of *individuals* (as, for example, in his own theories of supplying and demanding); and in our

modern, relatively loosely-articulated economic and social conditions, there is a strong case for preferring the less ambitious to the more global denomination. This consideration is reinforced by a *second*, that economic science is not practical politics and must not be defined in a manner such as to invite confusion between the field of study (economics) and the field of activity (statesmanship): though 'largely directed by practical needs, economics avoids as far as possible the discussion of those exigencies of party organization, and those diplomacies of home and foreign politics of which the statesman is bound to take account in deciding what measures that he can propose will bring him nearest to the end that he desires to secure for his country. It aims indeed at helping him to determine not only what that end should be, but also what are the best methods of a broad policy devoted to that end. But it shuns many political issues, which the practical man cannot ignore: and it is therefore a science, pure and applied, rather than a science and an art.' (*PE*, p. 36). The fact that economic science is not to be confused with practical politics, needless to say, does not mean that the economist should abstain from a study of the relationships between economics and politics – a study which Marshall undertook as an economist with great enthusiasm.

3. *PE*, p. 243.
4. L. Robbins, *An Essay on the Nature and Significance of Economic Science* (London: Macmillan, 1932), p. 16.
5. N. Senior, *An Outline of the Science of Political Economy* (1836) (London: George Allen & Unwin, Ltd., 1938), p. 6.
6. J. R. McCulloch, *Principles of Political Economy* (London: Longman and Co., 1825), p. 1.
7. J. B. Say, *Traité d'Economie Politique* (Paris: Deterville, 1803), p. i.
8. Mill, *Principles of Political Economy*, p. 1.
9. 'The Present Position of Economics' (1885), in *Memorials*, p. 158.
10. *PE*, p. 13.
11. *PE*, p. 32.
12. *PE*, p. 12.
13. 'The Present Position of Economics' (1885), in *Memorials*, p. 157.
14. *PE*, p. 532. As may be observed, say, in the equilibrium market price, the product of 'two opposing sets of forces, those which impel man to economic efforts and sacrifices, and those which hold him back' (*PE*, p. 270). Here, assuming individuals are rational and do not act at random, the balancing of motives which produces inertia generates a monetary measurement of the strength of those motives – the Benthamite calculus of pleasures and pains. It is worth noting that the measure is operative only at the margin (it does not pick up totals or the utility/disutility associated with intra-marginal units) and that it leads to misleading inferences in disequilibrium states (since in such instances remuneration/expenditure are not precisely proportional to subjective costs/benefits and windfalls/shortfalls are possible).
15. *PE*, p. 13. Note that the comparison being made is entirely static and the consumer is here being asked merely to make choices at a single moment in time. The comparison may be static but reality is dynamic –

and, just as 'the pleasures which two persons derive from smoking cannot be directly compared', so neither 'can even those which the same person derives from it at different times': 'No one can compare and measure accurately against one another his own mental states at different times' (*PE*, p. 13). Over time, after all, the consumer's tastes and preferences are subject to change (so that *ceteris paribus* cannot legitimately be assumed when making inter-temporal comparisons), and there is also some confusion as the status of the law of diminishing marginal utility where six months elapse between the drinking of the first cup of tea and the purchase of the second.

16. *PE*, p. 13. Marshall specifies that the men must be in the 'same rank of life' (by which he appears to mean roughly the same cultural *milieu*) and – the more important variable – must have 'the same means' (so as to hold constant possible differences in the subjective meaning of money as between different income-earning groups in society). The latter provision is intended to correct for the fact that 'the same sum of money represents different amounts of pleasure to different people' (*PE*, p. 106) – although in this interpersonal comparison as between rich and poor, Marshall is apparently infringing his former criterion, that the individuals being compared belong 'to the same classes of people' (*PE*, p. 108). The former provision is intended to correct for the fact that all 'normal' behaviour varies as between peer-groups and is 'relative to the members of a particular class at a given place and time' – witness 'the normal willingness to save, the normal willingness to undergo a certain exertion for a certain pecuniary reward, or the normal alertness to seek the best markets in which to buy and sell, or to search out the most advantageous occupation for oneself or for one's children' (*PE*, p. v), all of which vary from one reference-group to another. Only when these two conditions are satisfied, Marshall is saying, can the economist begin to draw reasonable inferences of a comparative nature with respect to highly subjective and psychological variables such as gratification and discomfort.
17. *PE*, p. 15. And child A might love a holiday in the countryside whereas child B would loathe it.
18. *PE*, p. 15. The sample must be 'sufficiently broad' so as to include 'people of every variety of temperament' (*PE*, p. 108) – but not excessively broad lest it thereby represent a group so heterogeneous in 'temper and character' (*PE*, p. 21), so disparate in terms of income-levels, as to generate a meaningless average, a spurious representative. Clearly, a sampler's lot is not a happy one.
19. *PE*, p. 16.
20. *PE*, p. 13. Your expected utility led to your expenditure. Your expenditure may accordingly be taken as a measure of your expected utility.
21. *PE*, p. 108. This assumption is not logical. It is, however, necessary for the internal consistency of his argument.
22. Letter to A. C. Pigou dated 19 March 1903, in *Memorials*, p. 433. Marshall's statement that the utility-function for a commodity *cannot* be constructed *save* on the assumption that people of 'different incomes'

and 'different sensibilities' are 'evenly distributed' through the consuming group is an important one but also a source of some difficulty. It is easy enough to cite instances where it simply does not hold (caviar is one, dog-racing another) but, more fundamentally, it is also profoundly ambiguous – since the condition requires the presence in the market of a good cross-section of the consumerhood while leaving indeterminate the economic significance of the respective purchases made by the various groups. Nor is it at all clear what subjective meaning attaches to aggregated estimates of the national income, or what 'elaborate mathematical formulae' Marshall had in mind when he declared that 'the task of adding together the total utilities of all commodities, so as to obtain the aggregate of the total utility of all wealth, is beyond the range of any but the most elaborate mathematical formulae' (*PE*, p. 109n). Marshall evidently thought that aggregative statistics on national economic welfare, subjectively-perceived, could in practice be collected, but he does not take the reader into his confidence when it comes to specifying the techniques of aggregation that are to be employed. In view of the difficulties to which he draws attention with respect to the construction of the demand-function for a single commodity, the reader is bound to be somewhat sceptical about the meaning of aggregate numbers embracing all commodities. Guillebaud says that Marshall, wishing as he did to reach a wide audience, 'omitted much that he regarded as being of purely theoretical interest' (Editorial Introduction to Guillebaud II, p. 29); and it is possible that a more extensive discussion of the aggregation problem was rejected for that reason.

23. *PE*, p. 700.
24. 'Mr. Mill's Theory of Value' (1876), in *Memorials*, p. 125.
25. *PE*, p. 17.
26. *PE*, p. 17.
27. *PE*, p. 18.
28. *PE*, p. 17n.
29. *PE*, p. 17. This statement – that today's habitual reflex is frequently based upon yesterday's rational calculation – is similar to Marshall's analysis of the inductive method as embodying (consciously or unconsciously) an analytical framework carried over from the past. Looked at statically, my reliance on the crutch of convention and on the raw data captured by my camera suggests that I am remarkably lacking in intellective faculties. Looked at inter-temporally, however, the inference is different – since what emerges then is that I rationally formulated my conventions and worked out what to photograph, but did so yesterday and thus do not need to do so again today.
30. *PE*, p. vi.
31. *PE*, p. vi.
32. *PE*, p. 20.
33. 'The Old Generation of Economists and the New' (1897), in *Memorials*, p. 299.
34. *PE*, p. 645.
35. 'The Present Position of Economics' (1885), in *Memorials*, p. 159. In

such a case, provided the alternative counter (e.g. honours) were quantitatively unambiguous, economics could exist even if money did not. Economics could, of course, not exist if there were genuinely no way of measuring the exchange ratio between extra service and extra reward.

36. *PE*, p. 19. It would be wrong to underestimate the importance of the approbation motive, as economists are coming increasingly to appreciate: 'The economists of to-day ... go beyond those of earlier generations in believing that the desire of men for the approval of their own conscience and for the esteem of others is an economic force of the first order of importance.' 'Some Aspects of Competition' (1890), in *Memorials*, p. 285. Social and social-psychological variables, it is clear, are to be regarded as an intrinsic part of the economist's subject-matter, if his objective is genuinely to be not the playing of intellectual games but the understanding of human problems.
37. 'The Present Position of Economics' (1885), in *Memorials*, p. 159. Marshall, as is well known, said that 'ethical forces are among those of which the economist has to take account' (*PE*, p. v) and that 'whenever we get a glimpse of the economic man he is not selfish' ('The Present Position of Economics (1885), in *Memorials*, p. 160). Marshall, in other words, was far from identifying the economic orientation as being one of 'sordid selfishness' (*PE*, p. 19). Of particular interest is his praise for the archetypical critics of the 'dismal science', namely Carlyle and Ruskin, paying tribute as he does to their 'brilliant and ennobling poetic visions' (*PE*, p. 39), their 'fine inspirations and intuitions' (*PE*, p. 643n), their 'splendid teachings ... as to the right aims of human endeavour and the right uses of wealth' (*PE*, p. 19) – even if not to their technical competence when interpreting how the economy actually worked. It would only be partially true to say that these references indicate a felt need to defend the discipline against the criticism that it eulogized greed in a manner that was anti-social, narrow-minded and immoral. A fuller explanation would stress the essential similarities between Marshall's teachings on economic chivalry and those of Carlyle and Ruskin on topics such as the aristocracy of industry and the nobility of labour. As Grampp says: 'Why did Marshall concern himself about something which in "Marshallian" economics as it is defined today does not even exist? He did so, I suggest, because the critics of classical economics had an influence he could not ignore. Indeed he was partly persuaded himself.' W. D. Grampp 'Classical Economics and its Moral Critics', *History of Political Economy*, Vol. 5, 1973, p. 359n.
38. *PE*, p. 12. The best inventors, for example, 'are stimulated by a noble emulation more than by any love of wealth for its own sake'.
39. *PE*, p. 22.
40. *PE*, p. 17.
41. *PE*, p. 20. The passage continues by stating that 'But still the family affections generally are ... a form of altruism'. Marshall, recognising just how easy it would be to define all of other-regarding action as essentially selfish, is evidently anxious to draw the line lest the other-regarding category be defined out of existence altogether.

42. *PE*, p. xii. Economic science, in other words, is concerned with action which is regular, normal, capable of being reduced to a 'general rule' (*PE*, p. vi). This explicit exclusion of the random and the unexpected in favour of the predictable builds positivism rather than historicism into the model save where the 'general rule' obtains – and this is not Marshall's sense – exclusively in the past.
43. *PE*, p. viii.
44. *PE*, p. 632n.
45. *PE*, p. 20.
46. *PE*, p. 20. Marshall's reasoning is that action based on self-interest displays greater regularities than does action emanating from duty or affection. Arguing *a priori*, however, there is no reason to suppose that this is the case. On the one hand moral absolutes, if rigidly adhered to, give a great deal of information about reaction to stimulus precisely because that reaction is in the absence of any trade-off always the same. On the other hand even self-interested action is subject to numerous constraints on rational calculation and optimising behaviour that are imposed by limited information. Thus Marshall, introducing the law of substitution, adds the qualification that it is of relevance only as far as the knowledge and business enterprise of the producers reach; while elsewhere, describing how 'every business man . . . *according to his energy and ability* . . . estimates *as best he can*' (*PE*, pp. 336–7, emphasis added), he in effect reminds the reader how much even business reality can diverge from theoretical models. Besides that, only a very naive observer would conclude that economic life, dominated as it is by speculators with expectations and human beings with hunches and biases, is the last word in predictability of response – as is illustrated by the supply function of savings: 'It is conceivable even that a person may discount future pleasures in an irregular random way; he may be almost as willing to postpone a pleasure for two years as for one; or, on the other hand, he may object very strongly indeed to a long postponement, but scarcely at all to a short one.' (*PE*, p. 692). The question then becomes an empirical one, whether the economist loses or gains in 'simplicity', 'definiteness' and 'apparent lucidity' (*PE*, p. 633) when he studies action motivated by love of children as contrasted with action motivated by love of money. Marshall, it must be said, does not present the empirical evidence which is needed if credence is to be granted to his assertions.
47. *PE*, p. 22.
48. *PE*, p. 22.
49. *PE*, p. 14.
50. *PE*, p. 27. The reference to 'money price' confuses the issue.
51. *PE*, p. 27.
52. *PE*, p. viii. And elsewhere, referring explicitly to change over time: 'The progressive nature of man is one whole. It is only temporarily and provisionally that we can with profit isolate for study the economic side of his life.' (*PE*, pp. 71–2). All in all, therefore, it would be best to drop altogether the hypothetical construct of the 'economic man'. As Marshall wrote to J. N. Keynes on November 17, 1889: 'I now differ

from you . . . in holding (what I did not always hold) that the economic man does so little good service and causes so much trouble that on practical and tactical (not theoretical) grounds, it is best to do without him.' Cited in J. M. Whitaker, 'John Stuart Mill's Methodology', *Journal of Political Economy*, Vol. 83, 1975, p. 1045.

53. *PE*, p. 643.
54. *PE*, p. 636.
55. 'The Present Position of Economics' (1885), in *Memorials*, p. 163.
56. *PE*, p. 636.
57. 'The Present Position of Economics' (1885), in *Memorials*, p. 164.
58. *PE*, p. 636.
59. 'The Present Position of Economics' (1885), in *Memorials*, p. 164.
60. *PE*, p. 69.
61. *PE*, p. 69.
62. *PE*, p. 107.
63. 'Mr Mill's Theory of Value' (1876), in *Memorials*, p. 121.
64. 'Mr Jevons' Theory of Political Economy' (1872), in *Memorials*, p. 96.
65. *IT*, p. 214.
66. *IT*, p. 680.
67. *IT*, p. 680. So the economist may after all employ specialist jargon where there is genuinely no alternative. Even so, however, he must continue to exercise the greatest caution while doing so. For one thing, he runs the risk of losing his readership and ending up writing exclusively for his brothers in the mystery. That would be unfortunate in view of the intrinsic importance of the subject-matter; and the action clause is that economics wherever possible should 'endeavour to conform itself to the familiar terms of everyday life', utilising 'language that is intelligible to the general public' (*PE*, p. 43) so that its reasonings might be widely understood. Again, 'bold and rigid definitions . . . lull the reader into a false security' (*PE*, p. 43) and, while repelling some, might have the unexpected and undesirable outcome of filling others 'with the vain imagination that they have mastered difficult economic problems, when really they have done little more than learn the language in which parts of those problems can be expressed, and the machinery by which they can be handled. When the actual conditions of particular problems have not been studied, such knowledge is little better than a derrick for sinking oil-wells erected where there are no oil-bearing strata.' Caution must evidently be exercised when economic jargon is employed; but, after all, 'the technical language and machinery of every science are liable to a similar misuse; and this evil, though not unimportant, is not to be weighed against the aid which clear-headed and careful students continually derive from them'. ('On Rent' (1893), in Guillebaud II, p. 501n).
68. *PE*, p. 107. Whether Marshall's own use of jargon does really serve his own declared objectives is more controversial; and more than one commentator has criticised him for being woolly, vague, unclear and ambiguous, for employing definitions which are as elastic as the context, for shifting his terminology in a manner which is more confusing than comprehensible. As MacGregor says, commenting on

the observation that 'it's all in Marshall': 'There is a sense in which many ideas may be "in" a book, but do not come out of it.' D.H. MacGregor, 'Marshall and his Book', *Economica*, Vol. 9, 1942. In Wood II, p. 126. Friedman, similarly, notes that Marshall's definitions are 'characteristically given parenthetically and implicitly', and that Marshall is careless and/or evasive about the precise content of the relevant variables to be assumed away under *ceteris paribus* in a given instance. See M. Friedman, 'The Marshallian Demand Curve', *Journal of Political Economy*, Vol. 57, 1949 and in his *Essays in Positive Economics* (Chicago: The University of Chicago Press, 1953). In Wood III, p. 187.

69. *PE*, p. 32.
70. *PE*, p. 302.
71. *PE*, p. 482. The economist obviously has a great deal to learn from the businessman, practical men of affairs being 'those from whose guidance economic students have profited most in recent years, and may hope to profit increasingly in the future' (*IT*, p. 12). Thence the case for remaining intelligible to the representative reader, relegating technicalities and *minutiae* to footnotes and appendices lest lack of clarity impede communication. The economist must, in other words, be a good writer as well as a good thinker since the reader of a book cannot ask the author questions concerning interpretation and, therefore, 'the written word must carry with it all necessary explanation' (*IT*, p. 680).
72. *PE*, p. 32.
73. 'The Present Position of Economics' (1885), in *Memorials*, p. 164. 'It is', Marshall said, 'a British habit to leave much to be supplied by the common sense of the reader' (*PE*, p. 645), and evidently a good one – since a scientific study of facts and normal conditions can in the last analysis 'never finish off a problem for practical purposes: the finishing touches must always be given by common sense, as the products of even the finest machinery need to be finished off by handicraft'. ('On Rent' (1893), in Guillebaud II, p. 502). Factual knowledge and technical brilliance are simply not enough in the absence of sensitivity, flexibility and a pragmatist's approach to the search for truth.
74. *PE*, p. 36.
75. *PE*, p. 38.
76. *PE*, p. 38.

7.2 Induction and Deduction

1. Pigou, 'In Memoriam: Alfred Marshall', in *Memorials*, p. 88.
2. 'The Present Position of Economics' (1885), in *Memorials*, p. 171.
3. 'The Graphic Method of Statistics' (1885), in *Memorials*, p. 179.
4. 'The Present Position of Economics' (1885), in *Memorials*, p. 166.
5. 'The Old Generation of Economists and the New' (1897), in *Memorials*, p. 298. And elsewhere, emphasising the importance of theory if laws are to be induced and inferences drawn, he writes: 'Facts by themselves teach nothing. History tells of sequences and coincidences; but reason

alone can interpret and draw lessons from them' (*PE*, p. 32).

6. *PE*, p. 638.
7. Quoted in R. Coase, 'Marshall on Method', *Journal of Law and Economics*, Vol. 18, 1975. In Wood I, pp. 410–11. He makes a similar point in defence of mixed methodology in a letter of 1899 to W. A. S. Hewins, the first Director of the LSE: 'It seems strange to me to be asked my views as to the study of pure economic theory; as tho' that were a subject on wh. I were fit to speak . . . . The fact is that I am a dull mean man, who holds Economics to be an organic whole, and has as little respect for pure theory (otherwise than as a branch of mathematics or the science of numbers), as for that crude collection and interpretation of facts without the aid of high analysis which sometimes claims to be a part of economic history.' Quoted in A. W. Coats, 'Alfred Marshall and the Early Development of the London School of Economics: Some Unpublished Letters', *Economica*, Vol. 34, 1967. In Wood IV, p. 133. The inclusion of 'interpretation' in the inductivist category of fact-gathering is perhaps surprising but it is also fully in keeping with Marshall's own common-sensical interpretation of what inductivists actually do.
8. 'The Old Generation of Economists and the New' (1897), in *Memorials*, p. 309.
9. 'The Present Position of Economics' (1885), in *Memorials*, p. 153. Continuity with the classicals there certainly was, but it has also rightly been observed of Marshall that 'taken as a whole, his writings contain more historical material of one kind or another . . . than those of any orthodox economist before or since, Adam Smith always excepted.' See S. Collini, D. Winch and J. Burrow, *That Noble Science of Politics* (Cambridge: The University Press, 1983), p. 322.
10. 'The Old Generation of Economists and the New' (1897), in *Memorials*, p. 303.
11. *MCC*, p. 308.
12. *MCC*, p. 273.
13. *IT*, p. 466.
14. 'The Old Generation of Economists and the New' (1897), in *Memorials*, p. 301. But the nineteenth century had, he felt, made great strides in other areas, notably in 'qualitative analysis' (by which he presumably has in mind the subjectivist revolution).
15. *PE*, p. 634. Marshall himself was a great gatherer of facts, even in his *Principles*. As Schumpeter says of that book (and of the wealth of historical and sociological material which it contains), 'full justice cannot be rendered to it by going straight to the core of the analytic apparatus the *Principles* present. For behind, beyond, and all around that kernel there is an economic sociology of nineteenth century English capitalism which rests on historical bases of impressive extent and solidity. Marshall was, in fact, an economic historian of the first rank, though he may not have been much of an historical technician. And his mastery of historical fact and his analytic habit of mind did not dwell in separate compartments but formed so close a union that the live fact intrudes into the theorem and the theorem into purely

historical observations.' (Schumpeter 'Alfred Marshall's *Principles*: A Semi-Centennial Appraisal' (Chapter 2, note 4), p. 102). The 'real Marshall', Schumpeter argues, was in truth far more of an inductivist than the 'traditionalized' or 'simplified Marshall' against whom critics such as the institutionalists directed their attack. A similar point is made by Shove, who (while not denying the presence of abstract theory in Marshall's work) concludes that 'if any school of thought outside the Ricardian tradition set its mark on the *Principles* it was the Historical School, rather than the marginal utility school, that did so'. G. F. Shove, 'The Place of Marshall's *Principles* in the Development of Economic Theory', *Economic Journal*, Vol. 52, 1942. In Wood II, p. 143. The descriptive element, needless to say, is even more marked in *Industry and Trade*, in evidence to Royal Commissions, and in other places which reveal Marshall as anything but a dogmatic deductivist clinging doggedly to his *a priori*.

p. 302.

17. 'The Present Position of Economics' (1885), in *Memorials*, p. 168.
18. *PE*, p. 644. The present never exactly reproduces the past, but this is no reason for the economist to despair about the possibility of prediction. At the level of ends, Marshall said, 'a chief purpose of every study of human action should be to suggest the probable outcome of present tendencies; and thus to indicate, tacitly if not expressly, such modifications of those tendencies as might further the well-being of mankind.' (*IT*, p. 7). At the level of means, moreover, there are good grounds for optimism concerning our ability to anticipate future events based on records of past: 'Probability is the only guide of general use in life. There are few matters, on which mere reasoning avails. There are a good many more, in which the observation of current events is both necessary and sufficient' (*IT*, p. 6). A characteristic conclusion is the following: 'Explanation is simply prediction written backwards: and, when fully achieved, it helps towards prediction' (*IT*, p. 7). Such a view of explanation and prediction as being essentially the same has been challenged by sceptics such as Shackle, who points to the 'contrasting nature' of the two operations and argues as follows: 'To be allowed to taste a cake and be asked what were the ingredients is not the same thing as to be given some ingredients and be asked what can be made of them. In practice, history can be "explained", after a certain style, without any acceptance of determinism, and without any insuperable difficulties in finding sets of materials which will compose into an ordered structure. But prediction, obliged to select its own materials and assumptions, is hardly more than theorizing in a vacuum. To ask: How did that traveller get here? is *not* the same as to ask: Where may that traveller go from here?' G. L. S. Shackle, *Epistemics and Economics* (Cambridge: The University Press, 1972), p. 347. Marshall's reply would no doubt be a sympathetic one, but he would also, one suspects, take the view that Shackle is being rather extreme in speaking of 'theorizing in a vacuum'. Certainly the danger is there, especially where long term forecasts are concerned, but some knowledge of the future is nonetheless possible. Marshall's position is perhaps most

clearly presented in his preface to the fifth edition (of 1907) of the *Principles*, where, speaking of the scope and purpose of his book, he says: 'Its motto, *Natura non facit saltum*, does not deny the existence of earthquakes and flashes of lightning. It is designed merely to indicate that those manifestations of nature which occur most frequently, and are so orderly that they can be closely watched and narrowly studied, form the foundations of economic as well as of all other scientific work; while those which are sudden, infrequent, and difficult of observation, are commonly reserved for special examination at a later stage.' In Guillebaud II, pp. 46–7. Marshall's point is neither that we can predict everything nor that we can predict nothing but, simply, that we can predict what we can predict, no more and no less. This is in effect what one would have expected from a man who was in so many ways a moderate and a pragmatist.

19. *MCC*, p. 310.
20. 'The Old Generation of Economists and the New' (1897), in *Memorials*, p. 309.
21. *PE*, p. 628n. Smith combined facts (chiefly those 'that were within everyone's knowledge') with theoretical abstraction; and for that reason 'his book, though not well arranged, is a model of method'. Gerbier's comment on yet another attempt by Marshall to link himself with Smith is apposite in the present context: 'Cette vision n'est cependant pas pour nous surprendre tellement Marshall avait pour habitude de lire chez ces autres ce qu'il pensait lui-même.' Gerbier, *Alfred Marshall: Théoricien de l'action efficace et critique radical de l'économie pure*, p. 182.
22. *PE*, p. 640.
23. Letter to *The Times* of 19 August 1910, p. 4, referring to Professor Pearson's 'facts' on the relationship between alcoholism and efficiency.
24. *IT*, p. 673.
25. *IT*, p. 676n.
26. *IT*, p. 673. In truth, 'absolute certainty is possible only in regard to (1) particular individual facts; and (2) deductions by strict reasoning from axiomatic premises, such as those of pure mathematics' – and in inferring generals from particulars the economist (like any other experimental scientist) is seldom on such secure ground.
27. *IT*, pp. 673–4.
28. *IT*, p. 674.
29. *IT*, p. 674.
30. *MCC*, p. 190.
31. Hutchison, *Review of Economic Doctrines*, p. 62.
32. *OP* (1903), p. 377. So the most one can reasonably say is that the room is warmer than it *otherwise* would have been.
33. *OP* (1887), p. 187.
34. *PE*, p. 319.
35. *IT*, p. 679. This aggregation problem imposes constraints on inference based on common sense. What is reasonable for one is not in effect reasonable for all; 'direct practical experience of particular events' is inadequate for purposes of prediction so long as we lack knowledge

concerning the expectations formed by others; and the induction-from-introspection approach in such situations evidently, by itself, 'reaches but a very little way towards the great task of deducing general guidance for the future from the instruction of the past' (*IT*, p. 680).

36. *MCC*, p. 310.
37. *MCC*, p. 189.
38. *MCC*, p. 313.
39. *MCC*, p. 189.
40. Letter to Louis Fry dated 7 November 1914, in *Memorials*, p. 484.
41. *MCC*, p. 274. The 'difficult problem of the interaction of countless economic causes' (*PE*, p. 306) is, it is clear, a complexity which simply cannot be ignored; and, despite the fact that it is 'the natural tendency of the human mind to be impressed by striking coincidences' (*OP* (1887), p. 184), the economist should never neglect to probe deep beneath the surface of things.
42. *MCC*, p. 309. Such selective use of data to support a favourite conclusion is a real danger, and not least where interested partisans are seeking to influence government policy. Thus Marshall notes that 'the worst instances of recklessness in this particular are to be found in the writings of the Protectionist school' ('The Theory of Foreign Trade' (1873–7), in Whitaker II, p. 53), and contrasts such carelessness of expression with the measured scepticism of the scholarly economist: 'Exaggerated notions of the scope and cogency of economic doctrines have been less frequent in calm academic discussions, than in heated political controversies' (*IT*, p. 760).
43. *IT*, p. 839.
44. *PE*, p. vii.
45. 'The Present Position of Economics' (1885), in *Memorials*, p. 166.
46. 'The Old Generation of Economists and the New' (1897), in *Memorials*, p. 306.
47. 'Some Aspects of Competition' (1890), in *Memorials*, p. 268.
48. *PE*, p. 637.
49. *PE*, p. 678. The whole thrust of the argument in Chapters Two, Three and even Four of the present book is that any model in the social sciences which does not allow for evolutionary change as time passes is likely to be misleading in its predictions concerning effects and their causes, and likely in addition to turn up the meaningless result and the spurious correlation. The economist should, in other words, never underestimate the significance of structural alterations brought about by the 'progress of wealth and knowledge' (*PE*, p. 584): 'For instance a small addition to a man's income will generally increase his purchases a little in every direction: but a large addition may alter his habits, perhaps increase his self-respect and make him cease to care for some things altogether' (*PE*, p. 637). Such an appreciation of structural alterations if intelligent predictions are to be made is itself a sound argument for the employment of the institutional and evolutionary methodology in economic investigation.
50. 'The Present Position of Economics' (1885), in *Memorials*, p. 169.
51. *PE*, p. 637.

52. *MCC*, p. 106. Time means change, change means uncertainty, and uncertainty means exceptional problems in the field of prediction. Our data refers, sadly, to the past and not to the future.
53. 'The Present Position of Economics' (1885), in *Memorials*, p. 154. Marshall is speaking here explicitly about the stages of development of a science, but what is implicit is the development of the phenomena that that science seeks to analyse. As he puts it a few pages later (on p. 159) in the same essay: 'We may not assign any universality to economic dogmas. For that part of economic doctrine, which alone can claim universality, has no dogmas. It is not a body of concrete truth, but an engine for the discovery of concrete truth.'
54. Letter to C. R. Fay dated 23 February 1915, in *Memorials*, p. 490.
55. Fragment dating from 1922, in *Memorials*, p. 360.
56. *IT*, p. 506.
57. *IT*, p. 656.
58. Letter to F. Y. Edgeworth dated 28 August 1902, in *Memorials*, p. 437.
59. *IT*, p. vi.
60. *IT*, p. 723n.
61. 'A Reply to "The Perversion of Economic History" by Dr Cunningham' (1892), in Guillebaud II, p. 739n. Marshall says that Jones's book, presumably the *Essay* of 1831, was 'one of the first on economics that I came across'. Elsewhere, he praises the 'wholesome influence of the criticisms of the historical school' (*PE*, p. 641), despite the opposition between the main drift of its work and his own, both for forcing economists to collect more factual data and for compelling them to be sceptical about the universality of theoretical propositions.
62. 'The Present Position of Economics' (1885), in *Memorials*, p. 163.
63. 'The Present Position of Economics' (1885), in *Memorials*, p. 166.
64. *PE*, p. 639.
65. 'The Present Position of Economics' (1885), in *Memorials*, p. 171.
66. 'Distribution and Exchange' (1898), in Guillebaud II, p. 72.
67. 'The Present Position of Economics' (1885), in *Memorials*, p. 164.
68. 'The Present Position of Economics' (1885), in *Memorials*, p. 171.
69. Letter to F. Y. Edgeworth dated 28 August 1902, in *Memorials*, p. 437. Marshall, in his essay on 'Distribution and Exchange' (1898), in Guillebaud II, p. 72, actually boasts that only a part of his *Principles* is actually devoted to pure theory, namely Book V (which is devoted to 'the eternal opposition of forces impelling people to do, and forces holding them back'): The 'theoretical backbone of our knowledge of the causes which govern value, on its two sides of distribution and exchange, is put together in my Book V. The word "Theory" appears in the title of that Book alone. It deals with abstractions; and refers to realities for the purpose of illustration only, not of construction.'
70. 'The Present Position of Economics' (1885), in *Memorials*, p. 153.
71. 'The Present Position of Economics' (1885), in *Memorials*, p. 154.
72. 'The Present Position of Economics' (1885), in *Memorials*, p. 162.
73. 'Some Aspects of Competition' (1890), in *Memorials*, p. 258.
74. 'Some Aspects of Competition' (1890), in *Memorials*, p. 258.
75. 'The Present Position of Economics' (1885), in *Memorials*, p. 159. And

yet Marshall elsewhere defines 'classical' ideas in economics as those original ideas 'which, once created, can never die, but are an existing yeast ceaselessly working in the Cosmos' (Letter to James Bonar dated 27 September 1898, in *Memorials*, p. 374). He appears therefore to have believed, at least at one point, that there was something of eternal relevance in the ideas of the men of 1770–1820 (the period he explicitly cites). Similarly, in the *Principles* he speaks of Mill's 'power of doing that kind of work which influences the course of thought in future generations' (*PE*, p. 210n).

76. *PE*, p. 638.
77. *PE*, p. 637.
78. *PE*, p. 637.
79. 'The Present Position of Economics' (1885), in *Memorials*, p. 153. It was, as we have already noted, precisely this mix of evidence and analysis, fact and formalism, Marshall declared in a letter to L. L. Price dated 19 August 1892 (in *Memorials*, p. 379), which had at an early stage attracted him to Adam Smith; for Smith's contribution is in truth to be found 'more in the general conspectus which he presented than in particular doctrines. And as regards this, the more I knew of him, the more I worshipped him. It was his balance, his sense of proportion, his power of seeing the many in the one and the one in the many, his skill in using analysis to interpret history and history to correct analysis . . . that seemed to mark him out as unique; very much as similar qualities have more recently given a similar position to Darwin. . . . His high prerogative comes from his having shown how inseparable induction and deduction are.' As early as the *Economics of Industry* Marshall adopted the position that 'Inductions continually suggest new Deductions; . . . Deductions continually suggest new Inductions' (p. 3n) and that therefore 'the science of Economics progresses step by step, alternately applying theory in the search for and explanation of new facts, and applying new facts in correcting and broadening and strengthening theory' (p. 149). In a sense the interdependence between *ex ante* interpretive schemata and *ex post* observation is most marked in *Industry and Trade*; but the same ingredients of classification, presentation, example, illustration are to be found in the *Principles* as well, even if the mix is different. No one knows the *Principles* who knows only Books III and V. As Keynes said, pointing to the myriad qualifications and the implicit intricacies: 'It needs much study and independent thought on the reader's own part, before he can know the half of what is contained in the concealed crevices of that rounded globe of knowledge, which is Marshall's *Principles of Economics*.' (Keynes, 'Alfred Marshall, 1842–1924', in *Memorials*, p. 48).
80. 'The Old Generation of Economists and the New' (1897), in *Memorials*, p. 309.
81. 'The Pure Theory of Foreign Trade' (1879), in Whitaker II, p. 119.
82. 'The Pure Theory of Foreign Trade' (1879), in Whitaker II, p. 118.
83. *PE*, p. 453.
84. *PE*, p. 326n.
85. *PE*, p. 644.

86. 'The Graphic Method of Statistics' (1885), in *Memorials*, p. 180.
87. *PE*, p. 71.
88. *PE*, p. 688.
89. *PE*, p. ix.
90. *PE*, p. ix, where he also says of diagrams: 'Experience seems to show that they give a firmer grasp of many important principles than can be got without their aid'. The 'grasp', it must be stressed, is, like that yielded by the apparatus of mathematics, essentially expositional in nature: 'It is to be remembered that graphical illustrations are not proofs. They are merely pictures corresponding very roughly to the main conditions of certain real problems. They obtain clearness of outline, by leaving out of account many considerations which vary from one practical problem to another' (*PE*, p. 129n). And in the 'Pure Theory of Foreign Trade' (1879), in Whitaker II, p. 133, he writes as follows in praise of quantitative argumentation by means of diagrammatic exposition: 'Diagrams present simultaneously to the eye the chief forces which are at work, laid out, as it were, in a map; and thereby suggest results to which attention has not been directed by the use of the methods of mathematical analysis. The method of diagrams can be freely used by every one who is capable of exact reasoning, even though he have no knowledge of Mathematics . . . . Diagrams are of great service, wherever they are applicable, in interpreting to the eye the processes by which the methods of mathematical analysis obtain their results. It happens that with a few unimportant exceptions all the results which have been obtained by the application of mathematical methods to pure economic theory can be obtained independently by the method of diagrams.'
91. Letter to A. L. Bowley dated 27 February 1906, in *Memorials*, p. 427. In his letters to Hewins (see note 7, *supra*), describing pure theory as 'elegant toying' (p. 137) and the mathematical method as an aid to precision of expression for those who 'happened to like mathematics', he is slightly more merciful about the future of the intermediate stages once they had been carefully translated back into English: scholars, he suggests, might care 'to keep a few specimens of such work in an old curiosity shop' (p. 134).
92. *PE*, p. 671.
93. *PE*, p. 297n.
94. *PE*, p. 85n.
95. *PE*, p. 386n. See also *PE*, p. 399n for a similar statement.
96. *PE*, p. 644.
97. *PE*, p. 701.
98. Letter to J. B. Clark dated 24 March 1908, in *Memorials*, p. 417.
99. Letter to A. L. Bowley dated 3 March 1901, in *Memorials*, p. 422. Such modesty with respect to mathematics is an essential part of Marshall's economics, if not always of the textbook tradition which he fathered. Mathematics, he consistently argued, is first and foremost to be regarded as didactic scaffolding, as a guide to logical reasoning intended to 'give the mind strength': 'It is the special work of mathematics to give the power of reasoning correctly and of knowing when a thing is

proved. There is not, and as far as we can see there cannot ever be, a study which can do this work nearly as well as mathematics can... Mathematics is to the mind what bread is to the body.' (Public lecture intended for delivery in Bristol in 1877. Quoted in Whitaker, 'Alfred Marshall: The Years 1877 to 1885' (Chapter 3.2, note 14), p. 146.) Marshall's point is that mathematics in essence should be looked to for training rather than results. He also warned, in 'The Pure Theory of Foreign Trade' (1879), in Whitaker II, p. 162n, of the dangers that face the mathematical economist: 'The use of mathematical analysis has been found to tempt men to expend their energy on the elaboration of minute and complex hypotheses, which have indeed some distant analogy to economic conditions, but which cannot properly be said to represent in any way economic laws.' An economist who allows himself to be so far removed from the world of economic reality is clearly not of much service either to his discipline or to his society.

100. *PE*, p. 700. The subjective, the expectational, the intuitive, the empathetic are only some of the important economic variables that are lost in this way, in addition to the time-related, organic and genetic relationships which Marshall explicitly mentions.
101. *PE*, p. 700.
102. *PE*, p. 644, emphasis added.
103. *PE*, p. 656. The problem of indeterminacy rather than equilibrium is what Marshall seems to have had in mind when opting not to follow Edgeworth and Pigou (and, for that matter, Lardner's *Railway Economy* of 1849) in incorporating 'slight touches of mathematical reasoning' into his discussion of imperfect competition as applied to the field of transportation: 'Their route is not followed here: for mathematical analysis cannot easily be applied to *conditional* monopoly: it is almost constrained to start with the hypothesis of *pure* monopoly, and gradually to introduce successive limitations, corresponding to the various limitations and restrictions which are imposed on railways by various circumstances, and especially by the guiding and restraining influences of public opinion and authority' (*IT*, pp. 449n, 450n). In a letter to Edgeworth dated 28 August 1902 (in *Memorials*, p. 435) he appears to make a similar point about contingency in expressing reservations about the theory of demand and supply: 'Ox for market values measures a stock and not a "flow"; and I found that, if I once got people to use Demand and Supply curves which discussed *stocks* along the axis of *x*, they could not easily be kept from introducing the notion of stock when *flow* was essential.' This reminds us once again that 'length of time' has been conspicuously absent in 'mathematical and semi-mathematical discussions of the theory of value' (*PE*, pp. 414–5), and that this lends a spurious precision to a subject-matter which is anything but constant, universal and easily predictable. Shackle's view is eminently apposite in the present context: 'Economics cannot be a precise science of calculable effects. Its nature is to be the subject-matter of critical imagination, a subject-matter suited to an essentially literary expression, like history itself' (Shackle, *The Years of High Theory*, p. vi).

104. *PE*, p. 306.
105. *PE*, p. 699.
106. Letter to Edgeworth dated 28 August 1902, in *Memorials*, p. 435. Two decades earlier Marshall had made the same point not *to* Edgeworth but *about* Edgeworth, in his review in *The Academy* of 18 June 1881 of *Mathematical Psychics*: 'This book shows clear signs of genius, and is a promise of great things to come .... It will be interesting to watch the development of his theory, and, in particular, to see how far he succeeds in preventing his mathematics from running away with him, and carrying him out of sight of the actual facts of economics.' In Whitaker II, pp. 265, 267.
107. 'The Pure Theory of Foreign Trade' (1879), in Whitaker II, p. 163. And elsewhere: 'When a force moves the thing on which it acts, it thereby changes the force which that thing afterwards exercises' ('Mechanical and Biological Analogies in Economics' (1898), in *Memorials*, p. 313). The passage, which deals with interdependencies, 'complications' and 'reciprocal influences' between dynamic phenomena, concludes on a note of caution with respect to the use of mathematics: 'The most helpful applications of mathematics to economics are those which are short and simple, which employ few symbols; and which aim at throwing a bright light on some small part of the great economic movement rather than at representing its endless complexities.'
108. 'The Present Position of Economics' (1885), in *Memorials*, p. 154.
109. Pigou, *Alfred Marshall and Current Thought*, pp. 11–12.
110. Letter to A. L. Bowley dated 3 March 1901, in *Memorials*, p. 422.
111. 'The Graphic Method of Statistics' (1885), in *Memorials*, p. 180.
112. 'Social Possibilities of Economic Chivalry' (1907), in *Memorials*, p. 324.
113. 'Social Possibilities of Economic Chivalry' (1907), in *Memorials*, p. 323.
114. Letter to A. L. Bowley dated 20 December 1901, in *Memorials*, p. 424.
115. Letter to A. L. Bowley dated 21 February 1901, in *Memorials*, p. 421.
116. Letter to A. L. Bowley dated 3 March 1901, in *Memorials*, p. 423.
117. 'Mr Jevons' Theory of Political Economy' (1872), in *Memorials*, p. 99. Marshall clearly took his own advice in the work he was then doing on international and domestic trade.
118. L. E. Fouraker, 'The Cambridge Didactic Style (A. Marshall and J. M. Keynes)', *Journal of Political Economy*, Vol. 66, 1958. In Wood I, p. 276.
119. *Ibid.*, pp. 279–80. As the argument in the Chapter indicates, however, there is no reason to think that Marshall, in his desire to be useful and to persuade, actually compromised on *necessary* rigour so as to be comprehensible to a wide audience of general readers.
120. Pigou, *Alfred Marshall and Current Thought*, p. 6.
121. Pigou, 'In Memoriam: Alfred Marshall', in *Memorials*, p. 86.
122. F. Y. Edgeworth, "Reminiscences", in *Memorials*, p. 66.
123. J. A. Schumpeter, *History of Economic Analysis* (Oxford: Oxford University Press, 1954), p. 838.
124. Schumpeter, 'Alfred Marshall's *Principles*: A Semi-Centennial Appraisal' (see note 15, *supra*), p. 104.

125. 'Mr Jevons' Theory of Political Economy' (1872), in *Memorials*, pp. 98, 99.
126. Letter to A. L. Bowley dated 27 February 1906, in *Memorials*, p. 427.
127. 'Mr Jevons' Theory of Political Economy' (1872), in *Memorials*, p. 99.
128. *PE*, p. ix.
129. Letter to A. L. Bowley dated 27 February 1906, in *Memorials*, p. 428.
130. 'Mr Jevons' Theory of Political Economy' (1872), in *Memorials*, p. 99. Keynes (in 'Alfred Marshall, 1842–1924', in *Memorials*, p. 24) goes so far as to call Marshall 'the founder of modern diagrammatic economics'. Marshall was also, and to the same extent, the father of modern mathematical economics. As a Wrangler, of course, he had no need for conspicuous display of symbolic pyrotechnics, and was able to afford the luxury of wearing his learning lightly.
131. *PE*, p. viii.
132. *PE*, p. 642.
133. PE, p. 306.

7.3 Organicism and Economics

1. *PE*, p. xiii.
2. 'Mr Jevons' Theory of Political Economy' (1872), in *Memorials*, pp. 94–5.
3. *PE, p. xii.*
4. K. E. Boulding, *Evolutionary Economics* (London: Sage Publications, 1981), p. 17.
5. *Ibid.*, p. 84.
6. T. Veblen, *The Place of Science in Modern Civilisation and Other Essays* (1919) (New York: Russell & Russell, 1961), p. 173. Nor does Wesley Clair Mitchell manage to find any significantly institutional elements in Marshall. See his *Types of Economic Theory* (1949) (New York: Augustus M. Kelley, 1969), Vol. II, Chapter X. It is genuinely mystifying why evolutionary economics has failed to find in Marshall so important a forebear as he in truth would seem to have been.
7. J. M. Keynes, *A Treatise on Money* (1930) (London: Macmillan, 1960), Vol. II, p. 406.
8. *PE*, p. 382.
9. *PE*, p. xii.
10. *PE*, p. xiii.
11. 'Mechanical and Biological Analogies in Economics' (1898), in *Memorials*, p. 318.
12. Blaug, *Economic Theory in Retrospect*, p. 420.
13. *PE*, p. 269. The law of gravity and the bowls in the basin reappear on p. 674.
14. 'The Old Generation of Economists and the New' (1897), in *Memorials*, p. 300.
15. *IT*, pp. 5, 6. The motto itself comes from Leibniz.

16. *PE*, p. xi.
17. 'A Fair Rate of Wages' (1887), in *Memorials*, p. 226.
18. *IT*, p. 81.
19. 'Remedies for Fluctuations of General Prices' (1887), in *Memorials*, p. 188.
20. *PE*, p. vi.
21. *PE*, p. v.
22. *PE*, p. 631.
23. *PE*, p. 42. Marshall is using the term 'state of economic development' in a loose sense in the present context. Elsewhere, however, his approach to the term and the concept is more precise – as when, noting List's 'well-known doctrine that economic development in the past has generally shown three clearly marked stages', he comments: 'That doctrine, taken broadly, appears to be securely established' (*IT*, p. 697). This comment may, as a matter of factual accuracy, indicate a greater commitment to the phases-of-development theory than was actually the case. In a set of notes dated 18 April 1923 (and thus of the same vintage) Marshall included a section on the theory but then scrawled over it 'go into this matter carefully or avoid it altogether' (see Marshall Papers, Red Box 1 (3), envelope entitled 'Progress and Ideals'); and the references to the stages-theory in his published work are conspicuously few in number. And there are even more important problems that arise in connection with the theory. List's three-stage model involves a continuous process of evolution from a concentration on primary products (stage I) through simpler forms of manufacture (stage II) to advanced manufacturing (stage III). It is hard to see why Marshall regards such an expansion-path as 'securely established' in view of the fact, as he himself points out, that the theory fails to account for the economic strength of a country such as Holland whose comparative advantage lies in commerce rather than industry. Marshall seems to think that List's theory is a reasonable account of the British experience (historically considered) but he also says: 'It is no longer reasonable to assume, as a matter of course, that an increase in a country's manufactures must be welcomed more heartily than other developments of her economic activity' (*IT*, p. 699). For someone whose objectives were clearly so ambitious, it is remarkable how vague Marshall can be on quite important issues associated with the theoretical underpinnings of economic history. There is much truth in Glassburner's observation about Marshall that 'he argued that one could not avoid implication of a theory of history, but he really felt that no general theory of history could be written. He never offered an explicit one of his own nor ever really analyzed the implicit theoretical factors in his personal attitude toward history . . . . The social organism was occasionally supplied by him with a suggestion of vertebrae, but on most occasions in his hands it resembled most nearly a jellyfish.' B. Glassburner, 'Alfred Marshall on Economic History and Historical Development', *Quarterly Journal of Economics*, Vol. 69, 1955. In Wood I, p. 269.
24. *PE*, p. vi.

25. *PE*, p. v.
26. *PE*, p. 642.
27. *PE*, p. v. As with the theory of value, so with the theory of wages, that it is all in the classical economists and continuity rather than cleavage is the order of the day: 'We hear a great deal about the supplanting of old-fashioned theories of wages by newer and truer doctrines. But in fact the change in the theory itself has not been very great. Although a good deal of new work has been added, and the old work has been developed, yet but very little has been destroyed. Almost everything that was ever said by the great economists of the first half of the century is true now if properly understood.' (*IRC*, p. 186.) Few if any other economists would have selected the debate about the wages-fund as an illustration of continuity in economic thought. One is tempted to speculate on what, if anything, Marshall would have regarded as an intellectual revolution. Since he acknowledged the possibility of political revolution, his obsessive *natura non facit saltum*ism in the field of ideas suggests a genuine and unexplained asymmetry in his thinking.
28. *PE*, p. viii.
29. *PE*, p. 339n.
30. *PE*, p. 694.
31. *PE*, p. 269. The use of the word 'equilibrium' in this context is an unusual one since it refers not to the (physical) balance of forces but to the (biological) turning point – to that historical point on the time axis, in other words, which separates growth (which has ceased) from decay (which has not yet set in). It is worth adding that, precisely because the horizontal axis is a time as well as a quantity axis, the U-shape of the cost curve itself reflects organic variables – as when average cost rises due to the inflexibilities and loss of initiative of age.
32. *PE*, p. 200.
33. *PE*, p. 200.
34. *PE*, p. 12. Hence 'economics cannot be compared to the exact physical sciences' of which the subject-matter is inert. It is perhaps worth recording that Marshall in one place makes a pedantic but useful distinction between human *nature* and its external *manifestations*: 'In the modern age human nature remains very much as it was in former times: but intellectual habits have changed fast and progressively' (*IT*, p. 400). This distinction points to interesting linkages between psychology and economics which could profitably be followed up.
35. 'The Old Generation of Economists and the New' (1897), in *Memorials*, p. 311.
36. *PE*, p. 631.
37. See Chapters Two and Three of the present book.
38. *IT*, p. 797.
39. *EI*, p. vii.
40. *IT*, p. 748n. What this means is that a socially-valued custom will simply cease to be socially-valued where that long-established way of doing things is perceived to be inappropriate in the new material conditions. Evidently even custom can be explained if sufficient facts are collected;

and once that is done considerations of economic and social rationality are likely to loom large in the account of its causes. This, however, leaves important questions unanswered, such as why different countries develop different customs in broadly similar circumstances – and why some demonstrably show no interest in rationality, progress or even growth. The reason could, of course, be that those cultures are following a path which is genuinely alternative to that which Marshall anticipated would be the normal one.

41. 'The Present Position of Economics' (1885), in *Memorials*, pp. 169–70.
42. See *IT*, pp. 197–8.
43. *IT*, p. 163.
44. *IT*, p. 163. In the case of the pigeon the centrepiece of the theory of action is to be sought not in freedom and deliberateness but in instinctual response and conditioned reflex. Much of man's action too is instinctual (the relationship between the sex drive and the procreation of children) and automatic (as in the case of conformity to custom) – but much is based on intellective qualities such as imagination and conscious choice in which the pigeon is known to be weak.
45. *IT*, p. 9.
46. *IT*, p. 6.
47. 'Mechanical and Biological Analogies in Economics' (1898), in *Memorials*, p. 317.
48. *PE*, p. xi.
49. *IT*, p. 206.
50. The comparative method is thus historical in nature to the extent that today's savage is yesterday's Englishman – a not uncommon assumption in Marshall's day. See on this J. W. Burrow, *Evolution and Society* (Cambridge: The University Press, 1966).
51. Parsons, 'Wants and Activities in Marshall' (Chapter 2.1, note 53), p. 218. Parsons' general point is valid but his example of socialism is not entirely felicitous for the reasons which we considered in Chapter 4.1.
52. 'Some Features of American Industry' (1875), in Whitaker II, p. 355.
53. *PE*, p. 622.
54. *PE*, p. 623.
55. 'Some Features of American Industry' (1875), in Whitaker II, pp. 357, 358. And on p. 357, speaking of the manner in which character is endogenous to economic processes, he once again places great stress on the influence exerted by the 'daily occupations of men': 'This influence has I think in general been underrated. I think it is enormous, because people occupy the greater part of their time in their daily occupations. There are no thoughts, or actions, or feelings, which occupy a man, and which thus have the opportunity of forming the man, during so large a portion of his life as those thoughts and actions and feelings which make up his daily occupation.'
56. 'A Reply to "The Perversion of Economic History" by Dr Cunningham' (1892), in Guillebaud II, p. 737.
57. *PE*, p. 623.
58. *PE*, p. 225.
59. *PE*, p. 225. But in fact he does not say a great deal about Great Men,

save to note the possibility of their existence.

60. 'Mechanical and Biological Analogies in Economics' (1898), in *Memorials*, p. 313.
61. 'Mechanical and Biological Analogies in Economics' (1898), in *Memorials*, p. 317.
62. 'Mechanical and Biological Analogies in Economics' (1898), in *Memorials*, p. 313. Major new discoveries constitute a definite problem: 'The difficulty of forecasting the future . . . is increased by the growth of these ideas' (*IT*, p. 159).
63. 'The Future of the Working Classes' (1873), in *Memorials*, p. 116.
64. *IT*, p. 103. The explanation becomes even more organic when he attributes the rapid American growth rate in part to its inheritance of sound English genes.
65. *PE*, p. 284.
66. *IT*, p. 2.
67. *IT*, p. 4. This observation reflects Spencer's prediction of perceived harmony of interests in an exchange ('industrial') society.
68. *IT*, p. 2.
69. H. Spencer, *First Principles*, 5th ed. (London and Edinburgh: Williams & Norgate, 1890), p. 307.
70. *Ibid.*, pp. 342–3.
71. *PE*, pp. 20–1.
72. *PE*, p. 27.
73. *PE*, p. 23.
74. *PE*, p. 601.
75. *PE*, p. 334.
76. Spencer, *First Principles*, p. 318.
77. *PE*, p. 344.
78. *PE*, p. 448. Similarly, an entry-restriction or strike on the part of one grade of labour causes widespread ripples throughout the entire labour force and the economy. See, for example, *PE*, p. 580.
79. 'The Graphic Method of Statistics' (1885), in *Memorials*, p. 178.
80. *PE*, p. 564.
81. *IT*, p. 652.
82. *IT*, pp. 22, 23.
83. *IT*, p. 600.
84. *PE*, pp. 200–1. Another very good illustration of the same typically Spencerian proposition is the following: 'The world money market has become an agency, at once firmly unified and highly specialized. It is unified, in that the different parts of it are so closely connected that claims of any one kind can be used indirectly to balance claims of any other: and it is specialized, in that different financial houses give themselves to dealing in particular classes of international drafts, bills and other claims.' (*MCC*, p. 151). Economists interested in the dialectical method will no doubt find evidence of it in constructions such as these.
85. *PE*, p. viii.
86. 'The Present Position of Economics' (1885), in *Memorials*, p. 161.
87. *PE*, p. 672.

88. *PE*, p. 674.
89. *PE*, p. 334.
90. *EI*, pp. 147–8. In the example given, we in fact know both A and B. Real life is more complex since so many relationships are indirect and easily neglected – the impact on British exports of improvements in Italian railways, for example, or on British imports of the introduction of protective duties, of which 'the indirect are often much more important than the direct effects; in some of them the economic element predominates, and in others the ethical and the political. It is impossible to discuss fiscal policy without reference to all these elements.' (*OP* (1903), p. 367). The economist must accordingly strive 'to select the true causes of each event and assign to each its proper weight; and above all to detect the remoter causes of change' (*PE*, p. 640). Clearly, if the economist is truly to grasp 'the hidden springs of the economic order of the world', intuition, imagination and the power to make meaningful generalisations are as important as collection of data. This reminds us of the case of mutual causality which we considered in the previous section, namely the interdependence of induction and deduction.
91. 'Mechanical and Biological Analogies in Economics' (1898), in *Memorials*, p. 314.
92. 'Mechanical and Biological Analogies in Economics' (1898), in *Memorials*, p. 314.
93. *IT*, p. v. Some of the changes over time are caused by variables endogenous to the closed system or model, but others are the result of exogenous factors, outside shocks which cause us radically to alter predictions which on the basis of *ceteris paribus* seemed eminently reasonable. For example: 'Opening the sluice of a reservoir tends to lower the level of water in it; but if meanwhile larger supplies of water are flowing in at the other end, the opening of the sluice may be followed by a rising of the level of the water in the cistern' (*PE*, p. 584). Nor are such shocks, although coming from outside the system, entirely unexpected: it is, after all, to be expected that scientists will invent and innovate, and that entrepreneurs will strive to steal a march on their competitors in an environment characterised by survival of the fittest. Needless to say, the longer the time period under consideration, the greater the likelihood of such developments.
94. *PE*, p. 442.
95. *PE*, p. 290.
96. Schumpeter, *History of Economic Analysis*, p. 836.
97. *PE*, p. 637. And elsewhere he says: 'The fact that the general conditions of life are not stationary is the source of many of the difficulties that are met with in applying economic doctrines to practical problems' (*PE*, p. 289). Which, of course, did not prevent Marshall from attempting – albeit with caution – such applications.
98. A. Smith, 'The History of Astronomy', in *Essays on Philosophical Subjects* (1795), reprinted in J. Ralph Lindgren, ed., *The Early Writings of Adam Smith* (New York: Augustus M. Kelley, 1967), p. 100.
99. *PE*, p. vii.

100. *PE*, p. 482.
101. *PE*, p. 678. It must be remembered that some classical economists, due to their belief in the wages-fund doctrine, had denied that there was such an intrinsic homogeneity.
102. See *EAM*, Chapter 10.4.
103. *PE*, p. vii. Another instance of homogeneity within the labour force is Marshall's rejection of the classical doctrine that there was a significant difference to be drawn between productive and unproductive labour. See, for example, *EI*, p. 7.
104. *PE*, p. 523. Note his use of terminology drawn from biology.
105. Letter to L. L. Price dated 19 August 1892, in *Memorials, p. 379.*
106. Only in the Stationary State are actual values equal to normal values in all markets simultaneously; but even then change is taking place in the sense that some of the trees of the forest are growing while others are decaying. The forest itself is 'full of movement' despite the fact that the representative unit is of constant size – a result which suggests that Marshall, even when trying to think statics, was in the event compelled by the logic of his own temperament to relapse into dynamics.
107. L. Rogin. 'Davenport on the Economics of Alfred Marshall', *American Economic Review*, Vol. 26, 1936. In Wood II. p. 72n. The footnote in question may be found at *PE*, p. 339n. Marshall in no way says, 'implicitly' or otherwise, what Rogin asserts he does – rather the opposite, in fact.
108. Kerr, *Marshall, Marx and Modern Times*, p. 1.
109. *Ibid.*
110. H. Scott Gordon, 'Alfred Marshall and the Development of Economics as a Science', in R. N. Glere and R. S. Westfall, eds., *Foundations of Scientific Method in the Nineteenth Century* (Indiana: Indiana University Press, 1973). In Wood IV, p. 270.

7.4 The Mission of the Economist

1. 'Social Possibilities of Economic Chivalry' (1907), in *Memorials*, p. 324.
2. *PE*, p. 626.
3. *PE*, p. 116.
4. *PE*, p. 1.
5. *PE*, p. 116. Given that poverty is a bad thing and thence our resolve 'that the present evils shall no longer be allowed to exist' (*PE*, p. 601), the teleology and the normative orientation would seem to follow as if guided by an invisible hand; and Marshall therefore expressed much sympathy with the idea that 'the well-being of the whole people should be the ultimate goal of all private effort and all public policy' (*PE*, p. 39).
6. 'The Present Position of Economics' (1885), in *Memorials*, p. 172.
7. *PE*, p. 39. So in that sense economics is not value-free precisely *because* it is economics and thus *by its very nature* concerned with economising.
8. *PE*, p. 1.

9. *PE*, p. 40. Economics is about change, and that is why economists must be great evaluators of the costs and benefits associated with new departures. Change itself, after all, whether the result of policy or of the market mechanism, is an evil. Naturally, 'the greater the evils of change, the more important it is to inquire thoroughly whether any proposed scheme is the best possible.' ('Remedies for Fluctuations of General Prices' (1887), in *Memorials*, p. 188).
10. *PE*, p. 440. See also *PE*, p. 38.
11. 'The Present Position of Economics' (1885), in *Memorials*, pp. 172, 173.
12. 'Social Possibilities of Economic Chivalry' (1907), in *Memorials*, p. 323.
13. Letter to Mrs Bosanquet dated 2 October 1902, in *Memorials*, p. 445.
14. A. C. Pigou, review of the fifth edition of Marshall's *Principles of Economics*, *Economic Journal*, Vol. 17, 1907. In Wood II, p. 56. Emphasis deleted.
15. 'Social Possibilities of Economic Chivalry' (1907), in *Memorials*, p. 346.
16. 'Social Possibilities of Economic Chivalry' (1907), in *Memorials*, p. 339.
17. Lecture delivered in Bristol on 9 October 1877. Quoted in Whitaker, 'Alfred Marshall: The Years 1877 to 1885' (Chapter 3.2, note 14), p. 138. See also *EI*, p. 212. The media contribute as well in so far as they give union leaders a more general and a clearer appreciation of the remoter consequences of a given course of action: no sensitive man wants public opinion to identify him as a cad and trades unionists are sensitive men.
18. See on this Chapter 6.4 – a clear illustration of the way in which the collection of information actually has power to alter the course of events.
19. *IT*, p. 676n. See also *PE*, p. 407.
20. 'Some Aspects of Competition' (1890), in *Memorials*, p. 264.
21. 'The Present Position of Economics' (1885), in *Memorials*, p. 162.
22. 'The Present Position of Economics' (1885), in *Memorials*, p. 162.
23. 'Social Possibilities of Economic Chivalry' (1907), in *Memorials*, p. 346.
24. 'The Old Generation of Economists and the New' (1897), in *Memorials*, p. 306.
25. 'The Old Generation of Economists and the New' (1897), in *Memorials*, p. 303.
26. 'Some Aspects of Competition' (1890), in *Memorials*, p. 290. Marshall states in numerous places his conviction that sensitivity to social pressures is of considerable importance. In 'Some Aspects of Competition' (1890), for example: 'Unquestionably, the economists of to-day do go beyond those of earlier generations in believing that the desire of men for the approval of their own conscience and for the esteem of others is an economic force of the first order of importance, and that the strength of public opinion is steadily increasing' (In *Memorials*, p. 285; see also pp. 289–90, *IT*, p. 634 and *OP* (1893), p. 245). Once public opinion becomes 'an informal Court of Honour', then 'wealth, however large, would be no passport to social success if got by chicanery, by manufactured news, by fraudulent dealing, or by malignant destruction of rivals: and that business enterprise which was noble in its aims and in its methods, even if it did not bring with it a

large fortune, would receive its due of public admiration and gratitude' ('Social Possibilites of Economic Chivalry' (1907), in *Memorials*, p. 343). Such pressures can be mobilised for the social good, and in doing this – in creating social constraints, in other words, which to some extent obviate the need for political directives – the economist, like other opinion-leaders, has a useful social role to play. Thus in the *Principles* (p. 35) Marshall recommends the following question to the attention of the economist: 'What scope is there for the moral pressure of social opinion in constraining and directing individual action in those economic relations in which the rigidity and violence of government interference would be likely to do more harm than good?'

27. Lecture delivered in Bristol on 5 March 1883. Quoted in Stigler, 'Alfred Marshall's Lectures on Progress and Poverty' (Chapter 2.1, note 50), p. 173.
28. 'The Old Generation of Economists and the New' (1897), in *Memorials*, p. 310.
29. 'The Old Generation of Economists and the New' (1897), in *Memorials*, p. 310.
30. 'The Old Generation of Economists and the New' (1897), in *Memorials*, p. 304.
31. *PE*, p. 39.
32. *PE*, p. 38.
33. *PE*, p. 622.
34. *PE*, p. 622.
35. 'The Present Position of Economics' (1885), in *Memorials*, p. 163.
36. 'The Old Generation of Economists and the New' (1897), in *Memorials*, p. 305.
37. Keynes, 'Alfred Marshall, 1842–1924', in *Memorials*, p. 11.
38. Quoted in Keynes, 'Alfred Marshall, 1842–1924', in *Memorials*, p. 41.
39. Keynes, 'Alfred Marshall, 1842–1924' in *Memorials*, p. 37.
40. Pigou, 'In Memoriam: Alfred Marshall', in *Memorials*, pp. 82, 84.
41. C. J. Dewey, '"Cambridge Idealism": Utilitarian Revisionists in Late Nineteenth-Century Cambridge', *Historical Journal*, Vol. XVII, 1974, p. 63. Dewey continues: 'Where the utilitarian individual was (or seemed to be) an economic man automatically maximizing the pleasure and minimizing the pain he experiences, without concern for others, the rationalist-idealist individual was a moral being whose appetities and aversions, far from being constant or purely self-regarding, were set by the consensus of the society of which he was a part. Where utilitarian society was an aggregate of such self-maximizing individuals, held together by the haggling of the market and the coercion of the courts, rationalist-idealist societies were more than the mere sum of their individual constituents: they possessed a volition independent of the individuals of whom they were composed, and instruments of social control extending beyond the market and the courts to include the interaction of individual conscience and social consensus.' Dewey cites (p. 70) the following passage from *The Methods of Ethics* (2nd ed., 1877) to demonstrate the importance in Sidgwick's thought of concepts such as sympathy, disinterested duty, the love of esteem and the social

actor's commitment to the public good, together with Sidgwick's conviction that excessive hedonism and obsessive egotism makes it impossible for a man adequately to share the pleasures and pains of others: 'The perpetual prominence of self that hence results tends to deprive all enjoyments of their keenness and zest, and produces rapid satiety and *ennui*; the selfish man misses the sense of elevation and enlargement given by wide interests; he misses the secure and serene satisfaction that attends continually in activities directed towards ends more stable and permanent than one's own happiness can be.' Marshall held Sidgwick in high esteem, describing him as 'my spiritual father and mother' (quoted in Keynes, 'Alfred Marshall, 1842–1924', in *Memorials*, p. 7), and the shared interest in moral community is one which is of considerable significance in understanding the thrust of his life's work – as, indeed, the present book has sought to show. For a demonstration that Marshall grew increasingly sceptical about the utilitarian calculus, see G. W. Guillebaud, 'The Evolution of Marshall's *Principles of Economics*', *Economic Journal*, Vol. 52, 1942. In Wood II, pp. 176–8. Terence Hutchison discusses the influence of Sidgwick on subsequent Cambridge thinking in his *The Politics and Philosophy of Economics* (Oxford: Blackwell, 1981), Chapter Three; while Alon Kadish brings out clearly just how important in Oxford economics were the ideas widely associated with Green (participatory democracy, the supremacy of moral over material progress, the reliance on public opinion, to mention but three). See A. Kadish, *The Oxford Economists in the Late Nineteenth Century* (Oxford: Clarendon Press, 1982).
42. Richter, *The Politics of Conscience*, p. 297.
43. *PE*, p. 3.
44. A. C. Pigou, *Economic Science in Relation to Practice* (An Inaugural Lecture given at Cambridge, 30 October 1908) (London: Macmillan, 1908), pp. 12–13.
45. Letter to A. W. Flux dated 19 March 1904, in *Memorials*, p. 408.
46. *IT*, p. 675.
47. 'The Present Position of Economics' (1885), in *Memorials*, p. 165.
48. *IT*, p. 675.
49. *PE*, p. v.
50. Letter to Bishop Westcott dated 23 January 1901, in *Memorials*, p. 397.
51. T. Levitt, 'Alfred Marshall: Victorian Relevance for Modern Economics', *Quarterly Journal of Economics*, Vol. 90, 1976. In Wood I, p. 434. John Maloney detects 'an unhealthy give-and-take between Marshall the economist and Marshall the private citizen' in view of the fact that, in Marshall's perspective, 'the economist as private citizen had much to do. And Marshall the private citizen was everywhere. He attended Professor Marshall's lectures doggedly; his constant interruptions must have been very frustrating to the latter, who had not come along to tell students that one of the best ways to use their wealth was to buy pictures, exhibit them and leave them to the nation, or to tell them that keeping up with fashion was "a crime" or the *nouveau riche* was a trial to himself and to his friends.' (Maloney, *Marshall, Orthodoxy and the Professionalisation of Economics*, p. 198). Even so, and despite the

'unhealthy' give-and-take, Maloney ultimately reaches what is essentially the same conclusion as that of Levitt: 'Marshall the moralist, dressed up as Marshall the economic biologist, egged on Marshall the ordinary citizen to speak out in public by telling him he was speaking more or less professionally after all' (*Ibid.*, p. 200). For, after all, 'Marshall's *Principles* begins by trying to *show* that what is good for economic man is normally good for "total man"' (*Ibid.*, p. 184), so strong was the impulsion towards Social Darwinism in Marshall's make-up.

52. 'Mr Mill's Theory of Value' (1876), in *Memorials*, p. 125.

Index

Note: Most references are to Marshall's theories and writings and to Britain unless otherwise stated.